France

at its best

BY ROBERT S. KANE

The World at Its Best Travel Series
BRITAIN AT ITS BEST
FRANCE AT ITS BEST
GERMANY AT ITS BEST
HAWAII AT ITS BEST
ITALY AT ITS BEST
MEXICO AT ITS BEST
SPAIN AT ITS BEST
PARIS AT ITS BEST
LONDON AT ITS BEST

A to Z World Travel Guides
GRAND TOUR A TO Z: THE CAPITALS OF EUROPE
EASTERN EUROPE A TO Z
SOUTH PACIFIC A TO Z
CANADA A TO Z
ASIA A TO Z
SOUTH AMERICA A TO Z
AFRICA A TO Z

Robert S. Kane

France
at its best

 PASSPORT BOOKS

Trade Imprint of National Textbook Company
Lincolnwood, Illinois U.S.A.

For George L. Hern, Jr.

Published by Passport Books, Trade Imprint of National
Textbook Company, 4255 West Touhy Avenue,
Lincolnwood, Illinois 60646–1975.
© 1986 by Robert S. Kane. All rights reserved. No part of
this book may be reproduced, stored in a retrieval system,
or transmitted in any form, or by any means, electronic,
mechanical, photocopying or otherwise, without the prior
written permission of National Textbook Company.
Manufactured in the United States of America. Library of
Congress Catalog Card Number: 85–63112

67890 ML 987654321

Contents

Foreword   France: La Grande Image   **ix**

1   **France**   A Mini A to Z   **1**

2   **Paris**   The Continent's Great Capital   **23**

    FRANCE AT ITS BEST, ALPHABETICALLY

3   **Aix-en-Provence**   The Quintessential Provence   **106**

4   **Angers**   Evoking the Plantagenets   **113**

5   **Annecy**   Savoie's Best-Kept Secret   **119**

6   **Arles**   Caesar's Legions and Van Gogh   **129**

7   **Avignon**   Medieval Papal Stronghold   **136**

8   **Beaune**   Burgundy's Ancient Wine Center   **145**

9   **Biarritz**   and the Basque Country   **154**

10   **Bordeaux**   City behind the Wine Label   **163**

11   **Bourges**   Heartland of France   **175**

12   **Caen**   Bayeux and the Beaches   **180**

13   **Cannes**   Queen of the South Coast   **189**

14   **Chamonix**   In the Shadow of Mont Blanc   **202**

15   **Colmar**   and Alsace's Route du Vin   **208**

16   **Deauville**   Elegance on the Channel   **216**

17   **Dijon**   and the Beauties of Burgundy   **222**

18   **Grenoble**   Edging the Alps   **232**

19   **Honfleur**   Normandy's Enchanted Village   **240**

20   **Loire Valley Châteaux**   Tours to Orléans   **245**

21   **Lyon**   France's Second City   **257**

22   **Marseille**   Mediterranean Metropolis   **271**

23   **Monaco**   Big Things in Small Packages   **279**

24   **Montpellier**   Ancient Languedoc Updated   **290**

25   **Nancy**   What Duke Stanislaus Hath Wrought   **297**

26   **Nice**   and the Riviera Hills   **302**

27 **Nîmes** Ancient Rome in Provence **317**

28 **Pau** Vive Henri IV! **323**

29 **Poitiers and La Rochelle** East-Central Duo **330**

30 **Rennes** and Beyond in Brittany **338**

31 **Rouen** Core of Normandy **350**

32 **St.-Malo** and Eastward to Mont-St.-Michel **358**

33 **St.-Tropez** Hedonism on the Côte d'Azur **367**

34 **Sarlat** By Huffle and Truffle through Périgord **373**

35 **Strasbourg** Showplace of Alsace **383**

36 **Toulouse** Diversions to Albi and Carcassonne **392**

Acknowledgments **402**

Index **404**

Map of France **v**
City Maps
  Paris **30-31**
  Bordeaux **165**
  Lyon **259**
  Nice **304**

Foreword

France: La Grande Image

Paris problematical? It is, indeed. As the continent's ranking metropolis—with a name so magical that it has been synonymous over long centuries with the country of which it is capital—Paris has sufficient magnetism to preclude even the well-traveled among us from venturing beyond its core and environs.

Make no mistake. There are reasons. Enough of them for me—admittedly a longtime Paris partisan—to open this book with an in-depth Paris chapter that profiles not only the grand hotels (not everyone can stay at the Bristol or the Meurice), but good-value mid-category and smaller houses in quantity; that counsels not only the occasional splurge meal in glossy restaurants, but recommends a wealth of reasonably priced places for lunching and dining in the style of rank-and-file Parisians themselves; that brings to your attention well over a score of treasure-filled museums to complement the Louvre and the Pompidou; that steers you to quite as many history-and-art-filled churches, the better to appreciate that spiritual Paris is infinitely more than Notre-Dame Cathedral; that fills you in on a miscellany of monuments, Sorbonne to City Hall, Invalides to Bois de Boulogne; that appraises an extraordinary shopping scene—*grands magasins* (the department stores) to typically Parisian boutiques; that counsels excursions not only to the obligatory Versailles and Fontainebleau, but to châteaux whose names may be less familiar—Chantilly and Compiègne, St.-Germain-en-Laye and Vaux-le-Vicomte.

Then comes what the non-Parisian French—who constitute, I want to emphasize, some 52 million of the republic's total population of around 55 million—often call "The Other France": 34 chapters evaluating not only the two areas beyond Paris—Riviera and Loire Valley—where foreigners traditionally fear not to tread, but points France-wide, from Alsace in the northeast, next door to Germany, where locals speak

German about as fluently as they do French, and sauerkraut is the basis of the most famous food specialty, to the Basque country of the southwest, adjacent to Spain, with the Spanish language widely understood, and the bullfight a spectator sport.

You find yourself fascinated, as you move about provincial France, with the way Bretons cling to their folk costumes and, for that matter, their Celtic tongue; the way Normans to this day take pride in the long-ago duke who became king of a conquered England; the way southwesterners in Périgord keep their towns small and their fare rich; and the way citizens of Nice—masses of visitors notwithstanding— preserve as a landmark their city's venerable core.

Even bigger surprises are the cosmopolitan aspects, not to mention cultural resources, of the big provincial cities—Lyon's Gothic cathedral dominating a charming Old Town, the amazing wealth not only of Old Masters, but of post-Impressionists in Grenoble's Musée des Beaux-Arts, the remarkable caliber of the furniture and other antique objects in the opulent townhouse that serves as Marseille's decorative-arts museum, the world-class opera house that is but one example of the eighteenth-century architectural elegance of Bordeaux, and delightful quarters that are throwbacks to the Renaissance, in such cities as Dijon, Rouen, and Strasbourg.

In no country that I know do smaller places produce bigger treats. Bourges is as notable for its all-Europe ranker of a cathedral as for smart shops. (You soon learn, as you move about, that provincial France's shopping facilities can match those of Paris in quality, if not quantity.) The Riviera offers a veritable network of museums, each devoted to the work of a modern master—Matisse, Chagall, Picasso, to name three. You expect vineyards, of course, in the neighborhood of Bordeaux's St.-Émilion and Burgundy's Beaune—but they are centers of Middle Ages art and architecture, as well. The globally celebrated Loire châteaux? Chambord and Azay-le-Rideau—among many—of course. But they have France-wide competition from, say, Fougères in the north, Meillant in the center, Castries in the south—three of many. Provence's Nîmes remains an architectural outpost of ancient Rome, and so many other superb Roman remnants dot the landscape.

No matter where in France you travel—uncelebrated albeit stimulating cities like Caen and Rennes in the north, Périgueux and Pau in the southwest, Annecy and Vienne in the east, Alpine Chamonix, the Mediterranean's Cannes, lakeside Évian, the port-resort of La Rochelle on the Atlantic, Bayeux near the English Channel's World War II landing beaches—you are engulfed by the culture of France. By that, I mean you find yourself speaking the French language (is there a more beautiful tongue?) even if you've not studied it, relishing the French cuisine (is there a more delicious one?), savoring French wines (are there any finer?), observing French midday closings, staying in French-style hotels, and queueing up to pay cashiers for your purchases in French *supermarchés*. If you afford your hosts a chance to know you, the while giving yourself the opportunity to know them (always remembering the ages-long formality with which strangers greet each other and become acquainted in France), you come to admire a remarkable people who are, at their best—which is often—well educated and well organized, intellectually curious and conversationally loquacious, good fun and good friends.

ROBERT S. KANE

France

A Mini A to Z

ADDRESSES: *French Government Tourist Office* has its American head-quarters at 610 Fifth Avenue, New York, NY 10020, with branches at 645 North Michigan Avenue, Chicago, IL 60611; 9501 Wilshire Boulevard, Beverly Hills, CA 90212; 1 Hallidie Plaza, San Francisco, CA 94102; and World Trade Center, 2030 Stemmons Freeway, Dallas, TX 75258. There are FGTO offices, as well, at 1 Dundas Street, Toronto, Ontario, and 1981 Avenue McGill College, Montreal, Quebec, in Canada; and at 178 Picca-dilly, London. These offices—whose function is to provide the prospec-tive traveler in France with gratis information and literature—are part of a worldwide network, whose headquarters—*Direction du Tourisme*, attached to the French Government's *Ministère du Commerce, de l'Arti-sanat et du Tourisme*—is in Paris, where it operates a center providing information on travel throughout France; it is called *Agence Nationale pour l'Information Touristique* (A.N.I.T.) and is located at 8 Avenue de l'Opéra. Beyond the capital, throughout France, the traveler's best infor-mation source is the local *Office de Tourisme*, upon occasion termed *Syndicat d'Initiative*. Addresses of these offices appear in chapters fol-lowing.

BREAKFAST—*petit déjeuner*—is nothing more than the term (trans-lated as "little lunch") implies. Unless you specify otherwise, it will consist of *café au lait*—a pot of intense black coffee served with an equal-sized jug of hot milk, the idea being that you mix the two, more or less half and half. Accompanying the coffee will be a *petit-pain* (crusty roll), a *croissant* (for some reason or other, these are at their flakiest in Paris), and/or a *brioche*, along with butter and jam. This is a *café complet* or Continental breakfast, upon occasion served with fruit juice. Where that is not the case, juice, as well as eggs, bacon, and ham may be ordered additionally, at least at better hotels. (If a Frenchman ever has anything more than *café complet*, it is a single boiled egg served *à la coque* —in the shell—with salt, but rarely pepper, which must usually be specially requested. In virtually all cases, no matter how simple the hotel, breakfast is served in bedrooms, as well as in the hotel's dining or special breakfast room. And in certain instances—I indicate these in pages following—hotels offer the option of breakfast buffets; those of the Crillon and Ritz hotels in Paris are quite the grandest such of any that I know in France; links of the Novotel chain serve generous buffet breakfasts, too.

BUSES: Given a choice, I prefer the train—especially in France, where they are so good (see S.N.C.F., below)—to the long-distance bus. Still, for the very occasional town that is not served by rail (Honfleur in the north and St.-Tropez in the south are two such), buses fill the gap. They are, as well, a pleasant way to traverse the Riviera, which is of course served by train, also. The bus system is France-wide and, in my experience, efficient and inexpensive, although drivers—while usually helpful—tend to speak only French. Although you mightn't do so at home, it's considered polite to greet them with a *bonjour* upon boarding; they'll reply in kind, often wishing you *bonne journée*, when you exit. Bus stations—the term is *gare routière*—are often, but not always, near the just plain *gare*, or railway station.

CASINOS: Slot machines are *interdit*, forbidden by law, in France (although you'll find them in independent Monaco, Chapter 23). But casinos—with such games of chance as roulette, trente et quarante, and baccarat—are dotted about the republic; I indicate a number of them in chapters following. As a general rule, foreigners are required to show passports upon entering, and gents are expected to wear jacket and tie in the evening.

CHIENS: Although they do not vote (at least, to my knowledge), dogs come close to being full-fledged French citizens. I have no figures, but there simply has to be a higher proportion of dogs—vis-à-vis the human population—in France than in any other country. Certain restaurants deny them entry, but they go shopping with masters and mistresses, and rare is the hotel in France that does not have special rates *pour les animaux*. I have yet to meet a French dog that I did not like (they are invariably friendly and quite prepared to charm the pants off you). Which is not to say they all have been properly trained. *Caveat:* Watch where you walk.

CLIMATE: You are, of course, in a temperate-zone country, but a relatively mild—albeit erratic—temperate-zone country. By that, I mean Paris summers may be gray, nasty-rainy, and Paris winters may be glorious and crystal-clear, with spring and autumn—France-wide—delightful, if you're lucky with respect to rain clouds. In Paris, winter (late November through March) averages in the high thirties and forties, with January and February the coldest months. Spring (April and May) is likely to be in the fifties. Summer (June through early September) averages in the sixties, with July and August the hottest months, averaging in the mid-seventies—but capable of being much hotter. Autumn (late September through October) is apt to be fiftyish. Down south, along the Mediterranean coast, expect temperatures that average 10 degrees above those of the capital, with the Riviera the sunniest sector of the republic year-round (although its winters can be moist and chilly). Brittany and Normandy tend to have the coolest summers, and, not surprisingly, Savoie and the Alpine regions, the coldest—albeit sunniest—winters. Rain can fall at any time of year; don't travel without a collapsible umbrella.

CLOTHES: Although its capital is *couture* capital of the world, France—taken as a whole—is neither as well dressed as Italy nor as clothes-conscious as Britain, which is hardly to imply, however, that you want to pack only jeans. Paris and the principal provincial cities—Lyon, most especially—make a point of looking extremely good on business and more festive social occasions, by which I mean opera, ballet, concerts, and theater, as well as both lunches and dinners in better-category restaurants. Côte d'Azur resorts are smartly casual the day long, but dressier—especially at glossy eateries and casinos—after dark. Throughout France, the best and simplest rule is to clothe yourself informally in the course of daytime explorations, less so in the evenings.

CONFÉRENCIERS are university-educated specialists in art history and architecture—*not*, I want to emphasize, ordinary guides—who lead individuals, as well as groups, on day-long and halfday tours, coordinated by the French Government's Caisse Nationale des Monuments Historiques et des Sites, at some 40 of the cities, towns, and châteaux about which I write in later chapters of this book—Paris and environs, of course, included. Upon occasion, they are English-speaking. You learn a lot this way. Local Offices de Tourisme have details.

CREDIT CARDS are accepted in many—but by no means all—restaurants, chain department stores, and shops. But they are not yet as widely accepted as in the United States. Most popular are Visa, American Express, Diners Club, and MasterCard—in that order.

CRUISING BY BARGE: You either like the concept of traveling in smallish, hardly luxurious barges along a country's inland waterways, or you do not. I do not, for a number of reasons. First is accommodations:

although better companies' boats have private facilities attached to all cabins, space is, of necessity, limited—to understate. A single main cabin usually serves as restaurant, bar, and lounge. Deck space is so tight that there's room only for sit-up chairs—no recliners on which to lie back, as on a proper cruise ship. There is no choice of courses, for the most part, at meals, nor, for that matter, of wine served with lunch and dinner—usually included in the rate. You are bound by the company's prearranged itinerary. A lot of time is spent making small talk with fellow passengers in close quarters. And rates are high. For what a barge-tour costs, you can stay in comfortable, first-class hotels with decent beds and full-sized bathroom facilities (large people can have difficulty fitting into barge-cruise shower stalls, and sinks can be the size of a dinner plate), dine in restaurants ordering from multichoice menus and wine lists, and set your own schedule. That said, and you're still game, I have one firm to recommend: *Continental Waterways*. Its tours—of varying duration in several areas—are bookable through travel agents.

CURRENCY: The franc is subdivided into 100 centimes, with coins in 10-franc and lower denominations (always keep a supply of ever-so-handy one-franc coins) and notes in higher denominations. Inquire as to rates from bank and currency-exchange firms before departure; you may want to buy some in advance. In France, best rates are obtained at banks and *bureaux de change*—change offices (you absolutely *must* have your passport with you)—but hotel cashiers also change money. Take the bulk of your funds in traveler's checks—they're the safest—with plenty in 20-dollar denominations; they're the most convenient.

CUSTOMS: *Entering France.* Coming from non-Common Market countries such as the United States, you're allowed a carton of cigarettes and a couple of bottles of alcohol, as well as your own personal effects, including, of course, cameras and a reasonable amount of film. Coming from Common Market countries, the ante is raised by a third in the case of cigarettes and doubled in the case of alcohol. French immigration officers tend not to stamp passports, indicating dates of entry into and exit from France, unless you so request.

Returning to the United States. Each individual may bring back $400 worth of purchases duty free. That is allowable once every 30 days, provided you've been out of the country at least 48 hours. If you've spent more than $400, you'll be charged a flat 10 percent duty on the next $1,000 worth of purchases. Remember, too, that antiques, duly certified to be at least 100 years old, are admitted duty free and do not count as part of your $400 quota; neither do paintings, sculptures, and other works of art, of any date, if certified as original; it's advisable that certification, from the seller or other authority, as to their authenticity accompany them. Also exempt from duty, but as a part of the $400 quota:

one quart of liquor. And—this is important—there is no restriction on how much one may bring in beyond the $400 limit, so long as the duty is paid.

DEPARTMENT STORES, SHOPS, AND SUPERMARKETS: Paris is a department-store city of consequence: I detail facilities in Chapter 2. Its two major *grands magasins—Galeries Lafayette* and *Printemps*—have branches in a number of other cities. There are other chains, exclusively provincial, such as *Nouvelles Galeries* and *Dames de France*. There are nationwide budget-category chains, as well, such as *Monoprix*. Even the British-origin *Marks & Spencer* is on scene, as is the occasional locally owned department store. I make shopping suggestions in some detail, and by category, not only in Chapter 2 (Paris) but in chapters on a number of other important cities and towns around the country. The supermarket—*supermarché*—is happily ubiquitous and a source not only of grocery items, but of wines for hotel-room aperitifs.

DRIVING: Take your own car, rent one in advance of arrival or on the scene, or buy a new French car. You need a valid driver's license of your country of residence, as well as the international green card indicating that you are insured. (Home insurance companies can assist in this regard.) Of course, you know that gas is sold by the liter, but it's worth noting that an American gallon equals just over three and three quarter liters, and an Imperial gallon is four and a half liters. Kilometers? One km = 5/8 of a mile; conversely, one mile = 1.6 km. *Automobile Club de l'Île de France* (8, Place de la Concorde, Paris; phone 4266-43-00) answers questions 24 hours a day. On the road, in case of accident, breakdown, or an empty gas tank, contact the nearest *Gendarmerie* or *Poste de Police*. Rental firms? *Avis, Hertz,* and *Budget-Rent-a-Car* are on scene, as well as a number of French firms. France has some 930,000 miles of roads, of which more than 3,000 miles are superhighways. You may, for example, cut through the country by this means, on a north-south route taking you from Burgundy through the Rhône Valley and Provence to the Mediterranean—with rest areas every 10 miles, frequent emergency phones, motels and cafés along the way, and an 80-mile-per-hour speed limit.

ELECTRIC CURRENT: 220 volts AC. Take along a transformer for your shaver or hair dryer and an adapter-plug to be attached to prongs of your appliance, so that it will fit into holes of the French outlet. American department stores sell kits containing a transformer and a variety of variously shaped adapters. Alternatively, you may buy a French-made appliance, for use during your journey, upon arrival in France—recommended if your stay will be lengthy.

GEOGRAPHY: Texas is bigger—by a fifth. Still, France's area, exceeding 210,000 miles, is considerable; of the European countries, only the Soviet Union (partly in Asia) is larger. Bordered on three flanks by water—English Channel (*La Manche,* to the French) on the north, Mediterranean to the southeast, Atlantic to the west—France shares land frontiers with half a dozen countries: Belgium, Luxembourg, Germany, Switzerland, and Italy to the east; and Spain to the south. It lacks neither mountains (Mont Blanc, the Alps's highest peak, with a tunnel cut through it to neighboring Italy; the northeasterly Vosges range; the aptly named Massif Central; and formidable Pyrenees on the frontier with Spain) nor gently rolling plains (extending over its northern and western territory). Each of the Big Four rivers is celebrated: Seine, because it bisects Paris; Loire, because of the châteaux on its shores; Garonne, because it's the core of Bordeaux wine country; and Rhône, which cuts through Burgundy and Lyon into Provence and the Mediterranean, wherein lies Corsica, metropolitan France's sole island of consequence.

There are some 55 million Frenchmen living in a democratic, multiparty republic, led by a president (the term is seven years) who appoints No. 2—the premier—and a cabinet. The two-house legislature is big—491-seat Assemblée Nationale (terms are five years) and 318-member Sénat (terms are nine years). France is divided into 95 Départements (four of them overseas, including Guadeloupe and Martinique in the Caribbean). Départements are grouped into more than a score of administrative Régions and approximating—but only *approximating*—territory of the ancient provinces that were officially abolished during the Revolution but remain, two centuries later, France's traditional geographic and cultural subdivisions.

HISTORY: Chapter 2 (Paris) deals the most extensively with what has gone before, the better to appreciate what remains today; in succeeding chapters, I capsulize, but sufficiently, I hope, to provide you with perspective for intelligent on-scene exploration. At this point, let me compress the succession of dynasties and other governmental entities that France has known, following the first five centuries of the Christian era when it was Roman-governed *Gaul. Carolingian kings*—the dynasty was named for eighth-century Charlemagne—reigned until the mid-tenth century. There were more than a dozen, with both Louis the Debonair and Louis the Stammerer and both Charles the Bald and Charles the Fat, among them. *Capetians*—named for King Hugh Capet, founder of the line—were quite as numerous as Carolingians; their numbers included the sainted Louis XI, Robert the Pious, and Philippe the Fair; and they were in power until the beginning of the fourteenth century, when the dozen-plus sovereigns of the *Valois* dynasty succeeded, starting with Philippe VI and including the debonair arts-patron François I, not to mention Charles the Well Beloved and Louis XII, the Father of His

People. *Bourbons*—to us foreigners, the most celebrated dynasty—took over in the sixteenth century, with the accession of Henri IV, France's all-time favorite sovereign. Henri's successors—Louis XIII, Louis XIV, Louis XV, Louis XVI—are the stuff of familiar history courses. The late eighteenth-century *Revolution* abolished the ancien régime. Following were the *Convention* and, later, the *Directoire*. Then came the *Consulat*, headed by Napoleon Bonaparte, who declared himself *Emperor Napoleon I*, ruling from 1804 to 1815 and twice exiled. Two of Louis XVI's brothers, Louis XVIII and Charles X, followed Napoleon with their reigns (1814-1830) jointly dubbed the *Bourbon Restoration*. *Louis-Philippe*—Bourbon partly (on his mother's side)—was proclaimed King by the Assemblée Nationale after Charles X was forced to abdicate; Louis-Philippe himself abdicated in 1848. An ambitious nephew of Napoleon I—at first President as Louis Napoleon, later *Emperor Napoleon III*—ruled France from 1848 to 1870, only to be deposed as a consequence of the *Franco-Prussian War*. Ever since (*World War II Nazi occupation* under the puppet Pétain regime excepted), France has been a republic. *Charles de Gaulle* became provisional President for two years in 1944, returning as President for the decade 1959-1969, a momentous period that saw France reemerge as a universally respected world power.

HOLIDAYS: As in every country, they're a pleasure for residents, but major ones can be a bother for visitors, who do well to plan around them, noting the likelihood of closed museums and other places of interest, certain shops, and some restaurants. Besides Christmas and New Year's, take note of Easter Monday, Ascension, Whit Monday, Labor Day (May 1, with parades in the cities), Bastille Day (July 14, joyous celebrations France-wide), Assumption Day (August 15), All Saints' Day (November 1), and Armistice Day (November 11).

HOTELS: *About the hotels in this book.* I have either lived in, dined in, drunk in, and/or thoroughly inspected the hotels carefully selected for evaluation in these pages; I disregard the complexities of the official French Government star-system and have divided hotels (and restaurants) into three price groups: *Luxury, First Class,* and *Moderate*. Bear in mind that I am fussy. In towns of any size and cities, I concentrate on *centrally situated* hotels, including country hotels only when they are exceptional and will be of interest to travelers with cars. All hotels in my *Luxury* and virtually all in my *First Class* categories have television and mini-bars (stocked with liquor, wine, soft drinks, and sometimes snacks, for purchase) in all rooms, as well, of course, as private baths. Air-conditioning is standard in better modern hotels and many, but not all, traditional-style houses, and is, of course, more prevalent along and near the Mediterranean than in the cooler north; inquire when booking. My *Moderate* category hotels are *better*-Moderate, very often with TV and/or mini-bars and with baths attached to most or all rooms; I indicate the proportion in each case. The French rank with the very top-rung European hoteliers—Germans, Italians, and Swiss. I want to make clear that, by and large, at least in my not inconsiderable experience, they take as much pride in running modest hotels as in running luxury houses. (This is important to note in the case of Paris, which has more budget hotels than any other European city, with relatively few lemons in the lot; of the provincial cities, Nice is No. 2 in this respect.) When a French hotel is well operated, everything works well, reception to room service. I don't know of a hotel in the republic (except perhaps in the Basque country [Chapter 9]) without English-speaking personnel or without crackerjack housekeeping; French hotels, by and large, are shipshape. My principal caveat is with respect to showers. Outside of Paris—where they are fairly common, especially in better hotels—expect only hand showers attached to tubs, except in some hotels where single rooms may have stall showers in lieu of tubs. (In a small residue of lower-category French hotels, a "private bath" might consist of only a sink and a tub—with the toilet a public one, down the hall; happily, not many such arrangements remain, but in modest places it pays to ask in this regard.)

Hotels operated by crack United States-based international chains, such as *Inter-Continental* (heaviest represented, with three historic Paris hotels and a fourth—still another landmark—on the Riviera) and *Hilton International* (with three lovely luxury houses) will not be unfamiliar to transatlantic visitors. But there are other chains, French and international—with hotels France-wide—for which orientation is warranted. *Hôtels Concorde* is, on the basis of my experience, No. 1 of the lot, beyond any question; it is by no means the biggest, but the best, with half a dozen Paris houses—Crillon and Lutétia are the top rankers—and a dozen additional hotels in provincial France, Cannes's Martinez and Nancy's Grand, among them. There are a number of chains whose hotels are dominantly stark French Contemporary, more functional—they are principally for business travelers on overnight missions and for groups—than charming, albeit with delightful exceptions to the rule in the case of each. This group includes *Frantel, PLM-Etap, Mercure, Novotel,* and *Sofitel,* all dominantly *First Class*; and *Ibis,* which is *Moderate.* There are, as well, a number of associations of privately operated hotels, banded together for purposes of promotion and central booking. Of these, in the First Class/Moderate categories group, I consistently have the most satisfaction with *Mapotels,* associated with U.S.-based *Best Western.* There remains *Relais et Châteaux,* without question, cream of the French crop, of the associated privately operated hotels. They're located in the countryside more than in cities, often occupying fine antiques-furnished houses of considerable age—and frequently with distinguished restaurants. They are represented in North America by David B. Mitchell & Co., 200 Madison Avenue, New York, NY 10016.

Last—but hardly least—is aptly titled *Leading Hotels of the World* (head office: 747 Third Avenue, New York, NY 10017), an extraordinary association of extraordinary hotels around the planet that become affiliated only by invitation and after careful screening. Its dozen French affiliates number some of the finest hotels in the land; the range, to give you an idea, is Paris's George V and Ritz through Nice's Négresco and Évian's Royal. *A final note:* Especially beyond big cities, French hotels often, if not always, close for *fermeture annuelle*—vacation, usually during their slackest season; check before you go.

LANGUAGE: It's true that many Frenchmen are impatient with the less than perfect French spoken by foreign visitors, and that, indeed—more in Paris and on the Riviera than elsewhere—they'll often rudely reply in English (if they speak it) to your French. But it is increasingly true that these same Frenchmen—themselves studying foreign languages more than has been the case and traveling increasingly abroad—realize that speaking a strange tongue is no easy matter. There is, as a consequence, more tolerance with foreigners' pronunciation than was the case a decade or so back. What is important in Franco-foreign relationships are the polite niceties of conversation. To say simply, "Thank you," to a woman is enough in English; in French it is not. One says, "Merci, madame" or "Merci, mademoiselle," and, with a man, "Merci, monsieur." It is the same with a *bonjour* or an *au revoir;* you tack on *madame, mademoiselle,* or *monsieur*—no matter how impersonal or brief the exchange has been, and no matter the occupation or station in life of the person with whom you are speaking. It helps, believe me. And one more point: By no means everyone in France speaks even *un petit peu d'anglais.* Your French will be very useful with this vast majority; don't be bashful about using it. Conversely, don't hesitate about venturing forth without French. After all, English is France's most popular language, after the native tongue; 80 percent of the country's secondary and college language students are studying it. *Tip:* Before you go, pick up a copy of *Just Enough French,* one of Passport Books' excellent *Just Enough* phrasebooks; or study the language in advance of departure, with Passport's *Just Listen 'n Learn French*—a three-cassette and textbook kit.

OPEN HOURS: Quite sensible. *Museums* operated by the French Government traditionally close on Tuesdays and major holidays; many other—*but by no means all*—museums operate similarly. For example, the considerable clutch of museums operated by the City of Paris (Carnavalet, Petit Palais, Cognacq-Jay are but three) close on Mondays. Most—again, not all—museums close for approximately two hours at midday, as do *historic houses* and *palaces* operated as museums, *cathedrals,* and *churches,* especially beyond Paris. *Department stores* have the longest hours, usually Monday through Saturday from 9:00 A.M. to 6:30 P.M., with one or two late-opening nights in Paris and major provincial cities. *Other stores* generally open between 9:00 and 10:00 A.M., shuttering between noon and 2:00 P.M., and reopening until 6:30 or 7:00 P.M., Tuesday through Saturday. *Banks* are exceptionally generous with open hours: 9:00 A.M. to 4:30 P.M., Monday through Friday, closing at noon the day before a holiday. *Hairdressers and barbers* close on Monday.

OPERA, BALLET, CONCERTS, AND FESTIVALS: France and the performing arts have been synonymous these many centuries. I make a point of bringing particulars to your attention in chapters following, but I want at this point to emphasize that quality remains high beyond the capital and that settings for performances can be positively opulent. Festivals take place year-round but are most prevalent in summer. Be on the lookout for them as you move about, noting such festivals of consequence as those of *Paris* (Festival du Marais, Festival d'Été— summer), *Aix-en-Provence* (July), *Antibes* (late April and May), *Avignon* (July), *Bordeaux* (May), *Dijon* (July), *Île de France* (mid-May through mid-July, at many points), *Lyon* (Berlioz Festival, September), *Marseille* (August), *Montpellier* (June-July), *Orange* (July), *Périgueux* (August), *Poitiers* (May), *Strasbourg* (June), *Tours* (late June–early July), and *Vienne* (July).

PAN AM AND FRANCE: Pioneering Pan American World Airways— which, as long ago as 1927, was the first American airline to operate a permanent international air service—selected France as the termination point for the very first scheduled transatlantic flight. On May 20, 1939, a Boeing 314 flying boat, dubbed *Yankee Clipper*, took off from Port Washington, New York, with a cargo of airmail. It touched down en route in the Azores Islands, mid-Atlantic, and at Lisbon, before arriving the following day in Marseille.

Less than a month later, Pan Am's first passenger flight to France—a Boeing 314 named *Dixie Clipper*—flew the same route, arriving in Marseille June 30, 1939. A decade ensued before Pan Am inaugurated service to Nice via Lisbon and Marseille, with a Lockheed Constellation, on December 2, 1949. Then, a week before Christmas 1950, Pan Am linked New York with Paris, via Boeing Stratocruiser service. On September 10, 1957, Pan Am carried a group of journalists over the Polar Route—from San Francisco via Seattle and London—to Paris, aboard a Douglas DC-70, following with scheduled service from the West Coast immediately thereafter.

On October 26, 1958, Pan Am flew the then brand-new Boeing 707— on that aircraft's historic maiden commercial flight—from New York to Paris. And its first Boeing 747 linked New York with Paris on March 1, 1970.

Currently, Pan Am offers the only nonstop service from the United States to the Nice-Côte d'Azur International Airport, heart of the French

Riviera. It serves Paris with nonstops from New York, Washington, San Francisco, Miami, and Chicago, the while offering convenient single-carrier service to Paris from its gateways in 25 American cities.

Ever innovative, it was Pan Am that introduced economy-class service, as far back as 1948. Its management appreciates that that's how most of us fly and has always made a point—in my long experience as a Pan Am passenger—of making economy passengers comfortable, feeding them well, and treating them graciously, which is hardly to say that it is not expert at First Class—where menus are delightfully French accented (they're printed in both the French and English languages), and the wine cellar is never without a superb selection of Bordeaux, Burgundies, Beaujolais, an Alsatian white or two, of course Champagne, and a range of postmeal digestifs.

Pan Am's Business Class—relatively recently refurbished at a cost of a million dollars per plane for its entire 747 fleet—is equipped with seats that are larger than those that used to be in First Class, prior to the introduction therein of *chaise-longue*-like Sleeperettes. And if you're traveling First or Business with Pan Am via New York, you're treated to complimentary helicopter hops between the city and the airport. (*Air France*, *American*, *Delta*, *Pakistan International*, and *Trans World* also fly between the U.S. and France, and a number of airlines provide domestic service within France.)

PASSPORTS: Necessary for admittance to France and to be presented to U.S. Immigration upon your return. Apply at Department of State Passport Offices in a dozen-plus cities (look under U.S. Government in the phone book) or—in smaller towns—at the office of the clerk of a Federal Court and at certain post offices. Allow four weeks, especially for a first passport (valid for 10 years), for which you'll need a pair of two-inch-square photos and birth certificate or other proof of citizenship. There's a $42 fee (subject to change) for first passports; renewals are cheaper. If you're in a hurry when you apply, say so; Uncle Sam will usually try to expedite if you can show documentation indicating imminent departure. Upon receipt of your passport, sign your name where indicated, fill in the address of next of kin, and keep this valuable document with you—*not packed in a suitcase*—as you travel. In case of loss, contact local police, nearest U.S. Embassy or Consulate, or Passport Office, Department of State, Washington, D.C. 19524.

RATES for selected hotels (where I've stayed or which I've inspected) and restaurants (where I've eaten) are categorized as *Luxury, First Class,* and *Moderate;* these translate pretty much into what they would mean in the U.S., adjusted, of course, to the purchasing power of the dollar, with respect to the French franc at the time of your visit.

RESTAURANTS/CUISINE: There are two key qualifying adjectives: traditional and *nouvelle*. The latter—*cuisine nouvelle* in French, *nouvelle cuisine* in English—continues to be controversial, although, with each passing season, it is no longer all that *nouvelle*. Interview chefs as you travel France, and they tell you it's done with, finished, *terminé*. It does, to be sure, take on new appellations—*post-nouvelle* and cuisine légère are two such—and describes itself variously as creative, progressive, and original. But—a rose by any name—it remains. Although the French themselves maintain that the overwhelming majority of their countrymen never touch the stuff, *nouvelle* cuisine retains a certain snob appeal, and before booking at a *First Class-* or *Luxury-category* restaurant—the latter, especially—do a little advance homework. In essence, *nouvelle* is based first on presentation. It must look good, and its adherents adore symmetry, arranging dibs and dabs—portions are invariably minuscule—like petals of a flower. Its next premise is based on nutrition: Butter and cream are *interdit*. You must not expect to encounter the ingenious sauces indigenous to France's classic cuisine. Potatoes are looked at askance; likewise, most soups. Meats are offered thinly sliced, albeit fastidiously garnished. Vegetables appear in bland and custardy *timbales*. A plain, steamed serving of string beans? Never! Salads are artfully composed, often looking better than they taste. Worst of all, combinations can be absurd and bizarre, especially oddball mixes of sweet and savory. Only desserts remain rich; even they can be peculiarly composed. *Nouvelle* chefs tend to be young, photogenic, publicity-conscious, and ambitious, often naming their restaurants after themselves. You will find a sprinkling of *nouvelle* restaurants in this book— good ones, I believe; there is, after all, something to be said for the *nouvelle* concept of innovation and lightness in cooking. By and large, though, restaurants in these pages serve traditional dishes and, very often, superb regional specialties, the kind of food that is responsible for France's having achieved a deserved reputation as the country with the world's finest cuisine, the very same we cross oceans to experience on home territory.

Not that traditional fare is necessarily overrich or highly caloric. A typical meal will open with hors d'oeuvres or soup, go on to an entrée of meat or fish or a seafood dish, with a green salad dressed with oil, vinegar, salt, and pepper following: thence, cheese selected from a platter, fresh fruit or dessert, and postmeal coffee. If the meal is unfestive, one wine will accompany it—red, if with meat; white, if with fish. The French have far less aversion to the consumption of water than do, say, the British; feel free to request it.

Meal hours are sensible; lunch service in restaurants starts between noon and 12:30 P.M., continuing until about 2:00 P.M.; between 8:00 and 9:00 P.M. (often as late as 10:00 P.M. in Paris and on the Riviera) is the preferred time for dinner, although restaurants begin serving between

7:00 and 7:30 P.M. It's advisable to *reserve in advance*, except in simpler places (hotel concierges will do this for you, or phone yourself), noting that many restaurants observe a weekly closing day as well as a *ferme-ture annuelle*, or annual vacation.

Menu specifics: Hors d'oeuvres might include relishes like scallions and radishes, black and green olives, and celery *rémoulade*. There might be, as well, eggs-mayonnaise, lentils or beans, tiny shrimp or other shellfish, and snails served piping hot in their shells, with a parsley-butter and garlic sauce; various *pâtés* and *terrines*, and, the supreme opener, *foie gras* —poached fattened duck or goose liver. *French soups*—the widely exported onion, of course, but even simple *potages du jour*—are invariably delicious, as, indeed, are creamy *bisques* based on lobster or crab. *Meats* are masterfully prepared. Beef appears as steak *(entrecôte, châteaubriand)*, roasted on skewers, and in stews as *ragoûts* and *daubes*. *Blanquette de veau* is the veal stew par excellence. But look also for veal *escalopes*, as well as chops *(côtelettes)*, sweetbreads *(ris de veau)* and brains *(cervelle)*. Lamb appearing roasted, as *gigot d'agneau avec flageolet*-type beans is a favorite. Pork specialties are no less good, from *charcuterie* (sausage and specialty pork products) to *jambon* (ham) and roasts. *Fish and seafood:* If simply grilled with a squeeze of lemon or accompanied by a delicate sauce, fish in France is a winner. Likewise, such seafood as crab, crayfish, lobster, and oysters. Nowhere is *poultry* more imaginatively prepared; chicken, of course, but duck and goose, as well. If you haven't tried frog's legs *(grenouilles)*, you're missing a treat. In non-*nouvelle* restaurants, fresh *vegetables* still are served in decent-sized portions and never are overcooked. The *cheese* course is important in France. You know Camembert, Brie, and Roquefort, but try Pont-l'Évêque, Reblochon, Port-Salut, Chèvre (goat cheese, several species of which often appear on a single tray), and any number of others, varying by region, not unlike wine. *Pastries* are at their most enjoyable mid-morning or mid-afternoon, with coffee or tea in a *pâtisserie* that doubles as a *salon de thé*, or simply purchased by the bag from shops whose windows prove irresistible. They're always available as *desserts*, along with gargantuan *ice cream* sundaes, called *bombes* or *coupes*, hot *soufflés* —chocolate, lemon, vanilla, Grand Marnier—and so are *crêpes*, the thin pancakes of Breton origin. French wines rate a section of their own at the end of this chapter. Remaining are the delights of *regional cooking;* I make specific suggestions in chapters following.

My favorite restaurants? I note, in evaluations that follow in succeeding chapters, 26 restaurants which are, in my opinion—based on cuisine, service, and ambience—among the best restaurants in France. My honor list follows, alphabetically:

Allard, Paris
Auberge du Père Bise, Talloires
Au Fer Rouge, Colmar

Château du Domaine St.-Martin Hôtel Restaurant, Vence
Chez Dufour, Rouen
Chez La Mère Ticket, Grenoble
Ciro's, Deauville
De France Hôtel Restaurant, Auch
De La Poste Hôtel Restaurant, Beaune
Ferme St.-Siméon Hôtel Restaurant, Honfleur
Jacques-Coeur, Bourges
Jules Verne, Paris
L'Atre, St.-Malo
La Crémaillère, Orléans
La Merenda, Nice
La Rotisserie du Chambertin, Gevrey-Chambertin
La Tupina, Bordeaux
Léon de Lyon, Lyon
Le Grand Véfour, Paris
Le Petit Landais, Montpellier
Le Prieuré, Villeneuve-lès-Avignon
Le Relais de Saulx, Beaune
Le Vieux Castillon, Castillon du Gard
Les Ambassadeurs, Crillon Hôtel, Paris
Paul Bocuse, Collonges-au-Mont-d'Or
Vanel, Toulouse

SALES TAXES of up to 20 percent can be refunded, if you buy a specified minimum—the amount varies—from any given shop. Department stores are experts at explaining intricacies of an operation that involves filling out a long form at point of purchase, presenting it upon your departure from France to customs officers based at a special airport counter, who rubber stamp it and return it to you along with the stamped envelope the merchant has given you, so that you may drop it in a mailbox adjacent to the counter. It is thus returned to the seller, who only then draws a French-franc check for the amount of the tax, and posts it to your home address. Upon receipt of these foreign funds, you take them to your bank, where—unless you have a very friendly banker—charges for conversion to dollars may equal (or exceed) the amount of the check. Unless—and this "unless" is important—you make your purchase with a credit card, in which case request that the refund be credited to the card, obviating the return to you, in francs. Note, too, that in certain cases—ask on the spot—refund can take place at the time of purchase. Complicated? You bet. *Bonne chance!*

SHAKING HANDS: Everybody does it, toddlers onward; don't hesitate—it's appreciated. Bear in mind, too, that nonromantic kissing in France—in the nature of a greeting or a farewell—is on both cheeks. And note that the French are positively compulsive wipers of shod feet on doormats, even in fair-weather, slush-free situations; follow suit.

S.N.C.F.—*Société Nationale de Chemins de Fer Français* = French National Railroads. You're not going to ride any better trains in any country; in Europe, those of Germany and Switzerland come close. But the French distinguish themselves on the rails because they are such innovators. TGV—the world's fastest trains—are theirs. The relatively recent Nouvelle Première Classe—New First Class—is theirs. Loisir-rail—entertainment-on-board sightseeing tours—is theirs. The easy-to-use advance-purchase France Vacances ticket is theirs. So are smartly updated stations country-wide; handsome air-conditioned coaches; restaurant cars with good meals, smilingly served; polite conductors; an amazingly comprehensive network; and—hardly to be underestimated—trains that run on time, but *à la minute* on time (in my not inconsiderable experience, at least), 95 percent of the time.

TGV—Train à Grande Vitesse—translates, in effect, as Very High Speed, 169 miles per hour. The TGV network, ever expanding, connects Paris with such southeastern points as Dijon, Lyon, and Grenoble (with connections to Chambéry and Savoie ski resorts), and to Provençal cities down south like Avignon, Marseille, Nîmes, and Montpellier. All seats are reserved in either First or Second classes for these premium-fare trains, with supplements waived for holders of *France Vacances*. This is an advance-purchase ticket good for unlimited travel in either First Class (which I counsel) or Second Class, for a week, 15 days, or a month (and for periods of 9 or 15 days, if you buy the somewhat pricier France Vacances Spécial—with extra features). France Vacances may be bought from French National Railroads offices at 610 Fifth Avenue, New York, NY 10020; 360 Post St., San Francisco, CA 94102; 9465 Wilshire Blvd., Beverly Hills, CA 90212; 11 East Adams St., Chicago, IL 60603; 2121 Ponce de Leon Blvd., Coral Gables, FL 33134; 1500 Rue Stanley, Montreal, Quebec; 409 Granville St., Vancouver, B.C.; and 179 Piccadilly, London W1.

Train travel tips: Travel overnight, on a sleeper or *couchette*, and you save the cost of a hotel room. Except for the very rare Toonerville Trolley-type train, you'll find snack bars, refreshment carts rolled through the trains, and—on crack runs—restaurants. Even so, it's good practice to carry snack food with you, as the French do. And, if you're traveling eastward from Paris to Nancy (Chapter 25) or Strasbourg (Chapter 35), book in advance for the extra-fare *Nouvelle Première Classe*, with interiors designed by a leading Paris decorator (in a style reminiscent of Scotland's turn-of-century architect, Charles Rennie MacIntosh), meals catered by a pricey Paris restaurant (men must wear coat and tie for dinner), and a lounge car with a brass bar that could be fin de siècle—but isn't. Reserve seats in advance, even in first class, particularly on popular fast trains en route to major cities—Paris most especially. And, if you've a yen for beyond-the-capital exploration in the course of a Paris stay affording you limited time, consider a day-long *France-shrinker* excursion; these are escorted tours with English-speaking guides that include lunch, and are essentially by rail but make use of buses, as well, in the course of visits to points in Burgundy and Normandy—to cite a pair of destinations. Mind, you hit only certain highlights, adhering to a rigid schedule. But if you're a believer in the maxim that half a loaf is better than none, then a Franceshrinker—bookable through French National Railroads and travel agents in advance of departure—can prove convenient.

SON ET LUMIÈRE: The French invented *Son et Lumière*—sound and light—at Château de Chambord in the Loire Valley (Chapter 20). The idea was to tell its story to an audience seated in the shadow of the castle by means of the play of lights on features of the building and its grounds, coordinated with a spoken, dramatized commentary. The technique spread like wildfire, not only to neighboring Loire châteaux, but to points that stand out architecturally, scenically, and historically, throughout France. When well done, it effortlessly blends entertainment with education. Summer only.

STEAMSHIP SERVICE, transatlantic, is almost—but not quite—ancient history. Cunard Line's luxurious flagship, *Queen Elizabeth 2*, valiantly maintains scheduled sailings—about two dozen per year—between New York and the English Channel port of Southampton (see *Britain at Its Best*), with calls, as well, at the French port of Cherbourg—across the Channel—on selected westbound sailings. For France-bound passengers, Cunard arranges charter flights Southampton-Paris; alternatively, there is the option of crossing the Channel by the ferry service linking Southampton and Le Havre, in France.

TELEPHONES: Wherever possible, I have included the telephone numbers of hotels and restaurants selected for evaluation under Settling In and Daily Bread, respectively. If you are calling from Paris to anywhere else in the country, you need to first dial 16 and then the eight-digit number. If you want to call Paris from the rest of the country, you must first dial 16, then 1, then the number.

TIPPING is relatively effortless, thanks to the French system of adding a service charge—usually 15 percent—to restaurant bills and to café tabs, as well. (*Service Compris* on menus translates as service included; so does *Prix Net.*) There's no need to tip a hotel concierge unless he has performed special services, beyond handing you your key. Hotel porters who carry your bags to and from your room expect the franc equivalent of half a dollar per bag, more if the hotel is especially grand. Tip moderately to theater ushers if they escort you to your seat, 10 percent to barbers and hairdressers. Tip Paris and Riviera taxi drivers 10 to 15 percent of what's on the meter; elsewhere, they don't expect tips. In all events, tips are for cordial, efficient service. At no time are they obligatory in France—or anywhere.

TOURS, TOUR OPERATORS, TRAVEL AGENTS: Agents, first: Select one who is affiliated with the *American Society of Travel Agents* (ASTA) and, ideally, who knows France firsthand. For a first trip, some travelers are happy with a package; tour operators making a specialty of France—whose packages may be booked through travel agents— include (among many) *American Express, Auto Venture, Caravan Tours, Cortell Holidays, Extra Value Vacations, The French Experience, Globus-Gateway, International Weekends, Maupintour, Pan Am's Holiday Tours, Passport to France, Travcoa, Travel Time,* and *World of Oz.* In studying brochures, note *location* of hotels—in cities, you want to be *central*—not out in the boonies; places *actually visited* (not simply passed by, on the bus); *free time* at your disposal, especially in cities; and—in the case of meals—whether they're prix fixe or à la carte. An introductory package behind you, you're ready for return visits on your own—to where *you* want to go, at *your* speed.

WINES OF FRANCE, by Max Drechsler: Wine in France is, traditionally, a facet of daily living—the natural accompaniment to food. As such— except for rarefied vintages sought out by connoisseurs—it is not something to be reverenced with awe. It is true, of course, that some of France's wines are the greatest and most noble in the world. But it is by no means necessary to be an expert to enjoy drinking wine in the course of a French journey. Although some wines are drunk as aperitifs, by and large they augment and enhance meals. My maxim, while traveling in France—and my advice to you—is to be inquisitive and try, whenever possible, the regional wines, so often a part of experiencing the regional cuisine itself. There are hundreds of delightful wines encountered in the course of provincial wandering that are not ordinarily come upon in Paris. Discover them!

Always ask to see the wine list; read it over. You learn a lot from these carefully prepared compilations as you go from restaurant to restaurant. Conscientious restaurateurs—even in smaller places—give a great deal of thought, attention, and consideration to their wine lists. And lists of bigger restaurants are frequently publications deserving of far more careful reading than can usually be devoted to them in advance of a restaurant meal. If your interest in wine is such that you would like one of these lists, don't hesitate to ask, offering to pay for it if it appears to have been costly to produce.

As far back as the Middle Ages, the French recognized the need for legal controls to offer guarantees of origin and method of production. But it was not until 1935 that the government created the world's first comprehensive wine legislation. Termed *Appellation d'Origine Contrôlée* (A.O.C.), or Controlled Place of Origin, it covers every aspect of wine-making from soil and vine to bottle. Though not necessarily a guarantee of quality, A.O.C. regulations insure that the consumer knows what goes into the bottle he or she may purchase, where it came from, and how to identify it; there are some 400 A.O.C. wines. In addition, there are two categories of wines that meet less rigid classifications: *Vins Délimités de Qualité Supérieure* (V.D.Q.S.)—developed in 1945—and the even more recent *Vin de Pays*. Wines in these two last-mentioned categories are worth trying and can be very good value. There remains *vin de table*—not officially designated—made in vast quantities around the Mediterranean and often with little but its low price as a plus. In all events, it's the label that tells the story. Don't hesitate, in a restaurant of any quality, to ask to see several different bottles before making a decision; when in doubt, pose questions to the waiter, captain, or *sommelier*—the specialist wine-server (wearing a silver necklace containing a *tastevin*, or wine-tasting mini-cup), to be found in better spots. Invariably they're happy to be helpful. French table wines—reds and whites in quantity, fewer rosés—are usually dry, fruity, or flowery, but never sweet. Here's a breakdown by principal areas:

Alsace's wines are almost entirely white. Alsace (Chapters 15 and 35) is unique among French wine regions in that all of its wines are sold under the name of the grape from which they're made and with but one A.O.C. (Alsace), albeit broken down as *Riesling* (dry, clean taste, rich bouquet); *Gewürtztraminer* (spicy, fruity, pungent, with a flowery bouquet); *Sylvaner* (agreeable, fruity, and dry); and *Tokay* (not to be confused with the sweetish Hungarian Tokay, dry and full bodied).

Bordeaux (Chapter 10) has been a wine center since the beginning of the Christian era. It's regarded as the area of the planet that produces the greatest wines (although Burgundy partisans might quarrel with this). This southwestern region, dominated by the city of Bordeaux and bisected by the Garonne River, divides itself into sectors that have given their names to the various types of Bordeaux. The *four major areas* are *Graves, St.-Émilion, Médoc,* and *Pomerol;* from these come the most noted red and white table wines. A fifth, *Sauternes,* produces the most celebrated of the French sweet whites. There are two additional types of Bordeaux. One, named for an area called *Entre-Deux-Mers,* is a type of dry white wine. The last is *Bordeaux Rouge*—moderate-priced reds that come from throughout the Bordeaux area.

There are two broad types of bottled Bordeaux: château bottled and regional bottled. Château designates wine produced on the estate of a specific château or grower (a real castle may or may not be part of the grower's estate). *Château-bottled* wine is entirely a product of that vineyard—the grapes have been grown and tended there, then harvested and processed into wine, and finally bottled and labeled on the premises. Among the most expensive and famous are: Château Latour, Château Margaux, Château Lafite, and Château Mouton Rothschild, but there are 84, all told. *Regional-bottled* wine comes from a broader area rather than a single vineyard; they include Graves and St.-Émilion. Wines are taken to various shippers' cellars in the city of Bordeaux, processed, and bottled. Besides the name of the area of production on the label, that of the shipper is indicated (rather than the individual vintner or château owner-grower). Quality tends to be good—and consistent.

Bordeaux *reds* are usually firm and delicate, yet sturdy when young, and mellow and full bodied when mature. They grow better as they age—traditionally 10 years, sometimes sooner. At their best, they are subtle, with elegant flavor and brilliant color, the while being generous but neither heavy nor strong. Among the more important reds from the Left Bank of the Garonne River are Médoc, Haut Médoc, Moulis, Listrac, St.-Julien, St.-Estèphe, Pauillac (home of three of the five Premier Crus—or top rankers—Château Lafite, Château Latour, and Château Mouton Rothschild), Margaux (noted for Château Margaux), and Graves Rouges (noted for Château Haut-Brion). Important Right Bank reds include St.-Émilion, Pomerol (smallest of the leading Bordeaux districts), Fronsac, Côtes de Blaye, Côtes de Bourg, and Premières Côtes de Bordeaux.

Bordeaux *whites*—constituting about half the region's total output—include Graves, Entre-Deux-Mers, noted for light, crisp vintages; and —continuing south, where wines are less dry and more mellow—Premières Côtes de Bordeaux, Graves de Vayres, and St.-Macaire. The sweet Sauternes dessert wines (Château d'Yquem is the most noted) and those of Barsac are the most southerly; these last double as aperitif wines and go well with *foie gras frais*.

Burgundy (Chapters 8 and 17), southeast of Paris, produces some of the greatest of the world's wines, with its reds full, elegant, vigorous, big, and complex. Geographically, from north to south, it embraces *Chablis* (with France's most celebrated whites), *Côte d'Or* (divided into northerly *Côte de Nuits* and southerly *Côte de Beaune*), *Mâcon*, and *Beaujolais*. Originally attached to monasteries, the region's vineyards were secularized after the French Revolution and subdivided; the system of small owners prevails. In the Côte de Nuits, Côte d'Or area, they include Fixin, Gevrey-Chambertin (with eight Grand Cru vineyards), Morey St.-Denis (with four Grand Crus), Chambolle-Musigny, Clos Vougeot, Vosne-Romanée (with the ranking Romanée-Conti, La Tache, and Richebourg), and Nuits St.-Georges. Some of the best-known Côte de Beaune wines are Aloxe Corton (only Grand Cru of Côte de Beaune), Savigny, Pommard, Meursault, and Chassagne-Montrachet (lighter reds);

Santenay and Côte de Beaune-Villages. Mâcon produces some light reds but is known mainly for whites. Beaujolais, at Burgundy's southern tip, produces one of the best-known red wines—light and fruity and at its best when young and slightly cooled. Beaujolais Nouveau is drunk in the fall just after being made; the better Beaujolais include Brouilly, Chénas, Chiroubles, Côte de Brouilly, Fleurie, Morgon, and Moulin-à-Vent. Beaujolais is the favorite wine of Lyon (Chapter 21)—France's gastronomically reputed No. 2 city.

Best whites? Those of Chablis—crisp, fruity, extremely dry, with a refreshing acidity—embrace four categories: Petit Chablis (drunk young), Chablis (green-tinged, fruity), Chablis Premier Cru, and Grands Crus (with such labels as Blanchots, Les Preuses, and Valmur). Côte de Beaune ranking whites include Aloxe-Corton (Grand Cru Corton-Charlemagne), Meursault, Puligny-Montrachet, Bâtard-Montrachet, and Montrachet (considered one of the best dry whites extant). Mâcon whites—Mâcon, Mâcon Supérieur, Mâcon Villages, Pinot-Chardonnay-Mâcon—are invariably light, crisp, and good value. The best-known Mâcons are Pouilly-Fuissé (slightly green-tinged, very dry), Pouilly Vinzelles, and St.-Véran.

Champagne—from the region based in Reims (Chapter 2) that constitutes the most northerly of France's A.O.C. areas—produced still wines until, in the seventeenth century, a Benedictine monk (of course, you will have heard of Dom Perignon) began corking bottles, the better to keep the bubbles therein for an indefinite period. All Champagne is blended wine, and most of it is nonvintage. Each of the firms in the area has created its particular *cuvée*, or characteristic blend, and knowledgeable Champagne drinkers choose by the producer's name. Champagne may be called Champagne—in France, at least—only if it's from Champagne (otherwise, if made in the same manner, it is *vin mousseux*, created by the *méthode champenoise);* the French are sticky about this. According to how dry it is, it is categorized Brut (driest of the lot, and for most champagne drinkers the preferred type), Extra Dry (next to the driest, despite its always-in-English designation), Sec (medium sweet), Demi-Sec (even sweeter), and Doux (the sweetest). Champagne is the all-occasion wine, and Brut champagne is the one wine that is good served throughout a meal, with each and every course (omitting the salad, with which no wine is preferable). There are close to a score of top-rank Champagne firms, with Moët et Chandon, Mumm, Piper-Heidsieck, Taittinger, and Veuve Clicquot among the best known; all adhere to rigid standards set by Comité Interprofessionel du Vin de Champagne (C.I.V.C.).

Languedoc-Roussillon—the Mediterranean area around Montpellier (Chapter 24)—produces red, white, and rosé, but the best are reds—Corbières, Minervois, Côtes du Roussillon, Fitou, and Costières. There is an exceptional white—Clairette du Languedoc.

Loire Valley (Chapters 4 and 20) output includes white wines (both still and sparkling and accounting for three-quarters of the production), reds, and rosés. Better-known wines include such whites as Muscadet, Quincy, Sancerre, Saumur, Pouilly Fumé—clean, dry, crisp, and occasionally fresh and fruity; such sparkling whites as Vouvray and Saumur; such reds as Chinon, Bourgueil, Sancerre, and Saumur-Champigny; and two pleasant rosés: Rosé d'Anjou and Rosé de Cabernet.

Provence (Chapters 3, 6, 7, 22, and 27) provides a fascinating array of white, rosé, and red wines—with rosés especially celebrated and including Bandol (of which there are reds and whites, as well), Cassis (not to be confused with the black currant liqueur of Burgundy and a good white wine, as well), and Bellet (red and white, as well as rosé). Also worth trying (and not widely available beyond the area of production): Côtes de Provence, a red with rosé characteristics.

Southwest (Chapters 9, 28, 34, and 36): Beyond Bordeaux is a less famous wine region, but one that produces large quantities of very drinkable wines, especially well suited to the local cuisine. Reds include Bergerac, Côtes de Bergerac, Côtes de Duras, Pechermant, Madiran, and Cahors—the excellent "black" wine, so called because of its dark hue. Southwest whites of consequence include Montravel, Côtes de Haut-Montravel, Bergerac, Rosette, and Montbazillac—an excellent Sauternes-like, sweet wine, good with dessert.

Savoie and Jura (Chapters 5 and 14)—the Alpine regions: Savoie wines have the tang of their bracing environment. They are mainly whites, which can be excellent—such as Crépy and Seysel (both still and sparkling). Reds and rosés include Arbin and Cruet. Jura is famous for its *vin jaune*, or yellow wine; as well as Château-Chalon—reminiscent of sherry; L'Étoile—a sparkling white; and the sweet, highly alcoholic *vins de paille*, or straw wines.

Côtes du Rhône may well have been the very first region of France in which grapes were cultivated for wine, and production was spurred by the medieval popes' seat in Avignon (Chapter 7); indeed, the most famous Rhône red—Châteauneuf-du-Pape, the Pope's New Castle—celebrates the Provence papacy. That wine—strong and pungent—is the best known of the area's southern vineyards, along with Côtes du Rhône and Côtes du Rhône Villages (both red and white) and Tavel and Lirac (fine rosés). From the region's northern vineyards come Côte Rôtie (red, white, and rosé), Hermitage and St.-Joseph (red and white), Cornas (red), and Condrieu (white).

Cognac and Armagnac are the most noted of French brandies, which is to say, the best extant. Like Champagne—which may be so called only if from Champagne—Cognac may be so designated only if it is from the well-defined Cognac region, based on the little town of Cognac, north of Bordeaux. Cognac is made in traditional stills from Charentes wine and matured in oaken casks. There are several categories, designated by stars, and in the case of the finest, with initials VSOP for Very Special Old Pale. Armagnac comes from the Gascony region of the southwest around Auch (Chapter 36); like Cognac, it is protected by government controls. Best type is Bas-Armagnac. But all Armagnacs are made from distilled grapes by an ancient process that continues largely to ignore the machine. To experience it is to enjoy it. *Marc*, less known abroad, is a robust brandy, emanating principally from Burgundy and—somewhat more refined—from Champagne. It takes getting used to.

Eaux-de-Vie are highly distilled brandies made, by and large, from fruits of Alsatian orchards. They are clear and colorless and served icy cold as digestifs—after meals—with positively irresistible aromas redolent of the fruits from which they derive. Not unlike ice cream, they come in a variety of flavors, including framboise (raspberry), poire (pear), fraise (strawberry), mirabelle (plum), and kirsch (cherry).

Aperitif wines—nowhere better than in France—are worth becoming acquainted with, particularly if one is to follow the cocktail hour with a meal that will include wine and that may be followed by still additional variations on the alcoholic theme. It is not for nothing that Europeans prefer them to the transatlantic custom of more potent premeal cocktails. Best known is *vermouth*—excellent on the rocks with a twist of lemon. Popular, too, is *vermouth cassis*—the cassis being black currant syrup out of Burgundy. Noilly Prat, Boissière, and Martini are among the leading vermouth brands. (Note: *un Martini* means simply a glass of vermouth; *martini-gin* is what you ask for when you want a dry martini cocktail—and then only in better-category hotel bars accustomed to American and British tastes.) *Kir*—the most popular aperitif with the French—blends the earlier-mentioned cassis syrup with white wine; *Kir Royal*—esteemed by those French with higher drinks budgets—substitutes Champagne for the white wine. *Pastis* is the French national café drink—a Gallic variation of the Turks' raki and the Greeks' ouzo, anisette in flavor and so constituted that it turns cloudy when diluted with water; Pernod and Ricard are leading makes. *Dubonnet, Byrrh, St.-Raphaël,* and *Lillet* are aperitif wines of the vermouth family—sweetish but not cloyingly so, and good on the rocks and/or with soda.

Liqueurs: Orange-based *Grand Marnier*, widely exported, is known to many visitors in advance of arrival, as are *Bénédictine* and less-sweet *B & B*—brandy and Bénédictine combined; it emanates from the Norman town of Fécamp (Chapter 31). *Chartreuse*, which comes in two colors (green and yellow), is the only liqueur still made by monks (Chapter 18). Which leaves . . .

Bière: Foreigners are often surprised to learn that beer is popular with the French. Draft is cheaper than bottled; to order it, specify *à la pression*. Top brands, mostly out of Alsace, are Kronenbourg, Mutzig, Champigneulles, and Kanterbrau. Imports, too.

2

Paris
The Continent's Great Capital

BACKGROUND BRIEFING

The surprise of Paris is that it asks the visitor to meet it halfway. It presupposes a special kind of familiarity even though, as Continental Europe's premier city, it is by no means an unknown quantity. We grow up with Notre-Dame and the Eiffel Tower. Even the basic geography—division by the Seine into Right and Left banks—is a schoolchild commonplace. Many of us have studied the French language and acquired a taste for the masterful French style of cooking and of France's wines.

But once the basics of the usually abbreviated initial stay are completed, we are likely to say ho-hum and want to move right along, even though the encounter to date has been only with the tip of the iceberg. I very much suspect that Paris deserves a much better break than seven or eight out of ten transatlantic visitors afford it. This may or may not be because their orientation has been superficial, if not downright ooh-la-la stereotyped. Whatever, a few tightly scheduled days are not enough. Paris unravels only for the tourist who unwinds.

So often, the trouble with the visitor new to this city is that he or she knows so much less about it—and the country of which it is the capital—than he or she thinks. We know Jeanne d'Arc and Chanel No. 5 and Napoleon and the Folies-Bergère, of course. But we are hard put, without a little research, to distinguish between Louis XV and Louis XVI (the monarchs, not the furniture styles, although they can put us off, too). It has to do with our schools. We have been taught disproportionately much about Queen Victoria and Oliver Cromwell. We are sadly weak on, say, the Second Empire of Napoleon Bonaparte's nephew and on King François I, who rebuilt the oldest part of the ancient Louvre to use as his palace.

All those Merovingians and Carolingians and Capetians: Is it because Shakespeare didn't get around to writing plays about the French dynasties that they remain mostly beyond our pale? The only fairly early sovereign of whom we have some knowledge is Mary Queen of Scots, although I suspect many fewer of us realize that she was a Queen of France and married her first husband in Notre-Dame-de-Paris, than that she was imprisoned the second half of her life by Elizabeth I in a series of drafty English castles.

It is entirely possible to have the holiday of a lifetime in Paris without the faintest idea of what transpired before Charles de Gaulle. But not every country can also boast a King Clodion the Hairy (so called because he ordered his Frankish subjects to wear their hair long) or a Queen Clotilda (who was sainted because she converted her husband—King Clovis, the sovereign who designated Paris as France's capital—to Christianity) or a King Pepin the Short (his son was Charlemagne) or a King Charles the Fat or sovereigns of such distinctive dispositions that they are remembered as Louis the Quarreler and Charles the Affable.

THE PARIS BEFORE CHRIST

Early Paris goes back to the century before Christ, when Caesar conquered it and its residents—a tribe called the *Parisii*, whose name gradually replaced the earlier Lutetia. But before that happened, Lutetia, with its Seine location, became the tie-up point for ships sailing past, toward Rouen, which it gradually passed in importance, thanks to the ingenuity of transplanted Romans, who cleared its swampy environs. These same Romans built a temple to their deities on Île de la Cité, and later the area developed as the town center. But in 451, Attila's Huns might well have taken the town had not a young woman named Geneviève inspired the people to resist, to the point where the Huns were driven away, and the young heroine of the battle is the same Ste.-Geneviève who has been the patron saint of Paris down through the centuries.

Charlemagne, who in 800 went to Rome to be crowned the first Holy Roman Emperor by Pope Leo III, is known as a military-minded monarch and as a much-married one. (He does not quite measure up to England's Henry VIII, but four wives is a record not to be lightly dismissed.) Between spouses and battles, Charlemagne made Paris a seat of learning to be reckoned with.

At the end of the tenth century, with the start of King Hugh Capet's Capetian dynasty, Paris had become a handsome, substantial city. Hugh Capet and his successors made it even more so. This was the era of the founding of the University of Paris, the paving of streets, the founding of a police force, the first city wall, and substantial progress in the building of Notre-Dame by another very military and much-married monarch, Philip Augustus.

Louis IX—later to become St. Louis—embellished Paris with the exquisite Ste.-Chapelle, and by the time Philip the Fair added even more to its beauty, Paris had become the biggest and richest of medieval cities. Albertus Magnus and St. Thomas More contributed theological eminence to the Sorbonne's already established industrial reputation. The rich merchants and guilds set up their own municipal government, with their provosts on an equal footing with the provost of Paris, who was the King's own man.

JEANNE D'ARC AND THE RENAISSANCE

The Hundred Years War—that near-interminable series of struggles waged by the French to drive the English from their shores—saw the burning of Jeanne d'Arc at the stake two years after her unsuccessful siege of Paris, an English-occupied Paris in which the English Henry VI had been crowned king in Notre-Dame. The Renaissance came in with a bang with François I, who substantially rebuilt the Louvre, founded the Collège de France, started the first royal printing press, and set the stage for continued royal patronage of architecture and the fine arts, as well.

Under Louis XIII, Cardinal Richelieu made Paris the intellectual, as well as the political center, of Europe. The succeeding Louis—the Fourteenth—began his reign in 1643 and moved his court to the palace he built at suburban Versailles, a palace that was to be copied by monarchs all over Europe for the next two centuries.

Louis XIV reigned an astonishingly long time—72 years. It was a period of tremendous cultural, political, and military accomplishment for France. It was, after all, Louis XIV who stated—apocryphally, if not in fact—"L'état, c'est moi" ("I am the state"). The move to Versailles benefited Parisian industry immeasurably; indeed, it was from that period that Paris became a world center for luxury goods, which it remains to this day. Architects like Mansart, under Louis XIV, and Soufflot, under Louis XV, created works that added to the splendor of Paris. This was the period, too, of the plays of Molière and Racine, of scientists like Lavoisier and Buffon, of brilliant salons, of Gluck operas, and of powdered wigs.

"L'ÉTAT, C'EST MOI"—AND THE REVOLUTION

But the poor were getting poorer. If isolating his courtiers from his people was politically expedient for Louis XIV, it was also the beginning of the estrangement of the sovereign from the people. The succeeding reigns of Louis XV and Louis XVI culminated in the Revolution. Mobs forced the Royal Family from Versailles to Paris and stormed the Bastille. One may still visit the cell in the gloomy Conciergerie in which Marie-Antoinette, the excessively extravagant Austrian-born wife of Louis XVI, lived just before being guillotined at a public execution on what is now Place de la Concorde.

Paris was a turbulent city in the years that followed. The Reign of Terror, as the Revolutionary period was called, was followed by the First Republic, proclaimed in 1792. In 1795, the stormy Directory began its rule. There was a sweeping change in matters esthetic—from the elaborate Louis XIV, Louis XV, and Louis XVI decors of the monarchy to a neo-classic simplicity in architecture, furniture, and even clothes, with women in severe high-waisted dresses and men—the *incroyables*, or "unbelievables"—in tight trousers.

Politically, the severity was equally *incroyable*. The Directory was bankrupt, and its personnel were at such odds with each other and so intrigue-laden that, on November 9, 1799—a fateful day in French history—a bright young Corsican army officer, who had distinguished himself in foreign engagements, played a major role in a *coup d'état*.

THE CORSICAN NAMED BONAPARTE

The Consulate had replaced the Directory. It was actually a dictatorship, with the Corsican Bonaparte the No. 1 of the three consuls. In 1802, he was made first consul "for life." In 1804, we are back in historic Notre-Dame for the coronation of Emperor Napoleon I. As he set about conquering Europe and brilliantly reforming French domestic institutions, he found time to begin the Arc de Triomphe and to erect the Arc du Carrousel in the Tuileries, the arcaded Rue de Rivoli, and the splendid column in the Place Vendôme. Most important, he expanded the collection of the recently founded Louvre with loot that his troops had gathered in military campaigns. Those artistic spoils had to be returned to their rightful owners after the Congress of Vienna in 1815, but no matter. The concept of great public museums had been popularized. The Congress of Vienna was, of course, the aftermath of Napoleon's earlier and final defeat by Wellington at the Battle of Waterloo.

LITTLE-KNOWN KINGS AND LOUIS-PHILIPPE

The Bourbon dynasty restored itself rather briefly after Napoleon's exile, in the persons of two monarchs we hear little about these days—Louis XVIII and Charles X. (Louis XVII, if you are wondering, was the son of Louis XVI and died in prison at the age of ten in 1795.) Charles X was forced, as a result of the so-called July Revolution, to abdicate in 1830, and in came Louis-Philippe, who was proclaimed King, in a rather complex run of affairs, by the National Assembly. His "July Monarchy" (called after the revolution that brought him to the throne) was a big-business reign. He even dressed like a businessman, walking the boulevards, umbrella in hand. He had no comprehension of the working class's plight, though, and was attacked from both right and left.

All the same, France prospered materially (the Arc de Triomphe was completed), and the romantic movement flowered. Victor Hugo made his reputation as a writer. Delacroix painted. Berlioz composed. Still, Louis-Philippe went out as had Charles X before him, by abdicating. The Second Republic followed—but only for four years. Louis Bonaparte (an ambitious nephew of Napoleon Bonaparte), who had been elected President, managed to get his title changed. In 1852, he was proclaimed Napoleon III, although he was also known as Louis Napoleon. (Napoleon II, Bonaparte's son, was better known as the King of Rome; he never reigned and died at the age of 21 at Schoenbrunn Palace, Vienna.)

THE LATER NAPOLEON—AND HAUSSMANN

The 18-year reign of Napoleon III (who was emperor for precisely as long as Louis-Philippe was king) proved a significant period for Paris. The emperor appointed Baron Eugène Haussmann to convert Paris into a modern city. With the authority of the imperial command behind him, Haussmann was ruthless in the changes he made. Indeed, there are students of art, architecture, and town planning who still have not forgiven him. In order to build the wide arterial boulevards and the great squares that typify Paris today, he had to destroy much that dated back to medieval times. Notre-Dame, for example, was fronted by a cluster of venerable houses, all of which were razed to make way for the broad open space that Haussmann considered an improvement. Much of the facade of the Paris we are so accustomed to today—the grandiose Opéra is a prime example—dates from the Second Empire.

That epoch came to a dreary culmination with the siege of Paris, which was a consequence of the Franco-Prussian War, and the Commune of Paris. The Third Republic saw recovery. Paris escaped damage during World War I, after which the victorious Allies met in the palace that Louis XIV had built in Versailles. They imposed harsh terms on the vanquished Germans, who—never forgiving—invaded Paris and the rest of France in 1940.

THE TWO WORLD WARS—AND DE GAULLE

The government temporarily left the capital for the thermal resort of Vichy, where the guiding Pétain regime was a German puppet until 1944. That was when Paris was liberated by France's own remarkable resistance force. American forces entered the city thereafter, and the city—though austere and hungry in the early days of peace—quickly regained its brilliance.

The postwar years saw Charles de Gaulle as President in 1945 and 1946 and later from 1958 to 1969 under a new, strong-executive constitution. France voluntarily relinquished its vast Black African empire, as well as Tunisia and Morocco, and eventually—after much blood was shed—Algeria. The great student-worker uprisings of 1968 alerted France to the need to update its institutions even more rapidly than they already had. Under de Gaulle's successors, Georges Pompidou, Valéry Giscard d'Estaing, and François Mitterrand, it has been happening. Beyond central Paris in the industrial suburbs and in the cities of the provinces, France has come to terms with the technology of the late twentieth century (so much so that there are those who fear that proliferating skyscrapers may damage the traditional skyline of central Paris). But it is not necessarily wisdom, in a country with so great a past, to make arbitrary breaks with such a rich tradition. France is not moving recklessly—which is as it should be. One hopes that at least another century will elapse before another Baron Haussmann bulldozes his way through this still supremely beautiful capital.

ON SCENE
Lay of the Land: No great city is easier to find one's way about in than Paris. We may regret that Baron Haussmann destroyed much of medieval Paris when Napoleon III commissioned him to redesign Paris—with the installation of the wide boulevards and great squares—a little over a century ago. But there is no gainsaying that Haussmann's Paris is sensible and practical—and supremely walkable, despite its considerable size. Let me try to orient you by delineating what I consider the thoroughfares and landmarks that are essential to a basic geographical understanding of Paris.

Start with the *Rive Droite* (Right Bank) circle that was for long *Place de l'Étoile* but is now officially *Place Charles-de-Gaulle*. (Like New York's Avenue of the Americas—still Sixth Avenue to natives—Place Charles de Gaulle remains "Étoile" to those who have so known it.) No less than 12 streets radiate from the Étoile (thus the name *étoile*—star), whose landmark is the Arc de Triomphe. The most important of these is the *Avenue des Champs-Élysées*—the broad, café-cinema-boutique-auto-showroom boulevard that leads directly into the square that is the most beautiful in the world and the most difficult to negotiate in traffic, *Place de la Concorde*. Continue around Concorde, and you are in the heart-of-Paris park that is *Jardin des Tuileries*, with *Palais du Louvre*—the onetime royal residence turned museum. Tuileries and Louvre are bordered on the south by the *Seine River* and on the north by arcaded *Rue de Rivoli*.

One may leave this Concorde-Tuileries-Louvre area for *Place de l'Opéra*—heart of the Right Bank—by any one of three routes. *The first:* From the Concorde, take Rue Royale directly north to the Parthenon-like *Church of the Madeleine*, turn right at the Madeleine on the *Grands Boulevards* (comprising Boulevards de la Madeleine, des Capucines, and des Italiens—one street with three successive names). Walk, then, for a few blocks to Place de l'Opéra and the opera house for which it is named. *Two:* Walk from Rue de Rivoli, bordering the Tuileries, onto short, albeit shop-lined, *Rue de Castiglione,* and a couple of moments later emerge into extraordinarily beautiful *Place Vendôme,* easily identifiable because of the column in the center—erected by Napoleon and with a statue of none other than himself at its summit. Pass through Vendôme to celebrated *Rue de la Paix,* and within a few moments you have reached the Opéra by a second route. *Three:* Continue walking down Rue de Rivoli, bordering the Louvre, until reaching broad *Avenue de l'Opéra.* Turn left on that thoroughfare, walking north to the Opéra at its far end.

Now to the *Rive Gauche* (Left Bank) via the greatest landmark of them all, *Notre-Dame,* which is situated on an island—*Île de la Cité*—in the Seine. Return to the Louvre-flanking Rue de Rivoli. Pass Avenue de l'Opéra and continue east on Rivoli, beyond the entrance to the *Palais Royal,* until you reach *Rue du Pont-Neuf.* Turn right here; this street leads directly onto the famous bridge for which it is named. Over the bridge and there you are: on Île de la Cité, with twin towers of Notre-Dame just beyond. An even smaller island, *Île St.-Louis,* is directly to the rear of Notre-Dame, gained by little *Pont St.-Louis.* But you want to continue from Île de la Cité to the Left Bank. The most direct way is to proceed via the same Pont Neuf you took from the Right Bank to the island; it continues in the Left Bank.

Or, if you would rather orient yourself on main thoroughfares, go this way: After arriving on Île de la Cité, walk toward Notre-Dame to the first broad thoroughfare you hit. It will be *Boulevard du Palais.* Turn right, across narrow *Pont St.-Michel,* and voilà! Boulevard du Palais has changed names to become *Boulevard St.-Michel*—a principal Left Bank street. Spires of *Ste.-Chapelle*—another landmark—are to your right. But continue south on Boulevard St.-Michel—"Boule Meesh"—to the first principal cross-street. This will be *Boulevard St.-Germain.* Turn right on it, and you are in the core of *Quartier Latin,* with the landmark *St.-Germain-des-Prés Church,* shops, and cafés nearby. If you like, you may return to the *Right Bank* in roughly circular fashion. Continue along Boulevard St.-Germain, past St.-Germain-des-Prés, following the boulevard's curves. Before long, you will reach *Palais-Bourbon,* the colonnaded neoclassic landmark that is the National Assembly, facing the Seine, and the bridge that is *Pont de la Concorde.*

Before crossing, look up to your left at the Eiffel Tower. Make a note of it at this point, so you will realize its Left Bank situation. Behind it is the broad green called *Champ-de-Mars,* at whose other extremity is the *École Militaire,* or Military Academy. Still another Left Bank landmark—not at all far from where you are standing at Pont de la Concorde—is the complex of the *Hôtel des Invalides,* with the domed church where Napoleon is buried. Back you go now to the Right Bank—over Pont de la Concorde to familiar Place de la Concorde.

CHOICE DESTINATIONS, OR THE ESSENTIAL PARIS

Notre-Dame and the river islands: Notre-Dame, along with Westminster Abbey in London and St. Peter's in Rome, is the church we grew up with. It is part of our life—from history-book illustrations and travel posters and old movies—long before we ever see it. And when we do, it does not disappoint. Begun in the mid-twelfth century, it was not completed until the mid-thirteenth. It is one of the great Gothic cathedrals of Europe—conveniently placed smack in the heart of one of the great capitals—with its twin bell towers (you may climb up, as did Victor Hugo's hunchbacked *jongleur*, Quasimodo), its trio of arched portals, its exquisite rose window, its famed flying buttresses along the sides, and its needle-like spire over the transept. The apse, or altar area, behind the choir is perhaps the loveliest part of the always-crowded interior. The time to go—regardless of one's religious faith—is on Sunday for the 10:00 A.M. High Mass. Visitors from everywhere join Parisians in the packed pews. Celebrants of the Mass swing incense lamps from the high altar. The white-robed children's choir sings beautifully, organ music is richly sonorous, and Japanese tourists record it all with ever-clicking cameras. Outside, take note of two other visitable destinations: *Musée de Notre-Dame-de-Paris* (10 Rue du Cloître Notre-Dame)—crammed with paintings, prints, reliquaries, and historic documents associated with the cathedral; and *Crypte Archéologique de Notre-Dame*, entered by a not-easy-to-locate stairway on Place du Parvis, in front of the cathedral, which leads to a series of remarkable underground spaces, some dating to Roman-era Paris, others medieval.

The island in the Seine on which Notre-Dame is located—Île de la Cité—is the core of Paris, historically as well as spiritually, and has been from medieval times onward. It was only about a century ago that Napoleon III's Baron Haussmann removed the maze of house-lined streets from the front of the cathedral and otherwise altered the island, evacuating thousands from their ancient homes. The island's other principal monuments are the Conciergerie and its Ste.-Chapelle church, dealt with in later pages. Suffice it to say at this point that Île de la Cité is explorable walking territory, as is its smaller neighbor island, St.-Louis—essentially a Renaissance quarter, whose quiet streets are lined with graceful houses of that architecturally rich epoch.

Musée National du Louvre (Jardin des Tuileries) is synonymous with the history of France—or at least much of it, since medieval times. It began as a crenelated fortress punctuated by a maze of circular towers in the early thirteenth century. Charles V, a hundred years later, converted it into what was essentially a palace; he was its last royal tenant until the early sixteenth century, when François I set about knocking down towers and turrets and building a Renaissance palace. Catherine de Medicis expanded the complex with the construction of an adjacent Tuileries Palace and the formal gardens which remain a joy of Paris. Monarchs remained in residence through Louis XIV, who replaced the royal seat in Paris with his new suburban palace of Versailles. As the Revolution approached, the rundown palace was rehabilitated, and Louis XVI used it concurrently with Versailles. Indeed, it was from the Tuileries that he was arrested by the revolutionary mob in 1792. Decades later, Napoleon began a much-needed post-Revolution restoration, and his Bourbon successors—Louis XVIII and Charles X, not to mention the later Louis-Philippe and Napoleon III—all made contributions, for better or for worse, with still others to follow (as recently as those of President François Mitterrand) for a subterranean entrance in Cour Napoléon, excavations for which unearthed foundations of a twelfth-century fortress built by King Philippe Auguste and the fourteenth-century palace of Charles V.

The museum aspect of the Louvre dates to the same François I who razed the old Louvre and started the building of the new. His collection of a handful of old masters was the nucleus of the royal collection, which never stopped expanding through all of the later Louis—XIII to Louis-Philippe—beyond to Napoleon I. There are larger museums (the Hermitage in Leningrad has some two million objects), but the Louvre's 400,000-plus are of such exceptional quality that the museum, even setting aside its magnificent house, is one of the handful of the world's greats.

What most interests visitors are the fine arts collections. Leonardo's *Mona Lisa*—a part of François I's small but choice collection—is the Louvre's global trademark. But consider Fra Angelico's *Coronation of the Virgin*, the Raphael *Madonna* and her chubby *Christ*, Titian's much reproduced *Man with Glove*, Vermeer's lovely *Lace Maker*, and works by France's Ingres, David, Delacroix, and Corot. Sculpture is a Louvre specialty: *Winged Victory of Samothrace* and *Vénus de Milo*, both of classical Greece, but masterworks, as well, from medieval and Renaissance Europe—Michelangelo's *Slave*, Goujon's *Diana of Anet*, and an unknown Tuscan genius's wood-carved and painted blond head of a beautiful young lady of the fifteenth century. Get away from the heavily trafficked paintings and sculptures, and other departments of the vast Louvre are relatively quiet. Would that they made replicas of the mummylike pottery figure colored a strong blue, with black trim—or, for that matter, Coptic textiles that go back to the fifth century, in the Egyptian galleries. Also away from the crowds are a series of rooms full of the furniture and objets d'art of the periods Louis XIII, Louis XIV, Louis XV, Louis XVI (with treasures of the extravagant queen, Marie-Antoinette), Napoleon, the Directory, and the Restoration era of Louis XVIII and Charles X. An entire chamber is pure Napoleon—with his throne from St.-Cloud and his incredibly elaborate toilet kit, or *nécessaire*, and the majestic cradle of his son, the King of Rome. There is a rolltop desk that was Marie-Antoinette's, a bed with a red and white velvet canopy slept in by a marshal of Louis XIII, masterful Louis XV chairs, tapestries and tables, carpets and cupboards. Beyond are applied arts of the medieval and Renaissance eras. I have hit only some personal highlights; there are, after all, more than a couple of hundred galleries, and you will want to formulate your own plan of attack, ideally dividing it into several separate sessions. There's an enormous shop and a cafeteria.

Tour Eiffel (Quai Branly): The Eiffel Tower was completed in 1889, is nearly a thousand feet high, weighs some 7,000 tons, was almost razed in 1909, has three observation levels and, when reproduced in miniature, continues year after year as the most popular Paris souvenir. (I was given this rather sad intelligence by the Galeries Lafayette department store.) The level of the tower to head for is the top one, from whose platform—nearly 900 feet heavenwards—given a clear day, one can see for many miles. Even in winter, when the top level can be closed, the views are hardly to be despised, from the lower platforms, No. 2 at under 400 feet, No. 1 about half that high. There is, of course, an elevator, but if you want to shed some weight, you may walk; there are 1,652 steps to the summit.

Arc de Triomphe (Place Charles-de-Gaulle/Étoile) was begun by Napoleon I and finished by Louis-Philippe. Baron Haussmann, whom Napoleon III commissioned to make drastic changes in the city, added nine to the three existing avenues that lead from the Place Charles-de-Gaulle/Étoile—of which the arch is the centerpiece—making the total a magnificent, if rather confusing, 12 traffic arteries leading from the circle. (The chief of these is, of course, Champs-Élysées, which extends from the arch to Place de la Concorde; going in the opposite direction from the arch, it becomes Avenue de la Grande-Armée. The remaining 11 avenues radiating from L'Étoile are a blend of residences, shops, restaurants, and cafés, the lot comprising one of the most fashionable quarters of Paris.) There's a little museum relating to the monument upstairs in the arch, whose major attribute is the fine vista it affords (in many ways better than the one from the Eiffel Tower). It's fun being up there above the traffic.

Les Invalides (Rue de Grenelle): If you are wondering why Napoleon is buried in a place called Les Invalides, it is because the church with his tomb is but a part of an enormous veterans' hospital—probably the world's first—built by Louis XIV and with a 7,000-patient capacity, of which not a handful remains today. (Charles II's also-big Chelsea Royal Hospital went up contemporarily in London.) Les Invalides, today, embraces a pair of churches and a trio of museums. *Musée de l'Armée,* largest of the three, constitutes one of the world's major collections of arms, from the medieval period onward. *Musée de l'Ordre National de la Libération* tells the story of World War II anti-Nazi Resistance forces, and is not unlike similarly commendable museums in Copenhagen and Oslo, not to mention others throughout France. *Musée des Deux Guerres Mondiales's* exhibits relate to both world wars. The relatively uncelebrated *Church of St.-Louis-des-Invalides* is severe. In its chapel is the carriage on which Napoleon's remains started their long journey from the exile-island of St. Helena to the next-door *Church of the Dome*, where they repose under a topheavy cupola in an ambience at once overblown, graceless, and ostentatious.

Place Vendôme is an almost completely enclosed square that is the work of a single architect—Hardouin-Mansart. It has but two entrances, one on Rue St.-Honoré, the other on Rue de Castiglione. The shape is square, but with the charm of chopped-off corners. Palaces of the square are all early eighteenth century; one is now the Ritz Hôtel, and its next-door neighbor—with a near identical facade—is the Ministry of Justice. The towering column in the center is a shaft of stone decorated with a spiral of bronze that is a souvenir of the Battle of Austerlitz. It was erected by that battle's victor, Napoleon, with a statue of none other than himself atop it. This is rather a pity because the Bonaparte likeness replaces an earlier statue of Louis XIV, the original builder of the sublimely beautiful square to which not a few visitors make return pilgrimages within moments of arrival in Paris.

Place de la Concorde: Thank Louis XV for Place de la Concorde; it was begun during his reign and named for him—until Revolutionists tore down the central statue of him, called the square for their insurrection, and proceeded to set up their guillotine in its midst. When you try to cross today, as hundreds of cars block your way, think of earlier days. Louis XVI, his queen, Marie-Antoinette, and Madame Du Barry—successor to Madame Pompadour as mistress to Louis XV—were among those whose heads were chopped off in this beautiful spot. Indeed, the reputation of Place de la Révolution was so bloody that the Directory, when it took over the government, gave it its present name. The square, with its myriad of black wrought-iron lampposts, an Egyptian obelisk more than 3,000 years old as a centerpiece, a pair of fountains, and eight statues dedicated to as many French cities, is fronted on the river side by the bridge that takes its name. On the opposite side are twin structures, each a part of the original eighteenth-century design of the square. The palace on your left as you look inward from the Seine is Hôtel de Crillon, while the twin palace to the right is the Navy Ministry. Directly to the left of the Crillon, but not directly on the square, is the newer, albeit classic-style, American Embassy; like its counterparts in virtually every capital around the world that I have visited, it has one of the most enviable locations in town. In this case it has views of the Concorde, the Tuileries, and the Seine from its front windows; to the rear and a hop and a skip away is Palais de l'Élysée, official residence of the President, not to mention the house in which the U.S. envoy resides, as distinct from the main Embassy building, known as the Chancellery. But I have not quite finished with Place de la Concorde. As if views, toward and away from the Seine, are not enough, the other two are quite as spectacular—one looking way beyond, up the wide Champs-Élysées to Place Charles de Gaulle and the Arc de Triomphe, and the other toward the formal gardens of the Tuileries and the little *Arc du Carrousel,* a kind of mini-Triomphe that is—you will see for yourself when you look from one to the other—perfectly aligned with the Arc de Triomphe.

Théâtre de l'Opéra (Place de l'Opéra) is the great neo-Baroque structure that dominates the square that takes its name. The work of the same Charles Garnier who designed the similar but smaller theater in the Casino of Monte-Carlo (Chapter 23), the Opéra is remarkable in that its red and gold auditorium is but a small part of its interior. There is an enormous backstage area (decades ahead of its time) and a promenade area above the grand staircase that must have been a perfect foil for Second Empire audiences. Even with today's relatively casual audiences, the Promenade Salon and its adjacent refreshment rooms are quite the classiest of any theater in Europe.

Musée National des Thermes et de l'Hôtel de Cluny (6 Place Paul-Painlevé): The Cluny is, along with the Louvre, the most Parisian of museums, embracing both Roman-era and Medieval-era Paris. Its building is part Gallo-Roman baths, part Middle Ages monastery. You see the immense, high-ceilinged and extravagantly arched Frigidarium—Roman-built in the second century. And you visit, as well, the later monks' chapel and a couple of dozen additional chambers rich with medieval art, the most noted piece of which is the *Dame à la Licorne* tapestry. Take your time as you go through, noting sculpture and stained glass, altars and paintings, and exquisitely detailed rooms of the period, the brilliantly vaulted chapel—dating to 1500—most especially.

Place des Vosges is the most celebrated treasure of the Renaissance-era Marais district, the Right Bank area near Place de la Bastille that has recovered from a long period of neglect and is the subject of additional comment on later pages. Henri IV had the square built in the early seventeenth century. Houses surrounding it are of basically uniform design. No. 6 is where Victor Hugo lived and is now a Hugo museum. But the Place des Vosges is at its nicest on a sunny day in spring, when the old trees have their new leaves, and you have time to sit back on one of the benches and relax with the neighborhood locals—early enough in the day so that the kids are still in school, and this remarkably unspoiled, authentically Parisian antique is still quiet enough to savor and be grateful for.

Montmartre, way up in a detached area of town in the shadow of Sacré-Coeur, is the romanticists' Paris. No visitor who knows Utrillo's paintings will rest until he or she has had a walk through it. Montmartre, even today, is hilly, narrow streets, with very paintable old houses, funny little squares, and broad vistas. Remove the blinking signs and the mod clothing, and Utrillo could go right back to work. What I suggest you do is take the Métro up to *Place Pigalle,* or a nearby stop, and amble about. You will take the funicular up in that absurdly designed old chestnut of a landmark, Sacré-Coeur (see Ecclesiastical Paris, on later pages of this chapter), and after taking in the view of the town from its terrace, you'll walk over to still-charming *Place du Tertre,* pop your head into lovely old *St.-Pierre-de-Montmartre* (see Ecclesiastical Paris), look at the delicious food shops of *Rue Lépic,* lunch in a local restaurant, work your way down the steep streets to *Place des Abbesses,* gradually gaining broad *Boulevard de Clichy* and Place Pigalle. Memories of such past Montmartre folk heroes as Toulouse-Lautrec and the people he immortalized in his paintings—like Yvette Guilbert, Jane Avril, and La Goulue— die hard. Still, it is to Montmartre's credit that, even though its artistic greats have long since departed, the charm remains.

HISTORIC PARIS

Bridging the Seine: By my count, the river that flows through Paris is crossed by some 30 bridges—representing a mix of the city's epochs. Most significant: *Pont Alexandre III,* my favorite—with wrought-iron lampposts evoking its Second Empire origin—traverses the Seine at the point where Grand and Petit palaces face Les Invalides. *Pont Neuf,* way to the east, is the oldest bridge—early seventeenth century. It's the first bridge on Île de la Cité, as you approach from the west, and is worth crossing slowly to savor the views—in all directions. *Pont de la Concorde,* joining Place de la Concorde with the Left Bank frontage of Assemblée Nationale, is eighteenth-century and rewards with memorable vistas. *Pont d'Iéna* links the Eiffel Tower on the Left Bank with Palais de Chaillot on the Right; sightseeing boats depart from its Left Bank extremity. *Pont de Grenelle,* noteworthy for its miniature Statue of Liberty, a thank-you in kind from New York City to the French in appreciation of the French gift of the original Miss Liberty, is west of Palais de Chaillot, near the circular O.R.T.F. building—headquarters of French TV. *Pont Marie,* way east, makes for a pleasant approach—amidships, so to speak—to Île St.-Louis, when you come from the Right Bank. To gain the Left Bank, the bridge continues, renamed *Pont de la Tournelle.*

Château de Vincennes: Take the Métro often enough and the names of the lines—bearing the destination at either end—become familiar to you. One that had long intrigued me was Neuilly-Vincennes. I knew Neuilly—a suburb to the north of the Bois de Boulogne. And, on a recent visit, I took the Métro all the way in the opposite direction to Bois de Vincennes (see Verdant Paris, on a later page) and the château for which it is named. The castle is the only medieval royal palace in the Paris area. It goes back to the fourteenth century, so that there is no question but that it is respectable. What it is not is beautiful. The most impressive of the remaining structures is the Dungeon, a gawky medieval skyscraper that had known royal tenants, then took to boarding the more respectable of the kingdom's prisoners, with the nastier of the lot reserved for the Bastille. The interior is what might be termed Grim Gothic, not terribly unlike much vaster chambers of the Conciergerie. Opposite the Dungeon and in great contrast to it is a church with a lovely, lacy Gothic exterior, Ste.-Chapelle. Its interior is in somber contrast, for it is completely without furnishings. The other principal buildings are the newer, Renaissance-era King's and Queen's pavilions, partially restored from earlier desecrations. Someday—not too long off, one hopes—enough skilled restoration of the entire Vincennes Château complex will have been achieved so that we will have a less depressing, fuller, more joyous, and more lifelike idea of what the medieval royal courts of France were all about.

Conciergerie (Quai de l'Horloge)—the vast Île de la Cité palace with its matchless round towers themselves a Paris landmark—is the one ancient building in Paris, with which I am familiar, at least, that is more interesting outside than within. Guides take groups through darkish, depressing spaces of cavernous size, the only exception being the simple little cell—now a chapel—where Marie-Antoinette lived before she was carted to her death on Place de la Concorde. She was by no means the only prisoner of the Revolution. The old Conciergerie—originally a part of the royal palace when kings lived on Île de la Cité and named for the palace caretaker—had served as a prison before the Revolution and was pressed into service for that purpose during the Terror. More than 2,500 enemies of the Revolution were incarcerated in its Gothic depths, most passing from there to the Tribunal, which heard their cases and then sent most to their execution. Of the Conciergerie's toured chambers, the Men-at-Arms' Hall is the least depressing. There are, as well, an enormous kitchen, guards' quarters, and courtyards of both men and women prisoners. The place served as a prison long after the Revolution for a succession of monarchs—the murderer of a nephew of Louis XVIII, a pesky bomber of the Louis-Philippe era, and still another, who attempted to take Napoleon III's life. Cheery place, this. Adjoining it is *Palais de Justice*, all of whose law courts (save Juvenile and Divorce) are open to the public. This massive maze embraces a variety of epochs, much eighteenth and nineteenth century, some considerably older. There are gowned, briefcase-bearing, scurrying *avocats* all about, to liven the place up. And there is the treasure of the complex that is the *Ste.-Chapelle*, dealt with on a later page.

Le Marais: We are creatures of habit, even in strange cities. Take Rue de Rivoli. We walk it, and upon return visits rewalk it, but only between Place de la Concorde, where it begins, and as far in the other direction as theater-flanked Place du Châtelet, where we invariably turn toward the Seine, Notre-Dame, and the Rive Gauche. By staying right on Rivoli, though, walking past the landmark ruin that is Tour St.-Jacques and the marvelously neo-Gothic Hôtel de Ville, Paris's City Hall, we come to the beginnings of the Marais, the heart of fashionable Paris in medieval and Renaissance times.

Toward the end of the sixteenth century, aristocrats put up grand mansions—*hôtels particuliers*, as they still are called—which became the prototype of the French townhouse, in an area which had long been a center of artisanship and commerce. But, after a century, the smart set gravitated toward the other side of the river. The posh Marais once again became the artisans' Marais. Esthetics of the great houses were forgotten by shopkeepers and craftsmen, who altered them for their own purposes.

After World War II, a civic group that translates as the Association for the Preservation and Enhancement of Historical Paris went to work to right matters. Legislation was enacted to encourage rehabilitation. Upwardly mobile Parisians have moved into the old houses. Nonprofit organizations lease others. Specially trained guide-scholars—*conférenciers*, as they are called—offer visitors detailed commentaries. *Hôtel de Sully*, an early seventeenth-century masterwork with a courtyard through which you may pass right into Place des Vosges, has some beautifully restored interiors.

Hôtel de Marle (11 Rue Payenne) is also easy of access, at least on afternoons; it houses the Swedish Cultural Center. *Théâtre Sylvia Montfort* occupies an immense old palace—modernized, to be sure—at 8 Rue de Thorigny. There are two Marais churches of special interest. Both have double names. They are *St.-Gervais–St.-Protais* (Place St.-Gervais) and *St.-Paul–St.-Louis* (90 Rue St.-Antoine). Three Marais houses shelter museums and are included in the Museums section, following: *Hôtel Carnavalet* (23 Rue de Sévigné), *Hôtel de Soubise* (60 Rue des Francs-Bourgeois), and *Hôtel de Guénégaud* (60 Rue des Archives).

Palais-Royal is a tranquil oasis of striking beauty smack in the heart of town—at the Louvre-Tuileries end of Avenue de l'Opéra, next to the Comédie-Française. Originally built by Louis XIII's prime minister, Cardinal Richelieu, the palais was actually royal for only two brief periods—when Louis XIV lived in it as a youthful monarch and later when it was inhabited by Philippe II of Orléans, Regent of France during the minority of Louis XV. Palais-Royal looks today much as it did in the late eighteenth century, when it was converted from a relatively intimate residence to a great quadrangular mass of buildings that must surely have been one of Europe's first apartment houses of consequence. There have been more downs than ups in the Palais-Royal's history, but for much of the past century its flats have been a very good address, indeed, with the novelist Colette among the more celebrated of its tenants. The gardens of the quadrangle are open to the public. On a sunny day, in between sightseeing or shopping, there is no respite more pleasant than a pause on a bench in the odd seclusion of a palace lived in by the very same king who built Versailles—long before it was even a gleam in his eye.

Panthéon (Rue Soufflot, near Jardins du Luxembourg) is a good deal more recent than that of Rome—about 1,700 years. It is the somber, neoclassic, domed structure that Louis XV commissioned the noted architect Soufflot to design; it was finished in 1789. There is more to the building than at first meets the eye. Detail work—Corinthian columns, ceilings, arches and cupolas—is superb. And in the basement is a crypt containing tombs of such French immortals as Zola, Hugo, Rousseau, and Voltaire. You may see the crypt only in the company of a guide who takes groups as they collect. Because French civil servants have a way of staying on their jobs, it is conceivable that you will have the same guide who has been in the crypt these many seasons. No matter how elementary your French, his repartee results in the funniest running show in Paris.

OFFICIAL PARIS

Hôtel de Ville (Place de l'Hôtel de Ville) is City Hall, fronting a square named for it, with Rue de Rivoli on one side, a Seine-front street—with Notre-Dame just beyond—on the other, and the Marais just beyond. English-speaking visitors would call the Hôtel de Ville Victorian—giddy Victorian, at that. The French prefer the more appropriate Belle Époque label, an equally evocative description. The interior is quite as grand as the exterior leads one to believe it will be. The room to head for is the vast, high-ceilinged Salon Principal, in which no aspect of the decorative arts is absent; if anything, quite the reverse is the case.

Palais de l'Élysée (Rue du Faubourg St.-Honoré): You cannot go in, but it is worth passing by Palais de l'Élysée on modish Rue du Faubourg St.-Honoré; this is, after all, the President's official home. Guards and police on duty are used to people peering into the courtyard to see what they can see. When one considers that the Élysée was taken over by Madame de Pompadour not long after it went up in the early eighteenth century, it is not difficult to appreciate how beautiful it must be. Madame de Pompadour—long-time mistress of Louis XV—was a woman of keen intelligence and considerable taste in the fine and applied arts. Ever since her tenancy, the palace has known occupants of note. Napoleon abdicated there—for the second and final time; the third Napoleon—nephew to the first—lived there, and so have all the subsequent Presidents of France. You can get an idea of the size of the palace's gardens by walking past walls that enclose them, either on Avenue de Marigny, leading to Champs-Élysées, or Rue de l'Élysée, running parallel to it. Back on Rue du Faubourg St.-Honoré, don't confuse the also impressive—and neighboring—British Embassy with the Élysée, nor indeed the similarly designed mini-palace (No. 41) that serves as the residence of the American ambassador, whose offices are in the embassy's chancellery, just off Place de la Concorde, opposite the west facade of Hôtel de Crillon.

Palais du Luxembourg (Rue de Vaugirard): It is a measure of the admirable flexibility of the French that the home of one of the grandest of all French queens—Italian-born Marie de Medici—now houses a chamber of republican France's legislature. (Queen Marie, after becoming the widow of Henri IV in the early seventeenth century, yearned for a new home that would evoke her childhood.) Luxembourg is rather loosely based on Florence's Palazzo Pitti and has had a multitude of alterations over the centuries, right through to the middle of the nineteenth. Still, one wants to see the Senate Chamber, the reception rooms, and the Delacroix paintings in the elaborate library. The Senate president's official residence is next door in the house that preceded Queen Marie's palace as the original Luxembourg. The setting is a park worthy of space on its own, in pages following.

Palais-Bourbon (Quai-d'Orsay)—facing the Seine at Pont de la Concorde—is the home of Assemblée Nationale, the 491-member lower chamber of Parliament. Palais-Bourbon has a colonnaded, neoclassic facade not dissimilar to that of the Church of the Madeleine, way over on the Right bank. It was planned that way by Napoleon, so that you could look from one harmonious facade to the other and enjoy the way the two complement each other. Palais-Bourbon takes its name from a daughter of Louis XIV—the Duchess of Bourbon. Her early eighteenth-century townhouse got its present look in the early nineteenth century. To see the Assembly in session in their great half-circle of a hall is, indeed, a special Parisian experience.

Palais du Quai-d'Orsay (Quai-d'Orsay): Foreign offices in capitals around the world habitually occupy handsome old houses. (The State Department in Washington, in a modern, specially constructed building, is an exception to the rule.) The French Ministry of Foreign Affairs, in a venerable villa conveniently next door to the earlier-described Palais-Bourbon, admits visitors on hour-long guided tours. Chief lures are Louis-Philippe and Second Empire salons and the chamber where the Congress of Paris met and the Kellogg Pact was signed.

Maison de l'UNESCO (Place de Fontenoy on the Left Bank, near École Militaire) is the Y-shaped, glass-and-reinforced-concrete world headquarters of the United Nations Educational, Scientific and Cultural Organization and is among the most imaginative pieces of contemporary architecture in France. Certainly no modern building in Paris surpasses it, both as regards its own design and the caliber of the works of art decorating it. It was a joint international collaboration, and there are pieces by Picasso, Mexico's Tamayo, Japan's Isamu Noguchi, and America's Alexander Calder, to name a few. Visitors are welcome.

SCHOLAR'S PARIS

Académie Française (23 Quai de Conti) is the august body founded in the seventeenth century by Cardinal Richelieu. It is best known for the French-language dictionary it has compiled and revised eight times over the centuries. But it is, as well, a body of 40 elected leaders from various fields of endeavor—engineering and diplomacy, as well as writing and painting. The academy's headquarters are in Institut de France, a building only some decades younger. The Institut embraces half a dozen additional academies of various arts and sciences; one must make advance arrangements for admission. Rooms to see are the chambers in which the Académie Française and its fellow bodies deliberate and the Great Hall, where members of the academy are installed.

Bibliothèque Nationale (58 Rue Richelieu) occupies a substantial eighteenth-century complex, just behind Palais-Royal. A descendant of an earlier Royal Library, the National Library is at once a repository of books (some 7 million of them, including—like Washington's Library of Congress and London's British Museum Library—a copy of every new book printed in the country) and of rare old manuscripts, coins, and other antiquities. To see: short-term art exhibitions in the Mazarin Gallery and Salle Labrouste—the vast and exquisitely arched main *salle de lecture*, or reading room.

École Militaire (Place Joffre)—on the Left Bank and separated from the Eiffel Tower by the broad, formal expanse of green called the Champ-de-Mars—is substantially as it was when Louis XV founded it in the eighteenth century. Its students are no longer impoverished youths aspiring to army commissions (Napoleon Bonaparte was one such), but commissioned officers undertaking advanced courses. The symmetrical complex is among the more eye-filling of Paris and includes an open-to-the-public chapel, as well as other areas that may be viewed only upon special application.

La Sorbonne (Rue des Écoles) is the University of Paris. It is France's preeminent university and, academically, one of the great ones of the world, which is not to say that it is without the scruffy look that is inevitable in so aged and overtrafficked a facility. Location is Left Bank, between the Cluny Museum and the Panthéon. If you are tempted to enter, as many visitors are, on Place de la Sorbonne, don't. The gate you want is on Rue des Écoles, around the corner. There's a concierge there, and I suggest you request that someone lead you to the classical-style seventeenth-century University Church (it is usually kept locked) and the Main Hall. Otherwise, the university is a largely nondescript, mostly nineteenth-century maze of classroom and lab blocks interspersed by student-filled courtyards, their entrance passages adorned with the myriad bulletin boards that no university—in any land—can apparently survive without. Almost next door, on Rue St.-Jacques, is the *Collège de France*, whose roots go back to the Middle Ages and which functions today as an exclusive center of research, not unlike the Institute for Advanced Study in Princeton. Some distance away, at the Left Bank's extreme edge fronting Montsouris Park, is the remarkable *Cité Universitaire*, a campus full of dormitories—more than 35—housing 7,000 Sorbonne students. There is an International House, not unlike the similarly named dorm at New York's Columbia University, but a good many of the halls are for students of a single country. The grounds are green, extensive, and attractive, and the buildings—dating from the 1920s to the present—comprise an architecturally diverse mélange.

VERDANT PARIS

Bois de Boulogne is not very far from Arc de Triomphe, at the city's western flank. It is bordered by good residential neighborhoods, and within its 2,500 acres are a multitude of attractions. There is a pair of racetracks—better known Longchamp (the noted Grand Prix de Paris is an annual spring event—France's answer to Britain's Ascot) and Auteuil, a steeplechase track. There are, as well, a lake for rowboating; Jardin d'Acclimatation, which is at once amusement park (with a Paris-traditional marionette theater *pour les enfants*) and zoo; riding trails; picnic glades; ultramodern Musée National des Arts et Traditions Populaires (below); and, not surprisingly, good restaurants.

Bois de Vincennes fringes eastern Paris. Its landmark and namesake is earlier-described Château de Vincennes, but it has other lures; most recent is Jardin Floral. A broad expanse of gardens encircles a central lake. There's a restaurant-café and display areas for special exhibitions, as well as something called the Exotarium (what would the Académie Française think of that word?), with displays of tropical fish and reptiles. Better known and more fun is the park's big zoo, which is No. 1 in France and, like many of its contemporary counterparts around the world, has its residents living cageless lives in open terrain.

Champ-de-Mars is the front yard of École Militaire, or the back yard of the Eiffel Tower, whichever you prefer. Begun in the eighteenth century, along with the military school, this so-called Field of Mars is a formal garden in the French tradition. Proportions are extravagant; its fountains, arbors, benches, and paths are inviting. It's pleasant for a stroll in conjunction with an Eiffel Tower visit or a morning or afternoon at the Palais de Chaillot museums, just across the Seine.

Jardin du Luxembourg, the Left Bank's favorite playground, takes the name of the earlier-described palace originally built for Queen Marie de Medici in the seventeenth century. Not all of the park's sixty acres are as formally Franco-Italian as they were when it was laid out, but there are still a central allée; a great fountain; vivid, carefully manicured patches of flowers; and a popular marionette show, Théâtre du Luxembourg.

Jardin des Plantes (57 Rue Cuvier): I first visited the Jardin des Plantes when I had time to kill before departing on a train from nearby Gare d'Austerlitz, way at the eastern end of the Left Bank. This is at once a spacious and beautiful botanical garden and a zoo, with the latter—elephants, lions, tigers, and monkeys are resident—perhaps more diverting than the former. The whole complex is an agreeable way to brush elbows, on a balmy day, with Paris at its leisure.

Jardin des Tuileries: When we return home from a trip to Paris and begin to dream about it, it is the Tuileries Gardens that come to mind. They are the very essence of the city—big and bold and precise and elegant and ravishing in their beauty. The siting is matchless, with waters of the Seine on the south, arcades of Rue de Rivoli on the north, Louvre Palace to the east, and Arc de Triomphe perfectly aligned with smaller Arc du Carrousel to the west. The gardens were begun in the sixteenth century by Queen Catherine de Medici, but the great Le Nôtre—of Vaux le Vicomte and Versailles—redesigned them a century later. With their reflecting pools, sculpture, clipped lawns, and brilliant, multicolored flowerbeds, they cry out for walks—to remove the kinks, say, of a long Louvre afternoon or an expensive morning in the shops.

And there are the youngsters to be observed, sailing bathtub-boats in a great circle of a pond, watching Guignol and Gnafron in a marionette show, or cavorting on gaily painted merry-go-round chargers.

ECCLESIASTICAL PARIS: BEYOND NOTRE-DAME

Chapelle Expiatoire (Square Louis XVI, off Boulevard Haussmann, near Place St.-Augustin): With the Bourbon Restoration, King Louis XVIII moved the bodies of his ancestors, Louis XVI and Marie-Antoinette, from a Paris cemetery to Basilica of St.-Denis, on the outskirts of town. To mark the site of their city resting place, he began erection of this severe neoclassic chapel; it was completed by Charles X. Under its dome are somewhat fanciful statues of Louis XVI and his Austrian wife. Setting is an engaging little park whose benches are frequented by neighborhood locals. Go at midday and savor the delicious odors of lunch being cooked by the wife of the concierge in their apartment adjacent to the ticket office.

St.-Augustin (Place St.-Augustin, not far north of Place de la Madeleine) is included here for much the same reason as Église Polonaise—the Polish Church; lots of visitors pass by and are curious. St.-Augustin is mid-nineteenth century, and its exterior—with an oversized central dome surrounded by four towers—makes the interior anticlimactic.

Ste.-Chapelle (Île de la Cité), after Notre-Dame, is the most important church in town. Tucked into the vast Palais de Justice complex, it is a thirteenth-century masterwork built by Louis IX—later St. Louis. The slimness and elegance of its exterior proportions would be enough to make it a standout for the centuries, but its immense stained-glass windows are easily the finest in Paris and among the best in Europe. I only wish it did not close for lunch and, moreover, that there were no admission charge for what is, stained glass or no, a place of worship.

St.-Denis, ten miles north of town on Route A1, is much-restored Romanesque. The present basilica was built in the twelfth century, but five centuries before, in an earlier St.-Denis, Dagobert I became the first of a long line of French monarchs to be accorded a St.-Denis burial. Since he was interred there, every one of his successors has been, save a few monarchs of the medieval Capetian dynasty and successors to the post-Napoleonic era's Louis XVIII—Charles X, Louis-Philippe, and Napoleon III. The solitude of the St.-Denis crypts was interrupted by the Revolution, when coffins were removed and remains within unceremoniously disposed of. Tombs themselves were saved, though, and later returned. One sees them today empty but hardly unimpressive. They total 79—kings, queens, princes, and princesses.

St.-Étienne-du-Mont (Place Ste.-Geneviève and Rue Clovis, near the Panthéon, on the Left Bank) is very important to Paris, for it contains a shrine to Ste.-Geneviève, the city's patron saint. Beyond that, however, it is an exceptional Gothic structure, with the only rood screen of any church in town, handsome vaulting, fine stained glass, and splendid proportions.

St.-Eustache (Rue du Jour) is a landmark of the old Halles quarter, for long the produce center of town until those operations were removed to the drearily dull Rungis sector, beyond the city. St.-Eustache is big and beautiful, a meld of Gothic and Renaissance, with a rich history and an equally rich decor. Ceilings are high, with fine vaulting and elaborate columns in support. Much of the stained glass is good, and there are side chapels, one with a painting by Rubens.

St.-Germain-l'Auxerrois (Place du Louvre) is so overshadowed by its across-the-street neighbor, the Louvre, that it is more often than not ignored. This is a Gothic church that is among the loveliest in the city, which is not surprising when one considers that it had been the parish church of the Royal Family during periods when the Louvre was a royal residence. Bits and pieces of it are Romanesque and Renaissance, but it is essentially Gothic, with a pair of rose windows of that era and a handsome choir. Like St.-Eustache, this church is noted for its concerts.

St.-Germain-des-Prés (Boulevard St.-Germain at Rue Bonaparte) goes all the way back to the sixth century, but is mostly more recent; the bulk of it is eleventh century. Within, the Gothic sanctuary and choir are attractive, even if the unfortunate late nineteenth-century stained glass is not. This church's concerts are of high caliber.

St.-Gervais–St.-Protais (Place St.-Germain, behind Hôtel de Ville, in the Marais) rather oddly combines a Gothic interior with a Baroque facade—and gets away with it. There are surprises within—some art objects, an organ said to be the oldest in Paris, and lovely glass and vaulting.

St.-Julien-le-Pauvre (Rue St.-Julien-le-Pauvre, on the Left Bank) is so literally in the shadow of Notre-Dame that you find yourself sitting in its garden to have a look at Big Brother; from nowhere is Notre-Dame seen in finer perspective. From still another angle, the view is of nearby St.-Séverin Church, later described. But you must go inside St.-Julien-le-Pauvre; it is a millennium old, with a high, high nave, and an unusual-for-Paris inconostasis (the church is Malachite, an Eastern rite) from which hang paintings of saints and over which is suspended a great cross. Go for the Sunday morning service to hear the first-rate choir and smell the incense.

St.-Louis-en-l'Île (Rue St.-Louis-en-l'Île, Île St.-Louis) is a richly embellished Renaissance church, with a slim steeple and—of interest if you're from Missouri—a tablet from that state's St. Louisans paying tribute to the American city's namesake.

La Madeleine (Place de la Madeleine) is an enormous, late eighteenth-century neoclassic landmark that started out to be all manner of things, none of them a place of worship, and was almost a railroad station before the final decision was reached (one of the few we hear about, of the reign of Louis XVIII). It is the scene today of *haut monde* weddings. There are flower stalls in the surrounding square, whose food shops are in many ways more inviting than the austere interior of this church.

St.-Merri (Rue St.-Martin, just north of Tour St.-Jacques, near Hôtel de Ville) is an opulent Gothic church that has known some unfortunate tampering over the centuries, but there are the stained-glass windows, handsome vaulting, and a honey of a choir.

St.-Nicolas-des-Champs (Rue St.-Martin, near Place de la République) is about 900 years old and holding up very well, thank you. The interior appears a beautiful sea of pillars, and there are lots of paintings. While you are about it, go next door and visit *St.-Martin-des-Champs*, smaller, equally venerable, and reminiscent only in name of the much newer St. Martin in the Fields on London's Trafalgar Square.

St.-Nicolas-de-Chardonnet (Rue des Bernardins, just off Boulevard St.-Germain) is essentially late Renaissance, with a good deal of charm and exemplary paintings. It's rather a nice contrast to the cafés of St.-Germain, when you're exploring the neighborhood.

St.-Philippe-de-Roule (Rue du Faubourg St.-Honoré at Place Chassaigne-Goyon) is included here only because you might well pass it in the course of shopping the Faubourg St.-Honoré. The church is originally late eighteenth century—neoclassic, with a colonnaded portico that is at least as meritorious as any of the architectural or decorative aspects within.

St.-Pierre-de-Montmartre (Place du Tertre) is just the esthetic relief you are looking for after a pilgrimage to Sacré-Coeur, its near neighbor way up in the mountains of Montmartre. St.-Pierre is the genuine architectural article—Gothic, with bits and pieces that are even older Romanesque. This church goes back to the twelfth century, so that whoever was inspired to implant striking contemporary stained glass in its windows had courage. And taste: The combination is pleasing.

Église Polonaise (Place Maurice Barrès at Rue St.-Honoré) is a domed, Italianate-looking structure that shoppers frequently pass by and are curious about. It is seventeenth century and not nearly as impressive inside as out, despite frescoes covering the lining of the dome. The name derives from the national origin of most parishioners—Polish—in which language Masses are said.

St.-Roch (269 Rue St.-Honoré) is here included, first because it is in the heart of tourist Paris, and you might want to know what's inside. Second, its priests say Masses in English. This is a beauty of a Baroque church, with fine sculptures and paintings.

Sacré-Coeur (Square Willette, Montmartre): The world is full of churches built as acts of thanksgiving to God. Sacré-Coeur is quite the opposite: It was conceived as an act of contrition after France's emergence as the loser in the Franco-Prussian War, which was such a disaster that it led to the abdication of Napoleon III. It was not, however, until after still another conflict, World War I, that this enormous basilica finally opened. There is little one can appreciate as regards its esthetics. The best that can be said for it is that its white domed facade and its high Montmartre elevation make it stand out as a landmark of the Paris skyline and that the view from its dome is excellent.

St.-Séverin (Rue des Prêtres-St.-Séverin) is a near neighbor of earlier recommended St.-Julien-le-Pauvre, on the Left Bank. You begin liking St.-Séverin because of the garden that sets off its substantial Romanesque facade so well. And you like what you see inside, too: a mostly Gothic church of fine proportions and detailing, not the least of which are the stained glass and the unusually capacious, strikingly decorated area behind the altar.

Church of La Sorbonne (Rue des Écoles) is the University of Paris chapel and the only one of its buildings that is quite as it was when Cardinal Richelieu had it constructed four centuries ago. It contains the cardinal's tomb. Get the key from the concierge inside the gate on Rue des Écoles.

St.-Sulpice (Place St.-Sulpice, between Palais du Luxembourg and Boulevard St.-Germain) is still another Left Bank standout, with ancient origins, but with Baroque rebuilding, a twin-tower facade, and an absolutely immense interior, full of splendid art and artisanship, mostly eighteenth century. The surprise, in one of the chapels, is the mid-nineteenth-century murals by Delacroix.

Val-de-Grace (Rue du Val-de-Grace at Place Alphonse-Laurent, near Boulevard du Montparnasse) had its origins with Anne of Austria, mother of Louis XIV. She ordered it built (it is domed Baroque and so Italian that you pinch yourself to make sure you are not in Rome) after giving birth to her son, having been unable to conceive during the first 23 years of her marriage. Young Louis laid the cornerstone when he was still a tot, in 1641. The Italian motif continues within, with a St. Peter's-like baldachin—twisted columns and all—sheltering the altar. Then look up: The inside of the great dome is frescoed.

Cimetière du Père Lachaise: Cemeteries, even when their occupants are celebrated, are not to every sightseer's taste. This one, in eastern Paris away from the action, is named for the Jesuit priest who was a chaplain of Louis XIV. It has all sorts of historic associations but is best known for the personalities buried within: Molière, Chopin, Corot, Delacroix, Balzac, Bizet, Bernhardt, Proust, to name some from earlier times, and—more recently—Colette and Edith Piaf.

Some non-Catholic places of worship: *American Cathedral,* Avenue George V; *American Church of Paris,* Quai d'Orsay; *British Embassy Church* (Anglican), 6 Rue d'Agucasseau, near the embassy on Rue du Faubourg St.-Honoré; *Église Grecque* (Greek Orthodox), 5 Rue Georges-Bizet; *Église Russe* (Russian Orthodox), Rue Daru; *Institut Musulman et Mosquée* (Moslem—and in beautiful Moroccan style, with a pretty inner courtyard that is worth inspecting), Place du Puits-de-l'Ermite; *Temple Israélite* (known also as Synagogue Rothschild—for its benefactors), 44 Rue de la Victoire; *Temple Protestant de l'Oratoire,* 147 Rue St.-Honoré; *Temple Protestant de Ste.-Marie,* 17 Rue St.-Antoine.

MUSEUMGOER'S PARIS: AFTER THE LOUVRE AND THE CLUNY

Atelier de la Manufacture Nationale des Gobelins, de Beauvais et de la Savonnerie (42 Avenue des Gobelin) has royal origins—Louis XIV to be precise, who placed the Versailles designer-decorator artist, Charles Le Brun, at its head. Ever since, skilled artisans have been at work, one generation after the other, laboriously, slowly, and tediously creating tapestries that represent the time-honored techniques of their forebears. And there are completed specimens of their work displayed, museum-style.

Centre National d'Art et de Culture Georges Pompidou, a.k.a. Le Beaubourg (Rue Beaubourg): Ask Parisian friends for an opinion, and by and large they mostly appear no happier with the look of the Beaubourg—a brutally stark, six-level rectangle of unadorned glass and steel that is positively aggressive in its oil-refinery ugliness—than with its location. It's on the site of razed buildings in the beloved ex-produce center of Les Halles, adjacent to Hôtel de Ville, the city hall. Still, in the company of foreign and provincial-French visitors, locals mob the center's stadium-sized lobby-cum-bookshop, whose only decoration is a stylized portrait of the late President for whom it is named. Then they queue to ride its messy, glass-enclosed exterior escalators (similar to— but not as frequently cleaned, it would appear—as those at De Gaulle Airport) to the third-level exhibition area wherein are hung contents of the National Museum of Modern Art, for long housed in what is now dubbed the Musée du Palais de Tokyo (below). This area of the Beaubourg proved to be so esthetically unsuccessful as an exhibit space that it was subjected to a major redesign in 1985, for which, praise be! On display is an undeniably exemplary collection, by contemporary greats like Picasso, Bonnard, Vlaminck, Roualt, Gris, Modigliani, Chagall, Kandinsky, and Klee. Temporary exhibits take place on the second level; there's an eternally jammed café on the top level (affording views of Notre-Dame and the next-door Church of St.-Merri); and street entertainers perform frequently in the broad square outside, called La Piazza.

Galeries Nationales du Grand-Palais (Avenue de Selves, off Champs-Élysées, near Place de la Concorde). The Grand-Palais, with its neighbor, the Petit-Palais, are among the more maligned of Paris's public buildings, at least architecturally. I would surely rather have them than what might well go up today in their place, the Beaubourg (above), for example. They are relics of a turn-of-century world's fair, and I like their monumental scale. The Grand-Palais is put to intelligent use for special exhibitions, frequently arranged with skill and imagination. Watch papers for the current show.

Musée d'Art Moderne de la Ville de Paris (11 Avenue du Président Wilson) is the next-door neighbor of Musée du Palais de Tokyo (below) and, like it, attractive Art Deco. (They are wings of a building constructed for the Paris Exhibition of 1937.) In the old days, when the Tokyo housed the national modern art collection (now at Centre Pompidou, above), visitors took in both at a single clip. Contemporarily, this excellent city-owned cache is not as appreciated as it might be. Matisse, Dufy, Sonia, and Robert Delauney are but a quartet of painters in the permanent collection, and there are frequent temporary exhibitions.

Musée des Arts Africains et Océaniens (293 Avenue Daumesnil) is well worth the longish Métro ride. Housed in a Thirties-Modern pavilion is a sumptuous collection that the French—always appreciative of the cultures of peoples whom they governed during the days of empire— acquired during the colonial period. The African masks, headdresses, and other ceremonial pieces are among the finest extant.

Musée des Arts Décoratifs (107 Rue de Rivoli, in the separately entered Marsan Pavilion of the Louvre complex)—closed for a major refurbishing for a full two years before reopening in 1985—does justice to the Catherine de Medici-era palace it occupies. There are four treasure-filled floors of exhibits relating to the arts of decoration—a fifteenth-century wood canopied bed from Auvergne; the collapsible desk that traveled with Napoleon in the field, with lines so clean it could have been designed at the end of the twentieth century instead of the end of the eighteenth; and chairs of the three Louis periods; so that once and for all—if this trio of styles confuses you—you can sort them out to your satisfaction. There are, as well, porcelains, silver, jewelry, tapestries, sculpture, and painting—from Asia, as well as Europe. Best of all, though, are the period rooms. They evoke the look of French interiors from the seventeenth century through Art Deco of the twentieth, with the boudoir and bath of couturière Jeanne Lanvin an especial dazzler. Along with London's Victoria and Albert and Copenhagen's Decorative Arts, this is one of the Continent's great repositories of objects relating to the decorative arts, well complemented by counterparts in Bordeaux (Chapter 10), Lyon (Chapter 21), and Marseille (Chapter 22). There's a bookstore and shop selling pricey reproductions of museum objects.

Musée Rodin (77 Rue de Varenne) has one subject: Auguste Rodin and his sculpture. *The Thinker*, his best-known work, is in the garden. Smaller pieces are up a flight, with the ground floor devoted to medium-sized works. What makes this museum at least as inviting as its exhibits is the building itself—a honey of an early eighteenth-century *hôtel particulier* called after one of its relatively early occupants.

Musée Balzac (47 Rue Raynouard, in the Passy area, not far from Palais de Chaillot): Honoré de Balzac's novels had not been especially popular in the United States until a British dramatization of *La Cousine Bette* made its way across the water to American TV screens, sparking something of a renewal of interest in Balzac's extensive fictional series, *La Comédie Humaine*, a sharply delineated picture of French society during the reign of the bourgeois businessman, King Louis-Philippe, in the mid-nineteenth century. Balzac lived and wrote in this atmospheric house for nearly two decades.

Musée Carnavalet (23 Rue de Sévigné) is earlier recommended as a major monument of the Marais district. This is the Museum of the History of Paris, one of a number operated by the city government with great finesse. The main building is the sixteenth-century mansion of no less a personality than Madame de Sévigné, where she wrote her famous letters of social commentary. Choicest part of the museum is a group of rooms—the Henriette Vouvier Collection—furnished in the Louis XV and XVI styles of the eighteenth century. Elsewhere, you see what Paris was like in earlier eras, from specimens of citizens' clothes, documents, etchings, paintings, and all manner of bibelots—even including personal possessions left by Louis XVI and the extravagant Marie-Antoinette before they were beheaded. Take your time here, making sure to have a look around the courtyards and gardens; facades are noteworthy.

Musée Cernuschi (7 Avenue Velasquez) is recommendable on three counts. First, its contents are Chinese works of art collected by a rich turn-of-century Parisian, who bequeathed them to the City of Paris, along with his house, to be utilized for their display. Second, the house itself is a mansion in the grand style, on a block of similarly opulent houses. And third, the museum is near a smallish park relatively unknown to visitors—*Parc Monceau.* On a sunny day, a walk here is a pleasurable Paris experience. Of the museum's exhibits, the most memorable is an enormous Japanese Buddha in bronze; it dominates the main gallery, whose other standouts include spectacular screens and ceramics, of which a very ancient and sad-looking pottery pig is particularly appealing.

Musée de la Chasse et de la Nature (60 Rue des Archives) occupies an *hôtel particulier* of special beauty in the Marais and has been earlier recommended for that reason alone. As a museum, it is perhaps more limited in its appeal. Still, there is no denying the beauty of the paintings and tapestries—mostly eighteenth century—of hounds, with other hunting motifs, not to mention other art objects with the same theme. But it is the architecture of this house, its courtyard, and its interiors (be sure to go upstairs) that make it visit-worthy.

Musée Clemenceau (8 Rue Franklin, near Palais de Chaillot) is the apartment of Georges Clemenceau, who held the premiership of France both some years before and during World War I and whom we all remember from history books as France's vocal representative—and an antagonist of President Wilson—at the Versailles Conference. The irony of Clemenceau is that he criticized Wilson because he considered the Wilson-inspired peace treaty too moderate to assure France's security; yet, he was defeated in the postwar elections for being too mild in his attitude toward Germany. His apartment is hardly without interest, for the man was his country's most important early twentieth-century politician.

Musée Cognacq-Jay (25 Boulevard des Capucines): It is the location of this museum that makes it a sleeper. You just don't expect this sort of treasure trove to be located upstairs in an otherwise unexceptional building in the heart of the busy Grands Boulevards area. Downstairs, Parisians and their visitors go about their business. But within the quiet confines of the Cognacq-Jay, the matter at hand is France's eighteenth century and its art—applied and fine—the gift of the founder of the Samaritaine department store to the City of Paris. In a series of furnished rooms of the period, one finds some of the finest pieces of furniture and other objects of the era to be found in Paris, with a bonus of paintings by such masters as Fragonard, Chardin, Greuze, Boucher, Tiepolo, and Watteau. Special.

Musée Guimet (6 Place d'Iéna, off Avenue du Président Wilson, near Palais de Chaillot), severe and gloomy despite partial refurbishing comes to life only when you concentrate on its collection. It embraces choice works not only from big countries—Indian sculpture, Chinese jade, Japanese scrolls—but smaller ones, as well, with rare pieces from Indonesia, Cambodia, Korea, Nepal, and Tibet. Allow yourself time; this is a much bigger collection than, say, that of Musée Cernuschi (above).

Musée de l'Histoire de France (60 Rue des Francs-Bourgeois, in the Marais district) occupies the very grand and very beautiful Hôtel de Soubise (earlier described), whose interiors—a magnificent stairway and sumptuously decorated rooms—are in themselves reasons for a visit. But the subject matter of the museum—the history of the country as recorded in the National Archives' most precious documents, such as seals, treaties, manuscripts, and even marriage contracts—is absorbing on its own.

Musée de l'Homme (Palais de Chaillot, Place du Trocadéro) is the most important of the trio of Palais de Chaillot museums. The idea is to show us how anthropologists can dramatize the excitement of variations in the human condition. There are two floors of galleries. The Black African section is one of the better collections of African art and artifacts. There are Bambara headpieces from Mali, sculpture from Baoule in the Ivory Coast, and some of the finest bronzework of the ancient Benin civilization in Nigeria. There are fine North African pieces, as well—jewelry, metalwork, ceramics. See, too, galleries devoted to the folk art of Europe—a Lithuanian *St. George and the Dragon*, esoteric Swiss dance masks, processional figures from Flanders, and costumes from Iceland and Wales, Romania and Spain, Holland and Italy. There are, as well, exceptional works from India, Burma, Tibet—indeed, all of Asia—as well as the South Pacific, with a carved-wood Maori tomb from New Zealand. Surprises for North Americans are remarkable collections devoted to the folk art of the Indians and Eskimos of the New World.

Musée Jacquemart-André (15 Boulevard Haussmann, some blocks west of the big-domed Church of St. Augustin) is still another example—along with others, like the Cernuschi, Cognacq-Jay, and Nissim de

Camondo—of the legacy of a single wealthy Parisian family. In this case, founder-donors were a remarkable couple—Edouard André, son of a banker, and his wife, Nelie Jacquemart, a painter. They spent much of their lives collecting antiques with certain of them destined for their Boulevard Haussmann mansion. Monsieur André died in 1894, his wife in 1912, by which time the Haussmann house had become a repository of two types of art: eighteenth-century French and Italian Renaissance. House and collection were left to the Institut de France to be administered as a museum; President Poincaré officiated at the opening in 1913. There are fabulous treasures here. Downstairs is mostly French, and upstairs is mostly Italian. French paintings alone are memorable, with works by Fragonard, Chardin, Proud'hon, and Greuze among them. Tapestries are rare and beautiful. Eighteenth-century furniture is choice, too. Uccello's *Saint George Slaying the Dragon* is perhaps the most celebrated of the Italian works upstairs. But there are pieces by Botticelli, Mantegna, Carpaccio, and Titian, as well, with sculpture by Donatello, ceramics by Della Robbia, furniture, and accessories. Guards are among the friendliest in Paris, more often than not the only company one has, wandering through this beautiful, lonely house.

Musée National de la Légion d'Honneur et des Ordres de Chevalerie (2 Rue de Bellechasse): A special one, this, for history buffs. It tells the story not only of France's Legion of Honor and its various subdivisions, but of foreign orders of chivalry, as well. (More than 300,000 Frenchmen hold the Legion of Honor, while some 75,000 have been awarded the lesser Order of Merit.) Displays are not only of orders, medals, and ribbons. There is a considerable number of historic paintings, some good, some of historic interest; not to mention sculpture, etchings, drawings, and costumes.

Musée de la Marine (Palais de Chaillot, Place du Trocadéro) offers perhaps more than a lay person can absorb on matters maritime. Still, going at one's own pace, judiciously skipping here and there, it makes for a diverting visit. Ship models of all eras and ages are minor treasures. There are decorative objects taken from old ships, not to mention paintings, drawings, documents, and flags, evoking the romance of the high seas during the presteam era. Other sections are devoted to later periods; models of the ill-fated pre-World War II *Normandie* indicate what a masterwork that ship was.

Musée Marmottan (2 Rue Louis-Boilly) had always been a worthy enough destination; a fine home filled with the collection of its late owner, including Empire furniture and Renaissance tapestries. In later years, though, came two groups of paintings by Claude Monet. The second group was so large—65 works—that a special subterranean gallery was built to house it, along with paintings by Monet's contemporaries, including Pissarro, Renoir, and Berthe Morisot. Subject matter is mostly the flowers for which this first of the Impressionists is celebrated, but there is a good deal else: a Trouville beach scene with Monet's wife and cousin, sunset in the harbor of Le Havre, a Tuileries landscape, and, in contrast, smoky Gare St.-Lazare. Among the second group of Monets are many of water lilies painted at his Giverny home (later counseled as an excursion destination), as well as such diverse subjects as a Dutch tulip field and Rouen Cathedral. A brilliant collection.

Musée des Monuments Français (Palais de Chaillot, Place du Trocadéro) is an absolutely fabulous put-on; it is surely the only museum —serious museum, that is (I exclude waxworks)—that consists of nothing but fakes. Its exhibits are reproductions of sculpture and painting in the great cathedrals and churches of France. The main floor embraces one enormous arch, doorway, window frame, saint-in-plaster after another. The museum is late nineteenth century, and the idea was to see it as a teaching tool for students who were unable to get around their country as easily as they can now to see monumental art and sculpture. Anyone who has traveled France will see favorites, Amiens to Vézelay.

Musée National des Arts et Traditions Populaires (6 Avenue du Mahatma-Gandhi, near the kids' Jardin d'Acclimatation in Bois de Boulogne) occupies striking modern quarters. Besides sections on French folk and other costumes, there are exhibits concerning literature, music, dance, theater, and farm and city life. Objects on display are old and contemporary, fine and folk, rare and commonplace: the French museum profession putting its boldest foot forward.

Musée Nissim de Camondo (63 Rue de Monceau, near Parc Monceau, northeast of Arc de Triomphe) occupies the mansion of the parents of a young man who died while serving as a lieutenant in the French Air Force in World War I. His father and mother left the house as a museum in their son's memory. Though the structure itself is relatively modern, albeit in colonnaded Louis XVI style, interiors are of the eighteenth century. Aside from mostly Louis XVI furniture and accessories, there are exceptional paintings (Guardi, Oudry, Dupléssis, Vigée-Lebrun), gilded bronzework, porcelain, Beauvais and Aubusson tapestries. The most dazzling room is the rectangular Grand Salon—with gold and beige classic-style paneling and a suite of a dozen-odd chairs, all of whose seats are tapestry-covered, and a blue-and-gray Savonnerie carpet. Special.

Musée de l'Orangerie des Tuileries (Place de la Concorde)—the elongated, classic-style pavilion at the western edge of the Tuileries—served for many years as the site of short-term exhibitions, much like the Grand-Palais (above). Recent seasons have seen it transformed—after a thorough refurbishing—into the repository of a brilliant collection bequeathed to the French Government by Madame Jean Walter who put it all together over a long period, in collaboration with her first husband, dealer-collector Paul Guillaume, and her second husband, a wealthy architect. It comprises 144 paintings covering the period beginning with the Impressionists and continuing through 1930, either by French nationalists or foreigners who worked in France. It is difficult to fault the collecting trio's taste. There are a full two dozen Renoirs, 14 Cézannes, a dozen Picassos, and almost as many Matisses and Utrillos, with even heavier representation of André Dérain. Specifics? How about *Blonde à la Rose* by Renoir, *Odalisque à la Culotte Grise* by Matisse, *Pommes et Biscuits* by Cézanne, *Femmes au Chien* by Marie Laurencin, a Rousseau wedding party, the harbor of Argenteuil by Manet, and a Chaim Soutine pâtissier. Lovely.

Musée d'Orsay (15 Rue de l'Île) occupies the onetime main hall of Gare d'Orsay, the Seine-front railway station on the Left Bank that went up at the height of the Belle Époque era, in 1900. It came about as a consequence of a decision in the 1970s, when the administration of President Valéry Giscard d'Estaing—looking for a cultural project of consequence that would serve as a monument of the Giscard presidency, in the manner of President Pompidou's Centre Beaubourg and President Mitterrand's subterranean entry to the Louvre—earmarked the station as site of a museum of nineteenth-century art. The idea was to transfer exhibits of that era from the overcrowded Louvre and its dependencies and obtain still other works from other French museums. The space is monumental: a 453-foot-long room, magnificently barrel-vaulted and glass-roofed. Exhibits run a broad gamut. Stars of the show are great Impressionist paintings that had long been exhibited at Galérie du Jeu de Paume in the Tuileries—a Van Gogh self-portrait, Renoir's *Moulin de Galette*, Manet's *Déjeuner sur l'Herbe*, Monet's *Rouen Cathedral* and *Tour d'Abane*, Pissarro's *Red Roofs*, Cézanne's *The Blue Vase*, and paintings, as well, by Gauguin, Sisley, Toulouse-Lautrec, Mary Cassatt, and Rousseau—to name some. But there are, also, sculpture, graphics, posters, and photographs, with architecture and applied arts of the era represented.

Musée du Palais de Tokyo (13 Avenue du Président Wilson): Paris visitors who first knew the city a decade or so back and have pleasant memories of the old Musée National d'Art Moderne, will recognize this pleasing Art Deco structure. Alas, when the building's collection was transferred to the harsh quarters of the Centre Pompidou (above), authorities rechristened this building and displayed a cache of works long in storage—mostly from the period 1884–1904—too late in time for Impressionists at the Musée d'Orsay (above) and too early for the post-1905 group at the Pompidou. Works by Paul Signac and H. E. Cross and a goodly group of paintings by Vuillard are among them. These are all on the main floor. But don't leave without a trip to the basement, chock-full of masterworks by the likes of Braque, Picasso, Rouault, and Henri Laurent, whose original donors forbade their being transferred to the Beaubourg.

Musée Picasso (5 Rue de Thorigny): Picasso is hardly a stranger to museums in Paris or the French provinces. (The château where he once lived in Antibes [Chapter 13] is devoted to his work.) And Museo Picasso in Barcelona, with more than a thousand of his works (see *Spain at Its Best)* embraces major Picasso periods. Still, Paris's Musée Picasso, opened in late 1985, is hardly to be ignored. Occupying space in Hôtel Salé, an opulent seventeenth-century mansion, in the Marais quarter, that has been creatively restored (and that is not without an interesting history, having served variously as the Venetian Embassy and as the Archbishop of Paris's official home), the museum's nucleus is an extraordinary collection of works from Picasso's estate. It embraces well over 200 of his paintings (including a riveting 1901 self-portrait), more than a hundred sculptures, some 3,000 drawings and prints, as well as ceramics and paper collages—with the range 1901 to the artist's death in 1973. Included, too, is the painter's own cache of work by other masters—Seurat, Cézanne, Degas, Matisse, Dérain, and Rousseau, among them. Café and shop.

Musée du Petit Palais (Avenue Winston-Churchill, off the Champs-Élysées) is the fine arts museum of the City of Paris and is, as well, the site of frequent special shows. Like its bigger sister, across-the-street Grand Palais, it's a souvenir of a turn-of-century World's Fair, elaborate Belle Époque. Special shows get more public play than the permanent collection, although this is an eminently inspectable hodgepodge. Range extends from Etruscan and Egyptian through the Middle Ages and Renaissance up to the Romantics and the Impressionists of the last century. There are Maillol and Rodin sculptures; paintings by Toulouse-Lautrec and Cézanne, Courbet, and Delacroix; Beauvais tapestries and Louis XV furniture; Limoges china and medieval manuscripts. *Good* eclectic.

Maison de Victor Hugo (6 Place des Vosges, in the Marais district): Memories of Charles Laughton as the *jongleur* of Notre-Dame notwithstanding, this seventeenth-century house, inhabited by Victor Hugo between 1821 and 1848, should be of interest, if only for its advanced age, inspired Place des Vosges situation, and sumptuously furnished rooms. But there are bonuses—manuscripts of the author's works, letters, pictures, and all manner of Hugo memorabilia.

EXCURSIONIST'S PARIS: A SELECTION OF DAY TOURS

Chantilly (23 miles north of town, via Route A1) is the site of a pair of connected castles—originally Renaissance, but rebuilt—in the bigger of which are the painting collections of the Condé family. Raphael, Titian, Clouet, Lippi, and Perugino are among artists represented. There is a room full of antique jewels, not to mention ancient illuminated manuscripts and other treasures, as well as a stable that cared for several hundred horses two centuries ago. Grounds and artificial lake are splendid—surprising when one considers that they were laid out by the same Le Nôtre who played a major role in the design of the gardens of Versailles. Lunch is indicated at *Restaurant Relais du Coq Chantant* (21 Route de Creil; phone 457-01-28; *First Class*). A visit to nearby *Senlis* combines well with Chantilly. Special lure is Notre-Dame Cathedral, a twelfth-century masterwork with a soaring steeple that dominates the main square and is among France's finer Gothic specimens—from the intricate sculptured stone of the main period of the exterior to the transept, choir, and side chapels, in particular, of the interior. Senlis is not without other monuments of a rich past (it was a royal seat in medieval times)—remains of a onetime king's castle, a bishop's palace, a fifteenth-century town hall, Rue Vieille de Paris (filled with aged houses), and nearby Maison Haubergier, now the surprise-packed local museum.

Chartres (50 miles southwest of Paris) is for many visitors to France the first great out-of-Paris cathedral town. It has never been known to disappoint. I suspect this is because, tourist traffic notwithstanding, the town itself remains the same provincial capital it was long before the advent of day-trippers out of Paris. Approached from the front, with low-slung houses setting it off, the Cathedral of Notre-Dame reveals its proportions without any pretense. The vastness of the cathedral is immediately apparent. Two steeples—one Romanesque, one Gothic—flank a magnificent rose window. Length of the building is almost 400 feet, and the transept is almost half that in width.

Then one goes indoors to see the globally celebrated windows. There is no finer stained glass in France; peers of Chartres are the Cathedral of Bourges (Chapter 11) and Paris's much smaller Ste.-Chapelle. But Chartres's windows are never forgotten by the viewer: The rose windows flanking the facade and the transept are only starters; windows of the long nave are equally lovely. Special, also, are sculptures of the choir: 40 groups and 200 statues portraying great moments in the life of Christ and the Virgin Mary.

Beyond, fronting a quiet garden, is the Bishop's Palace; it shelters *Musée de Chartres*, rich with Renaissance tapestries and medieval ivories and enamels; and paintings and drawings by such French masters as Teniers, Hugo Robert, Rigaud, Boucher, and Fragonard, as well as foreign greats like Holbein and Zurbarán. Art-rich *Church of St.-Pierre* is nearby, with fine stained glass and a dozen enamels of the Apostles. Old residential Chartres is of interest, particularly houses on streets like Du Bourg, Du Pont, St.-Hilaire, and Des Écuyers. Lunch is lovely at *La Vieille Maison* (5 Rue au Lait; phone 3714-10-47; near the Cathedral; *First Class*); or stop for pastries-cum-tea at *A. Gilbert* on Rue du Cygne.

Compiègne (47 miles north of Paris), given its pedigree, is strangely incognito to most foreign visitors. It has not, to be sure, the beauty of other excursion destinations out of Paris—it is not and never was, Versailles or Fontainebleau—but it remains a place of considerable importance in the history of France: a touristic sleeper of no little interest. At journey's end is a château which knew many medieval and Renaissance kings of France. Charles V built a palace on the site in the fourteenth century. Jeanne d'Arc was taken prisoner nearby in the fifteenth. In the mid-eighteenth century, Louis XV commissioned the very same Gabriel whom he had design Paris's Place de la Concorde to rebuild the Compiègne castle. Its facade is the same today as it was from that time: a great neoclassic expanse with a colonnaded central portico. The whole, viewed from the formal garden it dominates, is not unlike a vastly widened White House.

Compiègne is the last—and newest—of the French royal palaces. From the time of its builders through to the third Napoleon and his empress, of just a century ago, it was made considerable use of. All manner of historic events have taken place within its walls. Louis XV and his grandson, the future Louis XVI, welcomed the young Austrian princess and future queen Marie-Antoinette to Compiègne upon her arrival in France in 1770. Napoleon I did likewise, with still another Austrian lady—his second wife-to-be, Marie-Louise, in 1810, concurrently redecorating the sovereigns' apartments in the style of the period. The later Napoleon—the third—and his empress, Eugénie, made Compiègne synonymous with fashion, with their annual autumnal "Series" of house parties. Several generations later, Marshal Foch signed the World War I Armistice on behalf of his country in a nearby wood; he used the castle as his headquarters.

A great part of the palace is given over to *Musée du Second Empire*, an era that the French know—and appreciate—more than does the outer world, particularly the English-speaking outer world, which concentrates on contemporary events across the Channel and calls the age Victorian. The Second Empire of Napoleon III and Eugénie was replete with overdecorated salons and bedchambers and portraits of royalty and beautiful ladies by the very same Winterhalter who painted Victoria.

There are a number of state rooms. Marie-Antoinette's game room is the most charming (along with Empress Eugénie's giddy bedroom). But I like the Napoleon I rooms, too—the ballroom, with its crystal chandeliers; and the library, with its Empire-style furnishings and fittings. The castle's biggest draw, with French youngsters at least, is a museum of old cars and carriages. But if your visit is for only a day, skip the antique autos and move on into town.

Hôtel de Ville is a Renaissance city hall. It contains a museum of toy soldiers; 90,000 of them, portraying melodramatic moments in French history. More requisite is the *Musée Vivenel*. It occupies a beauty of an early nineteenth-century house set in a serene garden. Within is a catch-all of exhibits—Old Masters' drawings, eighteenth-century furniture, ancient Greek pottery, medieval wood carvings, Renaissance enamels, and Limoges china. Lunch is excellent at *Hôtel du Nord*, Place de la Gare (phone 4488-22-30; *First Class*).

Fontainebleau (40 miles south of Paris), although on an equal historical footing with Versailles, is considerably less visited, thanks to a situation that places it farther from the capital than the Sun King's masterwork. This helps make a visit less enervating than a tour of visitor-jammed Versailles, especially in summer. No one would call Fontainebleau intimate. But in contrast to the competition—which was precisely what Versailles turned out to be—it is positively minuscule. It is, after all, the country palace that long preceded Versailles. But it was used concurrently with it. It had been a royal palace since the twelfth century. Louis IX—the same king who built the Ste.-Chapelle in Paris and was later canonized, becoming St. Louis—lived there. Louis XIII was born there. François I, the same who rebuilt the Louvre, largely rebuilt Fontainebleau, with the help of Italian artists and artisans. Succeeding monarchs—including Louis XV, who built an entire wing, and Napoleon I, who created apartments for himself and his empress—made contributions. Today's Fontainebleau, with its darkish, largely Renaissance facade, appears somber to the arriving visitor. But interiors—surrounding several magnificent courtyards—offer glittering surprises, with such rooms as a chapel, theater, François I Gallery, and ballroom (with a parquet floor to end all parquet floors). No soldiers could have clicked their heels in a more elaborate Guard Room. The chamber in which Bonaparte abdicated is among the more memorable. And the Queens' Apartments housed such illustrious royals as Catherine de Medici, Mary Queen of Scots, and Marie-Antoinette. For lunch, consider the excellent and elegant *Hôtellerie du Bas-Breau*, at nearby Barbizon (phone 6066-40-05; *Luxury*).

Giverny (45 miles north of Paris): You've seen the monumental collection of the Impressionist painter, Claude Monet, at Musée Marmottan in Paris; you've followed that up with Monet's matchless *Les Nymphées*, at Musée de l'Orangerie. Now, appetite whetted, you want to make a pilgrimage to Monet's lovely house at Giverny to the north, midway between Paris and Rouen (Chapter 31). Monet's home from 1883 to 1926, this classic-style house was opened to the public after a masterful restoration in 1980; it was an overnight success. The house, with a pale pink and white facade—complemented by green shutters at the windows—is at its best in the rooms hung with the painter's collection of Japanese engravings. His studio, in its own building, is visitable, as are the gardens that inspired so much of his work, most especially the Water Garden, whose weeping willows and pink-blossomed lilies became the subject matter of his best-loved paintings. You may go via commercial bus tour, but it's more fun on your own, via train from Gare St.-Lazare to the station of the little Seine River town of Vernon, a taxi ride from the Monet house. *Restaurant Beau Rivage* (13 Avenue Maréchal-Leclerc, in Vernon; phone 3251-17-27) is a satisfactory and *Moderate* choice for lunch.

Reims (78 miles northeast of Paris) is the city in whose cathedral Charles VII was crowned in the presence of Jeanne d'Arc, five and a half centuries back—at the conclusion of the Hundred Years War and following Joan's successful defense of Orléans from the English enemy. This is the city, as well, where a full two dozen kings of France were crowned, from an early Louis (the eighth) in 1223 to the final Charles (the tenth) in 1824. Depart early enough so that you have the bulk of the morning for an inspection of the *Cathedral* (Place des Six Dadrans). But tarry a bit before entering. This Gothic work, created between the thirteenth and fifteenth centuries, is at its most spectacular from without. The deep-set trio of portals—beneath a rose window surmounted by a frieze-like gallery of sculpted kings, surmounted by a pair of square towers—makes for one of the most impressive of cathedral entries in France. The apse is flanked by broad flying buttresses and delicate pinnacles delineating them. Only after entering do proportions seem skimpy; Reims Cathedral appears narrow, which is hardly to carp, given the quality of the stained glass (including some by this century's Mark Chagall). The adjacent ex-archbishop's residence, *Palais de Tau*—operated as a museum—displays half a hundred rich medieval tapestries, other treasures of the cathedral proper, and boasts an exquisitely scaled Great Hall. Move, then, to *Basilique de St.-Rémi,* a Romanesque-Gothic meld taking the name of the saint after which the city is called and dating to the eleventh and twelfth centuries; vaulting of both nave and altar stands out. Pause for lunch in the exemplary restaurant of *Boyer-Crayères Hôtel* (64 Boulevard Vasnier; phone 82-80-80), a *Luxury* category restaurant in a charming, park-encircled, 16-room *First Class* hotel affiliated with Relais et Châteaux; the owner-chef's roast baby squab and fish specialties are delicious. In the afternoon, work off lunch by pacing the galleries of *Musée des Beaux Arts* (a.k.a. Musée St.-Denis), with a group of portrait-drawings by Cranach and a collection of paintings by such masters as Philippe de Champagne (who was, alas, not a local but from Flanders), Poussin, Boucher, Daumier, Daubigny, Renoir, Monet, Gauguin, Dufy, and—special treat—a substantial clutch of works by Corot. And note that Reims' Champagne-producing firms—Krug, Mumm, Pommery, Piper-Heidsieck, Roederer, Ruinart, and Taittinger, among them—cordially welcome visitors to their *caves*. Still other Champagne houses in the not-far-distant town of *Épernay* also are open to the public; these include Martel, Moët et Chandon, Perrier-Jouet and Pol-Roger. *Royal-Champagne Hotel* (in Champillon; phone 2651-11-51) between Épernay and Reims is a good *Moderate* overnight selection, with an excellent *First Class* restaurant.

Malmaison (10 miles west of Paris) is the country house Napoleon built for his first empress, Josephine, who came from the still-French Caribbean island of Martinique (her Martinique birthplace is a popular visitor attraction). There is nothing *mal* about the sumptuously furnished, pure Empire-style *maison*, except its excessive expense. Josephine remained after her husband, wanting a male heir, divorced her to marry Austrian Archduchess Marie-Louise. Though left well off by her husband, Josephine still found it difficult to manage. Despite a settlement of more than three and a half million francs from the emperor, she was in debt after two years. But seeing what she spent her money on is easy on the eye. Malmaison is low-slung and set in a flower-garnished formal park. You enter a marble vestibule, full of busts, Roman style. The gilded salon is a maze of Empire-style armchairs. The dining room is simpler, with a black-and-white-checkerboard marble floor and Pompeian decor wall designs. The imperial couple's bedrooms are the most original interiors in the house. Josephine's resembles a luxurious desert chieftain's tent, an exception being her canopied bed topped with a gold eagle. Napoleon's room is the simplest and the handsomest in the house; beige moiré covers the walls and is draped over an unpretentious bed and a half-dozen odd chairs, as well. Throughout the house, the paintings are knockouts, most especially one of Josephine by Gérard, another of Napoleon as First Consul, arm in vest, and a third of the emperor on horseback, by David—the very same one you've seen in Courvoisier cognac ads. Book lunch at appropriately named (and aptly addressed) *Restaurant Pavillon Joséphine* (19 Avenue Bonaparte; (phone 1751-01-62. *First Class.*) Go by R.E.R., an extension of the Paris subway.

Rambouillet (35 miles southwest of Paris) is a little forest-surrounded town whose drawing card is the properly turreted and ever so venerable castle—a part of it dates to the eighth century—that has, since the reign of Napoleon III, belonged to the French Government, becoming, at the turn of this century, official summer house of presidents of the republic. When they're not on scene, Rambouillet keeps open hours. Thank Louis XIV, a onetime resident, for the opulent paneling of the series of Assembly Rooms within and his successor twice removed, Louis XVI, for a pair of oddball buildings in the surrounding park—a mock dairy and a house surfaced in shells—that were constructed as gifts for Queen Marie-Antoinette. Oddly unfamiliar to foreign visitors—not many remember that then President Valéry Giscard d'Estaing hosted a major summit conference in Rambouillet—the château has known historic moments. François I died there. It was from Rambouillet that Napoleon was taken to his initial exile on St. Helena. Charles I abdicated there and —to jump a few centuries—it was from this castle that General de Gaulle directed the liberation of Paris in 1944. *Restaurant Relais du Château,* 2 Place de la Libération (phone 3483-00-49) is a gala—and delicious—lunch choice. *First Class.*

St.-Germain-en-Laye (13 miles west of Paris)—like the earlier recommended Malmaison—is easily reached via the R.E.R. suburban line of the Paris Métro. It's attractive, with a charming core. What brings one to St.-Germain-en-Laye, though, is its castle—a formidable if substantial pile, dating to the mid-sixteenth century and largely the work of the builder-king, François I. There is, as well, a pre-François Gothic chapel of uncommon beauty, a park (grand and formal, as how could it not be, what with Versailles' Le Nôtre its designer?), and, as a surprise package, an unusual museum within the château. The exhibits at *Musée des Antiquités Nationales* are very antique, indeed, going back to the medieval Merovingian dynasty and earlier. The museum was originally a project of Napoleon III, but it was completely redesigned in 1968 and is now one of the handsomest in the land, with exhibits set off to advantage in rough-finished plaster-walled galleries. On display are pottery and metalwork objects. Louis XIV was born at St.-Germain-en-Laye, in a room of *Pavillon Henri IV* that had been the oratory of his mother, Anne of Austria, and is now the smart, 42-room luxury *Hôtel Pavillon Henri IV* where I suggest you have lunch (phone 3451-62-62).

Sèvres (five miles southwest of Paris): Porcelain has been keeping this town busy since the eighteenth century, when the Crown-sponsored china factory that had been at suburban Vincennes was moved. The visitor's Sèvres breaks down into two parts. *Musée de Sèvres* is an eye-opener for the porcelain-wise traveler. On display are specimens from the best-known factories of Europe—England, the Continent, both east and west—and Asia, as well, including Japan and China, where it all started. There is, also, the Sèvres factory, where visitors get a start-to-finish tour.

Vaux-le-Vicomte (30 miles southeast of Paris, near Melun) is the French country house at its pinnacle: grand in scale but not so large that it is dizzying to comprehend; brilliant in decor but never overtly so; splendidly sited—set off by gardens at once formal and capacious—but not so extensive that they create a feeling of isolation; and, most important, stylish, elegant, and—to this very day—livable.

Its very construction can be said to have altered the course of history. The man behind the château was Nicolas Fouquet (a contemporary of the young Louis XIV), who, after becoming the king's finance minister, set about building a house befitting his exalted rank. Fouquet was bright and rich and a friend not only of royalty but also of such luminaries as Molière (who performed his plays at Vaux-le-Vicomte) and La Fontaine. To build his house, Fouquet brought together three young geniuses: architect Louis Le Vau, painter-interior designer Charles Le Brun, and landscapist André Le Nôtre. They razed an older house on the site and put up what one sees today: a château in a formal garden that was the inspiration for the Versailles of Louis XIV—the palace that took the court of France out of the capital, isolating it from the people for most of three long reigns, during which time a court style developed that engendered a revolution.

Moreover, the builders of Versailles were the very same who created Vaux-le-Vicomte: the Le Vau–Le Brun–Le Nôtre trio. A visit to Vaux in 1661—the year he attained his majority—inspired Louis to outdo his finance minister. He not only built Versailles as his answer to Vaux, he had Fouquet arrested for embezzlement, to die two decades later in prison. In 1875, the rich Sommier family bought the place and began to restore it.

Vaux is an enchantment—from the moment one steps into the oval, high-ceilinged great hall. Each room—dining room, with its half-timbered Louis XIII ceiling; Muses' Room, with sumptuous Le Brun decor; gilded Games Room; Louis XIV-style King's Chamber-Cabinet-Library—is breathtaking. And the sculpture-dotted gardens are no less so. *Auberge Vaugrain* (1 Rue Amyot, in nearby Melun; phone 6452-08-23; *First Class*), with four-century-old quarters, is a good lunch-stop; build your meal around the house veal-stew specialty.

Versailles (a dozen miles southwest of Paris and easily accessible by train [a good, cheap way to go] or bus tour) was the residence of Louis XIV, Louis XV, and Louis XVI and is essential for an understanding of France's history and culture. Go first to Vaux-le-Vicomte (above), which, as I explain, was the inspiration for Versailles. Louis XIV visited it and lost no time in hiring its designers—architect Le Vau, landscapist Le Nôtre, and interior designer Le Brun—to build a castle that would make Vaux—the country house of Fouquet, his finance minister—appear inconsequential in contrast. A half-century went into the building of Versailles. Louis XIV changed architects in midstream, hiring the noted Mansart to replace Le Vau. At one point, more than 35,000 artisans and laborers were at work on the palace and its gardens. Moving-in day meant a lot more than the Royal Family and servants; something like a thousand courtiers came to call Versailles home, with as many additional settling in the area, the better to be near the powerful Sun King, his favorites, and his patronage. Louis played the divide-and-conquer game. He kept nobles and their wives and families living to the hilt, emulating his elaborate way of life and expensive tastes in food, furnishings, and fashion. And, by concentrating them all in and around Versailles, he could keep his eyes on intracourt intrigues and diversions, the while governing France with minimal interference, if not always maximum wisdom.

A full day is by no means too much time to devote to Versailles. Two days or at least part of two days is even better. Pick midweek days; there will be fewer visitors. Versailles is enormous. Getting about the château complex is complex; it is not well signposted, and in warm weather months it is mobbed. I suggest you begin with a *Visite Libre* ticket which will allow you to follow the crowds to and through *Galerie des Glaces*—the very same Hall of Mirrors where the World War I peace treaty was signed; the colonnaded *Chapelle Royale*, where crown and courtiers worshiped; a number of other seventeenth- and eighteenth-century rooms; *Musée de l'Histoire de France* (pictorial documentation of the seventeenth–nineteenth centuries); and—a fair-sized walk away— *Grand* and *Petit Trianons*, smaller mansions to which kings and their mistresses got away from the hubbub of the main palace. The Grand Trianon dates to Louis XIV and housed monarchs through to Louis-Philippe. Restored in the 1960s, it shelters official state guests now, much like Blair House in Washington; furniture is essentially Empire. The Petit Trianon is mid-eighteenth century, dating from the reign of Louis XV, and was a project of his first mistress, Madame de Pompadour, with her successor, Madame du Barry, the first tenant; Louis XVI's queen, Marie-Antoinette, was still another. The restoration—with superb furniture— is Louis XVI. Marie-Antoinette's exquisite theater—made of papier-mâché—is nearby, as is the ten-building complex called the *Hamlet*—a mock Norman village where Marie-Antoinette retreated for rustic respite.

Your second, separately purchased ticket, will take you on an expertly guided visit (in French or English, as you choose) to rooms of the château that have been refurbished by the French Government in recent years at staggering expense and with meticulous attention to historical accuracy—as part of a commendable, ongoing project. These include the king's and queen's private apartments; Madame du Barry's, Madame de Pompadour's, Madame de Maintenon's, and Madame Adelaide's apartments; and Louis XVI's library, the lot constituting interiors of the period—ceilings, mirrors, stucco work, marble, gilding, paintings, sculpture, furniture, textiles—unsurpassed anywhere in Europe. Allow time for sculptures and fountains of the vast formal gardens. Lunch is recommended in the delightful restaurant of lovely old-school *Trianon Palace Hôtel* (1 Boulevard de la Reine; phone 3950-34-12). *First Class*—and a splendid overnight spot as well.

Amiens (74 miles north of Paris) is visitable primarily because its *Cathedral of Notre-Dame* (Rue Henri IV) is not only the largest in France, but one of the most extraordinary: a ravishingly beautiful masterwork, begun in the early thirteenth century and completed more than two centuries later. Pause before entering at the entrance, itself reason enough for an Amiens excursion. Its dazzlers are a trio of portals, their deep frames a veritable museum of sculpture; stone-carved biblical stories appear in rich abundance. Go inside, then. Amiens visitors do not forget their first glance down an exquisitely Gothic-vaulted nave that is 336 feet in length, flanked by rows of elegant columns, 63 on each side. There are three sumptuous rose windows, a pair flanking the transept, another—you must look back—over the entry. The choir is Renaissance, a mind-boggling mass of carved small figures—lay as well as biblical—several thousand strong. And don't neglect the Treasury. Amiens's *Musée de Picardie* (not far from the cathedral, on Rue de la République) is at its loveliest, for me, at least, with a clutch of eighteenth-century portraits by the likes of Fragonard and Chardin, but there is notable sculpture, as well, and contemporary paintings, too. A good lunch spot is the *Nord-Sud Hôtel Restaurant* (11 Rue Gresset, phone 2291-59-03; *First Class*)—heart of town, near the cathedral, with prix-fixe menus, and a couple of dozen rooms, should you opt to stay overnight.

AFTER DARK
Opéra de Paris (Place de l'Opéra): The Second Empire opera house, one of the half-dozen world greats, is earlier recommended architecturally and herewith recommended artistically. Repertory is nothing if not diverse—with the range from such favorites as *Madama Butterfly*, *La Traviata*, and *Cosi Fan Tutti*, to such lesser-known works as Lully's *Alceste*, Gluck's *Iphigenia in Taurus*, and Berg's *Wozzek*. Productions—thanks to the commissioning of sets and costumes by internationally reputed designers—are anything but run of the mill. Performances of opera are interspersed with evenings of dance by the *Ballet de l'Opéra*, with works by such choreographers as Bournonville, Béjart, and Rudolph Nureyev danced by skilled stars and soloists, a crackerjack corps de ballet, and a repertory including *Swan Lake*, *Coppélia*, and *Raymonda*. For the first-timer who has never experienced Charles Garnier's masterwork, an evening at the Opéra is an adventure; it should include a stroll in the Promenade Salon, with a pause at a banister of the Grand Stairway, to take in comings and

goings, in the equally elaborate foyer. The auditorium (a jarringly inappropriate ceiling by Marc Chagall notwithstanding) embraces orchestra boxes (*baignoires*), first balcony (*balcon*), three higher balconies (called *loges*), the topside *amphithéâtre*, and the even higher-altitude *stalles-de-côté*. It's worth queueing up at the box office for tickets; English is spoken. (Hotel concierges deal only in the priciest seats, which they usually buy through agencies [for which there is a hefty commission] and to which they tend to add *their* commissions.) Additional opera is performed at several other locations, the most important of which is *Opéra Comique* (Rue Favart, just off Boulevard des Italiens), a turn-of-century house in the grand tradition, with an opulent interior.

Theater: There are several score legitimate theaters, albeit with appeal limited to visitors with enough command of the French language to understand offerings—the range Molière through musical comedy. Most significant is the *Comédie Française* (Place du Théâtre-Français, at the foot of Avenue de l'Opéra)—France's most historic theater. Although the present home is fin de siècle—and on the button, having opened in 1900—the company itself goes back to the reign of Louis XIV. Napoleon subsidized the troupe, and it remains government funded, with a repertory based upon classics: Racine, Corneille, Molière. The house is one of the most beautiful in Europe and reminds me, rather sadly, of the old Metropolitan Opera House—R.I.P.—on New York's Broadway. Productions are styled with considerable panache and, it is surely worth noting, tickets are considerably cheaper than those of the Opéra. Other major theaters include *Théâtre National de l'Odéon* (Place Paul-Claudel on the Left Bank), a nineteenth-century building that enjoyed contemporary fame during the post-World War II decades, when its company was led by the gifted man-wife team of Jean-Louis Barrault and Madeleine Renaud; *Théâtre Musical de Paris* (Place du Châtelet, on the Right Bank near the Seine), an elaborate house specializing in operettas and musicals; *Théâtre de la Ville* (another Place du Châtelet old-timer, often used for concerts); *Théâtre du Palais-Royal* (Rue de Montpensier), at the rear of the quadrangular Palais-Royal, with a handsome eighteenth-century interior, its principal fare variety and musicals; and *Théâtre National de Chaillot*, which shares the Art Deco-era Palais de Chaillot with a trio of museums (above) and gained fame in recent decades as home base of the *Théâtre National Populaire*. *What's-on publications:* Hotels give away *Allô Paris*—of some value, but it's worth going to any news kiosk and purchasing the inexpensive but extraordinarily comprehensive weekly, *L'Officiel des Spectacles*.

Concerts and recitals: *Orchestre de Paris* and *Orchestre National de France*—the principal Paris symphonies, both of them world-class—usually perform in *Théâtre des Champs-Élysées*, a charmer of an Art Deco house that is not—take note—on the Champs-Élysées, but on a street leading from it, Avenue de Montaigne. Concerts are played in several other halls, including *Salle Pleyel* (252 Rue du Faubourg St.-Honoré) and *Salle Gaveau* (54 Rue de la Boétie). *Olympia* (28 Boulevard des Capucines) is home to rock concerts and other pop programs, as is *Palais des Sports* (Porte de Versailles, at the southwest edge of the city). Note, too, that many concerts and recitals take place in beautiful churches—including *Notre-Dame Cathedral, St. Germain-des-Prés* and *St.-Sulpice.*

Movies: Parisians adore movies; they line up for hits, just like the rest of us. There are three principal movie sectors: Champs-Élysées, Quartier Latin (in and about Boulevard St.-Michel), and Grands Boulevards (Boulevard de la Madeleine, Boulevard des Capucines, Boulevard des Italiens). When movies are foreign made, they are sometimes shown with original sound tracks. When that is the case, ads and marquees say "V.O.," for *Version Originale.* This is worth bearing in mind if you've a yen for a movie from home or across the Channel, in its original English.

Music hall and cabarets: The former are places in which you watch a show from a theater-type auditorium, neither eating nor drinking, except at intermissions; the latter are night clubs in which you are obliged to eat and/or drink—paying dearly for the privilege—while you watch. Give one or two of the better places a go; shows are indeed spectacles— smashing costumes, perfectly beautiful women in the chorus (often with breasts exposed), and productions so elaborate that Las Vegas annually imports several. *Les Folies-Bergère* (32 Rue Richer; phone 4246-77-11) remains the all-time favorite, with good reason—atmospherically Belle Époque—with long-legged, high-kicking dancers carrying on, elaborate act after elaborate act, each more gorgeously costumed than the last. If you limit yourself to one such evening, this should be it; top-balcony seats are inexpensive. *Le Moulin Rouge* (Place Blanche, in Montmartre; phone 4606-00-19) is hardly what it was when Toulouse-Lautrec immortalized it with his paintings, but the cancan still is danced and the show—performed in a Las Vegas-style showroom, with visibility excellent from all over—is probably the best of all the cabaret offerings; sit at the bar and you've found yourself a bargain. *Le Lido* (116-bis Avenue des Champs-Élysées; phone 4563-11-61) is still another cabaret leader— and pricey. *Crazy Horse* (12 Avenue George V; phone 4223-32-32), also a cabaret, is the Wild West, or at least a rather fanciful—and amusing— Paris concept of the Wild West; as at Moulin Rouge, it's cheaper sitting at the bar. *Au Lapin Agile* (16 Rue de Saules; phone 4606-85-87) must surely have been around since the Renaissance reign of François I; it has unlimited staying power, thanks to the surefire formula of unpretentious Montmartre entertainment that's good-natured, fun, and less costly than the competition.

SETTLING IN

SELECTED RIVE DROITE/RIGHT BANK HOTELS

Ambassador Concorde Hôtel (16 Boulevard Haussmann; phone 4146-92-63): Consider this attractive, full-facility house, especially if you're a music buff (the Opéra is a hop and a skip distant) or a dedicated shopper (top department stores are just down the street). The Ambassador Concorde has 300 rooms, traditional style and recently renovated, as well as a creditable restaurant and friendly bar-lounge. Hôtels Concorde. *First Class.*

Astra Hôtel (29 Rue Caumartin; phone 4266-15-15) is middle sized, elderly, and modernized to the point where every one of its rooms has a bath. Equally commendable is the convenient location—on a street between Boulevard des Capucines and Boulevard Haussmann, with the Opéra to the east and the Madeleine to the west. Restaurant. *Moderate.*

Brighton Hôtel (228 Rue de Rivoli; phone 4260-30-03) is a comfortable, smallish, smartly located hotel. All 69 rooms have baths, although doubles can be smallish. Breakfast only. *Moderate.*

Bristol Hôtel (112 Rue du Faubourg St.-Honoré; phone 4266-91-45) comes closer to seeming like a palatial townhouse than any other luxury hotel in town. Public rooms are eighteenth century; crystal chandeliers illuminate spaces furnished with Louis XV and Louis XVI pieces, some of museum caliber. The Winter Restaurant is an exquisite oval, its oak panels hand-carved in Hungary for the hotel, when it opened in 1924. In summer, the restaurant—recommended on a later page—moves to an airy, rattan-furnished pavilion, whose glass walls give on to a capacious garden. The bar is dark-paneled, with striped Louis XVI chairs flanking its tables. There are 220 rooms and suites in two buildings, the more recent a one-time convent overlooking the garden and smartly traditional in look, with super marble baths. Remaining is the Bristol's special treat: a honey of a swimming pool on the roof, glass-walled and with a sauna and solarium adjacent. Location, on the smartest shopping street in town, just steps from Palais de l'Élysée, the presidential residence, is inspired. Member, Leading Hotels of the World. *Luxury.*

Burgundy Hôtel (8 Rue Duphot; phone 4260-24-12) is fortunate in its location (between Boulevard de la Madeleine and Rue St.-Honoré), its agreeable middling size, and its 90 good-looking rooms, all with bath, and in traditional style. There is a restaurant-grill-bar in connection and a capacious lobby. Conscientious owner-management. *First Class.*

Calais Hôtel (4 Rue des Capucines; phone 4261-50-28) is at the corner of Place Vendôme and Rue de la Paix and has been a favorite of mine these many years. The bigger of the 59 rooms, with their own bath, are comfortable and attractive. Breakfast only. *Moderate.*

Cambon Hôtel (3 Rue Cambon; phone 4260-38-09) is on a hotel-dotted street just off Rue de Rivoli, near Place de la Concorde. There are 45 rooms, a third of which have private baths; bar and restaurant. *First Class.*

Castille Hôtel (37 Rue Cambon; phone 4261-55-20): Overshadowed by the legendary Ritz just across the street, the Castille remains a too-well-kept secret. This is a stylish, 79-room house (a good number of accommodations are duplexes), with decor a meld of contemporary and traditional. There's a restaurant (that moves to a garden in summer), much frequented by locals, and a congenial bar. *First Class.*

Caumartin Hôtel (27 Rue Caumartin; phone 4742-95-95): Enviably well positioned between Opéra and Madeleine, this is a worth-knowing-about house that has been refurbished in contemporary style, with brown leather sofas in the lobby-lounge and light and airy looks to the 40 rooms, all with bath. Breakfast only. *Moderate.*

Concorde-Lafayette Hôtel (Place du Général Koenig; phone 4758-12-84) occupies a strikingly designed, 34-story tower adjacent not only to Palais des Congrès—Paris's principal convention center—but, of more immediate interest, next door also to Porte Maillot Air Terminal, from which buses depart for and arrive from De Gaulle Airport quarter-hourly. A kingpin of the France-wide Hôtels Concorde, along with the landmark Crillon on Place de la Concorde, the Concorde-Lafayette embraces a thousand pastel-colored rooms and suites, agreeably contemporary and full-facility, a trio of restaurants (the range is from haute-cuisine L'Étoile d'Or to casual Les Saisons), and as many bars, with that on the picture-windowed roof—all Paris lies below—an especial treat. And there's a bonus of shops—60 all told—adjacent. *Luxury.*

Crillon Hôtel (10 Place de la Concorde; phone 4265-24-24) is an intrinsic and original component of a monumental Paris square, with its next-door twin housing a ministry of the French Government. It is surely the only hotel extant with one of its original rooms—a Rococo boudoir—moved in toto for permanent display in a world-class museum (New York's Metropolitan). Like Place de la Concorde, both hotel and Ministère de la Marine date to the eighteenth century when, in 1758, King Louis XV commissioned architect Jacques-Anges Gabriel to design the north facade of the square; along with Place Vendôme and Place des

Vosges, it is the loveliest such in Paris. Some years after its construction, the building served as a residence of the Spanish ambassador. In 1788, it was purchased by Comte de Crillon, whose name it took and in whose family it remained until the turn of the present century. In 1909, along with two adjacent buildings, it became a hotel, passing relatively recently to control of the Taittinger family, producers of the esteemed champagne bearing their name and proprietors of Hôtels Concorde, of which the Crillon is flagship. Between 1981 and 1985, the Taittingers invested $10 million in a splendid refurbishing. Walls of the lobby, Grand Salon (a smart venue for tea and cocktails), and Restaurant Les Ambassadeurs (an appropriate name, what with the American Embassy just next door) are sheathed in gold-hued marble, a perfect foil for illumination provided by a network of crystal chandeliers and sconces. There's a snappy cocktail lounge paneled in warm walnut, its chairs covered in the same red velvet as those of the adjacent Obélisque, an informal grill with quick but stylish service. (I evaluate both Crillon restaurants on later pages, but at this point let me urge you to try the buffet breakfast at Les Ambassadeurs, even if you're staying in another hotel.) Rooms? A brilliantly proportioned formal staircase leads up a flight to the quartet of Grands Appartements—high ceilinged and with broad terraces giving onto Place de la Concorde. They have been painstakingly refurbished— Louis XV and XVI furniture, Aubusson carpets, Flemish tapestries, original stuccowork and sculpture; there is nothing else quite like them in France. Smaller suites—all told, there are 40—are hardly to be despised; with 140 bedrooms, no two quite alike, that are stunning in their simplicity. Eighteenth-century style furniture is set against pale-hued, paneled walls; high windows are hung with sumptuous draperies, and baths are elaborately equipped and marble walled. The Crillon is one of a kind: a unique experience. Member, Leading Hotels of the World and Relais et Châteaux. *Luxury.*

Daunou Hôtel (6 Rue Daunou; phone 4261-57-82) has location as its ace in the hole—on a street between Avenue de l'Opéra and Rue de la Paix. Nothing fancy here, mind you: 40 functional rooms, 30 with baths. Breakfast only. *Moderate.*

Duminy-Vendôme Hôtel (3 Rue du Mont-Thabor; phone 4260-32-80) is nicely situated on a convenient street a step or two from Place Vendôme. There are just under 80 traditional-style rooms with bath, and a friendly bar. Breakfast only. *Moderate.*

Edouard-VII Hôtel (39 Avenue de l'Opéra; phone 4261-56-90): Paris abounds in hotels named for British royals. I counsel on other pages hostelries called after George V, his son, Edward VIII (when Prince of Wales), and George's wife, Queen Mary. The Edouard-VII, whose title honors George V's papa, occupies a building dating to the Edwardian— or early twentieth-century—era, with just a hundred rooms, convenient Restaurant Delmonico, busy bar, and strategic situation just down the avenue from the opera house, corner of Rue d'Antin. *First Class.*

Etap St.-Honoré Hôtel (15 Rue Boissy d'Anglais; phone 4266-93-62) is just down the street from the American Embassy, with the celebrated Crillon just opposite and fashionable Rue du Faubourg St.-Honoré at the end of the block. The lobby is tastefully contemporary; ditto, an adjacent cocktail lounge. Accommodations embrace 104 clean-lined rooms, all with bath, and seven duplex suites. Breakfast only. *First Class.*

Étoile-Maillot Hôtel (10 Rue du Bois de Boulogne; phone 4506-42-60) is a winner, just off Avenue de la Grande-Armée, which is Champs-Élysées with a new name, substituted when it goes beyond Étoile. Rooms, all with bath, are spacious and tasteful, and there are some suites, good to know about if your Paris stay will be for some time and will involve entertaining. Only breakfast is served. *Moderate.*

Excelsior-Opéra Hôtel (5 Rue La Fayette; phone 4874-99-30) is a near neighbor to the Opéra, for which it is partially named. Behind its busy Belle-Époque facade, are half a hundred mod-look rooms, all with bath, and a bar-equipped lobby-lounge. Friendly. Breakfast only is served. *Moderate.*

France et Choiseul Hôtel (239 Rue St.-Honoré; phone 4261-54-60) is a heart-of-town oldie near Place Vendôme. There are 135 rooms, all with bath, although some appear smaller than one might like in a hotel of this caliber. Public rooms are traditional, Louis XV mostly. There's a smallish dining room, bar-lounge, and an agreeable patio. *First Class.*

Frantel-Windsor Hôtel (14 Rue Beaujon; phone 4561-04-04) occupies a turn-of-century building in a tranquil quarter between Étoile and Parc Monceau and is quite the most comfortable link of the Frantel chain at which I've stayed, France-wide. Public spaces—generous-sized lobby; cozy bar; excellent, weekdays-only Restaurant Clovis—are a deft meld of contemporary and Belle Époque, while those of the 135 rooms I've seen, including some big ones, are gracious old-school. Lovely service. *First Class.*

George V Hôtel (31 Avenue George V, just off Champs-Élysées; phone 4725-54-00) is a grand hotel in the grand manner, handsomely furnished (and recently, extensively, and superbly refurbished) in eighteenth-century style, with the genuine articles—tapestries, paintings, sculptures, clocks, boiseries—scattered about to add authenticity to the ambience. The restaurant moves to the lovely courtyard in summer. The bar is one of the most engaging in Paris, particularly at day's end, when it's time for an aperitif—or a scotch or dry martini. But what really makes the George V, when all is said and done, is service: skilled, quick, and gracious, and that includes concierges, room service waiters, chambermaids, doormen, and bellmen. This exceptional house is a part of Trusthouse Forte's Exclusive Division, and a member of Leading Hotels of the World. *Luxury.*

Inter-Continental Paris Hôtel (3 Rue de Castiglione; phone 4260-37-80): Talk about felicitous name changes: if your Paris experience extends back a decade and a half, you'll remember the Continental Hôtel —one of the great Second Empire houses. When Inter-Continental took over in the 1970s, all they had to do was add the prefix "Inter" to the original title. The traditional decor happily remains in the 500 deftly refurbished rooms and in public spaces, including a pair of fine restaurants (one later evaluated) and bar. Location is heart-of-town, with Inter-Conti's Meurice Hôtel just opposite. *Luxury.*

Lancaster Hôtel (7 Rue de Berri, just off Champs-Élysées; phone 4361-90-43) is surely among the more engaging of the deluxe hotels—the bedrooms are as big as the hotel is small; ditto, the baths. There is a cozy bar and first-class restaurant that in summer is transferred to the patio. Skilled management, too, which is not surprising; the Lancaster is a part of the London-based Savoy Hotels group. *Luxury.*

Le Grand Hôtel (2 Rue Scribe; phone 4268-12-13) was a key part of the master plan for the reconstruction of Paris by architect Baron Haussmann. An immense Belle Époque triangle, it is quite the oldest of the city's landmark luxury hotels, constructed as such. In July 1862 Empress Eugénie toured the completed building, remarking at the time that its splendor put her in mind of the pair of palaces she called home. (*"C'est absolument comme chez moi, je me suis crue à Fontainebleau ou à Compiègne."*) Alas, a succession of managements over the years did not do justice to the Grand's interiors. We must be grateful the original, brilliantly decorated restaurant, now called Salon Opéra and used for private parties, has mercifully been left intact; the same Charles Garnier who would later create the next-door opera house was one of its designers. And we must appreciate, as well, that the relatively recent landlord, Inter-Continental Hotels, which realizes that it has a national treasure, has set about on a long-range program of restoration, budgeted at $25 million. This is a big house; its 600 rooms and suites are being gradually renewed in traditional style. (When booking, request a room overlooking the Opéra; the view is fabulous.) The Grand's Café de la Paix, a history-laden Paris institution (about which I write more in a later paragraph) thrives as always, but the hotel's restaurant Opéra, one of the ranking luxury-hotel eateries in town (and reviewed on a subsequent page) is underappreciated. And still another restaurant serves good-value buffet lunches. *Luxury.*

Louvre Concorde Hôtel (Plaza André-Malraux; phone 4261-56-01): Talk about being heart-of-Paris: the Louvre Concorde is just opposite the Comédie Française, just down the avenue from the Opéra, adjacent to the Palais Royal, an immediate neighbor to the Tuileries and the Louvre. There are 220 rooms, a chatty cocktail lounge, and the commendable Restaurant Les Tuileries, whose terrace-café lies under arcades of the Palais Royal. Hôtels Concorde. *First Class.*

De Lys Hôtel (24 Rue Serpente; phone 4326-97-57) is venerable seventeenth century, furnished with fine, old French Provençal pieces and loaded with atmosphere. All 21 of its rooms have baths. Breakfast only. *Moderate.*

Madeleine-Palace Hôtel (8 Rue Cambon; phone 4260-37-82) is a fair-sized oldie that has been, as its management succinctly puts it, *entièrement renové*. That means all of the 116 rooms have their own baths, and there is a bar. Location is middle-of-everything. Breakfast only. *First Class.*

Marriott Prince de Galles Hôtel (33 Avenue George V; phone 4723-55-11) began life as the just plain Prince de Galles (doesn't *Prince of Wales* sound nice in French?) in 1929, as a next-door neighbor of the hotel (above) named for the father (George V) of the then Prince of Wales, who was to reign so briefly as Edward VIII. Though the Prince de Galles is considerably smaller than the George V (it has just over 170 rooms and suites, in contrast to its neighbor's near 300), their facades are both of the Art Deco era, and both have gracious inner courts. The Marriott chain, which purchased the "Prince" in 1984, completed an extensive and masterful renovation the following year. The look of the hotel is now essentially early nineteenth century, Directoire and Empire, with careful attention paid to luxurious textiles, wall-coverings, and lighting fixtures. (Bravo, interior designer Robert Lush, who also directed renovation of the Carlton Inter-Continental in Cannes.) Amenities include a striking-looking peach and ivory-hued, marble-accented restaurant (which moves to the flowering courtyard in summer) and a bar-lounge beloved of Parisians and visitors over the years, refurbished to be sure, but still with its original handsome paneling. *Luxury.*

Meurice Hôtel (228 Rue de Rivoli; phone 4260-38-60), with its inspired locale—as beautiful as it is convenient—at the intersection of Rue de

Castiglione and Rue de Rivoli, steps from Place Vendôme and the Tuileries—was built in 1816, the year Napoleon abdicated, and the ambience remains at once elegant and low-key, so meticulously have Inter-Continental Hotels (the Meurice is the costliest of their Paris trio) carried out a major restoration. The lobby and adjacent lounge—still with its original gilded paneling and crystal chandeliers and a smart choice for a drink or afternoon tea—are among the most atmospheric in Paris. Accommodations are super. Suites, mostly overlooking the Tuileries, are predominantly Louis XV, with antiques of that era among their furnishings. Standard rooms are smart, too, most overlooking Rue de Castiglione or an inner court; you must specify preference. (I have opted for the former on my visits.) Worth noting: the intimate Restaurant Meurice and its adjoining bar-lounge. *Luxury*.

Ministère Hôtel (31 Rue de Surène; phone 4266-21-93) is a pleasant selection in the central Madeleine quarter. Rooms can be smallish, but those with bath, 24 of 32, are comfortable. Management is accommodating; service, personal. Breakfast only. *Moderate*.

Molière Hôtel (21 Rue Molière; phone 4296-22-01): A hotel named for the playwright simply has to have something going for it, and the Molière does: an excellent location near the Opéra and good-looking rooms, all with bath, be they single, twin, or suite. Breakfast only is served. *Moderate*.

Mont-Thabor Hôtel (2 Rue du Mont-Thabor; phone 4260-32-77) is smack in the heart of things on a street that lies between Rue de Rivoli and Rue St.-Honoré, near Place Vendôme. The lobby and bar are agreeable; and those bedrooms I've inspected, likewise. Japanese restaurant. *First Class*.

Plaza-Athénée Hôtel (25 Avenue Montaigne; phone 4723-78-33) is, not unlike the George V, a relatively modern building with a fashionable off-Champs-Élysées location, perfectly beautiful eighteenth-century interiors (Relais Grill and the Bar Anglais are contemporary-look exceptions), and an inner patio that becomes a restaurant in summer. A special feature is Les Gobelins, a long gallery connecting the extraordinarily handsome Restaurant Régence with the lobby, which sees service as a tea lounge in the afternoon. Suites are sumptuous, but ordinary guest rooms are attractive, too; all are in the style of Louis XV or Louis XVI, with luxurious baths, and face either the quiet street or the courtyard; specify preference. Lavish attention to detail is evident throughout, with the budget for fresh flowers in excess of that for electricity—to give you an idea. A Trusthouse Forte Exclusive Division hotel that's also a member of Leading Hotels of the World. *Luxury*.

Queen Mary Hôtel (9 Rue Greffulhe; phone 4266-40-55) could have been named for Mary Queen of Scots, who was, after all, Queen of France before she was Queen of Scotland. But I suspect it was named after the more recent wife of the late George V. The only royal picture in the lobby is of none of these sovereigns, but of Edward VII, instead. At any rate, this is a smallish, nicely managed and located hotel (the Madeleine is nearby) that has been recently refurbished with a Louis XVI salon off the lobby. All 16 rooms have bath. Breakfast but no restaurant. *Moderate.*

Regina Hôtel (2 Place des Pyramides; phone 4260-31-10) is fin de siècle, albeit updated as regards baths and the like, but has retained its original decor. There is a long gallery of a lobby, cozy restaurant-bar, which extends into a patio in summer, and some of the best-looking bedrooms and suites in town. (The bedsteads are inevitably old-fashioned brass.) Those with a view of the Tuileries are special (and more costly, of course). Location is noteworthy on a square bisected by Rue de Rivoli, almost opposite the Louvre. *First Class.*

Résidence du Bois Hôtel (10 Rue Chalgrin; phone 4500-50-59) is a townhouse kind of hotel on a residential street just off fashionable Avenue Foch, which is one of the arteries leading from Étoile. The 20 suites and rooms and public rooms are period style and luxurious; you have the feeling that you're in the country. *First Class.*

Ritz Hôtel (15 Place Vendôme, with an entrance, as well, on Rue Cambon; phone 4260-38-30) has not, to its great credit, been content to rest on the laurels of a global reputation; it's the "original" Ritz, founded by the legendary César Ritz in 1898. Acquired by a new management team in the late 1970s, it has undergone a multimillion-dollar renovation—undertaken with extraordinary imagination, taste, and skill—that has been more a case of renewing and enhancing original decorative elements than of replacing them. The Ritz occupies one of the original eighteenth-century Place Vendôme palaces and extends through to an early twentieth-century Rue Cambon addition. The opulent Vendôme-side lounge is a splendid choice for afternoon tea or cocktails. But then you walk through the arcade that connects Vendôme with Cambon buildings, alongside a block-long series of windows displaying luxury goods from Paris shops (with a *vendeuse* on hand during daytime hours to make sales), and there is a pair of bars, both of which double as cafés, serving light but elegant meals and snacks. Restaurant Espadon (which I review on a later page) moves from Louis XV winter quarters to the garden in summer. Accommodations? There are just 200 suites and rooms. The suites—including one with a bed that had been Marie-Antoinette's, and with museum-caliber eighteenth- and early nineteenth-century furniture and accessories in most—constitute, in my view, the most beautiful of any that I know of in any hotel in Europe. But ordinary rooms, singles as well as doubles—at least those I have stayed in or inspected—are superbly appointed, as well. (Indeed, the Ritz is the only traditional-style hotel in town, to my knowledge, that has proper showers supplementing tubs in *every* bathroom.) Member, Leading Hotels of the World. *Luxury*.

Royal Monceau Hôtel (53 Avenue Hoche; phone 4562-76-87): Long reputed as one of Paris's smarter hotels—it is located on one of the very grand avenues that radiate, like spokes, from Place Charles-de-Gaulle—the Royal Monceau joined the crack Italian luxury chain, Ciga, a few seasons back and has emerged handsomer than ever, as a consequence of a $15 million renovation. There are close to 200 rooms and nearly 30 suites, decorated in the style of the Empire and the Directoire, good-looking lobby, welcoming bar-lounge, and pair of noteworthy restaurants. One, Le Jardin, is surmounted by a glass dome in the hotel's garden; the other, Carpaccio, is authentically—and deliciously—Italian. You may work out, too; there are both a swimming pool and a gym-cum-sauna. *Luxury*.

St. James et Albany Hôtel (202 Rue de Rivoli; phone 4268-31-60) went up, in part, toward the end of the seventeenth century as the *hôtel particulier* of Duc de Noailles. Half a century later, Marquis de Lafayette married a daughter of the Noailles clan, on premises; and not long thereafter, Queen Marie-Antoinette welcomed Lafayette at Château de Noailles upon his return from America. Later dubbed Hôtel St. James, the earlier structure was combined with the adjacent Hôtel d'Albany in the mid-nineteenth century, to open as a commercial hotel, which it has been ever since. The early 1980s saw refurbishing—traditional interiors, alas, became acceptable if undistinguished contemporary (each of the 145 units—some two-room suites, some duplex suites—has a fridge and electric plate, should you want to make coffee or tea). The restaurant moves to a pretty courtyard in summer, and there's a bar. But, in the process of renovation, there was a name change. The long-time stubbornly plural Hôtels St.-James et d'Albany became the singular Hôtel St. James et Albany, and the preposition preceding Albany disappeared in the process. *Alors*, such is *le progrès. First Class*.

St. Petersbourg Hôtel (33 Rue de Caumartin; phone 4266-60-38) is no more Old Russian—the name notwithstanding—than it is Old English. It is, however, an elderly house that has been spruced up to the point that all 120 rooms have bath. There is a neat little lobby, a convenient restaurant, and a dark-paneled bar that calls itself Anglais, perhaps because it sports a framed photo of Queen Elizabeth II and Prince Philip. The location, between the Madeleine and the Opéra, is good. *Moderate*.

Scribe Hôtel (1 Rue Scribe; phone 4742-03-40) is in the heart of the busy Opéra area. It's a big, comfortable old-timer that has been intelligently, expensively, and tastefully refurbished in appropriate Louis XVI style, in the course of recent seasons. The 200 high-ceilinged bedrooms are a highlight. There are a congenial bar-lounge and reputed restaurant in the basement. *Luxury.*

Sydney-Opéra Hôtel (50 Rue des Mathurins; phone 4265-35-48) is a honey—smallish, with a convenient Madeleine-Opéra location and 40 rooms, no two alike, each delightfully decorated and with bath. Breakfast, but no restaurant. *Moderate.*

Trémoille Hôtel (14 Rue de la Trémoille; phone 4723-34-20) is intimate and quiet—on the serene street for which it is named, off Champs-Élysées, parallel with Avenue Montaigne. Public rooms are Louis XV, and furnished with elaborate boiserie and tapestries. There is a dining room-bar-lounge, and the 112 bedrooms are capacious and comfortable. A Trusthouse Forte Exclusive Division hotel, affiliated with Leading Hotels of the World. *Luxury.*

Tuileries Hôtel (10 Rue St.-Hyacinthe; phone 4261-06-94): The Tuileries is on a tiny street that gives onto more substantial Rue Marché St.-Honoré, lying midway between Place Vendôme (to the west) and Avenue de l'Opéra (to the east), with Rue St.-Honoré a bit south. This is a gracious, late eighteenth-century mansion converted with panache, in the style of the epoch when it was built, into a 30-room hotel. Breakfast only. *Moderate.*

Vendôme Hôtel (1 Place Vendôme; phone 4360-32-34) occupies a house designed by Hardouin-Mansart, the architect who took over Versailles from Le Vau at midpoint and completed it for Louis XIV. The front facade of the Vendôme is original; the rest of the building, although less venerable, is hardly unimpressive. This is a smallish hotel. The intimate bar-café doubles as a restaurant, making a specialty of full-meal service in the 40 high-ceilinged bedrooms (all of whose beds are super brass ones). And location is A-1. *First Class.*

Warwick Hôtel (5 Rue de Berri; phone 4563-14-11): A step or two off Champs-Élysées, this long-on-scene house was purchased a few seasons back by the small chain whose name it takes and refurbished stem to stern. Result is a stunner of a hotel decorated in pleasing contemporary tones, with traditional accents adding warmth. There are just under 150 rooms and suites (if you're splurging, consider a suite-cum-garden-terrace, that looks out on the city), La Couronne Restaurant, an agreeable bar-lounge, and a bountiful breakfast buffet. *Luxury.*

Westminster Hôtel (13 Rue de la Paix; phone 4261-57-46) is an old-timer on a legendary street (Cartier adjoins its entrance) that was completely remodeled—84 rooms and suites with new baths, upgraded restaurant, bar-lounge, the lot smartly traditional—when taken over in the mid-80s by Warwick Hotels. *Luxury.*

SELECTED RIVE GAUCHE/LEFT BANK HOTELS

Abbaye St.-Germain Hôtel (a.k.a. Hôtel de l'Abbaye; 10 Rue Cassette; phone 4544-38-11) occupies what had been a convent when it was erected a couple of centuries back, not far east of Boulevard Raspail, with Boulevard St.-Germain-des-Prés a fairish walk north. Relatively out-of-the-way situation notwithstanding, the Abbaye has built up a loyal following, thanks to the good looks of its lobby, bar, and garden and the marble baths of its 45 smartly traditional rooms. Breakfast only. No credit cards. *Moderate.*

Angleterre Hôtel (44 Rue Jacob; phone 4260-34-72) is no more English than the Quartier Latin street on which it is situated. It is a delightfully middle-category, typical Parisian inn; all rooms have bath or shower, and the management is at once congenial and efficient. Breakfast only. *Moderate.*

Bonaparte Hôtel (61 Rue Bonaparte; phone 4326-97-37) is an unpretentious, worth-knowing-about oldie on a core-of-St.-Germain street that leads to the Seine. Management is professional, and all 33 rooms are bath-equipped (the smaller ones have showers instead of tubs). Breakfast only. *Moderate.*

Claude-Bernard Hôtel (43 Rue des Écoles; phone 4326-32-52) is a neighbor of the Sorbonne and Collège de France. It is simple but adequate; most rooms have private baths. Breakfast only. *Moderate.*

Danube Hôtel (58 Rue Jacob; phone 4260-34-70), strategically situated at the intersection of Rues Jacob and Sts.-Pères, boasts a winsome inner patio and lounge. Management is pleasant; 30 of the 45 rooms have baths. A heavy repeat clientele means that you must book in advance. Breakfast, but no restaurant. *Moderate.*

Derby Hôtel (5 Avenue Duquesne; phone 4705-12-05) has a fin-de-siècle facade—and ambience within, as well—on an attractive street near the École Militaire, the Invalides, and UNESCO, from whose global membership it draws much of its clientele. Virtually all of the 36 good-looking rooms have baths. *Moderate.*

L'Hôtel (13 Rue des Beaux-Arts; phone 4325-27-22) despite—or possibly because of—small capacity (there are but 25 no-two-alike, antiques-accented rooms, each with a marble-surfaced bath), has achieved a certain snob status. There is no denying its good looks, convenient location, or interesting past (Oscar Wilde died on the premises). Still, I have found its reception staff unwelcoming and its restaurant more attractive than delicious. *First Class.*

Lutèce Hôtel (65 Rue St.-Louis-en-l'Île; phone 4326-23-52): Although I arbitrarily place the Lutèce on the Left Bank, you are neither Right Bank nor Left Bank when you stay here, but smack between the two, on lovely Île St.-Louis, just behind the flying buttresses and apse of Notre-Dame on neighboring Île de la Cité. To stay on Île St.-Louis in this charming house—there are but 23 pleasant rooms—is to live in a small community surrounded by the larger city. Breakfast only. No credit cards. *Moderate.*

Lutétia-Concorde Hôtel (45 Boulevard Raspail, at Rue de Sèvres; phone 4544-38-10), with its brilliant, carved-stone facade, is an Art Nouveau landmark of Paris and has been since it went up in 1910. Hôtels Concorde, its proprietors, have refurbished it stem to stern, and, to their great credit, they illuminate that one-of-a-kind facade every evening. There are 315 rooms and suites, with the ones to ask for those with views of Les Invalides and the Eiffel Tower. There is a pair of restaurants; I am partial to the popular-priced Brasserie, reviewed on a later page. The bar is congenial. And the situation is super. *First Class.*

Madison Hôtel (143 Boulevard St.-Germain; phone 4329-72-50) is decidedly unpretentious, but with a good location opposite the Church of St.-Germain-des-Prés and with a view of it from the front. All 57 rooms have baths. Breakfast only. *Moderate.*

Montalembert Hôtel (3 Rue Montalembert; phone 4548-68-11) is an agreeable, old-school house of fairish size, with an equally agreeable core-of-Left-Bank situation. All 60 rooms have been modernized and have baths. Breakfast only. *First Class.*

Pas-de-Calais Hôtel (59 Rue des Sts.-Pères; phone 4548-78-74) is conveniently situated in the heart of the Left Bank, on one of its most attractive streets. It is smallish, spotless, and inviting. All 41 rooms have baths. There are a spacious lounge, congenial management, and breakfast (but no restaurant). *Moderate.*

Hilton International Paris Hôtel (18 Avenue de Suffren; phone 4273-92-00) was considered a sassy Yank upstart by the locals when I covered its brilliantly staged official opening in 1966. It was the first completely new hotel in Paris for decades, and it is to the everlasting credit of Hilton International that it pioneered here as it has in other areas of the world. At first, the French tended to be patronizing about the new '*Eel-tohn*, but they soon realized that it represented contemporary luxury hotel keeping. And so this hotel has thrived, despite a location that is more romantic than convenient (its next-door neighbor is the Eiffel Tower) and a look that is more functional than beautiful. There are fine views from riverside rooms; a restaurant called Le Western beloved of the Parisians for its thick, Yank-style steaks; a swank and very French rooftop restaurant—Le Toit de Paris—as well as a late-hours, Gallic-accented coffee shop. And I'll say this for the location. During my first visit, on the occasion of the opening, I made up my mind to take absolutely no taxicabs; I wanted to master the Métro. With the system map always in hand, I took it everywhere: it was a valuable experience, and I have been a Métro fan *and* a Paris Hilton fan ever since. *Luxury.*

Quai Voltaire Hôtel (19 Quai Voltaire; phone 4261-50-91) has a location that is nothing less than inspired, on the Seine, right across from the Louvre, between Pont Royal and Pont du Carrousel. This is a nicely freshened-up old building. There are fewer than 35 rooms, a good proportion with private baths. Breakfast only. *Moderate.*

St.-Germain-des-Prés Hôtel (36 Rue Bonaparte; phone 4326-00-19) is an aged building that has been sensibly modernized. Ambience is simple and spotless, with baths in all 30 rooms. Breakfast, but no restaurant. *Moderate.*

St.-Simon Hôtel (14 Rue St.-Simon; phone 4548-35-66), flanking a short street just off Boulevard St.-Germain, is a case of good things in small packages—just under 30 rooms, all with bath, and a welcoming management. Breakfast only. *Moderate.*

Scandinavia Hôtel (27 Rue de Tournon; phone 4329-67-20) may not sound like it from its name, which connotes Functional Modern, but it is a restored old inn, built during the seventeenth-century reign of Louis XIII when it was known as Auberge des Scandinaves. It is smartly furnished in period, with many antique pieces. There are but 22 rooms, all with bath; location is between Luxembourg and St.-Germain-des-Prés. *Moderate.*

Splendid Hôtel (29 Avenue de Trouville; phone 4551-55-98), a neighbor of École Militaire, UNESCO, and the Invalides, is worth knowing about. Most of the 45 simple but pleasant rooms have bath. There's an inviting lobby-lounge with a bar but no restaurant, although breakfast is served. *Moderate.*

Trianon Palace Hôtel (1 bis Rue de Vaugirard; phone 4329-88-10) is fair-sized—120 rooms—and situated near Boulevard St.-Michel and the Jardin du Luxembourg. Most rooms have baths, and breakfast is served. *Moderate*.

STAYING AT THE AIRPORTS

Hilton International Orly Hôtel (phone 4687-33-83) has the great advantage of being directly opposite Orly's main entrance. It is, of course, soundproofed and air-conditioned, with 379 comfortable French-modern rooms, moderate-tab coffee shop, smart restaurant, bar-lounge, and amenities, including barber and beauty parlor and gratis bus service to the terminals. *First Class*.

Holiday Inn Roissy Hôtel (54 Rue de Paris, Roissy; phone 4988-00-22) is typically Holiday Inn functional, with 250 rooms, each with a shower-equipped bath; convenient restaurant, comfortable bar-lounge, and a location adjacent to De Gaulle Airport. *Moderate*.

DAILY BREAD

SELECTED RIVE DROITE/RIGHT BANK RESTAURANTS

Ambassade d'Auvergne (22 Rue du Grenier-St.-Lazare; phone 4273-31-72) offers specialties of south-central Auvergne, rarely encountered in Paris. The prix-fixe dinner, to give you an idea, might embrace *soupe aux choux* (a cabbage potage), *petit salé aux lentilles* (a hearty pork dish), and the difficult-to-describe but delicious *aligot*. *First Class*.

Les Ambassadeurs (Crillon Hôtel, 10 Place de la Concorde; phone 4265-24-24): The approach to this restaurant is hardly to be despised. Place de la Concorde for starters, with the Crillon lobby following. You pass, then, up a couple of steps, to the hotel's high-ceilinged Grand Salon where you could do worse, if it's evening, than to pause for a predinner drink in one of the city's handsomest cocktail environments. The salon leads to Les Ambassadeurs: marble-walled, hung with crystal chandeliers, massed with great bouquets of flowers, its tables flanked by black-upholstered armchairs. Splurge with *foie gras* as an opener, or select a truffled omelet. Fish are special here—poached filet of sole with aïoli sauce, especially; chicken and beef filets are exceptional, too. Or you may fall back on grilled lamb chops, thyme seasoned, and served with a scrumptious *gratin* of potatoes. All the chocolate desserts are irresistible and so, for that matter, are the made-on-premises chocolates. Some will be served with your coffee, but you will do well to order a half-pound box or two from the obliging captain, to take with you. In my experience, one of France's best restaurants. *Luxury.*

André Faure (40 Rue du Mont-Thabor; phone 4260-74-28): You are not going to lose weight as a consequence of an André Faure meal. But it will have been worthwhile. This is a smallish place on a street leading from Rue de Castiglione, near Place Vendôme. You go for the warmth of the welcome and the satisfying à la carte, composing a meal that might, to give you an idea, start with a dozen snails, continue with *coq au vin* or a rich duck *confit* in the style of the southwest, concluding with a Norman-origin *tarte tatin. Moderate.*

Angelina (226 Rue de Rivoli) is for afternoon tea deluxe. China is fine Limoges. Decor is Belle Époque. Clientele is an amusing mix of ancien régime and moneyed younger Parisiennes. In what other tearoom might you see two handsome, albeit on in years, ladies order splits of champagne to revive them from the rigors of the boutiques? Mind, the waitress will bring only tea or coffee. Another staffer—a *pâtissier*—is the source of the irresistible pastries. *First Class.*

Androuet (41 Rue d'Amsterdam, near Gare St.-Lazare; phone 4874-26-93). The name of the Androuet game is cheese, glorious cheese. Its ground floor is a shop selling nothing but, in infinite variety. Up a flight you go—for a meal; I suggest you order "Le Grand Plateau." A hundred and fifty types of cheese are presented (they take up space on seven trays), with wine and bread to accompany. No better introduction to the cheeses of the world's No. 1 cheese country. *First Class.*

Bistro de la Gare (38 Boulevard des Italiens and several other locations; phone 4828-49-61) is a Parisian success story, thanks to its ingenious simplicity: an inexpensive menu embracing but a handful of combinations, that of steak (or broiled chicken) with *frites*, preceded by a salad, the most popular. Setting is bright, welcome, and cordial; service, efficient. (A competing operation, *Hippopotamus*, which also has several Paris outlets and is in the provinces, too, is diagonally opposite.) *Moderate.*

Bristol Hôtel Restaurant (112 Rue du Faubourg St.-Honoré; phone 4266-90-45): Go in winter, and the setting is an oval room superbly paneled and chandelier-hung. Go in summer, and you'll be seated in a rattan-furnished pavilion giving onto the Bristol's capacious garden. The menu blends traditional with *nouvelle*. You may, for example, begin with smoked Norwegian salmon or lobster *bisque* among the familiar starters, or a more innovative *salade* built around duck breasts and crayfish; continuing with roast lamb or filet of beef among old-school type entrées, in contrast to, say, *escalope* of turbot cooked with Sauternes, or *confit* of sweetbreads prepared with wild mushrooms. Desserts rate a separate card. And you will not go thirsty: 70,000 bottles are stored in the Bristol's cellar. Splendid service. *Luxury.*

Café Tuileries (Inter-Continental Paris Hôtel, 3 Rue de Castiglione; phone 4260-37-80) is called to your attention as a source of tasty, well-priced sustenance, breakfast into the evening; menus at lunch and dinner are good buys; onion soup is always a good bet, and there's an entrance on Rue de Rivoli. *Moderate.*

Cafés: Of the Right Bank cafés, most requisite is *Café de la Paix* (Place de l'Opéra), which has been a Paris institution for nearly a century and a quarter—from the time when Le Grand Hôtel went up alongside the Opéra, as part of Baron Haussmann's reconstruction of Paris. Nary a visitor, celebrated or not, who has passed through Paris over that long period has missed stopping for coffee, a drink, or a bite to eat, the better to take in action on the square. (Relais Capucines, adjacent to the café, is a proper restaurant counseled in a later paragraph.) *Café Royal Concorde* (7 Rue Royale) is a super spot to sit for a spell, observing broad Place de la Concorde, just beyond. *Café Pény* (3 Place de la Madeleine) is strategically situated, with the colonnaded Church of the Madeleine and the square's pedestrians as subject matter. If you're hungry, order *salade Niçoise* or an *assiette froide*, while seated at an outdoor table. *Fouquet's* (99 Avenue des Champs-Élysées) is as much restaurant as café, but it's to the tables out front, spilling around onto Avenue George V, that I direct you for observation of ambulatory action in this quarter. *Café Les Tours de Notre-Dame* (23 Rue d'Aréole): Take a table in the shadow of the cathedral's gargoyles; splendid views. *Café Wepler* (Place de Clichy) and *La Mère Catherine* (Place du Tertre and later recommended as a restaurant) are for people-watching in Montmartre. *Café Royal Vosges* and *Café Ma Bourgogne* are well situated on beautiful Place des Vosges. All of the foregoing are *Moderate.*

Caveau des Chevillards (1 Rue St.-Hyacinthe; phone 4261-19-74): Down you go, to the vaulted seventeenth-century cellar of an elegant house a bit north of Rue St.-Honoré and due east of Place Vendôme. Time to go is evening, when candles illuminate smartly set tables, and you sit at Louis XIII chairs, feasting on such traditional dishes as seafood mousse or a salad based on *confit* of duck, trout prepared the house's way, half a dozen beef dishes, or roast lamb, garlic scented. Menu at lunch is *First Class*; dinner, à la carte, comes closer to *Luxury.*

Cartet (62 Rue de Malte, north of Place des Vosges; phone 4723-12-24) is a smallish, narrowish place with tables packed together. You go for the food. Order a bottle of Côtes du Rhône and start with a selection of house terrines and sausages. There are half a dozen fish choices. Main courses? If you're two, order *gigot d'agneau* and wait for the arrival of an entire leg of lamb perfectly roasted, with *pommes de terre gratinées* in tandem. Or try *saucisson de Lyon chaud* or *daube* of beef. You'll be in no shape for a sweet, but persevere. Options include *profiteroles aux fraises*, a choco-strawberry sensation; *tarte au citron;* or *gâteau au chocolat*, with pears in its central regions. Memorable. *Luxury.*

La Chaumière (38 Rue du Mont-Thabor, near Place Vendôme; phone 4544-67-91) is mobbed at lunch with workers of the area, tucking into its good-value menus, three courses that typically include such entrées as chicken and steak. Cheerful service. *Moderate.*

Cochon d'Or (31 Rue du Jour; phone 4226-38-31) is about midway between Palais Royal and Centre Pompidou; stop in after a Pompidou morning, choosing a pork or beef entrée that might follow a tasty snail-and-mushroom appetizer. *First Class.*

Chez Gabriel (123 Rue St.-Honoré; phone 4233-02-39) comes through with flying colors by means of a three-course menu with a grilled veal chop and a mound of crisp *frites* indicated as the entrée choice. Old-fashioned in look, ditto the smiling service. *Moderate.*

Chez Pauline (5 Rue Villedo; phone 4296-20-70) straddles a short street just east of Avenue de l'Opéra, just north of the Comédie Française. It is at once small and smart, with paneled walls and silk-shaded table lamps. You are heartily welcomed and well fed; a dinner might run to *jambon persillé* (one of the best such I've had in France) or *bisque de homard*, continuing with *boeuf Bourguignon* or the house's deservedly reputed stuffed cabbage. Super sweets. *First Class.*

La Chope des Vosges (29 Place des Vosges; phone 4534-67-98): You've been touring the Marais of a morning and have just come from, say, Musée Victor Hugo. You're ready for lunch. At La Chope, it might consist of *soupe du jour*—usually a vegetable potage—a nicely grilled brace of lamb chops with *frites,* and a glass or carafe of the house red. With a view of the square as a bonus. *Moderate.*

Le Drouot (103 Rue Richelieu, just off Boulevard des Italiens; phone 4296-68-23): There's a neon sign on the corner to guide you to the Drouot's unimpressive entrance, which leads to an equally unimpressive stairway, which you ascend, to find yourself in a noisy, cavernous, utterly unpretentious space with the dimensions—if hardly the decor— of a ballroom. I don't know if this restaurant dates to the turn of the century, when Lautrec painted. Had it, he would surely have been on scene to record this panorama of working-class Paris. The lure is corking good bistro food at rock-bottom prices—the lowest such of any I know in Paris. Open with one of the best interpretations of *céleri rémoulade* you'll encounter, tomato or cucumber salads, a dozen snails, mayonnaise-dressed avocado, or an omelet. Your entrée might be roast chicken, *choucroute garnie* (which I counsel), or beef any number of ways. Cheeses are tasty; so are pastries and ice cream. Ditto, the house wine. And if you draw a waitress who doesn't speak your language, she'll cheerfully shout over to a colleague who does, for a translation. No credit cards. *Moderate.*

Entracte Opéra (1 Rue Auber; phone 4742-26-25) is easy to pass by, hovering, as it does, in the shadow of the Opéra. But locals working in the neighborhood patronize it with good reason: tasty food at good prices, with service on its two floors smiling and snappy. In summer, consider a range of salads and cold platters. At any time, onion soup is the indicated starter; then zero in on *saucisson chaud*, grilled sausages-cum-potatoes, with a *coupe*—or sundae—to conclude. *Moderate.*

Esapadon (Ritz Hôtel, 15 Place Vendôme; phone 4260-38-30) has been a personal favorite since a long-ago summer lunch was hosted by the late Charles Ritz in the garden. At other seasons, Espadon occupies high-ceilinged quarters within, its arched walls the palest green and tables pink-napped, with red roses and gleaming crystal. There's a daily menu—estragon-seasoned salmon or a refreshing salad to start; a hearty *navarin*—lamb stew—or a roast wheeled over on a silver wagon to be carved tableside, with a choice of fabulous Ritz desserts. The à la carte menu embraces traditional favorites, with *nouvelle* creations to add spice. Exquisite service. *Luxury.*

L'Écluse (64 Rue François 1er, near Champs-Élysées; 15 Place de la Madeleine and several other locations) just has to be the definitive Paris wine bar. Decor varies according to locale, but in each case tables are tight; decibel count, high; waiters, more efficient than you would dare hope, given the impression of turmoil at mealtime; and food, tasty. Bar signs identify principal wine choices; order *au verre* (by the glass), *à la bouteille* (by the bottle), or *en carafe*. Accompany with the *assiette charcutière*, a delicious cold meat platter; a generous order of smoked salmon, cold roast beef, or the house's *pâté*. End with cheese—preferable to the chocolate cake. *First Class.*

Fauchon (26 Place de la Madeleine): The city's most reputed fancy-food shop is a lunchtime magnet for Parisians who pack its self-service buffet. There are hot dishes—the moussaka is as savory as it is in its native Greece—along with sandwiches, salads, the celebrated Fauchon pastries, and sublime chocolate sodas. To order: Decide what you want, pay the cashier, *then* take the cashier's receipt to present to the counter attendant in exchange for your grub. And expect crowds. *First Class.*

Galeries Lafayette (Boulevard Haussmann): Lunch is invariably a pleasure at this behind-the-Opéra department store. No. 1 locale is the handsome *Lafayette Grill* on the sixth floor—a proper restaurant with a well-priced menu (salad, entrée, cheese, or help-yourself dessert buffet). The same floor's *Relais des Galeries* is a good-value cafeteria. And in the separate building housing Galfa Club (the men's store) is the up-a-flight *Le Pub*, with steaks the specialty and *plats du jour*, as well. *Moderate/First Class.*

Garnier (111 Rue St.-Lazare; phone 4387-50-40): It's odd how rarely visitors venture north of Boulevard Haussmann to the Gare St.-Lazare quarter—unless they're catching a train. Garnier, just below the station, is smart, its banquettes a mix of tan leather and chrome, its staff expert and cordial, its prix-fixe menu—oysters or snails, grilled sole (or other fish) with *beurre fondu* or *Béarnaise* sauce, with dessert following—the ideal way to become acquainted with the offerings of a premier seafood house. *First Class.*

La Grande Cascade (Bois de Boulogne; phone 4506-33-51): It's a glorious day, with the sun bright and clouds billowy. Why not lunch in the park, on the terrace of this delightfully Belle Époque restaurant? Open with a refreshing salad, concentrate on *tournedos* or roast partridge as entrées, ending with one of the Cascade's made-on-premises sherbets. *First Class.*

Le Grand Véfour (17 Rue Beaujolais; phone 4296-56-27): Louis XV was king when Le Grand Véfour opened in 1760. Its location then—fronting gardens at the rear of Palais Royal—was one of the choicest in town; two centuries later, it still is. The walk across the quadrangular garden is a joy at midday or in the evening, with a myriad of lamps lighting the way. For long bailiwick of the celebrated restaurateur Raymond Oliver—whose faded sign on the windows, "Sherry Cobblers, Lemon Squash, English Spoken," were an amusing put-on—the restaurant in recent seasons was acquired by the Taittinger champagne interests and exquisitely refurbished. (Alas, my only quarrel with the decor is the elimination of M. Oliver's window sign.) The menu, formerly grandly traditional, is now a happy mix of the conventional and the creative. Beneath the painted glass panels of the ceiling and from tables set with cut glass and old Limoges, you lunch or dine exceedingly well, opening with vichyssoisse laced with *confit* of lamb, mushroom-flecked poached eggs, a *foie gras terrine*, or *escalope* of salmon in aspic. Roast duck or *tournedos*

—among traditional entrées—are super, but there are *nouvelle* veal and sweetbread dishes that go down very well indeed. Conclude with either hot apricot tart or chocolate mousse. In my experience, one of France's best restaurants. *Luxury.*

Hachette-Opéra (Boulevard des Italiens at Place de l'Opéra) is the relatively recent name for long-on-scene Drugstore-Opéra, a catchall gift shop (if there is an actual pharmacy, it has long eluded me), with both a café (whose prix-fixe menus make for satisfactory on-the-run lunches) and a stand-up counter (open, traditionally at 7:00 A.M.) whose flaky croissants and good coffee are many times cheaper than when ordered from room service as a *café complet,* in neighboring hotels. *Moderate.*

L'Incroyable (26 Rue de Richelieu; phone 4260-41-23) is, indeed—to translate its title—unbelievable, or at least its prices seem so, for what you get: a three-course menu that might run to soup or *pâté, escalope* of veal or grilled pork chop, nicely garnished, as well as cheese or pastry. Just east of Avenue de l'Opéra. *Moderate.*

Lasserre (17 Avenue Franklin-Roosevelt; phone 4359-53-43). Time was, not so many seasons back, that when you wanted to dine at this gala and gorgeous spot, you picked up the phone and booked, a day or two ahead. Recent seasons have seen the matter of booking become so complex and long range that one wonders if it's worth it; there are, after all, countless outstanding restaurants in Paris, most of them less pricey and less patronizing than Lasserre and willing to let you pay for a high-priced meal with a credit card. That is not the case here. Should you be among the chosen, you'll be impressed by the show, although the attitude toward foreigners, in my experience, can be patronizing and the atmosphere distinctly chilling. Setting is a sumptuous townhouse. You have a drink in one of the ground-floor lounges. When the table is ready, poof! You're escorted upstairs to the dining room, whose roof—in summer at least—slides open to reveal the heavens. Food can be anticlimactic after all of this splendidly staged drama. Which is not to say it is not creditable; such classic standbys as *foie gras,* rich *terrines,* grilled lobster, and game birds are elaborately prepared. Remember, now, have a wad of franc notes or traveler's checks; no credit cards. *Luxury.*

La Mère Catherine (6 Place du Tertre; phone 4606-37-69), a Montmartre institution for generations, shows no sign of slacking. It remains a congenial locale for a dinner up on the hill. A *pastis* in the forward room—all red and white checked cloths and lampshades—is for premeal, with neighborhood locals invariably in attendance. Dinner out back is served to musical accompaniment and embraces an unchanging menu: appetizer, chicken or steak, cheese, dessert, and wine. *First Class.*

Au Lyonnais (32 Rue St.-Marc; phone 4296-69-04), with cozy, fin-de-siècle dining rooms on two floors, is proficient at preparing the fare of Lyon. Start with hot sausages, go on to lamb with *flageolet*-type beans or *coq au Beaujolais*, making certain that you do not fail to order a portion of *gratin Dauphinois*, the tastiest of potato casseroles. Drink Beaujolais—the wine of Lyon. *First Class.*

Mövenpick (12 Boulevard de la Madeleine; phone 4742-47-93) is accorded space here only because you may have encountered outlets of this chain in Teutonic nations of origin, as have I, and with satisfaction. The Paris version is something else again: a garish succession of connected basement spaces that makes an attempt at standard dishes like chicken, steak, and *paillard de veau*, without success. Environment and fare are coffee-shop caliber, albeit with steepish tabs and disagreeable service. *First Class.*

Monoprix (21 Avenue de l'Opéra): The up-a-flight eatery of this outlet of the nationwide budget-price department-store chain is a good bet for lunch on the run. *Moderate.*

Les Noces de Jeannette (14 Rue Favert; phone 4296-36-89) teams up well with a performance at the just-opposite Opéra Comique. This is an upstairs spot with somewhat excessive Second Empire decor, but reliable fare—*coquilles St.-Jacques* or a pot of *rillettes* (pork *pâté*) to begin, a chicken entrée or *steak marchand de vin* following, served as part of a prix-fixe menu that is sound value. *First Class.*

L'Obélisque (Crillon Hôtel, 10 Place de la Concorde, with its own entrance on Rue Boissy d'Anglas; phone 4265-24-24) is the less expensive—and more recent—of the Crillon's restaurant pair. This is a snappy grill room, all red velvet chairs and Lalique-like chandeliers, with wines offered by the glass or bottle and delicious comestibles, the lot of them speedily—and cheerily—served; the range, salads and omelets, pasta and *poisson* (there's always a fish of the day), smoked salmon and steak, with *gratin Dauphinois* the potato specialty, a super cheeseboard, and luscious desserts. Lots of locals and staff members from the next-door American Embassy are regulars. *First Class.*

Opéra (Le Grand Hôtel, 2 Rue Scribe; phone 4268-12-13) is so overshadowed in the public mind by the same hotel's historic Café de la Paix (above) that its premium restaurant—beautifully paneled and chandeliered, with a crackerjack kitchen and serving staff—is perhaps the least appreciated of the important hotel restaurants. Pity, this. You want to book for a dinner that might embrace the best vichysoisse in town or smoked Norwegian salmon served with Russian blinis, roast lamb, the house's chicken-breast specialty, with poached pears in a Poire William-flavored *sabayon* sauce as a festive finale. *Luxury.*

Pierre Traiteur (10 Rue de Richelieu; phone 4296-09-17, a hop and a skip from Palais-Royal) is intimate in scale, unspectacular—paintings of no special discipline punctuate pinky-buff walls—and staffed by a team of congenial waitresses uniformed in neat black and white. The menu is limited, but everything I have tasted is commendable. Starters include asparagus sauce *mousseline*, poached eggs in a piquant sauce, or a delicious *soupe à l'ail glacée*, which is Pierre's answer to Spain's gazpacho. *Steak au poivre* and *gigot d'agneau* are favored entrées, and, in all events, you must order the house's potato winner, *gratin Dauphinois*. Baked-on-premises fresh grapefruit tart is, to understate, unforgettable. *First Class.*

Pharamond (24 Rue de la Grande Truanderie; phone 4233-07-72)—in a house of yore that exudes ambience, near Centre Pompidou—is a touch of Normandy in the capital. You may not want to go so far as to order the Norman standby, *tripes à la mode de Caen,* but there are such satisfactory dishes as duck *terrine* and marinated salmon salad, scallops prepared with Norman cider, filet of veal in a rich sauce, and roast lamb. Pear *charlotte*, bathed in raspberry sauce, is the indicated sweet. *First Class.*

La Poularde Landaise (4 Rue St. Philippe du Roulle; phone 4359-20-25) is a charming spot between Champs-Élysées and Boulevard Haussmann, with a homely, chintzy look and kind waitresses in attendance. Specialties are of the southwest—*confit de canard*, preserved roast duck—especially. It's served with sautéed potatoes and a salad, but it is not, I caution you, as good as you'll get in the area of origin. *First Class.*

Printemps (Boulevard Haussmann, diagonally to the east of the Opéra), one of the preeminent department stores, is a spectacular setting for lunch, thanks to the situation of its complex of eateries—restaurant, grill, *salon de thé*—on the sixth floor of its Nouveau Magasin building (one of a trio that's closest to the Opéra) beneath an absolutely fabulous (and immense) stained-glass dome. *Moderate.*

Relais Capucines (Le Grand Hôtel, Place de l'Opéra entrance; phone 4268-12-13) is the often-neglected restaurant section of the Grand's celebrated Café de la Paix (above). It's a Belle Époque space adjacent to the outer café, with an extensive brasserie menu; the range, from oysters, soups, fish, and meat entrées to cold plates, hamburgers, and a selection of *coupes*, or sundaes; not to mention a half-dozen, changed-daily *plats du jour*. *Moderate/First Class.*

La Samaritaine (Rue du Pont Neuf, between Rue de Rivoli and Quai du Louvre) is a multibuilding, budget department store that has put its river-front location to good use with *Restaurant Terrasse* on the tenth floor of Building No. 1. Lures are cold plate lunches offered in combination with spectacular vistas of Paris. *Moderate.*

Self-Tuileries (205 Rue de Rivoli, east of the Meurice Hôtel) is a long-on-scene cafeteria, adequate for a snack or casual meal on the run. No credit cards. *Moderate.*

Tartempion (15 bis Rue du Mont-Denis; phone 4606-10-40) is an agreeable alternative to La Mère Catherine (above) for a Montmartre meal. Setting is a charming old house; lure is a well-priced menu based on beef and poultry entrées. *Moderate.*

Taillevent (15 Rue Lamennais; phone 4561-12-90) has had so much praise quite literally heaped upon it in recent years that prospective customers must set to work weeks in advance to gain entry, only to have to lay out considerable cash (or traveler's checks) for the privilege. When innumerable other restaurants of good repute are so glad of one's credit-card business, it's questionable if the effort is worthwhile. In a setting of oak-paneled walls, crystal chandeliers, and caned Louis XVI chairs, the ambience is, to be sure, engaging. Food is taken very seriously, indeed, and there's no denying that service is impeccable, with the menu a meld of *nouvelle* and traditional. A Taillevent lunch or dinner might embrace *foie gras* or truffled seafood sausage, a guinea-hen *pot-au-feu*, and a dessert representing the handiwork of the house's *pâtissier*. *Luxury.*

Aux Trois Quartiers (Boulevard de la Madeleine), a centrally situated and venerable department store, has a top floor café that's worth knowing about for a quick lunch when you're in the neighborhood or for afternoon tea, later on. *Moderate.*

Le Train Bleu (Gare de Lyon; phone 4343-09-06): Wow! That's what you say when you climb the steep flight from Gare de Lyon's main floor to this turn-of-century restaurant that is surely among the great Belle Époque environments in the republic. A series of ravishing circular murals, framed in heavy gold, embellish the ceiling. Additional murals are embedded in the walls, heavy gold frames setting them off. You are not surprised to learn that it was the President of France who inaugurated this restaurant in 1901, nor that it is still going strong. Start with *potage cressonnière* or smoked filet of mackerel, continue with *gigot d'agneau*, duckling *à l'orange*, or braised Provençal beef. Don't skip the cheese platter, nor, for that matter, a fruit tart to conclude. And turn the menu over. An excellent wine list is on the reverse. *First Class.*

W. H. Smith (248 Rue de Rivoli; phone 4280-37-97): If you know Britain, you know this bookstore chain. Its Paris outlet's second floor looks like a tearoom, with its stage-set mock-Tudor walls. But go for the good-value lunch (neighborhood residents and workers are regulars) that is no-nonsense French—soup to start, a chicken entrée, for example—and tasty. Friendly waitresses. No credit cards. *Moderate.*

SELECTED RIVE GAUCHE/LEFT BANK RESTAURANTS

Allard (41 Rue St.-André-des-Arts, off Place St.-Michel; phone 4326-48-23) is an old-timer with staying power. The look is Congested Quartier Latin; you enter a cramped barroom; there are low-ceilinged dining rooms on either side, with tables at close quarters. Old-school waiters are gracious. Fare is unpretentious—Paris bistro cooking at its delicious best, including the casserole that is *cassoulet*, an estimable *coq au vin*, a masterfully prepared *gigot d'agneau aux flageolets*, beef and lamb stews. What you start off with—*terrine de canard, escargots, salade de concombre* or radishes with butter—is excellent, too. Desserts are few but satisfying, with *tarte aux fraises* and fresh orange salad as house specialties. In my experience, one of France's best restaurants. *First Class.*

L'Assiette au Beurre (34 Rue St.-Benoît; phone 4222-49-76) is at once atmospheric and delicious—a salute to the glory of the turn-of-century Art Nouveau period, with a loyal following. There's a reasonably priced menu, centered around such entrées as *côtes d'agneau* (lamb chops) and *maigret de canard* (duck breasts) with *profiteroles au chocolat* a favored dessert. *First Class.*

Bistrot de Paris (33 Rue de Lille; phone 4261-16-83) is the bourgeois bistro at its smartest, most convivial, and most delicious, with such stick-to-the-ribs dishes as coarse and tasty house *pâtés*, among starters; entrées like *sauté de veau l'estragon* and *boeuf Bourguignon*. Desserts run to favorites like apple tart and chocolate mousse. *First Class.*

Blanc (26 Avenue de Tourville; phone 4421-38-82) is a sensible choice for a sensibly priced lunch when you're in the neighborhood of the Eiffel Tower; there's a wide variety of set menus, both midday and at dinner. Plain in look, but welcoming. *Moderate.*

Brasserie Lipp (151 Boulevard St.-Germain; phone 4548-53-91) has been a Quartier Latin institution these many years. The fin de siècle interior, with superb stained and cut glass and dark woods, is among the more engaging in Paris. Fare is Alsatian. Not surprisingly, *choucroute garnie* is No. 1 entrée. But consider also the specially prepared Baltic herring, pigs' feet, and sweetbreads, ending with *tarte maison*. No credit cards. *First Class.*

Brasserie Lutétia (Lutétia-Concorde Hôtel, 45 Boulevard Raspail; phone 4544-38-10): I don't know of a hotel restaurant in town with a larger proportion of neighborhood regulars among its clientele. Big and bright and humming, it works like a charm. By that, I mean the food is as satisfying as the service is kindly and swift. The menu, or *formule*, embraces thyme-scented *gigot* (roast lamb) garnished and served with a salad, wine or beer, and coffee. But the à la carte is extensive—omelets and terrines, snails and soups, with such entrées as *coq au vin*, *châteaubriand*, and *steak tartare*. And the chocolate *mousse* is justifiably celebrated. *First Class*.

Cafés: The Left Bank's Big Two are *Café des Deux Magots* (170 Boulevard St.-Germain) and *Café de Flore* (172 Boulevard St.-Germain): they're always packed with visitors, as well as Quartier Latin types. *Café-Select-Latin* (Boulevard St.-Michel at Rue des Écoles) is ideal for observation of the Sorbonne student populace, while *Café Quartier Latin* (6 Place Edmond Rostand) offers a fine view of the Jardins de Luxembourg. Beyond, in Montparnasse, position yourself at *Café la Coupole* (Boulevard Montparnasse at Boulevard Raspail). All are *Moderate*.

Chez Dumonet (117 Rue du Cherche-Midi; phone 4222-81-19) is unpretentiously traditional, with a menu to match. This is a honey of a Montparnasse dinner spot. Consider a meal that might consist of *salade paysanne*, *entrecôte* grilled on an open wood fire served with the potato masterwork, *gratin Dauphinois*; and *crème caramel* or *poire belle Hélène* to conclude. *First Class*.

Chez Maître Paul (12 Rue Monsieur le Prince; phone 4354-74-59) is located on a not-necessarily-easy-to-find little street near Place de l'Odéon and the theater taking its name. It's a tiny, neat-as-a-pin place, with Monsieur Gaugain the expert chef, Madame Gaugain the charming hostess, service expert, and fare perfectly delicious. I counsel starting with snails, opting for one of several chicken entrées, *entrecôte*, or veal chop. They come with tasty *pommes Pont-Neuf* and a well-dressed salad. *First Class*.

Dodin Bouffant (25 Rue Frédéric Sauton; phone 4325-25-14) is here accorded precious space only because its name is known to transatlantic visitors. Alas, success seems to have had a not very pleasant effect. A recent lunch was a disappointment—grim service throughout, a hot soup served cold; flat, overchilled *rillettes*, bland *poularde de Bresse*, the lot served in the company of an oddly unprepossessing clientele. *First Class*.

Au Gourmet de l'Île (42 Rue St.-Louis en l'Île; phone 4326-79-27) occupies ancient quarters on the pretty island to the rear of Notre-Dame and operates a first-rate kitchen. *Pâté* or stuffed mussels are ideal starters. Entrées are specialties of the Auvergne region—chicken with lentils, for example. You may order à la carte, but the menu is a better bet. No credit cards. *Moderate.*

La Grosse Horloge (22 Rue St.-Benoît; phone 4548-28-12) comes close to being the prototypical Rive Gauche bistro. By that, I mean you go for a convivial dinner with good friends, sticking to hearty standbys. If it's the season, begin with *asperges sauce mousseline* (I have had neither the vegetable nor the sauce any better prepared) and continue with steak/*frites* accompanied by a big *pichet* of the house red; fruit tarts are indicated for dessert. *First Class.*

Jardin de la Mouff (75 Rue Mouffetard, near the Panthéon; phone 4326-56-31) offers lunchers or diners a picture-window view of its neat rear garden and a value-packed set menu, with a choice of seven hors d'oeuvres and the same number of entrées. And everything that I've tried tastes good. *Moderate.*

Jules Verne (Tour Eiffel, second level; phone 4555-61-44): You want to book in advance for this one, and, when you approach the tower, look for signs that will direct you to its Pilier Sud, or South Column. There you'll find the restaurant's private elevator. Its attendant phones up to confirm your reservation, and then whisks you to a sleek, gray, black, and white environment, picture windowed, which is, in my view, the single best-looking example of modern interior design that I have come upon in France. It carries through to the glassware (black-stemmed), porcelain (black and white), soap in the washrooms (in black plastic boxes), and silk flowers on the tables (black-stemmed in black vases). Not surprisingly, staff is in tuxedos. The meal you'll be served from an extensive à la carte is *nouvelle* accented, but hearty and tasty. Start with mussel soup, puff pastry-topped (considering also smoked salmon, lobster salad, duck terrine, or half a dozen oysters). Entrées run a wide gamut—filet of salmon, filet of beef, a chicken-crayfish stew, a delicious veal specialty, tomato and basil flavored. Desserts are spectacular to look upon—and taste. I counsel accurately named Le Grand Dessert Jules Verne. Lovely service. In my view, one of France's best restaurants. (And with a bonus: If your meal has been lunch, walk down a flight to the bottom observation deck; you won't be charged the usual admission.) *Luxury.*

Lous Landès (157 Avenue du Maine, Montparnasse; phone 4543-08-04) makes a specialty of southwest cuisine. Open your meal with *coupe de garbure*, which could be an entire meal, if you let it. The *cassoulet* is one of the best in Paris. For dessert: *tourtière*—a meld of puff pastry, prunes, and armagnac. Gracious service. *Luxury.*

La Petite Chaise (36 Rue de Grenelle, near Boulevard St.-Germain; phone 4222-33-84) occupies two floors of a seventeenth-century house. Look is brocaded walls, brass chandeliers, paintings in original frames. Lure is one of the best set menus in town, both as regards taste and price. *Entrecôte aux frites*, for example, are first rate. *Moderate.*

Le Port Saint-Germain (155 Boulevard St.-Germain; phone 4548-22-66)—stucco-walled, with a beamed ceiling—is indicated for a reasonably priced seafood repast, with assorted mollusks served on stilted platters. But there are meat dishes as well. Not a few of your fellow diners will be tucking into lamb or beef accompanied by mounds of crispy *frites*. Solid value. *First Class.*

Le Récamier (4 Rue Récamier; phone 4548-86-58): You're welcomed with a smile in this good-looking restaurant (tables spill into Rue Récamier in warm weather). And, if you're attuned to the rich cuisine of Burgundy, this is the place—*oeufs en meurettes* (poached and served in a wine sauce) and *boeuf Bourguignon* are but two stellar specialties. With a wide choice of Burgundy wines to accompany. Very pleasant. *First Class.*

Tea Caddy (7 Rue St.-Julien-le-Pauvre) is the perfect respite spot when sightseeing Quartier Latin, Notre-Dame, or the neighboring Church of St.-Julien le Pauvre. Stop in, mid-morning or mid-afternoon, for coffee or tea served with a slice of the Caddy's own cake or pastry. Setting is a *very* old house, all beamed ceilings and paneled walls. *Moderate.*

Le Toit de Paris (Hilton International Paris Hôtel, 18 Rue de Suffren; phone 4273-92-22) translates as Paris's Roof—and is, indeed. Select a table on the Tour Eiffel side, and you can practically touch the tower's shaft. But, from any position, views are spectacular, and Hilton International sees to it that you dine well. Beef specialties are delicious, but consider lamb or veal options, lobster, or the day's fish catch. The hotel's *patissiers* are skilled; don't skip a sweet. Skilled service. Dinner only. *Luxury.*

Tour d'Argent (15 Quai de la Tournelle; phone 4354-23-31): If you're on an initial Paris foray, nothing is going to stop you from booking eons in advance for a meal in this Paris institution, which appears quite as tourist-populated as Centre Pompidou, though it's considerably pricier. You enter a venerable river-front structure and, reservation or not, are led into a ground-floor bar to while away time (awaiting your table upstairs) over a costly drink. A lift operated by a very small boy with a very big smile (which must net him an enormous nightly take-home in *pourboires*) then transports you to the rooftop dining room, whose picture windows, with vistas of the river and Notre-Dame, are used to good advantage. Serving staff, because moneybags Americans constitute a heavy proportion of its stock in trade, is English-speaking and—especially if they sense this is your first experience in a snazzy Paris eatery—patronizing. Order the satisfactory pressed duck, making sure that souffléed potatoes accompany it. Insist on seeing the wine list so that you may, if you like, select a relatively reasonably priced bottle (rather than simply following the unpriced verbal suggestion that may be proffered by the *sommelier*). Chocolate cake is a sensible dessert choice. And if you depart wondering what all the fuss was about, you will not have been the first. *Luxury*.

La Truffière (4 Rue Blainville; phone 4633-29-82), as its name suggests, specializes in truffled dishes from Périgord. *Escargots* stuffed with truffles and ham are a fine opener, as is the more traditional Périgordine specialty, *foie d'oie frais à la gelée*—fresh goose liver in aspic. *Brochette de truffes* or *cassoulet* are counseled for entrées. *First Class*.

Vagenende (142 Boulevard St.-Germain; phone 4548-44-96) is absolutely super-looking Belle Époque. But dark paneling, intricate mirrors, and brass fixtures are only a part of its appeal. Prime lure is sound-value prix-fixe lunches and dinners four courses in length and at two prices; each offers good choices within each category—steak *grillé*, liver and bacon, stuffed eggplant, *coquilles St.-Jacques*, for example, as one day's entrées of the cheaper menu. Although Vagenende is invariably packed, service is swift and polite. *Moderate*.

SHOPPER'S PARIS

Parisians are the planet's most glamorous shopkeepers. In no other city are merchants—large or small, expensive or modest—able to display wares more alluringly or make them appear more desirable. No matter how parsimonious, the visitor does well to savor the mercantile scene, if only to window-shop. On *Rive Droite/Right Bank*, my candidate for the all-around smartest street is *Rue du Faubourg St.-Honoré*, with its extension, *Rue St.-Honoré* (somewhat less fashionable); *Rue Royale* is the dividing line between these two. Also browseworthy are certain streets leading from the Champs-Élysées, such as *Avenue Montaigne, Rue François 1er* and *Avenue George V*. Avenues proceeding from the Étoile—*Wagram, Friedland, Kléber, Marceau, Iéna*—cater mainly to affluent Parisians and are not without interest. Relatively short *Rue de la Paix* has noteworthy shops, as do *Place Vendôme* (where the emphasis is on precious jewelry) and *Rue de Passy* (near Palais de Chaillot). *Place de la Madeleine's* forte is food emporiums (not to mention flower stalls), and *Boulevard de la Madeleine* is middle category. *Boulevard Haussmann,* behind the Opéra, is the site of two leading department stores. *Rue de Rivoli* is smartest at *Place de la Concorde* and becomes more popular as it extends east, becoming a center of low-priced schlock after it passes the Louvre and extends to the Marais—a venerable quarter centered by *Place des Vosges,* now filled with trendy clothes, in both men's and women's shops. *Place des Victoires,* a long-neglected Baroque beauty, a bit northeast of Palais-Royal, has in recent seasons become a center of avant-garde fashions. *Le Louvre des Antiquaires,* just east of Palais-Royal, is a multilevel mall with some 250 high-quality antique dealers. *Galeries Vivienne,* also near Palais-Royal, embraces a mix of fashion and gift boutiques. And *Forum des Halles,* near Centre Pompidou and with similarly bold contemporary lines, shelters some 250 shops.

On *Rive Gauche/Left Bank, Boulevard St.-Germain* is Main Street—with wares ranging from old books to *haute* clothes and superb antiques. Equally significant is *Rue de Rennes,* running south from St.-Germain and with fine shops, at least until it reaches *Boulevard Raspail. Boulevard St.-Michel* is another major Left Bank artery, with popular-priced shops, many dealing in books and shoes. A number of other Left Bank streets constitute a major antiques area, including *Rue des Sts.-Pères, Rue Jacob, Rue du Bac,* and riverfront *Quai Voltaire.*

DEPARTMENT STORES are a glory of Paris, quite on a par with those of big American cities, London, Copenhagen, and Tokyo and—given a pricing policy geared to a French clientele—constitute ideal shopping territory for the visitor, in contrast to pricey boutiques catering heavily to foreigners. The Big Two are both on Boulevard Haussmann, just behind the Opéra. Of these, *Galeries Lafayette,* perhaps the better-known, is a three-building complex: the center building is the main one, with multilingual interpreters, money exchange, travel agency, men's and women's hairdressers, watch repair; two of three restaurants, as well as several upper floors of women's and children's clothes, housewares, and kitchen equipment on five; and on main an immense perfume section, souvenirs, gifts and leather goods. Men's clothes and accessories have a building of their own, with Galfa Club (the store's house-label) and wares of ranking designers, as well, occupying three floors. A final building contains additional departments. *Printemps,* directly west, is another three-building complex, with its Welcome Service, hostesses, and women's and children's clothing and accessories in the building labeled Nouveau Magasin; home furnishings and kitchenware in Magasin Havre; and men's duds in a building to the rear of the Havre pavilion, called Brummel. (You'll see branches of both Galeries Lafayette and Printemps in cities throughout France.) Another chain—this one low-budget—called *Prisunic* has an outlet on Rue Caumartin to the rear of Printemps and still another branch on the Champs-Élysées; both have supermarkets. Still another France-wide cheapie chain, *Monoprix*, has two central outlets, one (with a giant supermarket) is a part of the Galeries Lafayette complex (above); another is on Avenue de l'Opéra, several blocks below the Opéra. *Aux Trois Quartiers* (Boulevard de la Madeleine) is a conservative old-timer, central as can be, with all departments in its main building, except men's clothing and accessories, in a detached building with its own name, *Madelios*. Across the river, again in a two-building complex, is the Left Bank's principal department store, *Bon Marché*, with the main entrance on Rue de Sèvres; don't miss the mouthwatering food department in Building No. 2. *La Samaritaine* (75 Rue de Rivoli) occupies no less than a quartet of buildings in a cluster east of the Louvre, with the emphasis on low-cost goods (have a look around for bargains) and a chief lure for visitors an on-high restaurant called to your attention on another page.

ANTIQUES: You are in a world-class antiques city. Ranking dealers—often with museum-caliber French seventeenth-, eighteenth-, and nine-teenth-century furniture, accessories, and paintings—include *Didier Aaron* (31 Avenue Raymond Poincaré), *Aveline* (20 Rue du Circle), *Étienne Levy* (178 Faubourg St.-Honoré), *Jacques Pérrin* (3 Quai Voltaire), and *Bernard Steinmitz* (4 Rue Drouot). Consider also *Galerie Vallois* (41 Rue de Seine—Art Deco); such dealers in *Le Louvre des Antiquaires* (2 Place du Palais-Royal) as *Flourens* (seventeenth- through nineteenth-century furniture); *Cordier* (Art Nouveau glass); *Alain Lesieutre* (antique oriental carpets); *Philippe Cézanne* (bronzes); *J. D. François* (eighteenth-century furniture); and *Galerie de l'Écaille* (seventeenth-century paintings and accessories). *Ors et Arts* (44 Rue des Sts.-Pères—antique silver); *Lucien Vigneau* (5 Rue des Sts.-Pères—antique porcelain); *Jacques Kugel* (135 Rue St.-Honoré—eighteenth-century furniture and accessories); *Éymery* (157 Rue St.-Honoré—Asian antiques); *Pinault* (27 Rue Bona-parte, autographs); *Pinault* (36 Rue Bonaparte—antique books), and *Jansen* (9 Rue Royale—antique furniture and accessories, as well as costly re-productions designed by the most celebrated of the city's interior design-ers).

ANTIQUES AUCTIONS: *Hôtel Drouot* (9 Rue Drouot) is the city's best-known auction house; it's enormous, and excellent buys are possi-ble. Sales take place Monday-Friday between 2:00 P.M. and 6:00 P.M., but you may inspect the merchandise in advance, daily from 11:00 A.M. to 6:00 P.M.

ART GALLERIES: Surely no city has more than Paris. Pop into any with works that appeal. General rule of thumb is established biggies on the Right Bank's Rue du Faubourg St.-Honoré, Avenue Matignon, and Boulevard Haussmann; less celebrated artists on the Left Bank's Boulevard St.-Germain and streets leading from it.

BARBERS AND HAIRDRESSERS: *Galeries Lafayette* (Boulevard Haussmann) has a staff of half a hundred, so that chances are you won't have to wait; no need to book ahead. Next-door *Printemps* is similarly good. *Henri Courant* (Avenue Franklin Roosevelt 61; phone 4359-14-40) is reliable for men. *Julie* (180 Boulevard St.-Germain; phone 4548-98-37) is unisex.

BOOKS: *Brentano's* (37 Avenue de l'Opéra) and *W. H. Smith* (248 Rue de Rivoli) have English-language books—huge stocks—as specialties. *Librairie Hachette* (20 Boulevard St.-Michel) has enormous stocks in all subjects—in French. *Opéra Hachette* (Place de l'Opéra at Boulevard des Capucines) is heavy on imported newspapers and magazines, including American. And bear in mind books on the fine arts in the *Librairie* of the *Musée du Louvre* (Tuileries); on the decorative arts in the *Librairie* of the *Musée des Arts Décoratifs* (107 Rue de Rivoli).

CHILDREN'S CLOTHES: Biggest selections are in department stores (above); also consider *Jones* (Avenue Victor Hugo) and—for toys, as well—*Au Nain Bleu* (406 Rue St.-Honoré).

COOKING LESSONS: *Club de Cuisine d'Hubert* is a school located in a restaurant where the teacher is chef-owner, offering individual and group classes, with English translations of lessons. Information: Monsieur Hubert, Bistro d'Hubert, 36 Place Marché St.-Honoré; phone 4268-03-00. And, of course, you will have heard of *Le Cordon Bleu* (24 Rue du Champs-de-Mars; phone 4555-02-77), easily booked on relatively short notice for a sample lesson—conducted in French.

CHOCOLATES: *Crillon Hôtel* (10 Place de la Concorde) vends its own made-on-premises chocolates—in my view, unsurpassed in France—in the same shop adjacent to the lobby wherein are also sold the hotel's porcelain, crystal, bathrobes, and the like. *Godiva* (11 Rue de Castiglione) and *Marquise de Sévigné* (32 Place de la Madeleine) are other tempting chocolate sources.

CRYSTAL: Department stores (above), of course, but for choice selections of Baccarat, Daum, and Lalique, head for *Limoges Unic* (12 Rue de Paradis); and check out *Christofle* (31 Boulevard des Italiens and 12 Rue Royale).

DUTY-FREE SHOPPING: Allow plenty of time upon departure for duty-free shops at *Aéroport Charles de Gaulle*. Besides a supermarket-type store with a big selection of French wines in varying categories and price ranges—as well as liqueurs, eaux-de-vie, liquor, chocolates, and tobacco—there are other shops selling French foodstuffs (remember, if you're bound for the U.S., that meat products—even canned—are *interdits*, more's the pity), silk scarves and neckties (those of Hermès are cheaper than in their Paris shop, and they're packed in Hermès' famous orange bags), perfumes and colognes, jewelry, leather, and other gifts.

FOOD SHOPS: They're everywhere: *boulangeries* (bread bakeries), *charcuteries* (French counterpart of our delicatessen, with cold meats, sausages, *pâtés*, *terrines*, salads), *pâtisseries* (wherein pastries are baked; when they have tables at which you may order, they double as *salons de thé*), *épiceries* (groceries), *fromageries* (cheese stores), and *supermarchés* (supermarkets, at which wines—nice for hotel-room aperitifs—are also sold). Have a look at the fabulous concentration of food shops on *Rue Lépic* (Montmartre) and *Rue de Seine* (Quartier Latin), also taking in the old-style open-air market—*Marché de la Mouffe* on Rue Mouffetard, near the Panthéon, on the Left Bank. And note these shops: *Fauchon* (26 Place de la Madeleine), the greatest retail food show in town, with a café (above) that's fun for lunch; *Hédiard* (21 Place de la Madeleine), a smaller-scale Fauchon, with vast varieties of tea, an excellent wine department, and a relatively new restaurant; *Caviar Kaspia* (17 Place de la Madeleine, with its own restaurant where you might enjoy caviar served with blinis); *Pétrossian* (18 Boulevard La Tour-Maubourg), celebrated for caviar and with its own caviar-restaurant in New York); *La Maison de Truffe* (19 Place de la Madeleine), for truffle addicts, but a full-fledged charcuterie as well.

FRENCH LESSONS: Long-established *Alliance Française* (101 Boulevard Raspail) teaches privately and in classes.

JEWELRY: Paris is one of the world's great jewelry cities, and it doesn't cost a sou to look at, for example: *Cartier* (12 Rue de la Paix) and the fabulous shops on Place Vendôme: *Aldebert, Boucheron, Gianmaria Buccellati, Chaumet, Van Cleef & Arpels*, and *JAR's* (in the arcade at No. 7).

KITCHENWARE AND TABLEWARE: *Déhillerin* (18 Rue Coquillière) is an old-timer, with copper pots (which they will ship) a specialty. Also try *Au Bain-Marie* (20 Rue Hérold)—tableware, table linens, cooking equipment; *Christofle* (31 Boulevard des Italiens and 12 Rue Royale) with its own reputed silver flatware, plus crystal and porcelain; *Culinarion* (99 Rue de Rennes)—a link of a mod-look national chain: clean-lined accessories for cooking, serving, dining; *Porcelaine Blanche* (108 Rue St.-

Honoré, 112 bis Rue de Rennes, and other locations), with well-priced white china the name of its game. (See also CRYSTAL above.)

LUGGAGE: I've had good luck at the big luggage department in *Printemps; Galeries Lafayette*'s good too. Consider also *Aux États-Unis* (229 Rue St.-Honoré), with dog collars and dog bowls with French legends for your Fido—*mais seulement s'il comprend le français;* and *Morabito* (1 Place Vendôme).

MARKETS: *Marché aux Puces* is the French for Flea Market. It's open Saturday, Sunday, and Monday each week, from 7:00 A.M. to 5:30 P.M., and it's a long Métro ride; get off at Porte de Clignancourt and allow yourself a good half day, as the market sprawls, there being some 3,000 dealers. Much of the stuff is elderly rather than antique. You must search diligently. A few dealers to look for: *J. Le Sault* (eighteenth- and nineteenth-century furniture); *Bernard Montalègre* (antique paintings and furniture); *Patrick Molina* (elderly accessories); and *Classic Art Deco*. And mind, you are expected to bargain over prices. *Marché aux Timbres* is French for Stamp Market, but note that old postcards are also on sale at this one. Location could not be more fashionable—corner of Avenue Marigny and Avenue Gabriel, just off Champs-Élysées, Thursday, Saturday, and Sunday, from 10:00 A.M. *Marché aux Fleurs* is the flower market lining the curbs of Place de la Madeleine on Tuesday, Wednesday, Thursday, Saturday, and holidays. And, on any day, take a walk on *Quai de la Mégisserie*, fronting the Seine just east of the Louvre, for a remarkable sidewalk market embracing birds, tropical fish, monkeys, and heaven knows what other lower-order representation.

MEN'S CLOTHING: I check out *Brummel*, the men's store at Printemps, and *Galfa Club* at Galeries Lafayette on each Paris visit; each stocks wares of name couturiers, but best buys are their house-label merchandise. *Daniel Crémieux*, a nationwide chain, is strongly influenced by classic American clothes and accessories; its Paris outlets are at 6 Boulevard Malesherbes, 24 Rue Marbeur, and 2 Place St.-Sulpice. *Façonnable* (whose Paris shop is at 1 Rue Royale) has stores France-wide, as well; its pricey clothes and accessories are Yank-influenced, too. *Cerruti* (3 Place de la Madeleine and 27 Rue Royale) sells its own-design clothes—smart, conservative, costly. *Marks & Spencer* (45 Boulevard Haussmann) is the very same you know from Britain—its sweaters and accessories can be good value (and there's an on-premises supermarket). *Hilditch & Key* (252 Rue de Rivoli) is from across the Channel, too—London's Jermyn Street—and sells elegant haberdashery. *Lanvin 2* (244 Rue de Rivoli) is quite possibly the smartest of the French-origin men's shops. *Charles Jourdan Monsieur* (12 Rue du Faubourg St.-Honoré)—clothes as well as shoes. *Yves St.-Laurent Homme* (38 Rue du Faubourg St.-

Honoré)—fashions not unlike those in foreign branches. *Hermès* (24 Rue du Faubourg St.-Honoré) has the most beautiful—and expensive—ties in town; other menswear, too. *Courrèges* (49 Rue de Rennes)—very trendy and pricey. *Givenchy Gentlemen* (3 Avenue Georges V)—smart and stylish, year in, year out. *Rodier Monsieur* (8 Rue Babylone; other locations)—sensibly priced shirts and sweaters. *J. C. d'Ahetze* (250 Rue de Rivoli)—good value neckties for as many years as I can remember.

PERFUMES: At every turn in this, the planetary perfume capital. Department stores and certain shops sell at list prices, albeit offering exemption from the government's 15% VAT tax if your purchases meet the legal minimum of the moment. At *De Gaulle Airport*'s duty-free shop you pay list but obtain VAT exemption regardless of the amount you buy—although variety of labels and bottle sizes can be limited. Trick, if your order will be at all substantial, is to buy at an in-town discount shop, offering diverse stocks, 20%–25% discounts from list *and*—if you meet the legal minimum—VAT exemption, as well, in which case savings are around 40%. *Michel Suisse* (15 Rue le la Paix) fills this bill, with huge selections, smiling staff, mail-order service, canvas bags gratis with bulky orders, and a manager—loquacious Max Cohen—who knows the scent scene, Balenciaga and Balmain through Weil and Worth.

SILVER: *Christofle* (31 Boulevard des Italiens, 12 Rue Royale) is the most esteemed; beautiful and expensive.

STATIONERY: *Armorial* (98 Rue du Faubourg St.-Honoré)—engraved note paper, personal/business cards, or invitations to your wedding.

WOMEN'S CLOTHING: Women's clothes in the couture capital of the world? Where begin? Where stop? Department stores devote by far the greater part of their selling space to female fashions; you want to check out *Galeries Lafayette, Printemps*, and *Marks & Spencer*—just opposite the Big Two on Boulevard Haussmann. But, to give you an idea of how easy it is to pop into the outlets of celebrated designers, I walked down Rue du Faubourg St.-Honoré with a notebook, and these are the shop names I noted: *Pierre Cardin, Louis Ferraud, Walter Stieger* (shoes), *Karl Lagerfeld, Chlöé, Hanae Mori, Courrèges, Yves St.-Laurent, Ungaro, Ted Lapidus, Guy la Roche, Léonard, Hermès*, and *Lanvin*. To these, add *Christian Dior* and *Valentino* on Avenue Montaigne; *Chanel* on Rue Cambon; *Maud Frizon* (shoes) on Rue des Sts.-Pères; *Charles Jourdan* (shoes), *Lancel*, and *Samantha* on Rue de Rennes; *Daniel Hechter* on Boulevard St.-Germain (and at other locations); *Kenzo* and *Thierry Mugler*—among many others—on Place des Victoires; and youthful, designer-owned boutiques like *Sierra* and *Point Fixe*, but a pair of the shops (both on Rue du Pont-Louis-Philippe) in the now-trendy Marais district.

INCIDENTAL INTELLIGENCE

Airport/Air Terminal: Pan Am and other transatlantic carriers use Aéroport Charles de Gaulle, at Roissy, 15 miles north of Paris. Efficiently operated buses that depart approximately quarter-hourly connect De Gaulle with Porte Maillot Air Terminal in the basement of the Palais des Congrès (Paris's Convention Center), not far northwest of Arc de Triomphe. From there you may take a taxi to your hotel, or vice versa. (Certain domestic flights take off from and land at Aéroport d'Orly, connected with bus service to Invalides Air Terminal on the Left Bank. Additionally, there is bus service between De Gaulle and Orly airports for passengers with connections, one to the other.)

In town, there are half a dozen *railway stations*, and it's important to ascertain the correct one, especially for departures. Four are on the Right Bank—Gare du Nord, Gare de l'Est, Gare St.-Lazare, and Gare de Lyon; while Gare d'Austerlitz and Gare Montparnasse are on the Left Bank. *Le Métro*—Paris's subway system—ranks with London's Underground, in my view, at least, as the world's best. I use taxis in Paris only for arrival to and departure from the air terminal, with baggage; otherwise, when not walking, I travel Métro. Pick up a map of the system, gratis, at any station. There are some 15 routes, each with terminus stations at their extremities. If you want to go from Place de la Concorde to Place Charles de Gaulle/Étoile, enter the Concorde station, buy a ticket specifying the class—first or second (difference in cost is minimal and facilities identical, but at rush hour first class is less crowded). Having studied your pocket map or wall maps, you know that you are to proceed to the platform of Neuilly-Vincennes line; you'll have noted on the map that your stop—De Gaulle/Étoile—is en route to the Neuilly end of the line, so you look for the track marked "Direction Neuilly," board the appropriate train, and exit at your station. Métro cars are equipped with maps of the route they travel, and signposting throughout the system is superb. Note, too, that some trips may involve a change of trains, or transfer. Key French word in this case is *correspondance;* by plotting out your route on a map in advance, you easily determine where to transfer. If you have bought a *France Vacances* train pass before leaving home, it will contain a *Paris Sésame* ticket, which allows you free Métro travel for a specified number of days. If not, or upon expiration of your Paris Sésame, buy a *carnet*, or packet of ten Métro tickets (at any station ticket window); it cuts the fare considerably. Carnets come first or second class; I counsel second. *R.E.R.,* which stands for *Réseau Express Régional,* is a suburban/exurban extension of the Métro and ideal for trips to such points as Malmaison and St.-Germain-en-Laye. Métro tickets are valid on buses, but bus routes are divided into fare-stages or *sections*. One ticket covers up to two sections; two tickets are valid for three or more sections.

Buses take a lot more getting used to than the Métro. Worth knowing about routes include No. 21, which takes you from Gare St.-Lazare, on the northern fringe of the Right Bank, through cores of both Right and Left banks, to Cité Universitaire, on the latter bank's southern edge; No. 73, connecting Place de la Concorde with the futuristic suburb of La Défense; and No. 82, which begins at Jardin du Luxembourg, passing one notable monument after another on both Left and Right banks, terminating at the American Hospital in the suburb of Neuilly. *Bâteaux Mouches* are the Seine River sightseeing vessels that first-timers often enjoy; they depart approximately half-hourly from Pont de l'Alma, at the foot of Avenue George V and have both open and glass-roofed decks. 1:00 P.M. and 8:30 P.M. departures are restaurant equipped. Competition includes *Vedettes du Pont Neuf* (departing from its pier on Pont Neuf, at Île de la Cité; and *Vedettes Paris-Tour Eiffel,* which departs from Pont d'Iéna on the Left Bank, just below the Eiffel Tower. *Bus tours* with varying itineraries are operated by such firms as *American Express* (11 Rue Scribe; phone 4266-09-99), *Cityrama* (4 Place des Pyramides; phone 4260-30-14), and *Paris-Vision* (214 Rue de Rivoli; phone 4260-31-25). An introductory half-day or day-long jaunt is never a bad idea, but before going off on longer, pricier tours, consider on-your-own excursions by train or rented car—of the kind I outline earlier in this chapter.

Visites-Conférences is French for guided walking tours conducted by extraordinarily well-educated specialists called *conférenciers* (who are not ordinary guides) to areas where they are experts, coordinated by the government's Caisse Nationale des Monuments Historiques; for information: Hôtel de Sully, 62 Rue St.-Antoine (in the Marais quarter); phone 4887-24-14. Tours are listed in issues of the What's On weekly, *L'Officiel des Spectacles.* Many firms provide sightseeing by guide-driven car; one that I can recommend from experience is *Service 3000,* whose president, Sylvain Deschamps, knows Paris—and all of France—very well, indeed; address is 35 Rue La Boétie; phone 4563-99-11.

Car rental: There are many options, among them *Avis* (phone 4609-92-12) and *Hertz* (phone 4788-51-51).

Press: English-language *International Herald Tribune* is published in Paris as a joint venture of *The Washington Post* and *The New York Times;* its news content is more international than Parisian, except in Saturday editions. Fluent in French or not, consult the leading dailies, *Le Monde* and *Le Figaro.*

Changing money: Hotels will, of course, but banks give better rates and are open from 9:00 A.M. straight through 4:30 P.M. weekdays, bless them. There are change offices at the airports, in-town air terminals, and all six railway stations; those at Gare de l'Est and Gare St.-Lazare remain open until 8:00 P.M. weekdays.

Paris Addenda: Police emergency phone is 17; police headquarters is at 9 Boulevard du Palais. Paris *Lost and Found* is at 36 Rue des Morillons;

phone 4531-14-80. *Main Post Office* (52 Rue du Louvre) is open 24 hours for phone calls, telegrams. . . . *To obtain a physician at night,* phone 4578-15-00; *day or night physicians:* phone 4542-37-00. *Pharmacie Dhéry* (84 Champs-Élysées, phone 4256-02-41) is open 24 hours. . . . *Ambulance* phone: 4887-27-50. . . . *United States Embassy* is at 2 Avenue Gabriel (phone 4296-12-02); *British Embassy:* 35 Rue du Faubourg St.-Honoré (phone 4266-91-42). *American Hospital* is at 63 Boulevard Victor-Hugo, in the suburb of Neuilly (phone 4747-53-00). . . . *British Hospital* is at 48 Rue de Villiers in the suburb of LeValois (phone 4758-13-12). *Further information: Office de Tourisme de Paris*, 127 Champs-Élysées, open daily with branches at Gare d'Austerlitz, Gare du Nord, Gare de l'Est, Gare de Lyon, and, in summer, Tour Eiffel; *Agence Nationale pour l'Information Touristique* (A.N.T.I.), at 8 Avenue de l'Opéra, is an all-France tourist information center.

3

Aix-en-Provence
The Quintessential Provence

BACKGROUND BRIEFING
It may perhaps be exaggerating to term Aix the quintessential Provence. But not by much. Arles (Chapter 6) is immediately associated with a foreign artist—Van Gogh. Nîmes (Chapter 27) technically—if not traditionally—in Languedoc, brings to mind memorable monuments of its ancient Roman period. Avignon (Chapter 7) has built its reputation on the palace of a succession of seven medieval popes. Marseille (Chapter 22), as a major metropolis, belongs as much to the entire south as to Provence.

Aix, though, is Provençal through and through, evoking the beauty of the region in a fountain-centered, boulevard-like main street and the Romanesque cloister of its cathedral, than which there is no lovelier in France. As seat of the Counts of Provence, it was the Provençal capital for much of the period embracing the formative twelfth through fifteenth centuries; toward the end of that period, the multi-titled René— variously King of Naples, Duke of Anjou, *Bon Roi* René de Provence— passed his final years in Aix, where his courtiers were writers and musicians; his pastimes, painting and poetry.

Post-René centuries saw Aix evolve as cultural center of Provence, even as it remained seat of the provincial *Parlement* until the *ancien régime* was no more, upon the advent of the Revolution. More recently, painters have replaced politicians. The most reputed was Aix-born Paul Cézanne, whose paintings of the neighborhood and its people motivate the Aix-bound visitor at least as much as the sculpture-embellished palaces lining Cours Mirabeau and the aromatic herbs—rosemary, thyme, marjoram—that distinguish Provençal cuisine.

ON SCENE

Lay of the Land: The landmark thoroughfare, *Cours Mirabeau*, cuts a horizontal swath through the city on a west-east axis, from a circle of a square called *La Rotonde* (a.k.a. *Place du Général de Gaulle*), flanked by the municipal casino, eastward to more modest *Place Forbin*, off which *Rue de l'Opéra* leads to the Théâtre Municipal. The *railway station* is south of La Rotonde on *Avenue Victor-Hugo*. Mansion-bordered *Rue du Quatre-Septembre* leads from Mirabeau past Musée Arbaud to *Place des Quatres-Dauphins*, named for sculpted dolphins of its Baroque fountain and flanked by Rococo mansions. Otherwise, most of what you will want to visit in Aix is a walk north from Mirabeau on *Rue Clemenceau* to *Place St.-Honoré* and the boutiques of the *Rue Marius-Reinaud.* Or go north on *Rue Nazareth* from Mirabeau to reach *Rue Aude,* smartest of the pedestrian shopping streets, which leads into shop-lined *Rue du Maréchal-Foch,* whose northerly terminus is *Place Richelme* just south of *Hôtel de Ville*—massively Baroque, but with a graceful Gothic clock tower. That square will take you into *Rue Saporta* which, as it continues north, becomes—when bisected by *Place des Martyrs de la Résistance*—*Rue Laroque,* locale of the cathedral and former archbishop's palace, now sheltering a museum.

Cathedral of Saint-Sauveur (Rue Laroque) spans a dozen centuries, with its oldest component part a sublimely beautiful octagon of a tower. The portal is Gothic; it frames a treasure: a pair of sixteenth-century carved-wood doors. Inside, beeline to a triptych, *The Burning Bush,* painted by the fifteenth-century artist Nicholas Froment. The nave's Flemish tapestries are standouts, too. But I've saved loveliest for last: the Romanesque cloister, each of its arches supported by a pair of pillars, no two of whose exquisite carvings are alike.

Musée des Tapisseries (Place des Martyrs de la Résistance) occupies a seventeenth-century palace that long served as residence of the archbishops whose seat was the next-door cathedral (above). Now, its second floor displays a collection of tapestries gathered by long-ago clerics. They occupy walls of a suite of high-ceilinged rooms, with the most arresting the series called *Les Grotesques,* a seventeenth-century Beauvais group that could be stage sets, peopled with dancers, musicians, and animals.

Pavillon Vendôme (Rue Vendôme, not far from Musée des Tapisseries) dominates a charming park and is the very model of a nobleman's townhouse, circa late seventeenth century; it bears the name of the Duc de Vendôme, a grandson of King Henri IV. There are two floors, with plasterwork walls and ceilings, paintings, and what furniture there is of high quality.

Musée du Vieil-Aix (17 Rue Saporta) is set in a Baroque mansion on a principal street that will lead you to the center of town. Halt, though, for lovingly tended memorabilia of Old Aix—paintings and prints, clothes and certificates, and, among much else, an exemplary collection of the carved-wood Provence figures called *Santons*.

Musée d'Histoire Naturelle (6 Rue Esparist): I'm not bringing this museum's collection to your attention, but rather its smashing Baroque facade, with a stone gate enclosing the courtyard and, within, original ceilings and carved-wood doorways and window frames.

Atelier de Cézanne (Avenue Paul-Cézanne): Cézanne was born in Aix and died here in 1906. You must visit Musée Granet (below) to see paintings by this major post-Impressionist in his hometown. Here, you'll find his studio carefully re-created, with a good bit of Cézanneiana exhibited, as well.

Musée Granet (Place St.-Jean-de-Malte) is, the cathedral and its cloister (above) excepted, a case of saving best for last. First things first: Cézanne paintings. By my count, there are five of that Aix-born Impressionist's works here, all small in size: *Bathsheba, Nature Morte, Madame Cézanne, Baigneuses,* and *Femme Nue*. Still another Granet painting, *Les Joueurs de Cartes*—a work of the Le Nain brothers dating to the seventeenth century—was used by Cézanne as a basis for his painting of the same name, at the Metropolitan Museum in New York. This museum is named for a nineteenth-century Aixois painter and contains a number of his works, none of them as good as a portrait of him, black-cloaked, by no less a master than Ingres. It's with Italians that the Granet starts you off—fine works by the likes of Vivarini, Giordano, and Guercino. Then comes a Rembrandt self-portrait to introduce the Dutch, with a De Hooch in this group, along with Seaghers and Paul Bril. Van Cleve and Rubens (the latter with handsome man-and-wife portraits) are the stellar Flemings. Cézanne aside, it is the late seventeenth-century and eighteenth-century French masters at which the Granet excels: Largillière and Philippe de Champaigne, Fragonard and Hugo Robert, Rigaud and Jacques Louis David. Take your time; this is one of the best art museums in provincial France.

Musée Arbaud (24 Rue du Quatre-Septembre): A visit to this museum—with its theme antique Provençal pottery, paintings, and prints, supplemented by antique books bound in leather—is killing two birds with one stone. You see the handsome Arbaud, occupying a Baroque mansion in the architecturally rich Quartier Mazarin. And, en route to it, you pass by facades of landmark neighboring houses.

Church of St.-Jean-de-Malte (Place St.-Jean-de-Malte), built by Knights of Malta in the thirteenth century, is distinguished by an extraordinarily wide nave. The high-altar painting is exceptional, and there are nineteenth-century replacements of original tombs of a pair of ancient Comtes de Provence.

SETTLING IN

Cézanne Hôtel (40 Avenue Victor-Hugo; phone 4226-34-73) is Aix's surprise package: a relatively recently refurbished house whose interiors are an exceptionally creative—and successful—mix of antique and contemporary furniture and accessories, teamed with an eclectic range of textiles and wallpapers. Even corridors are smashing: doors of each of the 44 rooms leading from them are taken from eighteenth-century armoires. Decor of each room is distinctive. One, for example, embraces a pair of canopied beds, plaid-spreaded, with beige club chairs; in another room, green-and-white wallpaper is complemented by white woodwork and crocheted white bedspreads, with furniture a mix of Directoire and modern. There's no restaurant, but both breakfast and a range of drinks—available at any hour—are served in rooms. And the staff is at once professional and cordial. *First Class.*

Nègre Coste Hôtel (33 Cours Mirabeau; phone 4227-74-22) has more than a central location going for it. This fine eighteenth-century mansion on the city's landmark street has been transformed into an exceptionally agreeable hotel with just three dozen no-two-alike rooms, accented with antiques of the period of construction. Breakfast only. *Moderate.*

Roi René Hôtel (14 Boulevard du Roi René; phone 4226-03-01) is a gracious old-timer with a welcoming staff, a capacious series of main-floor lounges, attractively Art Deco, a restaurant (cuisine is traditional style, with regional specialties featured) overlooking a terrace (to which it moves in summer), and a good-sized swimming pool. There are 64 rooms; nicest are period style, with toile fabrics, balconies overlooking the pool, and stall showers supplementing tubs in the baths. At the other extreme are smallish rooms on the top floor. The Roi René is not heart of town; you're a quarter-hour's walk south of Cours Mirabeau. *First Class.*

Des Augustins Hôtel (3 Rue de la Masse; phone 4227-28-59) is well worth knowing about; location is a pleasant street just off Cours Mirabeau. Setting is a onetime Augustinian monastery, still stone-walled, with soaring arches in public spaces. Original architectural details remain, as well, in certain of the 29 rooms. *Moderate.*

St.-Christophe Hôtel (2 Avenue Victor-Hugo; phone 4226-01-24) is neat as a pin, with a friendly reception area, mod-look bar-lounge, and half a hundred brightly contemporary rooms. Central as can be—edging Cours Mirabeau at La Rotonde—and good value. *Moderate.*

Le Manoir Hôtel (8 Rue d'Entrecasteaux; phone 4226-27-20): A hotel in a converted fourteenth-century monastery-cum-cloister should be a pleasanter experience than this turns out to be: Mattresses are saggy, even though the smallish rooms are antiques accented. There's a little lounge, and breakfast (the only meal available) is served in the now barren cloister. This house needs an intelligent and costly overhaul. Location is in a not-easy-to-find street north of Cours Mirabeau. *Moderate.*

Moderne Hôtel (34 Avenue Victor-Hugo; phone 4226-105-16) is small, efficiently run, and just down Avenue Victor-Hugo from La Rotonde; 22 rooms. Breakfast only. *Moderate.*

PLM Le Pigonnet Hôtel (Avenue du Pigonnet; phone 4259-02-90): Were it central, Le Pigonnet would top my Aix grouping. With a car, you can be very happy in this park-encircled good-looker of a hotel—a ten-minute drive from the center. Those rooms and suites I've inspected are antiques accented, with traditional design fabrics and wallpapers and, very often, big baths. Public spaces—lounge, bar, gardens, swimming pool—are a pleasure. So, indeed, is the restaurant, which moves to a terrace in summer and is evaluated on a later page. A PLM hotel. *First Class.*

Mas d'Entremont Hôtel (Route d'Avignon, several miles north of Avignon; phone 4223-45-32) is an attractive country house—rough walls, beamed ceilings, reproduction furniture in period style—with a restaurant and just eight rooms that, according to the proprietor-manager, are booked a year in advance by his French clientele. I received the distinct impression, in the course of my brief visit, that transatlantic guests are not welcome. *First Class.*

DAILY BREAD
Le Vendôme (Place du Général de Gaulle; phone 4226-01-00) is just the ticket for a gala Aix dinner (it's adjacent to the casino). Dine in the main salon, with a mural-topped fireplace; in an adjacent room highlighted by a stained-glass ceiling; or, in warm weather, on the terrace. Game is the specialty. There are three prix-fixe menus, with such openers as salmon *rillettes* or vegetable *terrine*, a fish course, *médaillon* of veal or filet of beef as entrées, cheese to follow, and a choice of desserts. *First Class/Luxury.*

L'Abbaye des Cordeliers (21 Rue Lieutaud; phone 4227-29-47) is especially inviting on a sunny day, when your table is set under shady trees in the garden, whose residents include two dogs, a cat, and an itinerant rooster. Order either of the prix-fixe menus, opening perhaps with *foie gras de canard* or a beautifully presented platter of *crudités*-cum-dips. *Brochettes d'agneau*—grilled cubed lamb on a skewer—is a favored entrée, one of a number. Super sweets. Charming. *First Class.*

Flambée des Bourres (22 Rue Lieutaud; phone 4227-69-69) is rustic stone-walled in look, with grills the specialties. Smoked salmon makes a nice opener. Choose *filet de boeuf, brochette Provençale,* or lamb chops; for dessert, the house's own sherbet. *First Class.*

Le Bouchon (19 Rue des Tanneurs; phone 4227-92-66): The open kitchen at the rear is appetite-producing. Well-priced menus might open with *piperade,* the masterful omelet of the Basque country; continue with *escalope de porc,* nicely garnished; and then conclude with *crème caramel.* *Moderate.*

Le Picotin (16 Rue de la Paix; phone 4227-95-44) makes a specialty of *confits*—the preserved meats and poultry of the Southwest. They come off only fairly well; highlight of a meal here is its conclusion: utterly delicious baked-on-premises sweets, including *mousse au chocolat* served with a fresh-orange salad; *tarte tatin,* the Norman upside down cake; and a chocolate cake smothered with the irresistible sauce called *crème anglaise.* Small and friendly. *First Class.*

La Gousse d'Ail (15 Rue des Tanneurs; phone 4227-94-25) is a happy choice for a modestly tabbed meal. The prix-fixe might open with sautéed shrimp, garlic accented, leeks and turnips puréed and baked in a deliciously crusted casserole; steak or *gigot d'agneau,* both served with *frites* are entrées; sweets follow. Cordial service. *Moderate.*

Malta (28 Place des Tanneurs; phone 4225-15-43) prides itself on being Aix's first pizzeria. The pies are indeed tasty, but you may have *entrecôte* or *poulet aux frites,* if you prefer. Take a table on the terrace. *Moderate.*

Le Pigonnet Hôtel Restaurant (Avenue du Pigonnet; phone 4259-02-90)—though away from the center—is worth the drive from town on a moonlit evening, when dinner is served al fresco. Prix-fixe menus are based on traditional specialties. Super soups—cream of mushroom and cream of asparagus, to name two—to begin. Seafood salad or a savory *tarte* might follow. Entrées—always with an interestingly prepared potato—are usually beef or lamb. Don't skip the cheese platter, nor, for that matter, dessert. *First Class.*

Arbaud (19 Cours Mirabeau; phone 4226-66-88) is up a flight, in a sumptuous Cours Mirabeau mansion dating back two centuries, with decor (brocaded walls hung with fine paintings and illuminated by crystal chandeliers) of the period. At lunch, salads are tasty. Go for afternoon tea. Or pop in for a dinner centered on *maigret de canard* (breast of duck) or *filet de boeuf*. *First Class.*

Café des Deux Garçons (27 Cours Mirabeau) is Aix's preeminent see-and-be-seen watering hole and has been since Émile Zola was an habitué. Take an outdoor table; order coffee, *pastis*, or a snack; and watch the passing parade. *Moderate.*

SHOPPER'S AIX
Printemps (Avenue des Belges) and *Monoprix* (Cours Mirabeau) are principal department stores. *Souleïado*, which makes a specialty of typically Provençal hand-blocked cottons (which are sold in the United States) is on Place des Tanneurs. Rue Aude is chock-full of fine shops, including *L'Herbier de Provence* (also in the U.S., with attractively packaged herbs), *Geneviève Lethu* (housewares, including Provençal linens, with china in matching patterns), *La Layette* (kids' clothes), and *Comptoir Anglais du Thé* (jams and other food gifts). Rue Marius Renaud is another chic street, with *Yves St.-Laurent, Charles Jourdan, Daniel Hechter, Lasserre,* and *MicMac*—essentially for women—all represented; and such men's shops as *Daniel Crémieux*. Rue du Maréchal Foch is strollable, too, with *Rodier* and *Georges Rech* but a pair of smart shops. *Paradox* is the name of an English-language book and periodical shop at 2 Rue Reine Jeanne.

SOUND OF MUSIC
Théâtre Municipal (Rue de l'Opéra) is Aix's eye-filling, four-tier opera house, still with original nineteenth-century decor. Besides opera, there are concerts, ballet, and plays. (The last three weeks of July is the traditional time for Aix's renowned summer music festival, with events scheduled at a number of sites, including the interior and the cloister of Cathedral Saint-Saveur and Hôtel de Ville's courtyard.)

INCIDENTAL INTELLIGENCE

This is a region well served by long-distance buses, as well, of course, as by train. Avignon (Chapter 7), for example, is less than an hour and a half from Aix by bus, and there are sightseeing bus tours—half-day and day-long—to regional points. *Further information:* Office de Tourisme, Place du Général de Gaulle, Aix-en-Provence.

4

Angers
Evoking the Plantagenets

BACKGROUND BRIEFING
Consider a visit to this humming, handsome, history-rich city—at the western edge of the Loire Château country—and you must, at the same time, consider the Plantagenets. The extraordinary Anglo-French dynasty—whose early nickname, a derivative of *planta Genista*, a species of bush, bits of which the clan's progenitor wore as a part of his head-dress—is more properly named Angevin, connoting Angers origins. Angevin is to this day what you are called if you are fortunate enough to live here, as, indeed, did Counts of Anjou, starting in the tenth century.

One of those counts, the very same Geoffrey who wore twigs of *planta Genista* in his hats, unwittingly commenced an English relationship of consequence when he married Matilda, daughter of English King Henry I. Their son became Henry II, first of a considerable clutch of Plantagenet rulers (Richard I, John, Henry III, Edward I, Edward II, Edward III, and Richard II). But more to the point of this chapter, Henry II took as his wife no less formidable a personage than Eleanor of Aquitaine, at once daughter of the powerful Duke of Aquitaine and divorced wife of the French King, Louis VII. These first Plantagenets, whose remarkable realm came to include much of France, as well as England, not only based themselves in Angers, but lived in and expanded the castle that remains today this city's principal—and most visited—landmark. Later centuries saw dukes of Anjou, successors to the counts, rule from an increasingly wealthy Angers, with the fifteenth-century's learned, militarily cunning, and well-liked René, the last of the line.

ON SCENE
Lay of the Land: The *Maine River* flows through Angers, north to south, but does not bisect it evenly, in the manner of, say, the Seine with respect to Paris. Bulk of the city—its core—is on the east, or Right Bank,

in a quadrangular area bounded by the river to the west, *Boulevard du Général-de-Gaulle* (which becomes *Boulevard de Roi-René*) to the south, and *Boulevard Carnot* to the north. *Rue des Lices*—midships in this area— is Main Street, with big department stores like Nouvelles Galeries and Dames de France. It leads into *Place du Ralliment*, ideal starting point for a leisurely walk through *Vieux-Angers*—along atmospheric streets, lined by Renaissance and medieval houses. Still another square—this one distinguished by a half-timbered sculpture-embellished, fifteenth-century house, Maison d'Adam—is *Place Ste.-Croix*. The landmark cathedral is adjacent, and the city's multitower château is nearby, edging the river.

Château d'Angers (Place du Président-Kennedy) is the catchall name for a thirteenth-century complex flanking the Maine River, whose walls are punctuated by 17 perfectly splendid towers, some nearly 200 feet high, and surrounded by moats, partially surfaced as formal gardens, partially the venue for a herd of deer. This longtime seat of the Counts of Anjou—almost razed in the sixteenth century, but mercifully spared— is one of the great French fortresses. There are a number of visitable interiors—a mini-château where King René of Anjou was born half a millennium back; a charming chapel of the same era; royal apartments; and, most spectacularly, *La Tenture de l'Apocalypse*, commissioned by Duke Louis of Anjou in the fourteenth century and to this day a record holder: largest tapestry extant—551 feet long, 16 feet high. With its theme the Apocalypse—it embraces seven sections, each with a dozen subdivisions—this masterwork, in shades of red, blue, and gold, was woven in Paris over a half-decade period, beginning in 1375. It reposes in a modern pavilion constructed for the purpose, some 350 feet long. But the Apocalypse tapestry has company. Others, only somewhat more recent, are on display in the chapel and other castle spaces.

Cathedral of Saint-Maurice (Place Freppel) has a smashing situation atop stone steps that climb a fair-sized hill, ascent of which brings into perspective a building of impressive symmetry. Two bold steeples of this essentially twelfth- and thirteenth-century church flank an incongruous third, added several centuries later. The cruciform-shaped interior makes much of a splendid transept bordered by superb rose windows. The Gothic nave is handsomely vaulted and the colonnaded and gilded altar—though as recent as the eighteenth century—manages to fit well into its surroundings. Observe the stained glass created over a four-century span, starting with the twelfth. Departing the cathedral, pop into *L'Ancien Évêché* (2 Rue de l'Oisellerie), a nineteenth-century rebuilding—for the most part—of the medieval bishop's palace, still with a twelfth-century chapel, chapter room, and sixteenth-century staircase.

Musée des Beaux Arts (10 Rue du Musée) is headquartered in Logis Barrault, a turreted palace erected five centuries ago by the man whose name it takes—a rich noble who was thrice mayor of the city. Beeline for the French eighteenth-century work. Watteau's *Les Concerts Champêtres* is the most celebrated single painting. But such masters as Chardin, Boucher, Greuze, Van Loo, and Lancret are represented, too.

Hôtel Pincé (a.k.a. Musée Turnin de Crisse; 12 bis Rue Lenépeveu, near Place du Ralliement) is a knockout of a Renaissance palace fronted by a formal garden that had for long been seat of a distinguished Angers family. Within, architectural and decorative features—coffered ceilings, massive fireplaces, well-proportioned staircases—are at least as interesting, to me, as displays of Oriental art.

Hôpital St.-Jean (4 Boulevard Arago): You cross the river to visit this hospital, dating to the twelfth century and used for the purpose for which it was built, to care for some 200 patients—half men on one bay of the main ward, half women on the other—until as recently as 1865. There are a cloister, a chapel still with original stained glass, a wine museum in the basement, and—star of the St.-Jean show—a set of tapestries by a contemporary weaver, Jean Lurçat, collectively titled *Le Chant du Monde.*

Church of St.-Serge (Avenue Marie-Talet) is an Angers treasure—visitable principally because of the magnificent Gothic nave and pair of side aisles, an also-venerable choir, and stained glass as old as the twelfth century.

Église Reformée (12 Rue du Musée) was not, of course, a Protestant church when it went up in the twelfth century. Happily, the original architecture—that of a small, severe chapel built during the transition period between Romanesque and Gothic—remains, the capitals of columns supporting vaults the only embellishments.

Musée David d'Angers (34 Rue Toussaint): This thirteenth-century church, no longer sanctified and with a decidedly contemporary glass roof, houses works by the nineteenth-century local sculptor whose name it takes. The architectural mix of the building—opened by President Mitterrand in 1984—is decidedly striking; you will have to decide for yourself whether David's sculpture was worth all the effort.

Saumur (25 miles southeast of Angers) is a pretty Loire River town dominated by *Château de Saumur* (Place du Château) whose profile of towers, turrets, slate roofs, and chimneys has been the subject of paintings—and later photographs—ever since it was erected five centuries ago by Duke Louis I of Anjou. There have been alterations over the years, none of them seriously damaging, and the castle was put to varying uses—prison, army barracks, military arsenal. At the turn of this century, the city of Saumur bought the place, set it to rights, and installed within a pair of delightful museums. The more important—*Musée des Arts Décoratifs*—embraces an entire floor filled with furniture, art objects, porcelain, and tapestries, with the range a thirteenth-century enameled crucifix through *fauteuils* (armchairs) of the Louis XV period of the eighteenth century; the Medieval Hall—chock-filled with tapestries, furnishings, and monochrome sculpture of the Middle Ages—is perhaps the loveliest room. An upper story is for equestrians—a veritable international museum of the horse.

A quartet of Anjou châteaux: The Anjou region surrounding Angers is rich in still-inhabited châteaux, none as celebrated as the Loire châteaux to the east (Chapter 20), but hardly to be passed by. Here are a selected quartet, each about a half-hour's drive east of Angers. *Château de Brissac* (Route N-748) is a veritable Renaissance skyscraper. Building seven stories skyward at the turn of the sixteenth century was by no means common. Its pair of formidable towers makes this a fortress, as well as a residence. Still, state rooms are not without amenities; the range is from Gobelin tapestries, Limoges porcelain, and frescoed walls to gilded ceilings, eighteenth-century furniture, and an amusing mid-nineteenth century theater. Your hostess is the Marquise de Brissac. *Château de Montgeoffrey* (Route D-74) is a celebration of the late eighteenth century, although it's flanked on one side by a medieval church and on the other by dramatic towers of the same period. The grand salon, within, is a felicitous mix of Louis XV furniture with Louis XVI paneling. And there are paintings by such artists as Poussin, Rigaud, Desportes, and Van Loo. La Famille Contades are your hosts. *Château de Montreuil-Bellay* (Route N-38) is surrounded by a high wall punctuated by circular towers, its inner precincts containing a splendid church and arcaded subterranean passages. Decor is based on furniture of the seventeenth and eighteenth centuries. And there is a fabulous kitchen. *Château du Plessis-Bourré* (Route N-23) is formidable from without—a veritable fortress, high-walled and with a conical tower at each of its four corners. Go inside, then, crossing the wide moat, and you'll note that this originally fifteenth-century construction is very comfortable as you pass through antique-furnished library, drawing room, and—most impressive—splendidly frescoed guard room.

SETTLING IN
Concorde Hôtel (18 Boulevard Foch; phone 4187-37-29) is a crackerjack modern house, core of town, that is one of the best equipped and best operated that I know in provincial France. There are 75 rooms and suites,

each of whose baths has a proper shower-cum-curtain attached to the tub, along with plenty of soap and towels. There are thoughtful touches in the rooms, like makeup mirrors over combination desk-vanities. Staff —reception, concierges, chambermaids—is quick, bright, and smiling. And the restaurant, about which I write more on a subsequent page, is an all-Angers leader. Hôtels Concorde. *First Class.*

D'Anjou Hôtel (1 Boulevard Foch; phone 4188-24-82) is meticulously owner-managed, with half a hundred attractive rooms, Louis XV-style bar-lounge, Louis XIV-style Restaurant La Salamandre, and central situation. Very nice. Mapotel/Best Western. *First Class.*

Mercure Hôtel (Place Pierre-Mendès-France; phone 4160-34-81), abutting the city's modern convention center complex and Jardin des Plantes, is itself contemporary. If it will not win a beauty contest, it is neat and functional, with 86 rooms, rust-hued bar-lounge, and pink and white restaurant whose picture windows give onto the Botanical Garden. Chaîne Mercure. *First Class.*

De France Hôtel (8 Place de la Gare; phone 4188-49-42) is elderly but has been thoroughly updated; there are 62 rooms with bath or shower, reputable restaurant, and pub-bar. Near the station. *Moderate.*

Du Progrès Hôtel (26 Rue Dénis-Papin; phone 4188-10-14): This 42-room house's interior designer felt no restraint with respect to the use of primary colors, nor any inhibitions with respect to restraint in the selection of wallpapers. Withal, it is spotless, welcoming, and convenient to the railway station. Breakfast only. *Moderate.*

Le Prieuré Hôtel (Chênehutte-les-Tuffeaux, near Gennes, which is four miles west of Saumur; phone 4150-15-31) is a pristine white château—dating to the fifteenth century—in its own 60-acre park, elevated from the Loire. Public spaces are handsome, and the 40 rooms and suites are partly in the main building, partly in detached pavilions, with the higher-up river-view accommodations the choicest. The restaurant—its cuisine is traditional, albeit nouvelle-accented—is exceptional; there are tennis courts and a swimming pool, and service is warm and welcoming. Member, Relais et Châteaux. *Luxury.*

DAILY BREAD

Le Toussaint (7 Rue Toussaint; phone 4187-46-20) is agreeably traditional—*rillettes de porc* or *foie gras* to start and entrées of beef or chicken. *First Class.*

Le Logis (17 Rue St.-Laud; phone 4187-46-15) has made a reputation on seafood; you will not regret ordering sole prepared Logis style. Very pleasant. Central. *First Class.*

Le Grand Cercle (Concorde Hôtel, 18 Boulevard Foch; phone 4188-52-37) is big, bustling, and welcoming, with a pleasant buzz, especially at lunch, when Angers business types come in to help themselves from the huge—and delicious—buffet, an Angers institution. You do well, too, with *soupe à l'oignon* to start, entrées like *brochette* or filet of beef, and grilled lamb chops. And don't skip the *gratin* potatoes. *First Class.*

Belle Rive (25 bis Rue Haute Reculée; phone 4148-18-70) is well named, given a situation overlooking the Maine River, a few minutes' drive from the center of town. Start with *soupe au poisson*, continue with *entrecôte Roquefort*, and conclude with the house's own *profiteroles au chocolat*—a rich, puff-pastry-and-chocolate confection. Friendly. *Moderate.*

Le Blé Noir (43 Rue Delaâge; phone 4187-03-81): You're just next door to Brittany—whence French crêpes originated. There's a big choice of them here, savory and sweet. *Moderate.*

Pâtisserie/Salon de Thé du Château (55 Rue Toussaint) is just the spot for a mid-morning or mid-afternoon pick-me-up; made-on-premises pastries accompany your tea or coffee. *Moderate.*

AFTER DARK
Théâtre Municipal (Place du Ralliement), elaborately Second Empire, with a frescoed ceiling, is the site of concerts, drama, and ballet.

INCIDENTAL INTELLIGENCE

Further information: Office de Tourisme, Place du Président-Kennedy, Angers.

5

Annecy
Savoie's Best-Kept Secret

BACKGROUND INFORMATION

Alpine peaks? They're for mountain climbers, skiers, and, of course, the rest of us who enjoy cablecar rides to their summits-cum-views (Chamonix, Chapter 14). But what of history-laden towns in Alpine valleys? In the case of France's Savoie region, they constitute treasure troves of art and architecture complemented by lakes that are inland seas and by backdrop mountains that have assured centuries-long insularity. Only in relatively recent years have outlanders like ourselves popped in to partake of their spectacular beauty.

The point about urban Savoie, if that it may be called, is that, unlike the winter resorts—which are a modern-times phenomenon—it considerably predates the mountaineers. Though it is compact—French Savoie is bordered on the north by Lake Geneva, on the west by the Rhône, on the south by France's Dauphiné country (which is centered on Grenoble—Chapter 18), and on the east by the massif along which lie its borders with Italy and Switzerland—it is not lacking in the patina that is a concomitant of advanced age. The range has been Julius Caesar through Burgundians, Holy Roman emperors, and later Savoy Kings in power through the middle of the last century.

In common with lesser nobles, the church, and a long-wealthy mercantile class, Savoie's governors have left their mark in these towns. None of them is big or of special contemporary significance. But they combine to present a dimension of France like no other in the republic. And Annecy—its castle out of the Brothers Grimm, its canals overhung with flowers and swan-populated, its lake a shimmering jewel—takes pride of place.

ON SCENE

Lay of the Land: Dominant landmarks make Annecy geographically quick to comprehend. *Lac d'Annecy*—nine miles long, two miles wide, and the third largest in France—edges its core to the east, with jagged, snow-dusted peaks backing it. *Thiou Canal,* flowing on a west-east axis into the lake, is flanked by a jumble of pedestrian streets like *Rues Ste.-Claire, Perrière,* and *Filaterie,* the lot of them lined by fine old houses, Renaissance through Rococo, with outdoor cafés at intersecting squares. *Jardin Public,* a public park occupying a peninsula jutting into the lake, is the point from which lake steamers depart. The railway station is northwest of the center on *Place de la Gare.*

Château d'Annecy (Place du Château) was home to counts of Geneva for most of the thirteenth century, until the last of the family line became Pope Clement VII and made his home in Avignon (Chapter 7). Dukes of Savoie were their successors through the mid-eighteenth century. You go to see it not only to appreciate its architecture—it is a maze of square towers with high-ceilinged inner spaces and a broad terrace affording panoramas of peaks, lake, and city—but also to take in *Musée d'Annecy.* Relatively recent—and utilizing contemporary museum presentation techniques—this is a compendium of Annecy history, at its best in the section relating to the town's Roman origins, with some superb sculpture; but with a plethora of antique furniture, pewter, and pottery, as well.

Cathedral of St.-Pierre (Rue Jean-Jacques Rousseau), originally a Franciscan church, severely facaded, is mellow within—boasting a fine Gothic nave and exuberantly Baroque altar, pulpit, and organ. St. François de Sales, Annecy born and canonized for his accomplishments in converting Protestants to Catholicism during the Counter-Reformation of the seventeenth century, lived across the street while he was Bishop of Annecy.

Church of St.-Maurice (Rue Granette), originally the chapel of a Dominican convent and enlarged in the fifteenth century, has as its prime lures a pair of Renaissance frescoes discovered quite by accident as recently as 1953, as well as a striking interpretation by the eighteenth-century painter Pieter Purbus, *The Descent from the Cross.*

Mont Veyrier, Lac d'Annecy, and Talloires: Mont Veyrier, some 4,000 feet over town, is easily ascended by cable car—departures are frequent; views, unforgettable. When you come down, allow time—several leisurely hours—for a boat tour of the lake. You may go for lunch or dinner on the water or on a boat sans restaurant. There are stops at villages along the way; if you've time to go ashore, select pretty little *Talloires,* with exceptional hotels and fare (below). Better yet, budget time for a stay of a night or two in Talloires—to completely unwind.

Aix-les-Bains (21 miles south of Annecy), though by no means out of business—everything's up to date in its popular thermal spa—just has to be a shadow of what it must have been a century and more back, when moneybags Victorians (including Victoria herself, with Avenue Victoria commemorating the royal visit) and even Americans (Boulevard Pierpont-Morgan is north of the core) came to take the waters, first put to therapeutic use by rheumatic Romans. But that is hardly to suggest that you not visit Aix. Taken as a period piece—alas, its grand hotels are no longer—it is not without interest. And Aix's setting—edging Lac de Bourget at the foot of Mont-Revard—remains spectacular. Indeed, a cable car ascent of the mountain—for an overall view of town and lake—makes for a proper introduction. Amble about the center of its pedestrian shopping area. *Palais de Savoie* (Rue du Casino) is the casino; you might like to try your hand at roulette, and there's a restaurant (with dinner-dancing) on the premises—fin de siècle, with a mosaic ceiling embellishing the lobby. *Thermes Nationaux* (Place des Thermes) is the spa. It was built in the last century, but it's gone through contemporary updating; you might be given a tour if you express interest at the reception desk. *Musée Lapidaire*, located in Hôtel de Ville, the town hall, is smallish but with choice sculpted remnants of Roman Aix. *Musée Faure* (Boulevard des Côtes) has as its trademark a Degas painting of a pair of tutu-clad ballerinas, but there are a number of other distinguished works, mostly nineteenth century, by the likes of Cézanne, Sisley, and Pissarro. Move along, then, to Boulevard du Lac, to take in small craft bobbing in the waters of *Petit Port*, which has both a public swimming pool and a bathing beach. Conclude with an excursion by lake steamer—there are frequent departures—of *Lac du Bourget*, zeroing in on a single destination like the pretty village of *Le Bourget du Lac* (whose originally eleventh-century *Prieuré*, a onetime cloistered monastery-cum-garden, welcomes visitors) or opting for the Grand Tour du Lac, an overall view of a beautiful segment of Savoie.

Chambéry (14 miles from Annecy), smallish and uncelebrated contemporarily, knew eminence in earlier centuries. As early as the fifth, it was the seat of a bishop. From the early thirteenth through the mid-sixteenth, its castle was home to Dukes of Savoy. It remained rich enough to have built, in the early nineteenth century, the elegantly arcaded street, *Rue de Boigné*, which cuts through town—passing *Place St.-Léger*, core of the pedestrian shopping precinct—from one principal monument to a second. The first is *Château des Ducs de Savoie* (Place du Château), a still splendid complex and locale of both *Cathedral of St. François de Sales* (Gothic with a lovely apse and cloister) and *Ste.-*

Chapelle (Gothic, as well, with its kicker a painted *trompe l'oeil* ceiling that looks stone-carved but isn't) and fine stained glass. The second, at the opposite end of porticoed Rue de Boigné, is *Fontaine des Éléphants* (Place Octagone), a nineteenth-century tribute to the same wealthy and generous local whose name was given to Rue de Boigné and who struck it rich in Asia; thus, its standout feature—life-sized, sculpted elephants peering out at pedestrians from each of the monument's four sides. *Musée des Beaux-Arts* (Place du Palais de Justice) surprises with its estimable collection. Italians are especially strong— Titian, Giordano, Guercino, and Uccello, whose *Portrait of a Young Man* is the star of the show. *Musée Savoisien's* (Boulevard du Théâtre) ranking exhibits are a clutch of medieval paintings—so-called Savoie Primitives—and sculptures; the setting is super: a onetime Franciscan monastery-cum-cloister.

Évian, an unassuming little spa town on the south shore of the Lake of Geneva (a.k.a. Lac Léman), just opposite the Swiss city of Lausanne (with which it is linked by frequent and fast—45-minute—ferry service), bases itself on *Rue Nationale,* a pedestrian-shopping core that parallels the lake, with adjacent and handsomely maintained public beaches and swimming pool. In a flower-embellished, park-like setting, you'll find a modern spa building where visitors drink the therapeutic water (not the same as the Évian bottled table water, a staple throughout France) and a surprisingly small, mod-look casino, without so much as a whiff of grandeur. Less costly hotels are in this area, with the two best atop the hill that backs the town. Excitement? Aside from the casino, there's a cable car at nearby *Thollon* (several miles east) that ascends to the summit of *Plateau des Mémises* (4,800 feet). And there's lots of golf, tennis, and sailing on the lake. You go to Évian to relax.

SETTLING IN

ANNECY

Carlton Hôtel (Rue des Glières at Rue St.-François; phone 5045-47-74) is at once central and agreeable, with half a hundred traditional-style rooms in tones of brown and gold, bar-lounge, and inviting lobby. Breakfast only. *First Class.*

Au Faisan Doré Hôtel (34 Avenue d'Albigny; phone 5023-02-46) is lakefront and attractive, with just over 40 rooms—those I've seen are pleasant, although beds can be narrow—a flower-filled lobby, and a reliable restaurant, counseled below. *Moderate.*

La Réserve Hôtel (21 Avenue d'Albigny; phone 5023-50-24) is a deftly converted residence of some years, with just a dozen inviting rooms in shades of rose and beige, nicely wallpapered; a bar-lounge; and, in a modern wing, a picture-window restaurant. Lakefront. *Moderate.*

Ibis Hôtel (12 Rue de la Gare; phone 5045-43-21) is heart of town, in the pedestrian shopping zone, with 83 rooms, which are functional, if hardly fancy; a restaurant; and a bar. *Moderate.*

Alp Hôtel (26 Rue Vaugélas; phone 5045-59-80) has as its plus a core-of-the-city situation. This is a plainly modernized elderly house with 40 minimally furnished rooms, whose beds are the narrowest I have encountered in France. Breakfast only. *Moderate.*

TALLOIRES, LAC D'ANNECY

L'Abbaye Hôtel (phone 5067-40-88) is precisely what its name implies, a seventeenth-century Benedictine Abbey—lakefront and cloistered. Monks' cells have been deftly converted into guest rooms—just 31, no two alike, each (of those I inspected) antiques-accented and with good paintings. Rooms lead from either the cloister or a two-story-high gallery; their windows give onto the lake. Public spaces, including a bar-lounge in the monks' *cave* and a restaurant about which I write in a later paragraph, are a pleasure; management and staff are delightful. This is certainly one of France's most beautiful hotels. Member, Relais et Châteaux. *Luxury.*

Auberge du Père Bise (phone 5060-72-01) is the only luxury hotel I know of whose glass-walled kitchen is just opposite the reception desk in the lobby, a reflection of the significance management wisely accords the justifiably celebrated on-premises restaurant, evaluated in a later paragraph. The hotel itself—there are 34 suites and rooms—spreads itself around its own lakefront park, occupying several pavilions, with decor of accommodations varying, from Louis XIII with beamed ceilings to quite grand Louis XV. There's a congenial bar-lounge with a player-piano (it doesn't need a pianist) that's fun. The third generation of the founding family is in charge of a skilled and friendly staff. Member, Relais et Châteaux. *Luxury.*

L'Hermitage Hôtel (phone 5060-71-17), straddling a Talloires summit, is a contemporary house with a good-sized swimming pool, congenial bar-lounge, 40 terraced rooms, a picture-window restaurant serving traditional cuisine, and absolutely fabulous views. *First Class.*

AIX-LES-BAINS

Ariana Hôtel (Avenue de Marlioz; phone 7988-08-00)—set back in an away-from-the-center park adjacent to Marlioz Spa, which is No. 2 in Aix after that in the core of town—is modern, with 60 terraced and tasteful rooms, swimming pool, and both bar-lounge and restaurant attractively Art Deco. Impersonal service. *First Class.*

Des Îles Britanniques Hôtel (Place des Thermes; phone 7961-03-77) retains the name it took when Aix was popular with the British at the turn of the century. It has, to be sure, seen better days, but it remains spotless and cheerful. There are 88 traditional style rooms, no two quite alike, as well as a restaurant and bar-lounge. Location is *far* atop a *high* hill, heart of town; you want a car, unless you're a mountaineer. *Moderate.*

Le Manoir Hôtel (37 Rue George 1er; phone 7961-44-00) is an old-timer with a look of flowered wallpaper and upholstery, and just over 70 rooms, some good sized and with terraces. Restaurant. Situation is the summit of a veritable mountain overlooking town; you need a car. *Moderate.*

CHAMBÉRY

Le Grand Hôtel (8 Place de la Gare; phone 7969-54-54) would be even more desirable if it were more into the center, which is, however, easily walkable. This is a gracious, good-looking house, with high-ceilinged public spaces and 55 suites and rooms; those I have seen are traditional style, smart, comfortable. Breakfast only. *First Class.*

Des Princes Hôtel (4 Rue de Boigné; phone 7933-45-36) is nicely situated on Chambéry's snazziest street. The lobby is welcoming, those of the 50 rooms I have inspected—decor varies—are agreeable, and the restaurant is worthy of space in an additional paragraph. *Moderate.*

ÉVIAN-LES-BAINS

Royal Hôtel (phone 5075-14-00) has the best location in town: high above the hill overlooking Évian and the Lake of Geneva (when the atmosphere is clear, you can see Lausanne), in its own 28-acre, deer-filled park. The building went up at the turn of the century, when ceilings were high, proportions grandiose, decorative detail extravagant. A few years back, the current owners—the Pomméry champagne people—set aside a multimillion-franc budget, hired architects and interior designers from Paris, and set about restoring this grande dame stylishly, but retaining the atmosphere of the era in which it was constructed. They succeeded. A series of extraordinarily handsome lounges lead from the lobby, along with a kicky cocktail lounge and an enormous formal restaurant. Upstairs, there are 200 suites and rooms; those I have inhabited or inspected are smashers—capacious and terraced (you want to specify lakefront) with decor luxuriously low key. There's a swimming pool in the garden (around which barbecue lunches are served in summer), tennis courts-cum-pro, eighteen-hole golf course, a health club with attached dietetic restaurant, shuttle-bus service to the casino in town, and skilled concierges. Affiliated with both Leading Hotels of the World and Hôtels Concorde. *Luxury.*

La Verniaz Hôtel (phone 5075-04-90) embraces an impeccably maintained garden complex up in the hills behind town, with suites, chalets, and rooms—no two alike, but those I have inspected, comfortable—located in a mix of pavilions dotted about the swimming-pool-centered grounds. Lounges are stone-walled, with a country look; the cocktail bar could be a mountain chalet; and the restaurant, which moves outdoors in summer, is exemplary enough to warrant later comment. Management is friendly; staff, professional. Member, Relais et Châteaux. *First Class.*

Bellevue Hôtel (Rue Nationale; phone 5075-01-13) is a lovely, old-fashioned house, heart of town, with capacious public areas, corking good restaurant, pretty garden, and half a hundred rooms, with lakefront ones the nicest. *Moderate.*

La Bourgogne Hôtel (Rue Nationale; phone 5075-01-05) belies its advanced age with exceptionally good-looking rooms and phone-equipped baths. Reputed restaurant in connection. *Moderate.*

De La Plage Hôtel (Avenue Général-Dupas; phone 5075-29-50) is indicated for swimmers; it's opposite the municipal pool and adjacent beach. Some rooms are lakeview, some face the garden; those I've seen are smart. Restaurant and bar. *Moderate.*

DAILY BREAD

ANNECY

Auberge du Lyonnais (Quai de l'Évêché at Rue de la République) is congenial, canal-bordering, and heart of town, with perfectly delicious things to eat. From the well-priced menu, a meal might run to smoked Savoie ham, a slice of the house's own *terrine de petits légumes,* or grilled trout, followed by roast lamb or roast duck, the latter served with *gratin Dauphinois;* both cheese and dessert courses are included. Friendly. *First Class.*

Auberge de Savoie (1 Place St.-François, adjacent to the landmark Annecy church for which the square is named; phone 5045-03-05) is intimate and nicely appointed, with a competent kitchen. Order from the good-value menu, choosing perhaps a fish soup, filet of veal, deliciously sauced, with *tartes aux fraises*—buried under an avalanche of whipped cream—to conclude. *First Class.*

Au Faisan Doré Hôtel Restaurant (34 Avenue d'Albigny; phone 5023-02-46) is a source of lake fish, skillfully prepared, with meat entrées, as well, the lot served in conjunction with well-tabbed menus. It is lakefront and *Moderate.*

Le Crocodile (Place Ste.-Claire; phone 5045-31-30) bases its reputation on specialties of the Savoie: the hot cheese and kirsch dip called *fondue; raclette,* a cheese dish you may know from Switzerland; and super Savoie sausages. *Moderate.*

MS. Libellule (reservations, phone 5051-08-40) is the sleek, white lake steamer that sails each evening at eight o'clock from its heart-of-town pier on a two-and-a-half hour Lac d'Annecy dinner excursion. A traditional, multicourse meal is served on white linen in a candlelit, picture-windowed dining room. A floor show follows dinner, and there's a piano-bar aboard. Lunchtime sailings, too. Fun. *First Class.*

Le Fidèle Berger (Rue Royale) is heart of the pedestrian shopping area and indicated for a coffee/tea and pastry stop. *Moderate.*

Pub Cheltenham (Passage de l'Évêché) is a waterfront café. Pause for something to drink, the while taking in the beauty of Annecy—and its crowds. *Moderate.*

TALLOIRES, LAC D'ANNECY

Auberge du Père Bise (phone 5060-72-01): As I indicate when evaluating the hotel part of this lakefront operation (above), the open-to-view kitchen is just opposite reception, as you enter—an indication of the importance attached to a well-regarded restaurant. You may order from an extensive à la carte, but there are three prix-fixe menus, too. The least pricey might include oysters prepared the house's own way or pigeon casserole, followed by cheese and *méli-mélo*—a fabulous mélange of fruits and ice cream—with baked-on-premises *petits-fours* to accompany coffee. Tarragon-flavored or truffled chicken, lobster grilled or as the basis of a Breton-origin stew; roast shoulder or saddle of lamb, a goose-liver masterwork (*escalope de foie d'oie Richelieu*)—these are a handful of other memorable entrées. Breakfast is special here, too, with the best croissants I have had outside of Paris, except for those at De La Poste Hôtel in Beaune. And service is as skilled as it is smiling. In my experience, one of France's best restaurants. *Luxury*.

L'Abbaye Hôtel Restaurant (phone 5067-40-88) presents a pair of four-course, prix-fixe menus. You might commence with a terrine of *foie gras de canard* served in tandem with a salad, continue with an unusual *escalope* of lake trout served with a confit of onions, follow with cheese from an oversized platter, and conclude with choice of desserts. *First Class*.

AIX-LES-BAINS

Lille (Grand-Port; phone 7935-04-22)—not surprisingly, given its gar-den-backed, lakefront setting—does very well by fish. There are well-priced menus and an à la carte, as well. Consider a meal that would open with *omble* (char—a type of salmon), champagne sauced; continue with the house's sautéed chicken specialty; and conclude with a mouthwater-ing raspberry *soufflé*. Congenial. *First Class*.

Brasserie de la Poste (32 Avenue Victoria; phone 7935-90-65) is old-reliable, heart of town, and satisfactory for a lunch of, say, *entrecôte aux frites* or *salade Niçoise*. If it's sunny, take an outdoor table. *Moderate*.

Le Verre d'Eau (Place de l'Hôtel de Ville): You're determined to be the first on your block to taste Aix's long-celebrated thermal water. As the title suggests, this café is the place. Outdoor tables. *Moderate*.

CHAMBÉRY

Des Princes Hôtel Restaurant (4 Rue de Boigné; phone 7933-45-36) makes its home in a delightful, traditional-style room and serves up essentially traditional-style fare. Open with a salad based on smoked breast of goose and choose grilled filet of beef—deliciously garnished and sauced—as your entrée. *First Class*.

Roubatcheff (6 Rue du Théâtre; phone 7933-24-01): There are three prix-fixe menus and an à la carte, including such specialties as smoked-trout salad; *brochette* of grilled fish, a kind of marine shishkebab; fricas-see of chicken, Roquefort sauced; and a luxuriant Grand Marnier *soufflé*. Attractive. *First Class/Luxury*.

La Venoise (44 Rue Pierre-Lanfrey; phone 7969-02-78) is tiny, cramped, and overdecorated, but food can be satisfactory, as, for example, a meal embracing fish soup or a casserole of baked mussels, filet of red snapper, basil scented, or a competently sauced *filet de boeuf* accompanied by *pommes Dauphiné*. *First Class.*

Taverne (Place St.-Léger) is heart of the action, on the square that anchors the pedestrian shopping zone. Take an outside table. *Moderate.*

ÉVIAN-LES-BAINS

La Verniaz Hôtel Restaurant (phone 5075-04-90) is at its best in summer, when tables are set in the garden. But the indoor restaurant—tables set in pink linen, with Louis XV chairs—is attractive, too. The two menus are both good value. A meal might commence with the house's own hot trout terrine or fresh *foie gras*, continue with saffron-scented steamed turbot or *aiguillettes de canard*, with cheese and dessert following. And note that grilled meats are a specialty—the filet of Charolais beef for two and grilled lamb chops, especially. *First Class/Luxury.*

SOUND OF MUSIC
Théâtre Charles-Dullin (Rue du Théâtre, Chambéry) is a regional showplace—nineteenth century—and based on the design of Teatro alla Scala in Milan. Go for opera, ballet, concerts.

INCIDENTAL INTELLIGENCE

Aéroport de Chambéry–Aix-les-Bains, is at Le Bourget-du-Lac, five miles north of Chambéry; scheduled domestic flights. *Further information:* Office de Tourisme, 1 Rue Jean-Jaurès, Annecy; Place Mollard, Aix-les-Bains; 24 Boulevard de la Colonne, Chambéry; Place d'Allinges, Évian-les-Bains.

6

Arles
Caesar's Legions and Van Gogh

BACKGROUND BRIEFING
The irony of this small Provençal town is that despite early eminence as a Roman colonial city founded by no less an emperor than Julius Caesar—with still-standing Caesar-commissioned constructions—it was not until after a prolific Dutch-born artist came for a 15-month sojourn some 900 years later, that it achieved a measure of global repute.

And the irony is compounded when one considers that even though Vincent Van Gogh created some 300 paintings, drawings, and watercolors during his Arles stay, not a single one of his works hangs in its art museum. The painter's association with the town is evident today only in postcard reproductions of works in distant galleries, for sale at the occasional news kiosk. A multilingual brochure, *Arles et Van Gogh*, published by the city tourist office, acknowledges the "hostile attitude of the Arlesian people" toward Van Gogh, but concludes that Arles "feels thankful to Van Gogh for having placed the name of the city in all the greatest museums of the world." As well it might.

The point of an Arles visit today is not, then, association with Van Gogh (of what he painted, only a rural road flanked by stone sarcophagi and a rebuilt out-of-town bridge, *Le Pont de Langlois*, remain), but, rather, the heritage of the Romans. They followed earlier Phoenicians and Greeks who had been attracted to this town's strategic situation at the mouth of the Rhône. Caesar's town dates to 49 B.C., and was heaped with perquisites accorded only those colonies in whose establishment he had a personal hand. Later emperors, like Constantine and Honorius, saw Arles only as the hub of the early Christian world, and it became the seat of regional archbishops. Now, though, its onetime cathedral is but a parish church.

ON SCENE

Lay of the Land: Although the Rhône flows through Arles, you've only to concern yourself with the larger right bank of town, whose core is marked by *Place de la République*, seat of a pair of landmarks: Hôtel de Ville, or city hall, and Church of St.-Trophime, the onetime cathedral. Commercial *Rue de la République* runs east-west, just below the square taking its name. What remains of the Roman theater edges *Place Pomme*, to the west, while the massive amphitheater is centered on *Rond-Point des Arènes*, directly to Place Pomme's north. *Boulevard des Lices* runs east-west and constitutes the southern edge of the city center; the railway station is at its northern tip.

Les Arènes (Rond-Point des Arènes): Some 1,900 years young, this amphitheater remains in use—not unlike its Nîmes counterpart—for the Provençal species of bullfighting, and you're in luck if your visit coincides with one of these spectacles. In any event, have a look at this remarkable monument, embracing 60 arches in its two remaining levels and built to accommodate 25,000 Roman-era Arlésiens, who came for the excitement of contests pitting gladiators against savage animals. The Middle Ages saw the amphitheater put to use as an enclosure for houses and shops, and the three towers built at that period—to fortify it—remain.

Théâtre Antique (Place Pomme): When they weren't watching gladiators at Les Arènes (above), ancient Arlésiens went to the theater, as, indeed, their descendants do many centuries later. Alas, much less of this theater remains than of the bigger amphitheater. A solitary pair of columns behind the stage—nicknamed Deux Veuves (Two Widows)—are reminders of what had been a fine portico, enclosed by a three-tiered arcade that surrounded a space large enough to accommodate 12,000 spectators. Arrive in Arles during July, and chances are the theater will be in use for a play or pageant.

Les Aylcamps (Avenue des Aylcamps, southeast of the center) is what, over long centuries, Arles has come to call this unusual cemetery originally named Champs Élysées—Elysian Fields. It is nothing more than an elongated thoroughfare, on either side of which residents, from the early Christian era through the Middle Ages, ordered elaborate sarcophagi containing their dead to be placed. Over the centuries, most of the best tombs disappeared; some, however, are now to be seen in the Musée d'Art Chrétien (below), while some—of lesser quality—remain in Les Aylcamps (not all that different today from when Van Gogh painted it). A ruined Romanesque Church, *St.-Honoré*, is at its terminus.

Musée Lapidaire (Place de la République) has as its inspired location the desanctified seventeenth-century Church of St.-Anne, its high and splendid Gothic-inspired vaults a fine foil for mint-condition Roman-era mosaics that line what had been the nave. The latter are flanked by other early Arles pieces—strikingly carved sarcophagi, fine busts, and full-length statues, as well.

Musée d'Art Chrétien (Rue Balze) is still another desanctified church seeing contemporary service as a repository of ancient art. Beautifully Baroque, originally built by Jesuits, it brims with lovely objects, most of them early Christian sarcophagi—many from Les Aylcamps (above)—with biblical scenes replacing those relating to Roman mythology in the sarcophagi at Musée Lapidaire (above). Take your time studying these; workmanship is exceptional. Before exiting, descend to the cellars—a 300 x 500-foot space built approximately 2,000 years ago as a granary of superb proportions.

Church and Cloister of St.-Trophime (Place de la République): A cathedral until the eighteenth century, St.-Trophime had a great deal of art lavished upon it, more than would appear from its modest-sized facade. Indeed, its portal, framed by a pediment, occupies easily half of that otherwise simple exterior. Pause before entering, to get an idea of the way sculptors set to work in the twelfth century, portraying the Old Testament for largely illiterate worshipers. The lunette above the door is Christ as the judge of the Last Judgment, with the angel of St. Matthew, the eagle of St. John, the ox of St. Luke, and a legendary St. Mark's lion being blessed. The frieze directly below is a representation of the twelve Apostles, while an assortment of saints stand in niches, between columns, on either side of the door. Inside, concentrate on finely worked sarcophagi dotted about an otherwise unexciting space. I save best for last: a separately entered Romanesque cloister (the cathedral was originally staffed by resident monks), which is the singlemost outstanding monument of Arles, along with Les Arènes (above). Give time not only to capitals above columns supporting arches ringing the cloisters, but to statues of saints at each of the four corners—especially on the east and north sides, which are twelfth-century—some 200 years older than the remaining work.

Musée Réattu (Rue Marius-Jouveau) is as good a reason as any for a walk through atmospheric older sections of the city to this utterly beautiful fifteenth-century palace, for long the Arles seat of the Knights of Malta and, since the early decades of the last century, repository not only of works—some of them interesting—by the Arles-born artist for whom it is named (and who became its owner), but of eighteenth-century furniture dotted about, in rooms graced by beamed ceilings and massive fireplaces; a onetime chapel is the handsomest. Paintings are mostly French, with a Simon Vouet self-portrait outstanding. There are works, as well, by the likes of Gauguin and Dufy, Marquet and Vlaminck, with the kicker of the collection a clutch of 50 Picasso drawings, many of them portraying clowns.

Musée Arlaten (Rue de la République) makes its home in a sixteenth-century palace. Its theme is the Arles life-style over the centuries. There are a couple score galleries, the best of which are period rooms, meticulously furnished and accessorized, even to mannequins appropriately costumed; a dining room set for a traditional feast and a kitchen are standouts.

Camargue is the name given to marshland flanking the Rhône delta as the river flows south from Arles to the Mediterranean; much of it is cultivated, principally with good-quality rice. There is, as well, a not inconsiderable population of horses and bulls, kept in check by what have come to be called Camargue cowboys. I can understand the fascination of French visitors with these wide, open, albeit somewhat soggy, spaces, but it has always seemed to me that France has points of considerably more interest, at least for transatlantic visitors familiar with the American West. Excursion boats make daily trips from Arles during the summer. There are bus tours, as well, and of course, you may go on your own. Essentials include *Musée Camarguais*—all that you wanted to know about the area, its people, animals, and agriculture—at Mas du Pont de Rousty; and the charmingly named village of *Stes.-Maries-de-la-Mer*, whose lure is a fortified Romanesque church with walkable ramparts.

Les-Baux-de-Provence (13 miles north of Arles) is the name of a village, half atop a table-like stone mountain, half at the mountain's base. And, thanks to smart hotels, reputable restaurants, and trendy shops, the elevated portion of Les Baux has become a destination of consequence for travelers in Provence and an easy excursion—ideally for lunch, if not overnight—from Arles, or from Avignon (Chapter 7) to the north. A part of the rocky mountain range known as the Alpilles, Les Baux (which, incidentally, gave its name to the mineral bauxite, mined nearby) has medieval origins, with both a castle and a village (eerily called La Ville Morte) to prove its age. What you especially want to visit, though, are the shops of *Grande Rue; Musée d'Art Moderne* in a Renaissance mansion; contemporary murals in *Chapelle des Pénitents-Blancs;* and, more impressive and much older, *Church of St.-Vincent,* a mini-Romanesque marvel.

SETTLING IN

Jules César Hôtel (Boulevard des Lices; phone 9093-43-20) was built as a Carmelite convent in the seventeenth century and converted with panache into a perfectly lovely 61-room hotel. The cloister has been glassed in, and the rooms are capacious, with excellent baths, and no two alike in their traditional good looks. The lobby-lounge is one of the biggest and best-looking of any such that I know in France. Management is astute, staff is blessed with sunny Provençal dispositions, and restaurant is worthy of comment in a later paragraph. Member, Relais et Châteaux. *First Class.*

D'Arlatan Hôtel (26 Rue du Sauvage, near Place du Forum; phone 9093-56-66) went up as the château of Comtes d'Arlatan de Beaumont. Credit them with building a substantial seventeenth-century house on an even older base. Stone-walled public rooms are atmospheric and welcoming, and there's a pretty garden that's pleasant for drinks. The hotel has just under half a hundred rooms; those I've seen are charming. Friendly owner-management. Breakfast only. *First Class.*

Forum Hôtel (10 Place Forum; phone 9093-48-95) makes good use of wallpapers, textiles, and antique accents in the decor of its public spaces and 43 bedrooms. Bar-lounge is cozy, and there's a swimming pool out back. *Moderate.*

Calendal Hôtel (22 Place Pomme; phone 9096-11-89) is a near-neighbor of the Roman theater. There are 17 neat rooms, a bar, and a welcoming garden. *Moderate.*

Cloître Hôtel (18 Rue Cloître; phone 9096-29-50) and the street on which it's situated take their names from the nearby cloister of St.-Trophime Church; you're heart of town in this 31-room-cum-bar house; breakfast only. *Moderate.*

Oustau de Baumanière Hôtel (Les-Baux-de-Provence; phone 9097-33-07) is an aged Les Baux dwelling in the shadow of the village's also-ancient château, with stone-walled public spaces, antique-accented accommodations (there's a high percentage of suites—11, in contrast to 15 regular rooms), panoramic terrace and swimming pool, pair of tennis courts, and restaurant worthy of comment on a later page. Member, Relais et Châteaux. *Luxury.*

Cabro d'Or Hôtel (Les-Baux-de-Provence; phone 9097-33-21) is owned and operated by the Oustau management (above). It, too, occupies venerable quarters, agreeably updated in traditional style: 22 rooms, delightful restaurant and bar, swimming and tennis. Member, Relais et Châteaux. *First Class.*

DAILY BREAD

Lou Marques Restaurant (Jules César Hôtel, Boulevard des Lices; phone 9093-43-20) sports classy, old-school good looks and gives onto a terrace where meals are served in warm weather, on tables set with pink linen. There is a pair of prix-fixe menus—sweetbread salad, a remarkable chicken stew, a homemade pasta, and cheese and desserts from a wagon might be the order of battle—and an extensive à la carte that includes fish soup, fresh *foie gras*, and a reputable *filet mignon*. Super service. *Luxury*.

Vaccarès Restaurant (Place du Forum; phone 9096-06-07): I retain pleasant memories of a delicious *navarin d'agneau*—old-fashioned lamb stew—at this long-on-scene restaurant. It has, since then, become more *nouvelle* accented but with the beef entrées and desserts quite special. No credit cards. *First Class*.

Tourne Broche (6 Rue Balze; phone 9096-16-03) is indicated for lunch after touring Musée d'Art Chrétien just opposite. Walk through a courtyard and you're in an elongated *cave*-like room, where the chef-owner serves up a prix-fixe menu that might run to fish soup with a dollop of hot *rouille* sauce atop it, pork filet teemed with endives, cheese, and a sweet. *Moderate*.

Arlésienne (Boulevard des Lices; phone 9096-40-72) terms itself a *grande brasserie*, which means you may order anything from coffee or a simple snack to a roast chicken with *frites*. Outside tables. *Moderate*.

Hippocampe (Rue Charles-Pelletan, Stes.-Maries-de-la-Mer; phone 9091-80-91): a reliable choice for a lunch based on seafood in the course of a Camargue outing. *First Class*.

Oustau de Baumanière Hôtel Restaurant (Les-Baux-de-Provence; phone 9097-33-07) is the celebrated dining room of a celebrated hotel; you lunch or dine beneath massive electrified lanterns and seated on Louis XIII chairs beneath stone arches. Open with *foie gras, bisque de homard*, or filet of red mullet in an unusual red-wine sauce; beef, duck, and the house's celebrated lamb chops are indicated entrées. And you'll not have an easy time with dessert choice. *Luxury*.

Riboto de Taven (Les-Baux-de-Provence; phone 9097-34-23) occupies a centuries-old stone house, antiques-filled and with a honey of a terrace. Fare is exceptional. Seafood openers are indicated here. Entrées of roast quail, rabbit, and shoulder of lamb are exemplary; so are sweets. Gracious service. *Luxury*.

AFTER DARK

Théâtre Antique (Place Pomme) is a beautiful Arles setting for plays and folklore performances: summer only. Also in summer, Les Arènes—the amphitheater—becomes *una plaza de toros,* with bullfights; your hotel or the tourist office (below) will have schedules.

INCIDENTAL INTELLIGENCE

Further information: Office de Tourisme, Boulevard des Lices, Arles; Office de Tourisme, Avenue Van Gogh, Stes.-Maries-de-la-Mer; Office de Tourisme, Grande Rue, Les-Baux-de-Provence.

7

Avignon
Medieval Papal Stronghold

BACKGROUND BRIEFING

Sur le pont d'Avignon, on y danse, on y danse . . . —Traditional song

The point about Avignon is not its long-sung-about, now-in-ruins, albeit still-visitable bridge, but popes.

After 13 centuries of Roman residence, an unlikely fluke of history—having to do with the especially prickly Italian political scene of the moment and the coincidence of there being a bit of papal-owned territory in southern France—saw His Holiness, Clement V, a Frenchman who had been Archbishop of Bordeaux, take himself and the papal entourage to oddly named Comtat Venaissin—a compact area centered on the little town of Venasque, northeast of Avignon. Facilities for the elaborate court were so limited there that Clement accepted an invitation to settle in at bigger Avignon, then within the realm of the Counts of Provence. The year was 1309.

John XXII, still another Frenchman—all seven Avignon-based popes were French-born—remained in Avignon. But it remained for his immediate successors, Benedict XII (originally a Cistercian monk) and Clement VI (an extravagant patron of the arts) to build the Palais des Papes—actually a joined pair of palaces, one Benedict's, the other Clement's—that we see today, either as casual visitors or, believe it or not, as conventioneers. The City of Avignon, owners of the palace, have annexed a Centre des Congrès to it, utilizing original palace halls—that had in the Middle Ages, when Avignon was center of the Christian world, been the scene of brilliant banquets—for contemporary badge-wearers' receptions beneath Gothic vaults of what is surely France's most curious historic site. It was that site—and the presence of not only popes in Avignon for most of the fourteenth century, but their successors, the

Cardinal Legates, and *their* successors, the Vice Legates, who were in charge until 1790, when the city became a part of France—that shaped Avignon's destiny. It not only fostered culture (there was an Avignon school of Renaissance painting), but encouraged construction of churches and chapels, convents and monasteries, elegant townhouses and formidable fortifications, in across-the-Rhône Villeneuve-lès-Avignon, as well as in the city proper, the while creating an ambience of vitality and sophistication that Avignon hallmarks to this day.

ON SCENE

Lay of the Land: Observed from Villeneuve-lès-Avignon, the satellite town across the Rhône, Avignon retains its matchless medieval profile: towers of irregularly contoured Palais des Papes coupled with the dome of its cathedral and the ruins of its legendary bridge, ending abruptly at midpoint in the river. But once one sets foot and ambles about, it is immediately clear that Avignon has known the hand of a good town planner; its layout is one of the easiest to master of the smaller French cities. Still surrounded by medieval ramparts, Avignon begins at the *railway station*. It is situated at the foot of the north-south thoroughfare that neatly alters the core of town—called *Cours Jean-Jaurès* in its southerly reaches, later becoming *Rue de la République* before it concludes at the nerve center called *Place de l'Horloge*. This square is flanked by the pair of nineteenth-century focal points, Hôtel de Ville and next-door Théâtre Municipal, with cafés spilling into its center. Go north a hop and a skip, and you're at *Place du Palais*, named, I need hardly point out, for the medieval papal residence dominating it. *Rocher des Doms*, directly to its north, is a rocky eminence serving as a city park that affords views of the Rhône, the city's celebrated bridge, and bastions of Villeneuve-lès-Avignon, beyond. Avignon's cathedral borders this park, and the so-called Petit Palais, now an art museum of consequence, is just beyond. Shopping? It's good in Avignon. *Rue Joseph-Vernet*—entered from Cours Jean-Jaurès and with its landmark the eighteenth-century palace housing one of the most beautiful art museums of the republic—has the smartest shops. Other streets, leading west from central *Place de l'Horloge*, constitute shopping territory as well; they are *Rue des Marchands* and *Rue de la Bonneterie*. Try to find time for strolls along central streets— *Rue du Roi-René* and *Rue du Four* are two such—lined with townhouses that attest to Avignon's centuries-long eminence.

Palais des Papes (Place du Palais): You are apprehensive as you climb steep stone steps at the entrance. Suppose the magnetism of Rome was not strong enough to have lured the popes back at just about the time when the Middle Ages were evolving into the Renaissance? What would the Italian capital be like today without the cachet of the Vatican? Would this smallish Mediterranean city, now simply the seat of one of 95 *départements* of the French Republic, have evolved into a metropolis, as headquarters of the globe-girdling Catholic church? Although it is not without disappointments—alas, its somberly gray and unfurnished interiors lack warmth, if not an extraordinary sense of proportion and scale—the palace is a history book, a century-long chapter in the affairs of a church whose evolution in the medieval epoch was intertwined with that of temporal powers like Italy, France, and the far-flung Holy Roman Empire. The palace is at its best when it is massive—the 135 x 30-foot *Grand Tinel*, where the papal court entertained state visitors at banquets, and the 166 x 45-foot *Chapelle Grande*, site of papal worship—both on the upper floor; and *Salle des Audiences*, similar in size to the chapel (just above it) and with Matteo Giovanetti's frescoes—the subject is a group of bearded prophets—among the palace's art treasures. There is, to be sure, other admirable art. In the ground floor's *Chapelle de St.-Jean*, Giovanetti has interpreted feats of the two most eminent of the sainted Johns, Evangelist and Baptist. The upper level's *Chapelle St.-Martial*, just above St.-Jean, is graced by still another clutch of Giovanetti works. *Chambre du Pape*—the pope's bedrooms, upstairs and relatively intimate as rooms go in this complex—retains its decoration, an overall painted wall design that may well be the predecessor of wallpaper. Save the best for last: *Chambre du Cerf*, called the Deer Room, after exquisite—and still exquisitely colored—murals, again by Giovanetti, surprisingly secular in theme, that of hunters-cum-dogs, against a lovely, leafy background.

Cathedrale of Notre-Dame-des-Doms (Place du Palais) is, not surprisingly, the palace's next-door neighbor. It is relatively small for a church of its status, but it's of a respectable age, with Romanesque portions dating to the twelfth century. There are features of note, most particularly an archbishop's throne in dramatic white marble and tombs of a pair of popes—John XXII, the second of the Avignon pontiffs, and his builder-successor, Benedict XII.

Musée du Petit Palais (Place du Palais)—originally a kind of satellite space, supplementing Palais des Papes, used to house VIP guests (King François I was reputedly among them)—saw architectural changes during the Renaissance. Centuries later, in the 1970s, the building was brilliantly refurbished to serve as setting for the nucleus of its exhibits—some 300 medieval Italian masterworks gathered by a sixteenth-century Roman nobleman named Campana. These are supplemented by a selection of works, many of the fifteenth-century Avignon school, from Musée Calvet (below). But it's the Campana paintings that make Petit Palais one of the best small-city museums in France. I would be a wealthy man if I had a 20-centime piece for each postcard sold in the museum's shop of Botticelli's luminous *Virgin* robed in red and blue and framed by an arch, with a chubby baby Jesus before her. There are a

Carpaccio *Sacred Conversation,* a Giorgione *Madonna and Child,* a Giovanni di Paolo *Nativity,* an *Annunciation* believed to be by Perugino, a Simone Martini *David,* and the museum's mascot painting—a hunter with his dog. The setting—there are 19 no-two-alike galleries—is as sumptuous as the art.

Musée Calvet (Rue Joseph-Vernet) is one of the most beautiful museum environments in France, an enchanter of an eighteenth-century palace, with peacocks in its garden; superb furniture in high-ceilinged, exquisitely detailed galleries (including a set of eight Régence chairs in the crystal chandeliered library); and lovely paintings. A view of Avignon from the Rhône by a local master named Robert Bonnart in 1700 is memorable; no less so is an eighteenth-century procession in Place du Palais. With works, as well, by the likes of Bourdon, Robert, Mignard, and le Nain, with an unexpected oil of England's King Henry VII by an unknown Renaissance portraitist.

Musée Lapidaire (Rue de la République) is quartered in a handsomely Baroque church, originally Jesuit, now desanctified, with the exhibits of sculpture embracing Avignon's Roman period—the capitals of columns are special—through the later periods of the popes and their successors.

A quartet of churches: *St.-Agricole* (Rue de la Petite-Fusterie) stuns with its enormous porch and Gothic portal, exceptionally wide nave, and charmer of a chapel under its side cupola. *St.-Didier* (Rue de la République) has a fifteenth-century fresco by the Sienese painter Simone Martini and a joyous, angel-studded Baroque altar. *St.-Pierre* (Rue de la République) greets you with a pair of engaging mini-steeples framing a Gothic facade. The interior is art-embellished Renaissance. *Chapelle des Pénitents-Noirs* (Rue Banasterie) represents Rococo Avignon, with exuberance typical of the eighteenth century, and the street on which it's located a scenic one.

Villeneuve-lès-Avignon, the town across the Rhône which developed handsomely as a consequence of the thirteenth-century papal period—warrants the inspection it is all too often denied by Avignon visitors. If you have the strength or the youth—or both—I would begin at *Fort St.-André* (Rue Montée du Fort St.-André), the very same medieval battlement whose fabulous twin towers you see from Avignon, a view of which is obtainable in exchange for your having ascended a considerable expanse of steps. Proceed, then, to *Chartreuse du Val de Bénédiction* (Rue de la République), a former Carthusian monastery of the same order as the closed-to-visitors mother house outside of Grenoble (Chapter 18). This is the only charterhouse in France where you may see the relatively capacious, two-room-cells-cum-gardens in which the Carthusians lead solitary lives. The cells open off a trio of cloisters; their chapel is visitable, too. *Église Paroissiale* (Place Meissonier) is a visit-worthy church, if only because of a pair of sculpted Virgins, one in marble— beautiful enough, to be sure; the other in ivory. End at *Musée Municipal* (Rue de la Foire, near the church), brimming with antique furniture, but with its masterwork a painting, *Couronnement de la Vierge*, by a fifteenth-century local—Charanton, by name.

Orange (18 miles north of Avignon) is a small town big in remnants of Roman Provence. Head first, upon arrival, to *Théâtre Antique* (Rue St.-Florent). You'll find it difficult to believe that this amphitheater, built 21 centuries ago (and still in use), remains in near-mint condition—the best preserved Roman theater extant, with the stone wall backing its stage graced by a statue of the building emperor, Augustus, and with elegantly contoured rows of seats (capacity 10,000) climbing a hillside. The theater edges a dramatically hilly park. *Colline d'Europe*, a ruined temple, is nearby, as is *Musée Municipal*, whose exhibits are of Orange-area Roman sculpture and fragments. And don't leave town without glimpsing a Roman-built *Arc de Triomphe*, on the avenue taking its name; not unlike the amphitheater, it's the best preserved of its kind in Europe.

SETTLING IN

D'Europe Hôtel (12 Place Crillon; phone 9082-66-92) is quite the handsomest of the urban Provençal hotels, occupying a high-ceilinged, sixteenth-century mansion. You enter through a capacious courtyard to which the restaurant is transferred on summer evenings, continuing to public spaces under whose beamed ceilings furniture is a mix of seventeenth century through the Directoire and Empire periods of the nineteenth. There are just over half a hundred distinctively decorated rooms (with hand showers only, attached to tubs in the baths) and a bar-lounge. Service is polite—but *just*, in my experience—and the restaurant disappointing, again, in my experience; it's reviewed on another page. Location is a 10-minute walk from Place de l'Horloge. *First Class.*

Sofitel Pont d'Avignon Hôtel (Rue Ferruce; phone 9085-91-23). Arrive by car, and you enter from a motor entrance to the rear, facing the town ramparts. Approach on foot and there's a conventional front door. In either event, you must not expect an esthetic treat. Advantages here are the kindest and most efficient management and staff of any in this national chain that I have experienced, as well as a central location. There are 66 rooms in mock-traditional style—more agreeable than the usual Sofitel rooms in vivid orange; a bar; and a restaurant available only to resident groups. For the rest of us, breakfast only. *First Class.*

Cité des Papes Hôtel (1 Rue Jean-Vilar; phone 9086-22-45) is the building with the striking modern facade just below Palais des Papes, that you cannot help but notice, given the divergence in architectural styles. There are just over 60 neat but graceless rooms, with the twins smallish and palace views from some. The hotel serves breakfast only, although there's a reliable restaurant—Le Bristol—adjacent. *Moderate.*

Du Midi Hôtel (33 Rue de la République; phone 9082-15-16) has its central location and the cleanliness of its nearly 60 plain rooms to recommend it. *Moderate.*

Bristol-Terminus Hôtel (44 Cours Jean-Jaurès; phone 9082-21-21), long on scene and central, offers the highest room capacity—91—of the in-town hotels which makes it of interest to groups. *Moderate.*

Le Prieuré Hôtel (7 Place du Chapitre, Villeneuve-lès-Avignon; phone 9025-18-20) was the palace of a cardinal in the court of John XXII, second of the Avignon popes. John had part of his palace converted into a priory—thus the hotel's name—and only in this century did it become a charming hotel, in its own park. There are two dozen handsome rooms; antiques-accented public spaces, including a restaurant (that moves to a terrace in summer) exceptional enough to warrant comment on a later page; and a good-sized swimming pool in the garden. Member, Relais et Châteaux. *First Class.*

La Magnaneraie Hôtel (37 Rue Camp-de-Bataille, Villeneuve-lès-Avignon; phone 9025-11-11), built in the fifteenth century, ivy-walled, and on a hill overlooking the town, welcomes with 20 pleasant rooms, bar-lounge, swimming pool in the garden, and a restaurant commendable enough for comment on a later page. *First Class.*

Les Frênes Hôtel (Avenue des Vertes-Rives, Montfavet; phone 9031-17-93) is just the ticket for a relaxing overnight, a honey of a nineteenth-century country house, set in its own garden-cum-swimming pool, with 18 elaborately decorated rooms and suites and a reputable restaurant. Avignon is six miles west. Member, Relais et Châteaux. *First Class.*

L'Auberge de Noves (Noves; phone 9094-19-21) is an oasis in a sea of vineyards, just eight miles south of Avignon. This is a rambling country mansion, with 20 traditionally furnished, good-sized rooms, charming lounges and bar, swimming pool in the garden that's covered with a plastic bubble in cool weather, and a commendable restaurant, al fresco in summer. Member, Relais et Châteaux. *First Class.*

DAILY BREAD

Hiely-Lucullus (5 Rue de la République; phone 9086-17-07) belies its eminence with a decidedly unpretentious setting: up a flight in a nondescript building on Avignon's main street. Bowls of flowers and tables meticulously set with pale pink linen are the only bright touches in an otherwise plain decor. But you're received with smiles, service is professional, and fare—happily based on traditional Provençal specialties—is excellent. You do well to order the carefully created prix-fixe menu. Openers might be fresh asparagus or artichokes, deliciously sauced. Entrées run to *escalope de saumon, maigret de canard*, or a typically Provençal *estouffade d'agneau*. Cheese platter is next, preparatory to a choice of the house's memorable desserts. Member, Relais et Châteaux. *Luxury*.

L'Auberge de France (28 Place de l'Horloge; phone 9082-58-86) is at once handsome (contemporary touches in an antique setting), cheerful (welcome is warm; service, a delight), and delicious. The prix-fixe is indicated, commencing with the likes of a *terrine de foie de canard* and continuing with salmon-trout *soufflé* or the house's rabbit specialty, with cheeses served prior to the arrival of dessert, either pastries from a trolly or a choice of ice-cream concoctions. *First Class*.

Les Trois Clefs (26 Rue Trois Faucons; phone 9086-51-53): Smartly set tables are framed by pink and ivory murals in this inviting restaurant, where there are three good-value prix-fixe menus, with chicken specialties counseled. *First Class*.

Vieille Fontaine (D'Europe Hôtel, 12 Place Crillon; phone 9082-66-92) is handsomely old-fashioned. Would that the fare matched the decor. Alas, it is essentially *nouvelle*, and in my experience by no means distinguished *nouvelle*. There are two prix-fixe menus; the cheaper of the two might consist of scallop *mousse*, sautéed lamb, cheese, and a pedestrian dessert. With correspondingly disappointing service. A pity, for so felicitous a setting. *First Class*.

Le Saint-Didier (41 Rue de la Saraillerie; phone 9086-16-50) is agreeable enough to look upon, with peach-hued draperies and linen and antique prints of horses on the walls. But the prix-fixe lunch menu can be slim pickings—a green salad or fish *pâté* to start, skimpy beef filet or seafood platter as entrées, and cheese or the dessert of the day, over which you have no choice. The considerably costlier dinner menu offers more choice. *Moderate* at lunch; *First Class* at dinner.

Chantegril (24 Place de l'Horloge; phone 9082-76-10)—a link of a national chain, with an attractive garden decor—makes a specialty of a buffet embracing all the *crudités* you can eat; ditto, desserts. With a slightly pricier and more conventional prix-fixe menu and an à la carte of grills. Good value. *Moderate.*

Helen (1 Rue Jean-Vilar; phone 9086-06-45) embraces a proper restaurant and a less elaborate café; the former has solid Provençal specialties; the latter, short orders. Central. Good value. Restaurant, *First Class*; café, *Moderate.*

Crêperie Bretonne (6 Rue de la Balance; phone 9085-20-99) is the genuine Breton article; *crêpes* savory (order a pair to start), *crêpes* sweet (order one for dessert). Satisfying and *Moderate.*

Simple Simon (26 Rue Petite Fusterie; phone 9086-62-70, and pronounced *sahm*-ple see-*mohn*) bills itself as *Le Salon de Thé Anglais d'Avignon*, but you'll need your best French to order its delicious cakes with a cup of tea or, for that matter, breakfast or a casual lunch. Attractive and central. *Moderate.*

Lou Mistrau (13 Place de l'Horloge; phone 9082-40-98) is at once a *brasserie*—order a simple, but satisfying, meal of, say, *entrecôte aux frites*—and a café, with its tables spilling onto the square, for coffee or a drink. *Moderate.*

Le Prieuré Hôtel Restaurant (7 Place du Chapitre, Villeneuve-lès-Avignon; phone 9025-18-20). If your visit is during the cool weather months, the setting for a meal will be a dark-beamed room, with country Provençal chairs surrounding tables set with great bowls of flowers to contrast with yellow linen. In summer, you're al fresco. A nibble served with your aperitif might well be *canapés tapinade*—the so-called *caviar du pauvre*—which is a *pâté* of black olives, anchovies, and capers bound with olive oil and garlic-seasoned. A shrimp-and-spinach salad might follow, with one of the house's poultry, beef, or lamb specialties as entrées, well garnished. The cheese platter is a requisite here. So are the chef's pastries. In my experience, one of France's best restaurants. *First Class.*

La Magnaneraie Hôtel Restaurant (37 Rue Camp-de-Bataille, Villeneuve-lès-Avignon; phone 9025-11-11): Tables are set in the garden in summer. Select one of the two well-priced menus, building your meal around a seafood or poultry entrée, with the house's own *crêpes fourrées*, to conclude. *First Class.*

La Maison (1 Rue Montée-du-Fort; Villeneuve-lès-Avignon; phone 9025-20-81) is as tasty as it is good-looking, traditional style, with its celebrated specialty—*maigret de canard au beurre rouge,* a duck delight—counseled. *First Class.*

Le Pigraillet (Chemin Colline St.-Europe, Orange; phone 9034-44-25) is strategically situated on the hill facing the amphitheater, an ideal spot for a lunch pause in connection with an Orange excursion; prix-fixe menus center on chicken and lamb. *First Class.*

SHOPPER'S AVIGNON

Department stores—*Nouvelles Galeries, Dames de France, Monoprix*—are on Rue de la République. Rue Joseph Vernet's classy boutiques include *Jean Christophe* (men's and women's accessories), *Jacques Hiely* (women's haute couture), *J. P. Palun* (classic-design men's clothes); *Henry Doux* (jewelry), *Alex Bretinière* (men's and women's shoes), and *Idées Formes-Fonctions* (leather, watches, jewelry). *Les Olivades* on shop-filled Rue des Marchands is a source of Provençal products, especially hand-blocked cottons by the bolt and fashioned into bags, skirts, aprons, placemats, and sachets. *Souleiado,* a link of a chain with similar specialties, is on Rue Joseph Vernet. And *La Taste* (Rue de la Balance) vends Provençal foods and wines.

SOUND OF MUSIC

Théâtre Municipal (Place de la Horloge) is the city's principal theater—opera, ballet, concerts, plays; there are others. (And in summer, July usually, the Avignon Music Festival takes place in historic sites—Palais des Papes included—all around town.)

INCIDENTAL INTELLIGENCE

This is a good point of departure for excursions—many of them day-long—to points throughout Provence: The tourist office (below) has details. *Further information:* Office de Tourisme, 41 Cours Jean-Jaurès, Avignon; Office de Tourisme, 1 Place Charles-David, Villeneuve-lès-Avignon; Office de Tourisme, Cours Aristide-Briand, Orange.

8

Beaune
Burgundy's Ancient Wine Center

BACKGROUND BRIEFING

You go to Beaune—small, congenial, and fortuitously situated in east-central France—for three reasons: Burgundy wines, first. (In no French city of my acquaintance is tasting, purchasing, and—most important—*understanding* more effortless.) Art and architecture share second billing. (However, in the case of non-wine buffs, they move up to first place.) And the classic cuisine of Burgundy is No. 3. Beaune is strong in restaurants serving regional specialties in tandem with wines that, with those of Bordeaux (Chapter 10), constitute the most esteemed on the planet.

Medieval Dukes of Burgundy favored Beaune. Until Louis XIV revoked the Edict of Nantes, guaranteeing religious freedom, Beaune's big Protestant community enriched it, as weavers whose textiles were coveted throughout Europe. Simultaneously, the town thrived as a shipping point for area vintners; Burgundy wine was hardly less sought after than Beaune-made cloth. All this occurred while Beaune developed as a cultural crossroads between France to the west and easterly Teutonic territories. Handiwork of these rich centuries remains—ramparts-cum-watchtowers that could be sets for adventure films; townhouses somberly stonefaced and townhouses ebulliently Baroque; a plethora of cloistered convents, some now put to clever secular use; and, not to be overlooked, centuries-old *caves* lined with casks of the wine that affords Beaune its livelihood and its celebrity.

ON SCENE

Lay of the Land: Beaune bases itself on a pair of central squares, southerly *Place Carnot* and northerly *Place Monge*—dominated by a fourteenth-century bell tower—which are joined by the principal pedestrian shopping street, *Rue Carnot*. *Rue de Lorraine*, leading north from Place Monge, is flanked by fine old houses and the visitable *Chapelle de* *l'Oratoire*, with *Porte St.-Nicolas*, an eighteenth-century ceremonial gateway, at its terminus. Place Carnot is almost contiguous with *Place de la Halle* and neighboring *Place Fleury*, both due west and focal points of a quarter redolent of *Vieux-Beaune*. Major monuments (below) are in this core and easily accessible on foot. The *railway station* is beyond the center, at the eastern end of *Avenue du 8 Septembre*. Although Beaune is principal trading center for wines of the entire Burgundy region, the vineyards surrounding it—some northerly, most to the south—comprise the area called *Côte de Beaune*, including such celebrated townships as *Savigny-lès-Beaune*, *Pommard*, *Meursault*, and *Puligny-Montrachet*, with the *Mâcon* and *Beaujolais* vineyards south of Côte de Beaune. These are conveniently visited on excursion from Beaune, while Burgundy's northerly vineyards are best inspected on tours out of Dijon (Chapter 17).

L'Hôtel-Dieu (Rue de l'Hôtel-Dieu) represents a mix of superlative Renaissance architecture and great Renaissance art. What happened was that in the fifteenth century, a local bigwig—Nicolas Rolin, by name—endowed the town with a paupers' hospital, the likes of which were unknown in the Europe of the period, or since, for that matter. (In my trans-Europe travels, I have encountered nothing comparable, with the exception of Hostel de los Reyes Católicos in the northwestern Spanish city of Santiago de Compostela; it was built by Ferdinand and Isabella for pilgrims arriving sick, after the long pilgrimage-trek to the tomb of St. James the Apostle, and is now a luxury hotel, which I recommend highly in *Spain at Its Best*.) L'Hôtel-Dieu—a Sisters of Charity-operated hospital to this day, albeit with its patients now in detached modern quarters—is a dazzler even from without. You start in a stadium-size courtyard whose steeply pitched roofs are tiled in a diamond pattern in shades of green, beige, and black, with a near-limitless maze of pinnacles surmounting a sea of turrets and gracefully framed windows. Eventually, it's your turn to go inside (crowds are such that batches of visitors are taken through on guided-in-French tours, with explanatory leaflets in major foreign languages passed around to non-French-speakers). The hospital's sole ward, 236 x 48 feet, could be a ballroom, with its vaulted ceiling—the shape of a ship turned upside down—measuring 66 vertical feet. And patients were not doubled up in beds—as they were, for example, in Lyon (Chapter 21), where a typical bed that accommodated four is on exhibit in that city's hospital-museum. Beaune's beds were canopied and curtained, and Beaune's ward doubled as a chapel, with the altar at the far end visible from all beds, so that patients could worship while confined; prayers were led by the nuns, whose no-longer-worn blue and white habits are displayed in an adjacent museum. Best comes last at L'Hôtel-Dieu: the altarpiece. Builder Rolin commissioned Roger Van der Weyden to paint for the ward a nine-panel interpretation of *The Last Judgment*, centered by a somber-visaged, white-robed Archangel St. Michael, exquisitely detailed and recognized as the most brilliant masterwork by a Flemish master who painted many such.

Basilique de Notre-Dame (Place Notre-Dame) is Beaune's showplace church, a Romanesque beauty begun in the thirteenth century, as handsome from out back (the three-level apse-cum-flying buttresses is exceptional) as from within, where the severe barrel-vault of its nave frames architectural features—the range, capitals of columns supporting it to a serene cloister. But standouts here are the tapestries, a series lining walls behind the choir, that date to the fifteenth century and are believed to have been woven in what is now the Belgian city of Tournai. Theme of the series—17 all told—is *La Vie de la Vierge.* You have, of course, seen many representations of the Virgin's life. But these panels—each in still-luminous color, framed by borders with overall designs embracing birds and flowers—will stay with you. *Presentation at the Temple, Marriage, Annunciation, Nativity, Visitation, Adoration of the Magi, Flight Into Egypt, Dormition and Crowning*—I wager you'll buy postcard reproductions of the lot as you exit.

Musée des Beaux-Arts (in Hôtel de Ville, the town hall, on Rue Oudot) is small and unexceptional, as such museums go in France. But there are some noteworthy paintings, especially a batch by Beaune-born Félix Zeim, a talented nineteenth-century master whose works are in the same vein as England's brilliant J. M. W. Turner, a contemporary. There are, as well, Flemish Primitives, to complement the Van der Weyden in Hôtel-Dieu; and eighteenth-century charmers by the likes of Greuze, Lancret, and Boucher.

Musée du Vin (Rue Paradis) makes its home in a multi-roomed mansion that goes back half a millennium and had been the Beaune residence of the Dukes of Burgundy. Exhibits may well tell you—if you give them enough time—more than you want to know about the history of wine, by means of considerable documentation and a vast array of implements.

Marché aux Vins (Rue Nicolas-Rolin, a street named for the builder of Hôtel-Dieu, nearby) is without doubt the best-organized regional wine-tasting/orientation/sales enterprise of any that I have come across in France, or in all of Europe, for that matter. Setting first: The main hall is a stunner of a desanctified Gothic church—Des Cordeliers, by name. And it is supplemented by extensive *caves.* Look at the exhibit of wines from throughout Burgundy (not just Côte de Beaune)—from Chablis up north through Mâcon and Beaujolais to the south. Then move about, sampling whichever wines you like, as many as you like, with you yourself doing the pouring into glasses available at each display. Close to 40 wines are on hand, ranging in age from three to ten years old. (The trick is not to get tipsy.) It's all free, and you are under no obligation to buy, but you may if you like: pick up whatever bottles interest you from their shelves (prices are indicated, and there are printed order forms), taking them in supermarket-type baskets to the cashier at the exit: the market ships overseas.

Visits to individual Beaune caves: Besides Marché aux Vins (above), you may visit any of a number of prominent Beaune wine firms' cellars. One that I have enjoyed is *Calvet* (6 Boulevard Perpreuil), whose *caves* are below atmospheric medieval ramparts, and which invites its guests to taste representative vintages. Other open-to-visitors *caves* include Léonce Bocquet (29 Boulevard Clemenceau) and *Patriarche Père et Fils* (Rue du Collège).

La Rochepot (12 miles southwest of Beaune): Regional vineyards and *caves* excepted, La Rochepot is the requisite Beaune excursion destination—a picture-book village in the hills, surrounded by vineyards, based on a single-steeple Romanesque church and dominated by a Middle Ages château on which patterned tile roofs are at least as intricate as those of L'Hôtel-Dieu (above). Of the state rooms within the castle, the Salle à Manger stands out, not so much for its dining table and chairs, but because of its marvelously painted beamed ceiling and a monster of a fireplace.

Côte de Beaune—the southern tier of Burgundy's Côte d'Or—makes for an agreeable excursion. A region of both red and white wines, its *vignerons*—smaller and less pretentious than the châteaux of Bordeaux—welcome visitors to their *caves*, where tasting is invited, and purchases may—or may not—be made, quite as you like. A nice routing might take in *Pommard* (whose reds are among the region's most prestigious and whose eighteenth-century *Château de Pommard cave*-vineyard is traditionally open daily the year round); *Meursault*, with world-class white wines and an eminently visitable Gothic parish church; *Puligny-Montrachet*, perhaps the most charming of the villages of this group and noted for its whites, as well as its reds; *Santenay*, whose Church of St.-Jean is a Romanesque-Gothic mix; and—en route back to Beaune—*Auxey-Duresses*, near La Rochepot and its château (above) and a good lunch stop. *Mâcon*, the neat-as-a-pin Saône River town, has given its name to the celebrated Burgundy wine region south of Côte de Beaune and just north of the Beaujolais area. *Musée Municipal* (Rue de Strasbourg) has as its setting a mellow seventeenth-century convent, and its ace-in-the-hole is a clutch of mostly French paintings by such artists as Greuze, Courbet, and Monet, with a Titian as a bonus. The nearby *Hôtel-Dieu* (Square de la Paix) is an eighteenth-century hospital with charming antique porcelain and furnishings in an open-to-visitors pharmacy. Note the detailed Renaissance facade of *Maison de Bois* (Place aux Herbes). Just beyond town, any number of *caves* welcome visitors: *Les Vignerons des Côtes Mâconnaises et Beaujolaises* at nearby *Cavaye* has representative vintages of a region whose wines include Pouilly-Fuissé and Chardonnay, both reputable whites, as well as Mâcon rouge.

SETTLING IN

De la Poste Hôtel (1 Boulevard Clemenceau; phone 8022-08-11) has been operated by several generations of the same family since the turn of the present century. I like the old-fashioned, high-ceilinged lobby-floor lounges, agreeable for drinks prior to a meal in the hotel's capacious restaurant—worthy of comment in a later paragraph. There are just 23 rooms and suites, no two alike, and those that I have either inhabited or inspected are delightful in period decor, with imaginative wallpapers and textiles, not to mention antique accents. Breakfasts are the most thoroughly satisfactory of any I have experienced in any French hotel. Taken either in your room or in one of the lounges, the first meal of the day comes on a big tray covered with a linen placemat and matching linen napkin of the same material, a vase of fresh flowers, a basket containing warmed-for-you brioches and croissants of the highest quality (hardly to be taken for granted in contemporary France, alas), generous-sized crocks of jam, honey, and butter, and a really jumbo pot of coffee. The hotel is a five-minute stroll from the core, and management is at once skilled and friendly. Demi-pension only; you must have lunch or dinner. *First Class.*

Le Cep Hôtel (27 Rue Maufoux; phone 8022-35-48) is an originally Renaissance mansion, core of town, that has been converted with considerable panache into a 21-room hotel. No two rooms are alike, but each—at least, those I have inspected—is furnished with superb antiques (Louis XV, Louis XVI, and Directoire), is stylishly accessorized, and has a modern bath attached. Breakfast is served in a stone-walled *cave* (or, of course, in your room) and drinks in a lovely lobby-lounge. Pity that there's neither elevator nor restaurant. *First Class.*

L'Auberge Bourguignonne (4 Place Madeleine; phone 8022-23-53) is aptly named. It is, indeed, an inn, of advanced age, although nicely—and traditionally—updated. There are just eight rooms; those I have seen are very pleasant, indeed. And the Auberge's restaurant—featuring Burgundy specialties, both à la carte and with a choice of two prix-fixe menus—is good value, good-tasting, and *First Class*, but the hotel proper is *Moderate.*

Central Hôtel (2 Rue Victor-Millot; phone 8024-77-24) is accurately titled. There are just under two dozen satisfactorily equipped rooms, but no elevator, and a nice looking restaurant. *Moderate.*

Le Home Hôtel (138 Route de Dijon; phone 8022-16-43) is not, to be sure, central. But it's pleasant—a garden-encircled house with 20 neat rooms and an inviting bar-lounge. Madame Jacquet, the patronne, makes everyone feel at—dare I use the word?—home. Breakfast only. *Moderate.*

La Closerie Hôtel (61 Route d'Autun, a few miles south of Beaune; phone 8022-15-07) is ultra-modern, with 30 comfortable rooms, all more or less alike, and an outdoor swimming pool. Breakfast only. *Moderate.*

Samotel (Route de Pommard, a few miles south of Beaune; phone 8022-35-55) is plop in the center of a vineyard. Its plus is an attractive restaurant. The 66 rooms—good sized and modern, like the rest of the hotel—are comfortable enough, but, mind, mattresses are soft. *Moderate.*

Frantel Mâcon (26 Rue de Coubertin, Mâcon; phone 8038-28-06) is not central, like most other hotels of the Frantel chain with which I am familiar. But it's nicely situated on the banks of the Saône, with 63 similarly decorated, contemporary-style rooms, bar-lounge (which expands to a river-view terrace in summer), and convenient restaurant. Nicely operated. *First Class.*

DAILY BREAD

De La Poste Hôtel Restaurant (1 Boulevard Clémenceau; phone 8022-08-11): You appreciate the significance of this dining room in relation to the rest of the hotel when you see how much space is accorded it. It's high-ceilinged, with plenty of space between handsomely set tables; a staff that smiles but at the same time knows its business; and a kitchen that turns out the Burgundy dishes we cross oceans for. Open, for example, with a dozen *escargots à la Bourguignonne*, expertly sauced, delicious *tranche* of *jambon persillé*, or an unusual veal *terrine*. Entrées, accompanied by a masterful *gratin Dauphinois*, include *filet mignon*, shallot-accented shoulder of lamb, chicken with a Beaujolais-laced stuffing and the mushrooms called *morilles*, and traditional *coq au vin*. Cheeses are accorded care; desserts wheeled over on a chariot are the handiwork of a master *pâtissier*. There are always a hundred-plus of *grands crus* Burgundies to choose from, and you may order à la carte or from either of two prix-fixe menus. In my experience, one of France's best restaurants. *Luxury.*

Le Relais de Saulx (16 Rue Louis-Very; phone 8022-01-35) comprises a pair of formal and contiguous rooms—Louis XV style in front, Louis XVI to the rear, both framed by Burgundy velvet walls and matching drap-eries. Every table is adorned with silver candelabra and a bowl of flowers. I suggest you order one of the three prix-fixe menus—traditional, but with the distinctive touch of a talented chef. Choose a Beaune-style *cassolette* of snails or a more unusual salad of marinated and minced sea bass and salmon, as openers. Entrées run a gamut—grilled lamb chops, sautéed pork, *confit* of rabbit with a mustard sauce, seafood fricassee. As you proceed, bear in mind that not one, but a pair of trolleys will be rolled up, each groaning with desserts. Choose samplings of two or three—not missing the *gâteau au chocolat*, hot *tarte tatin*, and *génoise aux fraises*. In my view, one of France's best restaurants. *First Class.*

Auberge St.-Vincent (Place de la Halle; phone 8022-42-34): Restaurants just opposite tourist-trod monuments of consequence tend to aim for mass markets; rarely are they top-category. St. Vincent, in an aged mansion opposite l'Hôtel-Dieu, is an exception. Brass chandeliers illumi-nate a room whose tables are set with gold linen. Order à la carte such tempters as smoked trout, crayfish, and string bean salad, with seafood *pot-au-feu* a reputable entrée. Or select the good-value menu of four courses, with poultry or beef the entrées and sweets from a wheeled-to-table cart. *First Class.*

Jacques Laine (10 Boulevard Foch; phone 8024-76-10) edges the core of town, just west of Porte St.-Nicolas. Its quarters are a nineteenth-century mansion, with walls graced by Louis XVI paneling. You lunch or dine in one of a suite of connected rooms or, if it's summer, in the garden. I counsel the prix-fixe menu—with starters like *pâté* of scallops in a lobster sauce, *escalope* of trout as the fish course, a pigeon *sauté* or the house's ham specialty, choice of cheeses *and* of Laine-prepared desserts. *First Class.*

Le Bistrot du Marché (11 Place Carnot; phone 8022-12-00) is indicated for a low-tabbed meal of, say, *oeufs en meurette*—eggs poached in a red-wine sauce, with *entrecôte aux frites* following. Central. *Moderate.*

Bouché (12 Place Monge): Make your selections from the main-floor counter of this *pâtisserie* before moving along to the upstairs *salon de thé*, where you may have coffee or tea to accompany. Ice cream, too. Central. *Moderate.*

Ouvrée Hôtel Restaurant (Savigny-lès-Beaune; phone 8021-51-52): The 17-room hotel, first: It's simple and unpretentious but worth remember-ing if you're in the area and can't find space in Beaune, four miles distant. If you've a car, the capacious restaurant is worthy of the drive out, for a hearty lunch. *Oeufs en meurette* are the best such I have enjoyed; ditto, expertly prepared trout, *meunière* style. Beef is good, too. Cheeses are Burgundian, sweets are made by the Ouvrée's chef, and wines are from the *patron's* vineyard constituting the backyard, and bearing the Savigny-lès-Beaune appellation. *First Class.*

André Parra (a.k.a. Ermitage de Corton, Route 74, two miles north of Beaune, at Chorey-lès-Beaune; phone 8022-05-28) makes for an appropriate lunch pause in the course of a drive through vineyard country north of town, in the direction of Dijon. Red-upholstered Louis XVI-style chairs surround carefully set tables in a formal room. Prix-fixe menus are good buys; fare is based on traditional specialties. Filet of beef in a Corton wine sauce and roast duckling whose sauce is Cassis based are entrée favorites. *First Class.*

La Crémaillère (Route 73, Auxey-Duresses; phone 8021-22-60) is a long-on-scene and sensible choice for lunch in the course of a half-day exploration of wine towns south of Beaune; base your meal on *coq au vin* or *boeuf Bourguignon;* your wine will come from an adjacent vineyard. *First Class.*

Georges Blanc (Vonnas, 10 miles southeast of Beaune; phone 7450-00-10) appears, as you approach, to be a comfortable country house on a canal, and, indeed, it is—an attractive hotel (with duplex suites, as well as conventional rooms and a swimming pool) but, more to the point, an exceptional restaurant, now in the third generation of operation by the Blanc family. You are expected to order a premeal drink in one of the lounges, the while perusing a menu that embraces a pair of table d'hôtes and an à la carte. To select the cheaper of the two menus is hardly to skimp; it might include wine-sauced snails and the house's specialty entrées: a cream-sauced breast of chicken, garnished with a rainbow of vegetables and followed by cheese and an extraordinary choice of desserts. Setting is a capacious room, its well-spaced tables illuminated by silk-shaded lamps and flanked by Louis XIII chairs. Service is at once impeccable and congenial. Member, Relais et Châteaux. *Luxury.*

Au Chapon Fin (Thoissey, edging the Saône River, 10 miles south of Mâcon; phone 7404-04-74) occupies a contemporary, three-story pavilion in its own garden (it is a looker of a 25-room hotel, as well as a restaurant of consequence). A capon—the kind of poultry for which the establishment is named—is the subject of a painting above the fireplace in the paneled dining room, whose tables are surrounded by caned Louis XV chairs. Order, over a drink in the cocktail lounge. And go with an appetite. A meal—either à la carte or from the prix-fixe menu—might open with poached perch, accompanied by a superb sauce Hollandaise;

continue with the No. 1 specialty: chicken fricasseed with *morille*-type mushrooms. Charolais beef in a *marchand de vin* sauce is satisfying, too. Continue with local cheeses. For dessert: Grand Marnier-doused chocolate cake or raspberry sherbet under a blanket of fresh raspberries. If it's summer, you'll lunch or dine in the garden. Member, Relais et Châteaux. *First Class.*

INCIDENTAL INTELLIGENCE

Further information: Office de Tourisme, Rue de l'Hôtel-Dieu, Beaune; Office de Tourisme, 187 Rue Carnot, Mâcon.

9

Biarritz
and the Basque Country

BACKGROUND BRIEFING
The point to be made about the southern tip of the French Atlantic—
delineating the relatively compact stretch constituting France's Basque
country—is not so much the exoticism of a people with their own conso-
nant packed, not-all-that-widely-spoken language, but rather, the exoticism of non-Latin visitors in their midst. What I mean to say is that the
English-speaking visitor in Biarritz, the once-fashionable resort that is
the most widely reputed Basque town, sticks out like a sore thumb. The
overwhelming majority of visitors in France's distant southeast corner
appear to be either *citoyens français* or Spaniards from just over the
border. (See *Spain at Its Best.*) Indeed, I don't know of any other quarter
of the republic where English is less widely spoken; muster all of the
French and/or Spanish at your command for Côte Basque exploration.
It was not always so. After Empress Eugénie, the Spanish-born consort of Napoleon III, created a vogue for Biarritz in the middle of the last
century (much like she did for still another coastal watering-hole, the
English Channel's Trouville [Chapter 16]), north-of-the-Channel royalty
joined Eugénie and her imperial husband in Biarritz, as today's visitor
is reminded, by streets named for such onetime holiday-makers as Queen
Victoria and her son, Edward VII. White, white-sand beaches and spectacular coastal vistas, a hearty cuisine and royal patronage of yore notwithstanding, Biarritz and neighboring Côte Basque points have not
been able to compete with the easier-of-access Côte d'Azur, to which
this volume devotes four chapters (13, 23, 26, and 33). Which is hardly
to say you don't want to have a look around, if you're in the neighborhood.

ON SCENE

Lay of the Land: A fishing village fronted by a still-magnificent beach—
Grande Plage—Biarritz, prior to its discovery by Empress Eugénie, was
known primarily to residents of adjacent Bayonne (the coast's art and
cultural center [below]). Ideally, you position yourself in a central Biarritz hotel, the better to absorb whatever action emanates from the quarter surrounding *Place Clemenceau*—café- and shop-lined, just inland
from *Boulevard du Général de Gaulle*, which flanks Grande Plage and is
the site of *Casino Municipal*—one of two such; and leading to shop-filled
Avenue Edouard VII. *Place Bellevue*, with *Casino Bellevue*, is a hop and
a skip west. To experience Biarritz at its most scenic, head west of the
center to *Plage du Port-Vieux*, from which I suggest a stroll to the edge
of a narrow promontory at whose terminus lies a rock formation, *Rocher
de la Vierge*, high above swirling surf, affording coastal panoramas, and
named for a statue of the Virgin Mary erected by Napoleon III in 1865.
Biarritz's landmark *Phare*, or lighthouse (erected in 1834), is north of
town, on a mini-peninsula at the end of *Avenue de l'Impératrice*, overlooking *Plage Miramar*. Still other beaches—*Plage de la Côte des Basques*,
Plage Marbella, and charmingly named *Plage de Milady*—are south of the
center. The railway station is quite central, on *Avenue de la Gare*.

Musée de la Mer (Esplanade du Port-Vieux), easily visited in tandem
with Rocher de la Vierge (above), houses an aquarium whose most
amusing exhibit is a clutch of loquacious sea lions in a pool of their own;
it is, otherwise, unexceptional.

Church of St.-Martin (Rue St.-Martin) is Biarritz's solitary venerable
monument—a mix of styles, Middle Ages onward, with an impressive
Gothic choir the best esthetic reason for a visit.

Bayonne—in effect, Biarritz's next-door neighbor to the east—is the
Côte Basque's surprise package: a substantial small city just inland from
the Atlantic, with the Adour River to its east, and a monument-filled core
based on Rue des Gouverneurs, whose landmark is atmospheric and
aptly-named *Château Vieux*, or Old Castle, whose inhabitants—now
army officers—have included kings Louis XI, François I, Charles IX, and
Louis XIV, an entrance plaque advises. Pedestrians-only *Rue Victor-
Hugo* is the big shopping street, with *Printemps* department store nearby.
The grandest square, *Place de la Liberté*, edges the Adour and is flanked
by a rather grand multipurpose structure at once the city hall and the
opera house.
    Cathedral of Ste.-Marie (Square Dubarat): Bayonne's cathedral—
erected between the twelfth and the sixteenth centuries—is a Gothic
structure of no little beauty. Twin steeples frame a felicitous stone porch.
The long, high nave is exquisitely vaulted; the high altar, with its grace-

ful baldechin, hardly anticlimactic. Gothic tracery of the galleries of the cloister—separately entered—is extraordinary. So, for that matter, is the perspective of the cathedral from the rear—flying buttresses of the apse, most especially.

Musée Bonnat (5 Rue Jacques-Laffitte)—not unlike the cathedral—is another Bayonne sleeper, in turn-of-century quarters that have been smartly renovated, and with a corking good collection of paintings—the best such that I know of in a town so small, anywhere in France, save for those of its counterpart in Pau (Chapter 28). Smashers of this collection are a clutch of canvasses by Rubens in a room of their own—as well they might be, given the total: 16. But there is, as well, work by the likes of Leonardo and Rembrandt, Michelangelo and Dürer, El Greco and Goya, with later painters on scene, too, including Géricault and Delacroix, Ingres and Degas. And there's a superb cache of Old Masters drawings, the lot a gift to the town by native-son Léon Bonnat, a nineteenth-century portraitist-teacher.

Musée Basque (1 Rue Marengo) has quarters in a pretty riverfront house architecturally typical of the region, maroon shutters complementing white walls. Subject matter is the Basque people and their culture, with exhibits running a delightfully diverse gamut—the Basque-created game, jai alai (*pelote*, on home ground), and Basque country furniture, Basque costumes, and Basque art. With exhibits relating to the history of Bayonne, as a bonus.

St.-Jean-de-Luz (10 miles south of Biarritz) played a not unimportant role in French history, and compensates with a plethora of good seafood restaurants for its lack of a solitary in-town, first-class hotel. Nature ordained that this town—flanking the wide, white sands of perfectly crescent-shaped *Baie de St.-Jean-de-Luz*—would be a beach resort. And geography is uncomplicated. *Rue Gambetta*—the main shopping street— runs parallel with the beach's flanking street, *Promenade de la Plage*, site of *Casino de la Pergola*. *Rue de la République* is Restaurant Row; it runs perpendicular to Rue Gambetta and leads directly to the sands. And *Place Louis XIV* edges the harbor; you want to position yourself at a café table in early evening when the town's fishing fleet returns, its boats brimming with the day's catch—for sale from the decks—of sardines and tuna.

Maison Louis XIV (Place Louis XIV) is the charming Baroque mansion—inhabited by descendants of the original owners and operated as a museum by them—where Louis XIV and his Spanish bride, Infanta María Teresa, spent their wedding night on June 9, 1660, after the knot was tied in a nearby church (below), after an elaborate procession through the town. You see several authentically furnished rooms, the wedding chamber, of course, but salon and kitchen, as well.

Church of St.-Jean-Baptiste (Rue Garat): Pause before entering, to read the plaque affixed to the somber facade of this late Renaissance-early Baroque, sixteenth-century church. It advises that after Louis XIV was married within—and France gained as a queen a daughter of Spain's King Felipe IV, born in the Escorial, outside of Madrid—the door through which the royal couple passed, was *murée*, or walled, after the ceremony conducted by the then Bishop of Bayonne. And it still is. You enter alongside, dazzled by the gilded splendor of the high altar, impressed with unusual dark-wood balconies on either side of the aisle, traditionally occupied only by Basque men. If you've not had a chance to aquaint yourself with the Basque language, this is the place: Have a look at prayerbooks in the pews.

SETTLING IN

BIARRITZ

Du Palais Hôtel (1 Avenue de l'Impératrice; phone 5924-09-40) is accurately titled. It was, indeed, a palace. Napoleon III built it in 1854 for Empress Eugénie, and it served for some years thereafter as an imperial summer residence. In 1893—more than two decades after the demise of the Second Empire—it was converted into a hotel, and rebuilt following a 1903 fire. Setting is core of town, in a park of its own, with the Grande Plage just out front. Beneath severe, steeply pitched Mansard roofs that were so dear to Belle Époque architects is an anything-but-severe interior that represents, more than that of any other hotel that I know in provincial France, what the turn-of-century grand hotel was all about. Proportions—high ceilings, immense windows, grandiose spaces—are in themselves extraordinary. Decorative details—original crystal chandeliers, bronze sconces, marble mantels, massive French doors, intricate stuccowork of ceilings, capitals of columns, gilded window frames—dazzle. It's difficult to believe that in this capacious environment there are no more than 120 rooms and suites. Seaview accommodations are the loveliest, but the standard rooms on upper floors are hardly to be despised. The formal restaurant, off the lobby, is worthy of an evaluation on a later page. A second, contemporary, with scrumptious buffet lunches, faces the swimming pool, itself flanked by a vast sun deck, at the Atlantic's edge. There is a pair of bars. And service is skilled and smiling. Hôtels Concorde. *Luxury*.

Miramar Hôtel (Avenue de l'Impératrice; phone 5924-85-20) is an undistinguished contemporary house, with capacious public areas, 126 smallish but well-equipped rooms, swimming pool, elaborate health spa in the basement, bar-lounge, and a pair of restaurants, one standard, the other for spa customers on diets. *Luxury*.

Régina et Golf Hôtel (52 Avenue de l'Impératrice; phone 5924-09-60) is dramatically situated, agreeably traditional in style, with 45 rooms, reliable restaurant, and Miramar Beach just below. *First Class.*

Carlina Hôtel (Boulevard Prince-de-Galles, phone 5923-03-86) is worth knowing about because of its central beachfront situation; there are just over 30 full-facility rooms, but no restaurant. Breakfast only. *Moderate.*

Eurotel (19 Avenue de la Perspective; phone 5924-32-33): You're away from the center, out at Plage du Port-Vieux, here—near Rocher de la Vierge (above). But if you've a car, you might find this house worthwhile, with smashing views from high-up rooms, kitchenettes attached to all 60 of them, and a closed-weekends restaurant. Contemporary. *First Class.*

Plaza Hôtel (Avenue Edouard VII; phone 5924-74-00): You're a bit inland from the beach here, but core of the shopping district. This is a comfortable, 60-room-cum-restaurant house. *Moderate.*

BAYONNE

Capagorry Hôtel (14 Rue Thiers; phone 5925-48-22) is traditional style, agreeably situated core of town. There are close to 50 well-equipped rooms, no two identical, bar and breakfast, but no restaurant. Mapotel/Best Western. *Moderate.*

Aux Deux Rivières Hôtel (21 Rue Thiers; phone 5959-14-61) is a near-neighbor of the Capagorry (above), attractive in thetraditional manner, with 63 functional rooms and pleasant public spaces. Breakfast only. *Moderate.*

ST.-JEAN-DE-LUZ

Chantaco Hôtel (Golf [course] de Chantaco, a mile and a half east of town; phone 5926-14-76): I rarely begin town hotel evaluations with a noncentral hotel, but this is St.-Jean-de-Luz's best, by far. Of course, you need a car, and if you're a golfer—18 holes are adjacent—you'll be especially content in this lovely country-house-type hotel. There's a strong—and delightful—Spanish influence in decor of the public spaces, which include capacious lounges, bar, and a fine restaurant that moves to a patio in warm weather. The 20 rooms are lovely, each of them distinctively decorated. And management is delightfully welcoming. Pity there's no swimming pool. Very nice, withal. *First Class.*

De la Plage Hôtel (33 Rue Garat; phone 5951-03-44): This is a modest house, but it is, indeed, *sur la plage* and has a reliable restaurant. Ask for an oceanfront room; 30 all told. *Moderate.*

Bel Air Hôtel (Promenade Thibaut; phone 5926-04-86) is a near-neighbor of both the casino and the beach. There are just 16 adequate rooms, and a dinner-only, summer-only restaurant, as well, of course, as breakfast. *Moderate.*

Madison Hôtel (25 Boulevard Thiers; phone 5926-35-02) is a little in from the beach, with 25 neat rooms. Breakfast only. *Moderate.*

DAILY BREAD

BIARRITZ

La Rotonde (Du Palais Hôtel, 1 Avenue de l'Impératrice; phone 5924-09-40): I can't conceive of a visitor coming all the way to Biarritz and missing the experience of a classic dinner in this very grand environment. Precede your meal with an aperitif in the Palais's positively palatial cocktail lounge—through which you pass en route to this room, flanked by mirrored marble fireplaces, illuminated by crystal chandeliers, with the great windows of a half-moon-shaped wall giving on to the sea. A massive flower arrangement atop it draws your eye to the hors d'oeuvres table as you enter. You begin with half a lobster mayonnaise or *foie gras frais*, proceed with a fish course, as a prelude to such classic entrées as *châteaubriand*—beef is nowhere more succulent in southwest France— one of the house's lamb specialties, or the duck-breast masterwork, *maigret de canard*. Desserts come wheeled over on a two-level trolley, and the wine list is one of the most extensive in the Basque country. Lovely service. *Luxury.*

Chez Albert (Port des Pêcheurs; phone 5924-43-84) is as essential to an understanding of maritime Biarritz as is La Rotonde (above), for the Biarritz of Empress Eugénie. This big, busy, waterfront house reflects the gregarious hospitality of its *propriétaire*, M. Albert, who darts about, invariably making menu suggestions for newcomers—and good ones. Take his advice and open with the definitive French seafood platter—a gargantuan assemblage of crustaceans: crayfish and oysters through octopus and mussels. Order grilled fish or boiled lobster as an entrée, or take advantage of Biarritz's proximity to Spain and opt for M. Albert's saffron-rice based paella—deliciously enough garnished so as to put it on a level with the Iberian peninsula's best such. Summer only. *First Class.*

L'Operne (17 Avenue Edouard VII; phone 5924-30-30) is stylishly contemporary, with tables on a terrace over the Grande Plage, for summer meals. You will have heard of Pipérade, the Basque scrambled-egg meld—onions, green peppers, tomatoes are major ingredients—and, with the obligatory accompaniment of sliced Bayonne ham, you'll not find it more deliciously prepared elsewhere. Open with it, following with grilled salmon or filet of sole *meunière*. Friendly. *First Class.*

Atlantic (10 Rue du Port-Vieux, 5924-34-08) lures mussels fans, myself certainly included. If you're one of us, open with a giant bowl of *moules marinières*, served with plenty of bread for dunking. *Poulet au vinaigre et à l'estragon*—the house's chicken specialty—is indicated as an entrée. Fun. Summer only. *First Class.*

Miremont (5 Rue Mazagran) seems unexceptional, as you enter from a heart-of-town shopping street. Look, then, at the caliber of its pastries in main-floor counters. Proceed up the rear stairway, and poof! You're in a *salon de thé* whose entire far wall is a picture window giving on to the Grande Plage. And the Miremont's pastries are as sumptuous as the view. *Moderate.*

Café Royalty (Place Clemenceau). I can't guarantee crowned heads among the clientele, but it's fun to take a table in this core-of-Biarritz location and watch the passing parade. *Moderate.*

BAYONNE

Victor Hugo (Quai Amiral-Dubourdieu at Rue Victor-Hugo; phone 5925-62-26) is a throwback to the last century, still with original furnishings, and a smashing situation, riverfront, just beyond landmark Place de la Liberté. Order the seafood-based prix-fixe menu. *First Class.*

L'Escabos (4 Rue Saubiole; phone 5959-70-17) is agreeable for a midday meal following a morning in nearby Musée Basque (above). Open with the house *terrine*, making sure you select either the lobster-based *zarzuela*—a casserole with origins in just-over-the-frontier Spain—or the platter of grilled assorted seafood. *First Class.*

Café du Théâtre (Place de la Liberté; phone 5955-19-92) is named for the opera-house/city hall building in which it's situated. Take an outdoor table on a sunny day, for a casual lunch, coffee, or a cold drink. Delightful. *Moderate.*

Cazenave (19 Arceaux Port-Neuf): A pity, while you're in this city that pioneered centuries back in the preparation and presentation of then-novel chocolate, not to sample it at Cazenave, both in its *salon de thé*—variously employed—and by the bag or box, from its counter. *Moderate/First Class.*

ST.-JEAN-DE-LUZ

Kaïku (17 Rue de la République; phone 5926-13-20) agreeably typifies the St.-Jean-de-Luz seafood restaurant—stone-walled, beam-ceilinged, with lamps fashioned of local wood-cum-checked shades illuminating tables, and an open kitchen, the better to watch your meal being prepared. Open with cream of crab soup, following with expertly grilled catch of the day or a tasty specialty—*gratin de moules aux courgettes,* a mussel masterwork. *First Class.*

La Ruelle (27 Rue de la République; phone 5926-45-47) offers a good-value prix-fixe in pleasant surroundings; open with the area's esteemed fish soup or nicely garnished Bayonne ham and continue with a *faux-filet* steak or breast of duck, with a choice of desserts to conclude. *Moderate/First Class.*

De la Plage Hôtel Restaurant (33 Rue Garat; phone 5951-03-44) is indicated for an ocean-view meal that might embrace *pipérade* to begin, *poulet Basquaise*—the region's premier chicken preparation—or grilled local tuna or sardines, with *gâteau Basque* to conclude. If you have the prix-fixe menu, *Moderate;* à la carte, *First Class.*

Dodin (17 Rue Gambetta) is both *pâtisserie* and *salon de thé;* stop in for a cuppa with a slice of cake, perhaps purchasing a bag of their chocolate/cherry candy specialty. *Moderate.*

Le Madrid (Place Louis XIV) is a café on the ground floor of Maison Louis XIV (above) and named for the city of origin of King Louis's bride, on the historic square that overlooks the port, and is the site, as well, of the City Hall; that term in French—Hôtel de Ville—is translated into Basque—*Herriko Etchea*—on its facade. For drinks or a snack. *Moderate.*

SHOPPER'S BIARRITZ
Nouvelles Galeries department store is on Place Clemenceau, as are *Cartier* (jewelry, leather), *Artéon* (diamonds, watches), *Bord* (still another pricey jeweler), and *Fancy,* with smart duds, men's, as well as women's. *Hermès* (Avenue Edouard VIII) is a branch of the Paris leather-silk-accessories house. *Silva* (Avenue Edouard VII) features haute couturiers' clothes—Guy Laroche, Ungaro, St. Laurent, among others. *Formen*—aptly named, *Lacaze* (super swimsuits, male and female), *Déclic's* (women's clothes), *L'Île au Trésor* (antique furniture), and *Bernadette Malaganne* (nineteenth-century paintings) are among Place Bellevue's shops.

SOUND OF MUSIC
Théâtre Municipal (Place de la Liberté, Bayonne) is the region's opera house—and a classy one, at that; concerts and ballet, as well. (And check with area tourist offices [address below] for dates and locales of bullfights prevalent in summer.)

INCIDENTAL INTELLIGENCE

Men wear jackets and ties to both Biarritz casinos (addresses above); foreigners must present passports to disagreeable guards, for admission. You may rent umbrellas on the Grande Plage, but bring your own towels. Biarritz abounds in golf courses and tennis courts; the tourist office has details. *Aéroport de Biarritz–Parme* is a mile and a half southeast of town, with flights to and from a number of domestic points. *Further information:* Office de Tourisme, Square d'Ixelles, Biarritz; Office de Tourisme, Place de la Liberté, Bayonne; Office de Tourisme, Place Maréchal-Foch, St.-Jean-de-Luz.

10

Bordeaux
City behind the Wine Label

BACKGROUND BRIEFING

It's the core of the most prestigious wine-producing region in the world, with the magically named quartet of principal vineyard districts—Graves, Médoc, Pomerol, and St.-Émilion—encircling it, in the core of southwest France.

Each year ships bearing five million bottles sail from its Gironde River docks into the nearby Atlantic, the better to please palates of discerning drinkers planet-wide.

But what of the city behind the labels on the bottles? Long centuries of development—since the Romans settled in the ancient town they dubbed *Burdigala*—have seen Bordeaux evolve into one of the most elegant cities in Europe.

This sixth largest of the French Republic's cities was, after all, seat of the early Dukes of Aquitaine. Its soaring Gothic cathedral was where strong-willed Eleanor of Aquitaine—later to become Queen of England as the consort of Henry II—married her first husband, France's Louis VII.

That was eight and a half centuries back. But, even then, wine was a Bordeaux staple, as, indeed, it had been since Roman colonists first planted vines in the neighborhood.

English control of the city, through the period of Queen Eleanor and King Henry's reign, coincided with its emergence as an international wine-shipping center, with the English major customers then, as now.

By the time Montaigne, the essayist, and Montesquieu, the philosopher—locals both—had given Bordeaux intellectual cachet in the Baroque centuries, it had become rich. Indeed, the architectural heritage of its greatest century, the eighteenth, remains of consuming interest, which is hardly to suggest a preoccupation with the past. Indeed, perhaps because of its grandeur rather than despite it, contemporary Bordeaux typifies urban France at its most diverting, animated, amusing, and good tasting, with respect, I should make clear, to solid, as well as liquid, nourishment.

ON SCENE

Lay of the Land: This city of broad boulevards and monumental squares is a walker's town, with its overwhelming bulk on the west bank of the Gironde River, and its railway station flanked by a number of hotels—inconveniently detached from the center, a good 10-minute drive south of the core. Ideally, you want to headquarter in the heart of the city near *Place de la Comédie*, backed by the colonnade of *Grand Théâtre* (below), the landmark opera house. *Cours du 30 Juillet* leads east from the square to nearby *Esplanade des Quinconces*, one of Europe's largest—and most beautiful—squares, from which *Quai Louis XVIII* (soon changing its name to *Maréchal Liautey*) proceeds south to multiwinged *Palais de la Bourse*—the stock exchange complex that is the eighteenth century's outstanding contribution to the city's neoclassic good looks. Mercantile Bordeaux is centered on one of France's longest pedestrian shopping streets—*Rue Ste.-Catherine*, which cuts across the core, north from the triumphal arch on *Place de la Victoire* to central Place de la Comédie. *Cours de l'Intendance*, leading north from that square, is Bordeaux's answer to Paris's Rue du Faubourg St.-Honoré; it's lined with classy boutiques. And it ends at *Place Gambetta*, on the northern fringe of a venerable sector of town, dotted with landmarks and based on *Hôtel de Ville*, a neoclassic eighteenth-century quadrangle on *Rue des Ramparts*. There's a charming little park out back, enclosed by extensions, that houses a pair of major museums, with the soldier-attended pillbox fronting formidable walls of the *Préfecture* on *Rue Jean-Fleuret*, just beyond the *Cathedral* (below), another near neighbor.

Grand Théâtre (Place de la Comédie), without peer in France—Paris's Théâtre de l'Opéra excepted—is outstanding enough to warrant attention at this point. Late eighteenth century, its magnificent colonnade not only fronts it but flanks its sides. Interiors—foyer-cum-grand staircase; opulent salons for intermission refreshment; cupola-topped, ceiling-frescoed, six-level auditorium illuminated by a massive crystal chandelier—are among the most dazzling of any opera house in Europe. Pop in during the day to see the lobbies; better yet, snag a ticket for a performance, there being no daytime open hours for public inspection.

Cathedral of St.-André (Place Pey Berland) was built over a sustained half-millennium period, with the consequence a felicitous Romanesque-Gothic mix. Unlike most, though, it's not the west—or principal—entrance that's the most art embellished. Here, you want to study Porte Royale, on the southern facade, for the tympanum—or sculpted overdoor—at its best in an interpretation of the Last Supper. The interior

BORDEAUX

is immense, with the fine rose windows flanking the transept and an especially lovely chapel behind the high altar.

Musée des Arts-Décoratifs (39 Rue Bouffard) is a walled palace displaying work of Bordeaux artists and artisans—paintings, sculpture, silver, china—and furnished quite as it might have been two centuries ago, at the apex of the city's Golden Age. Indeed, no other open-to-the-public interior space in town, save the Grand Théâtre, provides the visitor with so graphic a portrait of what Rococo Bordeaux was like. And in all of France only this museum's counterparts in Paris, Lyon, and Marseille are its peers. You go from one ravishing room to another—a Louis XV salon in pale gray and blue with gilded *boiserie*, furniture-filled with pieces of that epoch; a dining room whose armoire is packed with period porcelain; Louis XVI-furnished drawing room in delicate green; a severe Directoire sitting room; a walnut-paneled study. Scattered about are glass cases filled with decorative objects—miniature paintings and watercolors, bronzes and busts in marble, amusing antique posters and drawings (including some of the Grand Théâtre), silver tea services and clean-lined wine glasses, cameos and keys.

Musée des Beaux-Arts (Jardin de l'Hôtel de Ville), in an atmospheric and aged pavilion edging the tranquil garden behind the City Hall, opens up with a bang. You are greeted with Veronese's masterful *Madonna and Child*, along with a Titian of *La Madeleine*—and does not become anticlimactic as you move along. The Italians continue—an immense Perugino *Virgin Mary*, Palma il Vecchio's *Holy Family*, another Titian, and another Veronese. Rubens, Van Ruysdael, Snyders, and Brueghel are among the Low Countries artists, as is Van Dyck, whose *Marie de Medici* is in a black gown relieved only by stark white collar and cuffs. The eighteenth century—as always, in this, of all French cities—charms with portraits by Largillière and Nattier, among the French; and Hoppner and Reynolds, among the British, with a study by F. J. Konson of the then-Duc d'Angoulême against a background of Bordeaux. And so you progress—Delacroix, Corot, and Félix Zeim, as the nineteenth century evolved, beyond to Renoir and Boudin, Matisse and Marquet (with a painting of the port of Bordeaux), Soutine and Vlaminck. Nearby *Galerie des Beaux-Arts* on Place du Colonel Raynal houses special short-term exhibitions; the museum's desk or the tourist office (address below) can apprise you of what's on.

Musée d'Aquitaine (Jardin de l'Hôtel de Ville, just opposite Musée des Beaux-Arts) is a worth-perusing repository of the lore of the Aquitaine region (of which Bordeaux is the seat), with sculpture from Roman *Burdigala*, furniture and costumes, documents and weapons, the lot painting a picture of life in the region to this very day.

Centre National Jean-Moulin (Place Jean-Moulin at Rue des Frères Bonies) is Bordeaux's World War II Resistance Museum, named for a Resistance hero, and portraying—often movingly—the ways in which the underground worked against the Nazis; principal displays are of clandestine printing presses and the illegal broadsides that came from them. Do pay your respects.

Church of Ste.-Croix (Rue Savageau)—a souvenir of Romanesque Bordeaux—is most stunning before you step inside, with facade dating to the twelfth and thirteenth centuries. There is a pair of square towers flanked by a fine central portal and a severely impressive nave.

Basilica of St.-Michel (Rue des Faures, not far from Ste.-Croix above) is a Gothic treasure, impeccably restored after World War II damage. Have a look at its uncommonly high—and detached—bell tower (ascendable, if you're up to it) and, again, if you're up to it, at mummy-like corpses in its crypt.

Church of Notre-Dame (Place du Chapelet) is a seventeenth-century treasure, of which Bordeaux is proud. After its roof collapsed in 1975, it was meticulously restored as part of a cooperative project undertaken by city authorities in collaboration with National Historic Monuments Commission architects and the Ministry of Culture. The interior is a felicitous mix of late Renaissance and Baroque, barrel vaulted, its altar backed by a trio of paintings, with details of the decor throughout—wrought iron, carved wood, sculpted marble—exceptional. And a one-time Dominican monastery (that in earlier times had been united with the church) next door is now a looker of a public library.

Maison du Vin (1 Cours du 30-Juillet, just north of Place de la Comédie) is a wine information center operated by the Bordeaux producers through their Conseil Interprofessionel du Vin de Bordeaux, the umbrella that joins together both producers and shippers of wine from more that 7,000—yes, 7,000—châteaux in the Bordeaux region. Stop in for excellent free literature. Ask to see the upstairs tasters' laboratory, where professional *taste-vins* ply their trade. Make arrangements—and, where necessary, appointments—for visits to châteaux in the region.

St.-Émilion, one of the four principal Bordeaux wine-growing regions, is, as well, an enchanting medieval village—still walled—in the center of the vineyards that take its name. If you are going to visit a single area wine town, this one—high in the hills 25 miles east of Bordeaux—should be it. Allow a day, or even overnight, for St.-Émilion, especially if you're interested in visiting a château or two. A pair that I have thoroughly enjoyed are *Château Soutard* and *Château Pavié;* hosts at both provide tours of the vineyards and the *caves,* and, of course, there are tastings. But, as I indicate above, château visits are by appointment only, ideally made in advance through Maison du Vin in Bordeaux, but it's possible that *Maison du Vin de St.-Émilion* (Place Mayrat) can be helpful on the spot. And you will find, driving about, small châteaux selling their own wines and offering samples to prospective purchasers. The town itself, as handsome as it is hilly, is based on central *Place du Marché.* It is named for a wandering eighth-century monk, later sainted, who founded a hermitage around which the town eventually developed. It was fortified in the twelfth century, and its walls—punctuated with Gothic gates— remain, as do a number of monuments. Start with the most extraordinary *Monolithic Church* (Place du Clocher), a Romanesque chapel in the nether reaches of a rocky cliff, created by the Benedictine successors of St.-Émilion, probably using preexisting *caves,* beginning in the ninth century—with substantial proportions—more than a hundred feet long, sixty feet wide, thirty-two feet high, and gracefully vaulted. St. Émilion's subterranean hermitage and a maze of catacombs are adjacent. Proceed to the *Collégiale Church,* a Romanesque-Gothic mix (Place Pinceau), with a not-to-be-missed cloister. *Cordeliers' Cloister* (a.k.a. Franciscan Friary, on Rue des Cordeliers) dates to the fourteenth century and is now put to sensible use as a café for the consumption of sparkling wine by the bottle. This leaves little *Musée Archéologique* (Rue du Clocher); it's skippable. But you'll want to allow time for aimless wandering in this pretty environment.

Médoc: The Bordeaux region producing the most glamorous wines—a high proportion of which are *crus classés,* as classified at the request of Emperor Napoleon III in 1855—is immediately north of Bordeaux city, its west flank on the Gironde River estuary. Though embracing eight famous *appellations d'origine contrôlées*—St.-Estèphe, Pauillac, St.-Julien, and Margaux are perhaps the most prestigious—and despite production of some of the planet's priciest vintages, it has nothing to compete with the Middle Ages village of St.-Émilion (above). As in St.-Émilion, smaller châteaux post signs on the road if they're interested in selling to the public. A few of the important châteaux keep regular open hours, including *Château le Bourdieu* (near Vertheuil), *Château Prieuré Lichine* (whose proprietor is prolific wine writer Alexis Lichine), and *Château Lanessan* (the main feature of which is Musée du Cheval, whose subject is horses—all you ever wanted to know about horses). Other principal châteaux are open only by appointment. Of these, star of the show—usually open only on weekday mornings (and not in August)—is *Château Mouton-Rothschild,* where the kicker, if one dare employ so frivolous a noun, is a collection of art objects based on the theme—you guessed it—of wine, the lot amassed by resident Rothschilds. A cool, multilingual hostess receives visitors in a lobby in which postcards (costing twice what they do in French museums) and also-pricey books about the owning family, the château, and its wine are sold in an effort, one supposes, to gain a bit of revenue as compensation for what may well be a misguided policy of gratis admissions. On display are a series of amusing Château Mouton wine-bottle labels designed by such artists as Chagall, Kandinsky, Henry Moore, and Robert Motherwell. There are, as well, quite lovely silver pieces (flagons and the like), antique glassware, Renaissance tapestries (their subject the harvesting of grapes), as well as Delft pottery, Oriental porcelain, and wine-related paintings by Old Masters like Nicolas Maes and David Teniers and such moderns as Gris and Picasso. Afterward, the group is led to a *chais*—Médoc's own word for *cave*, or cellar—where 100,000 bottles are stored, their corks changed every 25 years. A peep is permitted of still another *chais* in which, beneath august portraits of the clan's rulers, a thousand barrels are aging, to be transferred at the proper time to 300,000 bottles. Needless to say, no samples.

SETTLING IN

Grand Hôtel (2 Place de la Comédie; phone 5690-93-44): The pity of the Grand, with a rich history and the best location in town opposite the landmark Grand Théâtre, is that it has stripped its once elaborate Belle Époque interior—a solitary and splendid private-party room mercifully excepted—and, over recent years, transformed itself, within, at least, into a contemporary house. It's respectable-looking contemporary, to be sure, but the patina of yore has all but disappeared. There are a hundred functional bedrooms—sizes differ—including a few suites, and a bar-café (with outdoor tables fronting the square), but, upon my last inspection, not even a proper restaurant. Would that this old-timer were Luxury category. But alas, Bordeaux has none such. *First Class.*

Majestic Hôtel (2 Rue de Condé; phone 5652-60-44), a gracious old-timer felicitously updated in traditional style, welcomes with a smart lobby and friendly reception staff. There are just 50 rooms, no two identical but those I have inspected are tastefully decorated, with attention paid to textiles, wallpapers, accessories—and bathrooms. Central. Breakfast only. *First Class.*

Normandie Hôtel (7 Cours du 30-Juillet; phone 5652-16-80) is quite obviously proud of the facade of the dignified turn-of-century building it occupies; maintenance is first-rate. There are a hundred agreeable rooms and a helpful staff. Central. Breakfast only. *Moderate.*

Des Quatre Soeurs Hôtel (16 Cours du 30-Juillet; phone 5648-16-00). I can't help you in identification of the quartet of siblings for whom the hotel is called. But it's central, has the name of composer Richard

Wagner on its guest rolls, and offers 35 rooms—decor is fairly modern blonde wood—five of which are really oversized. Good value. Central. Breakfast only. *Moderate.*

Royal Médoc Hôtel (3 Rue de Sèze; phone 5681-72-42) sports a spiffy, black-leather and pale-wood lobby, smiles at reception, and shelters 45 small but otherwise satisfactory rooms in a conveniently central location. *Moderate.*

De Sèze Hôtel (23 Allées de Tourny; phone 5652-65-54) is a small (25-room) but satisfactory house, a major plus its location on one of the city's most beautiful thoroughfares. Breakfast only. *Moderate.*

Frantel Bordeaux (5 Rue Lateulade; phone 5690-92-37) is a component part of an almost aggressively ugly complex of shops, office buildings, and assorted multipurpose structures, a 12-minute walk north of the center. To its credit, Frantel is the only one of the national hotel chains even edging the core; several others are located out in the boonies. Here, once you learn the way, you can walk to Place de la Comédie. There are close to 200 Frantel-severe-look rooms; a cocktail lounge in which you sink into the floor when you sit on its absurd, armless, cushion-like benches; a reception staff comprised of indifferent youngsters; and— later evaluated because it is exemplary—a restaurant worth the trip from downtown. *First Class.*

Terminus Hôtel (Gare St.-Jean; phone 5692-71-58) is convenient to the railway station to which it is attached, but not to central Bordeaux, which is a 10-minute taxi ride distant. A pity, because this is an attractive, originally Belle Époque house that has been modernized with a sense of style—main-floor lounge off the lobby in red-and-gold Empire style, bar in contemporary black leather, bright-look *brasserie*, traditional Provençal-style restaurant, and—hardly unimportant—90 rooms; those I have lived in or inspected are as attractive as they are comfortable. Pity about the location. Mapotel/Best Western. *First Class.*

Arcade Hôtel (Rue Eugène-le-Roy; phone 5690-92-40) has the same inconvenient railway station location as the Terminus (above) but is lesser category, albeit adequate, with 140 clean-lined rooms equipped with good baths, as well as the convenience of a restaurant and bar. *Moderate.*

De Plaisance Hostellerie (Place du Clocher, St.-Émilion; phone 5624-72-32): Overnight in charming St.-Émilion? Why not, with a honey of a hotel like the Plaisance? This aged mansion affords smashing views of vineyards encircling the town from each of its dozen rooms, none quite like any of its neighbors, but all with fabulous marble baths and inventive antiques-accented decor. Pretty public spaces, bar and terrace among them, not to mention a restaurant, later counseled. Friendly. *First Class.*

DAILY BREAD

La Tupina (6 Rue Porte-de-la-Monnaie, an easy taxi ride from central hotels, just off Quai Ste.-Croix; phone 5691-56-37): Bordelais cuisine —indeed, much of the cuisine of the southwest—is considerably less celebrated abroad than that of, say, Burgundy, to name another celebrated wine region. La Tupina—occupying attractive quarters redolent of earlier centuries, in an aged house on an aged street—makes a specialty of regional cooking. Congenial waiters start you out with marvelous, coarse *pain de campagne,* setting a basket on your table, which is covered in red, white, and blue striped linen. You look over to the kitchen— cooking is being undertaken in immense copper kettles on an open grill—and you order from an extensive à la carte. *Foie gras à la fondue d'oignon,* hot and in a *pipérade*-like sauce, is delicious. A seafood salad— heavy on the crayfish—is, too. Likewise, a starter of garlic-scented smoked breast of duck; ditto, a cubed roast duck salad dressed with a shallot-accented *vinaigrette.* Entrées are hardly less memorable: *cassoulet,* the baked bean dish based on *confits* of duck; time-honored *entrecôte Bordelaise,* its sauce rich with the wine whose name it takes; a *pot-au-feu* combining vegetables with braised duck. La Tupina's made-on-premises sweets are hardly to be ignored: prune and Armagnac ice cream, a giant poached peach bathed in caramel sauce, rich chocolate cake. Needless to say, wine plays a major role in a meal here. In my experience, one of France's best restaurants. *Luxury.*

Le Bistrot de Bordeaux (10 Rue des Pilliers de Tutelle; phone 5659-99-22) makes no pretense of being anything more than its name indicates: simple and clean-lined; with pink linens on tables; long, white aprons on the waiters. The name of the game is wine sampling, so that with the well-priced prix-fixe, a glass of wine—you choose from a dozen available—comes with each course. Select, say, a Domaine de Fussignac to accompany your duck *terrine* and a Château Conilh to be consumed with your richly sauced chicken breast. *Foie gras* or lentil salad, grilled lamb or beefsteak are another pairing of courses. Dessert wine or no, you will have done well to open with *vin de pêche* as an offbeat aperitif and to conclude with the *bistrot's* celebrated chocolate cake, unfrosted but served in a soup bowl, the better to accommodate the *crème Anglaise* with which it is heaped. Central. *First Class.*

La Mériadeck (Frantel Bordeaux, 5 Rue Lateulade; phone 5690-92-37) bears the name of the glitzy north-of-the-center shopping complex in which it is located. It's the most attractive interior of this modern hotel (above), with a kitchen superior enough to lure neighborhood business types, as well as us outlanders. The well-priced prix-fixe includes wines and might open with masterfully sauced fish of the day, accompanied by a glass of Sauvignon wine, followed by *confit* of duck served with a château-bottled Bordeaux red; cheese selected from a platter and desserts selected from a trolley, conclude the meal. Everything that I have had is excellent; service is skilled and smiling. *First Class.*

Dubern (42 Allées Tourny; phone 5648-03-44) is a smart townhouse on a landmark Bordeaux street. Fare served as part of the less pricey of two exceedingly expensive prix-fixe menus—asparagus soup with oysters unnecessarily added to it, *escalope* of salmon, turkey entrée, cheese, house-selected dessert—was competent. But the glass of wine accompanying each of the first two courses was actually only half a glass— chintzy, that. And the gilded Louis XV paneling and crystal chandeliers of the upstairs dining rooms are not compensation enough for the staff's patronizing attitude. (With a cheaper café called *L'Estaminet* on the street floor.) *Luxury.*

La Chaminade (20 Rue des Pilliers de Tutelle; phone 5648-13-74) is, to be sure, in a basement, but a basement gained via a marble stairway and with tapestry-surfaced walls. There are also tasty victuals: oyster stew, filet of sole, roast lamb, super sweets. Congenial. Central. *First Class.*

L'Entrecôte (4 Cours du 30-Juillet; phone 5681-76-10): Forget about Beefsteak Charlie's back home. You're in Bordeaux, and the name of Entrecôte's game is what the title implies: the steak called *entrecôte*, scrumptiously Bordelaise sauced and served with a heap of crispy *frites*. Nothing else on the menu. Upstairs. Central. *Moderate.*

L'Imprévu (11 Rue des Ramparts; phone 5648-55-43) serves up creditable fare, as part of two prix-fixe menus. The less expensive might include a nicely presented plate of *crudités*; grilled steak, *cassoulet*, or *confit* of pork; and dessert. Cordial. Central. *Moderate.*

Aliénor (27 Quai de Queyries; phone 5686-50-65) is nothing less than a Gironde River steamer, attractively fitted out for evening dinner-dances the while it traverses the waterway that—passing villages and vineyards—connects Bordeaux with the Atlantic. Fare is regional—and hearty: ham or seafood *terrines*, roast lamb, *entrecôte*, or sole in champagne; and what the menu terms *super-choix de desserts*. Board by 8:30; you're back at the pier before midnight. *First Class.*

Café du Théâtre (Grand Théâtre) was, long decades back, a pioneering Bordeaux restaurant. Privately operated today—not run by the theater management—it is but a café-*brasserie*, albeit with original decor: crystal chandeliers, graceful columns, elaborate ceilings. *Moderate.*

Café Français (Place Pey-Berland): Take an outdoor table here for vistas of the cathedral and Hôtel de Ville. *Moderate.*

La Pierre qui Vit (5 Rue du Parlement Ste.-Catherine) is a smart stop for a glass of wine or coffee, in an eighteenth-century setting. *Moderate.*

De Plaisance Hostellerie Restaurant (Place du Clocher, St.-Émilion; phone 5724-72-32) is no less handsome than other sections of the hotel in which it's situated (above). And it offers tasty, prix-fixe menus, which might include crayfish and asparagus salad to open, sautéed veal filet or roast lamb as entrées, and flaky fruit *tarte* among the sweets. *First Class.*

L'Emiliano (Rue Portrail Brunet, St.-Émilion; phone 5774-44-64) is an old St.-Émilion favorite, with hearty, prix-fixe menus. Begin with a mushroom omelet or snails, and continue with *confit* of duck or pork, saving some of your wine (it had just better be St.-Émilion!) to accompany cheese; with dessert following. *Moderate/First Class.*

Le Savoie (Margaux village, opposite Office de Tourisme; phone 5688-31-76) is an elderly house transformed into the neighborhood's busiest restaurant, with tables occupying several ground-floor rooms and a pair of generous, prix-fixe menus. Open with coarse *pâté de campagne*, continue with a *Béarnaise*-sauced *filet de boeuf,* accompanied by deliciously prepared carrots, and conclude with a rich sweet, with a château-bottled Margaux—from the house's capacious *cave*—to accompany. *First Class.*

SHOPPER'S BORDEAUX
Wine, first: *Vinothèque de Bordeaux* (8 Cours du 30 Juillet) has incredibly immense selections—bargains through collector's items—from 200-plus châteaux. With accessories, as well—decanters, glassware, *taste-vins,* aprons, and the city's candy specialty: *sarments,* Médoc-flavored chocolates; overseas shipping. *Hôtel des Vins* (106 Rue de l'Épée) offers worthy competition. *Printemps* department store is on Place Gambetta, while its competitors—*Dames de France, Monoprix, Prisunic,* and *Grand Quartier* —are on Rue Ste.-Catherine, principal pedestrian street. Ever-so-smart Cours de l'Intendance's boutiques include *Hermès* (ties, scarves, men's and women's accessories), *Fabricant* (jewelry), *Lancel* (leather, gifts), *Sasson* (furs), *Burberry* (British-made raincoats, other duds), *Cacharel* (women's wear), *Daniel Hechter* (both men's and women's), *Descamps* (linens), *Roll*

(women's haute couture), *Centmil* (smart men's wear), and—for bargains—*Intendance 51*, discounted designer clothes. Rue Bouffard is antiques row, with such top sources as *Galerie Noël* (prints), *Camille Rousseau* (Louis XIV and Régence furniture), *R. Navarre* (silver), *Pruich* (eighteenth-century pottery), and *M. Cantaloup* (eighteenth- and nineteenth-century furniture).

AFTER DARK
Grand Théâtre (Place de la Comédie) is a principal Bordeaux landmark, as I try to make clear above. Go for opera, concerts, ballets.

Conservatoire André-Malraux (Rue Peyronnet) is the site of concerts, recitals, and other musical events.

INCIDENTAL INTELLIGENCE

Aéroport de Bordeaux–Mérignac is seven miles north of town, with frequent scheduled service to Paris and other domestic points. *Further information:* Office de Tourisme, 12 Cours 30-Juillet, Bordeaux; Office de Tourisme, Place du Clocher, St.-Émilion.

11

Bourges
Heartland of France

BACKGROUND BRIEFING

Is it conceivable that a city can be *too* central? In earlier centuries, Bourges's smack-in-the-heartland location (the precise geographical center of France is but 20 miles distant) served it very well, indeed. Contemporarily, though, trans-France travelers tend to give it short shrift, concentrating instead on the Loire châteaux to the northwest, Bordeaux to the southwest, or Burgundy to the northeast.

A pity, this. Too much remains of a rich past—a Gothic cathedral that's an all-Europe ranker, most significantly—to pass by the town that the Romans made capital of the northern segment of their Aquitanian colony and that later became capital of the medieval province of Berry, during which time it was nothing less than a royal seat.

Charles VII—the very same who, with Jeanne d'Arc's support, forced the English to retreat from France in the mid-fifteenth century—headquartered in Bourges. His son, Louis XI, who organized France's first post office, brought printing to France, and founded an esteemed local university that thrived for three centuries (until the Revolution), was Bourges-born. So, indeed, was the fabulously rich medieval super-merchant called Jacques Coeur—financial brain in the reign of Charles VII, pioneer French trader in the Middle East, owner of factories and mines, and monetary backer of campaigns against the English in the Hundred Years War. Coeur, alas, died ingloriously on a Turkish island, having escaped after enemies falsely arrested him on a charge of having poisoned Agnès Sorel, the bright and beautiful mistress of his employer, Charles VII. But the house that Coeur built in Bourges—one of the most startlingly prototypical examples of nonreligious Gothic architecture extant—still stands in Bourges, there for us to visit.

ON SCENE

Lay of the Land: Aptly named *Rue Moyenne* (which translates as Middle Street) cuts through the center of this essentially oval-shaped town, from *Place André-Malraux*—honoring one of this century's great French writers—at its south edge, to *Place Cujas*, named for the seventeenth-century teacher who is considered the father of modern jurisprudence and who taught at Bourges's late, lamented university. The city's principal landmark, its cathedral, is due east of Place Malraux. *Rue d'Auron*, perpendicular to Rue Moyenne, is the sprightly nucleus of a pedestrian shopping zone (*Nouvelles Galeries* and *Aubrun* are the top two department stores, and there are smart boutiques in surprising abundance). Several streets— *Rue Branly, Rue Coursarlon, Rue Mirabeau*—make for lovely strolls, the better to take in an extraordinary residue of medieval houses, many of them half-timbered—*colombage* is the French term. These streets more or less surround the handsomest of the city's squares, *Place Gordaine*, with its cafés the ideal relaxation venue between hours of exploration.

Cathedral of St.-Étienne (Rue du Guichet): French cathedrals—even celebrated ones like Rouen and Reims, to name a pair—are rarely set apart, in parks of their own, like most English counterparts. The cities in which they are situated have been built up around them, sometimes allowing open space for perspective, sometimes not. Bourges Cathedral is fortunate in that a venerable formal garden edges it to one side and frames the onetime Palais de l'Archevêque, a Baroque mansion that housed long-ago archbishops and that is now Hôtel de Ville. The perspective of the cathedral from the park is ravishing. While there, take in its proportions: flying buttresses supporting a pyramidal-shaped apse and, around the side, each buttress pinnacle-topped, the while serving as a divider, enclosing windows whose stained glass ranks with that of the Cathedral of Chartres—no modest attainment. Still, the approach to the cathedral from narrow Rue du Guichet—itself ancient, as houses flanking it attest—is hardly to be despised. At the street's end, you are faced with the cathedral's west or main facade. Tarry here; the artisans who erected this church (completed about 1350) did not stint at the entrance; worshipers have a choice of entry through five portals. In the tympanum—or recessed arch—above each door, sculptors have interpreted biblical chapter and verse so forcefully that Bourges's entrance these many centuries later is still called *La Bible des Pauvres*, the Bible of the then largely illiterate poor. That designation has even more meaning within. Walk first down the 350-foot-long nave to the high altar. (Bourges has no transept.) Then patrol the aisles, the better to take in the stained glass; that illustrating the Apocalypse, portraying Christ with a two-edged sword between his teeth, is a standout; so are scenes in the life of St. Stephen, for whom the cathedral is named.

Palais Jacques-Coeur (Rue Jacques-Coeur): If politics was the undoing of King Charles VII's finance minister—he died in foreign exile—it was also the means through which he achieved great wealth in the dynamic fifteenth century. The house he built is, indeed, a palace, with a fancifully gabled and many-chimneyed facade, stone walls intricately carved, and windows of its four stories mullioned. There are no furnishings. You go, rather, to appreciate what medieval civil architecture was all about—stunningly proportioned rooms, superb fireplaces (the one in the dining room is two stories high), as well as a masterful kitchen, a running-water system, a sauna, a bathroom, and a lavatory with the same contours as contemporary successors.

Musée de l'Hôtel Lallemant (Rue Bourbonnoux): As compensation for empty interiors of the Palais Jacques-Coeur (above), this onetime *hôtel particulier*, or townhouse, of a canny Renaissance cloth merchant, is furnished and accessorized so beautifully—and extensively—that it is a veritable museum of decorative arts extending over three centuries, sixteenth through eighteenth. Collections of smaller objects—porcelain, enamels, figurines, and paintings—is exemplary enough. But it is period rooms—one Régence, with walls of blue brocade and a brass chandelier; one Louis XIII, with a coffered ceiling and heavy oak furniture; one Louis XIV, with tapestried walls and tapestry-covered chairs; and one Louis XV, with a magnificent suite of furniture of that era—that especially captivate.

Musée du Berry (Rue des Arènes) occupies still another *hôtel particulier* —Hôtel Cujas, dating to the sixteenth century, double-towered and with a courtyard. It runs a considerable gamut, with respect to the span of time represented in two floors of exhibits, some prehistoric, some the folklore of recent epochs, the most interesting those relating to Gallo-Roman Bourges—busts and sculpted fragments, especially.

Church of St.-Pierre-le-Guillard (Rue des Arènes) is of the same period as the cathedral—begun in the thirteenth century. In one of the chapels of its graceful Gothic interior—the nave is especially lovely—you'll find the tomb of Bourges's honored Renaissance professor, Jacques Cujan.

Château de Meillant and Route Jacques-Coeur. Smaller, less spectacular, and certainly less well known than the châteaux of the Loire to the north, 10 castles—most of them inhabited and furnished in period—of the so-called Route Jacques-Coeur, all in the neighborhood of Bourges, are eminently visitable. *Château Meillant*, the biggest, is a Renaissance beauty; its skyscraper of a tower extends to seven stories. The grand salon is tapestry hung, its furniture Louis XIV and Louis XV. *Château Ainay le Vieil* is surrounded by a wall punctuated with half a dozen towers; *Château Culan*—parts of it are as old as the tenth century—sheltered Jeanne d'Arc in the course of her military travels. Others in the neighborhood include *Châteaux de la Verrerie, Boucard, Menetou-Salon, Chapelle l'Anguillon,* and *Jussy-Champagne.* Bourges's Office de Tourisme (address below) can route you.

SETTLING IN

Angleterre Hôtel (1 Place des Quatre-Pilliers; phone 4824-68-51) is a comfortable old-timer, tastefully updated and professionally operated, with just over 30 well-equipped rooms (all but a few with bath), an attractive restaurant—Louis XVI style in blue and white—and a cozy bar. Location is heart of town. *Moderate.*

D'Artagnan Hôtel (19 Place Seraucourt; phone 4824-67-51) is more functional than charming, with its chief advantage a good-sized room capacity (73 chambers). Restaurant and bar-lounge. Away from the core. *Moderate.*

Christina Hôtel (5 Rue du Halle; phone 4870-56-50) is a so-so No. 3, neither central nor engaging, but with 75 rooms. Breakfast only is served. *Moderate.*

Tilleuls Hôtel (7 Place de la Pyrotechnie; phone 4824-57-32) is just outside of town, occupying a renovated house of yore, with 29 rooms—some really spacious. Agreeable management. Breakfast only. *Moderate.*

Château de Thaumiers (20 miles south of Bourges, at Thaumiers near Charenton-du-Cher; phone 4860-87-62) looks older—thanks to half a dozen medieval-style conical towers—but is eighteenth century and inhabited, with 10 rooms-cum-bath for paying guests; breakfast only. Château Meillant (above) is a near neighbor. *Moderate.*

Château de la Verrerie (Oizon, near Aubigny-sur-Nère, 21 miles north of Bourges; phone 4858-06-91) is the very same Verrerie above recommended for inspection on Route Jacques-Coeur. But you may stay overnight, as well; there are half a dozen rooms with bath in this romantic, fifteenth-century castle, fronting a lake and in the center of its own forested park. Breakfast only. *First Class.*

DAILY BREAD

Jacques-Coeur (Place Jacques-Coeur; phone 4870-12-72): Talk about staying power: I enjoyed the Jacques-Coeur for the first time on a visit some two decades back, reporting favorably, at the time, on a dinner embracing snails, roast lamb with *flageolet* beans, cheese, and a poached whole peach. More recently, I ate equally deliciously; my meal commenced with a salmon *terrine* and continued with the same *escargots* I had remembered fondly. These were followed by steak Jacques-Coeur, served with a tarragon-scented mustard sauce and accompanied by Provence-style tomatoes; a sampling of the house's own pastries followed. Setting is opposite Palais Jacques-Coeur (above), and service remains delightful. In my view, one of France's best restaurants. *First Class.*

Le Sénat (8 Rue de la Poissonnerie; phone 4824-02-56): A restaurant on what translates as Fish Market Street had just better serve good seafood. Le Sénat does. Beef and veal entrées, too. Central. *Moderate.*

Le Bouffetard (Place Gordaine; phone 4824-19-68) is strategically situated at the edge of the city's most picturesque square. Consider *entre-côte aux frites* or a snack. No credit cards. *Moderate.*

INCIDENTAL INTELLIGENCE

Further information: Office de Tourisme, 21 Rue Victor-Hugo, Bourges.

12

Caen
Bayeux and the Beaches

BACKGROUND BRIEFING

It is little wonder that so much English is spoken in Caen. The interchange between this ancient Norman port and England began nine centuries ago, when the then-resident Duke of Normandy departed his Caen château, crossed the Channel with his legions, won the Battle of Hastings, and became sovereign of the land he vanquished, as William I—the Conqueror.

That was in 1066. In 1984, a successor of William—many generations removed—also crossed the Channel, albeit in a southerly direction, on a mission of joyous commemoration. Queen Elizabeth II worshiped in Caen's Abbaye aux Hommes—built by William. The irony of the occasion was not missed: It was the fortieth anniversary of the World War II, British-led liberation of Caen from the Nazis.

Love-hate relationship? If you like. Caen benefited from William's Hastings victory with a marked increase in commerce—it is just inland from the sea with which it is linked by canal—with England. Later—it was the early fourteenth century, by which time the Duchy of Normandy had become part of the kingdom of France—pro-English sentiment soured when, on two occasions in the course of the interminable Anglo-French Hundred Years War, English forces subdued Caen. On the second, in 1417, they remained as occupiers for more than three decades.

Even in that role, there were positive aspects. King Henry VI—who had been crowned in both London and Paris and founded England's Eton College and King's College, Cambridge, before he was murdered in the Tower of London—created the University of Caen. It thrives these many centuries later, although it was rebuilt, as was so much of Caen, 80 percent of which was destroyed by World War II bombs.

The city's most spectacular historic monuments—including the pair of abbeys built by William the Conqueror and his consort, Matilda, as acts of contrition for having married, even though cousins—were spared. And the immediate region of Caen is a study in stark contrasts, from venerable little Bayeux, with its extraordinary tapestries depicting William's conquest, to the English Channel beaches, on which Allied soldiers struck the invasion of Nazi-held Europe on D-Day, June 6, 1944.

ON SCENE

Lay of the Land: Caen is among the more attractively reconstructed of the European cities heavily damaged during World War II. It is based on its historic Big Three complexes. William the Conqueror's *Abbaye aux Hommes* on the street named for him—*Rue Guillaume-le-Conquérant*—marks the western edge of town, while *Abbaye aux Dames,* built by William's wife, is terminus of the core at its eastern extremity on appropriately named *Place Reine-Mathilde.* Between the two—near the city's southern apex—is what remains of William's once-glorious château, with still-splendid ramparts enclosing a mix of cultural institutions housed in recycled structures of the castle complex. *Avenue du 6 Juin*—bearing the date of D-Day—cuts through Caen from the château through central *Place de la Résistance,* flanked by venerable *Church of St.-Jean,* to the railway station on *Rue de la Gare. Boulevard du Maréchal Leclerc* is focal point of the pedestrian shopping precinct (with both *Galeries Lafayette* and *Nouvelles Galeries* department stores) in the core of town, southwest of the château, terminating at *Place Gambetta.*

The château complex—elevated and enclosed by original eleventh-century ramparts—is not all that it once was, but comes off handsomely, with its mix of manicured lawns, museums, and monuments. Still to be observed are formidable foundations of the onetime dungeon; a deftly proportioned little Gothic chapel, *St.-Georges,* by name, which now serves as a memorial to World War II Resistance fighters; also-Gothic *Échiquier* (it's used for conferences and private parties, but you may peep in), and the Baroque-era *Logis du Gouverneur,* an official residence cleverly adapted to house *Musée de Normandie*—an absorbing ethnological mix—with regional lore. I intentionally save best for last: a completely contemporary pavilion that was opened in 1970 to house exemplary collections of the city's *Musée des Beaux-Arts.* There are, to be sure, bigger French provincial art museums, but none, in my experience, with a higher proportion of beautiful paintings. I don't think anyone would not concede that the trademark work is Roger Van der Weyden's ravishing *Virgin and Child*—Mary red-robed, with a breast exposed for presumably imminent feeding of the naked baby Jesus, gently held in her lap. An arresting Rubens, *Abraham and Melchissedech*—vibrant with people and animals, color and movement—is a ranker, too, along with Perugino's *Marriage of the Virgin* and Veronese's *Temptation of St. Anthony,* as much for its melodrama as for its anatomy. Move along, then, to

Strozzi and Giordano, Van Dyck and Jordaens, Poussin and Vouet, Panini and Tiepolo, Boucher and Rigaud, Courbet and Delacroix, Impressionists, including Boudin and Monet, and later painters like Bonnard and Dufy.

The royal abbeys: What happened was that William the Conqueror—then Duke William (a.k.a. Guillaume le Bâtard, for he was illegitimate)—wooed and won the Flemish Princess Mathilde, a descendant of Charlemagne. But there was a hitch. Though not first cousins, they were related, and the pope of the moment excommunicated them. To achieve papal forgiveness, William erected a Benedictine monastery, while his wife, equally contrite, put up a convent for Benedictine nuns. If you are a gallant traveler, it will be a question of Ladies First, and you will start at the *Abbaye aux Dames* (Place Reine-Mathilde). The convent part of the complex, to the rear, was inhabited by nuns until the Revolution, later became a hospital, and currently is being restored—slowly and carefully. You want to see the abbey church, Trinité, by name, twin-towered Romanesque, with a fine nave, a crypt made beautiful by the sixteen splendid pillars framing it, and Mathilde's black marble tomb in the choir. *Abbaye aux Hommes* (Rue Guillaume-le-Conquérant), by far the more elaborate of the pair, will take more time. Its Church of St.-Étienne stuns, right off, with a pair of needlelike spires framing a severely beautiful Romanesque facade. Go on in, first, to pay your respects (as Queen Elizabeth II did on her D-Day Anniversary visit) at the simple black-and-white marble tomb, inscribed in Latin, of *Guillelmus Conquestor Normannise Dux et Angliae Rex*, taking in the misericords—the stand-up seats of the choir—with scenes, both lay and secular, of the seventeenth-century period when they were carved, and the portrait of a shrewd-visaged William in the transept. Move, then, to the newer part of the complex, the monastery, which was reconstructed in the eighteenth century, put to use as a school by Napoleon in the nineteenth century, and refurbished after World War II to serve as Caen's Hôtel de Ville, or Town Hall. The formal garden out front is more palatial than monasterial. Within, it's interesting to see how city fathers have assigned secular functions to interiors built for monks. The priors' reception hall is the city council chamber. The mayor hosts official receptions in the refectory. Civil marriages take place—chances are you'll observe a wedding in progress—in the onetime monks' chapter house. But other rooms—art-filled sacristy, monks' parlor for guests, and superb cloister—happily remain quite as they were, to be admired by visitors.

Church of St.-Pierre (Place St.-Pierre) is a reminder of how rich Caen's medieval merchants were; they built this single-steeple, Gothic beauty, and you want to head down the strikingly vaulted nave to observe the exquisitely carved frieze above the altar.

Château de Fontaine-Henry (seven miles northwest of Caen): The fireplaces—massive and magnificent—of its Renaissance rooms are reason enough for a visit, but the stairways are no less so, in a series of chambers rich with antique furniture, accessories, and paintings. A bonus: the Romanesque chapel in the backyard.

Château de Lantheuil (nine miles northwest of Caen) is the seat of a family whose most illustrious ancestor was a minister of Louis XVI and whose descendants still are resident. It is charmingly furnished in period.

Château de Creuilly (12 miles northwest of Caen) is more a case of history and architecture (it's as much fortress as residence and, at its eldest, dates to the eleventh century) than of art-filled interiors. It had been inhabited by Louis XIV's minister, Colbert, and his family well into the eighteenth century. In June 1944, a resourceful BBC crew moved into one of its towers to broadcast the Battle of Normandy.

Bayeux (18 miles northwest of Caen) is surely, along with Honfleur (Chapter 19), the most charming of Norman towns, but with considerably more than cachet to recommend it. Geography is not complicated. The cathedral towers over the town and is dead center. A sleeper of a town museum is just next door; the globally celebrated tapestries—your principal reason for coming—are a short walk east. And there's a pedestrian shopping center on Place du Général de Gaulle—where General de Gaulle made his first speech on liberated French soil (Bayeux was the first town to be freed by Allied troops on June 14, 1944).
    Cathedral of Notre-Dame, mostly twelfth- and thirteenth-century Gothic, packs an esthetic—and usually unexpected—wallop. The facade is graced by a trio of portals, two of them richly sculpted, but hardly less so than the smasher of a nave or, for that matter, the transept. Take your time wandering, noting art-filled side chapels, richly embellished high altar, and extraordinary Romanesque crypt—among France's loveliest.
    Musée Baron-Gérard, the cathedral's next-door neighbor, shelters a mixed bag collection of uncommon delights. A Clouet portrait of a Renaissance noble is its star painting, but there are works, as well, by Philippe de Champaigne, Boucher, and Boudin; a cache of priceless Bayeux-made porcelain; displays of also-Bayeux-created lace; and a Louis XV salon furnished in period.
    Tapisserie de Bayeux (Centre Guillaume le Conquérant) is not, properly, a tapestry, but rather a massive embroidery—when I say "massive," I mean some 230 feet long, with a height of not quite 20 inches—that is believed to have been made in England to decorate Bayeux's cathedral. Created while memories of the Battle of Hastings were still fresh, it relates—in 58 panels, wool-embroidered on a linen ground, with cap-

tions for each graphic episode in Latin—not only to the battle events, but also to the political, military, and civil events leading to it. You may rent a portable tape recorder, with a commentary on the tapestry to carry with you as you move along—and I recommend that you do so. Little has been left out by the embroiderers, from historic events like the death of King Edward the Confessor (William's predecessor on the English throne) to mundane matters like loading wine and weapons onto vessels making the Channel crossing. And take your time; it's the details of the tapestry that make it a medieval masterpiece.

Musée Mémorial de la Bataille de Normandie (Boulevard Fabian Ware, a short drive southwest of the center) is good preparation for a trip to the landing beaches (below): a graphic presentation of the Battle of Normandy embracing the 76 days between June 7 and August 22, 1944, by means of dioramas, displays of military equipment and weapons, and even mannequins wearing uniforms, both Allied and German.

Normandy Landing Beaches (Plages du Débarquement): The so-called longest day—D-Day, June 6, 1944—was the start of the World War II campaign by Allied forces that liberated France and the rest of occupied Europe from the Nazis—and paved the way to victory in Europe. General Dwight D. Eisenhower, later to become President of the United States, was supreme Allied commander, with British Field Marshal Bernard Montgomery serving as commander of land forces. There were five principal landing beaches. From west to east, these were *Utah* (4th U.S. Infantry Division), *Omaha* (1st U.S. Infantry Division—and the most difficult of the lot), *Gold* (50th British Infantry Division), *Juno* (3rd Canadian Infantry Division), and *Sword* (3rd British Infantry Division). Many lives were lost, as the area's military cemeteries attest. There are two American cemeteries, as many Canadian, a Polish cemetery, no less than 16 British cemeteries, and even half a dozen German cemeteries. And there are a number of museums and memorials relating to the campaign.

The American Battle Monuments Commission operates the *Normandy American Cemetery and Memorial* (Memorial du Cimetière Militaire Américain) atop a cliff overlooking Omaha Beach. There are 9,387 American war dead; the remains of 14,000 others originally buried in the region were returned home at the request of their families. Graves—their headstones are of white marble, a Star of David for those of Jewish faith, a Latin cross for all others—are set in 10 plots, on smooth green lawns edging the beach. Walls of the semicircular colonnade of the memorial contain maps detailing the landings. I have noted the legend inscribed on the frieze between the maps: "This embattled shore, portal of freedom, is forever hallowed by the ideals, the valor and the sacrifices of our fellow countrymen. In proud remembrance of the achievements of her sons and in humble tribute to their sacrifice, this memorial is erected by the United States of America."

Musée du Débarquement (a.k.a. Museum of the Landings, in the village of Arromanches, in what was the area of Gold Beach) faces the sea, clean-lined and glistening white, with flags of all the Allied nations flying from it and a simple brass marker with the legend *D-Day—6 Juin 1944* on its black entry doors. The museum's site is where, over a seven-month period, Allied convoys landed supplies used in the invasion. René Coty, then the French President, opened the museum in 1954. Films, dioramas, documents, equipment, uniformed mannequins tell the D-Day story. But, for visitors of a certain age, it is the photos on a lobby wall that are as memorable as any of the exhibits. France's de Gaulle, Britain's Churchill, America's FDR, and Canada's Mackenzie King are on the top row, with military leaders—including Ike, "Monty" Montgomery, and General Omar Bradley—below. Quite a show.

SETTLING IN

Relais des Gourmets Hôtel (15 Rue de Geôle; phone 3186-06-01): You like the location, just below the château. You like the warm welcome at reception. And you fall, at once, for the smart look of this 32-room house, a successful mix of the antique and the contemporary, with attention paid to textiles and wallpapers. All of the rooms I inspected—no two are alike—are delightful, and the restaurant is worthy of comment on a succeeding page. *First Class.*

Moderne Hôtel (116 Boulevard Maréchal-Leclerc; phone 3186-04-23) is heart of town, on Caen's main pedestrian street. This is a bright and lively house, with 57 rooms. Those I have inspected are comfortable and traditional style, with good baths. And there's an attractive restaurant, popular with locals. Friendly. *First Class.*

Malherbe Hôtel (Place Foch; phone 3184-40-06) occupies substantial quarters on a central square. Reception is alert, and there are just half a hundred rooms; those I have inspected are comfortable. Breakfast only. *Moderate.*

Royal Hôtel (1 Place de la République; phone 3186-55-33) is strategically located on a square at once central and attractive. There are just 45 neat rooms. Breakfast only. *Moderate.*

Dauphin Hôtel (29 Rue Gemare; phone 3186-22-26) comprises a score of rooms in a nondescript, converted house southwest of the château and an easy walk to the center. It is, however, in my not inconsiderable experience of French hotels, quite the gloomiest I have encountered. My room—one of 20—reminded me of nothing so much as a railway sleeping compartment. Cheerless restaurant. *Moderate.*

Métropole Hôtel (16 Place de la Gare; phone 3182-26-76): You're way over by the railway station if you put up here; however, there are 70 functional rooms. Breakfast only. *Moderate.*

Château d'Audrieu Hôtel (Audrieu, 12 miles west of Caen, 7 miles east of Bayeux; phone 3180-21-52) is a looker of an eighteenth-century château, set in its own park, with 22 no-two-alike antiques-accented rooms and suites, public spaces that include a wood-paneled salon, intimate restaurant, bar-lounge, and a swimming pool in the garden. I had a delightful sojourn and delicious meals on one occasion, but a disappointingly ungracious welcome in the course of an inspection visit several years later. There was no denying, even then, however, that the château still *looked* great. Member, Relais et Châteaux. *First Class.*

Manoir du Chêne Hôtel (Nonant, 15 miles from Caen, 3 miles from Bayeux; phone 3192-58-81) is a stone-walled country house that's far less smartly furnished than its neighbor, Château d'Audrieu (above); but it's agreeable, with 19 rooms, restaurant, bar, and tennis. *Moderate.*

Lion d'Or Hôtel (71 Rue St.-Jean, Bayeux; phone 3192-06-90) is Bayeux's chief charmspot—a gracious old house, agreeably updated, with cordial management and staff, 30 traditional style rooms (those I have seen are handsome), and a restaurant of good repute reviewed in a later paragraph. Central. *First Class.*

Luxembourg Hôtel (25 Rue des Bouchers, Bayeux; phone 3192-00-04) has two dozen rooms; those I inspected are neat as a pin and have showers in their baths. There are, as well, a cozy bar-lounge and a reliable restaurant, attractively Louis XIII in style. Very nice. *Moderate.*

Arrouges Hôtel (21 Rue St.-Patrice, Bayeux; phone 3192-88-86) is away from the center, with 29 bath-equipped rooms. Breakfast only. So-so. *Moderate.*

Marine Hôtel (Quai du Canada, Arromanches; phone 3122-34-19) is indicated, should you be contemplating an overnight stay in connection with visits to the landing beaches. It's long established and seafront, with 22 bath-equipped rooms and a restaurant that does well by traditional-style Normandy seafood specialties. *Moderate.*

DAILY BREAD
Relais des Gourmets Hôtel Restaurant (15 Rue de Geôle; phone 3186-06-01): Rust and gold draperies and wallpaper in the same shades set the tone in this handsome Louis XV room, with silver candelabra illuminating tables at dinner. Fare is deliciously traditional and Norman accented.

Open with *pâté*, fresh salmon, *foie gras*, a dozen oysters, or the house's fricassee of snails and frog's legs. Seafood entrées—grilled lobster flambéed with whiskey or a platter of four grilled fish of the day, for example—are tasty. So are meat entrées like filet of beef or—if you're game, in the city of origin—*tripes à la mode de Caen*. Desserts come wheeled on a chariot, and choice is not easy. *Luxury.*

Bourride (15 Rue Vaugueux; phone 3193-50-76) is a near-neighbor of the château; it's agreeable for lunch after a morning of exploration in the neighborhood or for a candlelit dinner, with the setting an atmospheric house of yore. Open with soup of the day—seafood *bisque*, perhaps—or the house's crayfish salad. Fish entrées are reliable; roast pigeon, too. Super sweets. *First Class.*

St.-Andrew's (9 Quai de Juillet; phone 3186-26-80) does not, to be sure, sound very *Caenois*. But it is, indeed, strategically—and attractively— situated on the waterfront, with starters and entrées built around seafood. *First Class.*

Relais Normandy (Place de la Gare; phone 3182-24-58) serves traditional favorites: duck Rouen style through *tarte Normande*. Well-priced prix-fixe menus. *First Class.*

Mandarine (18 Rue Froide; phone 3185-39-97) is exuberant Art Nouveau; tables are set with striped linen; and there's a pianist at dinner, which might include a seafood platter to start, *entrecôte* served with *pommes dauphines*, and not-bad desserts. Central. *Moderate.*

Café des Touristes (3 Boulevard Maréchal-Leclerc; phone 3186-11-56): Don't let the name put you off; situation is heart of the shopping area, so you can have coffee or a snack and take in the crowds. *Moderate.*

Lion d'Or Hôtel Restaurant (71 Rue St.-Jean, Bayeux; phone 3192-06-90) is the Old Bayeux restaurant you're seeking—beamed ceilings, ladderback chairs, reproductions of the Bayeux tapestry on the walls. Open with oysters, fish soup, or the house's own duck *pâté*. The chicken fricassee is hearty; filet of sole, more delicate but no less tasty. Lovely desserts; ditto, the service. *First Class.*

Rapière (53 Rue St.-Jean, Bayeux; phone 3192-94-97) occupies quarters in a Renaissance townhouse, with grilled steaks and lamb chops entrée specialties, and *tarte Normande* the indicated dessert. You're core of town, so that lunch is convenient; at dinner, tables are candlelit. *First Class.*

Dentellière (Impasse Prud'homme, Bayeux; phone 3192-16-59): You're in *crêpe* territory; stop here for a lunch comprised of one or two savory crêpes as your main course, with a sweet one to conclude. Omelets, too. Central. *Moderate.*

SOUND OF MUSIC

Théâtre Municipal (Place de l'Ancienne Comédie) is the well-equipped modern house at which are presented opera, ballet, concerts.

INCIDENTAL INTELLIGENCE

Aéroport de Carpiquet is four miles west of Caen; service to London, domestic points. *Further information:* Office de Tourisme, Place St.-Pierre, Caen; Office de Tourisme, 1 Rue des Cuisiniers, Bayeux; Office de Tourisme, Rue Maréchal-Joffre, Arromanches.

13

Cannes
Queen of the South Coast

BACKGROUND BRIEFING

The kind of public recognition given the English for their role in establishing Nice (Chapter 26) as a resort—the sea-girdling Promenade des Anglais—is, alas, absent in this smaller city 20 miles to Nice's west. But Cannes, too, owes England a debt for the cachet that accrued to it as a consequence of an 1834 visit—accidental, as an unplanned pause in the course of a journey to Italy—by Lord Brougham, the British Lord Chancellor, who was so pleased he promptly built himself a villa, impelling winter visits by friends among the British aristocracy.

Unlike Nice—a substantial city before its beaches were discovered by holiday makers—Cannes, though ancient, was a small fishing port. Named for a reed called *cannae* that grew in nearby marshes, it long predated the Romans who occupied it, to be followed by invading Moors, long-ruling monks, Spanish soldiers, Revolutionary troops, and—in 1815—Napoleon himself, en route from Elba at the start of the One Hundred Days interval before his second exile.

But it was the British invasion set off by Lord Brougham that provided Cannes with its true vocation: tourism. The Second Empire of Napoleon III saw Cannes's crescent-shaped, ocean-front artery, La Croisette—its counterpart of Nice's Promenade des Anglais—lined with palatial hotels. One was, to be sure, called Des Anglais; the lone survivor of this lot is the Gonnet et de la Reine. But somewhat later houses, turn-of-century, like the Carlton and the Majestic, continue to thrive. And by the time the Martinez—relatively recently restored to its original Art Deco look—went up in the 1920s, north-of-the-Channel visitors had been joined by continental Europeans, Parisians and other northerly Frenchmen, and the species of wealthy American chronicled in novels by Fitzgerald and Hemingway. Post-World War II decades have seen a democratization of Cannes's clientele—you have your choice, now, of well over a hundred hotels in every category—and newfound celebrity as the venue each spring with the planet's premier film festival.

But the visitor must not expect a duplication of bigger Nice, where tourism is but an aspect of a multifaceted economy. Cannes makes no pretense of being anything other than a tourist town. If it lacks Nice's vitality and diversity, it compensates—at least for sun worshipers and swimmers—with the wide, white-sand beaches replaced in Nice by a narrow, pebble-surfaced strand. Unlike skyscraper-packed Monte Carlo (Chapter 23), its core remains horizontal. And it is distinct from ultracasual St.-Tropez (Chapter 33) in that it is neither barefoot nor big-city, but rather a compromise between the two—and a happy one, at that.

ON SCENE

Lay of the Land: Thank nature for the crescent-shaped beach on which Cannes is based. And thank the *Cannois* themselves for having had the good sense to base the city's Main Street, *La Croisette*, on the beach's contours, extending from *Pointe Croisette*, western extremity and site of the summer-only *Palm Beach Casino* across the sands—subdivided into hotel-operated and public beaches, with lunch-only restaurants and rentable cabanas and beach chairs—to the area of town where it all began: *Vieux-Port*, the ancient harbor. This is the site of *Gare Maritime*, from where boats depart for the nearby *Îles de Lérins* (below). Above Vieux-Port's *Place de l'Hôtel de Ville* and *Quai St.-Pierre* is the oldest part of town: high-on-a-cliff *Le Suquet*, with a pair of key Cannes destinations (below), and *Rue St.-Antoine*, lined with dinner-only restaurants. Overlooking Vieux-Port to its west is *Palais des Festivals et des Congrès*, futuristic convention center–winter casino-theater complex. Shopping? La Croisette, to be sure. But you want to explore, as well, *Rue d'Antibes*, running parallel and gained by a number of northbound streets, *Rue des États-Unis* and *Rue du Canada*, among them. Center-of-the-action hotels line La Croisette, but others are on interior streets, *Rue Hoche*, particularly. The railway station is west of the core, just off *Avenue Docteur-Raymond-Picaud*. And Cannes is a center for excursions to such nearby points as *Antibes/Juan-les-Pins* (six and a half miles east), *Mougins* (six and a half miles north), *Grasse* (ten miles north), and *Vallauris* (four and a half miles east), all evaluated in later pages of this chapter.

Le Suquet, Cannes's dramatically elevated Old Town, is at its most spectacular on *Place de la Castre*—from which there are breathtaking views of the city below, and the sea. Go inside *Church of Notre-Dame-de-l'Espérance*, representing a mix of epochs—originally twelfth-century Romanesque, with a later Renaissance portal, and a simple Gothic interior. Nearby *Musée de la Castre* will take more time. This medieval tower houses an unexpected jumble of lovely old objects—an antique Cypriot bust; an early Egyptian-Coptic gravestone; Greek kraters and vases, their terra cotta-hued designs in mint condition; and pieces from Iran to the east (a painted princess) and Peru to the west (pre-Columbian pottery).

Marché Forville (Rue du Marché) is so easy of access, a few blocks inland from Vieux Port, that it's a pity not to make an early morning stroll through its aromatic stalls, wherein farmers sell fresh herbs— rosemary and basil, dill and thyme—so typical of the south of France. Look, too, at fish and crustaceans on sparkling beds of ice, along with fruits and vegetables arranged as though by artists, for still-life paintings.

Îles de Lérins: Earmark half a day for a swift excursion by boat to the pretty pair of Lérins Islands. On bigger *Ste.-Marguerite*, walk from the pier, upon arrival, to Fort Vauban, named for a prolific seventeenth-century military architect, to see a prison from that era, with cells not only of recalcitrant Protestants incarcerated after Louis XIV's Revocation of the Edict of Nantes, but of that same king's mysterious *Homme du Masque de Fer*—the Man in the Iron Mask—who was held for 16 years, with his identity never revealed. (Louis Hayward played him in a Forties' movie that you may have seen on TV.) To inspect as well: a museum of local archeological finds (Greeks and Romans were early settlers), an aquarium, and the flora (including eucalyptus trees) and fauna (including pheasants) of a pretty island. Catch a boat, then, to the smaller island, *St.-Honorat*, but a mile long and part of the Cistercians' Abbaye de Lérins, successor to a monastery that was opened sixteen centuries ago by the saint whose name the island takes. You're welcome to the monks' museum, noted for its antique sculptures, and to their church as well. Then, walk over to the much older *Fortified Monastery* to see its Romanesque chapels and smashing double-decker of a cloister.

Antibes/Juan-les-Pins—a pair of disparate towns east of Cannes, with beautiful *Cap d'Antibes* between them—may be regarded as vacation destinations in and of themselves or taken in, in the course of excursions from Cannes. *Juan-les-Pins* is modern and essentially a case of hotels, restaurants, cafés, and discos; it revolves around a summer-only Casino on Square Gould, just in from the wide, white-sand beach flanked by Promenade du Soleil. *Antibes*—the ancient Greeks' *Antipolis*, then a Roman colony, later the seat both of bishops and of rulers related to the Grimaldis of Monaco (Chapter 23)—is more substantial, which is not surprising, given its advanced age, and has a charming, centuries-old core that warrants on-foot exploration. Begin at *Place Nationale* and wander the adjacent pedestrian area between it and ramparts edging the sea, along such streets as *Rue Glose, Rue Sade,* and *Rue Aubernon,* taking in *Marché Provençal*—the market brimming with herbs, olives, produce, and fish and stands selling slices of tasty *pissaladière*, southern France's version of Neapolitan pizza. Stop into the so-called *Cathedral of Antibes* (actually a parish church and not the seat of a bishop these many centuries)—multiepoch, with a neoclassic facade, Romanesque choir, and Renaissance altar. Move along, then, to the next-door Château de Grimaldi, the rulers' originally medieval castle edging the ramparts. Severe and squarish, it is now *Musée Picasso*, with two floors of works by the master for whom it is named (and who was, for a time, in residence). The range is from a 1935 *Minotaur* to 1970s tapestries, with a considerable cache of Picasso-designed pottery and such standout paintings as *Joie de Vivre*, *Satyre et Faune*, and *La Femmes aux Oursins*, augmented by a number of sculptures (including a larger-than-life goat) and drawings; many photos of Picasso; paintings by other artists (the most gawked-at is by David Hockney, portraying a nude Hockney at a table with a clothed Picasso); and an herb-planted, sea-view sculpture garden. Deftly tucked into nearby *Bastion St.-André* at the end of the ramparts is *Musée Archéologique*, exhibiting bits and pieces of ancient Antibes. Antibes's medieval, four-pointed *Fort Carré* is now a theater/sports center. And beyond town, on *Boulevard John-F.-Kennedy at Cap d'Antibes*, is *Musée Naval et Napoléonien*—invariably popular with avid Napoleon buffs.

Grasse, as hilly as it is handsome, is Perfumeville—center of France's scent industry for three centuries, surrounded by fields of lavender, roses, and jasmine, with a number of perfume factories open to visitors (*Molinard*, at 60 Boulevard Victor Hugo, and *Fragonard*, at 20 Boulevard Fragonard, both of which have museums in connection). Grasse's monuments attest to its wealth over long centuries, ever since the twelfth, when it operated as an independent republic. Though no longer seat of a bishop, the handsomely Gothic and handsomely situated *Cathedral of Notre-Dame* (Place de Petit Puy) retains its original name and boasts not only a trio of paintings by Rubens, but another by Fragonard, Grasse-born in the eighteenth century. *Musée Fragonard* (Boulevard Fragonard) is a honey of a Rococo mansion, with a number of the native son's works, and the distinction of having had one of its paneled rooms moved, in toto, to the Metropolitan Museum of Art, in New York, where it is on display. *Musée d'Art et d'Histoire de Provence* (Rue Mirabeau), another fine old house, displays quite the oldest perfume bottles you are likely to encounter and a range of objects relating to Provençal life, costumes through china.

Vallauris (two miles west of Antibes) is a pleasant enough little town that would be unexceptional were it not that a chap named Pablo Picasso was a ten-year resident. He impelled locals to restore their once-thriving production of ceramics and left some of his own handiwork. At *Musée National Picasso*, "La Guerre et la Paix," in the chapel of the village's château on Place de la Libération, hangs the master's enormous and highly charged mural on the theme of war and peace; the town's *Musée Municipal*, with prize-winning ceramics from competitions it sponsors, is adjacent. On *Place Isnard* is Picasso's eye-catcher of a bronze sculpture depicting a shepherd with one of his flock. In and about *Avenue Georges-Clemenceau*—for better or for worse—are myriad Picasso-inspired pottery shops, whereas pottery by the instigator of all this enterprise is displayed at Musée Picasso in Antibes (above).

SETTLING IN

Martinez-Concorde Hôtel (73 La Croisette; phone 9368-91-00): The Twenties were Roaring, and a savvy, Sicilian-born hotelier named Emanuel Martinez—who had managed classy hotels in Paris, London, and Monte Carlo—determined that the time was ripe for a Cannes house that would reflect the dash and spirit of the period. He organized capital, hired a Nice architect, coincidentally named Palermo—for the capital of his native Sicily—and the Martinez opened its doors in 1929, a smashing success. Making a post-World War II comeback was something else again. The Martinez had deteriorated, but retained its Art Deco facade, its interior architectural details, and even many of its original, custom-designed furnishings. However, in 1982, Hôtels Concorde, the chain operated by the champagne-producing Taittinger family—spurred by the success of its rehabilitation of Paris's legendary Crillon—bought the hotel, retained crack Paris interior designers and architects, and sank several score millions of francs into a major renovation of what is, be it noted, Cannes's largest hotel—with 400 rooms and suites. The restored building is sumptuous—a collector's item for Art Deco buffs. Suites and bedrooms sport geometric motifs in subtle shades of blue, peach, and pink, with stunning Carrara marble baths. Lounge chairs in the lobby are pure Twenties, the big cocktail lounge is a pleasure, and there is a trio of restaurants—one elevated and with seaviews (I review it on a later page), another indoor/outdoor casual, the third (smart for a summer buffet lunch) located on the Martinez's private beach just across La Croisette. And there's a new Croisette-view swimming pool as a bonus. Member, Leading Hotels of the World. *Luxury.*

Carlton Inter-Continental Hôtel (58 La Croisette; phone 9368-91-68): Pre-World War I years saw Cannes well established, but the time appeared propitious for a new and palatial Croisette hotel. The Carlton—with a hundred-yard facade flanked by conical towers, which is among Europe's most impressive such—opened in 1913 and, it would appear, not a moment too soon, with crowned heads of Belgium, Greece, Italy, Portugal, Spain, and Yugoslavia among its guests during the early years. Later, in 1939, the first Cannes Film Festival opened with a party at the Carlton; Tyrone Power, George Raft, and the film crowd arrived to compete with the royals on the Carlton guest register. Recent years have seen U.S.-based Inter-Continental Hotels sink $15 million into a meticulous, stem-to-stern refurbishing of this extraordinarily beautiful hotel, retaining the marble, gold-leaf plasterwork, and original frescoes; installing Le Petit Bar with 2,000 gold-leaf rosettes on its ceiling—off the very grand lobby; re-creating the Grill in Louis XIII style; opening an intimate haute cuisine restaurant (reviewed on a later page); renewing the 335 suites (Louis XV and sumptuous) and traditional-decor rooms; the while retaining the vast drinks terrace and the lunchtime buffet-restaurant on the Carlton's private beach across La Croisette. *Luxury.*

Majestic Hôtel (La Croisette; phone 9368-91-00) is a meticulously maintained old-timer—warm, friendly, gracious—with high-ceilinged public spaces, 300 traditional-style rooms and suites of varying sizes, congenial cocktail lounge, trio of restaurants, and palm-shaded garden based on an umbrella-bordered swimming pool. Proprietors are Chaine Lucien-Barrière, three of whose hotels I recommend in Deauville (Chapter 16). *Luxury.*

Gray d'Albion Hôtel (38 Rue des Serbes; phone 9348-54-54), though not directly on La Croisette, is well situated in a shopping-residential complex between it and Rue d'Antibes. One of the town's newest houses, it is clean-lined contemporary, with 173 rooms (alas, they are small) and a dozen-plus suites (there are phones in all the baths), as well as a trio of restaurants—one quite grand and reviewed on a later page; a second, good value and casual; and a third, for super buffet lunches on the Gray d'Albion's private beach. Service is smiling; management, astute. *Luxury.*

Frantel Cannes (13 Rue du Canada; phone 9338-22-32) is but a block inland from La Croisette, just across Rue du Canada from the Carlton (above). It's one of the more attractive links of the Frantel chain, with public spaces modified-Persian, their walls surfaced in blue and yellow tile. There are 95 rooms—by no means overlarge, but functional; bar-lounge, swimming pool, and restaurant open only to groups staying in the hotel. *First Class.*

Gonnet et de La Reine Hôtel (42 La Croisette; phone 9338-40-00) is *grande dame* of La Croisette—sole survivor of the palace-type hotels built during the heyday of the Second Empire. It remains stubbornly quiet and old-fashioned, with a period-piece lobby-cum-bar; half a hundred rooms, of which those with seaviews are the most spacious and desirable; and a restaurant open only to registered guests. *First Class.*

Grand Hôtel (45 La Croisette; phone 9338-15-45): Given its enviable location—behind an enormous lawn (not always neatly clipped) in the core of La Croisette—the Grand really *should* be grand. As it is, the look is inoffensive, albeit nondescript, modern. There are 75 rooms, restaurant, bar, and private beach. To me, disappointing. *First Class.*

Beau Rivage Hôtel (61 La Croisette; phone 9394-24-25) is a worth-knowing-about budget house not only on La Croisette, but right next door to the Carlton (above). There are just 20 traditional-style rooms (corner ones are nice), competent restaurant with rustic decor, and a garden where drinks are served in summer. *Moderate.*

Palma Hôtel (88 La Croisette; phone 9394-22-16) is, to be sure, away from the central portion of La Croisette, at the Palm Beach Casino end. But it has half a hundred neat rooms (book ahead for an ocean-view one—they have terraces). Breakfast only. *Moderate.*

Mondial Hôtel (77 Rue d'Antibes; phone 9339-28-70) is well located on the main shopping street, an easy walk from the beach. There are 65 compact rooms. Breakfast only. *Moderate.*

Savoy Hôtel (5 Rue François-Einesy; phone 9338-17-74) is centrally located (the Carlton is a near-neighbor), with 55 neat rooms—there are seaviews from some of the higher-up ones. Breakfast only. *Moderate.*

Splendid Hôtel (4 Rue Félix-Faure; phone 9399-53-11): The title exaggerates, but there is no denying the lovely location of this old-fashioned house that overlooks scenic Vieux-Port. There are 64 rooms, some with kitchenettes. Breakfast only. *Moderate.*

Sofitel-Méditerranée (2 Boulevard Jean-Hibert; phone 9399-22-75): You're at the far (by that I mean west) end of Vieux-Port in this pink-facade hotel, a fair walk from the core of town. Still, views can be striking from the best-placed of the 145 modern rooms, and, besides a restaurant and cocktail lounge, there's a swimming pool-sundeck on the roof. *First Class.*

Montfleury Hôtel (25 Avenue Beauséjour; phone 9368-91-50) would be higher up in my Cannes hotel evaluations, were it only closer to La Croisette. Location is atop a steepish hill, which makes views of town and sea possible, but it's quite a trek by foot. This is a clean-lined contemporary house (it was originally operated by Inter-Continental Hotels) with 235 comfortable rooms, a trio of restaurants (one haute cuisine, one casual, one al fresco), bar-lounge, and—the hotel at its best—a honey of a pool in a lushly landscaped garden. *Luxury.*

Du Cap Hôtel (Boulevard J.-F.-Kennedy, Cap d'Antibes; phone 9361-39-01) comes in two parts. The main building is a Second Empire mansion with exquisitely furnished and accessorized public spaces; and a hundred equally sumptuous, no-two-quite-alike rooms and suites furnished in period, with antique accents and extravagant textiles, not to mention terraces-cum-views. Breakfast comes to you via room service. But, for lunch and dinner, you descend to a considerably detached pavilion smack on the sea—the hotel occupies an enormous park of its own—and with two levels; upper is the restaurant, evaluated in a later paragraph; a bar and pool-cum-terrace flank the rugged shore below, with swimming possible in the sea, as well, via an approach along a specially built cement path that cuts through the rocks. The Du Cap appears to make a point of catering especially to an international repeat-clientele, with bookings made as much as a year in advance. Service is efficient and correct, but cool. This hotel—one of the most beautiful in Europe—takes itself very seriously and, moreover, does not accept credit cards. Member, Leading Hotels of the World. *Luxury.*

Tananarive Hôtel (Route de Nice, Antibes; phone 9333-30-00): If you've a car, this is not a bad spot to alight for a night or two; half a hundred contemporary-design rooms, swimming pool, tennis. Breakfast only. *Moderate.*

Belles Rives Hôtel (Boulevard Baudoin, Juan-les-Pins; phone 9361-02-79) has location as a plus: beachfront and convenient both to the core of Juan-les-Pins, as well as Cap d'Antibes. Public spaces are high ceilinged, light, and airy; bedrooms (there are 42 and you want to book a seaview one), likewise. The cocktail lounge is handsome, and so is the picture-windowed restaurant, at its best when it moves to a broad terrace for candlelit summer dinners at the edge of the Mediterranean. Very nice, indeed. *First Class.*

Juana Hôtel (Avenue Gallice, Juan-les-Pins; phone 9361-08-70) is an elderly house, compact but nicely updated in traditional style, with a bar leading from the little lobby, 42 not overlarge rooms, a swimming pool out front, as well as a private beach nearby, and good restaurant. No credit cards. *First Class.*

Beachotel (Avenue Alexandre III, Juan-les-Pins; phone 9361-81-85): The title might better be *Near the Beachotel;* the sands are a full block distant. Still, this is an agreeable house—contemporary, with just under 30 kitchenette-equipped terraced rooms, a restaurant that turns out a super buffet at lunch and dinner, and a friendly staff. *Moderate.*

DAILY BREAD

Le Royal Gray (Gray d'Albion Hôtel, 38 Rue des Serbes; phone 9348-54-54) starts with smiles. You are cordially welcomed to a relatively intimate space, contemporary and in tones of aubergine and pink, with great bowls of flowers at strategic points; and the large staff categorized by uniforms: captains and *sommeliers* in tuxedos, waiters in red jackets, busmen in red tunics—the lot of them alert and efficient. Order from either a five-course menu or a *menu de dégustation* embracing no fewer than 10 courses served in smallish portions. Fare is *nouvelle*—sensible and, by and large, delicious *nouvelle*. Your meal might, for example, open with a warm mussel-and-fresh-pasta salad or warm oyster-and-caviar salad, continue with a shrimp-and-lima-bean casserole as the fish course, and follow with an exceptional entrée—*escalope de foie gras de canard poêlée croustillante aux pétales d'artichaut*, a wordy way of describing an inspired combination of *foie gras*, duck, and artichokes. Pastries are memorable—a *millefeuille de pommes sauce caramel*, especially. *Luxury.*

La Palme d'Or (Martinez Hôtel, 73 La Croisette; phone 9368-91-00) smartly carries out the hotel's Art Deco design. It's a capacious, red and rose space, up a flight, with picture windows overlooking the hotel's pool to one side, and a terrace—you dine under the stars in warm weather—the only such on La Croisette that's elevated, affording smashing views of the sea. Getting to La Palme d'Or—named for the Cannes Film Festival's top award—is half the fun. Blown-up photos of Lana Turner, Humphrey Bogart, Gary Cooper, Deanna Durbin, and Elizabeth Taylor line its foyer's walls; photos from film festivals over the years are in the bar; and likenesses of French stars like Simone Signoret and Jean Gabin are in the restaurant proper. You do well to order the five-course-and-coffee prix-fixe. It might embrace rabbit casserole, grilled fish of the day in a lobster sauce, roast lamb, cheeses from a vast platter, and choice of sweets (the *pâtissier* is a star of this show), with scrumptious little *petits-fours*, here called *mignardises*, served with coffee. *Luxury.*

La Côte (Carlton Inter-Continental Hôtel, 58 La Croisette; phone 9368-91-68): You don't expect the leading restaurant of this grand hotel to be so intimate. The smallish scale appeals, as do the good looks—striped Louis XVI chairs surround flower-centered tables under a glass-domed ceiling. The à la carte is what might be termed creative-traditional, with favored openers including duck *terrine*, shrimp *bisque*, sautéed crayfish, or Provençal-style scrambled eggs; a seafood platter served with a basil-scented sauce, grilled sole, broiled lamb chops and steak *au poivre* are among the entrées. Desserts justifiably rate a card of their own. *Luxury.*

La Mirabelle (24 Rue St.-Antoine in Le Suquet; phone 9338-72-75) is indicated for a festive dinner in Vieux-Cannes under the beamed ceiling of an aged townhouse. Open with fresh asparagus served with the chef's special sauce, continuing with grilled salmon, filet of Charolais beef, or roast lamb. Luscious sweets. *Luxury.*

Le Bistingo (Palais des Festivals, Jetée Albert-Edouard; phone 9338-12-11): It's a starry night and you fancy a dinner al fresco, overlooking Vieux-Port. Book here, in this Convention Center restaurant, ordering the good-value, prix-fixe menu, based on such entrées as grilled turbot, mustard sauced, or an unusual duck casserole. And wait till the trolley of desserts is wheeled over! *First Class.*

La Mère Besson (13 Rue des Frères-Pradignac; phone 9339-50-24): I don't know who the Pradignac brothers were—other than that they gave their name to the street on which this restaurant is located—but La Mère Besson is female operated, front and back. Try for a table on the terrace in nice weather. Inside, movie posters line walls in recognition of the annual film festival. Fare has a Provençal accent, with the prix-fixe running to a garlicky green salad with croutons or sautéed mushrooms to start and delicious frog's legs or a not-very-Provençal *osso bucco*, among entrées. Skip the rum and chocolate *génoise* for dessert at your peril. *First Class.*

Vesuvio (65 La Croisette; phone 9394-08-28) has as its drawing card a selection of delicious pizzas. But there are good steaks and grilled fish, as well. The coarse-textured bread is a treat, and there are outdoor tables. *First Class.*

Gaston et Gastonette (15 Quai St.-Pierre; phone 9339-99-34) is agreeable for lunch at an outdoor table overlooking Vieux-Port; the menu, embracing mussels *marinière* style, roast duck, and cheese or dessert, is a good buy. *Moderate.*

Lunch on the beach: There are two dozen lunch-only, summer-only restaurants, with buffets (including hot entrées and a variety of salads, as well as a choice of desserts), and à la carte choices, in many cases. They range from those operated by leading hotels—Martinez, Gray d'Albion, and Carlton, for example—to those on public beaches like Esterel, which are less costly. Wear what you like, including, of course, swimsuits. *Moderate through Luxury.*

Rohr (63 Rue d'Antibes) is No. 1 *pâtisserie/salon de thé*, ideal for sustenance in the course of a morning in Rue d'Antibes's shops. *Moderate.*

Moulin de Mougins (a mile and a half south of Mougins village, on Route D2; phone 9375-78-24) is an atmospheric and ancient olive-oil mill converted into a charming, rustic-look restaurant in the late Sixties by chef-patron Roger Vergé and his wife, Denise. Over the years—as much because of M. Vergé's skill at promotion, as well as at cooking—it has become one of the best known of France's country restaurants, and is agreeable as a lunch or dinner excursion destination from nearby Cannes— but four miles distant. Order à la carte or from a prix-fixe menu embracing half a dozen courses, opening, to give you an idea, with an *escalope* of salmon; continuing with a crayfish fricassee, grapefruit sherbet to freshen the palate, an entrée of basil-sauced *noisettes* of lamb served with stuffed zucchini and a Vergé potato specialty, and following with cheese, in advance of a strawberry-and-pineapple dessert accompanied by *petits-fours*. Lovely service. *Luxury*. (Note that M. Vergé operates a *second* Mougins restaurant, *Amandier de Mougins*, edging the village; phone 9390-00-91, also located in a looker of an old house, but about a third less pricey than the Moulin; very nice, indeed, and *First Class*.)

Le Relais à Mougins (core of the village; Mougins; phone 9390-03-42), operated by chef-patron André Surmain in an attractive and aged Mougins house, gives M. Vergé (above) a good run for his money, offering a pair of well-priced, prix-fixe, lunch-only menus that include house wine. The less pricey might open with smoked-salmon *rillettes*, continue with M. Surmain's popular three-part salad, with breast of duck or sole with a *foie-gras* flecked cream sauce as entrées, house dessert, and made-on-premises chocolate truffles as a bonus. Dinner is more costly. Friendly and delightful. Member, Relais et Châteaux. *First Class*.

Eden Roc (Du Cap Hôtel, Boulevard J.-F.-Kennedy, Cap d'Antibes; phone 9361-39-01) occupies a detached pavilion edging the rockbound shore, in the Du Cap's park-like grounds. White rattan chairs, cushioned in green, surround tables laid with white linen, within the spacious, picture-windowed dining room and on an open deck, adjacent. If you go for but one meal, it should be lunch, for two reasons: Smashing views along the coast is the first, and hors d'oeuvres—salads in immense variety, cold meats, and relishes—which you yourself select from a groaning buffet, is the second. You order the rest of your meal from an extensive à la carte, with roasts and grills—*paillard* of veal, lamb chops, duck with sauce *Béarnaise*, sole, or turbot—counseled. Desserts rate a card of their own—and they are elaborate. Service is professional, albeit impersonal. *Luxury*.

La Côte à l'Os (290 Rue James-Close, Antibes; phone 9334-37-45) has the look of Vieux-Antibes—dark woods and antique accents. And the seafood is delicious—brochette of shrimp and grilled catch of the day, especially. Friendly. *First Class*.

Le Cameo (Place Nationale, Antibes; phone 9334-24-17) is a sensible choice for lunch at an outdoor table on this vibrant square. Order fish or *entrecôte aux frites*. *Moderate.*

Le Sorrento (67 Promenade du Soleil, Juan-les-Pins; phone 9361-18-34) is long on scene, central, seaview, and with a terrace from which you might enjoy a seafood repast. Fun. *Moderate.*

Café Pam-Pam (Carrefour de la Joie, Juan-les-Pins): Tarry as long as you like over coffee or a cold drink. *Moderate.*

Amphitryon (16 Boulevard Victor-Hugo, Grasse; phone 9336-58-73) is reasonably close to the center and pleasant for a lunch pause in the course of Grasse exploration. Well-priced, prix-fixe menus. *First Class.*

SHOPPER'S CANNES
Dames de France and *Monoprix* department stores are on Rue Maréchal Foch. Stroll La Croisette and you'll come across blue-chip establishments like *Hermès, Lanvin, Gucci, Léonard, Chloë, Yves St.-Laurent, Christian Dior, Karl Lagerfeld,* and *Valentino* (clothes and accessories); *Bruno, Claude Bonucci* (pricey men's clothes); *Cartier, Fred, Mappin & Webb* (jewelry); *Fauchon, Hédiard* (fancy foods); *D. Porthault* (linens); and *Select* (shoes). On Rue d'Antibes you'll find such stores as *Charles Jourdan* (expensive shoes), *Minelli* (moderately priced shoes), *Céline* (women's clothes and accessories), *Giorgio Armani* (women's and men's clothes), and *Le Jardin* (Limoges porcelain). *Cannes English Bookshop* is at 14 Square Merimée. *Glacier Filfeu* (Rue des Etats-Unis, just off La Croisette) has the best ice cream cones in Cannes; and *La Lorraine* (12 Rue Sade, Antibes) just has to be the most mouthwatering *charcuterie* on the Riviera.

SOUND OF MUSIC
The two halls of Cannes's *Palais des Festivals et des Congrès*—the convention center-casino complex—smaller *Théâtre Claude-Debussy* and *Lumière Grand Auditorium,* are venues for winter concerts and musicals. In summer, there are varied entertainments at *Casino Palm Beach.* And ballet and concerts are performed at *Palais Croisette.* (To enter the casinos, men need tie and jacket in the evening; passports are required of all foreigners; games are roulette, blackjack, and *vingt-et-un.*)

INCIDENTAL INTELLIGENCE ═══════════════

Further information: Office de Tourisme, Palais des Festivals et des Congrès, La Croisette, Cannes; Office de Tourisme, 11 Place Général de Gaulle, Antibes; Office de Tourisme, Boulevard Charles Guillaumont, Juan-les-Pins; Office de Tourisme, Place Foux, Grasse; Office de Tourisme, Avenue des Martyrs de la Résistance, Vallauris.

14

Chamonix
In the Shadow of Mont Blanc

BACKGROUND BRIEFING
Means of access can be important. You may—or may not—remember
arrival in a new place by train or plane or even sleek superhighway. But
I'll not forget my first view of Chamonix. The approach was by car.
Within half an hour after departure from the Italian resort town of
Courmayeur, I had driven through the seven-mile-long international
tunnel cut through the Alps's highest peak, cleared both Italian and
French customs, and arrived in France's premier mountain resort, nes-
tled in a breathtakingly beautiful valley.

Chamonix is framed by the snow-surfaced peaks that began luring
visitors, intrepid English adventurers, three and a half centuries back.
What drew them was 15,781-foot Mont Blanc and a range of positively
smashing satellite peaks. The year was 1741. Four decades later, a pair
of Frenchmen—Balmat and Paccard, by name—reached the summit of
Mont Blanc, to be followed, shortly afterward, by a third, Horace Saussure. They had pioneered French mountaineering, paving the way for
development of what has become France's best-equipped and most
scenically situated Alpine resort, hosting a million visitors each year.

This is the town that was the site of the first Winter Olympics—back
in 1924. It's the resort with the highest cable car in the world. It brims
with facilities for skiers (two cog railways, half a dozen cable cars,
as many gondolas, 10 chairlifts, a score of ski lifts) and with skiers'
locales— Le Brévent and Les Grands Motets for the highly skilled, La
Flégère for mid-level expertise, Les Houches for beginners—to name but
four. And it offers a bonus of easily reached destinations of visual splendor (even including a half-day mountain journey to a foreign country—
Italy—by a succession of cable cars) for the nonskiing sightseers among
us who come to inspect a corner of Europe as well equipped with
creature comforts as it is spectacularly endowed by nature.

ON SCENE

Lay of the Land: A pair of nearly contiguous squares—*Place de Saussure* and *Place Balmat* are the core of town; they're named for two of the three pioneer climbers of Mont Blanc, and the main street—*Rue Docteur Paccard*, extending south from Place Balmat—is named for the third member of that illustrious trio; it is lined with shops (Chamonix has no department stores), as is *Avenue Michel-Croz*—pedestrians-only at the point where it edges the main squares. It leads west to the Town Hall, tourist office, pretty, slim-steepled parish church, and the *railway station* at its eastern terminus. The town's fabulous *sports complex*—indoor ice skating (with rinks for ice hockey and curling), a three-pool swimming center, along with a clutch of adjacent tennis courts—is just north of the core, on *Avenue du Bouchet*, while the gracefully pedimented *casino* is on Place Balmat to the south, not far from departure points for major peaks and glaciers. The body of water flowing through town, north to south, is the *Arve River*. And even if you choose not to ascend to the peaks, you're already in the mountains; Chamonix's elevation is a respectable 3,000 feet.

Musée Alpin (Avenue Michel-Croz, heart of town) is the ideal introduction to Chamonix, a well-organized, three-level presentation that starts you off at the beginning—in the case of Chamonix, that was the eighteenth century—with furniture, clothes, maps, and documents of that period relating to historic early ascents; and prints, postcards, and photos of the ensuing century, along with exhibits of climbers' paraphernalia, early through contemporary, and some super antique posters for nostalgia buffs. Well done.

By cable car via Aiguille du Midi and/or tunnel to Italy: The 11-mile tunnel (opened in 1965) connecting Chamonix with Courmeyeur (see *Italy at Its Best*) involves half an hour to 45 minutes' drive either way, to and from your Chamonix hotel; have your passport with you, for both French and Italian customs, going and returning. It's agreeable to depart after breakfast, arriving in *Courmayeur* in time for a visit to its *Museo Alpino* (on Piazza Abate Henry, just opposite the Baroque *Parish Church* whose stone bell tower goes all the way back to 1392) and smart shops of *Via Roma*, stopping for coffee at that street's *Caffè della Posta*, staying on for lunch at *Le Vieux Pommier* (Piazzale Monte Bianco 25; phone 842-281; *First Class*), and returning by means of the tunnel.

Much more exciting would be to go one way—through Mont Blanc Massif—via a series of cable cars. First lap of the journey is easily the most extraordinary. You ride the highest cable car in the world to the peak called *Aiguille du Midi* (with an en-route stop at 6,900-foot *Plan des Aiguilles*, reached in 10 minutes from the Chamonix station). Twenty minutes later and you've arrived at Aiguille du Midi, wide-eyed while en route—views are trinational, of French, Italian, and Swiss peaks—for a pause at its restaurant-café, the while you come to grips with your situation: at an elevation of eleven and a half thousand feet, high above the vast region known, not inappropriately, as the *Vallée Blanche*. Aiguille du Midi is what the French term a *correspondance*, or transfer point (although, of course, you may opt to return from there to Chamonix), to an elevator taking you to still another cable car for a thrill-a-minute journey past Mont Blanc and other snowy peaks, as high as 13,000 feet, to *Pointe Helbronner*—through which the Franco-Italian frontier passes— and with a café and observation terrace. There you transfer to still another cable car for the final portion of the trip, descending to the terminal at *La Palud*, edging Courmeyeur. You've arrived in Italy, ideally in time for lunch, returning later in the day the way you came or through the tunnel by means of either rented car or taxi.

Other Chamonix excursions include the summer-only scenic rail journey to *Montenvers*, at an altitude of 4,200 feet, descending to the grotto of the immense *Mer de Glace* glacier, through a tunnel into the so-called salon, a space in which a furnished living room—four easy chairs, coffee table, piano, and even a fireplace—have been carved from the ice; cable car trips to *La Flégère*, a few miles west of town, with an altitude of 5,700 feet, a restaurant and fabulous overhead views of Mer de Glace; and *Brévent* (farther west of town, at an altitude of some 7,700 feet), with a restaurant at the intermediate cable car station called *Planpraz*, and with a terrace—on Brévent—affording vistas of Mont Blanc.

Alpine golf is, to understate, unexpected and is, for that reason, called to your attention at this point. The Robert Trent Jones-designed course (18 holes, par 72) attached to *Golf Club de Chamonix* in nearby Les Praz at the foot of Mont Blanc, is among the most beautifully situated on the planet. You may rent clubs and there's a restaurant.

Assy (a.k.a. Plateau d'Assy, 19 miles northwest of Chamonix) would be an unexceptional little mountain village were it not for the art of the architecturally undistinguished *Church of Notre Dame de Toute Grâce*, begun before World War II and finished a few years thereafter, which catches you up, first, with an enormous mosaic fresco occupying virtually its entire facade, by Fernand Léger, that is typically Léger in bold strokes and bright hues. Go on in to see works by such modern masters as Matisse (St. Dominick outlined in black on yellow tiles in the style of the Matisse-designed chapel at Vence, Chapter 26), Rouault (or at least a stained-glass window based on a Rouault design, *Flagellation of Christ*), Bonnard (St.-François de Sales in a purple cape), Chagall, and Braque, with an extraordinary tapestry by an artist named Lurçat, covering the apse.

SETTLING IN

Mont Blanc Hôtel (Place de l'Église; phone 5053-05-64) has a number of pluses: heart of town location, albeit in its own little park-cum-swimming pool, traditional with respect both to facade and interior that includes half a hundred cheerful rooms (some facing the peak for which the hotel is named), perky little bar, satisfactory restaurant, and pleasant staff. *Luxury.*

Auberge du Bois Prin (Les Moussoux; phone 5053-33-51) is a get-away-from-it-all choice. There are just under a dozen capacious, attractive, no-two-alike rooms, restaurant dominated by a stone fireplace that extends to the ceiling, congenial lounge, and marvelous mountain views. *First Class.*

Albert 1er Hôtel (Impasse du Montenvers; phone 5053-05-09), edging the core from which it is easily walkable, is set in a garden with swimming pool and tennis courts. There are 34 comfortable rooms, lounge-bar with a vast fireplace, agreeable restaurant. Same management as Auberge du Bois Prin (above). *First Class.*

Le Prieuré Hôtel (Allée du Recteur Payot; phone 5053-20-72) is not without the ambience of the mountains. All 100 of its mod-look, terraced rooms give onto Mont Blanc and have showers in their baths. There's a bar-lounge and *brasserie*-type restaurant, smartly rustic. Central. Same management as the Mont Blanc (above). *Moderate.*

La Sapinière-Montana Hôtel (Rue Mumméry; phone 5053-07-63) deserves credit for a situation just far enough from the center to be tranquil but still walkable. There are 30 terraced rooms, all facing south, with ravishing mountain views, and inviting public spaces that include a reliable restaurant and lounge-bar. *Moderate.*

Alpine Hôtel (Place du Mont Blanc; phone 5053-44-77), formidably futuristic from without, blends a touch of the mountains with contemporary interiors. The lobby needed refurbishing on my last visit, but those of the rooms I inspected—there are 133, all told—were neat and functional. There are a rooftop restaurant-cum-panoramas and a lobby bar-lounge. Central. Mapotel/Best Western. *Moderate.*

Park Hôtel (Avenue du Majestic; phone 5053-07-58) looks its best when you enter its rustic restaurant and stone-walled bar-lounge. Corridors upstairs are noticeably narrow, but those of the 60 rooms I have inspected—decors differ—are pleasant. Central. *Moderate.*

Hermitage et Paccard Hôtel (Rue des Cristalliers; phone 5053-13-87)—a short drive (or a long walk) from the action—is an elderly chalet that has been brightly updated, with a pair of bar-lounges, each distinctive; picture-windowed restaurant; and 29 terraced rooms, all but nine with their own baths. *Moderate.*

DAILY BREAD

La Tartiffle (Rue des Moulins; phone 5053-20-02) has the appropriate look of the Alps—woodsy and rustic—that one anticipates in Chamonix. This is a good spot for traditional specialties like the *crêpes* called *matafans*, chicken Savoyard style and *gratin Dauphinois*—sliced potatoes baked in a creamy casserole. *First Class.*

Le Crochon (Rue des Moulins; phone 5053-41-78), a near neighbor of La Tartiffle (above) draws your eye from the street: It's a log cabin. Not unlike its neighbor, the look is *montagnarde.* Typical sausages of the region—open with an assorted platter—are delicious; the grilled trout, a pleasure. And the fondue—bits of bread dipped by all those at the table into a common cauldron of bubbly, hot melted cheese with kirsch, reminiscent of Switzerland. *First Class.*

Le Bartavel (26 Cours du Bartavel; phone 5053-26-51) is a delightful touch of the southwest, high in the Alps. By that, I mean you want to open with *foie gras*, continue with the bean-sausage-smoked-goose casserole called *cassoulet* and conclude with a light dessert. Wine is sold not only by bottles, but by the glass, which makes Bartavel an excellent place to become acquainted with Savoie vintages, opening, say, with a white Roussette and continuing with a red Gamay. *First Class.*

Le Coquelicot (88 Rue du Lyrat; phone 5055-93-40): You are so close to Italy that it would be a pity not to enjoy an Italian lunch or dinner. Open with antipasto, minestrone soup, or pasta before tackling a platter of *carne mista*—an assortment of beef, veal, and pork. *First Class.*

Eden (Praz-de-Chamonix, a mile and a half from Chamonix; phone 5053-06-40) makes a specialty of fish—trout prepared *meunière* style, amandine, or simply grilled, as well as half a dozen additional species from mountain lakes; seafood, too. *First Class.*

Le Blanchot (at the foot of Aiguille du Midi cable car; phone 5053-30-80): Prix-fixe meals are good value (and include wine). If it's Monday, bear in mind that the plat du jour is the sauerkraut spectacular, *choucroute garnie*—especially good with local sausages substituted for those of Alsace, where the dish originated. *Moderate.*

La Taverne du Chamonix (69 Avenue de Michel-Croz) is at its best on a sunny day when you take a table on the terrace and watch the passing Chamonix parade, over coffee, a drink, or a casual lunch. If it's packed, consider next-door *Brasserie du Rond-Point*; both are *Moderate*.

INCIDENTAL INTELLIGENCE

Tour operators offer skiers a wide choice of Chamonix packages that can be excellent value. Aspiring skiers do well to be aware of Chamonix's *École de Ski Français* (Place de l'Église)—with 200 instructors (they teach classes and privately, as well) and a reputation as one of Europe's best ski schools. Nearest transatlantic airport is Geneva. *Further information:* Office de Tourisme, Place de l'Église, Chamonix.

15

Colmar

and Alsace's Route du Vin

BACKGROUND BRIEFING
It is difficult to believe that this small, quiet town, a hop and a skip from the German frontier—whose contemporary political eminence is limited to serving as seat of one of France's 95 *départements*—was designated administrative center (in effect, capital) of Alsace by no less august a sovereign than Louis XIV in the third quarter of the seventeenth century.

By that time, Colmar had worn more than a few hats. At first Celtic, later Roman, then under the Germanic Allemani, who were succeeded by the Franks, Colmar became a Free City of the Holy Roman Empire in the thirteenth century. In the fourteenth, it joined nine other towns in the pan-Alsatian federation known as the Decapole. It was during the Revolution, in the late eighteenth century, that it became a departmental seat. The following century—in 1871—as a consequence of the Franco-Prussian War, Colmar, with the rest of Alsace, was annexed to the German Empire, of which it was a part for nearly half a century—until the Allied Victory in World War I. (It was during the German period that Kaiser Wilhelm II designated the nearby medieval château, Haut Koenigsbourg, as an imperial residence; the Treaty of Versailles restored the castle to France in 1918. Precious contents of Alsatian museums were stored in it for safekeeping during World War II, toward the end of which it was occupied by American troops.)

Though it lacks the animation and sophistication of considerably larger Strasbourg (Chapter 35), some 40 miles to the north, enough remains of Colmar's earlier centuries—the Middle Ages when it became a spiritual center (an old convent houses one of Europe's most beautiful art museums), the Renaissance when it attracted painters, the Baroque era when builders came—to impel a visit. And its situation, at the southern edge of the Alsatian vineyards, which climb gentle slopes of the Vosges Mountains and are dotted with time-stood-still villages, makes Colmar a logical takeoff point for excursions into the Route du Vin, easily the most charming such in France. If you know German—speak it—virtually everyone you meet will be conversant in that language and in French.

ON SCENE
Lay of the Land: You can walk everywhere. Core of town revolves around *Rue des Clefs*, an east-west pedestrian street, off which *Rue des Unterlinden* leads to the museum whose name it takes. *Dames de France* and *Monoprix* department stores are on *Place des Unterlinden*. *Rue Rapp* leads a bit north to Hôtel de Ville; *Rue St.-Nicolas* leads a bit south to café-lined *Place de la Cathédrale* and the landmark *Church of St.-Martin*. Historic *Rue des Marchands*, site of several major monuments, is to the south. Two delightful quarters—each architecturally redolent of old Colmar, with half-timbered houses lining southeasterly streets—are *La Petite Venise*, so-called because it is cut through by the canal-like, bridge-crossed *Lauch River*, with *Quai de la Poissonerie* its most scenic thoroughfare; and, contiguous with La Petite Venise to its north, relatively recently restored *Quartier des Tanneurs*. That district's principal streets are *Rue des Tanneurs* with the Renaissance *Ancienne Douane* (Customs House) on the square linking it with atmospheric *Grande Rue*, at whose northern terminus is the originally Franciscan, now Protestant *Temple St.-Mathieu*, treasure filled. Westerly *Rue de la République* is the site of the railway station and several hotels; it's a 10-minute walk from the core.

Musée d'Unterlinden (1 Rue des Unterlinden) claims to be, with good reason, I am sure, the most visited museum in provincial France. What draws the crowds—and in the warm weather months you must be prepared for congestion, allowing a solid half day in the museum—is the sixteenth-century altarpiece known as *Le Rétable d'Issenheim*, for the monastery from which it was taken at the time of the French Revolution and brought to Colmar, ironically at the same period that the building in which it now reposes was being closed after half a millennium as a Dominican convent. (It was not to reopen—as a museum—until 1852.) Mathias Grünewald, the Issenheim's creator, was the quintessential Renaissance artist, as skilled at perspective and color as at anatomy and architecture, not to mention theology and drama. The problem is to get close enough in, what with guides lecturing to tightly packed groups eager to hear every word of the commentary. You may want to allow for a return visit, to determine which of the numerous panels of Grünewald's masterpiece are for you the most memorable; *Concert of the Angels*, *The Annunciation*, and *The Nativity* are my favorites. See if you agree.

Then give the rest of the museum your attention. The high vaulted space in which the *Rétable* is exhibited, formerly the nuns' chapel, displays a number of other works, as well. Gothic tracery in the arches of the gallery lining the cloister is reason enough for an Unterlinden visit. Medieval sculpture from Colmar churches fills the nuns' former cellar, sharing space with mammoth and ancient wine casks. Painters like Holbein and Cranach are on scene. Upstairs, take in the exquisite eighteenth-century drawing room, with its original ceiling fresco, wood carving, and superb Louis XV furniture. On that same floor are Strasbourg porcelain and furnished rooms, late seventeenth-century Régence through nineteenth-century Charles X. Then the basement: It dazzles as much with its mint-condition Roman mosaic floor as with paintings of our era: Monet and Rouault, Dubuffet and Léger, Braque and Robert Delaunay, Picassos in profusion.

Church of the Dominicans (Rue des Serruriers) is fine thirteenth-century Gothic, well proportioned and vaulted, with excellent stained glass. Principal motivation for your visit, though, is the altarpiece—on the same esthetic level as the Issenheim at Unterlinden (above)—painted in the fifteenth century by a Colmar-born master named Martin Schongauer. *La Vierge au Buisson des Roses* is, of course, *The Virgin of the Rosebush*, so called because roses climb a trellis forming the backdrop for a portrait of a red-robed Virgin, beautifully long auburn tresses covering her shoulders, a naked baby Jesus in her arms, a pair of protecting angels—black-robed—overhead. Have a look, too, at this church's cloister, entered through the Public Library, adjacent.

Collégiale of St.-Martin (Place de la Cathédrale) is Colmar's oldest Gothic house of worship, dating to the thirteenth century. Because it was the seat of a bishop—and therefore a cathedral—for a brief late eighteenth-century period, it sometimes still is referred to as such. A rose by any other name. . . . St.-Martin is lovely, at its best in the splendidly sculpted portal (*The Last Judgment, Adoration of the Magi*) on its west side. Within, it is the exceptional height of the nave that is striking, along with stained glass that bears study.

Musée Bartholdi (30 Rue des Marchands): The ground floor of this building offers a bit of Colmar history in its exhibits. You go up a flight for displays celebrating the nineteenth-century career of Frédéric Bartholdi, the Colmar-born artist who designed New York harbor's *Statue de la Liberté;* there are several sketches of Miss Liberty as M. Bartholdi conceived her, early on. Otherwise, pickings are mostly slim.

Route du Vin: There are easily half a hundred villages in the Wine Route extending north from Colmar, skirting the Rhine River and the Vosges Mountains, to its terminus in Strasbourg. Everywhere you go, vintners are happy to welcome you, show you through their wineries, invite you to taste their white wines (Riesling is the most popular;

Sylvaner and Gewurztraminer follow), and even sell you a three-pack. Here is a quartet of villages that I have enjoyed exploring. Take them in en route to Strasbourg or as part of an excursion from Colmar, allowing extra time for others you'll pass through, which appeal. Order is south to north.

Kaysersberg is a piquant jumble of twin-gabled houses with a ruined castle, a fortified bridge, and two special treasures: a parish church, part Romanesque, part Gothic, with a luminous triptych over its altar; and an impressive *Mairie*, or Town Hall, dating to the Renaissance.

Riquewihr appears to have stopped building by the end of the Renaissance. With the exception of Rothenburg on Germany's Romantic Route (see *Germany at Its Best*), I don't ever recall being so captivated by half-timbered houses and elegant fountains in handsomely embellished squares. Pop into *Musée Postal* as much for its setting—an ancient castle—as for its contents. Dark-green pottery, typical of the region, is for sale at every turn. There are towers—one has a torture chamber—and drawbridges and fortifications. And you find yourself wanting to look at every courtyard you pass by.

Barr's La Folie Marco is an eighteenth-century house with a deceptively plain facade that shelters eighteenth-century furniture, as well as porcelain and pewter typical of the Alsatian countryside, all of which is charming. Strategically located almost next door is the cluster of structures—with vineyards climbing the hills just out back—of the A. Willm winery—as representative as any in the region. The Willms, third generation owners, and their staff take you past meticulously tended vines into cool cellars where wine is stored in oaken casks, from fall through spring, when it is transferred to the green bottles that are an Alsace trademark. Hope that the rolls called *cressins*—part croissant, part saltstick—will be served with the wines that you'll be invited to sample.

Obernai greets visitors with monuments of a venerable past, a fifteenth-century Marché du Blé—or wheat market—for starters, an opulently Renaissance council chamber in its *Mairie*, and atmospheric streets and squares, capacious Place du Marché, most especially.

Château Haut Koenigsbourg (nine miles north of Colmar, near Kaysersberg, on the Route du Vin) is a Prince Valiant castle atop a misty mountain. It went up in the twelfth century and was restored at the turn of the present century, while Alsace was part of Germany, by Kaiser Wilhelm II. The ascent to its gate is made on a curvy road through wooded mountainside. At the top—2,266 feet up—is an elongated maze of towers, turrets, battlements, ramparts, and bastions, the lot connected by drawbridges and steep flights of crooked steps, interspersed by galleried courtyards and verdant gardens. Essentially—and, of course, originally—medieval and for long the home of a line of counts, the castle was burned by invading Swedes in the seventeenth century and lay in ruins until Wilhelm set it to rights, the better to let his Alsatian subjects understand what he perceived to be the glorious heritage of their empire. Work began in 1901, the job took seven years, and criticism of architect Bodo Emhardt's work has never quite stopped. There is no denying that liberties were taken with the original or that the interiors might not pass muster in today's Disneyland, the occasional piece of good furniture excepted. Still, credit where it is due: Koenigsbourg anticipated the Disney parks by three quarters of a century. And who would not opt for a mediocre re-creation of the genuine article than the fantasy castles that dominate contemporary funlands?

Mulhouse (27 miles south of Colmar and pronounced Mul-*ooze*) has almost twice Colmar's population (approximately 115,000) but trails behind it—and of course Strasbourg—with respect to tourism in Alsace. It is centered by *Place de la Réunion* whose landmarks are the Gothic-origin *Temple St.-Étienne*, with fine stained glass, and *Hôtel de Ville*, with a handsome Renaissance facade and—inside—galleries of *Musée Historique*, as well as the viewable City Council chambers. Pedestrian streets— *Rue Henriette*, *Rue des Boulangers*, and *Rue du Sauvage* surround the square. Nearby, on *Place Guillaume Tell*, *Musée de Beaux-Arts* occupies a Rococo mansion, with paintings by the likes of Boucher, Brueghel, Cranach, and Boudin. *Musée National de l'Automobile*, southwest of the center and gained by Avenue de Colmar, is packed with cars—more than 465 of them—representing 90 makes, foreign as well as French, antique through contemporary. *Musée Français du Chemin de Fer* (northwest of the center by way of Rue Franklin) vies with its English counterpart, the National Railroad Museum in York; biggest draws are cars created for Napoleon III's aides de camp, for a turn-of-century Grand Duchess of Luxembourg, and for Presidents of France—this last Art Deco style and in use until 1971.

SETTLING IN
Terminus-Bristol Hôtel (7 Place de la Gare; phone 8923-59-59) is an elderly house, apparently refurbished in stages over the years, with little coordination of styles or decor. However, it works well enough. Sixty-five of the 85 rooms have full baths; some of these accommodations are quite attractive. There's a bar-café, as well as a restaurant evaluated in a later paragraph. Location is just opposite the railway station, a quarter-hour's walk from the center. *First Class.*

Champ de Mars Hôtel (2 Avenue de la Marne; phone 8941-54-54)—set back in a city park, 10 minutes' walk from the center—is run-of-the-mill modern, with 75 adequate rooms, limited-menu café, and bar that expands to an outdoor terrace in summer. *Moderate.*

Park Hôtel (52 Avenue de la République; phone 8941-34-80) is relatively contemporary, closer to the core than to the Terminus-Bristol or Champ de Mars (above), with 40 bath-equipped rooms, restaurant, bar. So-so. *Moderate.*

Colbert Hôtel (2 Rue des Trois-Épis; phone 8941-31-05) is between the railway station and the core of town—10 minutes by foot. Fifty full-facility rooms. Breakfast only. *Moderate.*

Turenne Hôtel (10 Route de Bâle; phone 8941-12-26) offers 72 contemporary rooms and breakfast only, with its plus a central location. *Moderate.*

Ville de Nancy Hôtel (48 Rue Vauban; phone 8941-23-14) pleases shoppers; you edge the pedestrian shopping area, core of town. But only half of the two dozen rooms have baths. Breakfast only. *Moderate.*

Château d'Isenbourg Hôtel (Rouffach, eight miles south of Colmar; phone 8949-63-53) is indicated for a bit of relaxation in the course of Alsatian wandering. This romantic castle—high on its own vineyard-surrounded hill with a swimming pool and tennis court in the garden—has 32 no-two-alike, smartly styled suites and apartments; and a distinguished two-chamber restaurant (picture-window views from one part, vaults of a Renaissance wine cellar from the other) with hearty Alsatian specialties. *Luxury.*

Le Grand Hôtel (Trois-Épis, eight miles west of Colmar; phone 8989-49-80): Setting is a charming village up in the Vosges Mountains, with the panoramas memorable. The Grand is smart (there are 50 lovely rooms, each with a distinctive decor based on traditional mountain motifs) and well equipped. By that, I mean there's a picture-windowed restaurant that turns out as good a *choucroute garnie* as I've had anywhere in Alsace *and* a health club-cum-swimming pool—to work off all those calories. *Luxury.*

Frantel Mulhouse (4 Place Général-de-Gaulle, Mulhouse; phone 8946-01-23) has nearly a hundred full-facility rooms, convenient restaurant, and busy cocktail lounge, popular with locals. Near the railway station. *First Class.*

Wir Hôtel (4 Porte Bâle, Mulhouse; phone 8956-13-22) is less luxurious than the Frantel but more central; 40 rooms, restaurant, bar. *Moderate.*

DAILY BREAD

Au Fer Rouge (52 Grande Rue; phone 8941-37-24) occupies a landmark building of advanced age on one of Colmar's landmark-filled streets. There is a pair of intimate dining rooms, with tables set in yellow linen, beneath original beamed ceilings. And walls are hung with small but excellent paintings by contemporary Colmar artist Jean-Claude Allenbach. Choose from one of the four prix-fixe menus (there's an extensive à la carte, as well). Fare is a mix of traditional Alsatian with just enough *nouvelle* twists—*sensible* twists—to distinguish it. A typical meal might open with caviar-topped poached eggs in crayfish sauce, *terrine de foie gras*, or rich mushroom soup; and continue with such entrées as duckling roasted with wild mushrooms, the house's own filet of beef deliciously sauced, or *médaillons* of lamb sautéed in a basil sauce, accompanied by baby fresh vegetables. The cheese board is exceptional. No less so are desserts, one of which—a baked half-apple doused with caramelized almond sauce and topped with coconut ice cream—is in and of itself worth the trip to Colmar. Delightful service. In my experience, one of France's best restaurants. *Luxury.*

Rendez-vous de Chasse (Terminus-Bristol Hôtel, 7 Place de la Gare; phone 8923-59-59) has an agreeable hum to it, especially at lunch when Colmar business types mix with the hotel's international clientele. Menu is essentially traditional, with Alsatian favorites—onion tart or snails to start, perhaps a sautéed trout to follow, with such entrées as *coq au Riesling* and filet of venison, this last the restaurant's most respected specialty. Super sweets. *First Class.*

Maison des Têtes (19 Rue des Têtes; phone 8924-43-43): If you haven't paused before this seventeenth-century house in the course of Colmar exploration, do so before entering. It's called House of Heads because of the plethora of busts that distinguish its facade. Hearty Alsatian grub is the name of the Têtes game—*foie gras* in a *brioche* frame or the day's soup as starters, followed by *choucroute garnie*—the sauerkraut and sausage specialty of the region—or, in season, roast pheasant. Apple pastries are indicated for dessert. *First Class.*

Au Trois Poissons (16 Quai de la Poissonnerie; phone 8941-25-21): Don't leave Colmar without having enjoyed a meal in the old Petite Venise/Quartier des Tanneurs sectors. Here, the setting is a centuries-old house; the specialty is fish (I suggest the local trout, either *amandine* or *meunière*) with traditional openers and lavish desserts. *First Class.*

Helmstetter (7 Place des Dominicains) is a *pâtisserie* and *salon de thé;* pause for coffee with a slice of the yeast-dough confection called *kugelhopf. Moderate.*

Gilg (Mittelbergheim, a mile and a half outside of Barr, on Route du Vin; phone 8908-91-37) is indicated for a festive lunch-pause in the course of exploring the vineyards and villages north of Colmar. An ancient *wein-stub* on scene since 1614, it serves up delicious victuals. Lunch might open with Monsieur Gilg's delicate fish *soufflé* or his also-celebrated *pâté de foie gras en brioche*; proceed with *tournedos*, Vieux Strasbourg style, or a poultry specialty. Distinguished desserts. *First Class.*

Auberge de l'Ill (Illhaeusern, near Ribeauville, 10 miles north of Colmar; phone 8971-83-23) is cool—very cool. Setting is a handsome house in a broad park-like garden, alongside the Ill River, with picture windows in the contiguous main-floor rooms constituting the restaurant. Reception, in my experience, is correct but distant; service, likewise; fare, competent, albeit—again, in my experience—unexciting. A meal might open with salmon *soufflé*, continue with filet of beef in a wine sauce, and conclude with a fruit-based sweet. Caveat: *Way*-in-advance bookings are usually required. *Luxury.*

Guillaume Tell (1 Rue Guillaume-Tell, Mulhouse; phone 8945-21-58): No bow, no arrow, no apple. Tasty Alsatian specialties, though, with a heart-of-town location. *First Class.*

La Tosca (6 Passage de l'Hôtel de Ville, Mulhouse) is just the *salon de thé* you're seeking, for a pause-cum-pastry between museums. *Moderate.*

SOUND OF MUSIC
Théâtre Municipal (Rue de la Sinne, Mulhouse) is the area's leading venue for opera, ballet, and concerts.

INCIDENTAL INTELLIGENCE

Aéroport de Bâle–Mulhouse is a remarkable example of Franco-Swiss cooperation, 17 miles from town, serving Switzerland's Basel, as well as Mulhouse, with service to a number of French points. Mulhouse is the area-city with the swiftest train service to Paris. *Further information:* Office de Tourisme, 4 Rue Unterlinden, Colmar; Office de Tourisme, 9 Avenue Foch, Mulhouse.

16

Deauville
Elegance on the Channel

BACKGROUND BRIEFING
Beach resorts develop either as a consequence of celebrated patronage, or they are deliberately created. Deauville's next-door neighbor on the English Channel coast that constitutes Normandy's northern flank, Trouville, is in the former category. Napoleon III's fashionable consort, Empress Eugénie, took a fancy to it in the middle years of the last century; the Imperial presence drew Imperial courtiers who in turn drew the bourgeoisie—and crowds packed Trouville.

Indeed, business was brisk enough to attract the attention of the canny Duc de Morny, who rounded up capital and partners and set to work creating Deauville, even erecting a racetrack as bait to draw holiday-makers. Period was the decade of the 1860s. It was a start. But the Second Empire fell in 1870, and Deauville limped along until the turn of the present century. By 1912, another entrepreneur, Eugène Cornuché, emboldened by the continued success of Trouville, where grand hotels encircled a casino edging the sea, put up a pair of luxury hotels—the Royal and the Normandy, both still Deauville leaders—and followed with the casino that remains, contemporarily, the smartest on the coast.

With the Roaring Twenties came cachet: Big names—the Dolly Sisters, the Rothschilds, the Cognac-producing Henessys, Indian maharajas, Middle Eastern pashas, British and Spanish royals—became synonymous with Deauville. The beach-flanking boardwalk, Les Planches, became northern France's spiffiest promenade; new hotels went up. Alas, they were requisitioned by the Germans as officers' quarters during the World War II occupation. But post-World War II decades saw Deauville emerge as Paris's seaside suburb, with fast trains and new highways linking it with the capital to the south.

Irony of ironies, while Deauville prospered, Trouville became more plebeian. Movers and shakers ignored it—Imperial origins notwithstanding—to the point that today it has not a single luxury hotel. This is hardly to say, however, that Trouville is out of business. Its market is mass—the old casino remains in operation, though it's no longer big-league—while that of Deauville is class. You'll want to compare the two.

ON SCENE

Lay of the Land: Deauville is delightfully easy to get about in. *Boulevard de la Mer* flanks *Les Planches*, the celebrated boardwalk, which in turn borders the wide, white-sand beach. In season, the latter is massed with umbrellas and changing *cabines* and edged by cafés and restaurants. Area just inland from the beach's central sectors embraces such facilities as a giant, covered swimming pool complex (Maurice Chevalier came up from Paris to declare it officially open in 1964), tennis courts in abundance, mini-golf (which the French adore), a sailing club, and Club Enfants—with activities for kids. *Boulevard Eugène Cornuché,* named for the resort's turn of the century developer, runs parallel to this beach area, framing it from the south. The casino fronts this boulevard, between *Rue du Général-de-Gaulle* and *Rue Gontaud. Rue Casino*, to the casino's rear, is lined with pricey boutiques. *Hippodrome de Clairefontaine*—the racetrack dating to Deauville's origins a century and a quarter back—is at the western edge of town; still another track, *Hippodrome de la Touques* (with a polo field), is inland, to the south. The railway station is at Deauville's eastern edge, a hop and a skip from *La Touques,* the estuary separating Deauville from Trouville, with *Port Deauville,* a marine-yacht basin complex, at its northern flank.

Trouville's focal point remains its *Casino,* on *Quai Albert 1er*, partially facing La Touques, partially open to the sea, and where fishermen still tie up their boats, as their ancestors did, over long centuries. Not unlike Deauville, its sands are framed by a boardwalk, *Promenade des Planches.* An enormous municipal *piscine,* or swimming pool, is just opposite the casino in the beach area, with tennis and other facilities nearby. Commercial Trouville begins at *Place du Maréchal Foch,* just west of the casino, spilling into adjacent *Rues Paul Basson, Charles Mozin,* and *Victor Hugo.*

Casino d'Été (Boulevard Eugène Cornuché)—immense, high ceilinged, and crystal chandeliered, shelters not only gaming rooms (slot machines are illegal in France, but how about roulette, chemin de fer, trente-et-quarante, or blackjack?), but also a theater, restaurant, and bar. Take your passport with you, and, gentlemen, wear a tie and jacket in the evening. (This is the so-called Summer Casino; the smaller *Casino d'Hiver,* used in winter, is adjacent.)

Casino Municipal de Trouville (Promenade des Planches, Trouville) has, to be sure, seen better days, but its Second Empire facade—with a marvelous mansard roof—redeems it, and the Salle de Jeux, or gaming room, within—silk-shaded lamps over the tables—could be right out of an old movie.

Musée de Trouville (Villa Montbello, 64 Rue du Général Leclerc, Trouville) is a still-imposing townhouse dating to the mid-nineteenth century, when Empress Eugénie was a frequent visitor to Trouville, and Impressionists painted it. Its eight galleries are a testament to the epoch, with photos and prints, ship models and Norman peasants' costumes, paintings and postcards. Evocative.

Aquarium Écologique (Promenade des Planches, Trouville): Don't let the pretentious title keep you away from what is probably the best-designed aquarium in France. Emphasis is on fish and shellfish from the Atlantic and the English Channel, but there are species from other regions of France and the tropics, not to mention a selection of crocodiles and giant snakes to scare the hell out of you.

Cabourg (11 miles west of Deauville) is a charming little resort with its core—a fabulous Belle Époque hotel and adjacent casino—the hub of a wheel-like area from which a score of turn-of-century streets, the wheel's spokes, fan out. The hotel is the very same at which Marcel Proust wrote *Within a Budding Grove*. His room was reproduced in the 1970s film, *Le Banc de la Désolation*, directed by Marcel Chabrol, and Cabourg's seafront boulevard is dubbed Promenade Marcel Proust. Go for lunch, perhaps taking in also the nearby town of *Dives-sur-Mer*, the historic point at which Guillaume le Conquérant—William the Conqueror—mustered the fleet with which he crossed the Channel to vanquish the English in 1066; William's officers' names are carved into a wall of Dives's venerable *Church of Notre-Dame*. There's an ancient *Halles*, or market, and an equally aged restaurant, later counseled.

SETTLING IN
Royal Hôtel (Boulevard Eugène Cornuche; phone 3188-16-41) is the very model of a grand seafront hotel of the old school, spanking white and colonnaded, with heroically proportioned public spaces—chandeliered lobby: rust-and-ivory Le Royal restaurant, later evaluated: à-la-carte-only grill, earth-toned bar-lounge, wherein there is always a choice of 25 brands of whiskey; a terrace on the lawn, its tables shielded with yellow umbrellas; and just over 300 suites and rooms, no two quite alike, the style, throughout, traditional. Those I have inspected are handsome and capacious and have excellent baths; terraced seafront accommodations are the choicest. The Royal is the flagship of the small but excellent Chaîne Lucien Barrière, which has the top trio of Deauville hotels, among others. *Luxury.*

Normandy Hôtel (38 Rue Jean-Mermoz; phone 3188-09-21)—with mock-Norman facade, shingled, gabled, and half-timbered—is appropriately named. Inside, decor is more typical of the turn-of-century period of construction—high-ceilinged and neoclassic—with perhaps the handsomest dining room in town (later recommended), a clublike bar-lounge, and potted plants alongside easy chairs in the lobby. There are 332 suites and rooms—attractive, well equipped, capacious. Chaîne Lucien Barrière. *Luxury.*

Golf Hôtel (just off Route 278, two miles from Deauville; phone 3188-19-01): Given proclivities toward golf (there are 18 holes at the door) and seclusion (you are away from the fleshpots of town), you can be happy in this 165-room house. It's half-timbered without and traditional with respect to public spaces (a big porch, sprawling lobby, smart restaurant, and cozy bar). Those of the 165 rooms I've checked out are very pleasant. Chaîne Lucien Barrière. *Luxury.*

Helios Hôtel (19 Rue Fosserier; phone 3188-34-69) is one of the best-looking contemporary hotels I know in France—with a bar leading from its lobby and 44 rooms, eight of which are duplex and can accommodate families. Breakfast only; it's buffet style. With a little swimming pool as a bonus. And friendly management. Central. *Moderate.*

Port-Deauville Hôtel (Boulevard Eugène Cornuché; phone 3154-91-00) is in Port-Deauville, the modern marina quarter that edges La Touques, with Trouville just opposite. There are 70 modern rooms, a bar-lounge, and breakfast only. A PLM hotel. *Moderate.*

Beach Hôtel (1 Quai Albert 1er, Trouville; phone 3198-12-00) is Trouville's newest, with 125 neat rooms, bar-lounge, buffet breakfast, and a super situation between the casino and La Touques, with the municipal pool and beach just opposite. Friendly. *Moderate.*

Grand Hôtel (Promenade Marcel Proust, Cabourg; phone 3191-01-79) dates to the Belle Époque period of the last century, whose flavor and look it retains, thorough refurbishing notwithstanding. The Grand looks bigger than it is; there are just 68 rooms and two lovely suites, the lot of them good sized and—at least those I have inspected—charming. A tremendous crystal chandelier at the lobby entrance sets the tone of the public spaces, which include a red and gold bar-lounge and a duplex restaurant, later reviewed. The beach—wide and white sand—is just out back. And the hotel can make arrangements for guest privileges at the Sporting Club de Cabourg—with a pair of pools, five tennis courts, and a gym—nearby. A PLM hotel. *Luxury.*

DAILY BREAD

Ciro's (Promenade des Planches; phone 3188-18-10) occupies a cool, pastel-hued seaside pavilion whose picture windows and French doors give onto a warm-weather terrace and the sea. The specialty is seafood, and you could do worse than to order from the good-value prix-fixe, four-course menu, starting perhaps with an unusual filet of sole salad (served *tiède*, or warm) or *rillettes* of salmon and continuing with fish of the day simply sautéed or a platter of the day's assorted seafood catch. Norman cheeses in profusion are then offered from a wagon, with a choice of desserts—I counsel *fondant chocolat au nectar d'orange*—to conclude. Service is impeccable; lunch only. In my view, one of France's best restaurants. *Luxury.*

Les Ambassadeurs (Casino d'Été, Boulevard Eugène Cornuché; phone 3188-29-55) is indicated for a gala evening in the see-and-be-seen casino, with the menu a *nouvelle*-traditional mix and both seafood and beef entrées reliable. Dressy. *Luxury.*

Normandy Hôtel Restaurant (38 Rue Jean-Mermoz; phone 3188-09-21): If it's cool, you lunch or dine in the best looking of the town's restaurants—high ceilinged, classically paneled, and colonnaded and with superb crystal chandeliers. In warm weather, tables are set in the pretty courtyard, under boughs of a veritable orchard of apple trees. There's a good-value menu, which might run to soup, salad, or a fish specialty to start, roast lamb or a beef entrée, cheeses, and a sweet. Smiling service. *Luxury.*

Royal Hôtel Restaurant (Boulevard Eugène Cornuché; phone 3188-16-41): The town's poshest hotel offers a surprisingly good-value four-course meal—with choices ample—that might embrace fish soup to begin, roast lamb or a seafood entrée, cheeses from a great tray, and pastries *au choix. Luxury.*

Saratoga (8 Avenue Charles-de-Gaulle; phone 3188-24-33) has the advantages of a central situation near the casino and super seafood—its classic *sole Normande* is a winner—from the à la carte; a prix-fixe menu, as well. *First Class.*

Bar du Soleil (Promenade des Planches; phone 3188-45-67) is the favored spot for casual lunches on the beach, center of the action. Seafood and salads. *Moderate/First Class.*

Café Le Drakkar (77 Rue Eugène-Colas) is a heart-of-town stopping point for coffee or a cooling drink in the midst of a morning or afternoon in the shops. *Moderate.*

Petite Auberge (7 Rue Carnot, Trouville; phone 3188-11-07): a well-situated (near the casino), well-priced, and delicious source of seafood; fun for lunch. *Moderate.*

Grand Hôtel Restaurant (Promenade Marcel-Proust, Cabourg; phone 3191-01-79) is a compact duplex, with good-value prix-fixe menus at two prices; the less costly might include a shrimp appetizer, the house's own *blanquette de poisson*, a kind of fish stew, as well as cheese and dessert. *First Class.*

Guillaume le Conquérant (2 Rue Hastings, Dives-sur-Mer; phone 3191-07-26) is a four-century-old source of tasty fare, seafood accented, in a lovely setting, ideal for lunch in connection with local exploration. *First Class.*

SHOPPER'S DEAUVILLE
Smart shops are in and about Rue du Casino, behind the casino, and include—to give you an idea—*Hermès* (men's and women's clothes and accessories, with their neckties and women's scarves celebrated), *Cartier* (jewelry), *Jean-Louis Scherrer* (women's haute couture), *Brummel* (men's clothes), *Jules-et-Julie* (kids' clothes), *La Gadgetière* (china and housewares), and a good-sized link of the *Printemps* department-store chain.

AFTER DARK
Theaters of *Casino d'Été* (Deauville) and *Casino Municipal* (Trouville) offer seasonal entertainment; your hotel will apprise you of what's on.

INCIDENTAL INTELLIGENCE

Further information: Office de Tourisme, Place de la Marie, Deauville; Office de Tourisme, Place du Maréchal-Foch, Trouville; Office de Tourisme, Jardins du Casino, Cabourg.

17

Dijon
and the Beauties of Burgundy

BACKGROUND BRIEFING

If it is true that Dijon conveys the impression of basking in the reflected glory of its Golden Age as capital of the far-flung medieval Duchy of Burgundy—this is the least cordial of the principal provincial cities—it follows, too, that there is reason for its residue of arrogance. Burgundy, in its heydey, was a big deal, feared even by the crown of France. And its wealth and power emanated from Dijon, the seat of its dukes.

Still, there is no question but that this city's riches—archeological, architectural, artistic—warrant inspection; nor that Dijon's situation in the world-class wine region, Côte d'Or, makes of it a base for excursions to the vineyards and their villages, to which it shares access with smaller, friendlier Beaune (Chapter 8), historic commercial center for Burgundy wine producers. It is from Dijon, too, that delightful day trips may be undertaken to beauty spots of western and northern Burgundy —Auxerre and Fontenay, Semur-en-Auxois and Bussy-Rabutin, Vézelay and St.-Thibault. And what its hotels lack in finesse (only Nantes [Chapter 30] and Marseille [Chapter 22] among the big French cities are as disappointing in this respect), Dijon compensates for with cuisine; the lavish Burgundian fare does justice to its celebrated wines.

Although it knew Romans as long ago as half a century before the birth of Christ (and assorted other governors, including fifth-century people from southerly Savoie whose name, *Burgundii*, was given to the region), it was not until the eleventh century—when rulers of Burgundy made it their seat—that Dijon came into its own. It was then that history began to celebrate dukes whose names were followed by qualifying adjectives—Philip the Bold, John the Fearless, Philip the Good. They developed a realm that extended into what is now Belgium, Luxembourg, the Netherlands, and northern France, the while maintaining a court in Dijon, whose art, music, and literature made it the talk of

Europe. Alas, Duke Charles the Bold proved *too* bold, losing his life in a fifteenth-century battle against France's King Louis XI. The Duchy of Burgundy, shortly thereafter, was absorbed by the Kingdom of France. But Burgundian memories die hard.

ON SCENE

Lay of the Land: Two central squares anchor central Dijon. Westerly *Place Darcy* is identified by a triumphal arch, *Porte Guillaume*. From it, the principal shopping street, *Rue de la Liberté*, leads east to *Place de la Libération*, an elegant half-crescent that is dwarfed by multiwinged *Palais des Ducs de Bourgogne*, now housing both *Hôtel de Ville* (the city hall) and *Musée des Beaux-Arts* (below). *Place Rude*, north of Rue de la Liberté, at midpoint opens onto another shopping street, *Rue des Forges*, off which leads pedestrians-only *Rue Liégard*. Nearby *Rue Verrerie* is Antiques Row. The neighborhood's *Rue Chouette* is strollworthy because of its mansions—fifteenth through eighteenth century; so, for that matter, are *Rues Berbisey, des Bons Enfants*, and *Chabot-Cherny*. The railway station is at the western edge of town on *Avenue Maréchal-Foch*.

Cathedral of St.-Bénigne (Place St.-Bénigne): Dijon's cathedral, chapel of a Benedictine monastery until the eighteenth century, is not nearly as exciting as big-city counterparts in Rouen, Lyon, or Bordeaux. Still, it does convey a sense of atmosphere, setting the mood for Dijon exploration. This is an upstairs-downstairs exercise. The cathedral proper is attractive Gothic, its facade framed by twin, conical-topped towers backed by a slender steeple. After you've walked the nave, go below to the crypt, a Romanesque octagon that's a thousand years old, its surprisingly high ceiling supported by not one, but a pair of concentric rows of columns. Upon exiting, head next door to . . .

Musée Archéologique (Rue Docteur Maret) is an architecturally exceptional Gothic structure that served as living quarters of Benedictine monks whose chapel (above) is now the cathedral. You go as much for the main-floor space—a sumptuously vaulted room that was the monks' dormitory—as you do for exhibits that document Dijon's history, Bronze and Iron Ages beyond to Roman, with both a bust and full-length statue of St.-Bénigne, for whom the cathedral is named.

Musée des Beaux-Arts (Place de la Ste.-Chapelle) is, as I indicate earlier on, a part of the onetime ducal palace, sharing space in its confines with the city hall (whose quite grand eighteenth-century reception rooms in the palace's central section are open to visitors upon application to its concierge). You want to have a look, too, at Tour Bar, a veritable sky-scraper of a medieval tower, and the high-ceilinged and adjacent palace kitchens. Then head for a collection of paintings, sculpture, and applied arts that is one of the best in the republic and in as felicitous a setting as any in the provinces, save Strasbourg (Chapter 35). Elevated tombs, in Salles de Gardes, of Philip the Bold and John the Fearless—surrounded by hovering angels and with sculpted mourners on a lower level of each, created by a genius named Claus Sluter—is a tough act to follow. But as you carry on, you find the range—and the quality—of paintings remarkable. Specifics? Well, consider such canvases as Melchior Broederlam's fourteenth-century pair, with *Annunciation* and *Visitation* cleverly combined in one and *Presentation at the Temple* and the *Flight into Egypt* amazingly combined in the other; Van der Weyden's somber, black-robed *Philip the Good;* Luini's *Virgin and Child;* Colson's young lady, catnapping in *Le Repos;* and Nattier's much reproduced *Marie Leczinska* —Louis XV's pretty, bonneted consort; with Bassano and Titian, Brueghel and Rubens, Brouwer and Hals, Greuze and Natoire, as well; and moderns—Millet through Monet—to add spice; not to mention furniture; ceramics; objects fashioned of ivory, enamel, gold, and silver; Renaissance through Rococo.

Musée Magnin (4 Rue des Bons Enfants, near Place de la Liberté) is a seventeenth-century townhouse, whose late owner turned it over to the French Government with the proviso that it be operated as a museum, with paintings, other art objects, furniture, and accessories all left intact. It's fun to poke about on an expedition of discovery, coming upon canvases by Vouet and Le Nain, Bourdon and Géricault, Tiepolo and Boucher, the while taking in the interiors: a brilliant grand staircase, family sitting room, formal salon, the lot elaborately eighteenth century.

Musée d'Art Sacré (15 Rue Ste.-Anne) is a desanctified church that brims with religious art—sculpture, most especially; an immense Baroque altar by Dijon-born Jean Dubois is star of the show. Should there be an exhibition—there are several each year—at nearby *Musée de la Vie Bourguignonne* in an ex-convent at 25 Rue Ste.-Anne, pop in.

Palais de Justice (Rue du Palais) is monumental Baroque. Apply to the concierge for permission to have a look at the lavish ceiling of the *Assises* courtroom and adjacent public spaces.

Church of Notre-Dame (Place Notre-Dame): Stand back on the square and look up—over the broad, triple-arched porch—to the clutch of gargoyles (by my count, 17) topping as many slim pillars on each of two galleries of the facade, with a third, or bottom, row for good measure. Inside, walk to the transept for another upward glance at inner walls of a tower framing the transept.

Church of St.-Michel (Place St.-Michel) is still another Dijon church requiring consideration from without. Its facade of five symmetric levels, topped by a pair of octagonal towers, is a Renaissance masterwork. The tympanum, or carved overdoor, of the central portal represents *The Last Judgment*—and beautifully—while the interior is graceful Gothic.

Wine country—south to Nuits St.-Georges: A tour of the southern tip of the Côte d'Or, touching Beaune, Mâcon, and Beaujolais—is outlined in Chapter 8. From Dijon, a wine-country excursion, morning well into the afternoon, might follow the *Route des Grands Vins* that would include stops at *Fixin* (to visit an unexpected museum of Napoleonic memorabilia in Parc Noisot); *Gevrey-Chambertin* (for inspection of Château Gevrey-Chambertin, parts of it tenth century, small, privately owned, and in a pathetic state of repair); *Clos de Vougeot* (for inspection of a medieval château set in a 225-acre vineyard that thrives on admissions charged of masses of tourists, fascinated at the sight of venerable wooden wine presses, casks, and the like, the lot explained in an excessive French-language commentary); and *Nuits St.-Georges* (surely the most euphoniously named of French wine villages, welcoming and with a small museum of Roman and medieval artifacts excavated locally). Throughout this pretty region—at such towns along the way as *Marsannay-la-Côte, Brochon, Morey St.-Denis, Chambolle-Musigny, Flagey-Echézeaux,* and *Vosne Romanée,* invariably friendly growers welcome you to their *caves*—you'll note signs as you move along—for gratis tastings, tours (upon occasion), and sales of their wines; but they do not high-pressure you to buy. Whether you do so or not is up to you.

Chablis and Auxerre (each about 80 miles northwest of Dijon) are near-neighbors (nine miles separate them). You'll be curious about Chablis because, no doubt, you drink its crisp white wine—the most globally famous French white—or California whites that have appropriated the Chablis name. Chablis is an unexceptional village with the Serein River to its northeast, vineyards with its celebrated grapes all about, and a friendly core, with Romanesque-origin *Church of St.-Martin* (Rue des Moulins) its major monument. *Auxerre* is something else again, a substantial town on the Yonne River that is based on *Place de l'Hôtel de Ville* —dead center and named for a bishop's palace that is now the city hall—with two visitable churches. The elder, *Church of St.-Germain* (Rue Docteur Labosse), attached to a venerable Benedictine monastery, is Gothic at street level, but it's the remarkable pair of Romanesque crypts that you want to inspect, one superimposed over the other, with their most striking features—capitals of columns supporting vaults excepted— frescoes relating scenes in the life of St. Stephen (for whom the town's cathedral, below, is named) that date to the ninth century, the oldest such in France. Move, then, to *Cathedral of St.-Étienne* (Place St.-

Étienne), one of the most beautiful Gothic churches in the republic, with
a lavishly sculpted facade—note *Christ in Majesty* and *The Last Judgment*
in the tympanum of the central portal, *Coronation of the Virgin* over the
left panel, *The Life of St. John the Baptist* over the right portal—and,
inside, the thirteenth-century choir, stunning stained glass, and a frescoed crypt.

Vézelay (60 miles west of Dijon) is a tiny, walled village capping a hill
and itself capped by a thirteenth-century church—*Basilica of Ste.-
Madeleine*, so named for on-site presumed relics of St. Mary Magda-
lene—that just has to be the biggest village church in France and certainly one of its most magnificent, thanks not only to its original designers,
but to a nineteenth-century restoration by Viollet-le-Duc that respects
its Romanesque origins. The single-tower facade stands out because of
an unusual pediment with statues filling its niches and framing its windows. There are three portals, with the tympanum of the central one,
Christ in Glory, worthy of study, in preparation for still another tympanum—this one inside, infinitely more detailed, depicting *Christ and the
Apostles*. The interior—principally because of Romanesque vaults patterned in black and white, which frame the high nave supplemented by
sculpted capitals topping columns supporting the vaults—is one of the
most outstanding in France.

Château de Bussy-Rabutin (40 miles southwest of Dijon) is the prototypical Renaissance castle: cylindrical towers delineating its extremeties,
moat leading to a courtyard galleried on either side, central section
distinguished by a steep-pitched roof. Windows throughout—elegantly
oblong in the style of the period—are superb. State rooms are, too. One,
atop a tower, La Tour Dorée, is the most smashing; another, the bedroom
of a Comte de Bussy, has walls and canopy of identical scarlet damask.
All are distinguished by a plethora of portraits, as many of somberly
suited gents as of ladies with generous bosoms, their necklines low and
their foreheads ringed with the curls of elaborate coiffures.

Abbey of Fontenay (46 miles northwest of Dijon)—despite its cold
severity, not surprising as it was inhabited by abstemious Cistercians—is
an impeccably maintained Romanesque complex taken in by means of
guided, 45-minute tours. It is at its most likable in the twelfth-century
cloister, centered by a manicured lawn, surrounded by a gallery, each
of whose arches is supported by double columns. The church—more
than 200 feet long—is virtually without embellishment, capitals of the
columns flanking its nave and a statue of the Virgin Mary in the transept
excepted. And the dormitory—wherein the monks slept on the floor on
straw pallets—is even plainer, albeit with a superb barrel vault.

Semur-en-Auxois (38 miles northwest of Dijon) is, if visited in tandem with nearby, gloomy Fontenay (above), a barrel of laughs in contrast. This is a time-stood-still village, preserved quite as it was for centuries, amenities like electricity and plumbing excepted. All of the ingredients of a medieval movie set are present: high-on-a-hill situation, the Armançon River flowing through the core, with a stone bridge traversing it, quartet of towers that date to when the village was defended by archers, walkable ramparts, *Musée Municipal* in a Baroque convent filled with medieval sculpture, and—frosting on the cake—single-steepled *Church of Notre-Dame*, a Gothic jewel that is a joy from without: elegant apse at the rear, tympanum over the central portal of a facade protected by an immense porch, exceptional sculpture, and good stained glass.

St.-Thibault (32 miles northwest of Dijon): If Semur (above) is a village, St.-Thibault is a hamlet. The only game in town is *Church of Notre-Dame* —unusual Gothic in that its designers made of its apse a veritable skyscraping tower, easily the equivalent of five or six stories and visible for miles around.

SETTLING IN
Du Nord Hôtel (2 Rue de la Liberté at Place Darcy; phone 8030-55-20): In a city where hotels are not a strong point, the long-on-scene Nord— family-owned and operated, centrally situated, comfortable—stands out. There are two dozen rooms—some bigger than others, all in traditional style, with good baths; attractive cocktail lounge; restaurant worthy of comment in a later paragraph; and kindly, caring, efficient management. *Moderate.*

De la Cloche Hôtel (14 Place Darcy; phone 8030-12-32) is not as big as it looks, taking space in only part of the interior of an impressive Second Empire building fronting a major Dijon square. It was relatively recently refurbished and, no question, smartly, with good-looking public spaces, including a crystal-chandeliered lounge, leather-chaired bar, breakfast room giving onto a garden, and brick-walled *cave* sheltering a reasonably competent restaurant. There are two problems: A majority of the 80 rooms are small and cramped (agreeable rattan-look decor notwithstanding). And service—mostly by uncaring youngsters at reception, whose principal qualification is language skills—is impersonal and indifferent. The De la Cloche gives the unhappy impression of being operated without top-management supervision. *First Class.*

Châpeau Rouge Hôtel (5 Rue Michelet; phone 8030-28-10): There are 33 no-two-alike, traditional-style rooms, with those that I have seen tasteful, with respect to antique accents and interesting textiles, although some are, indeed, small. Public spaces, including a cocktail lounge and restaurant, are agreeable. And situation is central. Sadly lacking, though, are smiles on staff faces—an idea of what hospitality is all about. A pity, this coldness. Mapotel/Best Western. *First Class.*

Du Jura Hôtel (14 Avenue Maréchal-Foch; phone 8041-61-12) is an elderly house that has seen better days. But it's reasonably central—not far beyond Place Darcy—with a capacious lobby, a bar-lounge with a log-cabin look, 75 rooms, and a cordial reception staff. *Moderate.*

Ibis Central Hôtel (Place Grangier; phone 8030-44-00) was, when I first knew it—before its affiliation with the Ibis chain—a decent old-school house. Alas, times have changed. Rooms that I have seen (there are 90) appear even more sparsely equipped than they were, with inadequate seating and lighting. Reception staff does not growl when approached, but one feels that this just *might* happen. The self-service breakfast is the skimpiest and least appetizing of any that I have experienced in France. With its pluses—Belle Époque facade, central location and a restaurant (reviewed in a later paragraph) so outstanding it's difficult to believe it's part of this hotel—the Ibis *should* be a top ranker. *Moderate.*

Montigny Hôtel (8 Rue de Montigny; phone 8030-96-86) is a small, contemporary-look house that's reasonably central; 22 adequate rooms. Breakfast only. *Moderate.*

Frantel Dijon (22 Boulevard de la Marne; phone 8072-31-13) would be at the top of my Dijon grouping if only it were central. You're a quarter-hour drive from the core here, but there are advantages: a modern house with 128 well-equipped rooms, convenient restaurant, relaxing cocktail lounge, swimming pool in the garden that's a pleasure in summer, and—hardly to be underestimated in this, of all cities—a friendly welcoming staff. *First Class.*

DAILY BREAD
La Toison d'Or (18 Rue Ste.-Anne; phone 8030-73-52)—a fairish but scenic walk from Rue de la Liberté, near Musée d'Art Sacré—is the handsomest restaurant in town, a Renaissance house with original beamed ceilings, flagstone floors, stone and paneled walls, Louis XIII chairs at flower-centered tables, and a half-timbered facade giving onto a court-yard. Not surprisingly, fare is traditional Burgundy. There are several well-priced prix-fixe menus. One of these opens with duck *terrine*, continues with filet of trout, proceeds to a cheese platter, and concludes with a house-baked pastry or a frozen *coupe Cassis*. The à la carte includes a deliciously wine-sauced filet of beef. The cordial owning couple operates a wine museum on the premises and conducts tastings for groups that have booked accordingly. *First Class.*

La Porte Guillaume (Du Nord Hôtel, 2 Rue de la Liberté; phone 8030-55-20) has the look of old Burgundy—brass chandeliers, ladder-back chairs, candlelight at dinner—and the taste of old Burgundy. There is a pair of menus, and even the cheaper one is a winner; open with *jambon persillé* or half a dozen Burgundy-style snails and continue with Burgundy's own *coq au vin* or veal kidneys, Dijon-style, with dessert following. Everything I've had here is delicious, and service is super. *First Class.*

Le Pré aux Clercs/Trois Faisans (13 Place de la Libération; phone 8032-02-21): Considering its choice situation (just opposite the ducal palace, in heavily trod tourist territory), the Pré aux Clercs, over the sustained period that I have known it, maintains standards—fare is typically Burgundy-tasty—and a sense of decorum. You are welcomed cordially to this venerable stone-walled salon, and in the evening red candles in silver sticks illuminate your table. There are two prix-fixe menus—opening, for example, with smoked ham, a vegetable *terrine* or Burgundy-style lamb brains, with entrées of pork filet, breast of chicken in tarragon-mushroom sauce, or filet of beef; with cheese and pastries following. The à la carte—including *foie gras de canard, quenelles de brochet,* kidneys *flambés,* to cite a trio of choices—is commendable, too. *First Class.*

Le Rallye (39 Rue Chabot-Charny; phone 8067-11-55) pleases both with appearance—pale green draperies contrast with ivory-hued walls and table linens—and with cuisine. Select the prix-fixe menu based on such entrées as filet of beef, sauce *marchand de vin;* or *médaillon* of pork prepared with prunes, in the manner of the region. And order *meringues Chantilly* to conclude. *First Class.*

Central Grill (with its own entrance at the side of Ibis Central Hôtel, Place Grangier; phone 8030-44-00) is big and busy—locals pack it at lunch—and as good a place as any in town to try such Burgundy specialties as *oeufs en meurette* (eggs poached in a red-wine sauce), *soupe au vin* (vegetable flecked, wine-based bouillon) and *boeuf Bourguignon* —to name a few. Prix-fixe menus or à la carte. Excellent, and with sprightly service. *First Class.*

La Concorde (2 Place Darcy; phone 8030-69-43) is an old-fashioned *brasserie,* evocative of the turn of the century, with temptingly tabbed prix-fixe menus. Open with half a dozen snails or *jambon persillé,* continue with an excellent *coq au vin,* and conclude with cheese followed by a fruit tart; house wine is part of the deal. Friendly. Central. *Moderate.*

Breuil, a.k.a. La Chouette (1 Rue de la Chouette; phone 8030-18-10) occupies a smallish room in a half-timbered fifteenth-century house, sets a fussy-looking table—lace cloths over pink undercloths, with floral-patterned china and elaborately etched stemware—and offers a relatively skimpy prix-fixe—*blanquette de veau* (veal stew) and minced lamb casserole are typical entrées—which does not leave you especially content when you've concluded, no doubt because the cooking is competent but without flair; and service, though correct, is distinctly cool. *First Class.*

Caveau de la Porte Guillaume (7 Place Darcy; phone 8030-58-38) is appropriately brick walled, in the manner of a wine *cave*. And wine is the reason for your visit; you may taste nearly a score of vintages by the glass. Staple fare accompanies. *Moderate.*

Nouvelles Galeries (41 Rue de la Liberté): The café-*salon de thé* of the Dijon link of a national department store chain is convenient and central. *Moderate.*

Café de la Poste (43 Rue des Forges): Take an outdoor table and steep in the atmosphere of Old Dijon—and the passing pedestrian parade. *Moderate.*

Café le Glacier (19 Place Darcy): Ice cream is indicated here, but coffee or a drink are options. *Moderate.*

Rôtisserie du Chambertin (Gevrey-Chambertin; phone 8034-33-20): I have lunched in this stone-walled, tapestry-hung restaurant in the course of two Gevrey-Chambertin visits, and on each I have enjoyed perfectly delicious traditional fare. Order *foie gras frais*, snails, *oeufs en meurette*, or mussel soup as openers; grilled lobster, *tournedos* of beef topped with a trio of superb sauces, thyme-scented lamb chops, and an extraordinary *coq au vin* are among the hearty entrées. Opt for cheese to accompany the obviously excellent wine you're drinking. For dessert: the day's *soufflé*, floating island, or Cassis sherbet doused with Cassis. In my experience, one of France's best restaurants. *Luxury.*

La Côte d'Or (Nuits St.-Georges; phone 8061-06-10)—red walled, its windows smartly draped, Louis XV chairs at its tables—sets a super table. There is a trio of prix-fixe menus. Consider opening with the house's own pigeon *pâté*, snails in pastry, or smoked salmon. Fish dishes—a seafood platter, especially—are special here. But you are in Burgundy: Beef is excellent. And desserts are rich. *Luxury.*

La Cambuse (8 Rue Devret, Semur-en-Auxois; phone 8097-06-78): You're heart of town; come in for lunch after a visit to the neighboring Church of Notre-Dame, selecting a menu embracing snails or *jambon persillé*, *coq au vin*, or a beef entrée; pastry to conclude. *First Class.*

De La Poste et du Lion d'Or Hôtel Restaurant (Vézelay; phone 8633-21-23) is hardly as aged as nearby Basilique Ste.-Madeleine—your prime reason for a Vézelay visit. But it *is* a landmark. Open with a duck *terrine* or snails in a Chablis sauce, hoping that chicken fricassee will be among the rib-sticking entrées. *First Class.*

L'Étoile Hôtel Restaurant (4 Rue des Moulins, Chablis; phone 8642-10-50): If you're motoring from the north or west, Chablis may well be your point of entry in Burgundy—and you may well be famished. This long-on-scene spot will fill the bill for a nourishing lunch, ideally based on an entrée of, say, grilled trout, to be accompanied by wine bearing the village's name. *First Class.*

SHOPPER'S DIJON

Wine and mustard—the big Dijon specialties—first: *La Cour au Vin* (3 Rue Jeannin), though hardly in a league with Marché au Vin in Beaune (Chapter 8), conducts several daily tastings (at a charge), will ship wine it sells, and has a shop with accessories like glasses and *taste-vins*, as well as a restaurant. *Gray-Poupon*, a leading mustard manufacturer, maintains a retail shop at 32 Rue de la Liberté, which is elegant enough to be a *parfumerie*, and sells its product in ordinary jars and fancy pottery jugs, as well. *Nouvelles Galeries* and the delightfully named *Au Pauvre Diable* department stores are on Rue de la Liberté, along with such shops as *Mulot & Petitjean* (chocolates and Cassis-flavored candies typical of Dijon), *Maille* (mustard), *Minelli* (well-priced men's and women's shoes), and *La Rose des Vents* (perfume). Place de la Libération's stores include *Madeleine* (women's haute couture) and *Morizot* (furs). *Jacadi* (children's clothes), *Linvosges* (linens), and *Comtesse du Barry* (charcuterie) are on Rue des Forges. Rue Verrerie abounds in antiques shops, including *La Crédence Buisson* (nineteenth-century furniture), *Au Bûcheron* (eighteenth-century pieces), and *Au Vieux-Dijon* (small objects).

SOUND OF MUSIC

Théâtre Municipal (Place du Théâtre, Dijon)—strikingly neoclassic, with tall Corinthian columns fronting its facade—is for opera, concerts, and ballet. Monthly calendars of events are available from the tourist office (address below).

INCIDENTAL INTELLIGENCE

Further information: Office de Tourisme, Place Darcy, Dijon; Office de Tourisme, 2 Quai de la République, Auxerre; Office de Tourisme, Place Gaveau, Semur-en-Auxois.

18

Grenoble
Edging the Alps

BACKGROUND BRIEFING
It is no wonder that the committee organizing the 1968 Winter Olympics selected Grenoble. How could they do other than headquarter in this lively southeastern city flanking the French Alps, after noting its spectacular backdrop of always snowy peaks?

Grenoble's situation, at the foot of the Belledone massif, with the Isère River cutting through it, has been a magnet since Romans settled in, close to 2,000 years back. The city they called *Gratianapolis* gradually became the more Gallic Grenoble, passing successively to rule from Burgundy to the north, Provence to the south, the area's own Dauphins of Viennois (whose title eventually came into use as the name of the Dauphiné region, remaining so to this day) and, in the mid-fourteenth century—about the time the celebrated University of Grenoble was founded—the French crown.

Contemporarily, the university's sprawling suburban campus appears more successful at luring foreigners—it has more students from other countries than any other French university—than does the city proper, with respect to foreign tourists. This is a town that makes its money on industry generated by rich hydroelectric resources and on nuclear research. Wealth notwithstanding, there's not a single luxury hotel. Withal, the Grenoble restaurant and shopping scenes are substantial, and if the city's visitor attractions are relatively limited—the sole requisite, in my view, is an art museum that's one of France's best—an attractive core and the region surrounding compensate.

ON SCENE
Lay of the Land: Get to know Grenoble by starting at the top. Or, I should say, ascending to the top. Hie yourself to *Quai Stéphane-Jay*, adjacent to *Jardin de la Ville*, a square rather than a garden, just below

the Isère River as it flows past the core of town. This is the site of the station for the *téléphérique*, or cable car, from which you may descend to *La Bastille*, a onetime fortress at an elevation of 1,400 feet, affording vistas of city, river, and assorted Alpine peaks. (Ideally, select a clear day and arrive in time for a summit lunch-cum-panorama at a restaurant below recommended.) Back in town, orient yourself from *Place Grenette*, heart of the old sector of the city, *Vieux-Grenoble*, with café tables spilling into it. Extending northeast from it, pedestrians-only *Grande Rue* proceeds to historic *Place St.-André*, dominated by the church whose name it takes. Take *Rue de la République* leading southeast from Place Grenette, and you'll soon arrive at *Place de Verdun*, site of the art museum. Go southwest from Place Grenette along pedestrians-only *Rue Félix Putlat*, and you arrive at *Place Victor Hugo*, entry point for *Avenue Alsace-Lorraine*, the street with the city's smartest shops, which terminates at *Place de la Gare* and the railway station.

Musée de Peinture et de Sculpture (Place de Verdun): The important French provincial cities all have substantial fine-arts museums; Lyon, Bordeaux, Dijon, Rouen, Toulouse, Marseille, Strasbourg, and Montpellier are all top class in this respect, and smaller spots like Pau, Colmar, and St.-Tropez have stellar collections, too. None of these, however, surpasses Grenoble. The beauty of this museum—I refer to the paintings rather than the nondescript setting—is that it is strong in several areas. European Old Masters, the French seventeenth century, and, most especially, modern work—the Impressionists, post-Impressionists, and recent painters, as well. Consider such works as La Tour's kneeling *St. Jerome*, cross in hand; Vouet's *Rest on the Flight into Egypt*; Philippe du Champaigne's *Christ on the Cross* and his *St. John the Baptist*, direct and youthful; La Hure's *Supper at Emmaus*, oddly reminiscent of the work of Veronese; Le Brun's *St. Louis Praying for Christians Suffering from the Plague*; Jouvenet's multicharacter *Martyrdom of St. Ovid*; Largillière's portraits of a self-satisfied *Jean de Creponne* and of *Elizabeth de Beauharnais*; Desportes's opulent *Fruit, Flowers and Animals*; and the landmark painting of the group: Lorrain's *Roman Countryside: Morning*. Contemporaries of these Frenchmen are represented, too: Rubens and Jordaens, for example; a brilliant Zurbarán quartet; and a clutch of Dutch still-lifes and landscapes. Earlier Italians—Veronese, Tintoretto, Bassano—are present, as well. Later French painters are strong—Rigaud, Greuze, Vigrée-Lebrun, to name an eighteenth-century trio at random—with Italians of that epoch, like Canaletto, Tiepolo, and Guardi, to complement them. From the French nineteenth century, Ingres, Fantin-Latour, Courbet, and Corot are all on scene. You ascend a steep stairway to the top floor, then, for Impressionists and their successors: Monet, Sisley, Renoir, Utrillo. But it is the twentieth-century work that stuns: Chagall and Klee, Miro and Magritte, Cocteau and Tanguy, Van Dongen and Le

Corbusier, Modigliani and Soutine, Léger and Picasso, Gris and Braque, Vuillard and Bonnard, Matisse and Vlaminck. An all-Europe ranker.

Musée Dauphinois (Rue Maurice-Gignoux) is as good a reason as any to cross over to the Isère's North Bank. Indeed, the museum's quarters— a creatively converted seventeenth-century monastery perched atop a hill and affording fine perspectives of the river and the city—is at least as impressive as the exhibits. These fill a couple of floors that surround a grassy cloister. A mixed bag here: regional Roman mosaics, Merovingian soldiers' helmets, pottery running a range of centuries, prints and portraits and posters, furniture (some especially good eighteenth-century pieces) and frescoes, and an absorbing section on the life-style of people in the mountain villages and farms, labeled *Gens de Là-Haut.*

Vieux-Grenoble: A half-day's stroll might include visits to the *Cathedral of Notre-Dame* (Place Notre-Dame)—as old as the Romanesque tenth century, but with Gothic and Renaissance additions and later restoration, the lot adding up to a composite that is not a special esthetic treat; *Church of St.-André,* built by the Dauphins whose name the region takes in the twelfth century and with a fine Gothic interior—choir, especially—and a graceful spire; *Palais de Justice* (Place St.-André), for long, the Dauphins' palace/parliament, with superb woodwork; and *Musée Stendhal* (Jardin de Ville), on the ground floor of the onetime City Hall, with mementoes of the Grenoble-born author in and about a furnished-in-period eighteenth-century salon.

Musée de la Résistance (14 Rue Jean-Jacques Rousseau)—another single-room museum, not unlike the Stendhal (above) in that regard, but with its theme Grenoble's valiant Resistance movement during World War II. Pay your respects.

Parc Paul-Mistral, southeast of the center, is pilgrimage-territory for sports and modern architecture buffs, with structures built for the 1968 Winter Olympics, including the futuristic *Palais des Sports* (seating 10,000) and *Stade de Glace,* the ice stadium.

La Grande Chartreuse (near Voiron, 14 miles north of Grenoble) is the headquarters monastery of the reclusive Carthusian monks (and of a companion group of somewhat less reclusive brothers). It's a magnificently facaded Renaissance complex spanning an isolated forest-encircled high valley. Because of the nature of this nine-century-old contemplative order, the monastery proper is not visitable. However, adjacent to the nearby—and visitable—distillery where the Carthusians still make their celebrated Chartreuse liqueur, they have created a museum in *La*

Corrèrie, a complex used in the past by the order's brothers. Exhibits include a full-scale mockup of a typical cell, along with showcases of monks' habits, sacred art objects and paintings, the lot of these alongside a Carthusian-built chapel, open to visitors. I was told, by distillery executives—who market and distribute the monks' liqueur—that there are fewer than 50 monks resident from countries around the world, that they speak only on Sundays in the course of communal walks lasting several hours, and that close family members may visit them, albeit very rarely. From the excellent Carthusian-written, English-language guidebook to the museum, one learns that because the monks live out entire lives in solitude (except for morning, evening, and middle-of-the-night communal worship and the Sunday walks) their cells—hermitages, actually—are relatively capacious duplexes where they sleep, eat (meals are brought to them by brothers), pray, study, work (chopping wood, for example, in winter), and garden (each cell has a little plot). And—again, I quote the guidebook: "The [monks'] food is simple, but adapted to the conditions of the life, and normally Carthusians reach the age of 80 and even beyond."

Château de Berenger (Sassenage, four miles west of Grenoble) is closest to the city of several eminently visitable castles. Berenger, backed by mountains, severely mansard-roofed, is a seventeenth-century house, with a suite of reception rooms—salon, library, dining room—mostly eighteenth century in decor, shown on guided visits.

Château de Vizille (10 miles south of Grenoble), considerably more ambitious than Berenger—indeed, it is ranked as the premier Renaissance château of Dauphiné—dominates its own lake-centered park. State rooms—a magnificently paneled library, especially—are sumptuous. It was at Vizille that representatives of Dauphiné towns—450 strong—declared themselves in favor of the French Revolution in 1788. (Grenoble was strongly anti-royal during this period, and there's a *Museum of the French Revolution* in the castle.) For a period, the castle served as a summer residence of presidents, including Auriol, Coty, and de Gaulle.

Château de Touvet (18 miles north of Grenoble and the same distance south of Chambéry, Chapter 5) goes back, originally, to medieval times. But it is, today, essentially eighteenth century and very handsome, with a grand stairway dominating its entry hall, salons furnished with Louis XIV and Louis XV pieces, and formal gardens.

Crémieu (47 miles north of Grenoble) is a remarkably intact village that is a throwback to the days when dauphins ruled Dauphiné. Visit *Château Delphinal*, high on a hill over town and for long where the Dauphins lived; *Cloître des Augustins*—an ancient monastery—one of a cluster of mellow structures on *Place de la Nation;* a superb covered market, or *Halles,* of the fourteenth century; and twelfth-century *Chapelle de St.-Antoine.*

Chemin de Fer Touristique de La Mure is just what it sounds like: a made-for-tourists mountain railway that runs from *St.-Georges-de-Commiers,* 12 miles east of Grenoble—through a roller coaster-like maze of passes, tunnels, and bridges, past peaks as high as 10,000 feet, mirrorlike lakes, and jagged cliffs—to *La Mure,* journey's end. The line opened as long ago as 1888 and was electrified in the early years of this century, when the cars you will ride were built. Allow a day for the adventure, which may be booked through the Office de Tourisme in Grenoble (address below).

SETTLING IN
Park Hôtel (10 Place Paul-Mistral; phone 7687-29-11) represents the best Grenoble has to offer. The good-sized lobby is contemporary. There are 50 rooms, agreeably decorated in a mix of traditional and modern, with up-to-date baths; select superior-grade accommodations; and the manager sends you two pieces of fruit with his card. Below, there's a bar-lounge and a little limited-menu restaurant that can be a convenience, given the away-from-center location of the hotel, whose combination reception-concierge-cashier desk is staffed by well-intentioned, albeit not necessarily professional, young people. *First Class.*

Angleterre Hôtel (5 Place Victor-Hugo; phone 7687-37-21): Happiness in Grenoble is a room at the Angleterre, with French doors giving onto a terrace and Place Victor-Hugo out front. The lobby-bar-lounge of this elderly but refurbished house is clean-lined contemporary; decor of the 70 rooms—which can be small but are equipped with satisfactory baths— is country-rustic. Central and friendly. *Moderate.*

Ibis Hôtel (Îlot des Trois Dauphins; phone 7647-48-49) is heart of town, and one of the more attractive and better operated links of this France-wide chain that I have encountered. Decor embraces blond woods, pale walls, primary-color textiles. One could wish for thicker mattresses, but there is an agreeable restaurant (later counseled) as compensation. *Moderate.*

Alpotel (12 Boulevard Maréchal-Joffre; phone 7687-88-41) is a little closer to the center of town than the Park (above), but not all that much. Otherwise, it is commendable—with 90 modern, well-planned, and well-equipped rooms leading from its high-ceilinged lobby; a worth-knowing-about, good-value restaurant; and bar-lounge. Congenial. *Moderate.*

De l'Europe Hôtel (22 Place Grenette; phone 7646-16-94) is brought to your attention principally because of its situation on Grenoble's most historic square, heart of the city. But by no means all of its 44 rooms have baths. Breakfast only. *Moderate.*

Grand Hôtel (5 Rue de la République; phone 7644-49-36): You must not be swayed by the name. The Grand's ace-in-the-hole is a central location and 75 clean rooms with baths. Corridors are gloomy; reception staff, in the course of my inspection, disagreeable. Breakfast only. *Moderate.*

DAILY BREAD
Chez la Mère Ticket (13 Rue Jean-Jacques Rousseau; phone 7645-44-40) typifies the unpretentious bistros, invariably with female owner-chefs, that dot southern cities. There is, to be sure, pink linen on the tables of this narrow, two-floor spot. It is otherwise quite plain—until you order. Start with a platter of *charcuterie* that is bound to include slices of ham and a variety of superb sausages, with coarse bread accompanying. Continue with *truite meunière vivante*—the fish plucked live from a tank and prepared to your order. Go on, then, to *poulet aux écrevisses*, chicken and shrimp served with *gratin Dauphinois*, the region's brilliant potato casserole. And desserts—if you're up to them—are very good. In my view, one of France's best restaurants. *Moderate.*

La Poularde Bressane (12 Place Paul-Mistral; phone 7687-88-90) is away from the center, but worth the taxi ride, with decor a successful mix of Belle Époque and contemporary and cuisine a blend of traditional and *nouvelle*. Lean to the former, and there are such successful openers as crayfish-stuffed ravioli in a savory sauce, or mussel and shrimp salad. Entrées are more stick-to-the-ribs—*navarin d'agneau* (lamb stew with young vegetables), roast duck with mushrooms, filet of Charolais beef. Gracious service. *First Class.*

Le Pommerois (1 Place aux Herbes; phone 7644-30-02) has good looks as a major plus; it's quartered in a venerable house on a fine old square, with the ambience smartly rustic, a contrast to be sure, with the *nouvelle*-influenced cuisine. Best buy is the prix-fixe menu, which opens with *amuse-gueules*, tiny slices of salami, radishes, puff pastry *canapés;* continue with a rich *foie gras.* Sliced breast of duck is a good entrée, served with a quartet of vegetables. Hot desserts—an apple and almond *tarte*, for example—are memorable. *First Class.*

Pique-Pierre (St.-Martin-le-Vinoux, two miles north of the center of Grenoble; phone 7646-12-88): Would that this lovely restaurant were closer in. Still, its regional specialties make it worth visiting; a prix-fixe meal might run to *gratin de moules Florentine*—a spinach and mussels casserole, deliciously prepared veal or chicken entrées, and choices of cheese and dessert. Friendly. *First Class.*

À la Bastille (La Bastille, atop the *téléphérique*; phone 7642-09-74) is indicated for lunch on a clear, sunny day, which might be comprised of, say, *soupe* and *entrecôte aux frites*, with fruit tart to conclude. No charge for the view. *Moderate/First Class.*

À la Table Ronde (7 Place St.-André; phone 7644-51-41): Forget about associations with King Arthur that the title might imply. This long-established restaurant on a long-established square specializes in Alsatian cuisine; go with an appetite for the copious *choucroute garnie*. Fun. *First Class.*

Ibis Hôtel Restaurant (Îlot des Trois Dauphins; phone 7647-48-49) is just the ticket for an unpretentious lunch. Omelets, salads, roast chicken are reliable; *mousse au chocolat* is a wise dessert choice. Attractive. *Moderate.*

Le Boeuf Mironton (9 Avenue Alsace-Lorraine; phone 7646-01-64): Given its location on Grenoble's classiest shopping street, this restaurant's three-course prix-fixe menus are good value, indeed. Open with the house terrine, continue with *escalope de veau*, conclude with a sweet and, in fine weather, dine outdoors on the terrace. *Moderate.*

Café Le Grenette (Place Grenette): Seat yourself for coffee or a giant ice cream concoction, to watch the passing parade on the city's handsomest square. *Moderate.*

Café du Tribunal (Place St.-André)—a coffee stop on a scenic square. *Moderate.*

Beau-Site Hôtel Restaurant (St.-Pierre-de-Chartreuse; phone 7688-61-34) is appropriate for lunch, in combination with an excursion to La Grande Chartreuse (above). Order one of the prix-fixe menus, with such options as crayfish *mousse* to start, jugged venison as an entrée, and cheese to follow, with the house's own black currant sherbet, vodka-laced, for dessert. *First Class.*

La Petite Auberge (Crémieu; phone 7690-75-45) appeals after a morning's exploration in this venerable village (above). Order the menu, making sure *gratin Dauphinois* is included. *First Class.*

SHOPPER'S GRENOBLE

Dames de France (Grande Rue, off Place Grenette) and *Prisunic* (Rue Lafayette) are leading department stores. The heart-of-town daily produce market is eminently visitable, on aptly named *Place du Marché*. Rue Bayard and Rue Voltaire constitute, between them *Antiques Row*. Rue de Burdet has such fine shops as *Bally* (shoes), *Rodier* (women's clothes), and *Burdet* (porcelain). And chic Avenue Alsace-Lorraine's boutiques include *Terrier* (men's accessories), *Paul* (women's duds), *Imperial House* (leather), *Robert Detraz* (men's and women's clothes), and *Rivoire* (chocolates, with a *salon de thé* in connection).

AFTER DARK

Maison de la Culture (Rue Paul Claudel) is Grenoble's architecturally innovative, ever-so-modern, multifunction cultural complex, with its several theaters (one of them features a revolving stage) venues for plays and other entertainment.

Théâtre Municipal (Rue Hector Berlioz) presents opera and ballet, and— just opposite—*Salles des Concerts* is the leading location for classical music.

INCIDENTAL INTELLIGENCE ━━━━━━━━━━━

Aéroport Grenoble–St.-Geoirs is a substantial 27 miles from town, but is served by buses that depart in time for principal flights to major French cities. *Further information:* Maison du Tourisme Dauphiné-Grenoble, 14 Rue de la République, Grenoble.

19

Honfleur
Normandy's Enchanted Village

BACKGROUND BRIEFING

Credit Honfleur with resilience. Everyone—from transoceanic explorers of half a millennium back to contemporary explorers, strolling its horse-shoe-shaped inner harbor this very moment—has paid calls. And a clutch of the last century's Impressionist artists—headquartered in a farmhouse that is now a respected restaurant—interpreted the Honfleur scene in paintings that hang in museums from Chicago to Copenhagen. Withal, Honfleur has accepted celebrity with good grace and good sense. Summer congestion notwithstanding, it remains, season in and season out, Normandy's enchanted village.

It was during the sixteenth and seventeenth centuries that Honfleur knew its Golden Age—hardly less than it deserved after nearly three decades of English occupation in the course of the earlier Hundred Years War. Then came the captains and their crews. No question but that the most celebrated was Samuel de Champlain, who first visited Quebec as early as 1604. But there were other pioneer explorers: Dinot Paulmier de Gonneville, who journeyed to Brazil in 1503; Jean Denis, who, in 1506, made it to the coast of Newfoundland and the mouth of the St. Lawrence River; and Pierre Berthelot, an early seventeenth-century wanderer in Asia.

As early as the start of the nineteenth century, descendants of the very same English who came as soldiers in the fifteenth century, arrived to paint. Richard Bonington, better known in Britain today than in the United States, and J.M.W. Turner—challenged by the clarity of the light and the beauty of villages flanking the Channel shore—joined such French painter-pioneers of the region as Corot and Daubigny and others of the so-called Barbizon school (named for the village where they had congregated, near Paris). Later, at mid-century, Honfleur-born painter Eugène Boudin served as a kind of catalyst for a movement of painters—

quartered at hospitable Mère Toutain's Ferme St.-Siméon, just outside of town—whose work of the period, as members of the so-called St.-Siméon school, influenced the paths of Impressionism. They included, besides the prolific Boudin (for whom an Honfleur museum is named and whose Norman harbor scenes are his trademark), such French talents as Claude Monet and Alfred Sisley, the American James McNeil Whistler, and the Dutchman Johann Jongkind. French writers came too—the poet Baudelaire, the best known.

ON SCENE

Lay of the Land: This is a small town, easily and delightfully negotiable on foot. Inner harbors are four in number—*Bassin de Retenue* (largest and most distant from the core), *Bassin de l'Est,* and the two most important: *Avant Port* flanked by strategically situated *Quai de la Quarantine* and *Place de l'Hôtel de Ville* (named for the nineteenth-century City Hall dominating it); and, most significant, most painted, and most photographed, *Vieux Bassin*—a rectangle formed by seventeenth-century houses on *quais Ste.-Catherine* and *St.-Étienne,* along with the landmark *Lieutenance,* a Renaissance mansion that long served as seat of the Lieutenant of the Port, and a charmer of a single-steeple, essentially fourteenth-century church, *St.-Étienne,* that's now a museum (below). *Rue des Logettes,* just west of Vieux Bassin, separates it from another landmark square, *Place Ste.-Catherine. Rue de la Ville,* a few blocks to the east, is the site of tiny *Grenière à Sel*—a salt warehouse dating to the seventeenth century. That street, in tandem with *Rue de la Prison,* constitutes the core of the pedestrian shopping area. Historic *Place Arthur-Boudin* is eminently inspectable, too, as are facades of venerable houses on such streets as *Rue Brûlée, Rue du Puits,* and *Rue de la Bavole.*

Musée Municipal Eugène Boudin (Rue de l'Homme de Bois) surprises, first off, with its modernity. It went up as recently as 1974, to honor the distinguished Honfleur-born Impressionist. Be assured that it displays works of his, including a pair of evocative cloudscapes of the beach at Trouville, with pastels and drawings, as well. Boudin's fellow Ferme St.-Siméon colleague, Jongkind, is represented, and so is Honfleur-born Dubourg, a talented watercolorist. Monet's painting of the local Church of Ste.-Catherine (below) is a special treat. So is work by Dufy that includes a self-portrait and a blue-and-orange Normandy wheatfield. Paintings by lesser-known artists are hardly less appealing; especially those with local settings, including harbor scenes by André Hambourg and Gelso Lagar. On your way out, take in the gallery of amusing nineteenth-century posters and still another display—of traditional Norman applied arts, furniture and costumes, particularly.

Church of Ste.-Catherine (Place Ste.-Catherine) is a one-of-a-kind wood structure, distinctive not so much for the material with which it was built, but because its Renaissance designer-constructors were shipwrights. Take a look at vaulting of the principal nave, and what you have is a downside-up hull of a venerable sailing vessel. Take your time as you stroll through; there is a second nave, lovely polychrome sculptures, an unexpected display of Renaissance musical instruments near the eighteenth-century organ, and in the detached, separately entered *Clocher de Ste.-Catherine*—the bell tower of the church—there's a mixed-bag exhibit of religious art, carved wood, and maritime regalia, which constitutes a branch of Musée Eugène Boudin (above).

Musée de la Marine (Quai St.-Étienne) has an inspired location: old St.-Stephen's Church (above). Model ship buffs are happy here; but displays run to all manner of objects relating to maritime Honfleur—prints and paintings, documents and drawings.

Musée du Vieux-Honfleur (Rue de la Prison) reproduces—and with a striking sense of realism—interiors of Norman houses: sailor's kitchen through merchant's salon, along with a superb cache of antique furniture, porcelains, and clothing. Setting is special, too: several joined structures of yore; one is Honfleur's ex-prison.

Church of St.-Léonard (Rue Cachin) is as good an excuse as any to explore the St. Léonard quarter. The church has a disproportionately bulky but pleasing octagonal tower and is mellow Gothic within.

Mont Joli is an eminence just west of town that affords absolutely smashing panoramas not only of Honfleur but of the Seine Estuary and the port city of Le Havre. Nearby is the charming little seventeenth-century *Chapel of Notre-Dame-de-Grâce*, site of annual pilgrimages by Honfleur sailors. Do go up.

SETTLING IN
Ferme St.-Siméon Hôtel (Rue Adolphe Marais, a mile from the center of Honfleur; phone 3189-23-61) is the very same that gave its name to the last century's St.-Siméon school of painters headed by Eugène Boudin (above)—an intricately gabled, brick-facaded, seventeenth-century mansion, perhaps better known contemporarily as a restaurant (below). But it contains in its main building nine no-two-quite-alike double rooms, each traditionally decorated with marble baths, whose tubs are supplemented by proper showers. A second building—Le Manoir—is a few hundred yards away, in a garden overlooking the sea, and has a dozen additional, similarly comfortable rooms. Relaxing and friendly. Member, Relais et Châteaux. *First Class*.

Cheval Blanc Hôtel (2 Quai des Passagers; phone 3189-13-49) is splendidly situated, heart of town. Its lobby-lounge is half-timbered; its bar is cozy and offers ladder-back chairs; its restaurant is smartly Louis XIII. There are three dozen rooms; those I have inspected are brightly papered and agreeable, and you do well to insist upon one with a harbor view. *First Class.*

Lechat Hôtel (3 Place Ste.-Catherine; phone 3189-23-85): Ivy covers two of the three stories of this ancient stone structure. There are just over two dozen rooms with bath, as well as a commendable restaurant, later evaluated. Super situation. *First Class.*

Écrin Hôtel (away from the center, at 19 Rue Eugène-Boudin; phone 89-32-39): Madame Blais, whose ebullient personality this immediately likable 20-room house reflects, is partial to the primary colors. No two rooms are alike—red-walled reception; main salon in blue and gold; emerald green-walled, coffered-ceiling library; bedrooms in a veritable rainbow of hues, with furnishings from sixteenth through nineteenth centuries. And yet it all comes together, thanks to Madame Blais's good humor and expertise. Breakfast only. Fun. *Moderate.*

Tour Hôtel (3 Quai de la Tour) is heart of the Honfleur action, with close to 50 functional rooms. Breakfast only. *Moderate.*

DAILY BREAD
Ferme St.-Siméon (Rue Adolphe Marais, a mile from the center of Honfleur; phone 3189-23-61) is both hotel (above) and restaurant. The latter occupies several connected rooms—each with beamed ceilings, antique prints, good paintings—taking up most of the space of the main floor, with a pretty terrace out front for warm-weather meals. Cuisine has for long been—and happily continues to be—authentic and traditional Norman, typical of this region, whose name is synonymous with superb cooking. At dinner, you order from an extensive à la carte menu (each dish, printed first in French, is accurately translated into English). Starters include a tasty fish soup, eggs scrambled in a shrimp sauce, and a refreshing seafood salad. Seafood entrées—grilled lobster with *sauce Béarnaise*, truffled *escalope* of salmon, classic *sole Normande* with mussels, mushrooms and shrimp in a cream sauce—are in themselves worth a Ferme visit, but roast duckling, saddle of lamb, and saddle of rabbit are tempting, too. Dessert choice is fabulous—there's a table full of tempters. What I counsel, though, is the house's celebrated hot apple tart served with a generous pitcher of heavy Norman cream. Bear in mind that there are solid-value prix-fixe menus weekdays at lunch. In my view, one of France's best restaurants. *Luxury.*

Lechat Hôtel Restaurant (3 Place Ste.-Catherine; phone 3189-23-85): Aged Norman apple presses are fashioned into lamps on the attractively laid tables of this heart-of-Honfleur eatery. Lobster, served in a number of ways, is the big specialty. But you do well, too, with such entrées as seafood *au gratin* and *coq au vin*. Prix-fixe menus are good value. *First Class.*

Deux Ponts Restaurant (20 Quai de la Quarantine; phone 3189-04-37) is enviably placed, heart of the harbor, and with seafood (including mussels and oysters) in abundance; *sole Normande,* of course, but the day's catch, simply grilled, if you so order. Temptingly tabbed menus. *Moderate.*

Au Bon Cidre (17 Quai de la Quarantine; phone 3189-04-24) is the ideal setting for an introduction to Norman cider; you'll find it cool, tart, and refreshing. And you do well to drink it in tandem with a savory *crêpe* or two, the species called *Normande* is filled with ham and cheese. *Moderate.*

Café de la Voile au Vent (Quai St.-Étienne) is indicated for close observation of the ambulatory Honfleur scene. *Moderate.*

INCIDENTAL INTELLIGENCE

Alas, trains, do not serve Honfleur. Nearest railway stations are at Pont-l'Évêque (10 miles south) and Pont-Audemer (14 miles southeast), from both of which towns there is scheduled bus service to Honfleur. There is frequent bus service, as well, between Honfleur and points along the coast, including Deauville and Caen. *Further information:* Office de Tourisme, 33 Cours des Fosses, Honfleur.

20

Loire Valley Châteaux
Tours to Orléans

BACKGROUND BRIEFING

Beginnings were not all that different from beginnings elsewhere in France. The wooded hills that sloped to the shores of the Loire—the nation's longest river, swinging southwest at Orléans, past Tours to the port of Nantes (Chapter 30) at its Atlantic estuary—knew early Romans, whose handiwork still is to be seen in regional museums. There were early Christians—St. Martin of Tours is surely the most celebrated—and the inevitable invading Barbarians.

Then, with the advent of the Middle Ages, the Loire Valley's situation and terrain attracted feudal baronies, each with its own derring-do castle atop a riverview hillock. Counts of Blois opposed Counts of Anjou, and Plantagenets became so aggressive that one of them (Henry II) assumed the throne of the English enemy.

It was only the twelfth century. Some two hundred years later, the English were back again, a thorn deep in France's side for the long, difficult span of the Hundred Years War. Its end came about only when a woman still in her teens—who was to become patron saint of France— routed the English from the Loire Valley city of Orléans (which celebrates that occasion each spring).

Jeanne d'Arc's miraculous victory paved the way for a clutch of Italian-influenced kings—charming, well-educated, meticulously organized François I was the most brilliant of the group, which included Louis XI, Charles VIII, and Louis XII—to build a network of Loire Valley castles wherein, with courtiers—whose ranks included painters, writers, musicians, philosophers, architects, landscapists and, yes, chefs, as well as couturiers—they developed a life-style that saw the national culture reach a zenith that to this day evokes admiration and awe; they brought to fruition the French Renaissance.

ON SCENE

Lay of the Land: Nobles and wealthy merchants followed kings to the Loire Valley, building smaller, but not necessarily less beautiful, dwellings along the river. There are, today, some 300 eye-filling residences in the valley, and, if you seek guidance on the lot of them at this point, you are reading the wrong book. My suggestion is that you settle for what I single out as the top 10—taking in two or three a day over a period of several days—in an area that stretches about 130 miles, from westerly Angers (Chapter 4) to easterly Orléans, with the region's most engaging city—history-laden Tours—a geographical midships, and for that reason the indicated headquarters for exploration of a relatively compact region that has no equal anywhere in Europe and that draws more foreign visitors than any region of provincial France, save, of course, the Riviera. With good reason.

Tours, Roman founded, was celebrated as early as the fourth century, when its Bishop Martin became St. Martin, and again in the sixth century, when its Bishop Gregory became St. Gregory. Two hundred years thereafter, its troops held off invading Moors in the course of what might have been a pan-European conquest. Renaissance kings, starting with Louis XI, used Tours as a supplemental meeting point beyond the confines of nearby châteaux. The proximity of those castles lured theologians and artists, sculptors and weavers to Tours. And, briefly, during the course of two much later wars—Franco-Prussian and Second World—it served as the French capital. It's well planned. The *Loire River,* its northern boundary, parallels busy *Boulevard Heurteloup,* its southern flank, with leading hotels and *Le Printemps* department store, as well as both *Palais de Justice* and *Hôtel de Ville,* at *Place Jean Jaurès,* from which *Rue Nationale* (with *Nouvelles Galeries* and *Monoprix* department stores, as well as many shops) cuts north to *Place Anatole France* and a pair of nearby museums. Still another north-south thoroughfare is *Rue du Petit Roi,* connecting Boulevard Heurteloup with *Place de la Cathédrale,* around which are centered the cathedral, fine-arts museum, and *Château de Tours,* housing the relatively recent *Musée Historial.* Eminently walkable streets of *Vieux Tours*—gained by *Rue du Commerce,* leading west from *Rue Nationale*—include *Rues Brettoneau, Grand Marché, Rôtisserie,* and *Châteauneuf,* based on *Place Pluméreau,* with its lures splendid Renaissance mansions, many half-timbered.

Musée Historial de Touraine (Rue Lavoisier) gets you in the mood—in effect, sets the stage for Loire wanderings. Setting—Château de Tours—is the well-restored fifteenth-century castle that was inhabited by two kings—Charles VII and his son, Louis XI. Idea is to tell the story of the region by means of a series of marvelously detailed dioramas that bring the region's history to life, 31 all told, beginning with St. Martin of Tours blessing a young priest—he will become St. Patrick—en route to Ireland;

moving through the centuries with tableaux evoking the eighteenth-century Battle of Poitiers; the eleventh-century visit of King Richard Coeur de Lion to Château de Chinon; Jeanne d'Arc receiving the Tours-crafted breastplates she later wore in battle against the English; Charles VII, with his beautiful mistress, Agnès Sorel, at Château de Loches; Charles VIII marrying Anne of Brittany at Château de Langeais; Leonardo da Vinci with his patron, François I, at Clos-Luce; the writer Rabelais and the poet Ronsard in local settings; Diane de Poitiers with her lover, Henry II, at Chenonceaux; and Mary Queen of Scots, while she was Queen of France, with the first of her three husbands, François II, and his mother, Catherine de Medici, at Amboise.

Tours's *Cathedral of St.-Gatien* is, like the city itself, underappreciated—a great Gothic beauty, with an intricately detailed facade embracing a trio of sculpted portals, beneath a rose window, itself surmounted by twin belfries, each topped by an octagonal tower, or lantern. The scale of the interior staggers, with superior stained glass, art-filled chapels, and the adjacent Psalette Cloister, an unexpected treasure.

An utterly beautiful palace in its own garden, adjacent to the Cathedral (it had been the archbishop's residence), serves with distinction as Tours's *Musée des Beaux-Arts*. Before you so much as glance at a painting, you envy long-ago clerics their opulent quarters in this building that was erected during the seventeenth and eighteenth centuries. Sculpture is exemplary, with works by Houdon and Bourdelle, among others. Precious eighteenth-century furniture is dotted about. Even the original floors are works of art. Then you observe paintings. There is a pair by Mantegna—a *Resurrection* and *Christ in the Garden*—that stick in your memory. But so many other artists are represented—Frenchmen like Largillière and Nattier, Boucher and Delacroix, and foreigners like Rembrandt and Rubens.

Make time for two more of a number of Tours museums. *Musée Archéologique* (Rue du Commerce) makes its home in an elegant townhouse; while the city's *Musée des Arts Décoratifs*—antique furniture is its forte—is located in another mansion on Rue Émile Zola.

The city surveyed, you're ready for country castles. Because you'll want to work out your own order of precedence according to the time you've available, my top 10 are presented alphabetically. Châteaux most popular with visitors are Chenonceaux (800,000 per year) and Chambord (400,000 per year), with Cheverny, Blois, Villandry, Amboise, and Azay-le-Rideau following; in other words, plan on sharing the sights with crowds, especially in summer.

Amboise surmounts a plateau, surrounded by high walls, a complex dramatically dominating the agreeable river-front village that takes its name. Quite the most interesting part of the interior is the suite of state rooms—this is one of the châteaux in which François I lived, but so did kings Charles VIII and Louis XI. The single most important element of the château remaining is the Chapel of St.-Hubert (honoring the patron saint of hunters and therefore of interest to Renaissance royals, virtually all of whom hunted avidly)—quite striking flamboyant Gothic. Note, too, a pair of towers, Tour Minimes and Tour Hurtault, one within the other, with an entry ramp—at first for horses, now for cars—to the château. Beyond, on Rue Victor-Hugo, is *Clos-Luce*, the gracefully gabled, brick manor house where François I installed Leonardo da Vinci, his imported-from-Italy artist-in-residence. The most interesting interior is the room in which Leonardo died in 1519, but there is a lovely chapel and a fair sprinkling of Da Vinciana.

Azay-le-Rideau, detached from the charming village taking its name and—unlike Amboise—completely intact, is set, rather ingeniously, partially straddling the Indre River, partially alongside it. It is sublime in scale, restrained in ornamentation (turrets and chimneys are relatively limited in number; state rooms are dominated by splendid fireplaces), and handsomely furnished. Allow time for a walk about the grounds; Azay is a joy from every angle.

Beauregard went up originally as a hunting lodge for François I, but was later enlarged—and made a considerably more substantial mansion—by a minister of Henri II. It is one of the most serenely situated châteaux of our group of 10—in a vast, green park. You see a number of rooms in the course of a visit—paneled and beamed reception salons, the original kitchen. But you go particularly for the Galerie de Portraits, where attention was paid to ceiling (with exquisitely decorated beams), floor (paved in Delft tiles), and—most especially—walls, hung with 327 portraits of French luminaries, from early Valois dynasty kings and nobles to Louis XIII.

Blois—not unlike Amboise in that it is a town, as well as a castle—is a lesson in early architecture, part Gothic, part Renaissance, part Baroque, the lot in four immense wings enclosing an also immense courtyard, where the *chef d'oeuvre* is the so-called François I staircase, an inspired octagonal spiral that climbs five stories, on each of which it is intricately sculpted. The royal apartments' architecture compensates for the lack of furniture, with the room used by Catherine de Medici—intricately paneled and with closets hidden behind some of those panels—the dazzler of the lot. And a museum of French paintings is a surprise. A pair of in-town destinations is noteworthy: *Cathedral of St.-Louis* (Place St.-Louis)—Gothic but with a Romanesque crypt—and especially for chocoholics, *Chocolaterie Poulain*, for long a Blois institution.

Chambord—in a walled deer park of more than 13,000 acres adjacent to an oddly administered village that is government property (none of its houses is privately owned)—is the most painted, the most photographed, the most chronicled, the most romantic, and also the largest of the Loire châteaux, with well over 400 rooms. You need not enter to be enraptured. Chambord is François I's jewel—elongated, with a circular tower defining each end, its roof an extravagant jumble of pinnacles and turrets, chimneys and domes. Not unlike Blois, Chambord charms with a main staircase. One of but half a hundred, its kicker is a design whereby two spirals are superimposed, with each going its own way, so that if I am going up and you're en route down, we don't see each other. Chambord remained popular long after the Renaissance. All of François I's kingly successors made use of it, including Louis XIV, during whose reign Molière's *Le Bourgeois Gentilhomme* had its first performance; and Louis XV, whose father-in-law—a deposed King of Poland—lived in it until he became Duke of Lorraine (Chapter 25). Napoleon gave the castle to a courtier; it did not fare well thereafter, but was repurchased and restored by the French Government in 1932. Have a walk around, taking in Chambord from a variety of exterior angles before you depart.

Chenonceaux is No. 1 in the Château Sweepstakes because it is as beautiful without (it appears to float on the Cher River, and it is set off by formal gardens) as within, and because historical figures most associated with it (Catherine de Medici, Diane de Poitiers, François I) are so well known. You enter on a drawbridge. Look right to Catherine de Medici's garden; look left, and the garden is that of Diane de Poitiers. Look at the Cher, and you see it flowing under six exquisite arches that support the château's rectangular wing. The interiors—including bedrooms of both Catherine and François, chapel, library, salons affording river vistas—are unsurpassed in the valley, with furniture, paintings, and tapestries sublime throughout. Allow enough time.

Chinon is as exciting from the Loire River—it dominates the village below it, taking its name—as from within. You go because it is the valley's most celebrated link with the Middle Ages. It is actually a trio of moated forts in partial ruins, with the central part, Château de Milleu, the site of a museum whose subject is the visit made to Chinon by Jeanne d'Arc; it was there that she met the Dauphin—not yet Charles VII—in 1429. Chinon village is at its best in and around Grand Carroi, the core of the old quarter, with adjacent streets lined by aged houses; the house at 15 Rue de la Lamproie was inhabited by the monk-writer-physician Rabelais, whose patron for a time was François I.

Cheverny's Grand Salon—with the sumptuously worked panels of its walls and ceiling, its paintings and its Régence furniture—is reason enough for a visit. But this sixteenth-century mansion, set back in its own verdant park, pleases on other counts: the fine details of its facade, the breadth of its central stairway, the canopied state bed, the frescoed ceiling and tapestried walls of its Chambre du Roi, the sword collection of its armory, and the fine paintings—with a number by Clouet and Rigaud—throughout.

Langeais is an appealing mix of moats and battlements and conical towers, set back from carefully tended flowerbeds. But what makes this castle special is the brevity of its period of construction. It went up in less than half a mid-fifteenth-century decade under the aegis of a minister of King Louis XI, in the center of the village that takes its name. A consequence is that it is of a piece, consistent in its architecture and decor and—significant, this—graced by splendid furnishings, in monumentally scaled state rooms, with high, wide, and handsome fireplaces and tapestried walls.

Villandry: If you've an interest in gardens, it seems to me there are three in France you don't miss: the Tuileries in Paris, to one of whose benches I repair for a tranquil pause in the course of every visit; Versailles, of course; and Villandry, in many ways the most spectacular of the trio. The château itself is interesting in that it was the last of the big ones to be built on the Loire shore. A minister of François I was first owner, but interiors are mostly eighteenth century. The following century, the nineteenth, a gifted Spanish physician, Joachim Carvallo, and his American-born wife bought Villandry (which is why there are fine paintings by such Spaniards as Goya and Zurbarán within) and set about redesigning the vast garden, which had been allowed to deteriorate over a long period, to its original Renaissance style. Horticulturists now consider it an all-Europe ranker. Skip the house, if you insist, but not this extraordinary trio of vast terraces: kitchen garden, fragrant with jasmine and with giant decorative cabbages, lowest down; ornamental garden at mid-level—the most magnificent, with clipped box and yew trees, heart- and fan-shaped (the theme is love); and, at the top, a maze of moats fed from a central lake and by fountains interspersed throughout.

Orléans—flanking the châteaux at its eastern edge—was badly bombed during World War II, not felicitously reconstructed, and nothing like as well equipped for visitors as Tours (above). Stay long enough, though, to have a look at *Cathedral of Ste.-Croix*, on central Place du Martroi, unusual in that it is essentially a reconstruction—begun in the seventeenth century but not finished until the nineteenth—of a Gothic structure substantially razed by seventeenth-century Protestants. Scale is stupendous, twin towers impressive, flying buttresses dazzling, nave high and long, decorative woodwork elaborate. This same square, with a statue of the city's beloved liberator, Jeanne d'Arc, is the site also of the relatively recent—and handsome—replacement quarters of a long-established *Musée des Beaux-Arts*; the collection cannot touch that of Tours (above) or of many other provincial museums—it appears more a case of quantity rather than quality—but there are some fine portraits, including a Drouais of *Madame de Pompadour*, a Pourbus of *Anne of Austria*, and a De La Tour of *St. Sebastian*. At least as absorbing, it seems to me, is *Musée Historique* (Rue Ste.-Catherine), located in a nineteenth-century mansion and brimming with sculpture and fragments from regional Roman ruins. And there are dioramas depicting events in her short but exciting life in *Maison de Jeanne d'Arc* (Place du Général de Gaulle).

SETTLING IN
De l'Univers Hôtel (5 Boulevard Heurteloup, Tours; phone 4705-37-12) is a Tours institution, easily dating back a century, with—I must caution at the outset—some of its 88 rooms by no means as nicely or anywhere as recently updated as others. You must specify accommodations that have been given a coat of paint, a layer of wallpaper and new bathroom fixtures in recent seasons. That accomplished, you can be happy in this centrally situated, professionally staffed house, with agreeable public spaces that include a restaurant and bar-lounge. *First Class.*

Bordeaux Hôtel (3 Place Maréchal-Leclerc, Tours; phone 4705-40-32) is quite as central as its near-neighbor, the Univers (above), though it's smaller (there are just over half a hundred full-facility rooms) and more modern. The two-part restaurant is so good that I accord it space in a later paragraph. *First Class.*

Gambetta Hôtel (7 Rue Gambetta, Tours; phone 4705-08-35) is an agreeable old-timer, core of Vieux-Tours, with 40 traditional-style rooms of varying sizes (those I have inspected are pleasant), many surrounding an ivy-walled courtyard. Breakfast only. *Moderate.*

Des Châteaux de la Loire Hôtel (12 Rue Gambetta, Tours; phone 4705-10-05) is a charming, old-school, Vieux-Tours house, with a handsome lobby-cum-bar and 32 rooms; those I have seen are delightful. Breakfast only. *Moderate.*

De France Hôtel (38 Rue de Bordeaux, Tours; phone 4705-35-32) is conveniently located, near the railway station and Boulevard Heurteloup, off which is the core of town. There are thirty-five neat rooms. Breakfast only. *Moderate.*

Château d'Artigny Hôtel (Veigné, seven miles south of Tours; phone 4726-24-26) is, *sans doute*, grande dame of the region, an early twentieth-century replacement—built by François Coty, of perfume fame—of a much older castle. Set in its own park and fronted by formal gardens, its high-ceilinged public spaces include the handsomest cocktail lounge in this part of France; oval-shaped restaurant, green-walled and with gilded paneling; and a smasher of a stairway that leads from the long gallery of a lobby to upper floors. Sizes and locations differ but all 60 rooms are Louis XV style, with fine baths. There's a swimming pool in the garden, a pair of tennis courts, and nearby golf and fishing. Service is at once professional and cordial. Member, Relais et Châteaux. *Luxury.*

Le Grand Monarque Hôtel (Place de la République, Azay-le-Rideau; phone 4743-30-08): I can't imagine a more charming venue to overnight, in the course of exploring the valley, than this delightful old-timer, in the village adjacent to the château whose name it takes. Public spaces are welcoming. More than half of the 30 rooms—those I've inspected are very pleasant, indeed—have baths. There's a caged wild boar in the garden (who sleeps most of the time), and the restaurant is exemplary enough to warrant comment in a later paragraph. Friendly. *Moderate.*

Domaine de Beauvois Hôtel (Luynes, eight miles west of Tours; phone 4755-50-11)—set back in a forest-bordered park—is a Baroque château with handsome public spaces, 40 smartly furnished and accessorized rooms and suites, reliable restaurant, and diversion including swimming, tennis, and fishing. Member, Relais et Châteaux. *Luxury.*

Château de Pray Hôtel (Route 571, just outside of Amboise; phone 4757-23-67) is a small but choice château of respectable age, framed by a pair of circular towers, in its own garden, with splendid river views. There are 16 no-two-alike rooms, reliable restaurant, bar-lounge, welcoming staff. *First Class.*

Le Choiseul Hôtel (36 Quai Charles-Guinot, Amboise; phone 4730-45-45), on the banks of the Loire, just opposite Château d'Amboise, is special—a mini-château embracing 20 Louis XV-style rooms of varying sizes and spacious lounge, off which are a bar and picture-windowed restaurant that overlooks the Loire and moves to the garden in summer. *First Class.*

Novotel Amboise (17 Rue des Sablonnières, Amboise; phone 4757-42-07) is a fair distance from the center of Amboise, but so situated that there are panoramic views of the château from half of its 82 clean-lined rooms giving onto the town. This is a contemporary house, with restaurant, bar, swimming pool. *First Class.*

Domaine des Hauts-de-Loire Hôtel (Onzain, near Chaumont-sur-Loire, midway between Tours and Blois; phone 4720-72-57) is a honey of an ivy-walled manor house set in a spacious park, with swans paddling about in the pond out front; antiques-furnished public spaces that include congenial bar and an esteemed restaurant; and just under 30 rooms and suites, no two identical; each of those I have inspected, delightful. Member, Relais et Châteaux. *First Class.*

Du Château Hôtel (22 Rue Porte-Côte, Blois; phone 4778-20-24) is heart of town, just below the château. There are baths in 34 of its 47 rooms and a convenient restaurant. *Moderate.*

D'Orléans Hôtel (6 Rue Adolphe Crespin, Orléans; phone 3887-35-34) has the advantage of a central situation in the shopping area, a hop and a skip from the cathedral. The look is agreeably contemporary, and there are 18 well-equipped rooms. Breakfast only. *Moderate.*

Des Cèdres Hôtel (17 Rue du Maréchal-Foch, Orléans; phone 3862-22-92) is closer to the railway station than to the core of town; 28 of its 32 rooms have baths. Breakfast only. *Moderate.*

Sofitel Orléans (44 Quai Barentin, Orléans; phone 3862-17-39) is considerably away from the center, in a nondescript—and by no means attractive—residential quarter. There are 110 functional rooms, smallish restaurant, bar adjacent to the garish lobby, and, in my experience, the most inept staff—reception through room service—of any that I have encountered in the French Republic. *First Class.*

DAILY BREAD
Bordeaux Hôtel Restaurant (3 Place Maréchal-Leclerc, Tours; phone 4705-40-32): For long, known as the "Garden of France" (and with good reason), Tours is skilled at putting raw ingredients—produce, poultry, meats, cheeses—to expert use. Nowhere is this talent more evident than at the pricier of the Bordeaux Hôtel's pair of restaurants. Handsome to look upon—furniture is Louis XV style, with sconces and chandeliers of crystal and murals on the walls—and with an expert staff, this restaurant offers one of the most delicious—and best-value—prix-fixe menus that I have come upon in France. You might, for example, open with the traditional *saucisson chaud*—sausages-cum-potatoes. *Truite meunière*, perfectly prepared, would follow. Entrée would be a hearty *coq au vin*. Then cheese from a platter, with a choice of tasty desserts to follow. *First Class.*

Les Tuffeaux (19 Rue Lavoisier, Tours; phone 4747-19-89) offers you either a very pricey prix-fixe or à la carte, with the cuisine a competent, if hardly exciting, mix of *nouvelle* and traditional. I suggest sticking to such safe standbys as *foie gras frais de canard*, fileted fish of the day simply grilled, or *filet de boeuf*. Desserts are this house at its best; *nougat glacé aux framboises*—a frozen raspberry confection—is very good. The look is quietly antique. Central. *Luxury*.

Charles Barrier (101 Avenue de la Tranchée, Tours; phone 4754-20-39): You need a car for Barrier, located north of the center, across the Loire, and convenient if taken in tandem with a morning visiting area châteaux. Look is formal—crystal chandeliers, masses of flowers, marble floors, silver candelabra at tables. There are good things to eat, traditional with contemporary touches, from either a prix-fixe menu or à la carte. You might open with truffled eel *terrine*, consider Loire salmon in a *beurre blanc* sauce as a fish course, with either the house's special duck or pigeon entrées to follow, and frozen fruit *soufflé* as a sweet. *Luxury*.

La Rôtisserie Tourangelle (22 Rue du Commerce, Tours; phone 4705-71-21) edges the Vieux-Tours quarter, is as good a place as any to open with *rillettes*—Touraine's own coarse pork *pâté*—continuing with a freshwater fish or poultry entrée. Desserts are reliable; prix-fixe menus, good value. Congenial. *First Class*.

Château de Beaulieu (Route Villandry, Joué-les-Tours, two miles southwest of town; phone 4753-20-26) is an eighteenth-century manor house, set back in its own capacious garden, that is at once a country inn (there are 17 traditionally furnished rooms) and a restaurant worth knowing about, in the course of touring the châteaux. There is a couple of decently priced prix-fixe menus, with traditional specialties; local salmon, deliciously sauced, is a highlight, with the house's own cherry dessert counseled. *First Class*.

Le Grand Monarque Hôtel Restaurant (Place de la République, Azayle-Rideau; phone 4743-30-08): Happiness in the Loire Valley is a sunny morning spent touring Château d'Azay le Rideau, with lunch following in the garden of Le Grand Monarque. Prix-fixe menus are good value, and fare is heartily traditional. Build your meal around duckling, Bigarade style, or fresh salmon expertly prepared. Don't skip the cheese course and conclude with a made-on-premises sweet. The owning Jacquet family are gracious hosts. *First Class*.

Monseigneur (12 Quai Charles Guinot, Amboise; phone 4757-08-09): You're just below the château, riverfront. Order the prix-fixe, commencing perhaps with pork *rillettes* or a game *pâté*, with an entrée of chicken and *chanterelles* mushrooms, and a fresh fruit tart to conclude. *Moderate*.

Chez Tantine (on the grounds of the château, Blois) could not be more casual or more fun. Madame Tantine, *la patronne*, runs the show, darting about from table to table, barking orders to bar and kitchen. There is a couple of inexpensive prix-fixe menus—unpretentious but tasty. Open, for example, with *crudités*, a tasty sauce accompanying; continue with grilled pork chops; and conclude with a pastry. *Moderate.*

St.-Michel Hôtel Restaurant (opposite the château, Chambord; phone 4720-31-31) could not be more scenically situated, and it's nicely combined with a château visit. Well-priced prix-fixe menus, with local standbys like *rillettes de porc* to start, grilled trout or perhaps a game entrée; satisfying sweets. *First Class.* (With 40 *Moderate* category rooms upstairs, should you want to stay the night.)

La Crémaillère (34 Rue Notre-Dame-de-Recouvrance, Orléans; phone 3853-49-17) has the old-fashioned look that becomes an ancient Loire Valley city—Louis XV armchairs in the cocktail area as you enter and a capacious dining room, beige walled, luxuriantly draped, brass chandelier-hung, with meticulously appointed tables, illuminated at dinner by pink candles. You may order à la carte, but the prix-fixe menu is excellent value. Open with a *terrine* made from a trio of Loire River fish species or the smoked salmon specialty. Go on then to talented owner-chef Paul Hyart's crayfish-stuffed ravioli. As an entrée, choose *pièce de boeuf*, an unusual rice-and-veal kidney preparation, or breast of chicken, *foie gras* garnished. Cheeses are served from an immense platter. M. Hyart's *crème brûlée* is indicated for dessert—one of a number of tempters. Sprightly, amicable service. In my view, one of France's best restaurants. *Luxury.*

L'Aviation (473 Faubourg Bannier, Orléans; phone 3888-71-92) entices with good-value prix-fixe menus. You want to make sure you have such house specialties as fresh-water fish in a *beurre blanc* sauce, medallion of lamb prepared with the mushrooms called *cèpes*, or the shrimp-sauced omelet. *Moderate.*

AFTER DARK
Son et Lumière—whereby historic monuments (châteaux in the case of the Loire Valley) are settings for evening entertainments in which piped actors' voices play out local history, the while spotlights focus on architectural details—is a French invention; it had its birth in the decade following World War II in the Loire Valley's Château de Chambord. Contemporarily, some 40 châteaux present Sound and Light, traditionally June through August, with commentary usually alternating, one night to the other, between the French and English languages. At its best—when professionally staged and lighted, with ranking actors—Son et

Lumière is at once good theater and an effortless lesson in history, as well as architecture.

INCIDENTAL INTELLIGENCE

The Loire Valley is too often taken in by means of day-long bus excursions out of Paris. I am a firm believer in the maxim that half a loaf is better than none; still, day-tripping the Loire is the coward's way. Come and stay awhile. *Further information:* Office de Tourisme, Place Maréchal-Leclerc, Tours; Office de Tourisme, Quai Général-de-Gaulle, Amboise; Office de Tourisme, 3 Avenue Jean-Laigret, Blois; Office de Tourisme, Place Albert 1er, Orléans.

21

Lyon
France's Second City

BACKGROUND BRIEFING
Whatever Lyon has done, it has done well.

Roman Lyon—*Ludgunum,* founded in 43 B.C.—was more than a colony. It prospered so that the emperors decreed it capital of all Gaul. (And enough of it remains for contemporary Lyonnais to have created one of the great European archeological complexes.)

As early as 12 B.C., Lyon's leaders hosted chiefs of the Gallic tribes at a kind of Parliament whose delegates discussed—for the first time—the idea of the confederation that would become France.

A century thereafter, Christians were martyred in Lyon, from where their religion was introduced into France; indeed, it was archbishops who ruled Lyon until 1308 when, during the reign of Philip IV, it became part of France. To this day, the Archbishop of Lyon is styled *Primat de Gaule*—Gaul's Primate.

As the Middle Ages became the Renaissance, Lyon pioneered with cultivation of silkworms, becoming the silk center of Europe, the while its merchants and traders (who opened France's first stock exchange as early as 1506) dominated Continental finance, even providing funds for French kings like Henri IV and François I—among the era's visitors to a still-thriving Old Town that ranks with that of Rouen (Chapter 31) as the most important such in today's republic.

Succeeding centuries saw the city expand eastward—from across the hills west of the Saône River, to the elongated strip between the Saône and the Rhône, thence eastward over the Rhône. This city, during the World War II Nazi occupation, was capital of the French Resistance movement. Contemporarily, it is a world-class innovator in scientific research, an extraordinarily rich cultural center, and with a cuisine tradition so fabulous that it's known to have visitors who come only to eat. But there are other reasons for a Lyon sojourn, as I try to make clear in the pages following.

ON SCENE

Lay of the Land: Lyon is a west-to-east city, historically as well as geographically. It began on the slopes of *Mont Fourvière*, east of the Saône, and still with Roman monuments. It moved down the hill, then, during medieval and Renaissance periods to the area now called *Vieux-Lyon*, dominated by a Gothic cathedral, with a principal street that takes the cathedral's name—*Rue St.-Jean*. Came the Baroque, Rococo, and Second Empire centuries and the city expanded eastward across the Saône to the quarter that is now its core—dominated by *Place Bellecour* (Europe's largest traffic-free square). *Rue Victor-Hugo* leads south from the big square to Gare Perrache, one of the railway stations. (And *Rue Auguste-Comte*, running parallel to it, is Lyon's Antiques Row.) Go north from Place Bellecour, along *Rue de la République*—through *Place de la République*—and you will be strolling one of the longest pedestrian shopping streets extant. Still another street leading from Place Bellecour, *Rue du Président Herriot*, is the venue of the city's smartest shops. These shopping streets lead to northerly squares edged by the *Opéra*, churches, and museums; *Place des Terreaux*, site of *Hôtel de Ville*, is the most important. Just as there are several bridges that traverse the Saône to Vieux-Lyon, so are there additional bridges that cross the Rhône to the biggest-in-area sector of the city—site of multipurpose *Palais des Sports* to the south—as well as the contemporary quarter called *Part-Dieu*, easily identified by a conical-topped cylindrical skyscraper, *Tour de la Part-Dieu*, and a shopping center that shelters a second railway station (Part-Dieu by name) and a clutch of decidedly noncentral hotels.

Musée de la Civilisation Gallo-Romaine and Roman Lyon are reached by a funicular from Avenue Adolphe-Max. The museum (entered at 17 Rue Cléberg) is one of the best-looking and best-designed contemporary structures in France; it's built on a hillside with the entrance on an upper level and the collections below. Not that you go only for the architecture. Dramatically displayed exhibits are from Gallo-Roman Lyon: mosaic floor after mint-condition mosaic floor; a bust of a goddess, a tiara in her neatly coiffed hair; silver goblets and a bronze tablet—*La Table Claudienne* —on which is inscribed the Latin text of a speech by Lyon-born Emperor Claude, delivered in the year 48 A.D.; sarcophagi and jewelry—the lot set against walls of poured concrete—with picture windows giving onto a complex embracing the still used *Grand Théâtre Romain*, built in 15 B.C. by Emperor Caesar Augustus to seat 10,000 and enlarged a century later by Emperor Hadrian; with a second, smaller theater, *L'Odéon;* as well as remains of *Temple Cybèle* (dating to 160 A.D. and the largest of its kind, along with that of Ostia, outside Rome).

Cathedral of St.-Jean, Musée Historique, and Vieux-Lyon: The cathedral (Place St.-Jean)—with a Romanesque apse and transept, but which

is otherwise essentially Gothic—was built over three centuries, twelfth through fifteenth, and has known its share of historic moments (it was the site of two medieval Catholic Church conclaves—the First and Second Councils of Lyon, the crowning of a pope (John XXII), and the marriage of a king (Henry IV, with Marie de Medici). But it is, as well, a place of beauty, with a facade graced by superbly sculpted portals, a treasury of Limoges enamels and exquisitely carved ivories, outstanding stained glass in rose windows flanking the transept, an impressive bishop's throne, and an extraordinary astronomical clock—indicating feast days beginning with the fifteenth century through the year 2000—which goes into its act daily at noon, 1:00 P.M., 2:00 P.M., and 3:00 P.M.

Musée Historique de Lyon (Place du Petit-Collège)—as good a way as any to inspect the interior of a townhouse typical of the quarter (it went up between the fourteenth and sixteenth centuries)—and its courtyard, with four floors of galleries, is a stunner, the while taking in mementoes of the old city. Furniture-filled rooms, up one flight, constitute the museum at its handsomest, with canopied beds made for Napoleon and Josephine—they came to Lyon in 1805—the most spectacular exhibits. But eighteenth-century rooms are lovely, too. Collections of porcelain and medieval sculptures are top rank, and there are antique marionettes as a bonus. Allow time to stroll Vieux-Lyon streets, noting especially their unique *traboules*—passages that cut through old houses providing routes to streets that run parallel to each other; one such leads from 3 Place St.-Paul (the site of Romanesque-Gothic *Church of St.-Paul*) to 5 Rue Juiverie. You'll come across a number of others in the course of a stroll through this relatively compact quarter, which should embrace the facades of *Place du Change, Place de la Trinité*, and *Rue du Boeuf*, not to mention shops, restaurants, and cafés of *Rue St.-Jean*, Vieux-Lyon's Main Street.

Musée des Beaux-Arts (Place des Terreaux): An obviously wealthy order of nuns, Dames de St.-Pierre, built a convent toward the end of the seventeenth century that could have been an Italian Baroque palace, its rooms cavernous, its ceilings high, its staircases not for the easily short of breath. You enter through what was the cloister and is now a tranquil public park. If the main floor sculpture collection—most of it in what was the sisters' refectory—were not so outstanding, I would not suggest that you pause. But there are fine things—Greek heads, Roman sarcophagi, medieval fragments, polychrome saints, carved-wood biblical scenes, Baroque busts, and works by later sculptors, Canova through Maillol, with Chinard's *Madame Récamier*—isn't she winking her left eyelid?—surely the single most fetching of the lot. Upstairs, then, to the paintings, a veritable survey of European art, Flemish Primitives through post-Impressionists: a Quentin Matsys *Virgin*—in cloth of gold—*and Child*, Zurbarán's *St. Francis of Assisi*, Veronese's *Bathsheba at Her Bath*, and Rubens's *Adoration of the Magi;* with such other masters represented as David and Tintoretto, Van Cleve and Cranach, Bassano and Vouet; portraitists, French, as well as English (Boucher and Lawrence, Lancret and Romney); pre-Impressionists like Corot, Millet, and Daumier; and beyond to Monet, Sisley, and Degas. Later work, too: Vuillard and Bonnard, Matisse and Picasso, Dufy and Van Dongen.

Musée des Arts Décoratifs (30 Rue de la Charité) is right up there with the best of its French counterparts—in Paris, Marseille, and Bordeaux. Setting is a garden-backed mansion designed by the same eighteenth-century architect, Soufflot, responsible for Paris's Panthéon. This museum celebrates the eighteenth century. There are, to be sure, galleries with display cases—of porcelain, glass, silver, clocks, and other small objects. But major excitements are period rooms, paneled and chandeliered and tapestried and exquisitely furnished with Louis XV and Louis XVI masterworks. Special.

Musée Historique des Tissus (34 Rue de la Charité), conveniently visited with neighboring Musée des Arts Décoratifs (above), pays tribute to Lyon's eminence as a silk center, with fine exhibits—in a jewel of a Rococo house that was official residence of governors of Lyon—not only of luxurious local silk, but of foreign textiles, as well. You'll see Coptic Egyptian tapestries, Islamic patterned cloth, Italian and Spanish silks from the Renaissance, and Turkish and Persian carpets, with the silk-savvy Orient represented, too.

Musée des Hospices Civils (Hôtel Dieu, Place de l'Hôpital): It is not often that public museums are located within the confines of working hospitals. But this museum—up a flight in the originally twelfth-century hospital known as Hôtel Dieu—is appropriately situated, given its theme: hospital care over the centuries. The exhibit that draws the most comment is a canopied bed that was shared by five patients until 1787—and was by no means atypical. Indeed, the museum catalogue points out that "often one was dead among them." There are, as well, surgical instruments covering a range of centuries, ancient syringes and urinals, a pill-making apparatus and microscopes, early patient ID bracelets, the costume and birdlike mask of a physician, worn during a plague epidemic, and even a padded cell used for mentally ill patients into the nineteenth century.

Musée de la Résistance (5 Rue Boileau) is, in effect, a tribute to France's anti-Nazi underground, as directed from Lyon during the World War II occupation: posters, blown-up photos, documents, newspapers, and other objects that chronicle the mission of a brave citizenry during a tragic period.

Hôtel de Ville (Place des Terreaux)—Lyon's magnificent city hall—went up originally at the height of the Baroque era, in the mid-seventeenth century. It was rebuilt, in period style, two centuries later and given a skilled 1980s refurbishing. If there are no attendants on hand to direct you, simply find your way to a stairway and ascend a flight to the high-ceilinged second floor. Then guide yourself through a series of unbelievably opulent reception rooms—each with coffered ceilings, gilded stucco, monumental murals, fireplaces tall enough to warm giants' hands, exquisitely patterned parquet floors, and crystal chandeliers of especial splendor. In one room, Salon de la Conversation, I counted a dozen of these mammoth chandeliers; in still another, Salon Louis XIII, there are 17. Have a look.

Musée de l'Imprimerie et de la Banque (13 Rue de la Pouaillerie) may tell you more than you want to know about printing presses (the range is five centuries) and of the history of banks, especially those of Lyon. But there are stunning displays that delineate the evolution of typography, Gutenberg onward, with choice antique books, woodcuts, and engravings. And the setting is a honey of a house: Hôtel de la Couronne, built in the fifteenth century and headquarters of the City Council during the first half of the sixteenth century.

Church of St.-Bonaventure (Place des Cordeliers) is a landmark, heart-of-town Gothic masterwork, with an immense—and immensely high—nave, a fine rose window gracing its facade, and an especially handsome apse.

Vienne—a charming, smallish Rhône River town 17 miles south of Lyon—rivals Arles (Chapter 6), Nîmes (Chapter 27), and Orange (Chapter 7), with its remarkable Roman monuments. Go for a day's excursion, beginning your exploration core of town, at *Cathedral of St.-Maurice* (Place St.-Maurice), which impresses with the detail of its Gothic facade—the three portals' tympanums are splendidly carved—very grand nave, and exemplary stained glass. *Temple Romain d'Auguste et Livie* (Place du Palais) is the only remaining temple, except for similar-appearing Maison Carrée in Nîmes, built by the Romans in Gaul and still standing; it's a stunner, still with the original fifteen columns—topped by Corinthian capitals—framing its facade and sides. *Church of St.-Pierre* (Place St.-Pierre), parts of it dating to the fifth century (making it Gaul's oldest church), is now desanctified and a museum of Roman artifacts from Vienne and the neighborhood. Beautiful mosiac floors now surface what was the nave, with sarcophagi, sculptures, and fragments to either side. *Church of St.-André-le-Bas* (Rue des Clercs) is mellow Romanesque—dating to the twelfth century and eminently visitable in its own right, but with a cloister that is at once an architectural treasure and a repository of early Christian art. *Théâtre Romain* (Rue du Cirque) climbs Mont Pipet on the west side of town and was excavated only in 1938 after having been buried under heavy layers of soil for centuries. Its original capacity was 15,000, and it's still used for summer performances. *La Pyramide* (Route N-7, south of the center) is Vienne's trademark monument; it's actually a slim column—wider at its base than its summit and dating to the second century—that surmounts a fourth-century arch. *St.-Romain-en-Gal* (across the Rhône, on the Right Bank) is a relatively recently excavated Roman city; digs continue, but already a lot has been uncovered—foundations of houses and baths, market and artisan's quarter, with heating and drainage systems, as well. And by the time of your arrival, there will no doubt be more.

Pérouges (23 miles south of Lyon) is an enchanter of a medieval fortified village, protected not only by the French Government as a national monument, but by its own Comité de Défense. A few movie companies have discovered it—a version of *The Three Musketeers* was filmed on location—but far too many visitors give it short shrift. Based on central *Place du Tilleul*, it expands ovally, on radiating streets. Visitors who do nothing but stroll, planning their visit to coincide with an atmospheric restaurant (below) are happy enough. But there is a trio of visitable interiors: fortified *Church of Ste.-Marie-Madeleine* (Rue des Trois Rondes) is a Gothic marvel—its inner walls faced with flagstone, its principal embellishment the vaults of a narrow nave. *Musée Municipal* (Rue des Princes), in a galleried mansion (ivy climbs its stone walls) is filled with Pérougiana—furniture and weapons, looms and weathered documents, domestic implements and costumes, prints and paintings. Neighboring *Maison des Princes* (Rue des Princes) is a beauty of a mini-palace in which long-ago princes of Savoy lived and is furnished in period. It's next door to the equally aged house sheltering a restaurant I recommend below for a lunch pause. After, it's fun to walk the ramparts along *Promenade des Terreaux*, past the series of towers that had for long protected this anachronism of a village—quite unlike any other in this region of France.

SETTLING IN
Grand Hôtel Concorde (11 Rue Grolée; phone 7842-56-21) is Lyon's grand dame, dating to the last century's Second Empire, but with all the comforts of the late twentieth century and—never to be underestimated in a city as big as this one—a superbly central situation. Although the entrance is on Rue Grolée—actually at the rear of the hotel—the Grand runs lengthwise out front, along Quai Jules-Courmont, fronting the Rhône. So, when you book for one of this hotel's 140 delightfully traditional-style rooms—many retaining original, albeit refurbished, Second Empire furnishings—you want to ask for a riverview room, so that

upon waking, you may step onto your terrace and take in the splendid Lyon skyline. The Grand's Le Fiorelle Restaurant is worthy of evaluation on a later page. The comfortable lounge off the lobby doubles as a bar, and the staff is one of the kindest and most efficient that I know of in France. Hôtels Concorde. *First Class*.

Royal Hôtel (20 Place Bellecour) is an agreeable old-timer that has wisely retained traditional ambience, the while tastefully updating facilities. There are 90 no-two-quite-alike rooms, a reliable restaurant, a friendly bar, and a core-of-town location. Mapotel/Best Western. *First Class*.

Sofitel Lyon (20 Quai Gailleton; phone 7842-72-50) is contemporary, with 196 full-facility, clean-lined rooms and a pair of restaurants and bars, centrally situated. *First Class*.

Carlton Hôtel (Place de la République at Rue Jussieu; phone 7842-56-51) is at its smartest in those of its 90 rooms which it has remodeled in Art Deco style. But remaining accommodations are comfortably traditional, although of different sizes and, of course, situations. Breakfast only. Central. Mapotel/Best Western. *First Class*.

Beaux-Arts Hôtel (73 Rue du Président Herriot; phone 7838-09-50) is enviably well located on the city's toniest shopping street. Marble-walled lobby is engaging Art Deco, and the 80 rooms are about half in that style, half conventionally traditional. Bar and breakfast only. Mapotel/Best Western. *First Class*.

La Résidence Hôtel (18 Rue Victor-Hugo; phone 7842-63-28) is nicely placed on a principal shopping street. All but three of its 63 rooms have baths or showers. Breakfast only. Friendly. *Moderate*.

Des Étrangers Hôtel (5 Rue Stella; phone 7842-01-55) offers half a hundred functional rooms, most with bath or shower, bar-lounge, breakfast, and the advantage of a central situation. *Moderate*.

Globe et Cécil Hôtel (21 Rue Gasparin; phone 7842-58-95) is on a street parallel with cushy Rue du Président Herriot, heart of town. Lobby-lounge is contemporary, rooms traditional style; 45 of the 49 have baths or showers. *Moderate*.

Bayard Hôtel (23 Place Bellecour; phone 7837-39-64): You ascend a stairway to reach the lobby, but it's worth the climb, if a small, core-of-town hotel is what you seek. Look is attractively Belle Époque; 15 bath- or shower-equipped rooms. Breakfast only. *Moderate*.

Des Terreaux Hôtel (16 Rue Lanterne; phone 7827-04-10) is named for a central square that's but a block distant. Though modest, its location is a plus; 37 of its 50 rooms have bath or shower. Breakfast only is served. *Moderate.*

Celtic Hôtel (5 Place St.-Paul; phone 7828-01-12) is worth noting, should you be intrigued by the idea of headquartering in Vieux-Lyon. Not quite half of this house's rooms have baths or showers. *Moderate.*

La Part-Dieu—ultra-mod, multifunction complex well away from the center, on the east bank of the Rhône—has as much of the flavor of Lyon, as would, say, a shopping mall in Carson City, Nevada. I say this despite its being the location of the railway station used by TGV high-speed trains and slews of stores. You must take two subways, changing trains en route, to reach the heart of town. Withal, three national chains have Part-Dieu hotels: *Frantel,* with 245 rooms, with a good restaurant and bar on top floors of the quarter's skyscraping circular tower; *Mercure* (at 47 Boulevard Vivier-Merle), with 124 rooms, restaurant serving buffet breakfast, and bar; and *Ibis* (on Place Renaudel), with 144 rooms and a restaurant. The first two are *First Class;* the third, *Moderate.*

Central Hôtel (7 Rue de l'Archevêché, Vienne; phone 7485-18-38) is, indeed, central—well placed for exploration of the core of Vienne—and is, as well, comfortable. There are 26 no-two-quite-alike rooms. Breakfast only. *Moderate.*

DAILY BREAD

Léon de Lyon (1 Rue Pleney; phone 7828-11-33): Restaurants with catchy names don't always live up to expectations. This one does. It *looks* like what we outlanders seek in Lyon: dark wood, stained glass, hanging copper pots, plentiful flowers, waiters in navy blue shirts and trousers protected by long navy aprons. And it *tastes* Lyonnais. Talented patron-chef Jean-Paul Lacombe splits his menu in two; the left is traditional cuisine; the right is M. Lacombe's. Or you may order from a prix-fixe. In either event, it's a good plan to sample both sides of the card. *Saucis-son chaud*—hot sausage served with lentils and boiled potatoes; *quenelle de brochet*—fingers of minced pike—served with *sauce Nantua; entrecôte* accompanied by *sauce marchand de vin;* and *blanquette de veau* —veal stew—typify Lyonnais fare. And M. Lacombe does innovative things with salmon, *foie gras,* chicken, rabbit, and lamb. Chocolate *mousse,* presented in tandem with an orange salad in an orange sauce—along with house-baked *madeleines* served warm—is one of the masterful desserts. Expert, smiling service. Central. In my experience, one of France's best restaurants. Member, Relais et Châteaux. *Luxury.*

Commanderie des Antonins (30 Quai St.-Antoine; phone 7837-19-21): Not for nothing has the Commanderie—situated in the arched, stone-walled *salle capitulaire* of a thirteenth-century monastery—been declared a *Monument Historique*. At dinner, when illumination is almost entirely by candles, I doubt there's a restaurant in town with a more evocative setting. And it tastes as good as it looks. Grills are the big thing here. I suggest opening with *foie gras frais de canard*—fresh duck liver served with hot toast, following with T-bone steak (which is what it's called on the menu) accompanied by sautéed mushrooms, a perfectly baked potato, and, perhaps, artichokes, with lemon tart rum flamed, to conclude. *First Class.*

La Tour Rose (16 Rue du Boeuf; phone 7838-25-90) combines the best of two worlds: a Renaissance-origin, Vieux-Lyon house behind a pink tower—thus its name—as its setting and *nouvelle*-influenced cuisine as its forte. Go at lunch for the good-value prix-fixe menu (not available at dinner), which might open with saffron-scented mussel soup or chicken and avocado salad and continue with *filet mignon* in a ginger sauce accompanied by honey-sauced turnips or a chicken and cabbage stew, with cheese and a choice of luscious desserts to conclude. Friendly. *Luxury.*

Nandron (26 Quai Jean-Moulin; phone 7842-10-26) is lovely and luxuriant—an up-a-flight room fronting the Rhône, with silk-shaded lamps illuminating exquisitely appointed tables. Skilled M. Nandron is in charge of the kitchen. Congenial Madame Nandron is in command out front. Fare is deliciously traditional. Madame Nandron is unhappy if you ask for mustard to accompany your *saucisson chaud*, but they're tasty without it; oysters on the half-shell and *quenelles de brochet* are options. Entrées might be grilled filet of sole, chicken and sweetbread stew that comes off well, roast lamb, or the house's special *tournedos*. And desserts: *Crêpes flambées* Grand Marnier and chocolate *soufflé* should be ordered at the start of the meal and do not disappoint; nor does *chocolat glacé*—mousse in a sponge crust slathered with whipped cream. Member, Relais et Châteaux. *Luxury.*

Chez Dussaud (12 Rue Pizay; phone 7828-10-94) is a typical Lyonnais *bouchon;* these are small, unpretentious restaurants usually operated by female *chef-patronnes*, with hearty Lyonnais fare. In this case, it's Madame Monique who's in charge. There are a few tables out front—her husband is maître d'hotel and waiter. Or you may be seated at one of three tables in the cramped, albeit impeccably organized, kitchen where Madame operates as though she had all the space in the world. Open with *jambon persillé*—a thick slice of parsley-flavored ham served with lentil salad, *rillettes de porc*—a coarsely ground pork *pâté*—or warm potato salad served with a filet of herring. Good entrées are *boeuf Bour-guignon* or filet of veal with mushrooms. Cheese follows (a local St. Marcelin, perhaps), with Madame's still-warm-from-the-oven chocolate cake to conclude. And a bottle of Beaujolais—Lyon's favorite wine. Booking is essential, as there must be a minimum of 20 reservations, and lunch is the only meal. Central. *Moderate.*

Café des Féderations (8 Rue du Major Martin; phone 7828-26-00) is still another *bouchon,* although it's larger than Chez Dussaud (above) and serves dinner, as well as lunch. Hearty, congenial, tasty. Central. *Moderate.*

Orsi (3 Place Kléber; phone 7889-57-68) is rather grand: walls hung with good paintings, nineteenth-century chandeliers, and tables elaborately set and attended by waitresses in long gowns who look as though they might be trendy Smith College students spending their junior year abroad. And if you speak American-accented English—or, for that matter, American-accented French—a set of flags, one French, one the Stars and Stripes, is placed on your table, an unusual touch in France. The four-course-cum-*petits-fours* menu is a good deal, with fare an agreeable *nouvelle*-traditional mix. You might open with potted snails or the house's own *foie gras,* follow with filet of beef, grilled *confit* of duck, or a fish dish. Cheese—you select from a generous-sized platter—is next, with imaginatively prepared desserts to conclude. Member, Relais et Châteaux. *First Class.*

Le Fiorelle (Grand Hôtel Concorde, 11 Rue Grolée; phone 7842-56-21) has a nice, intimate quality; you sit at ladder-back chairs and order corking good Lyonnais fare from either of two menus or à la carte. Vegetable and fish soups are hearty; duck *terrine,* exemplary; entrées like *steak au poivre* and *médaillons* of veal with sautéed mushrooms, excellent. And there's always a *plat du jour* to please neighborhood regulars who are patrons. Friendly. *First Class.*

Le Bistrot de Lyon (64 Rue Mercière; phone 7837-00-62) has the flavor of fin de siècle Lyon. Have a hearty meal of, say, the sausages called *andouillettes,* nicely prepared *grenouilles* (frog's legs), or a *poulet aux morilles* (chicken with mushrooms). Open until 1:30 A.M., with management the same as Léon de Lyon (above). *First Class.*

Le Savoy (20 Rue de la République at Place de la République; phone 7837-69-35) is as much outdoor café—go for coffee or a cold drink—as brasserie, with *quenelles sauce Nantua* and seafood as specialties. Central. *Moderate/First Class.*

Vettard (7 Place Bellecour; phone 7842-07-59) has as a major attribute its situation on Lyon's No. 1 square. It's small, with brown and ivory walls and Louis XVI-style chairs at tables set with Limoges china. There are two prix-fixe menus and—considering this restaurant's steepish prices and exalted reputation—a surprisingly limited à la carte. Fare is uninspired *nouvelle*, and portions tend to be small. One entrée specialty, to give you an idea, consists of modest slices of three grilled meats, each dabbed with a different sauce. But you may fall back on such standbys as *quenelles de brochet*. Disappointing. *Luxury*.

Les Adrets (38 Rue du Boeuf; phone 7838-24-30) is a less pricey alternative to La Tour Rose (above), when a Vieux-Lyon meal is your objective. Order from either of a pair of well-priced prix-fixe menus, both based on typically tasty Lyonnais entrées. Fun. *Moderate*.

Paul Bocuse (Place d'Illaeusern, Collonges-au-Mont-d'Or, six miles north of Lyon; phone 7822-01-40): There is no denying that Paul Bocuse is a genius at self-promotion—surely the cleverest such among the celebrated French master chefs. He anticipates your arrival with giant directional markers and billboards with his likeness, en route. His restaurant, a three-story white house with a giant sign bearing his name atop it, is unabashedly florid. There's a touch of kitsch and show-biz upon arrival; you're greeted first by a smiling page in a scarlet uniform, next by the maître d'hôtel in tails, who turns you over to a tuxedoed captain for the final lap of the escorted trip to your table. Depart the gents' after washing your hands, and pouff! There is M. Bocuse's shop—with cookbooks he has authored available for purchase in the French, German, Spanish, and English languages; Paul Bocuse-brand chocolates, Paul Bocuse-label tea, aprons with Paul Bocuse's name and face reproduced on them, and postcards of the restaurant, which are the most expensive I have encountered in France, save those at the museum operated by the Rothschilds in Médoc (Chapter 10). Back at the table, you remove your napkin from a disposable paper ring with M. Bocuse's *toque-blanche*-topped visage printed on it, sip water from a goblet bearing his name, and, when your meal arrives, eat from porcelain similarly identified. But there's a rub. M. Bocuse produces. His cuisine is, to be sure, innovative, but logically and sensibly. He is not afraid to cook with cream, butter, and wine. Nor to serve you more than you may be able to eat. With flair, with smiles, with love. There are two prix-fixe menus and an extensive à la carte. Under no circumstances would I counsel omitting *soupe aux truffes noires*—the pastry-topped, packed-with-truffles, Bocuse-created *consommé*, first served by the master for a 1975 dinner at Élysée Palace, the Presidential residence in Paris. A typical Bocuse repast might continue with filet of sole presented on a bed of noodles in a light cream sauce, accompanied by mushrooms, peas, and carrots. Cassis-flavored sherbet, a palate cleanser, would arrive next. *Médaillon* of veal crisscrossed with vegetables, tarra-gon-flavored lamb chops, Charolais beef, and roast duckling are typical entrées. Vegetables are served in proper portions, not teaspoon-sized *nouvelle* dabs—and include recognizable peas and spinach and a superb *gratin Dauphinois*, the potato casserole. Cheese? *Three* trolleys are rolled up for you to make a selection. And when you're ready, three *more* trolleys of desserts make their appearance; chocolate *mousse*, *crème brûlée*, *oeufs à la neige* are among them, or you may order *crêpes* to be prepared at table. As if that were not enough, several plates of *petits-fours* and made-on-premises chocolates accompany coffee. If M. Bocuse is present—not always the case, as he travels a lot—chances are, he will come and say hello in the course of this extraordinary gastronomic adventure. In my experience, one of France's best restaurants. *Luxury.*

Pyramide (Boulevard Fernand-Point, Vienne; phone 7453-01-96) is a long-on-scene restaurant founded by a universally acknowledged pio-neer chef. It is a measure of the admiration held for the late Fernand Point that the street on which his restaurant is situated—it occupies an attractive house in its own garden, edging Vienne—was renamed for him, posthumously. Fare remains deliciously traditional, albeit with Point-created variations. A meal might open with a warm scallop salad gar-nished with fresh asparagus tips, followed by *suprême de turbot*, cham-pagne sauced, as the fish course; roast lamb accompanied by *gratin Dauphinois*, string beans, and artichoke hearts as entrée; cheeses in pro-fusion; and such dessert options as Grand Marnier *soufflé* and fruit tarts. Service is gracious and professional. A delightful experience. *Luxury.*

Bec Fin (7 Place St.-Maurice, Vienne; phone 7485-76-72) is conveniently central and indicated for a well-priced lunch after a morning's rounds in Vienne. Select one of the prix-fixe menus. *Moderate/First Class.*

Ostellerie du Vieux-Pérouges (Rue des Princes, Pérouges; phone 7461-00-88)—a beautiful and beautifully appointed thirteenth-century house in a village (above) that is, in toto, a protected national monument—makes a specialty of hearty regional cuisine; take your choice of entrées, making certain, though, that you open with *panache Pérougien* (mushrooms sautéed in a crayfish sauce) and that you con-clude with *galette Pérougienne*, the village's celebrated dessert pancake. (You may overnight in the same management's charming, traditional-style *Manoir Hôtel.)* First Class.

SHOPPER'S LYON

Printemps, the big department store in the center of town, is on Place de la République. *Galeries Lafayette* has a one-floor women's store on Place des Cordeliers, with its major Lyon outlet—multidepartment—in Part-

Dieu. *Grand Bazaar de Lyon*, a long-on-scene department store, is on Rue de la République, the principal shopping street, with such other stores as *Christofle* (silver and china), *Samari* (tapestries and Persian rugs), *Patek Philippe* (watches), *Pierre Cardin* (men's duds), *Lancel* (women's accessories, leather), and *Broliquier* (jewelry). On Place de la République you'll find *Bally* (shoes), *Burberry* (raincoats), and *Voisin* (chocolates). Rue du Président Herriot has the smartest boutiques, including *La Souris* (fancy paper goods and desk sets), *Okapi* (women's handbags), *Léonidas* (chocolates), *Muscade* (women's sportswear), *Rizal* (furs), *Sauté Mouton* (pricey kids' clothes), *Ophélie* (kitchen equipment), *Georges Rech* (haute couture), and *Geneviève Lethu* (crystal).

SOUND OF MUSIC

Opéra de Lyon (Place de la Comédie, Lyon) is the city's Belle Époque opera house; look up from the square, at eight free-standing statues surmounting the facade. Its resident troupe presents a varied repertory, ranging from Rossini's *Barber of Seville* through Weber's *Oberon*, with works, as well, by *Ballet de l'Opéra de Lyon* and visiting troupes.

Auditorium Maurice Ravel (Rue de Bonnel)—strikingly contemporary—is the city's principal concert hall for performances of *Orchestre de Lyon* and other musical groups. (The two major Lyon festivals—International every June, and Berlioz every September—take place in these venues, as well as at *Théâtre Romain*, the ancient amphitheater.)

INCIDENTAL INTELLIGENCE

Stations of Lyon's spanking modern *Métro*, or subway system, are recognized by orange signs. Method of operation is based on that of Paris (Chapter 2), except, of course, that Lyon's network is infinitely smaller. There are two main railway stations—*Gare de Perrache*, adjacent to the center of town, and *Gare de la Part-Dieu*, considerably east of the center; ascertain in advance from which station your train will depart. *Aéroport International de Satolas*, 17 miles southeast of town—and connected with Gare de Perrache by frequently departing buses that make the journey in 45 minutes—is No. 2 in France after Paris's De Gaulle, serving more than 80 destinations: domestic, European, African, and Middle Eastern. *Further information:* Office de Tourisme, Place Bellecour, Lyon; Office de Tourisme, 3 Cours Brillier, Vienne.

22

Marseille
Mediterranean Metropolis

BACKGROUND BRIEFING

Credit where it is due: Ancient Greeks came upon a massive Mediterranean crescent of a beach—backed by high hills—some 2,600 years ago, and in establishing their colony of *Massilia*, they created what has come to be France's oldest city. And, I might add, its most beautifully situated.

It was the scheme of things for Romans to follow, and it was logical that, given its location, medieval Marseille would benefit from traffic between its port and the Middle East during the long Crusades period. Enough so for it to have attracted attention in the ancient Kingdom of Provence, which vanquished it in the thirteenth century, only to be conquered two centuries later by a more powerful France.

Today's Marseille is a fascinating fusion of cultures and peoples and ideas. Call it what you will: metropolis of the south; premier city of Provence; major port of the Mediterranean. Marseille is good-looking, good fun, and a distinctive dimension of the French experience.

ON SCENE

Lay of the Land: Aptly named Vieux-Port–the old harbor whose finger-like contours attracted the ancient Greeks—was the core of the original *Massilia*. It protruded from the Mediterranean into the heart of the city, protected by venerable *Forts St.-Jean* and *St.-Nicholas*—one on either side of its entrance—and is ringed by a café and restaurant-lined promenade variously called *Quai du Port, Quai des Belges,* and *Quai de Rive Neuve. Notre-Dame-de-la-Garde,* a nineteenth-century church that looks better from a distance than close up, straddles an eminence to the harbor's west, and with its high tower is a Marseille landmark. More easily visited *Hôtel de Ville*—the City Hall—is a splendidly scaled Baroque palace at water's edge (you want to ascend its grand staircase for a view from the harbor-view reception room). Inland makes easy geographic sense, thanks to the broad boulevard, *La Canebière*, that proceeds north from Quai des Belges. *Rue St.-Ferréol*, perpendicular with it and jutting east, is Marseille's smartest shopping street; others in the neighbor-hood—*Rue du Paradis, Rue de la République, Rue de Rome, Cours Belsance*—are shop-lined, too. *Gare St.-Charles*, the railway station, is northwest of the center. The modern harbor, which has long since supplemented Vieux-Port, edges the western flank of town, while *Corniche J. F. Kennedy* follows the scenic coast east of town, eventually becoming *Promenade de la Plage*—lining the beaches where Marseille spends its summer lei-sure.

Exploring Vieux-Port: Marseille's geography is such that visitors tend to concentrate on the core, ignoring the Vieux-Port area, redolent of earlier centuries. Of the unexpected pair of *Cathédrales de la Major* (Quai de la Tourette), the elder (and no longer used) is lovely twelfth-century Romanesque, but you must ask for the key in the sacristy of its next-door, nineteenth-century successor. *Fort St.-Jean*, with a landmark, fifteenth-century tower, is a hop and skip distant. *Basilica of St.-Victor* —on the other side of the harbor, adjacent to seventeenth-century *Fort St.-Nicholas*, on Rue Neuve Ste.-Catherine—is a fabulously fortified church with a pair of crenelated towers replete with crypt and catacombs: It's nine hundred years old. Beyond Vieux-Port, out in the harbor, you can't help but admire the profile of the small, walled island atop of which are battlements of the very same *Château d'If* you recall from Dumas's *The Count of Monte Cristo*. King François I built it in the sixteenth century and excursion boats make tours.

A Trio of Ancient-Marseille Museums: Newest of this extraordinary group is *Jardin des Vestiges* (Rue Barbuse), an area more or less the size of a stadium that was accidentally uncovered in the course of construct-ing the adjacent—and graceless—Centre Bourse shopping complex as recently as 1967. Amble about Greek/Roman Marseille in this pretty garden quite literally studded with fragments—bits of walls, ruined ramparts—of the ancient city. *Musée d'Histoire de Marseille* (Centre Bourse, Cours Belsance) adjoins Jardin des Vestiges and shelters treasures found in its confines during the 1960s excavations. They are presented chrono-logically, 600 B.C. (the Greek settlement) through 400 A.D. (the Ro-mans), with quite the most amazing exhibit comprised of the contents of a Roman ship wrecked in the third century. *Musée des Docks Romains* (Place Vivaux) is on the actual site of piers dating to the early Roman trader-settlers, with displays ranging from oil jars to boat fragments.

Musée du Vieux-Marseille (2 Rue de la Prison) makes its home in Maison des Diamants, so called because of the striking diamond design of its sixteenth-century facade. Two floors of galleries constitute one of the best—and most amusing—of French museums of municipal history, with the range high-caliber furniture and superb engravings through fetchingly displayed costumes and the carved-wood figures—typical of Provence—called *santons*.

Musée de la Marine (Palais de la Bourse, Quai des Belges) is of interest not so much for its exhibits—models of sailing ships and early steamers—as for its setting: the very grand neoclassic hall of a onetime stock exchange erected at the peak of Marseille's nineteenth-century Golden Age, now the Chamber of Commerce and with occasional special shows.

Musée Cantini (19 Rue Grignan, in the shopping district) makes for a serene diversion in the course of a morning's exploration. The setting is felicitous, and the contents consist mostly of pottery and porcelain, seventeenth and eighteenth century—and quite beautiful.

Musée Grobet-Labadie (140 Boulevard Longchamp): I save this all-France ranker of a museum (and its neighbor—Musée des Beaux-Arts, below) for the end of this section only because they are farthest away from the center. Named for the woman who lived within—born Mlle. Labadie, later Madame Grobet, who, first with her industrialist father, later with M. Grobet, collected and arranged its contents—the Grobet-Labadie is a museum of decorative arts on a level with counterparts in Paris, Bordeaux, and Lyon. But, possibly because its name does not signify its subject matter, it remains nothing like as celebrated. With the exception of certain of the collections—musical instruments, some decorative ironwork, a room full of sculptures—what you encounter is a series of rooms occupying two floors of a mid-nineteenth-century mansion, each furnished and accessorized in period by the onetime owners, the lot constituting a compendium of what was best in the decorative arts of the seventeenth and eighteenth centuries. There's not a room in the house you wouldn't want to live—or at least entertain—in: Louis XIV salon, with a spinet and Aubusson tapestries; Régence-furnished, paneled dining room; Louis XV bedroom, with paintings by Murillo and Nattier; upstairs sitting room, Louis XVI furnished, its walls with paintings by Boucher, Fragonard, Watteau, and Greuze; music room, its ceiling coffered, with an eighteenth-century harp, needlepoint-covered furniture, art on its walls by England's Constable and France's Daubigny.

Musée des Beaux-Arts (Boulevard Longchamp) went up in the Napoleon III period, when museums were supposed to look palatial. This one is gained by flights of steps that frame a reflecting pool and sculpted fountains, with a colonnade at the summit and the *palais* beyond. It's worth the climb. Paintings most relevant to Marseille are a pair by a local artist, Michel Serre, who lived through the city's eighteenth-century plague epidemic and recorded its suffering citizens—in one picture, before still-standing Hôtel de Ville, in the other, on a local boulevard. There are more celebrated works, as well. Simon Vouet's olive-complexioned *Virgin and Child* is surely the most memorable, but you are bound to be drawn, as well, to Rubens's exciting *Wild Boar Hunt*, Vigée-Lebrun's coquettish *Duchesse d'Orléans*, Signac's pointillist interpretation of the city's Vieux-Port. And so much else: Tintoretto and Perugino, Carracci and Bassano, Zurbarán and Antonio Mor, Oudry and Panini, Fragonard and Tiepolo, David and Millet, Courbet and Corot.

Cassis (14 miles east of Marseille) was pretty enough for Dufy and Matisse to have painted it. Proximity to the big city notwithstanding, it remains so. The inner harbor—a still paintable mix of seafood restaurants and bobbing fishing boats—is indicated for an excursion-cum-lunch out of Marseille, after which it's fun to take a boat ride to *Les Calanques*, the coastal area just west of the village and bordered by dramatic high cliffs.

SETTLING IN
Beauveau Hôtel (4 Rue Beauveau; phone 9154-91-00) is a nineteenth-century house with the best location in town: directly facing Vieux-Port, with the core of town to its rear. Hope that some needed refurbishing will have taken place by the time of your arrival; on my last visit such was indicated. There are 72 rooms, nicely furnished and accessorized in period, with those higher up and in front affording spectacular harbor views. A bar named "1920"—but which looks 1890s and is delightful—adjoins the lobby. Breakfast, the only meal served, is either from a generous buffet, or you may have it in your room. Friendly. A PLM hotel. *First Class.*

Noailles Hôtel (68 La Canebière; phone 9154-91-48): The days when luxury hotels lined the boulevard-like Canabière are, alas, gone. But the Noailles—no longer with its Louis XV restaurant—carries on, contemporarily updated, with 70 full-facility rooms and a congenial bar-lounge. Breakfast only. Mapotel/Best Western. *First Class.*

De Genève Hôtel (3-bis Rue Reine Elisabeth; phone 9190-51-42) has a convenient, near-Vieux-Port location and welcomes with an attractive and capacious lobby-lounge and half a hundred rooms, some traditional style (with brass beds), others plainly contemporary. Breakfast only. *Moderate.*

Grand Modern Hôtel (5 La Canebière; phone 9190-15-60) is more modern than grand, with a clean-lined lobby, friendly reception, and just under 50 neat rooms. Location is excellent—foot of La Canebière, facing Vieux-Port. *Moderate.*

Résidence du Vieux-Port Hôtel (18 Quai du Port; phone 9191-91-22) could have done with a bit of sprucing up on my last inspection, but there is no denying the fabulous views from its front rooms. Some have terraces, and from all of them the Vieux-Port is just out front. Les Santonniers Restaurant is on the premises. *Moderate.*

Concorde Palm Beach Hôtel (2 Promenade de la Plage; phone 9176-20-20) was just as sprightly-modern and attractive on my most recent visit of inspection as on an earlier occasion when I stayed overnight. Indeed, it would head my list, were it central. Still, if you've a car, you can combine its beachfront locale with the city—a quarter-hour's drive distant. There are 161 good-sized, well-equipped, terraced rooms—you want to specify a front seaview one—as well as an excellent restaurant, cocktail lounge, and big, sundeck-surrounded swimming pool. Chaîne Concorde. *First Class.*

Frantel Marseille (29 Place St.-Thibault, in the massive Centre Bourse shopping center; phone 9191-91-29) has as its principal attribute a heart-of-town location. Each of its 200 minimalist-decor rooms has but one small window. I mention this only because Marseille can be steamy-humid spring through autumn (when most pleasure visitors are in town), and when the Frantel's air-conditioning breaks down—as it did in the course of my stay, not to be repaired, management advised, for four days—I am here to tell you there is precious little ventilation available from a single, compact window. Restaurant, bar. *First Class.*

Sofitel Marseille Vieux-Port (36 Boulevard Charles-Livon; phone 9152-90-19) is, it should be made clear, at the *far end* of Vieux-Port, so that the center of town is a 15-minute walk away. There are 222 rooms and a choice of restaurants and bars. In the course of my first visit, I returned to my room before eleven o'clock the morning of my departure to find my baggage missing (I was to have left at noon—checkout time). After making anxious inquiries at reception, I learned that management, expecting a new arrival for my room, had decided to pack me up and move me out—without consulting me and while the room was still mine. On a return visit to inspect the hotel, with the best of good will, reception staff was at once inept, disagreeable, and unwelcoming. I am not a fan. *First Class.*

Le Petit Nice Hôtel (Anse de Maldormé, off Corniche Kennedy, a 20-minute drive from Marseille; phone 9152-14-39) is a country inn, with 16 vividly decorated suites and rooms—much orange, royal blue, and emerald green velvet—the lot of them antiques accented and with excellent baths, some with stall showers. There are, as well, swimming pool, bar, and restaurant. Vibrant-hued decor aside, the impression I am left with is ambience so chilling, you could cut it with a knife. Indeed, no other Relais et Châteaux member-hotel has, in my experience, appeared so frigid in the course of inspection. Except in winter, lunch or dinner—*demi-pension*—is obligatory. *First Class.*

DAILY BREAD

Le Chaudron Provençal (49 Rue Caisserie; phone 9191-02-37) is small, plain as an old shoe, with Monsieur Paul the skilled chef and Madame Paul out in front, welcoming each customer and, preparatory to taking orders, carrying over an immense basket full of the day's catch, so that you know just what it is you're going to have for lunch or dinner. This is a super spot to sample *bouillabaisse*, the celebrated seafood soup/stew of Marseille. Its preparation and service has become so codified in recent years that a dozen-odd restaurants who make it a specialty have combined to publish a brochure indicating what its component parts should be. There must be four out of a possible eight coastal species of fish and either *langouste* or *cigale de mer*, of the crayfish family. There are 10 additional ingredients—including saffron, garlic, potatoes, and olive oil; and the hot sauce called *rouille* should be an accompaniment. The restaurateurs are more permissive when it comes to service, although they make it clear they prefer that *bouillabaisse* be ladled out in two parts—the fish and shellfish separated from the soup. Try it here at Chaudron Provençal. Or order a seafood dinner embracing oysters on the half shell and a fish you've selected from Madame's basket. *First Class.*

Les Santonniers (18 Quai du Port; phone 9120-44-63) is indicated, if you're determined to follow first-timer-in-Marseille tradition and be served *bouillabaisse* on an outdoor table in Vieux-Port. Service is pleasant; the view, likewise; the *bouillabaisse*, only middling. *First Class.*

Le Jambon de Parme's (67 Rue de la Palud; phone 9156-37-98) setting is a neoclassic, quite formal room with brown suede walls, ivory paneling, crystal chandeliers, and a profusion of fresh flowers. It's staffed by tuxedoed waiters, smiling and cordial, and a chef who turns out pasta quite as delicious as any you are going to be served over the frontier to the east in Italy. *Tortellini alla Modenese, tagliatelli al pistou,* and *ravioli* are masterful. So are entrées like *piccata* of veal, Cassis-sauced duckling, and *châteaubriand*. For dessert: *zuppa inglese*, as you remember it from Rome or Florence. A delightful experience. *First Class.*

L'Oursin (14 Cours Ballard; phone 9133-34-85)—given its name, sea urchin—had just better serve seafood, and, of course, does. Oysters and other crustaceans from a big ice-surfaced buffet are indicated as openers, with grilled fish of the day to follow. *Moderate.*

Le Charpentier (22 Rue de la Paix; phone 9154-22-89) is mod-look and central; Provençal specialties are tasty, and if you go on Friday or Saturday evening, ooh-la-la! The chef will have prepared a multicourse *menu gastronomique*. *First Class.*

La Samaritaine (2 Quai du Port; phone 9199-31-41): Take an outdoor table, and watch ambulatory Marseille pass in review with Vieux-Port just beyond, while you order an omelet or *steak/frites* lunch. In the afternoon: tea and pastries. *Moderate.*

Le Petit Louvre (19 La Canebière; phone 9190-17-44) is worth knowing about: two daily prix-fixe menus. *Moderate/First Class.*

La Boutique du Glacier (Place Général de Gaulle) is an ice-cream parlor *extraordinaire*. So long as you're prepared for a bit of congestion—all Marseille seems intent on a *boule fraise* or a *boule citron* on a hot day—you can't help but be content. *Moderate.*

Lieutaud (on the harbor in Cassis; phone 01-75-37) is just the spot for lunch on a Cassis excursion; the *bouillabaisse* is celebrated, and there are other seafood options, as well. Take an outdoor table. *First Class.*

SHOPPER'S MARSEILLE
Le Marché aux Poissons (Marché des Capucins at the foot of La Canebière) is the daily seafood market, with more species of for-sale fish and seafood than I venture you'll have seen anywhere else in France. Best time to have a look is the morning; more fun than an aquarium. Major department stores—*Galeries Lafayette, Nouvelles Galeries, Dames de France*—are all on Rue St.-Ferréol, a shopping street with such other stores as *Cacharel* (men's and women's clothes), *Le Must de Cartier* (jewelry), *Bally* (shoes), and *Burberry* (raincoats). Rue Grignan makes a point of menswear shops, including *Daniel Crémieux, Alain Figaret, Façonnable*—all links of smart chains. The massive and confusing Centre Bourse has such shops as *Dans un Jardin* (a perfume chain), *Descamps* (linens), *Alain Manoukian* and *Rodier* (women's clothes), and *Paparazzi* (men's and women's sportswear).

SOUND OF MUSIC
Opéra de Marseille (Place Revyer): You'll have passed this neoclassic landmark. Book a seat, if you can, for the opera (which averages a dozen productions each winter season, ranging from Richard Strauss's *Salomé* to Joseph Strauss's *Vienna Waltzes*, Rossini's *Barber of Seville* to Milhaud's *Christophe Colomb*). This theater is home base, as well, to Roland Petit's *Ballet de Marseille*; concerts, too. (Office de Tourisme—address below—can advise you of programs in this and other theaters.)

INCIDENTAL INTELLIGENCE ═══════════════════

Aéroport de Marseille–Marignane (18 miles north of town); both international and domestic services. *Further information:* Office de Tourisme, 4 La Canebière, Marseille; Office de Tourisme, Place Baragnon, Cassis.

23

Monaco
Big Things in Small Packages

BACKGROUND BRIEFING
There is something to be said for a ruling house that has been in business since the twelfth century. At the back of the little guidebook they used to sell at the Prince's Palace in the 390-acre Principality of Monaco, there is a genealogical table of the House of Grimaldi, which indicates that it was founded in 1133 by one Otto Canella, whose son gave his name, Grimaldi, to the clan. Rainier III, the current reigning prince, came along 30 Grimaldis later, Rainier II—according to that table—having concluded his reign in 1407.

Succession? Prince Rainier shared his throne with the late Princess Grace, who, as Philadelphia-born Grace Kelly, gave up a successful film career to marry Rainier in 1956; she died following a 1982 auto crash. They had three children. The youngest and eldest are princesses: Caroline, divorced and remarried (born 1957), and Stéphanie (born 1965). Their blond brother, Prince Albert (born 1958), educated in Europe and America and resembling his late mother more than do either of his sisters—is heir to this ancient, if hardly impoverished, throne.

The Monaco that the world knows today as a tiny enclave surrounded on three sides by France, on the fourth by the Mediterranean, with a pair of solid gold casinos as its trademark, was impoverished to the point of bankruptcy something over a century ago. It was during the reign of Prince Charles. The principality had to give up territory to France—the nearby towns of Menton and Roquebrune, with the small settlement atop the rocky promontory of Monaco constituting the bulk of the remaining territory.

But Prince Charles—a handsome, intelligent-looking man, if the portrait of him in the palace is a guide—had an idea. Better to say he adapted an idea—the scheme of the Duke of Baden, who had opened a profitable casino at Baden-Baden, his German spa (see *Germany at Its*

Best). Charles decided to do likewise. Success did not come overnight, so in 1860 he hired a pro to take over the enterprise. Before 1870 there was rail service from Nice, and business at the casino was so good that the prince did away with direct taxes (as have all of his successors).

Before long, the Riviera had its most fashionable resort. The rich English came over from older, neighboring communities, to what they termed "Montie," and royalty made its way to the gaming tables, too. Although the Principality of Monaco retained its name, the area of the principality in which the new casino was situated had its name changed from hardly glamorous Les Spélugues to Monte Carlo, the Italian for Mount Charles, in honor of the enterprising man on the throne.

Until as recently as 1911, Monaco's princes were absolute rulers. A new constitution in that year set up a representative government, under a chief minister and an 18-member National Council. Women were given the vote only in 1962 (an American-born Princess may have had something to do with this). In the interim—in 1918—Monaco signed a treaty with France in which it agreed that the French Government would have to approve succession to the throne; that with cessation of the monarchy, Monaco would become a part of France, and that its for long untaxed citizens would become subject to French taxation. Needless to say, there has never been a republican movement in Monaco, and so long as Monégasques enjoy the bliss of freedom from taxes, it is not expected that there will be moves in that direction.

Not everyone living in Monaco is Monégasque. By no means. Something like 6,000 out of an estimated population hovering at the 30,000 mark, are citizens. A great majority are French, and must pay French taxes unless they were Monaco residents prior to 1957. And not a few other residents are successful foreign nationals come to live in the Riviera sunshine—and save paying high income taxes in their native lands. They populate seaview condominium apartments in an ever-increasing mass of skyscrapers; Monaco is the Riviera at its most decidedly vertical.

The buildings' construction reflects the aggressive development policy Prince Rainier adopted when, in 1967, his government bought out—for $8 million—Greek shipping tycoon Aristotle Onassis's controlling 52 percent of the Société des Bains de Mer, the euphemistically named company formed by Prince Charles in the last century to run the casino and which had become owner of hotels, clubs, restaurants, and cafés.

In control of their own ship, Monégasques charted a new course, welcoming foreign hotels (America's Loews and Britain's Trusthouse Forte are on scene), constructing a giant of a convention center to attract congresses, and making a strong bid for middle-income visitors to supplement a traditionally blue-chip clientele, the while encouraging development of high-rise condos. Even allowing for some 75 additional acres gained by reclamation of land from the sea, it has not been possible to preclude congestion.

Monaco's situation—straddling an irregular Mediterranean shore, with rugged hills and distant snowy peaks as a backdrop—will always be a magnet. So will its feisty people, stubbornly clinging to the anachronistic form of government that allows them independence, even as they are hemmed in by a herculean neighbor. The Casino de Monte Carlo remains the most glamorous extant, and the long-on-scene leading hotels, De Paris and Hermitage, remain two of the most beautiful in Europe. The guard changes, day in and day out, at the palace, high on a rocky eminence over the blue-green sea. A white- or even black-tie gala at the Opéra or the Sporting Club, the thrust toward egalitarianism notwithstanding, remains as gala an evening as one is likely to come across along the coast. (It must be remembered that Monégasques take their Royal Family and its titles *very* seriously, indeed, as do the French.) Still, when all is said and done, a price is being paid for financial gains and burgeoning real estate. Monaco's charm quotient diminishes with the arrival on site of each new construction crew.

ON SCENE
Lay of the Land: Terminology first. The country—area is less than 500 acres—is termed *Principauté de Monaco*, the Principality of Monaco. Its oldest sector is called either *Monaco* or *The Rock*, for it is an elevated stony peninsula that juts into the Mediterranean. It overlooks the principal harbor to its east, the Port of Monaco, which is flanked by a sea-level commercial and residential area, *La Condamine*, which separates Monaco from *Monte Carlo*, due east and site of the casinos, leading hotels, most shops, and beaches. The other harbor, *Port de Fontvielle*, is west of the Monaco promontory, flanking an area embracing the *Héliport* (from which scheduled helicopters connect Monaco with Nice) and the relatively recent *Louis II Stadium*, with a pair of French villages, each called *Èze*, not far distant. The Monte Carlo sector is based on *Place du Casino*, named for the Casino dominating it, with *Centre des Congrès*, the principal convention complex due south, edging the sea; *Avenue des Beaux-Arts*—lined with classy shops—to its west; and a block-long green boulevard—*Allée des Boulingrins*—leading north to shops of *Boulevard des Moulins*, an east-west thoroughfare. Eastern Monaco's precincts are gained by *Avenue Princesse Grace*, which leads from the core to wide, white sands of *Plage de Larvotto*, *Monte Carlo Sporting Club* straddling a green peninsula just beyond, with the sands and cliffs of *Roquebrune* on France's *Cap Martin*, immediately to the east.

Casino de Monte Carlo (Place du Casino): Mock Baroque, in the best traditions of the Second Empire, the casino's portico—surmounted by a pair of mini-towers backed by a glass dome framed by a pair of maxi-towers—gives on to the carefully tended floral core of the square taking its name. Opened in 1863, it retains original frescoes, sculpture, stained glass, gilded woodwork, and silk-shaded lamps hung from high ceilings over the gaming tables. It has, to be sure, reflected changes in gamblers' tastes—slot machines, for example, and more recently, an informal dress code for the onetime Salon de l'Europe, rechristened the American Room and with American roulette, blackjack, and craps—not to mention English-speaking, Nevada-trained croupiers. Withal, though, the casino remains the essence of Monte Carlo grandeur. The European Gaming Rooms—Salle Touzet, Salon Privé, and, if you please, Salon *Super*-Privé (where stakes are *very* high and whose open hours are by appointment only)—persist in requiring passports for admission and jackets and ties for gents (the American Room does not). They are devoid of slots, concentrating, as has long been the case, on European roulette, trente et quarante, and baccarat; with quite good restaurants and bars in connection.

As they have for as long as I can remember, the European Gaming Rooms open at 10 in the morning, continuing unshuttered through the wee hours. A part of the Casino's complex, Monte Carlo's opera house—called *Salle Garnier* in honor of its designer, the very same Charles Garnier who created the Opéra in Paris—does not, more's the pity, keep daytime hours; it is open only for performances. I don't know of a small-space theater anywhere in Europe that is more beautiful; whatever the performance during your stay, go. (Monte Carlo's second casino is Las Vegas-on-the-Mediterranean—a ballroom-sized space in neighboring Loews Monte-Carlo Hotel [below], with the same games as in the Casino de Monte Carlo's American Room, and—fear not—masses of slot machines.)

Palais Princier (Place du Palais) is essentially a Renaissance building with strong overtones of just-down-the-road Italy; the palace gained some crenelated towers in the late nineteenth century during the rich Prince Charles era. Architecturally, it is at its best in a stunning galleried courtyard (wisely put to good use for summer concerts). Nor do the state rooms disappoint: frescoed vault of the *Galerie d'Hercule*, busts of past princes in *Galerie des Glaces*; princely chair on a dais surmounted by a canopy topped with a crown in the *Throne Room*; a gilded bed behind a likewise gilded rail beneath opulent ceiling frescoes, in *Chambre d'York*, so called because an eighteenth-century Duke of York—brother to George III—died in it; eighteenth-century paintings of France's Louis XV and his consort, in *Salon Louis XV*; superbly decorated seventeenth-century walls and furniture of that epoch in *Salle Mazarin*. *Art note:* It is curious that the wealthy Grimaldis, reigning over long centuries, have not endowed the principality with a museum of fine arts. But there *are* good paintings on the walls of Palais Princier's state rooms; be on the lookout, as you move about, for works by Sebastian Bourdon, Philippe de Champaigne, Lebrun and Mignard, Largillière and Rigaud, Giorgione and Giordano.

Traditionally, the *Changing of the Guard* takes place every morning at the palace; you must not—I caution—expect anything like the spit and polish of the ceremony at London's Buckingham Palace (see *Britain at Its Best*). The palace proper—by that I mean the state rooms—again, traditionally, are open to visitors only from July through September. *Musée du Souvenir Napoléonien* (in the Palace complex) keeps year-round hours; its exhibits are uniforms, weapons, and documents of the Napoleonic era collected by a nineteenth-century prince, with some historic Monaco displays, as well.

Musée National Automates et Poupées d'Autrefois (Boulevard du Larvotto, above Larvotto Beach) may—or may not—be your cup of tea. It's a collection of dolls—400 all told—animated and otherwise, mostly eighteenth and nineteenth century.

Cathedral of Monaco (Rue de l'Église) is late nineteenth-century mock-Romanesque and hardly beautiful, albeit with a pair of altars painted by a respected area artist, Louis Brea, in the sixteenth century; and with tombs of Monaco princes.

Èze: There are two French villages called Èze, each about five miles west of Monte Carlo. Èze-Bord-de-Mer is a pleasant seaside village. But it's to just plain Èze—a onetime medieval fortress, on the summit of a mountain 1,200 feet above the sea, to which I now direct you, either for an excursion that would coincide with lunch or, better yet, an overnight stay. The views from on high—all along the coast—are spectacular. And it's fun to wander the narrow, hilly streets, flanked by ancient stone houses, poking about myriad shops in which are sold handmade jewelry, knitwear, leather, pottery, glass, Provençal cotton, and Riviera olives. But you want also to have a look at thirteenth-century *Chapelle de Ste.-Croix* (one of a number of charming churches), trek through pretty cactus-filled *Jardin Exotique*, and inspect locally created Renaissance paintings in *Musée d'Histoire et d'Art Religieux*.

SETTLING IN
De Paris Hôtel (Place du Casino, Monte Carlo; phone 9350-80-80) was a New Year's gift to the principality when it opened on January 1, 1864. Its original two stories have expanded to eight. But the ambience of this grande dame of the coast remains nineteenth century. A crystal chandelier, affixed to a glass dome, illuminates the amber-toned lobby. The adjacent bar-lounge is a study in Art Nouveau. Salle Empire, the principal restaurant, retains its original massive murals, with gilded capitals on Corinthian columns supporting its high, arched ceiling. A hundred and ten of the 300 rooms have been refurbished relatively recently in contemporary style, with white lacquer furniture upholstered in soft

pastels. Indeed, the refurbished suites—especially the one often frequented by Churchill and named in his memory—are, in my view, the most beautiful in France (if I may be permitted to so link Monaco with France at this point), along with those of the Crillon and Ritz in Paris. But less exalted accommodations are hardly to be despised; baths throughout are smashing, and many rooms have balconies. When you book, specify seaview (priciest), Place du Casino view (second priciest), or Avenue des Beaux-Arts (least pricey). A second restaurant, the rooftop-cum-view Grill, rates additional comment on a later page. The De Paris is flagship of the SBM group—and deservedly so. *Luxury.*

Hermitage Hôtel (Square Beaumarchais, Monte Carlo; phone 9359-67-31) might better be called the Belle Époque. This is an enchanter of a turn-of-century period piece. The original gingerbread facade—with a painted frieze extending the length of the top of the building and with sculpted angels and bearded gents' heads supporting wrought-iron balconies—is impeccably maintained. Public spaces include a winter garden topped by a stained-glass dome and a restaurant (evaluated in a later paragraph) that is one of the handsomest in Europe. Fifty-two of the 200 rooms have been refurbished in a smart, Art Nouveau motif as part of a multimillion-franc renovation program; they're lovely. And the health-club-cum-pool, which the Hermitage shares with the De Paris, is café equipped. I wish, though, that service was more spontaneous and smiling. But you can't have everything. An SBM hotel. *Luxury.*

Beach Plaza Hôtel (22 Avenue Princesse Grace, Monte Carlo; phone 9330-98-80) went up a decade or so back as a Holiday Inn. A few seasons ago, Trusthouse Forte, the ranking British chain, took it over and did it over stylishly and tastefully, in a contemporary-traditional mix. The beauty part of the BP is that it's one of but two Monte Carlo hotels beachfront. (The other is farther-from-the-center Monte Carlo Beach Hotel, below.) And it has a good-sized pool, as well. The 300 rooms are capacious and terraced, with good baths; precisely half are seaview—the ones to aim for. There is a pair of restaurants (one of which I review on a later page) and a poolside café that's a pleasure for lunch. Cozy bar-lounge, too. Friendly. *Luxury.*

Mirabeau Hôtel (1 Avenue Princesse Grace, Monte Carlo; phone 9325-45-45), newest of the SBM hotels, is unprepossessing from without; the facade is almost too severe, and it's a bit tricky of access if you're a pedestrian, although it is conveniently central, below Place du Casino. Once inside, you perceive that the Mirabeau has a nice, intimate quality; modern, but not too big. There are a hundred rooms (those I've inspected are immense, with super baths); seaview rooms are the most in demand. The pool is surrounded by a big sundeck, the bar-lounge congenial, the restaurant convenient, and the staff cordial. *First Class.*

Loews Monte-Carlo Hôtel (Avenue Spélugues, Monte Carlo; phone 9350-65-00) is ingeniously designed. Only a really talented architect could have fitted this 636-room giant into the core of Monte Carlo—just below Place du Casino, adjacent to the Convention Center and straddling the sea—with a profile so low that it defers to (and does not conflict with) the nineteenth-century architecture of the square up the hill. The casino leading from the massive lobby is Las Vegas style (see above). The seaview swimming pool is good sized, as are bedrooms, which have excellent baths. There is a trio of restaurants and as many bars, including one edging the lobby with a sea view. *Luxury.*

Du Louvre Hôtel (16 Boulevard des Moulins, Monte Carlo; phone 9350-65-25) has the advantage of a location on a principal shopping street, core of town; 32 functional rooms with bath. Breakfast only. *Moderate.*

Balmoral Hôtel (12 Avenue de la Costa, Monte Carlo; phone 9350-62-37), elderly and central, with an agreeable lobby-lounge and 72 rooms; those I have inspected have soft mattresses. Chilly atmosphere. Restaurant. *Moderate.*

Monte Carlo Beach Hôtel (Roquebrune/Cap-Martin, France; phone 9378-21-40): Though actually across the frontier in France—just barely—this hotel is one of the Monte Carlo-based SBM group; indeed, it's that company's elderly Old Beach Hotel thoroughly refurbished and with a new name. This is the only hotel on the beach, other than the Beach Plaza (above), closer in to town. There are just half a hundred comfortable rooms—furniture is white rattan and every room is seaview, with a terrace—as well as a restaurant and bar-lounge. Olympic-size swimming pool overlooking sand and sea. Within walking distance of the center. Closed in winter. *First Class.*

Vistaero Hôtel (Grande Corniche, Roquebrune/Cap-Martin, France; phone 9335-01-50) is a modern house quite literally perched atop a Grand Corniche cliff a thousand feet above the sea. You can imagine what views are like from the 25 terraced rooms and suites: Those on the west overlook Monaco; those on the east have equally fabulous coastal vistas. Restaurant, bar-lounge, swimming pool/sundeck. *Luxury.*

Château de la Chèvre d'Or Hôtel (Èze-Village, France; phone 9341-12-12)—of medieval origin—is stone-walled, with an antiques-accented lounge, swimming pool hugging the edge of an eminence that affords smashing coastal views, pretty courtyard where breakfast is served, half a dozen rooms and three suites, no two alike, and a reputable restaurant—seafood is a specialty—that's enjoyable for a candlelit dinner, as well as for lunch in the course of an excursion from Monaco. An enchanter. Member, Relais et Châteaux. *First Class.*

Le Cap Estel Hôtel (Èze-Bord-de-Mer, France; phone 9301-50-44) straddles an elevated park-like promontory jutting into the Mediterranean and is so situated that there are sea views from all 37 terraced rooms. Public spaces are gracious and in traditional style. The restaurant—picture windowed and Louis XVI accented—moves either to a broad terrace or under trees on the lawn in warm weather. And there is a pair of big pools—one, enclosed for cool periods; the other, al fresco and with a sundeck. *Luxury.*

DAILY BREAD
Le Grill (De Paris Hôtel, Place du Casino, Monte Carlo; phone 9350-80-80): What I categorize as top-of-the-world restaurants—those with wide-angle panoramic views—do not always come off so well with respect to cuisine. The Grill atop the De Paris is an exception of consequence. (And it has a retractable roof for under-the-stars dining on balmy evenings.) But you are dealing here with a crew of pros, chefs through waiters. What the French call *grillades—châteaubriand,* served with a wine and shallot sauce, *paillards* of veal, filet of beef, lamb chops—are delicious and imaginatively garnished. But there are other good bets—lobster in champagne and *maigret de canard,* among them. Cream of watercress soup and seafood salad are good openers. And desserts deserve the separate card they are accorded. Be sure to peruse the wine list; the cellar of the De Paris (hewn out of rock in 1874 and open by appointment to guests) prides itself not only on quality, which would be expected here, but quantity: The bottle you drink is one of an inventory totaling 200,000, with a 1945 Château Mouton Rothschild Premier Cru rated as its rarest vintage. *Luxury.*

Belle Époque (Hermitage Hôtel, Square Beaumarchais, Monte Carlo; phone 9350-67-31) is as requisite a Monte Carlo dining experience as the Grill of the De Paris (above). Substitute turn-of-century ambience here for the Grill's Mediterranean views. Ceiling frescoes are framed by gilded stucco. A marble colonnade—each pillar topped with a gilded Ionic capital—wraps itself around the room, illuminated by crystal chandeliers. Silver candelabra grace dinner tables. And fare remains stubbornly traditional, albeit imaginative—truffled *foie gras* and smoked salmon, among appetizers; scallop-and-green-noodle casserole standing out among seafood entrées; with veal *piccata,* lamb filet with the chef's own sauce, and roast chicken with mushrooms other good bets. Warm desserts are a specialty here; consider ordering, say, a chocolate *soufflé* upon arrival, so that there will be time to prepare it. Or how about paper-thin *crêpes* combined with poached pears and then soaked with Poire William *eau-de-vie? Luxury.*

Dominique Le Stanc (18 Boulevard des Moulins, Monte Carlo; phone 9350-63-36)—in common with so many rising young chefs out to make a name for themselves—has called his restaurant after himself. Fair enough; he's cook as well as boss. The look is smart, with fine old still-lifes (food, naturally, is their theme) on the walls and a collection of aged mechanical toys for kicks. Louis XV-style chairs, upholstered in tiny patterned fabrics surround candelit, flower-embellished tables. Not surprisingly, M. Le Stanc's bent is *nouvelle*, although his training is solid Alsatian. He presents tiny *amuse-gueules*—fish and chicken in puff pastry—to whet appetites. A festive dinner might include sweetbread salad-cum-mushrooms, truffled lobster or filet of venison as entrées, pastries and house-made ice creams, among sweets. *Luxury.*

Le Gratin (Beach Plaza Hotel, Avenue Princesse Grace, Monte Carlo; phone 9330-98-80): There comes a time when transatlantic travelers crave beef as they remember it at home. *Zut, alors!* Le Gratin to the rescue. The beef is not American, but rather Black Angus imported from Scotland—hardly to be despised. An immense joint is roasted—rare and medium-rare, worry not—and wheeled to table for carving, with baked potatoes among accompaniments. You may substitute roast saddle of lamb for the beef. Open with avocado salad or turtle soup. *Vacherin à la myrtille*—a blueberry confection—is a favored sweet. Dinner only. *First Class.*

Chez Gianni (39 Avenue Princesse Grace, Monte Carlo; phone 9330-46-33): With Italy just a few miles down the *piste*, it should come as no surprise that cuisine of the peninsula has found its way to Monaco. There are easily a dozen reliable Italian restaurants; Chez Gianni is among them. What Gianni calls *hors d'oeuvres maison* is actually a platter of assorted *antipasto*—an indicated opener, as might be a bowl of minestrone or the shredded raw beef specialty, *carpaccio*. There are a dozen pasta choices; spaghetti *au vongole* is, of course, *alla vongole*—in a clam sauce; *penne aux quatre fromages* is the classic quill-shaped pasta with a four-cheese—*quattro formaggi*—sauce. And *saltimbocca alla Romana*—the sliced veal and smoked ham specialty—is among entrées. *First Class.*

Le Bistroquet (Galerie Charles III, Monte Carlo; phone 9350-71-68) is a heart-of-town, al-fresco café—ideal for people watching—and a *brasserie*-type restaurant with substantial things to eat, lunch or well into the late hours. *Rillettes de porc*—traditional coarse pork *pâté*—is a good opener. *Salade Niçoise* goes down well on a hot day as a lunch entrée. So does *entrecôte aux frites*. Omelets are a specialty. And Gallic-accented cheeseburgers are tasty. Friendly. *Moderate/First Class.*

Café de Paris (Place du Casino, Monte Carlo) is the long-on-scene center of the action, midday through midnight—and beyond. Go for coffee, a drink, a snack. Views from the square tables are of the Casino, De Paris Hôtel, and Monte Carlo's ambulatory populace. *Moderate/First Class.*

SHOPPER'S MONACO

Avenue des Beaux-Arts, leading from Place du Casino, is nothing if not blue chip. By that, I mean there are outlets of such firms as *Bulgari, Piaget, Cartier* (jewelry), *Adriano Ribozzi* (antique furniture), *Hermès* (men's and women's accessories), and such women's fashion houses as *Céline, Yves St.-Laurent,* and *Givenchy. Christian Dior* and *Emilio Pucci* (women's clothes) are in the Hôtel de Paris, along with *Harry Winston* (jewelry). *Fred* (jewelry) is in Loews Monte Carlo Hôtel. Boulevard des Moulins is another interesting street, with *Christofle* (Baccarat, Daum, and Lalique crystal, Limoges porcelain), *Trussardi* (a smart, Italian clothing chain), *Charles Jourdan* (costly women's shoes), and *Salganik* (fabulous furs).

SOUND OF MUSIC

As if to compensate for its lack of fine-arts museums, Monaco does very well indeed by the performing arts. I allude, with enthusiasm, on an earlier page to *Salle Garnier*—the treasure of an opera house that is attached to the Casino de Monte Carlo (Place du Casino); it's the principal venue for opera, *Orchestre Philharmonique de Monte-Carlo,* and the relatively recently formed *Ballet de Monte Carlo,* a successor to the pioneering Ballet Russe de Monte Carlo of Serge Diaghilev, from the early decades of this century. Such now-classic ballets as *L'Après-Midi d'un Faune, La Spectre de la Rose,* and *Le Sacre du Printemps* had early performances in Salle Garnier; while operatic composers, including Berlioz, Massinet, Saint-Saens, Ravel, and Puccini presented works there, as well. *Auditorium Rainier III* (Centre de Congrès, Boulevard Louis II) sees Philharmonic and other performances, too. *Monte Carlo Sporting Club* (Avenue Princesse Grace) is the site of a variety of galas—a black tie dinner, for example, with Sammy Davis, Jr. entertaining; floor shows with dancing and other special events, invariably dressy and pricey. In summer, the Philharmonic presents a season of concerts in the courtyard of *Palais Princier* (Place du Palais), and there are open-air concerts at *Théâtre du Fort Antoine* (Avenue de la Quarantine).

INCIDENTAL INTELLIGENCE

Monte Carlo Golf Club (La Turbie, France)—high over Monaco and the Mediterranean and, as you will note, over the border in France—is beautifully situated, with a restaurant-equipped clubhouse; 18 holes, par

70. Good *tennis*, too. Helicopter service, via *Heli-Air Monaco*, is worth knowing about; it connects the principality with Nice; flying time is eight minutes, and there are frequent departures. *Further information:* Monaco Government Tourist & Convention Bureau, 845 Third Avenue, New York, NY 10022. Direction du Tourisme et des Congrès de la Principauté de Monaco, 2 Boulevard des Moulins, Monte Carlo.

24

Montpellier
Ancient Languedoc Updated

BACKGROUND BRIEFING
If Montpellier is unusual among French cities in that it has absolutely no Roman roots—there was, also, no *Montpellierensis* or anything of the kind—it is almost as unusual in that it passed through a medieval period when it was the property, successively, of the Spanish kingdoms of Aragon and Majorca. It has been quite French, ever since, fear not. Indeed, it was strongly Huguenot-Protestant French until the early seventeenth century, when Louis XIII sent troops south and took control of this city—midway between Marseille and Toulouse—an ostensibly military tactic that spurred economic development.

That was the period that saw construction of a substantial clutch of *hôtels particuliers*, opulent mansions that remain landmarks of a city that became even richer when the next reigning Louis—the Fourteenth, in whose honor Montpellier's Arc de Triomphe went up in 1691—decreed it official seat of the ancient province of Languedoc. To this day, dynamic Montpellier, as proud of a university that dates to the thirteenth century as of its contemporary flair for industry, persists in bilingual street signs. Every thoroughfare is labeled in Languedoc, as well as in French—the better to remind its citizens and its visitors of an extraordinary heritage.

ON SCENE
Lay of the Land: *Place de la Comédie* is the nerve-center of town, dominated by the mock-Baroque opera house whose name it takes, cafés that spill onto the pavement, and but a singular lapse—an all too contemporary McDonald's that sticks out like the proverbial sore thumb. *Rue de la Loche*, a principal commercial artery, extends northwest from this square until it reaches *Place des Martyrs de la Résistance*, off which another major thoroughfare, *Rue Foch*, extends west through the earlier mentioned seventeenth-century *Arc de Triomphe* into the capacious—

and gracious—*Promenade du Peyrou,* an eighteenth-century mix of paths and pools. Its western edge is flanked by an utterly beautiful water tower—still another eighteenth-century souvenir called *Château d'Eau,* six-sided, double-tiered, and supported by Corinthian pillars. The tower flanks a reservoir that is the eastern terminus of yet one more manifestation of Montpellier's eighteenth-century Golden Age—fabulous *Aqueduc St.-Clément,* built to carry water from a source ten miles distant. The two principal pedestrian-shopping streets are *Rue de l'Ancien Courrier* and *Rue de l'Argenterie,* perpendicular to each other, core of town. Eastern precincts of the city are dominated by futuristic *Centre Commercial du Polygone,* a mix of hotels, department stores, and shops; with the also-recent *Antigone apartment complex,* wherein an innovative architect has deftly melded classic and contemporary motifs, nearby.

Musée Fabre (Boulevard Sarrail): If Montpellier is a sleeper of a city, Musée Fabre is likewise a sleeper of a museum, one of the most art-rich of the repositories of beaux-arts in the republic. My notes are punctuated with exclamation marks: Veronese's *Marriage of St. Catherine* and a Carracci *Pietà;* Reni's *St. Agnes in Agony* and Houdon's bust of a young Molière; Italian fantasy scenes—architecturally detailed, albeit ethereal—that typify Hugo Robert's work; Vernet landscapes and a still life of books by Oudry—departing from his usual animal scenes; a riveting study of hands and feet by Géricault; decorative portraits by Ingres and Delacroix; lovely landscapes as interpreted by Corot and Courbet (with a bonus of Courbet portraits—not usual subjects by that master); Rubens's *Martyrdom of a Saint* and Steen's *Traveler Resting;* and a host of other Baroque Dutch works by the likes of Van Ruysdael and Van Goyen, Ter Borch and Cuyp. Spaniards are present—Zurbarán and Sánchez Coello. More recent painters are on scene, too—an exquisite Bonnard landscape, a Matisse still-life, Marquet and Degas, Robert Delauney and Utrillo; and the great sculptors of the last century—Canova, Bourdelle, Maillol, Carpeaux. Allow half a day.

Musée Atger (Faculté de Médecine, Rue École de Médecine): You need an advance appointment for the Atger; the city tourist office (address below) can arrange it for you. Setting in and of itself—the main building of the University of Montpellier's celebrated Medical School—is noteworthy; a tablet in the lobby honors all of the school's deans and rectors starting in the year 1220. Up you go to the second floor museum, where still another tablet advises that its collection of drawings was a gift from "Monsieur Xavier Atger, Amateur Montpelliérain." Once you are admitted, a curator takes you in hand, opening drawers of the cabinets in which prints are stored as a protective measure, commenting upon them (in French) as you move along. There are Renaissance Italians like Tiepolo (his *Head of an Old Man* is a star of the show). But most drawings are by such French eighteenth-century masters as Fragonard (a bucolic landscape), Natoire (*Madonna and Child with Angels*), Oudry (*The Birds' Christmas*), and Fragonard (*Portrait de l'Abbé*). A treat.

Musée Sabatier-d'Éspeyran (6 Rue Montpelliéret) is a mammoth nineteenth-century *hôtel particulier* that was the home of the family for which it is named. This is Montpellier's repository of the decorative arts. It's operated by Musée Fabre (above), whose information desk arranges guided tours. There are two floors, and the contrast is nothing if not instructional. The second is a suite of reception rooms furnished locally in the last century, mostly ostentatious Second Empire. You ascend one more flight, then, to the top level, and it is as though you have moved to another house. These rooms are superb eighteenth century—Louis XV and Louis XVI—furniture and accessories that were originally in the owning family's Paris home. Vive la différence!

Cathedral of St.-Pierre (Place St.-Pierre) is by no means one of the great ones. Withal, a visit to it by foot—through the core of town, perhaps with detours past courtyards of mansions on such atmospheric Vieux-Montpellier streets as Rue Jacques-Coeur and Rue des Trésoriers de France—makes for an agreeable excursion. The cathedral is at its best from without; its stone porch is flanked by two turreted towers out of the fourteenth century. The Gothic nave is of the same period, and rose windows flanking the transept are very old, too; but most of the rest of the building is a consequence of eighteenth- and nineteenth-century restoration.

Crypte Notre-Dame-des-Tables (Place Jean-Jaurès) occupies subterranean portions of a desanctified Gothic church whose exhibits relate the history of the city. Have a look.

Musée Fougau and Musée du Vieux-Montpellier (Hôtel de Varenne, Place Pétrarque, off Rue Embouque d'Or): Each occupies a separate floor in a townhouse, parts of which have original Gothic vaulting. The building's architecture is at least as absorbing as the mini-museums' collections.

Château country: Earmark a good half day for a trio of châteaux north of town, checking open hours, before departure, with the Montpellier tourist office (address below). *Château de la Mogère* (two miles north) is a classic-style mansion set back from a formal garden whose Rococo wall of shells frames a fountain. State rooms include a salon with stuccoed walls and ceiling and yellow and blue Louis XVI furnishings; a drawing room, dramatically scarlet accented; and a dining room with original tables and chairs, not to mention a Rigaud portrait over the buffet. *Château Flaugergues* (five miles north) resembles nothing so much as a seventeenth-century Tuscan villa. The entrance hall is dominated by a tapestried stairway. The reception rooms' vaulted ceilings frame Louis XV and Louis XVI furnishings, with Aubusson rugs on the floors. The ex-chapel—neo-Gothic—is a library, and your hosts, Brigitte and Henri de Colbert, descendants of Louis XIV's finance minister, own a vineyard; you may buy their wines. *Château de Castries* (eight miles north) is the most important of our trio—and the oldest, essentially sixteenth century, albeit with eighteenth-century refurbishing. Its magnificent park and formal garden were designed in 1666—and irrigated by water from a still-extant aqueduct four miles long—by the very same Le Nôtre whose work you know from Versailles. The still-resident Castries family has played a major role in regional history. And we are in its debt for opening the state rooms. A majestic stairway leads from the entrance hall to the second floor's Salon Bleu, Louis XVI furnished, with a memento-filled library; the dining room, with family paintings on its half-paneled walls; Chambre Rouge, so called because of its red-upholstered canopied bed; and a ballroom-sized drawing room called Salle des États du Languedoc, with both historic and esthetic significance.

Palavas-les-Flots (8 miles south of Montpellier) is where Montpellier swims and suns, straddling a long, wide Mediterranean strand with beachfront hotels and restaurants, an amusing *Aquarium* (317 Avenue St.-Maurice), and even a casino. Spend the day.

Pézenas (29 miles southwest of Montpellier) is a village whose core is a mass of tile-stone houses that constitute a medieval movie set. Position yourself at central *Place de la République*, wandering *Cours Jean-Jaurès* and adjacent streets, popping into *St.-Jean* and *St.-Ursule* churches, not missing *Musée du Vulliod St.-Germain* for its eighteenth-century furniture, tapestries, and porcelain.

SETTLING IN

Métropole Hôtel (3 Rue Clos-René; phone 6758-11-22) is an attractively updated turn-of-century house, with 92 no-two-quite-alike rooms and suites (those I've inspected are delightful); smartly paneled restaurant, with precisely half of its menu featuring *nouvelle* cuisine, the other half traditional; a delightful bar-lounge; and owner-management that is at once congenial and professional. *First Class.*

Sofitel Montpellier (Le Triangle; phone 6754-04-04) occupies lower floors of an ungainly contemporary apartment house, midpoint between Place de la Comédie and the Polygone shopping complex. There are 96 functional rooms, pair of suites, bar off the lobby and—the hotel at its best—a generous buffet at breakfast, the only meal served. *First Class.*

Noailles Hôtel (2 Rue des Écoles Centrales; phone 6760-49-80) charms with seventeenth-century ambience. The lounge is stone walled, barrel vaulted, with Louis XIII furniture. There are 30 rooms; all of those I've inspected are charmers, with good baths. Location is Vieux-Montpellier. Friendly. *Moderate*.

Frantel Montpellier (218 Rue du Bastion, in the Polygone complex, east of the center) is of modern design, not unlike the shopping center of which it is a part. There are 116 full-facility rooms, restaurant, bar-lounge. *First Class*.

Grand Hôtel du Midi (22 Boulevard Victor-Hugo; phone 6792-69-61) is an elderly house, centrally situated, with half a hundred rooms. Bar-café and breakfast. Okay. *Moderate*.

Palais Hôtel (3 Rue du Palais; phone 6760-47-38) thoroughly renovated its two dozen rooms relatively recently and is centrally situated. Good value. *Moderate*.

DAILY BREAD
Le Petit Landais (14 Rue du Palais; phone 6760-69-93) is small and friendly and operated by a delightful *patronne* who is at once hostess and chef. Cooking is regional, hearty, and delicious. Dinner might open with crab salad, followed by Madame's *foie gras de canard*, and continue with a superbly prepared magret—or breast—of *canard*; order baked-on-premises chocolate cake or *clafoutis aux cerises*, a cherry confection, to conclude. In my view, one of France's best restaurants. *First Class*.

Le Louvre (2 Rue de la Vielle; phone 6760-59-37) will remind you not at all of the Paris museum, but rather of 1940s movies you've enjoyed; decor is Art Deco. You do well to sample the house's own *cassoulet* —based on *confit de canard* and delicious—preceded by a light, but well dressed, tomato salad. Or have the prix-fixe menu; select a veal entrée. *First Class*.

Isadora (6 Rue du Petit-Scel; phone 6766-25-23): You descend the stone-walled cellar of an aged house to find Isadora (whose owner, to your surprise, is a gent) smartly styled and cheerily staffed, with a good-value menu that might open with shrimp-stuffed avocado, continue with a filet of beef or a poultry specialty, and conclude with a house-made sweet. *First Class*.

Le Ménestrel (Impasse Perrier, Place de la Préfecture; phone 6760-62-51) exudes ambience, given the high, stone vaults of its premises, a tremendous fireplace, red linen on the tables. The lower-priced of two menus features grilled lamb chops, with a hot Calvados-anointed apple tart to conclude. *Moderate/First Class.*

Chantegril (4 Rue Clos-René; phone 6758-14-15) is convenient to Place de la Comédie and a link of an attractive national chain—the lot with light, garden-like ambience—that specializes in good-value prix-fixe *formules* that open with *crudités* selected by you from a buffet and that continue with an appetizer and your choice of grill (steak, lamb chops, pork chops). *Moderate.*

Hôtel Montpelliérain des Vins du Languedoc (7 Rue Jacques Coeur; phone 6760-42-41) is operated by the Languedoc wine producers' promotion arm, primarily as a showcase for wines of the area. The menu, however, reads better than it tastes. Stick to simply broiled entrées, hoping for the best, the while you sample regional whites, rosés, and reds. Service is good-natured but slow. *First Class.*

Viguier (56 Rue de l'Argentier) is a *pâtisserie* that doubles as a *salon de thé;* order something scrumptious from the counter, to accompany coffee or tea. *Moderate.*

Café Riche (Place de la Comédie): While resting weary feet, observe ambulatory Montpellier; have coffee or a snack. *Moderate.*

Café de la Préfecture (Place Chabaneau) spills into the pretty square and is named for its next-door neighbor, the impressive structure housing the government of the *département. Moderate.*

SHOPPER'S MONTPELLIER
Galeries Lafayette, the No. 1 department store, is in the Polygone shopping center, along with *Parunis* and *C & A* department stores and such clothing shops as *Daniel Hechter* and *Rodier.* There's a big *Monoprix* on Place de la Comédie. It's fun to take in the *daily market*—food, flowers, clothes, you name it—on Place Jean-Jaurès. Of the pedestrian streets, Rue de l'Argenterie is the smartest, with such boutiques as *Georges Rech, Patricia Oresaud,* and *Via Condotti* (women's clothes), *Daniel Crémieux* (men's clothes), *André Roch* (leather), *Spiral* (jewelry), and *Cacharel Junior* (kids' clothes). Two good bookstores are *English Books* (9 Rue de l'École de Pharmacie) and *Le Maître Soldeur* (art books, 39 Rue de l'Aiguillerie). Montpellier is a major source of antiques. *Galerie du Peyrou* and *Galerie M. de B.* are two of a number of shops along Rue du Palais; *Centaure/Emanuel de Sauveboeuf* (5 Rue de la Petite Loge) is another well-stocked shop.

SOUND OF MUSIC

Théâtre Municipal (Place de la Comédie) is elaborately Belle Époque and the setting for opera, ballet, and concerts. There are a number of other theaters as well.

L'Esplanade is a city park that's popular in summer for its day and evening concerts. Central.

INCIDENTAL INTELLIGENCE

Aéroport de Fréjorgues is five miles southwest of town; flights to points throughout France. *Further information:* Office de Tourisme, 6 Rue Maguelone, Montpellier; Office de Tourisme, Mairie, Palavas-les-Flots; Office de Tourisme, Marché au Bled, Pézenas.

25

Nancy
What Duke Stanislaus Hath Wrought

BACKGROUND BRIEFING

It is, of course, outrageous to be so corny as to declare that Nancy is fancy. But it is.

Even, I hasten to add, when pronounced properly—*Nahn*-SEE—in the French manner.

If you except Paris, whose Place de la Concorde is of the same era, no French city of which I am aware has a Rococo square to equal that of northeastern Nancy—a hundred and seventy miles due east of the capital. For Place Stanislas—along with the palaces enclosing it and the monumental wrought-iron gates punctuating it—we must be grateful for what can only be termed the peculiar politics of the eighteenth century. What happened was that a man in need of a job, forced to step down as king of his native Poland, in the end settled for something less prestigious—the dukedom of Lorraine (of which Nancy has long been capital), which upon his death, and by terms of the deal he made with his father-in-law, King Louis XV, became a part of France.

Pre-Stanislaus Nancy had been seat of Lorraine's dukes since as early as the twelfth century. Neighboring Burgundians came from the south to annex it in a fifteenth-century battle, but Lorraine's Duke René II—a local hero to this day for valor—fended them off. The sixteenth century saw Duke Charles III lay out plans for a new city center. But the city did not really blossom until, in the early eighteenth century, the ruling Duke, François III, married Austrian Empress Maria Theresa and became an emperor. Imperial sleight-of-hand then saw François trade off Lorraine with Louis XV, in exchange for Tuscany. At that point, King Louis, married to Polish-born Maria Leczinska, turned over Lorraine to his then-idle father-in-law, the deposed Polish King.

Stanislaus and Nancy hit it off beautifully. An educated and enlightened man with a sure sense of style, he set about creating a new core

for his capital, commissioning the architect Hère and a designer of ornamental ironwork named Lamour to come up with a plan. Their square
so enraptured Nancy that its citizens named it for Stanislaus, last of the
Lorraine dukes. Nancy suffered in the nineteenth century (German troops
occupied it during the Franco-Prussian War—and again during World
War I). But its beloved square—exquisitely refurbished in recent years—
remains both its symbol and its soul.

ON SCENE
Lay of the Land: It should go without saying that the core of the city
is *Place Stanislas*, flanked by a clutch of palaces, not to mention
cafés, spilling onto the pavement. Adjacent is *Place de la Carrière*, gained
by a spectacular *Arc de Triomphe*, massed with trees in its center and
bordered by handsome houses, and the colonnaded *Palais du Gouverne-
ment*. *Grande Rue*, due north, is Nancy's Antiques Row, and the site, as
well, of the medieval *Palais Ducal*, now a museum complex. *Rue St.-Jean*,
the main street, is a hop and a skip from Place Stanislas and becomes
Rue St.-Georges in its easterly precincts. *Rue Stanislas*, parallel with Rue
St.-Jean, leads west to *Place Thiers* and the railway station.

Place Stanislas palaces warrant inspection. *Hôtel de Ville*, the city hall,
dazzles with a pair of second-story reception rooms, the bigger of which
was refurbished in the nineteenth century for a state visit by Empress
Eugénie. And getting to it is half the fun: The stairway's wrought-iron
bannister is a 27-yard-long masterwork by Lamour. Do your best to have
a look, too, at the elegant auditorium of the *Grand Théâtre*, by taking in
a performance, perhaps of the Ballet de Nancy—one of France's top
companies—or an opera. Another palace is occupied by *Musée des Beaux-
Arts* (below), and still another by the *Grand Hôtel Concorde* where—
especially if you are not in residence—a meal and/or drink are certainly
in order. Outside, amble about the square, taking in its gilded wrought-
iron gates and its pair of fountains, Amphitrite and Neptune, and concluding your tour over coffee or a drink at one of the square's cafés.

Musée des Beaux-Arts (Place Stanislas): The setting is so beautiful that
you half expect this museum's paintings to be anticlimactic; they are not.
If you are wondering whether the Lorraine-born Renaissance master,
Claude Lorrain (whose name was actually Claude Gelée), is represented,
let me reassure you. By one ethereal landscape: *Paysage Pastoral*. His
contemporaries, Poussin and Vouet, are on scene, as well. There are Old
Master Italians, a Lorenzo Lotto *Gentleman's Portrait*, a Perugino *Virgin*,
a Caravaggio *Annunciation*, Tintoretto, and Bassano—and later French-
men like Van Loo (with a likeness of Duke Stanislaus's father-in-law,
Louis XV) and Delacroix, with a massive interpretation of Lorraine Duke
René's decisive victory over the Burgundy forces of Duke Charles the

Bold in 1477. There is an enormous Rubens *Transfiguration* and more recent French work—Utrillo and Dérain, Signac and Manet, Vuillard and Dufy—as well.

Musée de Lorraine (Palais Ducal, Grande Rue): What could be more appropriate a setting for a repository of Lorraine lore than the château in which its dukes lived? It dates to the sixteenth century and is a marvelous mix of Gothic and Renaissance, on two splendid levels. Downstairs is a maze of medieval sculpture, stained glass, and swords. And how about those immense fireplaces? Upstairs is even more spectacular. There are paintings of the dukes, a series of sumptuous tapestries, works by Lorraine artists, including Claude Lorrain and Georges de la Tour, a cache of Renaissance furniture and of eighteenth-century porcelain from nearby Luneville. You move along then to the adjacent building, *Couvent des Cordeliers*, long since abandoned by Franciscan nuns and now *Musée des Arts et Traditions Populaires;* head for the second floor, where the kicker is a series of rooms from houses in the Lorraine countryside, furnished—and superbly—in period.

Church of the Cordeliers (Grande Rue): Franciscans often are called *Cordeliers* in France because of the white cords they wear as belts. This Franciscan church is at its best in the adjacent chapel and is so similar to the Chapel of the Medici (see *Italy at Its Best*) that you could be in Florence, substituting stone-carved tombs of Dukes of Lorraine for those of the ruling Medici.

Musée de l'École de Nancy (38 Rue du Sergent Blandan) wants its title explained, first off. It is called after the group, or movement, of celebrated turn-of-century Nancy artists and artisans—Majorelle (a cabinetmaker), Gruber (who designed stained-glass windows), and a number of others, whose specialties were tapestries, embroidery, jewelry making, bookbinding—who were brought together by glass-designer Émile Galle, the lot of them constituting the Art Nouveau period's École de Nancy. This museum is a onetime mansion with two floors of matchless Art Nouveau rooms—foyer, salon, music room, dining room below, bedrooms above; even an Art Nouveau-accented garden—that comprise a unique-in-the-world museum of an important period in the history of design. (The only other such that I know, on the same esthetic level is Hamburg's Museum für Kunst und Gewerbe [see *Germany at Its Best*], whose Art Nouveau period rooms rank with these.)

Cathedral of Nancy (Rue St.-Georges) is by no means one of the great ones. Still, there are not many eighteenth-century cathedrals in France. Nancy's is monumentally scaled—and not surprisingly—with fine, wrought-iron grillwork typical of that period in this city.

Parc de La Pépinière, east of Grande Rue, contains a statue of Claude Lorrain by Rodin and *Church of Notre Dame de Bon Secours* (at the foot of Avenue de Strasbourg), designed by Hère, who also created Place Stanislas, contains the tomb of Duke Stanislaus—should you want to pay your respects at either or both.

SETTLING IN

Grand Hôtel Concorde (2 Place Stanislas; phone 8335-03-01) is, as you've read above, one of the original eighteenth-century palaces of Place Stanislas. Hôtels Concorde, its owners, have sunk several million francs into an impeccable and very stylish restoration, with the consequence a hotel that is one of the most beautiful—and charming—in France. There are 60 suites and rooms, no two quite alike, the lot of them designed in period, with superb textiles, furniture, accessories, and, I might add, baths. The ones you want to aim for—always the first to go, not surprisingly—are those facing the square, with side rooms on which you can see the square by craning your neck, the next best. Public spaces are a pleasure. There's a lively bar—called Le Stan (what locals call the square)—and a restaurant worthy of additional comment in a later paragraph. And the staff is one of the best I've encountered in France. Along with the Crillon in Paris and the Martinez in Cannes, this is the Concorde operation at its zenith. *First Class.*

Frantel Nancy (Place Thiers; phone 8336-61-01) is, as far as I can perceive, Nancy's only skyscraper, with 192 full-facility rooms, cocktail lounge, and restaurant. Central. *First Class.*

Europe Hôtel (5 Rue des Carmes; phone 8335-32-10) has the advantage of a central situation; 80 functional rooms. Breakfast only. *Moderate.*

Portes d'Or Hôtel (21 Rue Stanislas; phone 8335-42-34) is another core-of-town house; intimate—just 20 rooms. Breakfast only. *Moderate.*

DAILY BREAD

Stanislaus (Grand Hôtel Concorde, 2 Place Stanislas; phone 8335-03-01) is intimate (seating capacity is limited), handsome (you're in an authentic eighteenth-century setting), and delicious. Open with the local pike prepared Nancy style, a seafood salad, or the day's soup. Beef entrées—*steak au poivre,* especially—are tasty and nicely garnished. Desserts are wheeled on a trolley and memorable. And service is impeccable. *First Class.*

Le Capucin Gourmand (31 Rue Gambetta; phone 8335-26-98) extends a warm welcome, in a luxurious setting. Open with *foie gras* prepared the house's way, consider game—a specialty—as an entrée, and on no account pass over desserts, ranging from made-on-premises ice cream doused with *eau-de-vie* to delicate pastries. *Luxury.*

Oxebon (85 Rue St.-Georges; phone 8332-00-42): Of course, you want to try *quiche lorraine* in Lorraine's capital; Oxebon makes a specialty of it. There's a wide range of entrées; frog's legs, among them. Central. *First Class.*

Nouveaux Abattoires (4 Boulevard d'Austrasie; phone 8335-46-25): Think what you will about calling a restaurant "New Slaughterhouses"; the fact remains that this is a long-established source of solid fare—filets of beef and *steak au poivre*, veal *escalopes* and veal chops, kidneys and sweetbreads. Chocolate *mousse* or *crème caramel* for dessert. *First Class.*

Café Jean Lamour (Place Stanislas): Take a table on the square and remain as long as you like over a single drink. If Lamour is filled, move along to the same square's *Café du Commerce* or *Le Glacier;* all are *Moderate.*

INCIDENTAL INTELLIGENCE

Further information: Office de Tourisme, Place Stanislas (where else?), Nancy.

26

Nice
and the Riviera Hills

BACKGROUND BRIEFING

Nice has an image problem with a double causative: sunshine and situation. Contemporary visitors understandably associate its—dare I say "nice"?—name with neighboring Riviera points like Cannes (Chapter 13), Monaco (Chapter 23), and St.-Tropez (Chapter 33), admire the action along the palm-lined crescent called Promenade des Anglais, deplore the pebbly strand edging the Baie des Anges, wonder what all the fuss was about—and move along.

They err. But it's neither their fault nor Nice's. With unabashed beach resorts—where the *raison d'être* is sun, sand, the spin of the roulette wheel, and the beat of the disco—flanking this city all along the Mediterranean shore, it's no wonder that today's traveler may be unaware that upon arrival he or she has reached a metropolis of a third of a million (only Paris, Lyon, Marseille, and Toulouse are larger) that was settled by the Greeks four centuries before Christ and was the scene of considerable activity—the lot contributing to Nice's vibrant life-style and underappreciated culture—between then and the middle of the last century, when the then-Italian city became a part of Napoleon III's Second Empire.

In between, there were few dull moments. Romans—whose name, *Nicaea*, has been changed little over the centuries—succeeded Greeks, making the still-visitable area called Cimiez (an amphitheater and ruined thermal baths remain) their town. Barbarians and assorted later invaders followed, by no means arresting this resilient city's development. Medieval Provence and then medieval Savoy were later landlords. François I's troops attacked Renaissance Nice. During the Revolution it was a haven for Royalists fleeing Paris, by which time it had also begun to lure wandering Britons partial to the mild climate and an idyllic location, with snowy mountains in the rear and the blue Mediterranean out front.

Indeed, it was a resident clutch of moneyed Englishmen who kicked in funds for the early nineteenth-century construction of the appropriately named Promenade des Anglais, the pioneer shoreline artery that inspired others in sea-girdling communities, planet-wide.

Today's Nice is an amalgam of these disparate influences. Elegance came with the eighteenth-century Parisians. The tradition of the grand hotel is surely English in origin. The lusty cuisine as much as high houses hung with clotheslines flanking alley-like streets of Vieux-Nice are Italian. And much of the extraordinary art in the museums is a consequence of Nice's having lured such masters as Chagall, Matisse, and Picasso, their curiosity piqued by nineteenth-century enthusiasts like the painter Delacroix, the writer Maupassant, and the composer Berlioz. No question but that Nice beaches are narrow and pebbly. But there are compensations.

ON SCENE

Lay of the Land: Nice is big; you can't walk everywhere. The central city is fronted by crescent-shaped, hotel-lined *Promenade des Anglais*, which flanks a baker's dozen beaches—some private (with access gained through your hotel), some public (your concierge will direct you to the closest)—extending the length of the *Baie des Anges*, at its smartest in central precincts, in and about landmark Hôtel Négresco at the corner of north-south *Boulevard Gambetta*, which leads to *Rue de France*, running parallel with Promenade des Anglais and, as it works its way east, becoming pedestrians-only *Rue Masséna*, terminating at massive *Place Masséna*, edged by Hôtel de Ville. Directly east is the splendid fountain-filled park-like area successively called *Espace Masséna*, *Square Leclerc*, and *Promenade du Paillon*. It constitutes the northern border of *Vieux-Nice*, the medieval/Renaissance quarter dominated by the cathedral and Palais de Justice in its center, just above an immense public market that flanks *Cours Saleya*, a thoroughfare parallel with the sea that is lined with typically Niçoise seafood restaurants. What remains of the ancient Roman colony of Cimiez is in a quarter retaining that name, a fair distance north of the center, with a pair of museums. Still other museums are in other sectors. By no means all of Nice's hotels line the waterfront; many are on attractive inland streets in and about Rue Masséna, *Boulevard Victor-Hugo*, and *Avenue Médecin*. The railway station is north of the core on *Avenue Thiers*, while the international airport is southwest of town, on *Promenade Édouard Corniglion*.

Roman Nice: Why not start in ancient Cimiez—the Romans' *Cemenelum*? Poke about what remains of their city, including a still lovely *amphitheater* and *baths*, detouring to the adjacent *Church of Cimiez*, whose treats are altars by the Renaissance-era Nice school's Louis and Antoine Brea. Both Dufy and Matisse are buried in an adjacent cemetery. But this

NICE

Baie de Anges

is Matisse territory; by that, I mean the upper floor of nearby *Musée Matisse* (entered at 164 Avenue des Arènes-de-Cimiez) exhibits works that are a survey of that artist's long career, 1890s through designs for the chapel in nearby Vence (below), with scores of drawings and not a few paintings, the 1944 *Lectrice à la Table Jaune* among the more memorable. The same building houses the city's *Musée Archéologique*, whose special treasure is a first-century statue in marble of Antonia, a niece of the Emperor Augustus, but there are half a dozen galleries displaying excavated treasures of Roman Cemenelum—capitals, busts, sculpted fragments, and sarcophagi.

Vieux-Nice, nerve center of the city from the Middle Ages well into the eighteenth century and still vibrant and engaging, is a pleasant walk east from hotels of the core. *Cathedral of Ste.-Réparate* (Place Rossetti)—among the relatively few Baroque cathedrals in France and certainly among the loveliest—is strongly Italianate, with statues in niches of its classic-style green and yellow facade, a smashing tiled dome, a detached bell tower in the Italian manner, and an interior not overlarge, but lavishly stuccoed and sculpted, with a fine marble pulpit. *Musée du Palais Lascaria* (15 Rue Droite) went up in the mid-seventeenth century, deteriorated sadly until municipal authorities, having purchased it just before World War II, completed restoration in 1969. Its coat-of-arms-centered stone facade is impressive enough. But high-ceilinged, stone-walled interiors are not anticlimactic, especially the second floor's state rooms, at their most opulent in a sumptuous suite embracing a frescoed sitting room furnished with Louis XV pieces and an adjacent space centered by a bed canopied in scarlet and white damask, with both ballroom and chapel down the hall. If you haven't paid attention to the sculpture-embellished stairway going up, do so when you descend. While you're in the neighborhood, pop into whatever churches you pass by—a number are Baroque and charming—and amble about squares like *Place St.-François* (centered by a fish market), as well as shop-lined streets like *Rue Ste.-Réparate,* making sure that you have at least one meal in a raffish *restaurant du quartier* (see below) on *Cours Saleya.* Note, as you move about, that Vieux-Nice street signs are in both French and Nice dialect; *Rue de Jésus,* for example, is also *Carriera dou Jeuse.*

Belle Époque Nice is perhaps best exemplified by *Musée Masséna*—a mansion of the period (it was built about 1900) on Promenade des Anglais, entered at 65 Rue de France. For me, its most evocative exhibit is a painting, *La Promenade des Anglais,* executed in 1921 by Angelo Garino, with the tower of Hôtel Négresco at the upper left, domed amusement pier (long since razed) on the right, and promenaders en masse (accompanied by leashed dogs, as, indeed, are successors today) *au centre.* But there's more in Musée Masséna. Its main-floor rooms are quite as opulent as they were in the early decades of the century (the City of Nice throws parties therein), and there's a mixed-bag collection of historical documents and drawings through regional folklore and antique jewelry.

Musée Chagall (Avenue Docteur Ménard, just off Boulevard de Cimiez, about halfway between the center and the northerly Cimiez complex, above) constitutes a big dose of Chagall, the biggest extant, for that matter. The museum was erected to house a group of massive canvases—nearly a score—that Marc Chagall (1907-1985) painted to illustrate biblical themes. *Adam and Eve Chased from Paradise* draws the largest crowds, but others—*Paradise, Moses Receiving the Ten Commandments,* and *Abraham and the Three Angels*—are compelling, too, as is the museum's auditorium into whose walls are set a series of Chagall stained-glass windows depicting *The Seven Days of Creation* and a quite brilliant and massive mosaic of the master's over a reflecting pool.

Musée Jules-Chéret (33 Avenue Baumettes, a pleasant 10-minute walk east of the central hotels)—not unlike Musée Masséna (above), installed in a Belle Époque palace, with guards quite as friendly as those at the Masséna—is Nice's Beaux-Arts repository. If it is not in a league with those of, say, Dijon, Strasbourg, Grenoble, or Lyon, it does not disappoint. The collection's range is from Van Loo and Fragonard to the Impressionists. Especially memorable are Allen Ramsay's portraits of both George III and Queen Charlotte; other Rococo works by a diverse group, Italy's Battoni through England's Lawrence; Renoir's nude *Bathers* and a solitary (and swimsuited) *Bather,* by onetime Nice resident Raoul Dufy.

Biot (15 miles southwest of Nice) is the pretty, stone village in the hills to which art devotees gravitate. Their destination: *Musée National Fernand Léger,* a rectangular pavilion—whose facade in ceramic tile is based on a Léger composition—that opened in 1960, five years after Léger's death at the age of 74. Fans of Léger—who began as a cubist but whose later work became more representational and which is universally popular because it is immediately recognizable, boldly colorful, and not without wit—have a field day here. There are more than 300 Léger works, tapestries and mosaics, as well as paintings. It is the latter—most in the upper-floor gallery—that linger with us. *The Builders,* a 1950 work as busy with construction workers as with steel girders—typifies the Léger genre. But other paintings with people in them—*Party in the Countryside, Leisure, The Big Parade*—are delightful, and of the abstract pieces the red, white, and blue *July 14, 1914* stands out. Take time to stroll Biot's core, peeking into *Musée d'Histoire Locale* (Place de la Chapelle)—a jumble of village lore, aged kitchens through costumes of yore; and Romanesque-origin *Church of Ste.-Madeleine* (Place des Arcades).

Vence (15 miles northwest of Nice) is still another enchanter of a hill village to whose principal monument contemporary-art buffs beeline. It is *Chapelle du Rosaire* (Avenue Henri Matisse), and one has the feeling that nuns of the convent in which this chapel is situated regret that their order commissioned Matisse to decorate it over a period of several years, concluding in 1951, just a few years before he died at the age of 85 in 1954. Unless they have a change of heart—hardly likely—open hours are, to understate, minimal: 10:00 to 11:30 A.M. and 2:30 to 5:30 P.M., Tuesdays and Fridays. Guardlike sisters, on duty within, exclaim "Shush" if you so much as utter a whisper to a companion, the while marveling at what Matisse created: a series of striking semi-abstract murals in stark black on equally stark white walls, painted tile edging the platform of the chapel's altar, stained-glass windows in joyous hues of blue and yellow; a wrought-iron cross—in effect the chapel's steeple, with a bell at its base—on the roof; even vestments for use by the priest celebrating mass.

The rest of Vence maintains civilized hours. Start in the core, on *Place Clemenceau*, in the multi-epoch *Cathedral*, which is Romanesque, by and large, albeit with a fine Renaissance choir. Move along *Rue de la Place Vieille* to fountain-centered *Place du Peyra*, mellow and medieval. Proceed along *Avenue Henri Isnard* to admire tiles in the cupola of seventeenth-century *Chapelle des Pénitents Blancs*. Conclude with a café pause, in *Place du Grand Jardin*. Unless you're settling in for a night or two—by no means a bad idea.

St.-Paul-de-Vence (a.k.a. just plain St.-Paul, 13 miles northwest of Nice and nicely combined with neighboring Vence on a day's outing) is proudly perched atop its own eminence—and fortified. The ramparts that surround it (commissioned by François I) afford wide-angle panoramas all the way to the Mediterranean. It is agreeable simply to stroll the street which cuts through the village—*Rue Grande*—pausing in crafts shops, idling in a café, taking in squares and gardens. But you want especially to note Rue Grande's urn-shaped and ancient fountain; step-like streets, including *Montée du Casse-Cou;* and the pretty Gothic parish church, expertly vaulted. Even if you are not lunching or dining there (see below), make it a point to ask politely if you may wander through the restaurant—not at mealtime, when it's busy—of the *Colombe d'Or Hôtel* to peruse paintings on its walls contributed by their creators—St.-Paul was a magnet for celebrated artists in the 1920s—among whom were Braque, Chagall, Calder, Dufy, Léger, Matisse, and Picasso (according to my notes; I may have missed some). And allow time for a visit to *Fondation Maeght* (north of the village)—a striking, contemporary structure designed by the late Spanish artist/architect Jose María Sert (the pair of poured concrete semicylinders on the roof are its trademarks)— which is a gold mine of modern art, with al fresco sculpture by the likes of Arp, Calder, Miró, and Giacometti; paintings by Bonnard, Dérain, Kandinsky, Léger, and Matisse; superb stained glass by Braque; even mosaics by Chagall.

St.-Jean-Cap-Ferrat (adjacent to Beaulieu-sur-Mer, six miles east of Nice) is a scenic finger of land jutting into the sea, dotted with mansions tucked behind impeccably manicured gardens. Your objective is one of those villas. It is styled *Fondation Ephrussi de Rothschild–Musée Île de France*, and is nothing less than the onetime Riviera home of a Rothschild baroness who had excellent taste in eighteenth-century furniture and made the collection thereof her hobby. There is furniture, as well, from the Renaissance and Middle Ages; superb antique carpets (Savonnerie) and tapestries (Aubusson and Beauvais); and—as a special treat— a ravishing clutch of eighteenth-century paintings by the likes of Hubert Robert, Lancret, Fragonard, and Boucher; not to mention works by such Impressionists as Renoir, Monet, and Sisley, along with French porcelain and Chinese lacquerware. When you've taken it all in, stroll the fountain-embellished, sculpture-filled gardens.

Cagnes-sur-Mer (nine miles west of Nice) comes in two installments: Cagnes-Ville, its lower-down sector, and elevated Haut-de-Cagnes, where, on Place du Château, is *Musée du Château*, a crenelated, originally fourteenth-century castle inhabited by Grimaldis related to the still-reigning Grimaldis of Monaco (Chapter 23). State rooms of the two lower floors are impressive, but you want to head for the top floor *Musée d'Art Moderne*, brimming with works of this century by artists who worked in the neighborhood, including Chagall; and another group of paintings—all portraits of onetime resident Marquise de Grimaldi—by such masters as Dufy and Marie Laurencin. Cagnes's other destination of consequence is *Maison de Renoir* (Avenue de Tuillères). Dubbed "Les Collettes" by the great Impressionist painter, it was his home for his last 12 years (he died at the age of 78 in 1919) and contains but two of his paintings (one is a charmer, of the house itself), along, however, with a number of his drawings and sculptures, including a bust of Madame Renoir, not to mention his workspace, furnishings in the rest of the house quite as they were when he died, and a pretty garden.

Other Riviera points: For Cannes, Antibes/Juan-les-Pins, Vallauris, Grasse, and Mougins, see Chapter 13; for Monaco (including Monte Carlo) and Èze, see Chapter 23; for St.-Tropez, Ramatuelle, and Gassin, see Chapter 33.

SETTLING IN

Négresco Hôtel (37 Promenade des Anglais; phone 9388-39-51): What happened was this: Rumanian-born Henri Négresco, after learning the hotel and restaurant trade in Paris, moved south to run the turn-of-century Casino Restaurant in Nice, decided that he wanted to house, as well as feed, the rich and the royal who were his customers at the casino, found a backer, and built this Promenade des Anglais house, immediately conferring upon it his own catchy, easily remembered family name. By the time the French Government designated the Négresco a national monument in 1974, the hotel had become synonymous with Nice. The beauty part of its story is that success has not produced the kind of arrogance that can result from such situations. Credit veteran Directeur-Général Michel Palmer with this happy situation. His presence—cordial, efficient, caring—permeates the hotel; nothing happens that he doesn't know about. The doorman smiles when you enter. The reception staff smiles when you sign in. The concierge knows the location of any restaurant you name—and then some. The chambermaids are not chintzy with either soap or towels. The barman does not patronize you when you order a vodka martini with a twist, rather than a kir royale; he prepares it expertly. And the look of the Négresco—bold hued, high ceilinged, widely corridored, with even the singles good sized—is a pleasure. All 140 rooms are distinctively decorated with antique accents, many from the last century's Second Empire; seaview suites and doubles are invariably sumptuous. There is a pair of restaurants, one amusingly casual (it emulates a carousel), the other quite grand and evaluated in a later paragraph. In the city which, after Paris, is the best-equipped hotel town in France, the Négresco is a standout. Member, Leading Hotels of the World. *Luxury.*

Westminster Concorde Hôtel (27 Promenade des Anglais; phone 9388-29-44) is a lovely Belle Époque oldie deftly updated and smartly staffed, with capacious traditional-style public areas that include a pair of restaurants (one with an al fresco, seaview terrace) and a bar-lounge. Of the 110 rooms—sizes vary but they're all comfortable—it's the front ones, some with terraces, facing Promenade des Anglais and the sea, that you want to aim for. Very nice, indeed. Hôtels Concorde. *First Class.*

West End Hôtel (91 Promenade des Anglais; phone 9388-79-91): If it is no longer the luxury house of its fin de siècle heyday, this Promenade des Anglais old-timer—so obviously named to attract Britons who flocked here when it was built—remains splendidly situated and grand of facade, with baths in all but 8 of its 96 rooms, the most desirable of which face the sea. Breakfast only. *Moderate.*

Mercure Hôtel (2 Rue Halevy; phone 9382-30-88), though entered on a side street, fronts Promenade des Anglais. There are 124 clean-lined, balconied rooms—you want to specify those looking out to sea—as well as a moderate-tabbed restaurant. Chaîne Mercure. *First Class*.

Plaza Hôtel (12 Avenue de Verdun; phone 9387-80-41) is handsomely facaded and attractively decorated, with 200 rooms, the nicest of which are good sized, with terraces capacious enough for breakfast-cum-panoramas of nearby Place Masséna and the sea beyond. Restaurant, cocktail lounge. Central. *First Class*.

Aston Hôtel (12 Avenue Félix-Faure; phone 9380-62-52) has location—near Place Masséna and overlooking the fountain-centered gardens adjacent to it—and facilities in its favor; there are 160 modern-design, well-equipped rooms (those on the top floor have terraces), restaurant, and cocktail lounge. *First Class*.

Ambassador Hôtel (8 Avenue de Suède et Gustave V; phone 9387-75-79) is modest sized—there are 44 full-facility rooms—but engaging, with a cordial staff, welcoming lobby, and super situation. *Moderate*.

Park Hôtel (6 Avenue de Suède et Gustave V; phone 9387-80-25), like the neighboring Ambassador (above), is at once scenically and strategically situated. There are 150 full-facility rooms—all terraced, with the higher-up affording nice views—as well as a restaurant-bar. *First Class*.

Sofitel Splendid (50 Boulevard Victor-Hugo; phone 9388-69-54) is king-pin hotel among a considerable quantity of inland houses, four or five pleasantly walkable blocks north of Promenade des Anglais. This is a rare—and most welcome—traditional-style link in the dominantly mod-look Sofitel chain. There are 150 tasteful rooms. Pluses include a rooftop pool/sundeck—views are fabulous—and an upper-floor bar, as well as a restaurant. Friendly, too. *First Class*.

Malmaison Hôtel (48 Boulevard Victor-Hugo; phone 9387-62-56) welcomes you with a crystal-chandeliered lobby-lounge; a Louis XVI-style restaurant is adjacent, and there are 50 traditional-style rooms. Very nice, indeed. *Moderate*.

Gounod Hôtel (3 Rue Gounod; phone 9388-26-29), a near-neighbor of Sofitel (above), charms with a smart decor that carries over from public spaces to half a hundred rooms. Breakfast only. *Moderate*.

Bedford Hôtel (45 Rue du Maréchal-Joffre; phone 9382-18-36) is contemporary and convenient; there are half a hundred full-facility rooms and a bar. Friendly. Breakfast only. *Moderate*.

Busby Hôtel (38 Rue du Maréchal-Joffre; phone 9388-19-41) is a neighbor of the Bedford (above) on a street parallel with busy Boulevard Victor Hugo. There are 76 rooms, all well equipped, and a delightful lobby. Breakfast only. *Moderate.*

Windsor Hôtel (11 Rue Dalpozzo at Rue du Maréchal-Joffre; phone 9388-58-35): You may or may not like the murals covering entire walls behind the beds of the Windsor's nearly 60 rooms; I think they're a nice touch. The big and welcoming lobby leads to a bar-lounge; a swimming pool is in the garden. *Moderate.*

Brice Hôtel (44 Rue du Maréchal-Joffre; phone 9388-16-44)—just opposite the Windsor (above) is, alas, without a swimming pool like its neighbor, but does boast both a garden and a restaurant. There are 60 functional rooms. *Moderate.*

Napoléon Hôtel (6 Rue Grimaldi at Rue du Maréchal-Joffre; phone 9387-70-01) is agreeably traditional, with gracious lobby, cocktail lounge, and 80 rooms, the better of which are as good sized as they are well equipped. *Moderate.*

Locarno Hôtel (4 Avenue des Baumettes; phone 9396-28-00) is nicely located in a quiet but easily gained quarter west of the business center. The lobby is welcoming, as, indeed, are those of the 50 traditional-look rooms I have inspected. Breakfast only. *Moderate.*

Carlone Hôtel (2 Boulevard François-Grosso, in the same western quarter as the Locarno, above, and but a block inland from Promenade des Anglais; phone 9344-71-61) has the look of a turn-of-century townhouse. The lobby-lounge is cozily Belle Époque, and 15 of the 18 traditional-style bedrooms have baths. The hotel management is cordial. Sound value. *Moderate.*

Beach Regency Hôtel (223 Promenade des Anglais; phone 9383-91-51) opened a decade or so back as the Hyatt Regency Nice, changing managements in the interim. It would be near the top of my Nice hotels grouping were it only closer in to the core of town. Despite a Promenade des Anglais address, it's *way* to the west, enough so that you want a car or taxi for excursions to the center. Withal, facilities are exemplary: 335 contemporary-design terraced rooms (seaview ones are, of course, preferred), with good baths; big swimming pool, with sundeck and lunchtime barbecue café; two additional restaurants; and as many bar-lounges. *Luxury.*

Château du Domaine St.-Martin Hôtel (Route de Coursegoules, Vence; phone 9358-02-02) is accurately named, a castle-like hostelry that went up as recently as the mid-1930s amidst atmospheric ruins of a medieval predecessor, in an elevated 35-acre park, just outside Vence village (above). There are just 25 rooms and suites; some of the latter are in cottages— *bastides* they're called—dotted about the grounds. Each is distinctively decorated with eighteenth-century antique accents, which are complemented by fine accessories and textiles. Public spaces are no less beautiful, the principal salon—giving onto a terrace affording splendid views— most especially, what with Flemish tapestries and medieval sculpture. Both swimming pool and tennis court are nestled among olive trees in the garden. And the picture-windowed restaurant is exceptional enough to warrant attention in a later paragraph. To sum up: one of France's most beautiful hotels. Member, Relais et Châteaux. *Luxury.*

Diana Hôtel (Avenue des Poilus, Vence; phone 9358-28-56) is adequate for a stay of a night or two in the heart of Vence village. This is an agreeable enough, 25-room house, a five-minute walk from the core. Breakfast only. *Moderate.*

Le Mas d'Artigny Hôtel (two miles west of St.-Paul-de-Vence; phone 9332-84-54) straddles a hill in its own 20-acre park, with views of St.-Paul across the valley. This is a rambling complex embracing half a hundred rooms and suites, with suites dominating—there are nearly 30, and each suite is fronted by a swimming pool of its own. Bedroom furnishings are wicker, while public spaces are more traditional. The restaurant is reputed, and there's a big central pool for the poor unfortunates who, alas, have none attached to their accommodations. You may well fall in love with Le Mas d'Artigny; I find it rather cold. Member, Relais et Châteaux. *Luxury.*

La Colombe d'Or Hôtel (St.-Paul-de-Vence; phone 9332-80-02) is intimate (there are but 14 rooms and 8 suites, the lot traditional style). There's a restaurant about whose extraordinary art I write (above) and about whose classic-style food I write (below), a swimming pool, and a casual, relaxing ambience. Central. *First Class.*

Le Métropole Hôtel (15 Boulevard Maréchal-Leclerc, Beaulieu-sur-Mer, adjacent to St.-Jean-Cap-Ferrat, six miles east of Nice; phone 9301-00-88) is a Riviera delight, situated in its own seaside park—flower-filled and with swaying palms—containing precisely half a hundred no-two-alike rooms and suites and a generous-sized, heated, seawater pool on a fabulous sun-terrace just above the hotel's beach. Public spaces are smart, and the restaurant is as attractive as it is delicious—with seafood a specialty. Member, Relais et Châteaux. *Luxury.*

La Réserve Hôtel (5 Boulevard Maréchal-Leclerc, Beaulieu-sur-Mer, adjacent to St.-Jean-Cap-Ferrat, six miles west of Nice; phone 9301-00-01) is just next door to the Métropole (above), but a standout in its own right. There are—again like the Métropole—just half a hundred rooms; you want to specify a front one—the higher up, the better the view. The restaurant's picture windows overlook the great rectangle of a pool-cum-terrace and the beach. Smart, very smart. *Luxury.*

DAILY BREAD

La Merenda (43 Rue de la Terrasse) is so popular with locals—who know that the only way to book a table is to stop in, and do so in person—that there's no telephone. Go early—at midday or in the evening—and hope that you'll be seated. Cuisine is traditional and hearty. Open with a plate of black olives served with coarse bread, the better to keep you occupied until a giant platter of assorted salamis arrives— and more of that marvelous bread. Next comes a Niçoise version of pizza (*pissaladière* is the local term), and it's superb. Or opt for *pâtes au pistou*, Nice's answer to not-far-distant Genoa's pasta, served with basil-flavored pesto sauce. But save space for *boeuf en daube*—a masterful beef stew—or any of several other entrées. Desserts are hearty, too. In my experience, one of France's best restaurants. No credit cards. *Moderate.*

La Cambuse (5 Cours Saleya; phone 9380-12-31) is one of a number of congenial seafood restaurants in Vieux Nice, opposite the big open market whose activity you may view from an outdoor table, at lunch. Open with the house's own *tarte aux poireaux*—a tasty leek tart—or a slice of *pissaladière*. I challenge you to eat, in its entirety, the gigantic mess of tiny fish that are a part of the *friture de poissons*, not to mention, the assortment of local specialties that accompany the fish—including *frites*, deep-fried onions, Provençal-style tomatoes, and eggplant served several ways. An adventure. *Moderate.*

Le Saleya (12 Cours Saleya; phone 9362-29-62) is somewhat less casual than La Cambuse (above) and serves up a tasty fish soup, as well as *gigot d'agneau*, France's classic roast lamb. Pasta—especially lasagna—is good here, too. Prix-fixe or à la carte. *First Class.*

Le Grand Pavois (a.k.a. Chez Michel, 11 Rue Meyerbeer; phone 9388-77-42): Once you make up your mind not to let the dreadful paintings affect your meal, you can be happy here. You're in Nice, so it makes sense to open with a *salade Niçoise*—based, as you know from back home, on black olives and tuna; fish soup or stuffed mussels are options, and you continue with either fresh trout *meunière* or a filet of *lotte* (monkfish) grilled with fennel. Cordial and central. *First Class.*

Le Mac Mahon (50 Boulevard Jean-Jaurès; phone 9362-39-71) sounds oddly Irish to be on the Côte d'Azur. But when you hear its smiling staff pronounce its name (I will not attempt a phonetic imitation), you know you're in France. At any rate, oysters are the principal specialty. The half-dozen on the half shell that are the usual order, transatlantic, are only half a portion here, and you've several types to select from. Follow with a fish or seafood entrée. Central. *First Class.*

Chantecler (Négresco Hôtel, 37 Promenade des Anglais; phone 9388-39-51): You're transported to the eighteenth century when you enter: antique crystal chandeliers, a marvelous Rococo armoire, Louis XVI chairs covered in red velvet encircling tables centered with flowers—to supplement giant arrangements of gladiolas dotted about the room. The enormous staff—in tails, tuxes, or scarlet jackets—is as congenial as it is professional. Diners, predominantly French, are as dressy a crowd as you'll come across on the coast. Fare? The grill here is unabashedly *nouvelle;* you want to be a *nouvelle* afficionado to appreciate a meal that might open with pigeon and almond salad and continue with truffled zucchini, followed by raw salmon seasoned with sea salt; with a *tian*—a Provençal mix of minced vegetables, in this case combined with lamb—as entrée. Desserts are more conventional, even including Black Forest cake. *Luxury.*

Le Farniente (Westminster Concorde Hôtel, 27 Promenade des Anglais; phone 9388-29-44): Opt to lunch or dine inside, and the setting is pastel-shaded Louis XV, but warm-weather lunches or starlit dinners on the adjacent terrace are hardly to be despised. The prix-fixe menu—opening with a shellfish *terrine* and embracing a grilled fish of the day or sautéed lamb chops accompanied by Nice-origin *ratatouille* (a kind of vegetable casserole), as well as cheese and dessert—is good value, and good-tasting. *First Class.*

Café Tordo (Place Rossetti): I can't imagine a more picturesque setting for an al fresco cup of coffee or a cold drink than the Tordo, opposite the handsomely facaded cathedral in Vieux-Nice. *Moderate.*

Auberge du Jarrier (Biot; phone 9365-11-68) typifies this venerable village—and serves traditional dishes, expertly prepared. Have the prix-fixe menu, opening with the house's own duck tart, continuing with *médaillon* of lamb in a garlicky sauce, and concluding with any of Jarrier's house-made pastries. *First Class.*

Café des Acadias (Biot) is core of the village and a delightful spot to pause over a bit of refreshment and take in the scene. *Moderate.*

Hôtel du Château du Domaine St.-Martin Restaurant (Route de Cour-segoules, Vence; phone 9358-02-02): You're so preoccupied with the picture-window view of the garden and the sea way beyond that the unobtrusive captain is hesitant to interrupt. You order, though, beginning with an almost wickedly rich *confit* of *foie gras frais de canard* and following with *goujonettes de sole*—mini-filets lightly breaded and deep fried, with an entrée of mushroom-garnished veal *médaillons*. Assorted cheeses come next. Dessert is chocolate cake, chocolate frosted, topped by delicately carved orange rind, with an orange filling between each layer. Flawless service. In my experience, one of France's best restaurants. *Luxury.*

La Colombe d'Or Hôtel Restaurant (St.-Paul-de-Vence; phone 9332-80-02): Paintings on the wall of this restaurant—by a mix of great artists of the era—are alluded to above. Herewith, I counsel the Colombe's traditional fare. Order your dessert—flaming Grand Marnier *soufflé* at the same time you select earlier courses, opening perhaps with vegetable soup or caviar and continuing with deliciously sauced *pièce de boeuf*, expertly prepared roast lamb, or a rich chicken fricassee. Green salads are a pride of the house. And there are other desserts, if you decide against the *soufflé*. Warm-weather terrace. *First Class.*

Café de la Place (Place du Général-de-Gaulle, St.-Paul-de-Vence) is a Vence institution. Nothing will do but that you pause here for coffee or a cold drink, the while watching villagers out front undertaking a game of bocci. *Moderate.*

SHOPPER'S NICE
Galeries Lafayette, the principal department store, is entered on Rue Jean-Médecin, just north of Place Masséna; it embraces six levels, with a supermarket/wine store in the basement and a bank on four. Rue Masséna, leading west from Place Masséna, is the main pedestrian street, with such shops as *Daniel Hechter* and *Barton* (men's clothes), *Fil à Fil* (men's/women's accessories), *Les Must de Cartier* (jewelry), *Hédiard* (fancy foods and wine), *Harmonie* (perfume), and a number of women's clothing shops, including *Cacharel, New Man, Alain Manoukian, Berty, Philippe Salvet*, and *Love*. Rue de France, a westward extension of Rue Masséna, has a strong concentration of antiques shops, including *St.-Michel, Occasions*, and *Récamier*, as well as a fabulous chocolate shop, *Ventadour*—which ships. Rue Paradis—still another pedestrian street—has such smart boutiques as *Chanel* (women's accessories), *Façon-nable* (men's Yank-style clothes), and *Jacques Andréolis* (Baccarat, Daum, and Lalique crystal, as well as Christofle silver and several makes of Limoges china).

SOUND OF MUSIC

Opéra de Nice (Rue St.-François de Paule)—with a dignified neoclassic facade and a five-level auditorium—opened in 1885 and maintains a repertory company that is among the best in the south of France. Works presented run an interesting gamut, from Mozart's *Marriage of Figaro* and Wagner's *Die Meistersinger* through Richard Strauss's *Daphne* and Lerner and Lowe's *My Fair Lady*. There are, as well, seasons of ballet and symphonic and chamber music concerts.

Salle Apollon (in the Acropolis, Nice's extravagantly equipped Centre des Congrès), which opened just a century after the Opéra—in 1985—is one of Europe's most architecturally innovative theaters, embracing three irregularly contoured levels, with a seating capacity of 2,500 and a stage that's the second largest in France, after that of the Opéra in Paris. It serves as an alternate venue for presentations of opera, concerts, both classic and pop, and other entertainments.

INCIDENTAL INTELLIGENCE ━━━━━━━

If you're driving about, via rented car, bear in mind that the Riviera has a trio of *corniches*—cross-country highways: *Grande* (or High), *Moyenne* (Middle), and *Basse* (Low); the top two are the most scenic. Nice is a major point of departure for bus excursions, both day and half-day, to such coastal points as St.-Paul-de-Vence, Grasse, Antibes, Cannes, Vallauris, Èze, Monte Carlo, St.-Tropez, and even Genoa in Italy (see *Italy at Its Best*). Nice's annual *Carnaval* takes place the two weeks preceding Lent—and is an all-Europe leader of its type. *Aéroport de Nice–Côte d'Azur* (four miles southwest of town) is served by Pan American, which flies nonstop to and from the United States, as well as by other carriers, international and domestic. *Further information:* Office de Tourisme, Avenue Thiers, Nice; Office de Tourisme, Place de la Chapelle, Biot; Office de Tourisme, Place du Grand Jardin, Vence; Office de Tourisme, Rue Grande, St.-Paul-de-Vence; Office de Tourisme, 59 Avenue Semeria, St.-Jean-Cap-Ferrat; Office de Tourisme, 26 Avenue Renoir, Cagnes-sur-Mer.

27

Nîmes

Ancient Rome in Provence

BACKGROUND BRIEFING

I thank Hubert Robert for first leading me to Nîmes. The prolific eighteenth-century artist, known more for interpretations in oil of idyllic Italian ruins than for works themed to his native France, quite obviously journeyed to Provence in order to paint two evocative works that now hang in Paris's Louvre—where, incidentally, he was an early curator. The one Robert to which I refer is of the Roman-built Maison Carré, in the core of Nîmes; the other is of the amazing Roman aqueduct, Pont du Gard, constructed 2,000 years ago to provide Nîmes with water. Provoked by Robert into a visit, I was to learn that the subjects of both paintings not only still stand, but are eminently visitable—but two of a number of monuments of the ancient Roman presence.

It was location that drew the Romans to Nîmes. They liked its situation at a convenient stopping-off point between colonies in Spain and home base, to the east, in Italy. Originally *Colonia Augusta*—the Emperor Augustus was partial to it and lavish in his construction budgets—and later the French *Nismes*, it was, in the early centuries of our era, a showplace not only of the Romans' Gallic colonies, but of their empire. The empire's fall saw Nîmes decline. Starting in the early fifth century, a succession of invaders—Visigoths, Arabs, Normans—looted and plundered.

The Middle Ages saw it aligned with Languedoc and, eventually, the French Crown, gaining a university under François I and a disproportionately large Protestant populace. If the Huguenots thrived as a consequence of Henri IV's Edict of Nantes—protecting them—they suffered when his grandson, Louis XIV, revoked that edict. Later, they constituted the core of red-shirted guerrillas in the early eighteenth-century Camisard Revolt—a case of Protestants quite literally protesting repression—against the royal army.

Still substantially Protestant—there are half a dozen-plus Protestant churches, a goodly number in a French city with a population of 140,000—Nîmes weaves textiles (the English word *denim* evolved from Nîmes-origin cloth—*de Nîmes)*, and receives visitors curious to experience not only the vestiges of Rome painted by Hubert Robert, but others as well.

ON SCENE
Lay of the Land: Nîmes revolves around the greatest of the Roman constructions, *Les Arènes*, on the square taking its name, *Place des Arènes*, more or less in the center of town. Directly east is another square of consequence, *L'Esplanade*, from which the main shopping street, *Boulevard de l'Amiral Courbet*, leads north—passing the old quarter to its west, *Vieux Nîmes*, centered on the cathedral—to the Roman-built gate named for the city's builder-emperor, *Porte d'Auguste*. *Boulevard Victor-Hugo*, running north from the Arena to the *Maison Carré*, on the square taking its name, constitutes the western border of the city center. The railway station is east of the core on *Boulevard Sergent Triaire*.

Maison Carrée (Place de la Maison Carrée): Though it translates as Square House, this miraculously well-preserved rectangle of a Roman temple—built some 1,900 years ago—remains from without quite as exquisite as it must have been when new: the perfect pediment of its forward facade supported by half a dozen Corinthian columns, with still additional columns—10 at each extremity—flanking side walls. If the interior is not as it was, we cannot carp, given the wealth of objects on display, the lot of them from Roman Nîmes. Consider, for example, a perfectly preserved mosaic floor in tones of blue, brown, rust, and white; a sculpted Roman fisherman; a full-length *Apollo* in marble, discovered in the eighteenth century; and the equally superb *Vénus de Nîmes*, the city's single most celebrated work of sculpture.

Les Arènes (Place des Arènes): The amphitheater of Nîmes ranks easily, at least to this viewer of Roman-era amphitheaters, with the Colosseum in Rome, the Arena of Italy's Verona, the Roman-built Colosseum of El Djem in Tunis, the Arena in Arles, and Théâtre Antique in Orange, as among the great ones of the onetime empire. Not unlike Maison Carrée, it is extraordinarily well preserved. Ideally, you want to see it in the course of a *corrida*, or bullfight, with the spectacle of the matador's entrance easily on a par with similar ceremonies in Spain. But, at any time, this masterwork impresses. In Roman days, spectators—come to marvel at feats of the gladiators or charioteers—were segregated by caste, their 20,000 seats on two dozen levels divided vertically into sections for various subdivisions of the citizenry, with a vast canopy shading the entire audience when the sun was strong.

Tour Magne (Chemin de Combret) quite accurately translates as Great Tower. Tallest of what had been a network of towers punctuating the city's walls, it straddles a substantial hill, Mont Cavalier, overlooking the city from the north. The tower, in three levels and octagonal at its base, is close to 150 feet high. If you're up to it, ascend its 140 steps by means of a contemporary stairwell; the view is spectacular.

Temple de Diane and Jardins de la Fontaine (Quai de la Fontaine) are a pair best taken in in the course of a descent from Mont Cavalier and Tour Magne (above). The temple, though in ruins and not actually dedicated to Diana when it was built in the second century A.D. (the name was appended in a later era), retains enough architectural detail— pedimented (albeit blocked up) windows, gracefully arched doorways, series of small but interestingly embellished side rooms, for example—to make it visitworthy. And surrounding Jardins de la Fontaine constitute a capacious eighteenth-century complex based on the town's ancient fountain, with an enormous reflecting pool—a perfect foil for the mix of sculpture, marble benches, and wrought-iron railings surrounding it.

Musée Archéologique (13 Boulevard Amiral Courbet) occupies a one-time Jesuit school. Its collection is considerably larger than the small group of Roman objects in Maison Carrée (above), if no less choice. Sculpture is first-rate, with the range, busts of curly-headed youngsters to busts of bearded warriors. Medallions carved in terra-cotta record the life of the era. There are tombs and mosaics, capitals and toys, bronze lamps and glass jewelry, with a room full of Greek and Etruscan pottery as a bonus.

Musée des Beaux-Arts (Rue Cité Foulc) is more often than not ignored by short-term visitors intent on the city's Roman aspects. Its most spectacular exhibit is very Roman indeed: the largest and surely the handsomest of Nîmes-origin mosaics, called *Les Noces d'Admète*, embracing 15 fabulous panels depicting scenes of a Roman wedding. Whip along, then, to the Renaissance—and later eras—for the hardly inconsiderable collection of paintings. Bassano, Giordano, Luini, and Panini are among the Italians, best represented of the foreign schools. And there are French works by Vernet and Moreau, Largillière and Rigaud, Natoire and Mignard, Boucher and Fragonard; not to mention sculpture by the likes of Rodin and Bourdelle.

Musée du Vieux Nîmes (Place de la Cathédrale) makes its home in a seventeenth-century mansion that was for long the palace of bishops of Nîmes. If, like me, you're partial to municipal historical collections, you'll have a good time here. Furniture alone is outstanding, chairs through chests, but there are, as well, paintings and prints, a wealth of ceramics, myriad assorted curios, and an extensive collection of objects—including toreadors' costumes—relating to Nîmes's bullfighting tradition.

Cathedral of St.-Castor (Place de la Cathédrale) is hardly among France's foremost. Still, its facade—top-heavy, with a formidable left-hand tower and a mix of epochs, Romanesque through Rococo—is not unimpressive, and you want to give a few minutes to the frieze, busy with gargoyles and griffons. Then amble about the neighborhood; you are in *Vieux Nîmes*, and it's worthwhile strolling past medieval and Renaissance houses—some beautifully embellished—on *Rue de l'Aspic, Rue des Marchands, Rue de la Madeleine*, and *Place du Marché*.

Pont du Gard (23 miles northeast of Nîmes) represents both engineering and architectural skills of the ancient Romans—at their most brilliant. They erected it in the nineteenth year of the first century A.D. to supply Nîmes with water from the Eure River, which it spans to this day. Even allowing for a nineteenth-century restoration commissioned by the government of Napoleon III (after a visit by the emperor), the resilience of this three-level construction is mind-boggling. To cite dimensions—three gracefully arched levels, 900 feet long by 160 feet high—is not to do the Pont du Gard justice. You'll appreciate the proportions of the aqueduct by having a look at it from either side of the river, ascending, then, for an ambulatory exploration, one side to the other.

SETTLING IN
Imperator Hôtel (Quai de la Fontaine; phone 6621-90-30) is a well-situated and handsome house of some years, kept nicely up to date, though in traditional style, with its ace architectural feature a pretty inner courtyard. There are 62 well-equipped rooms, a restaurant later counseled, and a bar. Service, in my experience, is unsmiling and chilly; hope that this situation will have ameliorated by the time of your visit. Mapotel/Best Western. *First Class.*

Cheval Blanc Hôtel (1 Place des Arènes; phone 6667-20-03) could not be more strategically situated—just opposite the Roman amphitheater, heart of town. This is an agreeable house with 50 rooms in the traditional manner, attractive restaurant (later recommended), and friendly bar. *First Class.*

Louvre Hôtel (2 Square de la Couronne; phone 6667-22-75) is central. There are 35 functional rooms, convenient restaurant, and bar. *Moderate.*

Vieux Castillon Hôtel (Castillon du Gard, just outside Rémoulins, a mile and a half from Pont du Gard and 15 miles northeast of Nîmes;

phone 6686-17-07) is set in a charmer of a village, embracing a complex of typically Provençal stone buildings edged by an elevated garden-cum-swimming pool. The highly reputed restaurant, with copper lanterns extending from a beamed ceiling, moves outdoors in summer. Drinks are served in a clutch of lounges. And there are just under two dozen rooms, no two alike, each antiques accented and smartly wallpapered and accessorized, with excellent baths. Member, Relais et Châteaux. *Luxury.*

Chemin de l'Hostellerie is the aptly named road a good quarter hour south of Nîmes on which are clustered relatively recently constructed outposts—functional, if hardly beautiful—of a number of hotel chains. On scene are *Sofitel (First Class), Mercure (First Class), Novotel (First Class),* and *Ibis (Moderate);* all but Ibis have restaurants and swimming pools.

DAILY BREAD
Imperator Hôtel Restaurant (Quai de la Fontaine; phone 6621-90-30) is a quiet but tasteful room—mural-like pictures of ancient Nîmes adorn its mocha walls; flowers are everywhere—with a commendable kitchen. A multicourse dinner might include such specialties as scallop and *foie gras* salad, the house's own *daube de sole* with artichokes, lamb steak with a creamed tarragon sauce, and a warm multifruit tart enveloped in raspberry sauce. Caveat: Unless matters have improved, do not expect smiles from the serving staff. *First Class.*

Lisita (2 Boulevard des Arènes; phone 6667-29-15) is at once central, reliable, and delicious. This might be just the spot to try such local dishes as *brandade de morue* (the Provençal cod and olive oil blend that tastes much better than it sounds), and *boeuf à la gardianne.* Nice sweets. *First Class.*

Mas (5 bis Rue de Sauve; phone 6623-24-71) is a wise choice for hearty specialties like filet of veal, Nîmes style; eels, garlic sauced; preserved duck with beans. *First Class.*

Brasserie le Courbet (18 Boulevard Amiral Courbet; phone 6667-25-23) is convenient, following a morning in the shops, for a substantial *entrecôte aux frites* lunch; other hearty dishes, too. *Moderate.*

Vieux Castillon Hôtel Restaurant (Castillon du Gard; phone 6686-17-07) is at its most romantic on a mild, summer evening, when tables are set around the pool, in the moonlight. Or go for lunch in connection with a visit to Pont du Gard. Consider a seafood salad or expertly prepared *foie gras* as openers; lamb chops, chervil-seasoned, and a platter of vegetables as an entrée; selection of cheeses; a sampling of, say, two of the house's celebrated sweets—poached whole fresh pears in a caramel sauce or a frozen *soufflé* scented with Poire William *eau-de-vie*. Expert service with a smile. In my view, one of France's best restaurants. *Luxury.*

INCIDENTAL INTELLIGENCE

Aéroport de Nîmes-Garons is five miles from town; scheduled domestic service. *Further information:* Office de Tourisme, 6 Avenue des Feuchères, Nîmes.

28

Pau

Vive Henri IV!

BACKGROUND BRIEFING

It is not an Italian River, in the course of a diversion into France. It is not Edgar Allen's last name, misspelled. It is not the word *poor*, as an American southerner might pronounce it.

It is, rather, a medium-sized southwest city so close to snowy Pyrenees peaks that they appear almost touchable from the core of town. And it is the birthplace—his fabulous castle is a museum operated by the French Government—of King Henri IV. Surely if a poll were to be taken today, four and a half centuries after his death, the likelihood is that Henri would come through, hands down, as France's favorite monarch. The very same Henri who wanted "a chicken in every pot" for all of his subjects was, as well, the very first of the dynasty of Bourbon monarchs that extended through his son, Louis XIII, beyond to Charles X in the post-Revolutionary period.

Given the complexity of his origins and, indeed, of his reign, Henri's kingly achievements are not always easy to appreciate. His father was, to be sure, a Bourbon duke, but his grandmother was the much-admired Queen Marguerite of Navarre, his great-uncle was French King François I, and his mother was Queen Jeanne d'Albret of Navarre, so that he became King Henri III of Navarre *before* becoming Henri IV of France.

His religion switches surely set some sort of record. He began as a Protestant, like his mother; became a Catholic after marrying his first wife (Marguerite of Valois); returned to Protestantism again during the Wars of Religion; leaned toward Catholicism later in the course of a conflict that translated as the War of the Three Henrys; reaffirmed his Catholicism—presumably by opining the oft-quoted "Paris is well worth a Mass" upon agreeing to enter the capital as king; and later came to the aid of Protestants with his proclamation of the Edict of Nantes, guaranteeing religious freedom. That edict was revoked by his grandson, Louis XIV, but Henri's reign saw other remarkable innovations.

Between the period of the annulment of his union with Marguerite of Valois and his second marriage—to Marie de Medici—he achieved a reputation as a leader with a sense of organization, fostering commerce and agriculture, signing trade treaties with foreign countries, and manifesting a concern for the welfare of his commoner subjects—not usual with monarchs of that era—or, indeed, of succeeding eras. Henri was an interesting man who obviously inherited the wit and sharp intelligence of his grandmother, Marguerite—as well as her Pau castle.

Switch, then, to Napoleonic Pau. The emperor himself is said to have inspired the still extant central boulevard that affords smashing Pyrenees panoramas. Word of the mountain views and of the city's other charms—a salubrious climate, among these—spread north of the Channel to England. The British started coming as tourists in the post-Waterloo years, and, although their numbers are not strong contemporarily, Pau acknowledges its debt to them for racetracks, hunt clubs, and what is believed to have been the first golf course on the continent of Europe.

ON SCENE
Lay of the Land: The sector of Pau with which you want to become familiar is its southwest corner, lying north of the *Gave de Pau River*. *Place Georges Clemenceau* and smart *Place Royale* are the central squares. The former lies amidships, with a wide street named for two military leaders cutting through it: *Rue Maréchal-Joffre* leads west into *Rue du Château* and the city's showplace castle, while *Rue Maréchal Foch* lies to the east in the direction of an all-France sleeper of a fine-arts museum. Smart shops are clustered on *Rue Louis-Barthou* to the north of Place Royale. To that same square's south is *Boulevard des Pyrénées*, aptly named; it was designed to bring the mountains into glorious perspective.

Château de Pau (Rue du Château): The setting is out of a fairy tale. A river, first, low down and with a properly picturesque bridge traversing it. A hill, next, as the appropriate site. Then, the castle, behind a bulky keep dating to the fourteenth century, with most of the rest of the facade—towers and turrets and high, gabled windows set into severe, black-slate Mansard roofs—two centuries younger. It is surely the supreme irony of this castle—which was the birthplace of Henri IV, first of a long line of Bourbon kings—that its restoration, after severe neglect that set in with the Revolution, was effected by a pair of non-Bourbon, nineteenth-century monarchs: King Louis-Philippe and Emperor Napoleon III. Credit them with a thorough and professional job. Using concepts of the nineteenth century, the two sovereigns' designers have given us a decidedly romantic series of Renaissance interiors, with furnishings an engaging mix of authentic pieces of the period, along with reproductions made at the time of the restoration and magnificent Gobelin tapestries. It works very well, indeed.

You see it on guided tours that depart periodically, with commentary in French. I think the state bedrooms—Chambre de la Reine and Chambre des Souverains, both with opulently canopied beds, paneled walls, marble mantels, and coffered ceilings—are the most elegant. But the vast Grand Salon, in which Henri IV was baptized, and the bedroom—with an interminably long plaque embedded in the wall above its fireplace, affording presumed details—where Henri was, by tradition, born on December 13, 1553, are of interest, too. So is the bedroom of his mother, Queen Jeanne d'Albret, principally because of the splendid flight-of-angels tapestry on one of its walls. And every visitor oohs and ahs in the dining room, a Louis Philippe creation, dubbed Salle aux Cent Couverts, its table comfortably seating a hundred for a regal meal.

Musée des Beaux-Arts (Rue Mathieu Lalanne) is nondescript architecturally, but you don't want its setting to discourage you from touring what is one of the most eye-popping of French provincial museums. You are engaged from the moment of entry. To your left is an open-to-visitors room that is hung with original works by *très jeune Palois*—Pau youngsters, more or less kindergarten age, enrolled in museum classes. Then you make the rounds of the galleries, for the permanent collection. For Americans, surely the most unexpected painting is one labeled *Bureau du Coton à la Nouvelle-Orléans*, portraying top-hatted traders at the New Orleans Cotton Exchange and painted by none other than Edgar Degas in 1873. But there are other treats—a solemn religious procession by Juan de Juanès, whose works rarely are seen outside of his native Spain; other Spaniards, including El Greco, Zurbarán, Alfonso Cano, and Ribera—the lot attesting to the proximity of Spain to Pau; rich Italian representation—Bassano, Giordano, Guido Reni, to name a trio of painters from that country; Brueghel and Jordaens, Rubens (with an extraordinary *Last Judgment*) and David Teniers, among the Flemings; British portraitists like George Romney and Sir David Wilkie. And a wealth of French art: a Boudin of Bordeaux harbor; an unexpected self-portrait of the sculptor, Carpeaux; a Corot landscape; a cluster of sailing ships by Daubigny; Largillière and Fantin-Latour; Marquet and Berthe Morisot; Nattier and Oudry, Rigaud and Robert; Van Loo and Vuillard. Wow!

Musée Bernadotte (8 Rue Tran): A funny thing happened in Pau on January 26, 1763: Jean-Baptiste Bernadotte was born in a middle-class Pau house. He went on to achieve distinction in Napoleon's army, becoming a general in 1794, married Désirée Clary in 1798, had a son named Oscar in 1799, and—through a chain of fortuitous political circumstances—was named Crown Prince of Sweden in 1810. He was officially adopted later that year by the childless Swedish king, Karl XIII, whom he succeeded as King Karl Johan XIV in 1818. His son by

Désirée—who broke her engagement to Napoleon to marry Bernadotte—
became King Oscar I upon his father's death in 1844; and the Bernadotte
dynasty they established continues as Sweden's Royal Family. If you
watch old movies on TV, you may recall the star-studded, 1956 Holly-
wood film, *Désirée*, which tells the Bernadotte story; Jean Simmons
played the title role, Michael Rennie was Bernadotte, Marlon Brando
was Napoleon, and Merle Oberon was Josephine. That background
behind you, enjoy this charming house-museum, brimming with Bernadotte memorabilia, including the bedroom in which Karl Johan XIV
was born. Visitors to the house have included the reigning Swedish
monarch, King Karl Gustaf XVI.

Parc Beaumont (at the eastern end of Boulevard des Pyrénées) is the
handsomest in town (Pau has three times been declared France's petti-
est garden city, in national competitions) with its ace-in-the-hole *Casino
Municipal*, along with the requisite lake and waterfalls.

Cathedral of Lescar (Place Royale, Lescar) is a quarter-hour's drive from
Pau. What makes the trip to the village of Lescar worthwhile is the
cathedral's Romanesque apse and altar. Other parts of the multiperiod
building—including a severe nave—are late Gothic, with the stained
glass nineteenth century.

Parc National des Pyrénées—embracing much of the countryside south
of town, in the beautiful mountainous region bordering Spain—makes
for a pleasant excursion, given its mix of lures: dense forests, snowy
peaks, mirrorlike lakes, and a wildlife population that includes bears and
eagles.

Lourdes (25 miles east of Pau) is the town in which Bernadette Soubir-
ous—later a nun and canonized in 1933—claimed to have witnessed the
appearance of the Virgin Mary on 18 occasions, beginning February 11,
1858. Pilgrims, many of them incurable invalids, have not stopped coming since, to pray at the grotto where Bernadette experienced her visions—*Grotte de Massabielle*—now the nucleus of a religious complex
embracing hospitals, as well as churches; most important of the latter is
Basilique Pie X, built in 1958 on the hundredth anniversary of the visions
and, to understate, massive, with a capacity of 20,000. The popularity of
Lourdes is a phenomenon of France; there are some four million pilgrims
each year, with Spain, Italy, and Ireland the heaviest represented countries, France following. Hotel capacity is extraordinary; room total is
17,000, with by far the majority in very simple hotels and pensions. And
the souvenir shops appear limitless. Permanent reception centers—*Ac-
ceuil de Pèlerins* (Pilgrims' Registration) and *Halls des Malades* (Patients'
Reception Rooms)—are at the railway station. Busiest times are at Easter,
August, and October.

Sauveterre-de-Béarn (35 miles northwest of Pau), a pretty village flanking the Cave d'Oloron River, is indicated, perhaps, for a lunch stop combined with a visit to *Château de Gaston VII*, with a splendidly situated terrace, and *Church of Ste.-Marie*—twelfth-century Romanesque, with a massive tower and panoramas of the Pyrenees from the perspective of a romantic ruined bridge jutting into the river.

SETTLING IN

Continental Hôtel (2 Rue Maréchal-Foch; phone 5927-69-31) is an immediately likable turn-of-century house that has been efficiently updated, the while retaining a traditional look. The 110 rooms include some attractive and commodious quarters with good baths, and there are both a restaurant—seafood is the specialty—and a bar-lounge. Smiling service. Mapotel/Best Western. *First Class.*

Grand Hôtel du Commerce (9 Rue Maréchal-Joffre; phone 5927-24-40) exaggerates, perhaps, with "grand" as part of its title, but it is agreeably traditional, with pleasant lobby, half a hundred rooms (accessories and wallpapers are tasteful; baths, modern), bar-lounge, and a Louis XIII-style restaurant recommended on a later page. *Moderate.*

Paris Hôtel (80 Rue Émile-Garet; phone 5927-34-39) is an elderly house whose management has modernized it: lobby bar-lounge, as well as the 40 rooms. Those rooms facing the hotel's courtyard are bath equipped. Breakfast only. Central. *Moderate.*

Roncevaux Hôtel (35 Rue Louis-Barthou; phone 5927-08-44) is ideal for shoppers, given a situation on Pau's heart-of-town boutiques street. There are just over 40 well-equipped rooms and a bar. Breakfast only. *Moderate.*

Gallis et Londres Hôtel (26 Avenue Bernadette-Soubirous, Lourdes; phone 5994-10-20) is No. 1 in Lourdes—with 90 full-facility rooms, restaurant, and bar. *First Class.*

DAILY BREAD

L'Aragon (18 Boulevard des Pyrénées; phone 5927-12-34): Though it is more *brasserie* than proper restaurant, L'Aragon has big pluses, especially in the case of the visitor with but time for a single Pau meal. You see the mountains as you enjoy your meal, thanks to the Boulevard des Pyrénées location. And your meal can be composed of such regional specialties as the local and delicious hard sausage, the also-local *rillettes* (a coarse *pâté*) or—in cool weather—the celebrated Béarn soup, based on vegetables, with the added flavor of preserved goose and a hambone, as starters; and fresh local salmon simply grilled and served with *sauce Béarnaise* (you are, remember, in Béarn), caught-in-the-neighborhood trout sautéed with almonds, or *confit de canard*—preserved duck—accompanied by *pommes persillées*, as entrées. Delicious, made-on-premises fruit tarts and wines of the region—from across-the-river Jurançon. No credit cards. *Moderate.*

St.-Jacques (9 Rue du Parlement; phone 5927-58-97) welcomes with a smiling staff and an inn-like interior with beamed ceilings, fireplace, and fresh flowers everywhere. The well-priced menu might embrace onion soup or smoked salmon, *entrecôte* served with a delicious *sauce Béarnaise* and crispy *frites*; or *maigret de canard*—sliced breast of duck—appropriately garnished. Near the château. *First Class.*

Les Pyrénées (Place Royale; phone 5927-07-05) attracts with a convivial Belle Époque ambience. There are tables out on the square in good weather and a downstairs bar-lounge, and the restaurant—up a flight—offers a prix-fixe menu that might be comprised of salad as an opener, *confit de canard* as an entrée, and *praliné mousse* for dessert, with wine included. Friendly. *First Class.*

Louis XIII (Grand Hôtel du Commerce, 9 Rue du Maréchal-Joffre; phone 5927-24-40) is brick-walled and candlelit at dinner, with ladder-back chairs flanking tables, at which you might be served a four-course menu of regional specialties, such as trout sautéed in Jurançon wine, *confit de canard,* and your choice of local cheeses or a made-on-premises sweet. *First Class.*

Café de la Coupole (Place Clemenceau), an atmospheric locale for coffee-cum-people-watching on a central square; also a restaurant. *Moderate/First Class.*

À Boste (Sauveterre-de-Béarn; phone 5938-50-62) is part of a complex embracing an eleventh-century tower that is pleasant for a lunch pause—fare is traditional—in connection with village exploration. *Moderate.*

SHOPPER'S PAU
Department stores—*Nouvelles Galeries* and *Prisunic*—are on Place Clémenceau, and Rue Serviez is a busy pedestrians-only street, but you want to stroll Rue Louis-Barthou for its boutiques, which include—to give you an idea of how smart a city this small can be—*Cacharel, Pierre Balmain, Chloë, Alain Manoukian, Natacha* (which features *Kenzo*), *Pérrineau* (with pricey jewelry), and *Olde England* (menswear).

INCIDENTAL INTELLIGENCE ═══════════════════

Further information: Office de Tourisme, Place Royale, Pau; Office de Tourisme, Mairie, Sauveterre-du-Béarn; Office de Tourisme, Place de Champ-Commun, Lourdes; Parc National des Pyrénées, Route de Pau, Pau. There is scheduled air service between Pau and Paris.

29

Poitiers and La Rochelle

East-Central Duo

BACKGROUND BRIEFING

Geography and tourism? Of course there's a correlation. Consider these two east-central cities: Poitiers—respectably aged and with its fair share of architectural treasures; and not-far-distant La Rochelle—most monument-rich port of France's long stretch of Atlantic coast between Brittany and Biarritz. They are both far enough south to be ignored, more often than not, by inspectors of Loire Valley châteaux (Chapter 20) to the northeast, and too far north to be considered visitable by travelers in more southerly Périgord (Chapter 34).

Poitiers, by far the elder of the pair, is one of the rare French cities whose modern name is unrelated to what ancient Romans called it—*Limonum*. It had turned Christian even before the Romans left, and—under its first bishop, the sainted Hilaire (whose name was given to a still-standing Poitiers church)—was the venue of a considerable clutch of convents as early as the fourth century. Later, it was ruled by Germanic Visigoths, who were followed by the Franks and eventually by Normans.

Eleanor of Aquitaine, the consort first of a French king (Louis VII) and then of an English one (Henry II), established a court of her own—and a glittering one, at that—in twelfth-century Poitiers. Two centuries later, during the Hundred Years War, Poitiers knew both English rule, for a period, *and* Jeanne d'Arc, as well; she was interrogated about the divine "voices" exhorting her to aid the Crown in the still visitable Great Hall of the city's ducal Palace prior to receiving a force of troops to battle the English enemy.

If you discount La Rochelle's contemporary eminence—among savvy French holiday-makers, for the most part—as a vacation destination, it has three claims to fame: as France's premier Atlantic fishing port; as departure point for many New World immigrants, especially the settlers of early Montreal; and as a focal point of Huguenot (i.e., Protestant) strength, vanquished by troops under the command of Louis XIII and Cardinal Richelieu, after a near-interminable, 14-month siege.

Half a century after this bitter defeat, Louis XIV proclaimed the Revocation of the Edict of Nantes, which lost French Protestants their religious rights, but had one positive effect: establishment of America's Rochelle—New Rochelle, New York—by refugees fleeing to the New World from the original French Rochelle, in 1688.

ON SCENE

POITIERS

Lay of the Land: *Place du Maréchal-Leclerc* is dead center, site of *Printemps* department store, with such pedestrian streets as *Rue des Cordeliers* (with *Monoprix* department store), *Rue Gambetta,* and *Rue du Moulin à Vent* in its vicinity, as are such other central streets—these strollable because of Renaissance houses—*Grande Rue* and *Rue de la Chaîne.* Everything you'll want to visit is more or less central and reached by foot. The railway station is west of the core on *Boulevard du Grand-Cerf.*

Church of Notre-Dame-la-Grande (Place Charles-de-Gaulle), an all-France ranker, is one of the most beautiful Romanesque churches in the republic. The facade is an uninterrupted mass of carving—above the central portal and the arches flanking it and in two upper levels of sculpture-filled niches; look carefully and you'll recognize *The Annunciation, The Nativity, The Visitation,* Old Testament prophets, the dozen Apostles. The interior is at its most sublime in the choir, surrounded by half a dozen columns—each with a magnificent capital—supporting a dome surfaced with a thirteenth-century fresco. And all of the chapels are art filled.

Baptistry of St.-Jean (Rue St.-Jean) is a mind-boggler. You step down—descending half a flight—at its entrance to find yourself in a massive space that was constructed between the fourth and sixth centuries and is, not surprisingly, given this pedigree, among the oldest Christian monuments in France. The baptismal font in its center is simple and beautiful; so are the frescoes.

Cathedral of St.-Pierre (Place de la Cathédrale) is anticlimactic after Notre-Dame and the baptistry (above), its near neighbor. But richly ornamented Gothic is hardly to be despised, given the quality of the carving of the tympanum framing each of three portals. The nave is high, wide, and handsome, and the thirteenth-century stalls of the choir are among the oldest in France.

Church of St.-Hilaire (Rue du Doyenne) is named for Poitiers's first bishop and surely does his memory justice. It is sublime Romanesque, parts of it dating to the eleventh century. Start out back, taking in the graceful apse, before you move along in to admire a long, cool nave and a severe transept—these in contrast to ebullient capitals of pillars framing the choir.

Palais de Justice (Place du Palais) represents the handiwork of centuries, twelfth through nineteenth. A courthouse today, it was, in earlier centuries, the home of counts of Poitiers and of dukes of Aquitaine. Head for the *Grande Salle*. A triple-compartment fireplace, with an intricately carved mantel surmounted by a massive Gothic window, occupies the entire far wall. The carved-wood ceiling is worth a little neck strain. And you will want to pause a bit when reminded that it was in this room that the Bishop of Poitiers quizzed Jeanne d'Arc about the visions that resulted in her leading French troops in battle against the English.

Musée Ste.-Croix (Rue Jean-Jaurès) goes on and on and on—high-ceilinged gallery after high-ceilinged gallery in rambling contemporary quarters, part archeological exhibits (bits and pieces of Roman Poitiers are the Ste.-Croix at its best) and with some paintings, none by celebrated masters or of any special distinction. Skippable.

LA ROCHELLE

Lay of the Land: Remember two words: *Vieux-Port*. The visitor's life in La Rochelle revolves around this romantic inlet of the sea, guarded these many centuries by a pair of battlements out of a fairy tale—*Tour St. Nicolas*, fifteenth century and the taller of the pair of towers; and somewhat older *Tour de la Chaîne*, so called because a chain was extended from it to its counterpart, as a way of closing the harbor. (Both of these towers are visitable; the Chaîne has a mini-model of medieval La Rochelle). Still a third tower—at times mistaken for a church because of the steeple topping it off—is *Tour de la Lanterne* nearby; take a walk up its spiral stairway to the summit for panoramas of town and sea. Cafés, restaurants, and hotels line Vieux-Port in and around *Cours des Dames*, *Quai de Carénage*, and *Quai Duperré*. The principal shopping street, *Rue St.-Yon*—perpendicular with Quai Duperré—passes a number of atmospheric thoroughfares intersecting it and lined with fine old houses. *Rue Gargoulleau*, at right angles to it, leads to *Place Verdun*, around which official La Rochelle is clustered, with its dominant monument *Cathedral of St.-Louis*, designed in the eighteenth century. The *Bourse* (now the

Chamber of Commerce) and *Palais de Justice* (courthouse)—also classic style, eighteenth century—are nearby. Beaches? *Promenade du Mall*, a 10-minute drive from the center, is a wide, mile-long, white-sand strand, centered by a casino, with cafés and restaurants dotted about. Or take a ferry from *La Pallice*, three miles north of town, to *Île de Ré*, lunching and/or overnighting in the village of *La Flotte*.

Musée du Nouveau Monde (10 Rue Fleurieu)—the Museum of the New World—opened its elegant doors on May 15, 1982. I mention the date because of its significance: the three hundredth anniversary of the founding of Louisiana. This museum, in this town with strong New World associations, was created as a cooperative venture of the City of La Rochelle, the Département of Charente-Maritime in which it is situated, and the French Government. Setting is an extraordinarily beautiful eighteenth-century mansion, Hôtel Fleurieu, refurbished for museum use, but with decorative details—fireplaces surrounded with gilt-framed mirrors, superbly paneled walls, a marble stairway, with masterful wrought-iron bannister—left intact. Exhibits reflect the museum's theme: commerce between and relations with what had been Acadia (now Nova Scotia), Quebec, and other areas of Canada, Louisiana, the French West Indies, and Brazil. Displays are more a case of quality than quantity. Only a selection of objects from the permanent collection is shown at any given time: Walls of one room are covered with panels of antique wallpaper depicting Indian life in the New World; an early nineteenth-century clock made of gilded bronze, its dial surmounted with a spear-carrying Indian, is placed atop a mantel. A Mohawk brave, European-drawn in the eighteenth century, is framed on a wall opposite. The bronze bust of a fine-featured chief wearing a multihued feather headdress occupies the panel of another wall. Caches of moccasins and snowshoes, sleighs and jewelry, wampum and hatchets fill cases. And pieces with decorative interest—a spear fashioned like a fleur-de-lis, an exquisitely carved powder horn, a framed map of sixteenth-century *Floride Française*, a watercolor of a banana leaf—are displayed with an eye to esthetics. There are, as well, fanciful painted interpretations of the New World and its people by artists who had never seen it. The only other comparable museum with which I am familiar—Museo de América, on the University of Madrid campus (see *Spain at Its Best*)—doesn't hold a candle to this one.

Hôtel de Ville (Place de la Mairie) is visitable by means of regularly departing guided tours; go along regardless of your fluency in French, to see this superb mansion, medieval without, elaborate Renaissance within, with one of its exhibits a plaque expressing the friendship of the people of New Rochelle, New York, toward the people of La Rochelle.

Musée d'Orbigny-Bernon (Rue St.-Côme) is a felicitous mix of history (exhibits that graphically portray the seventeenth-century Siege of La Rochelle) and the decorative arts (porcelain most especially), with the setting—an aged mansion—as appealing as the exhibits.

Musée des Beaux-Arts (Rue Gargoulleau) has a relative handful of known artists represented—Corot and Chassériau, out of the last century; Signac and Marquet, with post-Impressionist paintings of La Rochelle's Vieux Port; outstanding drawings; regional painters' works.

SETTLING IN

POITIERS

De France Hôtel (28 Rue Carnot; phone 4941-32-01) is your prototypical old-fashioned, small-city, French-traditional house. Public spaces are high-ceilinged and formal, the 86 rooms—no two quite the same—number some very agreeable accommodations among them, with good baths, and there are both congenial cocktail lounge and creditable restaurant. Core of town. *First Class.*

De l'Europe Hôtel (39 Rue Carnot; phone 4988-12-00) is quite as central as the De France (above)—just down the street. You enter through an aged courtyard, finding yourself in a pleasant lobby-lounge area. There are half a hundred full-facility rooms, and a restaurant that caters only to groups. For the rest of us, breakfast only. *Moderate.*

Domaine de Périgny Hôtel (Périgny, 18 miles northwest of town; phone 4951-80-43) is an isolated country complex, with lobby-bar-*nouvelle* cuisine restaurant in the contemporarily furnished main building and 40 antiques-accented rooms—differing in size and furnishings, some with little terraces—in a detached pavilion. Service is polite and professional, the restaurant—in my view—only middling; it moves to the garden in warm weather. Swimming pool, tennis. Member, Relais et Châteaux. *First Class.*

Royal-Poitou Hôtel (Route de Paris, seven miles north of town; phone 4901-72-86) can be faulted for vivid-hued decor of public spaces (lounge is royal blue, bar is purple, restaurant and poolside terrace-café are a relatively subdued red and white). But bedrooms—32 all told—are easy-to-live-with brown and beige, and staff is friendly. *First Class.*

LA ROCHELLE

Le Champlain Hôtel (20 Rue Rambaud; phone 4641-34-34) went up in the eighteenth century as the townhouse of a wealthy family and has retained much of its original decor—parquet floors and Rococo furniture in lounges that are set off by gilded Ionic columns and illuminated by crystal chandeliers. Those of the 32 bedrooms I've inspected are not without antique pieces—an armoire here, a chair there—and have good baths. Lovely. Breakfast only. *First Class.*

De France et d'Angleterre Hôtel (22 Rue Gargoulleau; phone 4641-34-66) is an essentially contemporary house, with both mod-look and traditional-design rooms (76 all told), a congenial cocktail lounge, and a reliable restaurant that moves to the garden it overlooks in summer. Central. Mapotel/Best Western. *First Class.*

St.-Jean-d'Acre Hôtel (4 Place de la Chaîne; phone 4641-73-33) is heart of the La Rochelle action, by which I mean, smack on the Vieux-Port. Public spaces and those of the 50 rooms I've looked at are contemporary and agreeable; you want, of course, to make sure your accommodations overlook the harbor. Vieux-Port Restaurant, a La Rochelle leader, is on the premises and later reviewed. *Moderate.*

Le Richelieu Hôtel (La Flotte, Île de Ré; phone 4609-60-70) makes for an agreeable respite, in the course of either a day's outing from La Rochelle (in which case, I suggest a seafood lunch in its excellent restaurant) or for a relaxing night or two; there are 22 traditional-style rooms with terraces giving onto the garden; attractive public spaces including a super bar-lounge; and a swimming pool, as well as the beach. *First Class.*

DAILY BREAD

POITIERS

Pierre Benoist (Route Nationale 10, Ligugé, a few miles west of town; phone 4957-11-52). A meal at Benoist may be likened to stopping by with friends in the country. Setting is a house in a garden: welcome is warm, cuisine traditional, service at tables on the terrace in warm weather. With the regional Poitou smoked ham, garlic-scented snails, or a lobster salad as openers, you may proceed with such entrées as *steak au poivre*, *châteaubriand sauce Béarnaise*, roast stuffed chicken, or a fish special. Desserts? Both *mousse au chocolat* and *profiteroles au chocolat* are special. *Luxury.*

Aux Armes d'Obernai (19 Rue Arthur Ranc; phone 4941-16-33) is relatively small, with the hearty cuisine of Alsace as its ace-in-the-hole. By that, I mean you may have the sauerkraut-based *choucroute garnie* or *poulet au Riesling*—Alsace's answer to *coq au vin*—preceded by *foie gras de canard* and followed with cheese and house-baked pastry—from the prix-fixe menu. Service is both cordial and professional. Central. *First Class.*

Le Poitevin (76 Rue Carnot; phone 4988-35-04) is smartly rustic, makes a specialty of regional dishes. Build your meal around the house's own chicken casserole, roast kid, or unusually prepared duck with peaches in a Sherry sauce. For dessert: frozen raspberry *mousse*. Central. *First Class.*

Taverne de Maître Kanter (24 Rue Carnot; phone 4941-07-74) is a *brasserie* with good salads, omelets, and steaks. Okay for a casual lunch. *Moderate.*

Crêperie Bretonne (51 Rue de la Cathédrale; phone 4988-81-74): The kind of *crêpes* you may remember from Brittany, both savory and sweet. *Moderate.*

Café Gambetta (Place du Palais): Take a table on the square and unwind in the midst of exploration, over coffee or something cold to drink. *Moderate.*

LA ROCHELLE

Au Vieux-Port (4 Rue de la Chaîne; phone 4641-73-33): If it's cool, you'll be served indoors, at tables set with pink linen and flanked by country chairs. But hope for sunshine; an al fresco meal is what Vieux Port is all about. The name of the game is seafood—a dozen oysters on the half-shell, crayfish with mayonnaise, half a cold lobster, or fish soup—among starters. Follow with sole grilled or prepared *meunière* style. Super sweets. *First Class.*

Claridge (1 Rue Admyrauld; phone 4641-35-71) is heart of Vieux La Rochelle, with antique chairs at tables set with beige linen. Open with the house's own smoked salmon or *foie gras*. Seafood is indicated as the entrée. *First Class.*

Les Flots (1 Rue de la Chaîne; phone 4641-32-51) is a Vieux-Port ranker, with *bouillabaisse* and grilled lobster, among specialties. *First Class.*

Richard Coutenceau (Plage de la Concurrence; phone 4641-48-19): Restaurants named for individuals usually are called after young owner-chefs out to make reputations with *nouvelle* cuisine. Such is the case with M. Coutenceau's establishment out at the beach; his fare has a solid seafood base. Open with this area's beloved *mouclade*—creamed mussels perked up with curry. And follow with fresh-caught fish, interestingly prepared. Good desserts. *First Class.*

De La Chaîne (5 Place Verdun) is not going to put you in mind of its Paris namesake; still, this is an agreeable venue for people-watching on the town's main square. *Moderate.*

INCIDENTAL INTELLIGENCE

Further information: Office de Tourisme, Place Maréchal-Leclerc, Poitiers; Office de Tourisme, 10 Rue Fleuriau, La Rochelle. There is scheduled air service between La Rochelle and Paris.

30

Rennes
and Beyond in Brittany

BACKGROUND BRIEFING
Relative proximity to the New World notwithstanding—France's
westernmost point is in this region—Brittany and its cities remain relatively terra incognita. The cities, especially.

Nantes, for example, though the largest and most important urban
center in western France, has not been thought about by most of us since
we learned about a proclamation protecting Protestants that was signed
there by Henri IV nearly five centuries ago. (Unless, of course, you
consider our familiarity also with its revocation by an even more famous
king—Louis XIV—and the urgent consequences thereof.) Oddly enough,
Nantes appears to appreciate that it is not celebrated; it has fewer good
central-city hotels than any other major French city of which I am aware.

Then consider Rennes, smaller but hardly of less historic significance.
There being no Edict of Rennes to afford it glory in the history books,
much less a Revocation, it is even less familiar—which is not as it should
be. Rivalrous in earlier centuries with Nantes—they both served as seats
of Dukes of Brittany—Rennes emerges contemporarily as far the more
sympathetic of the pair. And this is quite as it should be, given remaining
vestiges of eminence resulting as a consequence of the city's razor's edge
location on the border with France, when Brittany was a separately
governed duchy.

Developed by ancient Celts, later colonized by Rome, river-straddling
Rennes (situated where the Ille converges with the Vilaine) achieved
political power as long ago as the thirteenth century, when Breton dukes
settled in. Even after Brittany was united with France—as a consequence
of the marriage in Rennes of French King Charles VIII and Duchess
Anne of Brittany, in the late fifteenth century—the Bretons insisted upon
retaining an appreciable measure of self-government. Later, they set up
a legislature of their own—its opulent meeting rooms are a principal

reason for a visit to contemporary Rennes—with which they governed themselves until the Revolution. It was the century of the Revolution, the eighteenth, that was doubly significant for Rennes. With political changes came a rebuilding of much of the city's medieval/Renaissance core—following a disastrous fire—to designs by a neoclassicist architect named Gabriel, commissioned by Louis XV, as, indeed, was his better-known son, who created Paris's Place de la Concorde.

ON SCENE
Lay of the Land: Thank architect Gabriel for the essentially grid-design, eighteenth-century rebuilding of much of Rennes. The *Vilaine River*, running east-west, neatly separates northern from southern sectors, with the former—the northern half—the more visitworthy. A series of streets bearing different names—pedestrians-only, with shops lining them— run north of central, river-straddling *Place de la République* and are called, successively, *Rues d'Orléans, d'Estrées*, and easy to remember *Le Bastard*. Walk, then, not only to window-shop and for café pauses, but to reach major monuments fronting such squares as *Place de la Mairie*, named for the eighteenth-century City Hall fronting it (pop inside to see its very grand foyer), and even more significant *Place du Palais* (below), with medieval half-timbered houses on *Rue St.-Georges*, due east. But there's more to medieval Rennes: Walk west from Place du Palais to *Place St.-Sauveur*, and you're in *Vieux Rennes*, dominated by multiepoch *Basilica of St.-Sauveur* and the nearby cathedral and indicated for strolls past landmark houses—mostly half-timbered—on *Rues de la Psalette, St.-Sauveur*, and *du Chapitre*. If you've time to explore another district, walk east from Place du Palais, along to *Square de la Motte*. The Mansard-roofed palace with a masterful wrought-iron gate is the *Préfecture* of the department, and just north of it, on *Place Ste.-Melaine*, is the charmer of a cloistered church whose name it takes. The railway station is at the southern edge of Rennes's southern, more modern sector.

Palais de Justice (Place du Palais): Sensibly seeing duty today as the city's Palais de Justice, or courthouse, is the building that served as the Brittany Parliament from the time it went up in the early decades of the seventeenth century until the fall of the monarchy with the Revolution. During those final centuries of the ancien régime, kings of France within Brittany were styled dukes of Brittany and shared power with the duchy's legislature, which met in style, under coffered and frescoed ceilings, in the second-floor room still known—and hardly inappropriately—as *La Grande Chambre*; it constitutes one of France's more dazzling interiors. Credit a Paris *ébéniste* named Pierre Donis for wainscotting of the ceilings and walls that date to 1680. Of the ceiling's baker's dozen frescoes, it's the center one—on the theme of justice—that bears study. Gobelin tapestries woven in this century take the place of wallpaper, but the room is at its most unusual—and charming—with its loggias (little balconies framed in carved, gilded wood) on three of four walls, for the benefit of Baroque-era VIPs intent on watching parliamentary debates from on high.

Cathedral of St.-Pierre (Rue de la Monnaie)—twin-towered and with an essentially classic-style facade—is among France's newest, completed toward the middle of the last century. Major lure is a Renaissance altarpiece, depicting scenes in the life of the Virgin, in a chapel edging the transept. A secondary lure is not in the cathedral, but rather in the neighborhood surrounding it—the core of Vieux Rennes and delightful strollers' territory—north to *Place des Lices*, south to *Rue des Dames*, east to *Basilica of St.-Sauveur*, parts of it a century newer than the cathedral.

Musée des Beaux Arts (20 Quai Émile-Zola, on the south side of the Vilaine River, not far east of Place de la République) shares a building—Palais des Musées—with a fellow museum (below), but is by far the more significant of the pair. You'll encounter works by such foreigners as Veronese, Rubens, Jordaens, Bassano, and Tiepolo; by such Renaissance Frenchmen as De La Tour, Philippe de Champaigne, and Simon Vouet; by their eighteenth-century successors, including Chardin, Natoire, Desportes, and Greuze; nineteenth-century masters like Corot and Chassériau; by Impressionists like Monet, Sisley, Boudin, and Gauguin to the more recent Vuillard, Dufy, and Picasso.

Musée de Bretagne (also in Palais des Musées, 20 Quai Émile-Zola) is a World's Fair-like mix of audiovisual displays and exhibits of Brittany objects going back to the Gallo-Roman period, with its Middle Ages sections—including tombs and sculpted capitals—the most successful, along with sections featuring nineteenth-century furniture. There's an immense hall of costumes; this is a good place to get an idea of the remarkable variety of the traditional Breton women's *coiffes*—high, white, and lacy headdresses. A special bravo to the management for legends throughout in English, as well as in French—a courtesy to non-French-reading visitors rarely encountered in French museums.

Fougères and Vitré are castle towns not far east of Rennes that, combined, constitute an enjoyable excursion into the past. Start with 30-mile-distant Fougères. Its originally eleventh-century château—one of the biggest on the continent of Europe—is enclosed by a wall studded by no less than thirteen remaining towers. There were more, but not all have survived a history that saw the castle change hands often, especially during the Anglo-French Hundred Years War. Give yourself time enough to wander around this massive, multiacre complex—the walls are so thick that there's a sidewalk atop them—concluding your castle visit in a tower called Raoul, whose attraction is a museum exhibiting antique shoes, which is not as odd as it would appear after you learn that shoe manufacture has for long been a Fougères industry. Exit the castle for neighboring *Church of St.-Sulpice*, Gothic and with lovely altarpieces. There are fine old houses to be seen on nearby *Place du Manché*.

Pause, then, for lunch, continuing south to *Vitré* (22 miles from Rennes), smaller and better preserved than Fougères, as you can't help but notice on your approach from the north. You've a choice of castles. *Château de Vitré* is a fortified, multitowered triangle that evolved as the Middle Ages became the Renaissance. As at Fougères, you may walk atop the wall; do so, making your way to a trio of towers. *Tour de l'Argenterie* is skippable; it's a natural-history museum. But *Tour St.-Laurent* displays beautiful Renaissance sculpture, and *Tour de l'Oratoire* houses a charming chapel with a positively smashing altarpiece. Vitré's still formidable ramparts enclose atmospheric streets flanked with fine old houses—*Rue Beaudrairie, Rue Notre-Dame, Rue d'Embas* are three such—and Gothic-era *Church of Notre-Dame* is a lure.

But even more so is *Château des Rochers-Sévigné*, four miles south and the seventeenth-century seat of the redoubtable Madame de Sévigné, whose 1,500 witty and detailed letters to her daughter constitute a rich lode of information on life in France of that era. Many of the letters were written from this essentially seventeenth-century castle; only a few rooms are inspectable. One crammed with objects belonging to this very interesting woman highlights a visit.

Quimper (112 miles west of Rennes, just inland from the Atlantic) is small, friendly, and attractive, with its core flanking the north shore of the Odet River that cuts through it. *Rue St.-François* leading north from the river is one of a number of central, shop-lined streets. Passing east-west *Rue Kéréon*, it continues busily mercantile as *Rue des Boucheries*. Rue Kéréon's eastern terminus is *Place St.-Corentin*, named for the *Cathedral of St.-Corentin*, whose twin steeples date, surprisingly, only from the last century—appendages to an otherwise essentially Gothic structure with a long nave, exquisitely vaulted, an exuberant Baroque pulpit, with side chapels at either end of the wide transept, and a lady chapel edging the apse.

The town's *Musée des Beaux-Arts* (Rue de la Mairie) stuns with the quality and diversity of its collection—extraordinary in a town with a population of 60,000. Its specialty is the Pont Avon school of late nineteenth- and early twentieth-century paintings and similar to those of Gauguin, with a number by Émile Bernard. But there is so much more: Pannini and Piranesi, Giordano and Reni, among the Italians; Rubens and Jordaens, among the Flemings; Cuyp and Maes, among the Dutch; and a plethora of Frenchmen: Mignard and Vernet, Oudry and Fragonard, Boilly and Corot, Boudin and Marquet. A cache of drawings—by French masters like Vouet, Le Brun, Hubert Robert, Fragonard, and Watteau—is frosting on an already rich cake.

Musée Départemental Breton (Rue Ste.-Catherine) has quarters in the onetime Bishop's Palace, dating back four centuries. Certain of the exhibits—especially those from Roman Quimper—are considerably older, with a diverse range, wooden chests through peasant costumes.

Faïenceries de Quimper (Route de Benodet) calls itself a museum (admission is charged) but is simply a showroom of hand-painted Quimper pottery, alas, contemporarily without the good looks for which it was well known in past centuries, if this commercial display is typical.

Church of Notre-Dame-de-Locmaria (Place Benandier) is exceptional: severely beautiful Romanesque, little changed since it was erected in the eleventh century—even to the tiny, niche-like windows of that era—with a splendid wooden *Crucifixion* suspended from a beam over the main altar.

Locronan (11 miles north of Quimper) is a requisite excursion destination, an enchanter of a hill town, built in the fifteenth and sixteenth centuries of the local granite—and little changed since. The village is based on its central—and sole—square, with a combination church-chapel dominant, within whose precincts is a tomb of the namesake saint, Ronan, along with polychrome sculptures, including a very moving Pietà. There's a little museum of local lore and a shop with weavers, potters, and other artisans at work on their wares.

Pont-l'Abbé (13 miles south of Quimper) is a tradition-bound village bordering a channel, just inland from the sea, with miles of wide, white-sand beaches adjacent, which make it agreeable for a day's outing in the sun. In town, visit the Renaissance château that houses not only town hall and tourist office, but also *Musée Bigouden*—with local lore.

Loctudy (18 miles south of Quimper) is smaller than Pont-l'Abbé, with which it may be combined on a day-long excursion. It's the site not only of extensive beaches, but of a striking parish church, twelfth-century Romanesque and in mint condition.

Pointe du Raz (25 miles west of Quimper) is to France what Land's End is to Britain: its westernmost point—and delineated by a little lighthouse on a rocky eminence just offshore. Visit it from the nearby resort-village of *Audierne*, like Loctudy and Pont-l'Abbé, with splendid beaches.

Nantes (65 miles south of Rennes) is big (population is a quarter-million) and sprawling; you can't walk everywhere. Zero in on what interests you. Main shopping street of this lively Loire River metropolis is *Rue*

Crébillon (with Galeries Lafayette and Nouvelles Galeries department stores); classy Cours Cambronne, mostly early nineteenth century, and Passage Pommeraye, an also-classy shopping arcade that opened in 1843, are in the neighborhood. Nearby Rue d'Orléans leads to a pair of major monuments. One, Cathedral of Sts.-Pierre-et-Paul, is soaring Gothic, at its best out back, with flying buttresses framing a wide apse, and the superbly sculptured early eighteenth-century tomb of Duke François II of Brittany and his duchess highlighting the interior. The other monument is the Château des Ducs de Bretagne, somberly medieval without, exuberant Renaissance within. Kings Henri IV (come to promulgate the Edict of Nantes in 1598) and François I were among its residents, and today it houses three museums: Arts Décoratifs (mainly textiles), Art Populaire (with superb period rooms and quality furniture), and Salorges (matters maritime, including ship models). There is a trio of away-from-the center museums: Jules Verne (3 Rue de l'Hermitage, pertaining to the life and work of the Nantes-born author), Thomas Dobrée, and Archéologique (both on Place Jean V)—the former, an unusual mixed bag of paintings, drawings, illuminated manuscripts, and enamels; the latter with exhibits both domestic and imported, French and Greek through Egyptian and the New World. Still, Nantes's No. 1 museum is Beaux-Arts (10 Rue Georges-Clemenceau, near the cathedral). Ingres's Madame de Sennones is the museum's mascot painting, but the range is wide, the quality superior—Rubens and Perugino, Tintoretto and De La Tour, Lancret and Courbet—to name but a handful.

SETTLING IN

Frantel Rennes (Place du Colombier; phone 9979-54-54): I wish it were central—by that, I mean on the north side of the Vilaine River—but that reservation aside, this link of the Frantel chain is agreeable enough, contemporary in the not always logical Frantel style (by that, I mean a need for bedside lamps that would make reading possible and sink-faucets easier to operate, to cite two examples). The bar-lounge is comfortable and the restaurant is popular with locals—always a good sign. First Class.

Du Guesclin Hôtel (Place de la Gare; phone 9931-47-46): You're all the way south at the railway station. But the Du Guesclin is full facility; there are 42 modern rooms, agreeable restaurant, and bar-lounge. Moderate.

Anne de Bretagne Hôtel (12 Rue Tronjolly; phone 9931-49-49) is farther north than the Frantel, but still south of the Vilaine. There are 42 neat-as-a-pin, contemporary-style rooms. Breakfast only. Moderate.

Novotel Rennes Alma (Avenue du Canada; phone 9950-61-32) is in the boonies, three miles from town, but there are just under a hundred well-planned, comfortable rooms, a no-frills restaurant at its best with a generous breakfast buffet, and a bar-lounge. *Moderate.*

La Tour d'Auvergne Hôtel (13 Rue des Regulaires, Quimper; phone 9895-08-70) leads the Quimper pack. It's conveniently central, attractive in traditional style, with 45 rooms—those I have seen are pleasantly papered and have nice baths—as well as a cozy bar where you sink into deep, leather chairs and a looker of a restaurant with fare as agreeable as the hotel itself. Friendly. *First Class.*

Dupleix Hôtel (34 Boulevard Dupleix, Quimper; phone 9890-53-35) is on the south bank of the Odet River, but it's a relatively easy walk to the core of this smallish city. Decor is contemporary—in tones of tan and pale pink, with just under 30 good-sized rooms with okay baths, including some duplexes for three persons. And in summer there's a seafood restaurant. Very nice. *Moderate.*

Novotel Quimper (Route de Benodet, Quimper; phone 9890-46-26) is out of town—a 10-minute drive from the core. There are 95 good-sized, well-planned rooms, each with the same functional bath; a restaurant wherein is served an excellent buffet breakfast; and an efficient staff. *Moderate.*

Le Griffon Hôtel (Route de Benoît, Quimper; phone 9890-33-33), a little farther from the center than the Novotel (above), has the look of an American motel from without and a pleasantly contemporary decor. There are 54 full-facility rooms, a swimming pool, capacious cocktail lounge, restaurant operated by a concessionaire, and a shaggy dog attached to the friendly reception staff, who greets guests carrying one of his toys. *Moderate.*

Château de Karambleiz Hôtel (Plomelin, a 15–20 minute drive from Quimper; phone 9894-23-42) is a fairy tale château—turreted and towered and steep-roofed, in its own park (with fishing in a stream on the grounds) and smart interiors, including crystal-chandeliered restaurant, paneled bar-lounge, and a dozen traditionally furnished rooms. *First Class.*

Manoir du Stang Hôtel (La Forêt-Fouesnan, nine miles south of Quimper; phone 9856-97-37) is a sixteenth-century château, its management descendants of a long-on-scene family, its setting formal gardens, to the front; to the rear, a large private park, dotted with pools, with the sea not far distant. There are just 26 no-two-alike rooms, restaurant, bar-lounge, tennis, and fishing. *First Class.*

De La Plage Hôtel (Ste.-Anne-La-Palud, eight miles northwest of Quimper; phone 9892-50-12) is ideal for seaside respite—on the beach, as its title implies, with a pool-cum-sundeck to boot, picture-windowed restaurant looking out to sea (seafood is among the specialties), bar-lounge with deep brown-leather chairs, and 27 cheerful Louis XV-style rooms. Member, Relais et Châteaux. *First Class.*

Les Moulins des Ducs Hôtel (Moëlin-sur-Mer, 28 miles southeast of Quimper; phone 9839-60-73): How about a sixteenth-century windmill complex—stone-walled, antiques accented, with handsome public spaces that include a cozy bar and a creditable restaurant, as well as just under two dozen no-two-alike, imaginatively decorated rooms? With an indoor swimming pool, whose open-up picture-window-wall gives onto a sun terrace. Member, Relais et Châteaux. *First Class.*

Kastelmoor and Kermoor Hôtels (Benodet, 9 miles south of Quimper; phone 9857-04-48) are a kind of Mutt-and-Jeff operation. Kastelmoor edges a wide, white-sand beach and has 23 rooms, a swimming pool, and five tennis courts; Kermoor, a five-minute walk inland from the sea, is bigger, with 70 rooms and a restaurant that specializes in seafood. Stay in one, and you may use the facilities of the other; same management for both. Fun. *First Class.*

De France Hôtel (24 Rue Crébillon, Nantes; phone 4073-57-91) is the winner in Nantes: located on its main shopping street: handsomely traditional in style, with 80 no-two-alike rooms (those I have inspected are delightful; ditto, their baths); a welcoming bar-lounge; and a Belle Époque-style restaurant, later recommended. *First Class.*

L'Hôtel (6 Rue Henri IV, Nantes; phone 4029-30-31) is one of the more stylish of France's smaller, nonluxury hotels. Look is a meld of contemporary with traditional—overstuffed sofas and lounge chairs upholstered in smart fabrics and combined with smaller antique pieces. We do well with this style in the United States, as do the British. But the French can have difficulty with it. Not so here. A small but charming reception area is backed by a lounge wherein breakfast and drinks are served. Those of the 32 rooms I have seen are smart; aim for one with views of the cathedral and/or château; you are also close to Musée des Beaux-Arts and the railway station. But you're not in the central shopping district. *Moderate.*

Central Hôtel (44 Rue Couëdic, Nantes; phone 4020-09-35) has as its only plus—unless work has been done since my last visit—a central location. But public spaces and rooms I have inspected were, when I saw them, very much in need of refurbishing. Restaurant, bar. Mapotel/Best Western. *Moderate.*

Frantel Nantes (3 Rue du Dr.-Zamenhof, in the Beaulieu district of Nantes, a modern shopping center a couple of miles south of the center; phone 4047-10-58) is contemporary, with 150 full-facility rooms, restaurant, and bar-lounge. *First Class.*

Sofitel Nantes (Rue Alexandre-Millerand, in the same isolated Beaulieu quarter as the Frantel [above]; phone 4047-61-03) is ultra-mod, with a hundred rooms, restaurant, and bar. *First Class.*

DAILY BREAD
Le Palais (7 Place du Palais; phone 9979-45-01) borrows the name of the onetime parliamentary palace across the square; it is distinctly unpalatial, but rather cozy, with tables in a pair of contiguous rooms and its best bets either of two prix-fixe menus. You might, with one of these, commence with *trois petites salades*—a trio of the house's special salads; continue with rosemary-scented lamb or duck crisply roasted and served with turnips. Lemon *soufflé* is among desserts. Caveat: Service, though kindly, can be painfully slow. *First Class.*

Le Corsaire (52 Rue d'Antrain; phone 9936-33-69): You're north of the center here, but the seafood is so good that it's worth the excursion. Open with fish soup. Proceed with simply—but deliciously—grilled sole, the house's delicate *sole soufflé*, or, if you would rather, chicken and mushroom fricassee, a Breton standby. Baked-on-premises desserts. Friendly. *First Class.*

Ti-Koz (3 Rue St.-Guillaume; phone 9979-33-89) occupies a landmark Rennes house—half-timbered, with its facade unchanged for something like half a millennium. Behind white organdy tiebacks on the front windows lies an atmospheric dining room, wherein are served good things to eat, the range—to give you an idea—smoked salmon or *foie gras frais* among openers; *confit de canard* or filet of beef—deliciously sauced—among entrées; made-on-premises desserts. *First Class.*

Piccadilly Tavern (Place de la Mairie; phone 9979-30-88) retains its Anglo name as an amusing come-on. Situation is central, look engaging Belle Époque, clientele mostly local, fare *brasserie* style, with everything fresh and tasty. Open with warm Lyon sausage, hearty onion soup, or oysters, mussels, or clams—from the seafood bar. Entrées run to *filet mignon*, breast of chicken, even an Alsatian *choucroute garnie*. End, perhaps, with what the menu terms "L'Irish Coffee," made with *whisky Irlandais et crème fraîche. First Class.*

La Taverne (11 Place des Lices; phone 9979-27-28) is convivial and unpretentious, with a menu of all-French favorites, running to snails

Burgundy style, *entrecôte sauce Béarnaise*—the steak is grilled on an open fire—and fruit tarts to conclude. In Vieux Rennes. *Moderate.*

Café du Reynard (27 Rue St.-Georges) is indicated for coffee or a cool drink, on a table in this atmospheric street brimming with half-timbered houses. *Moderate.*

Les Voyageurs Hôtel Restaurant (Place Gambetta, Fougères; phone 9999-14-17) is a good choice for a substantial lunch—Breton chicken and seafood entrées are featured—in connection with a day-long outing to Fougères and Vitré. *First Class.*

La Rotonde (36 Avenue de la France Libre, Quimper; phone 9895-09-26) is at once welcoming, cheerful, delicious, and—not unlike a number of restaurants you'll no doubt encounter in Brittany—with waiters who have practiced their trade at French restaurants in New York (which are largely staffed by Bretons). Open with a seafood *terrine* or the house's stuffed oysters and clams specialty. *Confit de canard* with a Breton cider sauce is a delicious entrée. House-made *mousses*—lemon and chocolate—are super. And so is *fine de Bretagne*—a Breton brandy taken at meal's end as a digestif. *First Class.*

Le Capucin Gourmand (29 Rue des Régulaires, Quimper; phone 9895-43-12) is intimate and inviting, with a pair of prix-fixe menus. The simpler might start you out with an oyster specialty, the kicker being a dollop of *fine de Bretagne* brandy. Carry on, then, with veal *médaillons* in Breton cream and mushroom sauce, extravagantly vegetable garnished. Dessert is warm apple tart—of course with cream, if you can handle it. *First Class.*

La Tour d'Auvergne Hôtel Restaurant (13 Rue des Régulaires, Quimper; phone 9895-08-70) is the handsomest of Quimper eateries, with good-value fare. Select from one of the pair of menus, concentrating perhaps on a mixed hors d'oeuvres platter and following with roast chicken and rice or grilled fish of the day, with a caper-flavored *sauce au beurre* and choice of cheese or a sweet. *Moderate.*

Crêperie au Vieux Quimper (20 Rue Verdelet, Quimper; phone 9895-31-34) is as good a choice as you can make for a sampling of Brittany's celebrated pancakes. Setting is a stone-walled room in a venerable townhouse, with antique chairs at tables. Do as Bretons do: Open with a pair of *crêpes* with savory fillings—egg and sausage, for example, or ham and cheese (the menu offers scores of choices), and conclude with a sweet *crêpe*—hot banana is heartily counseled—as dessert, with Breton cider to accompany. At meal's end, move over to the open kitchen and watch pancakes being prepared. *Moderate.*

Holland (18 Rue Kéréon, Quimper) is at once a *pâtisserie* and *salon de thé*; stop in for pastry with tea or coffee. Near the cathedral. *Moderate.*

Café de l'Épée (29 Rue du Parc, Quimper) is river-front and pleasant for a mid-morning or mid-afternoon pause. *Moderate.*

Au Fer à Cheval Hôtel Restaurant (Place de l'Église, Locronan; phone 9891-70-74) is indicated for lunch in the course of an excursion from Quimper. Choose from a quartet of prix-fixe menus embracing country *pâté*, smoked ham braised in Port, and fruit tarts. Friendly. *Moderate/First Class.*

Le Gavroche (139 Rue des Hauts-Pavés, Nantes; phone 4076-22-49) is indicated for a candlelit dinner. Antique country chairs flank flower-centered tables. Open with *foie gras en gelée*, continuing with fish filet in the house's special sauce. Veal and poultry entrées are good alternatives. *First Class.*

La Tasterie (12 Rue Beauregard, Nantes; phone 4048-98-53) is central and reasonable, with a substantial three-course menu that might run to seafood salad, grilled lamb chops, and choice of desserts. *Moderate.*

L'Opéra (in Hôtel de France, with its own entrance at 4 Rue Molière, Nantes; phone 4073-57-91) is long-established, heart of town, and reliable, with three well-priced menus: even the least costly is satisfactory— *terrine de canard* or *crudités* to start, grilled sausage or the *plat du jour*, pastry, or *mousse au chocolat*. Friendly. *Moderate/First Class.*

La Cigale (Place Graslin, Nantes; phone 4089-34-84) looks better than it tastes. A National Historic Monument (it opened in 1895) with a marvelous Belle Époque look—its fabulous tiled walls bear inspection— it appears to have been spoiled by too much attention. *Brasserie*-style fare falls flat. Waiters are barely civil. *Moderate.*

SOUND OF MUSIC
Théâtre Municipal (Place de la Mairie, Rennes) is the city's principal venue for opera, concerts, and ballet.

Grand Théâtre (Place Graslin, Nantes) is very grand, indeed—opera, concerts, ballet.

INCIDENTAL INTELLIGENCE

There is scheduled service from the airports of Rennes, Quimper, and Nantes to domestic points. *Further information:* Office de Tourisme, Pont de Namours, Rennes; Office de Tourisme, Place Aristide-Briand, Fougères; Office de Tourisme, 3 Rue Roi-Gradlon, Quimper; Office de Tourisme, Place Change, Nantes.

31

Rouen
Core of Normandy

BACKGROUND BRIEFING

Rouen's problem is Paris.

Contemporarily, that is. This ancient estuary port, not far inland from the mouth of the Seine on the English Channel, is, in effect, the port of Paris—a plus, of course, in the burgeoning economy of a city with a metropolitan population of half a million. At the same time, though, it is close enough to giant Paris—the 80-mile distance is bridged by fast and frequent trains and by motor on modern highways—so as to be considered by Parisians and visitors alike as little more than a town in exurbia. Rouen is not, in other words, taken as seriously as would surely be the case if it were located where Bordeaux is, or Grenoble or Nice. (It is no doubt this proximity to Paris that has prevented it from becoming either a leading hotel or shopping city.)

It was not always thus. In centuries past, when communications were primitive and transport achingly slow, Rouen stood—and developed—quite on its own, to the point where, despite heavy destruction during the sixteenth-century Wars of Religion and this century's World War II, it remains an all-France showplace of Gothic and Renaissance monuments. (And not only churches and palaces. Eight hundred of Rouen's half-timbered houses have been restored—more than in any other French city—and 700 more are being restored.)

And Rouen's prominence in the evolution of France is hardly to be underestimated. The Romans' prosperous *Rotomagus* was the seat of a Catholic bishop as early as the fourth century. By the ninth, aggressive Viking raiders from the north—already called *Normands*—had become residents of the area surrounding Rouen, prosperous and powerful enough for the French king of the moment to declare their leader a duke, with jurisdiction over what has been known ever since as Normandy. It was, of course, one of this duke's successors, who, in 1066, as Guillaume le

Conquérant, vanquished the English and became King William I. Increasingly rich Rouen itself became English in the course of the Hundred Years War—for almost three mid-fifteenth-century decades. Indeed, it was in Rouen that Jeanne d'Arc was captured by the enemy from across the Channel, eventually tried, and executed on the central Rouen square where a contemporary memorial honors her memory.

ON SCENE
Lay of the Land: Be grateful for early—very early—planners who devised Rouen's grid layout. The *Seine River* running north and south, serves as the western edge of the *Rive Droite*—or principal—area. Three main thoroughfares run east from river-flanking streets: *Rue Jeanne d'Arc*, which extends past *Tour Jeanne d'Arc*—a circular medieval tower in which Joan was interrogated prior to imprisonment elsewhere in town— to *Gare Rive-Droite*, the main train station. (*Gare d'Orléans* is on the Rive Gauche.) Also on a west-east axis is central *Rue Grand-Pont*, which intersects *Place de la Cathédrale* (and Rouen's cathedral), continuing as shop-lined *Rue des Carmes* to Musée des Antiquités (below). The third major east-west street, *Rue de la République*, ends in massive *Place du Général-de-Gaulle*, site of the significant Church of St.-Ouen (below). Two other major museums, Beaux-Arts and Secq des Tournelles (below), flank the important north-south street, *Rue Thiers*. Even more trafficked is north-south *Rue du Gros-Horloge*, distinguished primarily because the landmark Renaissance clock—splendidly embellished, but with only a single hand to indicate time—is affixed to upper strata of buildings on either side of the street, one a Gothic bell tower, from which a nine-o'clock curfew has been tolled nightly since 1389. Rue du Gros-Horloge has contemporary distinction, as well, as the first pedestrians-only street in France. Other central shopping streets are *Rue Damiette* (with antiques shops), *Rue des Carmes*, and *Rue Croix-de-Fer*. Still other central streets— *Rue St.-Romain*, *Rue Malpalu*, and *Rue Eau-de-Robec*, to name three of many—make for meaningful strolls past medieval half-timbered houses (*maisons à colombage*) and no less handsome mansions of later eras.

Cathedral of Notre-Dame (Place de la Cathédrale): The Impressionist painter, Monet, chose well when he selected the cathedral of Rouen for the series of facade paintings that hang in a number of museums (Rouen's, below, included). It is an all-Europe Gothic ranker, built over four centuries, twelfth through sixteenth. Like Monet, you don't need to go inside. The west, or principal, facade—as wide as a generous-sized city block is long—is framed by a pair of irregular towers (the taller, the so-called Tour du Beurre, or Butter Tower, was named for a Lenten indulgence of the period of construction, permitting the consumption of butter) with a quartet of delicate pinnacles between them, these surmounting a rose window flanked by three rows of sculpted saints, above the church's three deeply recessed—and embellished—portals. Look at the cathedral from the rear, and your view is of a gracefully extended apse, with the *flèche*, or steeple, soaring into the sky. No cathedral in France, save Paris's Notre-Dame, has a more breathtaking nave. Two levels of arcades surmount floor-level arches and half a dozen columns with boldly carved capitals, which delineate the high altar. But tarry; the chapels and the tombs, dotted about, are works of art, each and every one.

Church of St.-Ouen (Place du Général-de-Gaulle) is quite as big as the cathedral and, again, like the cathedral, a Gothic jewel with a lovely, lacy facade dominated by a 242-foot-high tower, its outer walls braced by flying buttresses, a delicate pinnacle edging each buttress. Within, what appears most memorable is the perfect symmetry of the elongated nave.

Church of St.-Maclou (Rue Damiette) is No. 3—or No. 2, depending upon your preference—of Rouen's Big Three group of Gothic churches. It is distinguished by a disproportionately large steeple surmounting its transept and a fabulous west, or main, front, whose three intricately carved portals open into a nave flanked by a handsome chapel. But St.-Maclou's ace-in-the-hole is a carved-stone, circular stairway at the upper terminus of which is a rare Renaissance organ.

Âtre St.-Maclou (Rue Martainville, near the church) is a cloistered cemetery, part stone-carved, part half-timbered—and one of a kind.

Palais de Justice (Rue aux Juifs) is transitional—late Gothic/early Renaissance—with features like pinnacles and turrets of the former era and rectangular windows of the latter. The facade, as seen from the courtyard, is reason enough for a visit. The central sector was used as the Normandy Parliament, starting with the reign of François I. The west wing contains courtrooms leading from Salles des Pas Perdus—the Room of Wasted Steps—so called because of the plethora of nervously pacing *avocats*, awaiting trial of their cases. Peep inside—interiors are elaborate—noting the area called *Cryptes Juifs*, remains of what is believed to be a twelfth-century Jewish seminary, discovered when a courtyard was excavated as recently as 1976.

Church of Ste.-Jeanne-d'Arc (Place du Vieux-Marché): To commemorate Joan's death on this very square, heart of town—she was burned alive and the year was 1431—this modern church, distinguished by irregularly sweeping roofs that extend to a *porte cochère* over the entrance, was opened in the early 1980s. It may or may not be to your taste: best part, for me, at least, is the stained glass, a clutch of beautiful windows that were salvaged from a sixteenth-century church that was otherwise destroyed by World War II bombs. A covered market and a waxworks themed on Joan's life are adjacent.

Musée des Beaux Arts (Square Verdrel): Behind the undistinguished bulk of a late nineteenth-century facade is a collection of paintings that is one of the finest in provincial France. Clouet's *Bath of Diane,* a Poussin *Venus,* Gérard David's *Virgin and Saints* are among the French Renaissance greats. There are Italians like Veronese (*St. Roch and St. Sebastian*) and Bassano (*Adoration of the Shepherds*) not to mention Bronzino and Caravaggio. There are also Dutchmen like Steen, Van Goyen, and Ruysdael, no less than a handful of works by Rubens, and a Velásquez of a portly gent called *Democrite.* The French eighteenth century is on hand in strength: Nattier, Fragonard, Oudry, Hubert Robert, Vigée-Lebrun. This country's nineteenth-century painters? Consider Ingres's lovely *Madame Aymon,* a stern-visaged Géricault army officer, a clutch of Corots, works by Daubigny, Delacroix, and Rosa Bonheur. Of the Impressionists, Monet (who lived and worked at nearby Giverny [Chapter 2]) and Sisley are the most heavily represented, but Renoir and Boudin (from not far distant Honfleur, Chapter 19) are also present. And of later artists, Normandy-born Raoul Dufy figures heavily.

Musée des Antiquités (Rue Beauvoisine) is sheltered in an atmospheric old monastery, with its subject matter beautiful objects from no longer standing townhouses and churches—furniture and tapestries, reliquaries and weapons, jewelry and bronzes, not to mention sculpted fragments and mosaics from Roman Rouen. Special.

Musée Secq des Tournelles (2 Rue Jacques-Villon) occupies a smasher of a desanctified Gothic church—a perfect foil for its collection of wrought iron. You may feel the subject matter somewhat limited, but as you move about you get hooked. How about a sixteenth-century doorknocker, a circular stairway from a nearby château, a tree-of-life created in the sixteenth century, amusing signs with the symbols of shoemakers, florists, and butchers? Lovely.

Musée de Céramiques (Rue Faucon) is indicated for china and porcelain buffs, with a collection totaling some 300 objects, the lot of them Rouen-crafted between the sixteenth and eighteenth centuries.

Musée Corneille (4 Rue de la Pie): You don't have to have read *Mélite, Médée, Le Menteur,* or any other of the comedies or tragedies of this seventeenth-century playwright to enjoy an inspection of the house where he was born, with both a salon and study furnished in period.

Musée Flaubert (in Hôtel Dieu, a hospital at 51 Rue de Lécat): It is more likely that you have read Gustave Flaubert's *Madame Bovary* than Corneille's plays. At any rate, the nineteenth-century novelist was born in this apartment that is a part of the Hôtel Dieu complex (both his father and grandfather were surgeons on the hospital's staff). Flaubert's birth-place-bedroom is charmingly furnished. Exhibits relate both to the author and his works and to matters medical.

Fécamp (40 miles northwest of Rouen) is the little seaside town that the Bénédictine liqueur people have put on the map. Still, its principal lure is a positively gigantic abbey-church, *Abbatiale de la Trinité* (Rue Couturier), whose square Gothic tower—soaring to more than 200 feet—is the town landmark. Not that the length of the nave, close to 411 feet, is modest. If its proportions are what make it a standout—this is one of France's biggest churches—you want also to hike through the interior. Stroll down the nave to the altar, going behind it to the charming Lady Chapel. *Musée Municipal* (Rue Alexandre-Legros) is a mixed bag, city-operated repository of local lore, fishing paraphernalia through some quite nice furniture. *Musée de la Bénédictine* (Rue Alexandre-le-Grand): What you're no doubt most curious about is the liqueur operation. It is a long time since the Benedictine order had anything to do with it. Unlike Chartreuse (Chapter 18), the only liqueur still actually produced by monks, Bénédictine is a lay commercial operation. It is quartered in a mock-Renaissance horror of a building that went up in the last decade of the last century, with a museum whose exhibits relate to the founding of the distillery by a sixteenth-century monk and which includes some fine pieces from the old abbey—chalices and stained glass, ancient books and a sedan chair, a Renaissance carved-wood triptych and medieval sculptures. With tours of the distillery, if you like. (And note that there's a *casino* overlooking the public beach and next to the municipal swimming pool. *Rue Jacques-Huet* is the main pedestrian shopping street.)

SETTLING IN
Frantel Rouen (Rue Croix-de-Fer; phone 3598-06-98) is among the more satisfactory—welcoming, well equipped, well staffed, central—of any of the links of this all-France chain with which I am familiar. Quietly contemporary in design, it fits well into the core of the city. If you are lucky, you will draw a room (there are 108, including several suites) facing the cathedral. There's a convenient restaurant and a pleasant cocktail lounge. *First Class.*

Nord Hôtel (91 Rue du Gros-Horloge; phone 3570-41-41) is a few yards—quite literally—from Gros Horloge, Rouen's landmark, heart-of-town Renaissance clock. It has, in recent years, spruced itself up, to the point where all 60 rooms now have private baths. Friendly. Breakfast only. *Moderate.*

De la Cathédrale Hôtel (12 Rue St.-Romain; phone 3571-57-95) is heart of town, on a street lined with venerable houses. There are just 25 neat—but not elaborate—rooms, 19 of which have private baths. Breakfast only. *Moderate.*

De Dieppe Hôtel (Place Bernard-Tissot; phone 3571-96-00) is an across-the-square neighbor of Gare Rive-Droite—a fairish walk away from the historic core, the only reason it's not right up there with the Frantel at the top of my grouping. This is a professionally operated house—the same family has been running it since doors opened in 1880—with 44 rooms, some Louis XV style, some modern; those I have seen recently renovated are pleasant, as well as a restaurant (exemplary enough for me to evaluate it in a later paragraph) and a convivial bar. *First Class.*

Normandie Hôtel (19 Rue Bec; phone 3571-55-77) has location going for it—it's core of town and has just 23 neat rooms. Breakfast only. *Moderate.*

DAILY BREAD
Chez Dufour (67-bis Rue St.-Nicolas; phone 3571-90-62) epitomizes Vieux Rouen, given its location in a centuries-old house near the cathedral. Stone walls are hung with antique Rouen pottery and bits and pieces of medieval sculpture—including a likeness of St. Nick, who figures in the restaurant's address. There are half a dozen meat entrées. (*Toutes nos grillades sont faites au charbon de bois*—they're all charcoal-broiled.) But this should be your destination for an old-style Norman seafood meal—butter based and à la carte. (*Le beurre est à la base de notre cuisine.*) There are oysters in variety—Bretonnes, belons, or prairies—served with fresh lemon, an herbed sauce, and the traditional accompaniment, buttered rye bread. The morning's market determines composition of the seafood platter. If available, crayfish are served with the house's own mayonnaise. Stuffed clams are tasty; ditto, mussels *marinière.* Entrées? I defy you to find a more deliciously grilled sole, accompanied by *sauce Béarnaise. Brochette* of charcoal-grilled scallops are super. Or go for broke with a lobster. And on no account omit apple-based *tarte Normande* as your sweet. Service is sprightly and attentive. In my experience, one of France's best restaurants. *First Class.*

La Couronne (31 Place du Vieux-Marché; phone 3571-40-90) immodestly dubs itself "La Plus Vieille Auberge de France," indicating its opening date as 1345. Well, you can't quarrel with that pedigree—nor with a situation on the city's most historic square. Facade is appropriately half-timbered, interior mellow, service kindly. Order one of the three prix-fixe menus, each good value. The most ambitious, including Muscadet or Côtes de Bergerac wine, opens with half a melon, proceeds with a seafood *terrine* accompanied by a trio of sauces or with half a dozen oysters; and offers Calvados-flavored sherbet as a palate cleanser prior to a choice of entrées: *entrecôte* with *Béarnaise* sauce, Port-sauced roast squab, or seafood casserole. But you're not finished; cheeses are next, with *gratin de pommes et son sabayon*—apple tarts deliciously sauced, to conclude. *First Class.*

Le Beffroy (15 Rue Beffroy; phone 3571-55-27): I have never *not* enjoyed a female-operated French restaurant, especially when Madame is chef, as well as *patronne.* This restaurant is a charmer, in a traditional setting. Chilled scallop/crayfish/oyster soup is a refreshing starter. Fricassee of duck flavored with Norman cider is delicious; likewise, the house's own salmon, sole, and turbot specialties. Desserts deserve the separate card they are accorded, with *marquise au chocolat,* apples in puff pastry with a liqueur sauce, and caramel ice cream among the goodies. *First Class.*

Le Quatre Saisons (De Dieppe Hôtel, Place Bernard-Tissot; phone 3571-96-00): You will be seated, most likely, at a rust-hued *banquette* illuminated by fringed silk lamps overhead. I don't know of a more appropriate place to experience the city's renowned duck specialty, *caneton Rouennais*—red Burgundy, cognac, veal stock, butter, and a traditional quartet of seasonings are among its ingredients. *Foie gras de canard* is always among the appetizers, along with an unusual chicken-breast salad. Seafood platter is counseled, among entrées; so is *rognon de veau à la moutarde*—veal kidneys in mustard sauce. *First Class.*

Bertrand Warin (9 Rue de la Pie; phone 3589-26-69) is a smart spot—just off Place du Vieux-Marché—wherein the owner-chef presents a range of delicious comestibles, traditional, albeit upon occasion with Warin accents. First courses can be as classic as *terrine de foie de canard,* or novel—cream of watercress soup, pastry-topped, with mussels and vegetables. Continue with fish either simply grilled or with a Warin-created sauce. Roast rabbit, roast pigeon, chicken fricassee in a cider-based sauce, and grilled steak are entrée choices. I counsel Monsieur Warin's *trois tartelettes en bouchée*—a triple-threat dessert—to conclude. *First Class.*

La Cache Ribaud (10 Rue du Tambour; phone 3571-04-82) occupies half-timbered quarters on a street leading from Rue du Gros Horloge and is worth knowing about for its bargain-priced menu *rapide*—based on poultry, lamb, or beef. Friendly. *Moderate.*

Pasoline (5 Rue de la Potérue; phone 3589-67-44) welcomes with its Belle Époque decor, congenial staff, and choice of several inexpensive prix-fixe menus. Central. *Moderate.*

Dame Tartine (52 Rue St.-Romain) combines a lovely location—on a landmark street—with lovely things to eat, pastries especially, combined with coffee or tea. *Moderate.*

La Mirabelle (3 Place du Vieux-Marché) is indicated for coffee or a drink, combined with people-watching, in this principal square. *Brasserie*-type food, too. *Moderate.*

La Marine (23 Quai Vicomte, Fécamp; phone 3528-21-71) is indicated for a seafood lunch in the course of a Fécamp excursion, with views of the beach as a bonus. *First Class.*

SHOPPER'S ROUEN

Printemps department store is opposite the cathedral on the Rue des Carmes; *Monoprix* is on Rue du Gros-Horloge, principal pedestrian thoroughfare, with such interesting shops as *Newman* (men's and women's clothes), *Jean Druet* (perfumes), *Aumusse* (leather and furs), and *Jambon de York*, a mouthwatering *charcuterie*. Rue Rollon, parallel with Gros-Horloge, is shopping territory, too; there's a branch of *Hédiard*, the Paris food emporium, and a branch, also, of *Descamps*, the linen chain. Rue de Croix-de-Fer, near the cathedral, has smart boutiques, including *Toiles* (women's haute couture) and *Artisanat* (hand-crafted pottery).

SOUND OF MUSIC

Théâtre des Arts (Rue Jeanne-d'Arc, near the Seine) is Rouen's opera house and the venue also for concerts (especially of the Orchestre de Chambre de Rouen) and ballet. (This is a city for organ music, given a range of exceptional organs; watch for concerts in the *Church of St.-Ouen*, above, which has one of the best.)

INCIDENTAL INTELLIGENCE

There are about as many daily trains between Paris's Gare St.-Lazare and Rouen's Gare Rive-Droite as there are hours in the day; they take an hour and a half. *Further information:* Office de Tourisme, 25 Place de la Cathédrale, Rouen; Office de Tourisme, Place Bellet, Fécamp.

32

St.-Malo

and Eastward to Mont-St.-Michel

BACKGROUND BRIEFING

Canadians are familiar with St.-Malo because it was from this Breton port that Jacques Cartier sailed, in 1534, to discover their country. Englishmen and Channel Islanders know St.-Malo because they can—and do—sail to it from their shores, the summer long. The Welsh feel a bond with St.-Malo because it is named for a wandering seventh-century Welshman, sainted for miracles performed in the vicinity of the monastery he built in the neighborhood. Which leaves Americans, surely the last of the English-speakers to appreciate one of the most sparkling, and at the same time most monument-laden, of France's resort cities.

By the time St.-Malo became part of France in the late fifteenth century, bishops who doubled as its governors had moved it from what is now the quarter called St.-Servan to a nearby promontory that they proceeded to fortify with high walls topped with broad ramparts, punctuated at frequent intervals by defense towers and monumental gates. Its Corsairs, thriving as early as the fifteenth century and continuing their raids into the eighteenth century, saw St.-Malo feared by neighboring maritime powers, the English especially.

Cartier was but one of many long-distance mariners. By the time he established the colony of New France on the Gaspé Peninsula, St.-Malo-based fishing vessels had reached the cod-rich waters off the coast of Newfoundland. Their mariner-successors went even farther in the seventeenth and eighteenth centuries—along coasts of South, as well as North America, the West Indies, Africa, and even China.

Indeed, well into the fourth decade of the present century, St.-Malo's good fortune held. In 1944, World War II took its toll: 80 percent of the city within the walls was destroyed. But there was no stopping this valiant town. St.-Malo has been entirely rebuilt—meticulously and lovingly. The city you see today—walkable ramps, keeps and towers, ceremonial gateways, stone-walled houses, even the cathedral with Cartier's tomb—appears quite as it did pre-World War II. And there remains the bonus of beaches: white sand, hotel backed, casino equipped. St.-Malo is a winner.

ON SCENE
Lay of the Land: This town conveniently divides itself in two, with the aid of the Latin language. *Extra Muros* is the larger area, outside the walls. *Intra Muros*—within the walls—is what, elsewhere, might be called the Old Town. Its main entrance is through the walls at the splendid gateway called *Grande Porte*, into *Place du Poids-du-Roi*, which gives onto shop-lined *Grande Rue*, and extends north to the cathedral and *Place Châtillon*. This core-area is mercantile St.-Malo, with shops lining streets like *Rue Broussais*, west of the cathedral, and *Rue de la Ville Boucherie* running parallel with it, to the south, and extending to the square called *Marché Légumes*. To the north—and beyond the wall—are two major beaches, *Plage du Mole* and contiguous *Plage de Bon Secours*. The beaches wind around the northern tip of the promontory to the eastern shore and *Grande Plage*, site of the casino. The southeast corner of Intra Muros is flanked by restaurant and café-filled *Rue Jacques-Cartier* and centered by *Place Chateaubriand*, site of the château (containing a pair of museums and the city hall, as well), with the aquarium a near neighbor. Two additional quarters of interest are *St.-Servan*, with its beaches, restaurants, and a museum (below), and *Paramé*, southwest of Intra Muros, whose beaches are an extension of Grande Plage (above).

Les Remparts: Gain perspective by a walk along the ramparts, ascending them at the gate called Porte St.-Thomas. When the sun is shining, clouds billowy, tide in, and waves high, there is nothing else to compare with the experience in all France; when the tide is out, you may proceed to the offshore islands; there are guided tours of the historic fort on Petit Bé.

Le Château (Place Chateaubriand) shelters a pair of museums. One, *Galerie Quic-en-Groigne*, consists of a series of wax-figure tableaux, portraying the history of St.-Malo. You take them in, in the course of a self-guided tour, with piped commentary alternating between French and English. The second museum, by far the more significant—*Musée d'Histoire de la Ville*—occupies parts of several floors of the five-sided, seventeenth-century castle, giving you an opportunity to appreciate its architecture (most exhibits are in the circular ex-dungeon) the while taking in objects relating to St.-Malo's history: an eighteenth-century globe, model ships, parchment documents, figureheads and drawings, paintings by moderns like Signac, and by unknowns, of early St.-Malo mariners. Go all the way up, for the view from the top-level terrace.

Cathedral of St.-Vincent (Place Châtillon): The cathedral's spire dominates the skyline of Intra Muros; within, it is essentially Gothic, the result of an extensive postwar restoration that was completed in 1972. The contemporary stained glass is first-rate. You do not want to miss the severe but simple tomb of Jacques Cartier; the Canadian ambassador came from Paris to attend the mass at which Cartier was reinterred when the cathedral reopened: the tomb's plaque indicates Cartier's name, followed by the dates of his birth and death, 1491–1557, and the legend, *Découvreur du Canada.*

Musée International du Long-Cours Cap Hornier (Tour Solidor, in the St.-Servan section of town): The title is a mouthful but you go if only for the setting, a smashing skyscraper of a medieval château—it went up in 1382—that is half a dozen stories high, more vertical than horizontal, with a trio of graceful turrets topping it off. Stairs are steep, but exhibits—relating to explorers (Magellan is the best known) who rounded Cape Horn, from the sixteenth century through the nineteenth—are intriguing.

Aquarium (Place Vauban) concentrates on fish and other marine species native to Brittany waters. You will no doubt be in the company of not a few loquacious youngsters.

Dinard is St.-Malo's next-door beach resort, due west, just across the estuary called La Rance. It was popularized a century ago by Britons (*Le Temple Anglican*, on Rue du Temple, is a Church of England outpost) and remains popular today with their descendants. Dinard developed principally around crescent-shaped *Plage de l'Écluse*—a broad, white-sand beach dominated by a casino (whose facilities run a broad gamut, from gaming tables and restaurant to disco and a café and modern convention center; backed by hotels and edged by *Pointe du Moulinet* at the edge of a rocky promontory, with memorable views). Another beach, *Plage de St.-Énogat*, is to the north, while *Plage du Prieuré* is to the south. An enormous indoor swimming pool, a regional maritime museum-aquarium, and pretentious villas—mostly from the last century—are dotted about the coast, while the mercantile core of town is based on *Rue de la Pionnière* and *Boulevard du Président-Wilson*. The 18-hole, par 68 *Dinard Golf Course*, with a restaurant-equipped clubhouse, is at St.-Briac, four miles west of town.

Cancale (nine miles east of St.-Malo) typifies north coast fishing villages in that it is small and simple and fronts a crescent-shaped bay with gaily painted boats at anchor. The only monument of consequence is the *Church of St.-Méen*, from whose tower there are good views of the scenic coastline. The name of the Cancale game is seafood restaurants. They flank its waterfront and are popular with visitors from St.-Malo and residents of Breton cities like Rennes, to the south. Cancale makes for a relaxing lunch stop in the course of a day's exploration; two restaurants are recommended below.

Dol de Bretagne (15 miles south of St.-Malo, a little more distant from Rennes) is a Breton surprise-package, an utterly charming village with its ace-in-the-hole, *Cathédral St.-Samson*, which is as old as the ninth century—note Romanesque details of the facade—but is mostly thirteenth-century Gothic: the finest in Brittany. Indeed, the long, high, three-level nave is one of the loveliest such in France; it is lined by stained-glass windows that tell the story of Samson, and there is still more splendid glass in the apse, not to mention a fourteenth-century choir with interestingly carved misericords, or folding seats, and a bishop's throne. The village's mixed-bag *Musée Historique* is just opposite, in a house of advanced age. And you want to ascend the mini-mountain adjacent to Dol for a visit to its satellite village, *Mont-Dol*, and a landmark windmill.

Château de Combourg (21 miles south of St.-Malo, about the same distance from Rennes): Each of Combourg's four corners is defined by a fabulous circular tower-cum-turret. Windows are the kind of slits that archers used. The château's park is large enough to afford proper perspective; little Combourg village, adjacent, pales in contrast. You visit the castle's interior on guided tours taking less than an hour. They're essentially nineteenth century, a comedown from outside.

Mont-St.-Michel (28 miles east of St.-Malo): The point worth making at the outset is that precisely because it is one of a kind, and with its compact area unexpandable, St.-Michel is packed—uncomfortably jam-packed—spring through autumn, with an annual visitor count of two million. Understandably, of course. How many other Gothic abbeys do you know that are constructed on a fortified rock of an island that was accessible only at low tide, until so recently as a century back, when a causeway was built, joining it to the mainland? Of course you want to visit St.-Michel. But because of the congestion, limited hotel space, and overpopulated restaurants, I suggest you make it a day-excursion from your St.-Malo base, rather than overnighting in hotels at closer—but nondescript and boring—points. Or come in the dead of winter, when you'll no doubt have the little island pretty much to yourself—but when not a few of its hotels and restaurants are shuttered. My point is that you must take highly commercial Mont-St.-Michel on its own highly commercial terms.

With eighth-century origins, the Benedictine Abbey—mostly eleventh century but with a nineteenth-century spire—rises more than 450 feet and warrants your highest priority. The 90-step ascent is effort well expended: sublime Romanesque nave, late Gothic altar, sumptuously colonnaded cloister, the entire complex topping a mass of granite and embracing such auxiliary spaces—*La Merveille* (The Marvel), they are called—as long since disused official guest quarters, barrel-vaulted refectory, capacious halls, crypt, and chapels.

If you've devoted much of the morning to the abbey, it will be time for a lunch pause. Afterwards, stroll souvenir-shop-lined *Grande Rue* and pop into the pair of museums (there's a single admission ticket for both, but neither is of earthshaking consequence), the lovely fifteenth-century *Église Paroissiale*, a handsome church with a silver statue of St. Michael, and *Logis Tiphaine*, a venerable house with also-venerable furniture.

SETTLING IN

Central Hôtel (6 Grande Rue; phone 9940-87-70) is—as far as I am concerned—No. 1, assuming you want to headquarter in the historic Intra Muros part of St.-Malo. There are 46 rooms, not all of them over-large, but those that I have seen are attractive and full facility, the decor traditional. There's an on-premises restaurant (later recommended), bar where locals and guests mix, and the staff smiles. Mapotel/Best Western. *First Class.*

Des Thermes Hôtel (100 Boulevard Hébert, Grande Plage; phone 9956-02-56). If your prime St.-Malo mission is sun and sand, this turn-of-century beachfront house—tastefully updated—is indicated. There are 85 rooms, some really good sized, with the seaview ones the nicest—along with an attractive restaurant, glass roofed, and an indoor, seawater pool: a health spa—Thermes Marina—is adjacent. *First Class.*

De la Digue Hôtel (49 Chaussée du Sillon, Grande Plage; phone 9956-09-26) is a Grande Plage charmer: a delightful, 53-room house, with accommodations gracious, seafront bar and lounge congenial, and a honey of a terrace just above the sands, where breakfasts are a pleasure. No restaurant. *Moderate.*

La Villefromoy Hôtel (7 Boulevard Hébert; phone 9940-92-20): What happened was this: The owning La Villefromoy family bought this late nineteenth-century house (not far from the Grande Plage) and, utilizing expertise in period decor and antique furniture, refurbished it, stem to stern. There are 25 no-two-alike rooms, accessorized with lovely old pieces and in varying color schemes. Below, the main lounge and cocktail bar are quite the smartest public spaces of any hotel in town that I know. In a word: elegant. Breakfast only. *First Class.*

Le Valmarin Hôtel (7 Rue Jean XXIII; phone 9981-94-76) takes its guests back to eighteenth-century St.-Malo. Originally the home of a retired and wealthy corsair, it retains the ambience and furnishings of the period, with gracious public spaces and 10 thoughtfully equipped rooms. Near Grande Plage. Breakfast only. *Moderate.*

Alexandra Hôtel (138 Boulevard Hébert; phone 9956-08-75) welcomes guests with good-looking ground-floor lounges—popular for drinks and tea—that look out to sea and 15 smartly decorated rooms, the choicest those with terraces that overlook Grande Plage, an easy walk away. Congenial management. Breakfast only. *Moderate.*

Aux Ajones d'Or Hôtel (10 Rue des Porgeurs; phone 9940-85-03) is a handsome mansion, core of Intra Muros, that has been attractively converted into a two-dozen-room house that is friendly and comfortable. Breakfast only. *Moderate.*

Le Grand Hôtel (46 Avenue George V, Dinard; phone 9946-10-28)—on a street appropriately named for a British sovereign—evokes the Dinard of the last century, when Britons came south for respite in the sunshine. The Grand remains quite grand—with high-ceilinged public spaces, including a vast lounge and bar, restaurant with immense windows draped in scarlet, and a hundred terraced rooms, just half of them seaview. Central. *Luxury.*

La Plage Hôtel (3 Boulevard Féart, Dinard; phone 9946-14-87) is not, despite its name, directly on the beach, but rather a short block distant. There are just under 20 well-equipped rooms, cozy bar, good-value restaurant. *Moderate.*

Mouton Blanc Hôtel (Mont-St.-Michel; phone 9960-14-08)—small (with just 20 rooms) and good restaurant (below counseled)—is my sole hotel choice for Mont St.-Michel. *Moderate.* (Mère Poulard Hôtel, named for its original owner, who popularized the plebeian omelet a century or so back in her hotel's dining room, is the only hotel in the French Republic whose management would not allow me to inspect its public areas, not to mention bedrooms, unceremoniously directing me to leave as soon as I had entered in the company of a colleague who was a French Government official and who clearly explained our mission. Given that arrogant reception, I cannot recommend the Poulard to my readers.)

DAILY BREAD
L'Âtre (7 Esplanade Cadet Menguy, in the St.-Servan quarter of St.-Malo; phone 9981-68-39) positively hums at lunch—and with good reason. Tables are, to be sure, tightly spaced. But the staff is cordial and the

chef expert. The five-course menu yields memorable choices—a diverse platter of fresh seafood, oysters through mussels, to start; and grilled fish of the day, *au beurre blanc*, as the next plate. A smoked pork chop served with lentils and matchstick-thin *frites* might be the entrée. Then comes a salad dressed with a perfect *vinaigrette*. Desserts? You choose from a trolley—fresh strawberries in season, doused with Brittany cream, are among the possibilities. In my experience, one of France's best restaurants. *First Class.*

À la Duchesse Anne (Place Guy La Chambre, Intra Muros; phone 9940-85-33) occupies quarters in a house of substantial age. Tables are dressed in red and white polka-dot linen, the wine waiter wears a sailor suit, serving staff is attentive, and fare is utterly delicious. You order from an extensive à la carte; a meal might embrace fish soup and filet of sole *meunière*, accompanied by sautéed mushrooms and a mound of crispy *frites*. *Tarte tatin*, the house's dessert specialty, is as superlative as any you will find in neighboring Normandy, where this apple cake was invented. *First Class.*

Hôtel Central Restaurant (6 Grande Rue, Intra Muros; phone 9940-87-70) tempts with daily specials; in asparagus season, open with that vegetable in tandem with a sublime *sauce mousseline*. Skewered broiled scallops, with *beurre blanc* sauce, are a treat. So is filet of beef in the company of *sauce Béarnaise*. *First Class.*

Jean-Paul Delaunay (6 Rue Ste.-Barbe, Intra Muros; phone 9940-92-46) bears the name of its talented chef-patron, and you could do worse than to order half a duckling, prepared by him, with *calvados;* or lobster in a variety of styles. Tempting desserts. Location is a street just off Rue Jacques-Cartier. *First Class.*

La Croix du Sud (27 Rue Jacques-Cartier, Intra Muros; phone 9956-79-42) is at once well located and neat as a pin, with a good-value menu; open with the *crêpes* so popular in this region; continue with *coq au vin* or the day's fish catch, grilled; and finish with a fruit tart. No credit cards. *Moderate.*

Les Remparts (17 Rue Jacques-Cartier, Intra Muros; phone 9940-91-23) is smartly Old Brittany, with respect to decor and cuisine, as well. Choose from several prix-fixe menus, each built around well-prepared seafood, with *pre-salé* lamb—from animals nurtured on the salt marshes surrounding Mont-St.-Michel—also delicious. *Moderate/First Class.*

Tea-Time (4 Grande Rue, Intra Muros; phone 9940-89-12) could be across the Channel in England, with bacon-and-eggs breakfasts, salad-

and-omelet lunches, and made-on-premises cakes served with afternoon tea. Fun. *Moderate.*

Chez Gaby (2 Rue de Dinan, Intra Muros) is a typically Breton *crêperie;* make a meal of several, starting with savory and ending with sweet. Delicious. *Moderate.*

Café de l'Ouest (Place Chateaubriand): Take a table, and watch the crowds pass in review, with the walls of the château just opposite. *Moderate.*

Le Continental (Cancale, 9 miles east of St.-Malo; phone 9989-60-16) is, to be sure, a 21-room, moderate-category hotel located on the waterfront of this fishing village, but it is called to your attention here primarily because of its excellent restaurant. There are two prix-fixe menus based on seafood; the pricier—worth the relative splurge—might embrace a dozen of the esteemed local oysters, half a grilled local lobster, cheese, and choice of sweets. (Also worth sampling: just-caught fish, mussels, scallops.) Congenial. *First Class.*

Le Cancalais (Cancale, 9 miles east of St.-Malo; phone 9989-61-93) is still another of the many waterfront restaurants of this village—and an exemplary one. Order à la carte: mussels—either *marinière, à la crème,* or *farcies* (stuffed)—are a specialty; or pick one of four prix-fixe menus, on one of which *blanquette de poisson*—a fish stew—is always featured. *First Class.*

Mouton Blanc Hôtel Restaurant (Mont-St.-Michel; phone 9960-14-08) packs them in, especially at lunch, but never mind, the food is very good, indeed. Open your prix-fixe with a seafood platter packed with oysters, shrimp, clams, and sea snails; continue with a monster omelet—typically Mont-St.-Michel—which is preparatory to the entrée, *gigot d'agneau* (the lamb is *pre-salé,* fed on the salt marshes, adjacent) served with a mini-mountain of *frites. First Class.*

Terrasses Poulard (Mont-St.-Michel; phone 9960-14-09) presents a tempting prix-fixe menu with a variety of openers, the standard omelet as course No. 2, and—among entrées—sole prepared with Normandy cider. The *terrasses* of the title are the island's ramparts; no charge for the panoramic views. *First Class.*

SHOPPER'S ST.-MALO
Rue Broussais, in the Intra Muros section, is the main business street; *Aux Toiles de France* sells typical Breton lace. *Monoprix* department store is on nearby Rue St.-Vincent. *Jean Yves* (smart men's clothes) and *Guilbert*

(linens) are among Rue Barbinais's many boutiques. *Au Marin Breton* (with typical Breton fishermen's sweaters) and *Richard Yachting* (women's haute couture) are both on Rue de la Vieille Boucherie. *Le Mazagran* (white porcelain) and *Hélène Noël* (nineteenth-century antiques) are among Grande Rue's grander shops. *Villefromoy* (Place Châtillon) is the quality antiques shop owned by the family operating a hotel of the same name, recommended above.

AFTER DARK
Casino (Esplanade du Casino, Extra Muros) shares a contemporary, glass-fronted pavilion with a convention center. Assorted entertainments are presented in its theater; roulette and other games of chance, too; café-restaurant.

INCIDENTAL INTELLIGENCE

You may fly to the Channel Islands of Guernsey and Jersey, as well as London (see *Britain at Its Best*), on scheduled service from nearby *Aéroport de Dinard*. *Brittany Ferries* sail to Portsmouth from St.-Malo, and there is boat service, also, to the Channel Islands, provided by a number of companies. *Further information:* Office de Tourisme, Esplanade St.-Vincent, St.-Malo; Office de Tourisme, 2 Boulevard Féart, Dinard; Office de Tourisme, Port, Cancale; Office de Tourisme, 3 Grande Rue des Stuarts, Dol-de-Bretagne; Office de Tourisme, Corps de Garde des Bourgeois, Mont-St.-Michel.

33

St.-Tropez
Hedonism on the Côte d'Azur

BACKGROUND BRIEFING

It may not have seemed so when, many centuries back, this Roman-founded Mediterranean village—identified as much with the Riviera as with Provence—named itself after a Roman Christian martyr originally called *Torpes*. Nor, even later—in the Renaissance era—when it was virtually repopulated, after a period of decline, by a score of substantial Genoese families whose descendants constitute the nucleus of today's permanent populace.

No, it was not until much later—toward the turn of the present century—when long obscure St.-Tropez began to achieve celebrity. Maupassant exclaimed over its beauties in print. Matisse followed, pioneering among the painters, to be followed by a star-studded cache of colleagues: Signac, Bonnard, Henri Cross, and Marquet, to name a handful.

Colette joined this pre-World War I artistic contingent, following—by some decades, to be sure—Maupassant in printed praise. Pre-World War II St.-Tropez had become fashionable enough to attract the fashion and film worlds, innovating a casual, barefoot resort life-style on the French Mediterranean, nothing at all like more conventional fleshpots such as Cannes (Chapter 13), Nice (Chapter 26), and Monte Carlo (Chapter 23) to the east.

It took only a handful of talented publicists, after World War II, to chronicle St.-Tropez's hedonism as manifested by such regular visitors as actress Brigitte Bardot and novelist Françoise Sagan and to place St.-Tropez on the world-class resort map. And with reason. It is one of a kind.

None of this is surprising when you consider the setting. St.-Tropez straddles the inner shore of an enormous sheltered gulf—with the distinction of facing north (the better for afternoon sun) rather than south, as is common in seaside resorts of the region. The village climbs a château-topped hill and is backed by formidable mountains. Combine its situation with limited means of access—trains do not reach St.-Tropez, nor is there an adjacent airport—and the special appeal of the place becomes apparent.

St.-Tropez does not receive massive tour groups flying in on jumbo jets. There are no grand-luxe hotels in the traditional sense where gents change to jacket and tie for dinner. Restaurants are adequate, rarely exceptional, and, in no case I know, monumental. Sightseeing is not of the tour-bus variety. You shop in a way-out boutique rather than a department store. You dine very late and disco much, much later. The hotel social director is an unknown species; your daily schedule is of your own making. What I mean to say is that St.-Tropez is not for everyone. If the dictionary definition of hedonism appeals—"The ethical doctrine that the seeking of pleasure is the primary good"—it may just be for you.

ON SCENE

Lay of the Land: St.-Tropez juts into the waters of a placid gulf, facing the contemporarily created vacation village of *Port Grimaud*, if you look north, and the village of *St.-Maxime*, across to the east. Core of town is the horseshoe-shaped *Vieux-Port*, with restaurants and cafés tightly packed, one after the other, on ground floors of handsome old houses. *Rue François Sibili* is the more important of several streets leading inland from the harbor to a pair of atmospheric—and contiguous—squares: *Place des Lices* and *Place du XVᵉ Corps*. *Rue de la Citadelle* extends east from the harbor to *La Citadelle* (below), high over the village. *Rue Gambetta*, running parallel to Rue François Sibili, is boutique filled, as is *Rue Allard*, west of the harbor. Beaches are east of the center: *Plages des Graniers* is the closest; *Plages des Salins* is more distant. Hotels are dotted about, around the port, in hilly sectors overlooking the port, in the countryside, and in mountain villages. There is, of course, no railway station, but *Gare Routière*, the bus depot, is on *Place Banqui*, west of the center.

Musée de l'Annonciade (Place Georges Grammont)—an all-France sleeper—is a St.-Tropez surprise package of the first order. Quartered in the early sixteenth-century chapel whose name it takes, it is desanctified and beautifully adapted to its present function. It is the venue for exhibition of an extraordinary collection of post-Impressionist paintings by artists who have worked in St.-Tropez, beginning with the pioneering Signac's *Le Port de St.-Tropez* (painted in 1899); Marquet's similarly titled work of 1905, and Matisse's bare-breasted *La Gitane* of 1906. But there is so much more: a Braque mountain village, Seurat's twin-towered *L'Estaque*, a Dufy of northerly Honfleur, a Vlaminck *nature morte* (plums in a bowl alongside a blue pitcher), Van Dongen's *Femme à la Balustrade*, works by Dérain and De La Fresnaye, Gross and Rouault, Bonnard and Vuillard.

Musée de la Marine (Rue de la Citadelle): The medieval hilltop stronghold of La Citadelle is St.-Tropez's most impressive monument of yore, a formidable sixteenth-century battlement, the views from which—of town and harbor—are at least as impressive as the collection within, of ship models and other souvenirs of the village's maritime past, including documentation relating to its liberation by valiant Resistance forces after World War II occupation.

Excursions into the mountains might center on visits to the villages of *Ramatuelle* and *Gassin*, each seven miles out of town and affording spectacular panoramas of St.-Tropez and the region. If I had to choose one, it would be higher-up Ramatuelle, centered about a charming Baroque church. Although lower-down Gassin, with its even older church, is hardly to be despised. Indeed, the two can be nicely combined in a day's outing.

SETTLING IN

Byblos Hôtel (Avenue Paul-Signac; phone 9497-00-04): You may get lost, but you won't be bored in this extraordinary complex, which attempts—and not without success—to emulate a traditional Provençal village in this series of irregularly contoured (but mostly connected) pavilions in an essentially U-shaped layout. Location is a promontory high above town, albeit an easy walk to the core. There are 110 rooms and suites, and when I say no two are alike, I understate. Decor theme is essentially traditional—natural woods, heavy beams, a proclivity toward beds and storage space built into nooks and crannies, with those rooms (the overwhelming majority) in the older part of the complex far handsomer, to me, at least, than the newer (which feature jacuzzi-equipped baths adjacent to beds, with toilets in enclosed compartments). There are a pair of exemplary restaurants, below counseled, as many bar-lounges (one, out of the Arabian Nights), and two discos. Of these, the latter—Les Caves du Roi—illuminated by a quartet of giant, stylized, glass-leaved trees, can accommodate a thousand dancers. The swimming pool-terrace is inviting, and pricey shops are dotted about. As casual as Byblos appears—ambience is typically St.-Tropez-casual—this is a professionally and skillfully operated hotel. *Luxury.*

Résidence de la Pinède Hôtel (Plage de la Bouillabaisse; phone 9497-04-21; a five-minute drive from town) is low-slung and more or less traditional in look, with 40 thoughtfully equipped rooms (the ones to aim for are seafront, with terraces), an attractive restaurant with an al fresco extension on which informal lunches are served, and swimming either from the beach or in the pool. Management is astute and kindly. *First Class.*

Yaca Hôtel (1 Boulevard d'Aumale; phone 9497-11-79) is agreeably situated, halfway up the hill from the harbor, and pleases with its good looks—tile-floored lobby, 22 bedrooms whose beds and windows are covered in brown and white checks, and pretty pool flanked by a luxurious garden. Friendly staff. Breakfast only. *Moderate.*

La Ponche Hôtel (Place Revelin; phone 9497-02-53) attracts, first, with its situation on a landmark—and lively—square; then, with its agreeable ambience, club-like lobby, comfortable cocktail lounge, two dozen smartly styled rooms (the nicest those with seaview terraces), and a restaurant well known in its own right, later counseled. *First Class.*

Résidence des Lices Hôtel (Avenue Augustine-Grangeon; phone 9497-28-28) is at its most striking in a two-story, contemporarily designed lobby-lounge, fronting a big rectangle of a pool. There are 36 pleasant bedrooms, and you're central—just off Place des Lices. Breakfast only. *Moderate.*

Ermitage Hôtel (Avenue Paul-Signac; phone 9497-52-33) shares the same street—atop the hill overlooking the harbor—as the neighboring Byblos (above). Reception area/lounge are homelike, and there are 29 rooms, the most desirable those with views of town and sea. Friendly. *Moderate.*

La Maison Blanche Hôtel (Place des Lices; phone 9497-52-66) is not going to put you in mind of Washington's White House, which is hardly to say it is not worthy of consideration; this is an intimate house of but eight no-two-alike rooms, with the location a principal square. Breakfast only. *Moderate.*

Sube Hôtel (Quai Suffren; phone 9497-30-04) is called to your attention should you desire a modest hotel—not all of its 26 rooms have bath—directly on the harbor, heart of the action. Breakfast only. *Moderate.*

Le Jas d'Alexis Hôtel (Domaine de la Quessine, Ramatuelle; phone 9479-23-40) might be just the ticket, should you like the idea of a hotel high in the hills with a dozen pools fronting the long, low-slung pavilion that shelters 30 terraced rooms. Views—all the way to the sea—are fabulous. The hotel's Veranda Restaurant is reliable and indicated for lunch in the course of an excursion from St.-Tropez. *First Class.*

DAILY BREAD

Le Chabichou (Byblos Hôtel; phone 9497-00-04) welcomes with white stucco walls and country Provençal chairs, their seats padded in regional fabrics, with interesting paintings and sculptures as accents. Menu is *nouvelle* accented. You might open with lobster-chicken *terrine* served with a warm potato salad. Scalloped duck livers served on a bed of spinach and garnished with white onions and artichokes is a popular entrée. There's a traditional prix-fixe menu that might open with a truffled duck *pâté*, continue with sautéed lamb, and conclude with a choice of house-prepared sweets. Dinner only. *Luxury.*

La Ponche (Place de Revelin; phone 9497-09-29) is enjoyable on a mild summer evening, at a table set under the broad canopy in the square, elevated enough to afford seaviews. Order from the good-value menus, seafood accented, ranging from fish soup through the day's catch simply grilled and beyond to the house's own desserts. *First Class.*

La Pasquière and Le Mazagran are a pair of restaurants contiguous to each other on Place de Revelin, with the same management, same phone (9497-05-92), similarly pleasant panoramas of the harbor, and same reliable fare. The prix-fixe menu—start with mussels *marinière* or *pâté de campagne;* continue with grilled fresh sardines or a steak, accompanied by *frites* and tomatoes Provence style; and end with a choice of sweets—is tasty and well priced. *First Class.*

Bistrot de la Marine (7 Quai Suffren; phone 9497-04-07) is probably as satisfactory as any of the jumble of restaurants jam-packed into this street, directly on Vieux-Port. Do not count on space between tables in any of this group; the idea is sardine-like seating. Bistrot de la Marine makes some attempt at decor, however, with hurricane lamps on tables. The prix-fixe might include fish soup, filet of sole or *gigot d'agneau*, and dessert. *First Class.*

Les Mouscardins (Quai Jean-Jaurès; phone 9497-01-53) occupies fully enclosed quarters at the east end of Vieux Port. There is, alas, no terrace, so that even on fine evenings, when all of St.-Tropez dines al fresco, you're indoors. There are some good local dishes—*anchoïade* (anchovy paste served on toast) as an appetizer is among them. Grilled fish is a satisfactory entrée. By and large, though—mediocre. *First Class.*

Chez Nano (Place de l'Hôtel de Ville; phone 9497-01-66)—with its central location and nice-looking quarters—packs in the crowds at dinner, which is à la carte only and minimally tasty, with simpler entrées like lamb chops the safest. Waiters are inexperienced youngsters. I can't recommend this one. *First Class.*

Café Senequier (11 Quai Suffren)—massive and hardly distinguished to look upon—is St.-Tropez's see-and-be-seen congregating spot; go for *pastis* or coffee and take in the crowds. *Moderate.*

Bella Vista (Gassin; phone 9456-17-30) is accurately named, affording fabulous views of the sea, way below, and indicated for a lunch break in the course of an excursion into the hills. *Moderate.*

SHOPPER'S ST.-TROPEZ
Modish, youthful sportswear appropriate to the barefoot St.-Tropez dress code typifies the shopping scene, with branches of pricey chains as options. For example, *Hermès* (men's and women's accessories) and *Les Must de Cartier* (watches, jewelry) are on Rue de la Ponche. *Porcelain Blanc*—white housewares—is on Rue Gambetta. On Rue François Sibili and adjacent Passage Gambetta, emphasis is on wearables—*Kansai, Lady Wilson, Claire l'Insolite, Kenzo, Gianni Versace, Accessoire Diffusion, Stéfane Kélian,* and *Gas* (this last with costume jewelry)—for women; *Façonnable, Uomo,* and *Daniel Crémieux* are for men. *Galerie Suffren* (eighteenth-century antique furniture) and *Souleiado* (Provence textiles) are among shops in the Byblos Hotel. And there's a branch of the *Jacques Dessange* hairdressing chain on Rue Allard.

INCIDENTAL INTELLIGENCE

Nearest train stations are St.-Raphaël (to the east) and Toulon (to the west); regularly scheduled buses serve St.-Tropez from each of these points. *Further information:* Office de Tourisme, 23 Avenue du Général-Leclerc, St.-Tropez.

34

Sarlat

By Huffle and Truffle through Périgord

BACKGROUND BRIEFING

Locate the southwesterly city of Bordeaux (Chapter 10) on a map of France, fixing your eye in an easterly direction. The towns you'll note—Sarlat and Périgueux, especially—will be in small type. And it's not likely that, on an all-France map, many of the neighboring villages will appear at all. The point I make is that the region still termed Périgord, though lacking a single whizbang of a metropolis, compensates with a plethora of pretty towns where an overnight visitor is, to this day, an honored guest.

Périgord is a concentration of fortified castles on dramatic bluffs, elaborately facaded Renaissance mansions, and churches—more of them early, severe Romanesque than later Gothic—worshiped in over long centuries. And there is a pair of even more distinctive lures: caves in which Paleolithic man lived and painted, and an irresistibly rich cuisine—based on the truffle and the goose—that will never, *ever* come to terms with cholesterol.

Taking its name from ancient residents called *Petrocorii*, who date back to before the Roman occupation, Périgord evolved as a fiefdom of the dukes of Aquitaine and was English-held during the Hundred Years War, before becoming a part of Renaissance France. And although other parts of France have known quite as many battles and changes of land-lord and allegiance as Périgord, appurtenances of its past appear in greater abundance—and with less celebrity—than is the case elsewhere. A cardinal rule of Périgord tourism is this two-word maxim: *Go inside.*

ON SCENE

Lay of the Land: Périgord is, by and large, a region of overnight layovers. Ideally, it is traversed by rented car—although trains serve larger towns; buses, smaller ones. There are no time-consuming metropolitan centers, but as many utterly charming small towns (including medieval fortified villages called *bastides)* and country castles as you have time and inclination for; not to mention visitable prehistoric caves, of which the most significant cluster is at *Les Éyzies.* Distances are not great. By that, I mean a journey of, say, 30, 40, or 50 miles between Point A and Point B is a long one. I open this chapter with *Sarlat* because—though small and with no outstanding hotels or landmark restaurants—it is nothing less than one of the best preserved and most charming Middle Ages/Renaissance towns in France. And it's delightful to walk about. *Rue de la République,* which cuts through it north to south, is virtually its sole claim to modernity—and pedestrians-only in summer. The bulk of the town lies to its west, based on venerable *Place de la Liberté* (dominated by seventeenth-century *Hôtel de Ville,* with outdoor cafés), from which *Rue de la Liberté* runs south to *Place de la Cathédrale* and a clutch of important structures (below). *Rue Fénelon, Rue Landry,* and *Rue de la Montaigne* are but a trio of central streets, lined by beautiful old houses. The railway station is south of the center on *Avenue Thiers.*

Cathedral of St.-Sacrédos (Place du Péyrou) was built as the chapel of a substantially endowed abbey between the twelfth and fourteenth centuries, with Renaissance additions. The tremendous height of its nave impresses, as does a Baroque choir and a Rococo organ. The building is ingeniously tucked into a hill, with towering *Lanterne des Morts*—Lanterns of the Dead—out back, originally a chapel for funerals, with burials in the surrounding *Cimitière St.-Benoît,* and both a Romanesque chapel and tranquil cloister, adjacent. Just opposite is *Hôtel de la Boétie,* the house in which a noted writer whose name it takes was born, with the most celebrated Renaissance facade in town; note its carved stone window frames.

Musée de la Chapelle des Pénitents Blancs (Rue des Pénitents Blancs, just west of Rue de la République) is Sarlat's best-kept secret—a repository of sumptuous sacred art in an extraordinarily beautiful, desanctified seventeenth-century church. Every exhibit is handsome—gilded wooden angels, sculpted bishops, *Ste. Claire* as the subject of an eighteenth-century painting, and a seventeenth-century *St.-Jerôme* in polychrome constitute but a handful—and the lot are framed by the church's dramatic barrel vault.

Marché aux Oies is Sarlat's centuries-old goose market, in the square whose name it takes. Regional wines (from Bergerac, below) may be sampled and are sold at this square's *Maison du Vin de Bergerac. Cellier du Périgord* (Place de la Liberté) is a delicious source of the region's celebrated *foie gras, pâté, rillettes, tartines,* and *galantines.* Antiques shops—on Rues Émile-Faure, Fénelon, and other streets—can yield quality objects. And the principal department store is *La Grande Fabrique* (Rue de la République).

Château de Puymartin (six miles north of Sarlat) is essentially Renaissance and sports a pair of turreted towers. Resident family members take you through; Grande Salle, with a gorgeous fireplace, Aubusson tapestries, and Louis XIII chairs, is the showplace room.

Périgueux (38 miles north of Sarlat and capital of Dordogne département, which approximates the area of old Périgord) is a town of considerable beauty, compact enough for ambulatory exploration. *Place Bugeaud* is the central square, with *Monoprix* department store and good shops; these continue on adjacent *Rue de la République* (site of *Nouvelles Galeries* department store) and on *Rue du Président Wilson*. Nearby *Rue Limogeanne* is the core of the town's *Secteur Sauvegarde*, its meticulously restored old quarter, with Renaissance houses lining streets. Amble about for a bit to sense the flavor of Périgueux; then zero in on three interiors. *Cathedral of St.-Front* (Place Daumesnil) is one of the most curious such in France. It looks, as you approach it, for all the world like a southwest counterpart of Sacré-Coeur, above Montmartre in Paris—chock-filled with cupolas. These are nineteenth century, not unlike Sacré-Coeur's, but other parts of this impressively immense pile go back nine hundred years. Don't miss the cloister. *Musée du Périgord* (Rue Barbecane) is a surprise package of no little interest, with exhibits at once prehistoric (the skeleton of a 35-million-year-old neighborhood gent), ancient (neighborhood Roman mosaics), medieval (a carved stone griffon from the cathedral belfry dating to the twelfth century), and relatively recent (Rococo paintings and porcelain)—with later works by area artists. *Church of St.-Étienne de la Cité* (Place de la Cité) is severely Romanesque, a veritable fortress beneath an immense dome, with a lovely choir.

Bergerac (26 miles south of Périgueux and one of the region's Big Three towns, along with Périgueux and Sarlat): If, like me, you have read Rostand's classic *Cyrano de Bergerac* in French class or have seen it played, you want to pay your respects to the town of Cyrano and Roxanne, ringed by vineyards whose grapes are the basis of dry Bergerac and sweet Montbazillac wines. The town is centered by *Place de la République*, with shops on adjacent streets like *Rue Thiers* and *Avenue du Président Wilson* and a pair of museums in *Hôtel de Ville* (Rue Neuve d'Argenson), one of which, *Musée Municipal*, has exhibits of local prehistoric finds, as well as later Bergerac art and artifacts. *Château de Montbazillac*, two miles south of town in the hilly vineyards, compensates with Renaissance architectural details—crenelated walls, a quartet of towers, elaborate entrance—for what it lacks in size; museum exhibits within delineate, on the one hand, the story of the neighborhood's

wines, and, on the other, the neighborhood's historic Protestant ante-
cedents.

Les Éyzies (12 miles northeast of Sarlat): It is entirely possible to appreciate the global significance of the caves at Les Éyzies—and those nearby,
as well as exhibits in the national museum here—without being able to
relate to them as easily as to, say, a *paysage* by Poussin, a portrait by
Largillière, or a pool of water lilies by Monet. It is a question of time
frame. Prehistoric art and the science of prehistory can be difficult to
come to grips with, even in southwest France, where the evidence of
Cro-Magnon man—come upon only a century and a quarter back—is so
startling. Withal, this 30,000-year-old handiwork wants to be experienced. First stop should be *Musée National de la Pré-histoire*, built into
cliffs—in an originally medieval château, above the village. It is not
big—there are but eight galleries—but it is significant, and what one
most remembers is that its exhibits were the work of men who resem-
bled the Neanderthal figure just outside the museum entrance: It was
sculpted in 1930, using an actual Neanderthal skeleton as the basis of
its design. From the museum, opt for as many as half a dozen caves in
the neighborhood; those of *Font de Gaume*—but a third of a mile away—
are quite the most fabulous, with some 200 designs, in still discernible
color, of recognizable animals (bison, especially, but deer and horses,
too). If you've time for more, those of *Les Combarelles* (two miles distant),
some 300 extraordinary wall engravings, are important, too. If it's July
or August, when this area, I must caution you, is packed with visitors,
consider such alternatives as the *Caves of La Mouthe, Les Cent Mammouths, Bara-Bahau,* and *Du Sorcier. (Caveat:* Les Éyzies and surrounding
caves traditionally close mid-October through mid-April.)

Lascaux II: But what, you are about to ask, about the famous paintings
on walls of the prehistoric Cave of Lascaux? Alas, they have been closed
since 1960, only 23 years after they were discovered, the better to protect
them from destructive bacteria introduced by a plethora of visitors. But
the mid-Eighties saw the opening of Lascaux II—only a few hundred
yards away from the original, outside of the village of *Montignac*, 14
miles north of Les Éyzies. This second Lascaux is a scientifically re-
searched, carefully produced replica of the original; believe me, it is not
a variation on a theme of Disneyland. You enter an unlighted cave
whose contours are identical with the closed Lascaux, even to slippery
terrain and surfaces worn by centuries. A team of painters, sculptors,
engineers, and computer experts put it all together with amazing skill.
You wait your turn to be taken through in a small group by a staff expert,
watching your step as you move along in the dark, as the guide directs
a flashlight at frescoes of animals—bulls and horses, bison and deer,
delineated in earth tones of brown, beige, and goldish yellow—that were

executed in candlelight to re-create the level of illumination available to painters who created the originals 15,000 years ago.

Château de Beynac, in the Dordogne River village of Beynac-et-Cazenac, a few miles south of Sarlat, is a cliff-hanger—quite literally. It straddles an eminence at the river's edge, protected by formidably high, crenelated walls, part of a rebuilding as long ago as the thirteenth century. You cross a courtyard to reach state rooms—a sumptuous salon and oratory are the top two. But it's views along the river that are most memorable, and it's agreeable to amble through the atmospheric adjacent village.

Château de Bourdeilles (10 miles north of Périgueux), not unlike Beynac (above), is dramatically elevated, but on the banks of another river—the Dronne. It's actually two châteaux: medieval fortress and Renaissance palace. The former's kicker is an octagonal keep. But it's to the latter's Salle Dorée to which you beeline. This ravishingly decorated salon is the work of the same André le Nôtre who created Fontainebleau's interiors, a marvelous mix of fine furniture, splendid tapestries, paintings by the Fontainebleau school's Amboise Le Noble—and fabulously painted beamed ceilings.

Abbaye de Brantôme (seven miles north of Bourdeilles and nicely combined with it, edging the Dronne River, in a village whose name it takes) embraces a beautiful Gothic church, art filled, with a detached bell tower, eighteenth-century abbey buildings, and a garden from which there are river views.

Domme (11 miles south of Sarlat) is the prototypical *bastide*—or fortified village; if you visit but one such in Périgord, this should be it. Tucked into a cliff high above the Dordogne River, it was built in the late thirteenth century and is little changed since then, turbulent Hundred Years War battles notwithstanding. A trio of original gates and still formidable ramparts—a tower at each extremity—enclose the town. It's fun to stroll *Grande Rue*, taking in *Maison du Gouverneur*, the old governor's mansion on *Place de la Halle*, along with the colonnaded market hall, and to view the river from *Promenade des Falaises*, on the cliff, as you depart.

Château de Hautefort (20 miles east of Périgueux) is an essentially seventeenth-century masterwork—elevated, massively scaled, and multitowered, with three of its sides enclosing a capacious court; classic-style Grande Galerie and domed chapel, the highlights of its interior, with terraced gardens a visitor bonus.

Trémolat (20 miles west of Sarlat) is one of Périgord's prettiest villages, affording fine views of the Dordogne, on which it is oddly positioned in a kind of horseshoe contour. Its ace-in-the-hole is an unusual fortified church, quite as forbiddingly plain as it was when erected in the ninth century.

Limoges (though not in Périgord, but at its northeastern extremity, with Périgueux 60 miles to the south) is an industrial city—its name is synonymous with fine French porcelain—albeit with a trio of visitable destinations. *Musée Adrien-Dubouchée* (Place du Champ-de-Foire) is a celebration of porcelain, housing some 10,000 objects, from ancient ceramics to patterns being produced this very week in Limoges factories, with displays of such other French china as Sèvres and St.-Cloud, as well as foreign porcelains, Ming through Wedgwood. *Musée Municipal* (Boulevard de la Corderie), occupying a onetime archepiscopal palace built in the eighteenth century, stands out because of its Limousin—regional—enamels, medieval through modern, with the former (work of the Middle Ages and Renaissance) the most outstanding. Directly next door is *Cathedral of St.-Étienne*—thirteenth-century Gothic, with an impressively vaulted nave, sculpted tombs, and a treasury highlighted by locally created enamels. If you've time, stroll around the center of town, in and about pedestrians-only *Rue du Consulat* and neighboring streets lined with half-timbered Renaissance houses.

SETTLING IN

Hostellerie de Maysset (Route D-67, less than two miles from Sarlat; phone 5359-08-29) is not, alas, central. But it's so pretty that I can't resist leading off with it. If you've a car, you'll be content in this contemporarily constructed but traditional style inn. Public spaces—lounge, bar, nicely appointed restaurant—are delightful; ditto, the 26 no-two-alike rooms that look out onto the Maysset's park-like garden. *First Class.*

St.-Albert Hôtel (Place Pasteur; phone 5359-01-09)—at the south edge of town and an easy walk to the center—is unpretentious but comfortable enough, with 57 adequate rooms, a cozy cocktail lounge, congenial staff, and a restaurant worthy of additional comment in a later paragraph. *Moderate.*

La Madeleine Hôtel (Place de la Petite-Rigaudie; phone 5359-12-40) is an attractive, centrally located house. There are 22 traditional-style rooms, bar, and restaurant—an efficient operation that, alas, lacks spontaneity, warmth, perhaps even a smile. *Moderate.*

Salamandre Hôtel (Rue Abbé-Burguier; phone 5359-01-81) is a couple of blocks farther south of the center than the St.-Albert (above), with which it shares the same management. There are 21 adequate rooms, as well as five vividly decorated duplex suites. Bar and breakfast only. *Moderate*.

Domino Hôtel (21 Place Francheville, Périgueux; phone 5308-25-80) is an old house whose owning family has taken care to modernize it without losing an iota of the charm that has accrued in the century of its operation. Thirty-one of the 37 rooms are bath equipped, antiques accented—and delightful. There's a corking good restaurant that moves to umbrella-topped tables in the inner garden during warm weather, a bar whose clientele is a mix of locals and visitors, and skilled, congenial management. *Moderate*.

Bristol Hôtel (37 Rue Antoine Gadaud, Périgueux; phone 5308-75-90) is a relatively contemporary house, centrally situated and agreeable, with baths in 21 of its 28 rooms. Bar and breakfast only. *Moderate*.

Ibis Hôtel (8 Boulevard Saumande, Périgueux; phone 5353-64-58) is conveniently central—a near-neighbor of the cathedral, with 86 neat rooms, bar, and restaurant. *Moderate*.

Manoir le Grand Vignoble Hôtel (St.-Julien-de-Crempse, six miles north of Bergerac; phone 5357-92-44) is indicated as a headquarters for the Bergerac area. It's a manor house that dates to the seventeenth century, with high-ceilinged public spaces that include a beamed lounge-bar and a paneled restaurant. There are 26 distinctively decorated rooms, a good-sized outdoor pool, tennis, and an unexpected surprise—riding—either on the backs of horses or in the hotel's antique buggy. *First Class*.

Royal Vézère Hôtel (Place de l'Hôtel de Ville, Le Bugue; phone 5306-20-01) is a clean-lined contemporary house edging the Vézère River in a pleasant village not far south of Les Éyzies—and worth knowing about in connection with a visit to that area. There are 53 well-equipped rooms, bar-lounge, and a restaurant featuring regional specialties. Mapotel/Best Western. *First Class*.

Cro-Magnon Hôtel (Les Éyzies; phone 5306-97-06) is among the more thoroughly likable of Périgord's hotels—small enough for service to be personal, owner-managed, handsomely traditional, and set in its own swimming pool-equipped park. There are 30 no-two-alike rooms; each of those I have inspected is handsome. Bar-lounge, too, as well as an al fresco summer restaurant featuring truffle-based Périgord specialties. Charming. *First Class*.

Les Glycines Hôtel (Les Éyzies; phone 5306-97-07) is an agreeable house, with a reliable restaurant, friendly bar, and 25 full-facility rooms. *Moderate.*

Du Centenaire Hôtel (Les Éyzies; phone 5306-97-18) makes a point of being stylish, has 27 comfortable rooms and a *nouvelle*-cuisine restaurant. Member, Relais et Châteaux. *First Class.*

Le Relais du Soleil d'Or Hôtel (Montignac, near Lascaux; phone 5351-80-22) is modern, to be sure, but with nearly 40 rooms traditional in style, as is the attractive restaurant. Bar-lounge, outdoor pool. Congenial. *First Class.*

Rush Hôtel (Terrasson, 20 miles north of Lascaux, 30 miles west of Périgueux; phone 5350-03-74) is stark modern without and graciously traditional within. There are 50 rooms, some Louis XV style, some Louis XIII, and attractive public spaces that include restaurant and bar-lounge. *First Class.*

Les Îles Hôtel (Thonas, midway between Périgueux and Sarlat, near Lascaux and Les Éyzies; phone 5350-70-20) is well situated, rustic-attractive, with 10 rooms of differing sizes and facilities; and a stone-walled, beam-roofed restaurant featuring Périgord specialties, which moves outdoors in summer. *Moderate.*

Le Vieux Logis Hôtel (Trémolat, about midway between Sarlat and Bergerac, not far from Les Éyzies; phone 5322-80-06) is a long-on-scene, long admired stone manor house of yore, with 14 antiques-accented rooms, garden setting, and ranker of a restaurant with well-priced prix-fixe menus featuring Périgord classics. Member, Relais et Châteaux. *First Class.*

Le Panoramic Hôtel (Trémolat; phone 5322-80-42) is an unpretentious but comfortable 23-room house, with a bar-lounge and a reliable restaurant. *Moderate.*

Les Bruyères Hôtel (Route de Cahors, Villefranche-de-Périgord; phone 5329-97-97) is strategically situated on Périgord's southern frontier, just outside an aged *bastide*, or fortified town. Setting is an originally thirteenth-century house in a garden, with 10 agreeable rooms and a stone-walled restaurant. *Moderate.*

DAILY BREAD
St.-Albert Hôtel Restaurant (Place Pasteur; phone 5359-01-09): I don't know of a better restaurant in Périgord in which to become acquainted

with the rich cuisine of the region that's based on the goose, the goose's liver, and the delectable truffle. Order à la carte or from a prix-fixe in this expertly operated restaurant. Open, perhaps, with *foie gras frais* served with an onion sauce or *rillettes de confit de canard*—*pâté* based on preserved duck; with *confit de canard* as an entrée accompanied by sautéed potatoes flecked with the mushroom species known as *cèpes*. Filet of beef, veal, and poultry are options. *First Class.*

Le Moulin du Roi (Passage Henri-de-Segogne, 7 Rue Albéric Cahuet; phone 5331-01-38) is typically Vieux Sarlat—beamed ceilings and silk-shaded lamps in the intimate interior, tables set outside against aged brick walls in warm weather. There are four prix-fixe menus, one of which might embrace *pâté de foie gras* as an opener, a hearty *cassoulet Périgourdin* (truffle flecked), a regional cheese, and a pastry dessert. Friendly. *First Class.*

La Rapière (17 Rue Tourny; phone 5359-45-38) is indicated for an al fresco lunch in a scenic Sarlat quarter. The well-priced prix-fixe is based on *confit de canard*. Outdoor tables. *Moderate.*

Café de l'Hôtel de la Mairie (Place de la Liberté) is just the spot for coffee or a cold drink, the while you watch ambulatory Sarlat pass in review. *Moderate.*

La Flambée (Rue Montaigne, Périgueux; phone 5353-23-06) is small but smartly traditional, with tuxedoed waiters serving up tasty beef specialties grilled on an open-to-view fire. Open with the house's handsomely presented *crudités* or *foie gras frais* and continue, then, with *filet de boeuf* accompanied by *sauce Périgueux*—surely appropriate in the city of origin. Or select trout; the chef will come out and pluck a live one from La Flambée's tank, preparing it *à la meunière*, thereafter. Luscious desserts. *First Class.*

Le Tournepiche (2 Rue de la Nation, Périgueux; phone 5308-90-36) is atmospheric—as well it might be, given a location close to the cathedral, heart of town. Prix-fixe menus are based on grilled lamb chops, filet of beef, and sliced smoked duck breasts and include wine. *First Class.*

De l'Univers Hôtel Restaurant (18 Cours Montaigne, Périgueux; phone 5353-34-79) is at its most tempting in summer, when tables are moved to the street-view garden, so that you watch the passing parade, the while enjoying a prix-fixe menu built around *confit d'oie* or a steak. Lots of locals. *Moderate.*

Le Cyrano (2 Boulevard Montaigne, Bergerac; phone 5357-02-76): No quarrel with this restaurant's appropriate title, nor, for that matter, with its fare. Order the prix-fixe menu, making sure that you open with warm *foie gras* and artichoke salad and follow with duck—also a Cyrano specialty. *First Class.*

Frantel Limoges (Place de la République, Limoges; phone 5534-65-30) is on a central Limoges square—and is as recommendable for its Restaurant Renoir (with good-value prix-fixe menus) as for an overnight stay: there are 75 full-facility rooms. *First Class.*

INCIDENTAL INTELLIGENCE

Further information: Office de Tourisme, Place de la Liberté, Sarlat; Office de Tourisme, 1 Avenue de l'Aquitaine, Périgueux; Office de Tourisme, 97 Rue Neuve d'Argenson, Bergerac; Office de Tourisme, Place de la Mairie, Les Éyzies; Office de Tourisme, Place de Born, Montignac (near Lascaux); Office de Tourisme, Pavilion Renaissance, Brantôme; Office de Tourisme, Boulevard Fleurus, Limoges.

35

Strasbourg
Showplace of Alsace

BACKGROUND BRIEFING

Border cities—cities that have dealt with political, cultural, and linguistic crosscurrents over long centuries—are invariably appealing. Find Strasbourg on the map—with only the Rhine to separate it from Germany and Belgium, Luxembourg and Switzerland near-neighbors, this lot contrasted, of course, with the considerable territory of France to the west. Strasbourg's tale can be likened to a juggling act, practiced by experts over a 2,000-year span. Little wonder that its people speak German as fluently as French, along with a dialect of their own, and that so many of them speak good English, as well. Nor is it surprising, for that matter, that Strasbourg serves as seat of the European Parliament and the Council of Europe.

It was Celts who first settled Strasbourg at the dawn of the Christian era. Romans, who succeeded them, called it *Argentoratum*. Only with the influx of later Germanic settlers did the name change to *Strateburgum*. The tenth century saw Strasbourg part of the Holy Roman Empire. By the time it gained Free Imperial Status in the thirteenth century, it had become a medieval mercantile crossroads of consequence, with the German language dominant, to the point where it lured even Johann Gutenberg, who gave his name to a central Strasbourg street and square, remaining for a period in the fifteenth century before actually inventing the printing press in Mainz. (See *Germany at Its Best.*)

It was under Louis XIV's reign that Strasbourg became part of France in the seventeenth century, and it was after the French Revolution, in the late eighteenth century, that it became noticeably French, with respect to use of the language and adjustment to the culture.

There were, to be sure, two involuntary German relapses. As spoils of the nineteenth-century's Franco-Prussian War, Strasbourg, along with the rest of Alsace (see Colmar, Chapter 15) became German territory for nearly half a century, until the conclusion of World War I. The Second World War saw it German-occupied once again—and damaged. But Strasbourg has always bounced back. My only caveat with respect to a visit today is that you may not, at any given moment, be quite certain as to what country you're in. Strasbourg is by no means typical of urban France, nor of urban Germany, nor of rural Alsace. It is one of a kind, a city of extraordinary beauty that is comfortable with outlanders, knows how to have a good time, and—important, this—tastes as good as it looks.

ON SCENE

Lay of the Land: Strasbourg is old-fashioned enough to regard its palatial nineteenth-century railway station (*Place de la Gare*) as a focal point. Flanked by a clutch of hotels—including some very good ones—it's at the western edge of the city. *Rue du Maire Kuss* leads east to the core—crossing the *Ill River* just north of the scenic quarter, *La Petite France*—a delightful jumble of immaculately maintained medieval houses, half-timbered, their balconies giving onto the river and adjacent canals, with the view sublime from *Terrasse Panoramique* of the building known as *Barrage Vauban* on *Quai Mathias*. Area streets—*Rue des Moulins* (with the landmark *Maison des Tanneurs*), *Rue des Dentelles*, and *Grand Rue*—are lined with fine old houses, as is *Rue Fosse des Tanneurs*, which leads to big and busy *Place Kléber*, Strasbourg's premier square. From it, via shop-lined *Rue des Grandes Arcades*, the city's towering cathedral is a hop and a skip, on *Place de la Cathédrale*, with *Château des Rohan*—housing several major museums—adjacent, on *Place du Château*. Walk everywhere; Strasbourg comes up with surprises at every turn.

Cathedral of Notre-Dame (Place de la Cathédrale): Be glad of the cathedral's central location; you can pop in every time you pass by—which will be often—to experience a facet of its complex interior missed on earlier visits. Built over five centuries—it is, of course, essentially Gothic, from the thirteenth and fourteenth centuries—the cathedral lacks nothing but a tower on its right side to match that on its left, which, incidentally, is ascendable, if you're up to 300-plus steps. Halt at the west, or principal, facade. Tympanums, or carved overdoors, of its three portals are busy with sculpted likenesses covering a range of subjects—Wise and Foolish Virgins through Old Testament Prophets. Look up at the exquisite rose window, as you enter. Then move down the massively scaled nave to the transept, to pause between the unique-to-Strasbourg Angels' Pillar, with three rows of splendidly sculpted figures interpreting the Last Judgment. To be observed also in the transept is a plaque with this inscription: "In memory of American officers, non-commissioned officers and enlisted men who gave their lives to free Alsace 1944–45." Take in the pulpit, whose Gothic tracery makes it quite unlike any other. Enjoy the widely reputed stained glass. Note frescoes behind the high altar. Admire Romanesque capitals of the crypt—the remaining lower level of an earlier cathedral, over which this structure was built. Time your visit to conclude precisely at midday to watch the daily performance of the cathedral's Swiss-made, sixteenth-century astronomical clock, with Death—scythe in hand—striking the hour, while the twelve Apostles pass in review, beneath Christ blessing the audience, with a noisy cock crowing high in the background.

Musée de l'Oeuvre Notre-Dame (Place de la Cathédrale) is a repository of art objects associated with the neighboring Cathedral of Notre-Dame, including the Romanesque structure that preceded the present one, *and* of Alsatian art, medieval through Renaissance. It embraces some two score galleries, several courtyards, and a number of art-filled corridors. It's brilliant, and you want to give it some time. Entire rooms—their original paneled walls and decorated ceilings—have been incorporated in the exhibits. There are a transplanted seventeenth-century spiral staircase, doorways from Strasbourg mansions, stained-glass windows and wrought-iron architectural elements, glassware and pottery, tapestries and sculpture—including, among the latter, an intact stonecutters' guild meeting-room, with likenesses of saints in niches along four walls. There's also an entire cloister of a twelfth-century Alsatian monastery, scenes from the life of Christ carved into the capitals of its columns. You want not to overlook the courtyard designed as a medieval garden, with a stream winding through it. Paintings? You'll find several by Strasbourg-reared Hans Baldung Grien, with a complementary clutch by other artists of the same Renaissance period.

Château des Rohan museums (Place du Château) overwhelm with their treasures. Treasure No. 1 is the building itself, an all-France, early eighteenth-century masterwork, where Strasbourg's prince-bishops lived (Louis XV, Queen Marie Leczinska, Marie Antoinette, and Napoleon, on separate visits with each of his two empresses, were among its guests) in a setting of splendidly scaled, paneled, wainscotted, and furnished salons, themselves an integral part of a contemporary Rohan visit. Of the three actual Rohan museums, *Musée des Beaux-Arts* dominates, with a considerably larger collection than you might expect—in a single building housing several museums. There is, for example, a strong sprinkling of Spaniards—El Greco and Zurbarán, Ribera and Murillo; Italians like Lippi, Correggio, and the stellar portraitist Bronzino; the same Hans Baldung Grien whose work we see in Musée de l'Oeuvre Notre-Dame (above); Low Countries greats like Memling, Brueghel, Rubens, De Hooch, and Van Dyck; the early Renaissance Simon Marmion's moving *Pietà;* and a host of Frenchmen—Philippe de Champaigne through Renoir. *Musée des Arts Décoratifs* is a mix of Strasbourg-made furniture—

mostly eighteenth century, but some older—and locally manufactured porcelain, much of it by a firm named Hannong, with antique clocks as a bonus. *Musée Archéologique* takes you back—*way* back—to prehistoric Strasbourg. Pottery, utensils, weapons—that sort of thing; with more interesting Roman pieces: sculpture, fragments, and later objects, as well.

Musée Alsacien (Quai Alsacien) is fun: a 20-gallery collection of folk art in a seventeenth-century building that wraps itself around three sides of a cobbled courtyard. Period rooms—paneled parlor with seventeenth-century tile stove and furnishings, all-purpose farmhouse room with bed in a cabinet-like frame, country kitchen lined with gleaming copper *kugelhopf* molds—are the standout exhibits; toys and costumes, pottery and paintings, too.

Musée Historique (Rue du Vieux Marché-aux-Poissons), though not as amusing as Musée Alsacien (above), brims with documentation that tells the Strasbourg story. Spiffy soldiers' uniforms, some with their original breastplates, are the most colorful exhibits. But there's stained glass galore, historical prints, and etchings, as well.

Musée d'Art Moderne (Quai St.-Nicolas) contrasts its quarters—an antique customs house unused for centuries—with its contents: a corking good clutch of contemporary paintings that make for a nice change of pace in this tradition-laden city. Impressionists represented include Degas, Pissarro, and Monet, with later painters like Braque and Dufy and master-sculptors, Maillol through Arp.

Church of St.-Pierre-le-Vieux (Rue du 22 Novembre) is a Strasbourg contribution to ecumenism: Catholic and Protestant churches joined at right angles and dating to the Renaissance, with the Catholic part coming off with the more beautiful interior.

Palais de l'Europe (Avenue de l'Europe, a quarter-hour's drive northeast of the center) is a contemporary complex considerably younger (1977) and far less architecturally significant than the UN (1952) in New York—but reminiscent of it, with flags of the score-plus member European nations flying out front in the manner of the UN, and—again, like the UN—with a secretariat (headquarters of the Council of Europe) and an international legislature, the Parliament of Europe, which meets several times annually, with sessions usually lasting a week. Unlike the UN, which welcomes visitors without notice throughout the year, these chaps ask that you telephone (8861-49-61) first, to arrange a time for your tour.

SETTLING IN

Terminus Gruber Hôtel (10 Place de la Gare; phone 8832-87-00) is a lovely, old-fashioned house lining the vast square opposite the railway station—a seven- or eight-minute walk from Place Kléber. There are just a hundred no-two-quite-alike rooms, fussily but engagingly decorated, with good baths and—in some instances, good sized. Leading from the lobby are a cozy cocktail lounge; a rather grand, two-story-high, beamed restaurant that serves up a mighty tasty dinner, even at a late hour; and—facing the square—a *brasserie* as popular with locals as with guests. Reception-concierge staff—cordial, kindly, and efficient—is one of the best such that I know in France, for which, three cheers. *First Class.*

Sofitel Strasbourg (Place St.-Pierre-le-Jeune; phone 8832-99-30) is old enough—I suspect it goes back to the late Sixties—to antedate the newer crop of Sofitels that dot the republic and tend to be less felicitous in appearance. This one is tastefully contemporary, with a big lobby, 180 rooms (some, to be sure, smaller than others), restaurant, cocktail lounge, and a super situation: steps from Place Kléber. Friendly. *First Class.*

Bristol Hôtel (4 Place de la Gare; phone 8832-00-83) is an oldie, nicely updated, with 40 rooms, no two identical; restaurant, bar. Mapotel/Best Western. *Moderate.*

Grand Hôtel (Place de la Gare; phone 8832-46-90) is a turn-of-century house that has been nicely refurbished. The lobby is bright, the elevator leading to upper floors is glass-walled, and there are 90 rooms; those that I have inspected are very comfortable, and no hotel of my acquaintance gives the impression of being more squeaky-spanking-sparkling clean. *Moderate.*

Novotel Central Halles (Quai Kléber; phone 8822-10-99) has just under a hundred functional rooms and agreeable public spaces that include a restaurant and bar. Generous buffet breakfast. *Moderate.*

Ibis Central Halles Hôtel (Quai Kléber; phone 8822-14-99) is a next-door neighbor of the Novotel (above), also with just under a hundred rooms, restaurant, and bar. Tabs are cheaper, rooms smaller, and mattresses a bit thinner than those of Novotel. *Moderate.*

Arcade Hôtel (7 Rue de Molsheim; phone 8822-30-00) is one of a chain of agreeably mod-look, budget-tabbed, full-facility houses. There are 143 rooms, restaurant, and bar. Central. *Moderate.*

Le Pax Hôtel (24 Rue du Faubourg National; phone 8832-14-54) is no-frills but central, with baths in 84 of the 110 rooms, and a convenient, inexpensive restaurant. *Moderate.*

Hilton International Strasbourg Hôtel (Avenue Herrenschmidt; phone 8837-10-10) would head my Strasbourg grouping were it central. Location, however, is northwest of the center, out in the modern Palais de l'Europe quarter, a quarter-hour's drive from the center. This is a looker of a contemporary house, with just under 260 rooms and suites, whose decor is a restful, modified-modern mix and whose baths—bless U.S.-headquartered Hilton International—have real, honest-to-goodness, Yank-style showers over the tubs—a rarity, believe me, in provincial France. Smiles greet you as you reach Reception in the high-ceilinged lobby, off which are the Bar Bugatti, hung with prints of vintage Bugatti cars, a piano bar that draws evening crowds, a pair of restaurants later evaluated, and a terrace for warm-weather drinks. *Luxury.*

DAILY BREAD
Au Crocodile (10 Rue l'Outre; phone 8832-13-02) is subdued but handsome: Brown-leather upholstered Louis XVI chairs surround tables dressed in white linen, lighted by white-shaded lamps, with comfortable booths to the side. You are welcomed graciously, attended to punctiliously, and served deliciously. Crocodile has made its reputation on cuisine that's a deft mix of old-time Alsatian with *nouvelle*. You might, for example, open with a salad of *foie gras*—served warm—on a bed of endive, or cream of frog's legs soup. Seafood is exceptional—*gratin d'homard*, a lobster masterwork; a trio of *sole filets* in a truffled mushroom sauce, white-wine based. Chicken breasts are treated with skill; *blanc de volaille et noix de St.-Jacques*—the poultry melded with scallops, in a cream sauce laced with vermouth and Riesling—is a case in point. The house's duck and beef dishes are special, too. Cheeses are served in profusion, and *oeufs à la neige*—gossamer but satisfying—is an indicated dessert. This is the restaurant selected to cater the civic lunch for President Reagan at Château des Rohan (above) in the course of an official Strasbourg visit. With good reason. Central. *Luxury.*

Valentin Sorg (6 Place de l'Homme-de-Fer; phone 8832-12-16) is, like Au Crocodile (above), only steps from Place Kléber, but has the advantage of an elevated situation in a room lined with picture windows that give onto a cityscape dominated by the towering cathedral. Not that you come only for the view. Sorg cuisine is stubbornly—and satisfactorily—traditional. There are several prix-fixe menus, from one of which a meal might open with smoked trout served in tandem with celery *rémoulade*, continue with a *médaillon* of veal in a cream of mushroom sauce, and conclude with the house's own sherbet served with baked-on-premises *petits-fours*. Alternatives: Alsace's own *poulet au Riesling* served, as it should be, with broad noodles; *canard à l'orange*—duck in an orange-accented sauce; or roast lamb, Provençal style. Professional service. *Luxury.*

Maison Kammerzell (16 Place de la Cathédrale; phone 8832-42-14): You will have passed by this veritable skyscraper of a half-timbered medieval house—noting, particularly, the hand-carved wooden decorations between its windows—in the course of city strolls. It's a landmark, but it's also a corking good restaurant. There's no better spot to order the supreme Alsatian specialty, *choucroute garnie*—a vast platter with a generous base of sauerkraut, on which is piled pink *cervelas* sausage, white sausage, red Montbéliarde sausage, thick-cut slabs of bacon, the black "pudding" known as *boudin noir, saucisse de Strasbourg* (what we call knackwurst), sliced roast pork, liver dumplings, a ham shank, and—just so you won't leave the table famished—boiled potatoes. You don't attempt one of these every day, but you must have *choucroute garnie* at least once in the course of an Alsace visit. There are many other options here, grilled trout through roast pheasant, among them. *First Class.*

Maison des Tanneurs (42 Rue Bain-aux-Plantes; phone 8832-79-70) is quite what its name indicates—a onetime tanner's house, wonderfully atmospheric, overlooking the Ill River in La Petite France, with Alsatian specialties. Open, perhaps, with onion tart or *flammekueche*, a variation thereof with bacon, served hot. Snails are good here, too, as are smoked shoulder of pork and *coq au Riesling*. *First Class.*

Maison du Boeuf (Hilton International Strasbourg Hôtel, Avenue Herrenschmidt; phone 8837-10-10) is a good choice for a festive lunch combined with a tour of neighboring Palais de l'Europe (above) or for a candlelit dinner. The beef of the title is roast prime rib, rolled to your table on a silver trolley. But seafood is special, too. If you're not going to have it as an entrée, open with the chef's assortment of three species of smoked fish (salmon is one of them). You might follow with filet of beef served with marrow, in *sauce marchand de vin*. And conclude with a chocolate or lemon *soufflé*. Super service. *Luxury.* (And bear in mind that the Hilton's casual restaurant, *Le Jardin*, makes a specialty of Alsatian favorites, including onion tart and *coq au Riesling. Moderate/First Class.*)

Buerehiesel (4 Parc de l'Orangerie, out in the Palais de l'Europe quarter; phone 8861-62-24) is quartered in a Hansel-and-Gretel cottage, garden surrounded, with tables spilling into several small, primly decorated rooms. Welcome is chilly and service, likewise—at least in my experience. Cuisine is *nouvelle*, with a prix-fixe menu that might open with lamb salad, continue with roast rabbit, and conclude with ice cream enveloped in a coffee-flavored sauce. Disappointing. *Luxury.*

Du Dauphin (13 Place de la Cathédrale; phone 8832-86-95) is worth knowing about when you're in the core of town—and hungry. Hearty choices include *choucroute garnie, tarte à l'oignon,* and Riesling-sauced seafood stew. Outdoor tables. *Moderate.*

Pfifferbriader (9 Place de la Grande Boucherie, attached to Musée Historique; phone 8832-15-43): You want to sample at least one typically Strasbourg *weinstub* while you're in town. Build your meal around *baeckeoffe*—a pork, white wine, and potato casserole, *tarte à l'oignon,* or sausages, with a big pitcher of white wine to accompany. Everybody has a good time. *Moderate.*

Beyler (5 Place de la Cathédrale): Alsatians, I am told on good local authority, consume 25 percent more pastry than do Frenchmen in other regions of the republic and are, as well, the biggest ice-cream eaters in all France. If you want to understand why, select a plate of Beyler's baked goods, with or without frozen accompaniments. *Moderate.*

Café Tisza (14 Quai de la Bruche): It's a sunny day, and you could do with a cup of coffee al fresco; take it at Tisza. No finer views of La Petite France. *Moderate.*

Le Panoramic (Printemps, Rue de la Haute Montée): This café-cum-vistas—on the eighth floor of a department store—is accurately named. Have a casual lunch, snack, or coffee, bearing in mind that the store's excellent food—or *alimentation*—department is on five. *Moderate.*

Au Moulin (in the village of La Wantzenau, northwest of the center; phone 8896-20-01) is indicated for a sunny lunch or a relaxing country dinner. Au Moulin is situated in its own garden-centered plot, hospitality is warm, fare is Alsatian—and exemplary. A meal might open with *matelote aux nouilles*—fish stew with noodles, continue with *poussin*—young chicken—prepared in the house's style, and proceed to cheese (local Muenster, most likely), with plum tart smothered in whipped cream for dessert. *First Class.*

SHOPPER'S STRASBOURG
Magmod, Strasbourg's big nonchain department store, is on Rue 22 du Novembre; *Printemps* is on Rue de la Haute Montée, and good, old, thrifty *Marks & Spencer,* out of Britain but also in Paris and several provincial French cities, is on Place Kléber, site also of links of the *Daniel Hechter* (clothing) and *Lancel* (gifts and accessories) chains. *Gillman,* a fabulous *pâtisserie,* is at 6 Place du Temple Neuf and 20 Quai des Bateliers. *Frick-Lutz,* an also-fabulous *charcutier,* is at 10 Rue des Orfèvres. Both *Burberrys* (raincoats) and *Guy Laroche* (haute couture) are on Rue du Dôme. *Charles Jourdan* (shoes), *Menzer* (leather), and *Tedbury* (smart men's and women's duds) are all on Rue des Grandes Arcades. Rue des

Hallebardes is virtually lined with smart shops, including *D. Porthault* (linens), *Christofle* (crystal and silver), *Malbasa* (antiques), and *René* (classy men's shirts).

SOUND OF MUSIC

Théâtre Municipal (Place Broglie): If you collect theaters, this is one not to miss; early nineteenth century, handsome, and home of the regional Opéra du Rhin; concerts and ballet, too.

INCIDENTAL INTELLIGENCE

Aéroport de Strasbourg-Entzheim is seven miles west of town; scheduled service to a number of domestic points. *Further information:* Office de Tourisme, Palais des Congrès, Avenue Schutzenberger, Strasbourg.

36

Toulouse
Diversions to Albi and Carcassonne

BACKGROUND BRIEFING
It is not so much that Toulouse is underappreciated abroad; it is more a case of its being unknown. I would not hazard even an informal poll among friends as to its location, not to mention its significance. Still, this fourth largest of the French cities—150 miles southeast of smaller but better known Bordeaux and close both to the Mediterranean and to Spain—deserves more than passing acquaintance. It hums today as France's aircraft center (Caravelles and Airbuses you've flown were Toulouse-made). But it has always been busy at one sort of activity or another. Ever since Romans—calling it *Tolosa* and making of it one of the biggest of their Gallic colonies—set precedent, makers and doers have dominated the Toulouse scene.

Catholic bishops were present as early as the fourth century, following within but a hundred years the introduction of Christianity by the martyred St.-Sernin, whose name graces the city's all-Europe ranker of a Romanesque basilica. Germanic Visigoths came in the fifth century to make Toulouse capital of a kingdom that spread into neighboring Spain. The sixth century saw this city become seat of the wide-ranging kingdom of Aquitaine over a span of 300 years. In the mid-1100s, Toulouse was governed for the first time by the uniquely titled *capitoules* (from which the name of the current city hall, Le Capitole, derives).

By that time, counts of Toulouse ruled virtually all of Languedoc, competently and justly. They stood out because of their tolerance for Jews, many of whom settled in Toulouse, and they were hospitable to painters, writers, and philosophers, to the point where their court became a medieval culture hub celebrated throughout the continent. Simultaneously, Toulouse thrived as a spiritual center (Spanish-born St. Dominick established the Dominican order here) and as an educational center (the University of Toulouse opened in 1230 and is now the largest in

France, outside of Paris), as well as a mercantile *entrepôt* of no little significance. You have only to walk its core to observe still-standing mansions that bespeak its medieval and Renaissance wealth.

Withal, treasures of Toulouse must be assiduously sought out. This city lacks the hill-backed Mediterranean setting of Marseille; a core dramatically cut through by two rivers, like Lyon; a backdrop of snowy peaks in the manner of Grenoble. And, contemporary commercial eminence notwithstanding, there's nary a luxury-category hotel. Still, it pays to tarry in La Ville Rose—and so-called because red brick is the traditional building material—and to use it as a base for exploration of the nearby walled town of Carcassonne, Toulouse-Lautrec's native Albi, and the quiet little cathedral city of Auch.

ON SCENE
Lay of the Land: It's as though town planners knew we were coming and wanted to make it easy. Consider the *Garonne River* as Toulouse's southwest frontier. The bulk of the city to its west and north is what interests us. There are two central squares: northerly *Place du Capitole* (named for the eminently visitable city hall [below] overlooking it) and *Place du Président Wilson*, with cafés spilling into its center. As if the latter square, named for a U.S. President were not Yank association enough, the two squares are joined by *Rue Lafayette*—called after a French hero of the American Revolution. The principal shopping street, *Rue Alsace-Lorraine* runs through the two squares, concluding at southerly *Place Équirol*, through which the No. 2 street, *Rue Metz*, cuts, east to west. The neighborhood is crisscrossed by such pedestrian streets as *Rues Filatiers, des Changes,* and *St.-Rome*. Beyond the core is a pair of concentric boulevards—each of which is multinamed—ringing it. The railway station is at the northwest of the center on one of these outer arteries, called, at that point, *Boulevard de la Gare.*

Basilica de St.-Sernin (Place St.-Sernin): The French are often more niggardly than the English in the space they reserve in front of their great churches, the better to afford perspective. St.-Sernin is a case in point; it deserves a considerably more generous Place St.-Sernin than is the case. Still, this nine-century-old beauty catches you up as you approach, its five-story tower not a whit overbearing for the massive structure beneath—housing a 350-foot-long nave leading to the transept and high altar, beneath a sublime, 60-foot-high barrel-vaulted ceiling. Looking inward as you enter is an esthetic experience in and of itself. But other aspects of St.-Sernin warrant attention; the saint whose name it takes lies buried beneath a Baroque baldachin behind the eleventh-century marble high altar. Expressively carved capitals top columns in the transept; marble bas-reliefs of Christ and the Apostles grace the apse; below are a pair of crypts with half a dozen splendidly embellished chapels in the lower one.

Church of the Jacobins (Rue Gambetta) is like no other church you've seen before: a veritable Gothic tour-de-force, splendidly restored in the 1970s. The Jacobins is a successor to an earlier monastery complex established by St. Dominick and his black-and-white-robed preaching friars in the thirteenth century. It has three lures: pinnacle-like windows recessed into the facade of the church they ring; an utterly serene, poplar-planted cloister, and an abnormally high and elongated nave climaxed by a single pillar supporting the chancel, its vaults like the fronds of a palm tree.

Musée des Augustins (21 Rue de Metz) is a desanctified Augustinian monastery dating back seven centuries that was allowed to deteriorate pitifully—even after it became a museum in the last century—to the point where French Government experts, with a multimillion-franc budget, stepped in during the mid 1970s. They closed the museum's doors for half a decade, restored the complex to its original Gothic splendor, remounted its exhibits—many of them world-class—with flair, and reopened Musée des Augustins in 1980. You go as much for the setting— the high-vaulted onetime chapel's massive space devoted to paintings by Rubens, Murillo, Van Dyck, and a host of French masters; Romanesque sculpture in the refectory and chapter room—as for the art. And that is hardly to be despised, given works by such other French masters as Simon Vouet, Philippe de Champaigne, and Pierre Mignard, of the Baroque era; Largillière, Rigaud, and Oudry out of the eighteenth century; and the nineteenth-century's Delacroix, Corot, and Courbet. With Italian Old Masters Perugino, Lorenzo Monaco, and Guercino on hand, as well.

Cathedral of St.-Étienne (Rue Croix Baragnon): In a city without St.-Sernin, the Jacobins, and, for that matter, a cloistered monastery turned into an art museum (above), Toulouse's cathedral would be a stellar Gothic standout. As it is, even with the competition, you want to pop in, to see how it is actually two joined churches (built between the thirteenth and seventeenth centuries) with an oddly irregular but appealing facade, sublime tapestries, a rose window, and side chapels in near-limitless quantity.

Le Capitole (Place du Capitole) is City Hall, eighteenth century, with a dazzling classic-style facade stretching over some 400 feet. Pop through the courtyard to a grand staircase that will take you up a flight to the showplace reception room, *Galerie des Illustres*—it honors hometown lads who made good—lavishly frescoed with gilded capitals atop columns punctuating its walls.

Hôtel d'Assézat (Rue de Metz) is perhaps the most elaborate of a number of Renaissance townhouses. It was built by a sixteenth-century *capitoul*—or municipal legislator. Go beyond its classic-style facade for a peep at its courtyard. Look, too, at *Hôtel de Bernuy* (Rue Gambetta), early sixteenth century, with a fabulous nine-level tower.

Musée St.-Raymond (Place St.-Sernin) is nicely combined with the Basilica of St.-Sernin, its neighbor. It comprises an oddball mix of collections, with Roman emperors' busts and medieval sculpture its standouts.

Musée du Vieux Toulouse (7 Rue de May) makes its home in Hôtel du May, a sixteenth-century merchant princes' mansion, that brims with Toulousiana—high-quality furniture, most especially, but maps and prints, clothes and toys, domestic implements and pottery. Fun.

Albi (45 miles northwest of Toulouse) is surely the only city in France with a cathedral built to double as a fortress. Idea was to defend its bishop from communicants hostile to a kind of Inquisition he had instigated against believers in a peculiar medieval doctrine bearing Albi's name, called the Albigensian heresy. *Cathedral of Ste.-Cécile* (Place Ste.-Cécile) is severe and formidable without and lacks both flying buttresses and pinnacles. Yet, its look is pleasing and distinctive—and could not contrast more with the interior than is the case, once one enters. Bolognese artists were imported from Italy to fresco virtually every conceivable available surface, except a mass of niches that frame polychrome likenesses of saints. The west wall contains an extraordinarily detailed interpretation of The Last Judgment, notable as much for content as for size. And the mammoth choir—carved-stone pinnacles behind its wooden stalls, exuberantly painted panels between the gilded vaults of its ceiling—is extraordinarily beautiful. Switch, then, to *Musée d'Albi*, but a hop and skip geographically, that represents a leap forward of half a millennium to the year 1864, when Henri de Toulouse-Lautrec was born to a local noble family and, despite impaired growth as a result of a rare kind of dwarfism called pyknodysostosis, achieved immortality in the 37-year span of his lifetime as one of the great post-Impressionists. Toulouse-Lautrec is celebrated for penetrating studies, ranging from horses of his childhood to music hall habitués of later Paris years. He was as skilled at the brilliant-hued posters he pioneered as at drawings that reflected his gift for draftsmanship and at paintings—more formal but no less graphic. Few small towns do as well by native-son artists of stature as does Albi, in the case of Toulouse-Lautrec, in this attractive repository of his work, overlooking the Turn River. There are, to be sure, other masters represented—Rigaud, Boucher, Georges de la Tour from an earlier era; a pair of Vuillards, with their subjects Toulouse-Lautrec. But you go for the Lautrecs—an early painting of his mother, sketches of the

Moulin Rouge, Jane Avril—a favorite Lautrec subject—from the rear; studies of Paris types—train travelers, café-habitués, cabaret dancers, laundresses—in profusion; and studies you will not have seen before of Yvette Guilbert, La Goulue and—mascot of the collection—Bamboule, a bulldog drawn from life in 1897.

Carcassonne (53 miles southeast of Toulouse)—though extensively restored—remains nonetheless an originally thirteenth-century walled city that could be out of a fairy tale. There is a pair of concentric walls punctuated by towers and turrets, with entrance gained by a drawbridge over a moat. An overall view—in the course of your approach—is reason enough for a visit. But give this medieval marvel some time. Its *Musée Archéologique*, a part of the multiturreted château, brought to rights as part of the nineteenth-century ministrations of Viollet-le-Duc— the restoration wizard who worked France-wide—abounds in beautiful objects, the range busts and capitals and sarcophagi from the town's Roman period through murals, tombs, and bas-reliefs from Carcassonne's medieval Golden Age. Have a look, as well, at the stunning interior of *Basilica of St.-Nazaire*—noting especially capitals of columns flanking its Romanesque nave and its remaining, mostly Gothic, aspects especially stained glass above stone choir stalls behind the high altar, and rose windows on either side of the transept. It's fun, then, to amble about, noting the dozen-plus towers that punctuate each of the city's two concentric rings of walls, by means of a stroll along the lists, between inner and outer walls.

Auch (46 miles west of Toulouse and pronounced *Ohsh)* is a tranquil cathedral town in the gently hilly heartland of ancient Gascony, celebrated as the legendary home of D'Artagnan, leader of Dumas's *Three Musketeers.* Auch's conveniently compact center is based on *Place de la Libération*, dominated by Hôtel de Ville, a lilting Rococo palace of a town hall, from which lead a jumble of atmospheric streets, on one of which— *Rue Dessoles*—is located *Claude Laffitte*, a purveyor of the area's own brandy, Armagnac, along with food specialties. Nearby, too, is *Musée des Jacobins* (Rue Daumesnil) named for the long-disused monastery it occupies, and a repository of Gascon lore—paintings, prints, and local furniture with the patina of centuries. Which leaves best for last. *Cathedral of Sainte-Marie* is Gothic-vaulted with Renaissance embellishments: a severe, twin-towered facade; massive sixteenth-century choir stalls that are masterworks of the wood-carver's art (ranking with those of Amiens Cathedral [Chapter 2] as France's finest); and just under a score of 400-year-old stained-glass windows by a beloved local called Arnaud de Moles; each is beautiful, but search out *The Nativity*, *The Crucifixion*, *Moses and the Burning Bush*, and *The Flight into Egypt.*

SETTLING IN

Grand Hôtel de l'Opéra (1 Place du Capitole; phone 6121-82-66): You walk through the courtyard of a mellow Place du Capitole complex to enter the Opéra, passing its garden-centered swimming pool en route. This relatively recently refurbished house emerges as one of the handsomest in southwest France. The lobby is small but handsome, in smart period style. No two of the not-quite half a hundred rooms are exactly alike, but each that I have inspected is imaginatively decorated in period style, with varying color schemes, textiles, wallpapers, and furniture and fabulous marble baths. The cocktail lounge has the look of a winter garden on an old transatlantic steamer, and the restaurant is worthy of comment on a later page. *First Class.*

Frantel Wilson Toulouse (7 Rue Labéda; phone 6121-21-75) is a core-of-the-city old-timer that has been agreeably updated. There are 95 rooms of varying sizes, with good baths, as well as a cozy cocktail lounge and a staff at once cordial and professional. Breakfast only. *First Class.*

Concorde Hôtel (16 Boulevard Bonrepos; phone 6162-48-60) is a ranker of a house—tastefully contemporary, with a hundred thoughtfully fitted-out rooms with fine baths, a congenial cocktail lounge, and not one but a pair of restaurants—reviewed on a later page—and skilled management. Location is just opposite the railway station. Hôtels Concorde. *First Class.*

Mercure Hôtel (Rue St.-Jérôme; phone 6123-11-77) is central and modern and equipped with 170 full-facility rooms, restaurant, and café—qualities and facilities that apparently impel crowds to gather, to the point where the staff, at least to one observer, is impersonal and overworked. Chaine Mercure. *First Class.*

Victoria Hôtel (76 Rue Bayard; phone 6162-50-90) is delightfully old-fashioned and refurbished relatively recently with a sense of style; there are 75 rooms, some more capacious than others. But you're closer to the railway station than the core. Breakfast only. *Moderate.*

Royal Hôtel (6 Rue Labéda; phone 6123-38-70) is worth knowing about: first, because it's central and second, because it's inviting; the lounge is decked out in comfortable rattan furniture. Most but not all of the 25 rooms have baths. Breakfast only. *Moderate.*

La Capoul Hôtel (13 Place du Président-Wilson; phone 6121-51-87) could not be more central. There are 110 no-frills rooms and a *brasserie-café* on the square. *Moderate.*

D'Occitanie Hôtel (5 Rue Labéda; phone 6121-15-92) would be higher up in my Toulouse ranking were it not closed during the extensive period when French schools observe summer vacation, as well as during other school holidays. Reason is that it's a hotel-school. Which is what makes it otherwise desirable: Student staff really toes the line, under constant professional supervision. The 20 rooms are positively ship-shape, and, when you ask a question at reception, you half expect the youngster responding to stand at attention and salute in the course of his or her reply. Good restaurant in connection. *Moderate.*

Chiffre Hôtel (50 Rue Séré de Rivières, Albi; phone 6354-04-60) is a delightful, heart-of-town house operated by the third generation of its founding family, with 40 no-two-alike rooms in period style (Louis XVI dominates, with commendable attention to details like paneling, chandeliers, and coordination of wallpapers and textiles). There's a good-sized cocktail lounge and a restaurant evaluated on a later page. *First Class.*

Cité Hôtel (Place de l'Église, within the walls of Carcassonne; phone 6825-03-34) could not be more typical of Vielle Carcassonne, adjacent to the ramparts, with half a hundred well-equipped rooms, restaurant, bar, and pretty garden. *First Class.*

Du Donjon Hôtel (2 Rue du Comte Roger, within the walls of Carcassonne; phone 6871-08-80): Don't let its formidable name frighten you away; the Donjon is adequate for overnight. Breakfast only. *Moderate.*

De France Hôtel (Place de la Libération, Auch; phone 6205-00-44): The trim but simple lobby gives no promise of the smartness of this long-on-scene, 30-room hotel. Decor of each chamber differs, but count on Second Empire—or even older—furnishings, glazed chintz, antique prints on the walls, and marble-counter baths, some with stall showers, praise be. The cocktail lounge is charming; indeed, there is no better spot for a spot of the local Armagnac, served icy cold in heavy glasses designed so that they cannot be set down; idea is that, like it or not, you drink up in one fell swoop. The De France's restaurant is exemplary enough for comment in a later paragraph. *First Class.*

DAILY BREAD
Vanel (22 Rue Maurice-Fontvielle; phone 6121-51-82) is low key; a generous-sized space, with contemporary chrome-accented chairs at tables set with immaculate white linen and the only touch of color a range of good-quality, recent paintings on the walls. Lucien Vanel, the chef-patron, makes it a point to say hello to all of his customers at one point or other, in the course of a meal that cannot help but be extraordinary.

Monsieur Vanel has for long championed southwest cuisine, and he has stuck by it, the *nouvelle* vogue notwithstanding. You order à la carte from a full page of *plats du jour* or from among a group of standby favorites. Starters include truffled *pâté de foie gras* or *foie gras au naturel*, prepared in the house; or mushroom or truffled omelets and a scrumptious *cassoulet* of snails. Among entrées are *confit de canard*—served with Sarlat-style potatoes; *tournedos* in a pepper sauce, flamed with Armagnac; and stuffed goose neck. But M. Vanel's changed-each-day dishes are delicious, too. I recall, for example, opening with crayfish-flecked gazpacho, continuing with filet of beef with *sauce Bordelaise*, and concluding with a sweet from the separate dessert card—*mille feuilles aux fraises des bois*. And digestifs: M. Vanel's list includes a dozen *eaux-de-vie* and as many of the area's Armagnacs. Skilled, smiling, never-pretentious service. In my experience, one of France's best restaurants. *Luxury*.

Les Jardins de l'Opéra (Grand Hôtel de l'Opéra, 1 Place du Capitole; phone 6121-82-66) is as handsome as it is delicious. There are two well-priced menus, of which the pricier is the more interesting; a meal might embrace avocado *terrine*, the house's duck or rabbit specialties; and your choice of sweets. The à la carte features *cassoulet Toulousain*, the region's hearty, baked bean-based casserole, as well as filet of beef, *sauce Béarnaise*. Super sweets. Smiling staff. *First Class*.

Darroze (19 Rue Castellane; phone 6162-34-70): Once you resign yourself to the over-fussy, ever-so-grand ambience of this relatively small restaurant, you can enjoy the competent traditional fare. The cheaper of the two menus allows no choice—you open with the house's own *terrine*, garnished with a salad; continue with the day's fricassee, wine sauced; and conclude with a designated frozen sweet. The more expensive menu—billed as a surprise—is just that: you take what pleases the chef to serve you that noon or evening. Far better to select from the à la carte, opening perhaps with scrambled eggs-cum-truffles or seafood salad. Proceed with filet of sole or *médaillons* of lamb, as an entrée, terminating with *profiteroles au chocolat*. *Luxury*.

La Pomme d'Amour (1 Rue de Gorse, opposite Church of La Dalbade; phone 6153-34-88) is indicated for a hearty dinner built around *tranche de gigot grillée*—grilled lamb steak; or *confit d'oie*—preserved goose—deliciously garnished. They're served as part of a three-course prix-fixe, with lemon tart or champagne sherbet, among desserts. *First Class*.

Rôtisserie de l'Écluse (Concorde Hôtel, 16 Boulevard Bonrepos; phone 6162-48-60): Semiabstract, modern tapestries line the walls of this smart restaurant. The à la carte features tempters like smoked salmon, *crudités* presented with a dipping sauce, or hearty fish soup—to open;

with such entrées as *sole meunière*, grilled lamb chops, and a *cassoulet* of which the chef is justifiably proud. Gracious service. *First Class*. (And bear in mind this same hotel's *Brasserie*, zeroing in on the well-priced *plat du jour*, or the daily prix-fixe, with an à la carte *salade Niçoise* or an omelet good bets, too. Snappy service. *Moderate*.)

Les Jardins de Li (9 Rue Croix-Baragnon; phone 6253-00-14) makes its home in a Renaissance mansion, but its look is sprightly—with modern art on bare brick walls. Stick-to-the-ribs regional fare is the specialty— stuffed goose neck or mussel soup to start, *confit* or *maigret de canard* among a number of entrées; the house's own *tarte tatin* or Black Forest cake for dessert. *First Class*.

Pâtisserie Toulousaine (77 Rue Alsace-Lorraine) is, as well, a *salon de thé*, on the main shopping street. Stop in for pastry with coffee or a cup of tea. *Moderate*.

Le Cardinal (Place du Président-Wilson) is indicated for a pick-me-up— coffee or a drink, a casual lunch. Location is a principal Toulouse square. *Moderate*.

Chiffre Hôtel Restaurant (50 Rue Séré-de-Rivières, Albi; phone 6354-04-60) is a sensible choice for lunch, in the course of Albi exploration. The well-priced prix-fixe might be comprised of *foie gras*-stuffed goose neck, salmon *terrine*, roast lamb generously garnished; and a choice of house-made desserts. Central. *First Class*.

Auberge du Pont-Levis (just outside the main gate, Carcassonne; phone 6825-55-23) is a two-story, multiroom restaurant. I suggest you take a table upstairs and tackle the delicious prix-fixe, which might commence with a fresh filet of salmon served with a piquant sauce, follow with *confit de canard* or a filet of beef, and conclude with one of the house's fabulous desserts—chocolate cake, mocha, or orange tart, for example. Friendly. *First Class*.

De France Hôtel Restaurant (Place de la Libération, Auch; phone 6205-00-44) is a formal room in brown and beige, with high, chandelier-hung ceilings and French windows giving onto the square. The à la carte, typically and traditionally Gascon, is the creation of the hotel's owner-chef, André Daguin; everything that I have sampled has been delicious, and presentation is flawless. Consider a meal that might open with *foie gras d'oie et de canard avec un verre de Sauternes*—braised goose *and* duck livers served according to local tradition, with a glass of Sauternes; proceed with *cuisse de canard confits aux pommes Paillasson*—preserved duck presented with straw potatoes, delicately deep fried; and conclude with, for example, prune ice cream drenched with Armagnac or a trio of the house's own tart and grainy sherbets in primary colors, with *petits-fours*. Splendid service. In my experience, one of France's best restaurants. *Luxury.*

SHOPPER'S TOULOUSE
Department stores are spread around: *Nouvelles Galeries* on Rue Laperouse, *Dames de France* on Place Jeanne d'Arc; and a whopping big, cafeteria-equipped *Monoprix* on Rue Alsace Lorraine, which has still another department store, *Parunis,* and such clothing shops as *Daniel Hechter, Armand Thierry,* and *Kopetzki,* where suede is a specialty, and *Bally* (shoes).

SOUND OF MUSIC
Théâtre du Capitole (Place du Capitole) is a part of the historic, eighteenth-century City Hall complex (above), with a traditional horseshoe-shaped interior that has, more's the pity, been modernized over the years. It's the setting for diverse presentations of opera—Beethoven's *Fidelio* through Richard Strauss's *Arabella;* the operettas still popular throughout France; ballet, with classics like *Petrouchka* through to modern works; and concerts. Musical events take place also at the modern *Halle aux Grains* (Place Dupuy).

INCIDENTAL INTELLIGENCE

There is scheduled air service to points throughout France from *Aéroport Toulouse-Blagnac,* west of the center. *Further information:* Office de Tourisme, Donjon du Capitole (a towering medieval fortress), Toulouse; Office de Tourisme, Place Ste.-Cécile, Albi; Office de Tourisme, Boulevard Camille Pelletan, Carcassonne; Office de Tourisme, Place de la Cathédrale, Auch.

Acknowledgments

Of the continental European countries, it is France to which I have returned most often and reported on most extensively, over a quarter-century period. For a good part of that time—in the course of writing magazine and newspaper articles and a companion book—I have had the benefit of sound advice and cooperation from George L. Hern, Jr., who, as public relations director for the French Government Tourist Office in the United States, has made many friends for France, not to mention himself, among the American travel press. George was enthusiastic about this book from the start, and I am grateful for his counsel in preparation of the extensive principal research trip for it—a fascinating odyssey, which took me from Caen to Chamonix, St.-Malo to St.-Tropez, and on which—never, ever before speaking so much French—I made many new friends, learning in the process the scope and diversity of western Europe's largest land.

I am grateful, as well, to Jean-Marc Janaillac, director general of the French Government Tourist Office in the U.S., and other FGTO staffers, at scattered points, who are longtime friends—Jacqueline Moinot, Georges Sauvayre, André Moraillon, Jean-Michel Harzic, and Kajsa Agostini—as well as the crack press relations team at Direction du Tourisme headquarters in Paris—Nicole Garnier and Marie-Paule Bournonville—with whom it is a pleasure to work, on each trip to the French capital.

I am fortunate in having a publisher—Mark R. Pattis—who acquired his fluent French at the Sorbonne, and is a confirmed Francophile. Mark's support for this book is appreciated, as, indeed, is that of his National Textbook/Passport Books fellow executives, S. William Pattis and Leonard I. Fiddle, as well as that of Senior Editor Michael Ross, ever patient, sympathetic, and skilled. Three more French-speaking Francophiles who have been of immeasurable help are my research editor, Max Drechsler (to whom I am indebted, among much else, for his section on the wines of France); my agent, Anita Diamant; and my typist, Louise Fisher. To them all: *mes amitiés et mes remerciements.*

I want also to thank, alphabetically, the following friends and colleagues in France and on this side of the Atlantic, as well, for their personal kindness and professional cooperation: Henry Allavena, Marguerite Allen, Pierre Aron, François Beaussier, Roland P. Bennavail, Marie Bersot, Christine Birgé, Louis Blanchi, Kenneth Boone, Pierre Bord, Marie-France Bouchavon, Richard Bourgogne, Bernard Bouyer, Michèle Braccini, Lillian Braun, Alain Brière, Nora Brossard, Bunny Brower, Yann Caillère, Mary Carroll, Daniel Cavalli, Dominique Cesari, Michel Claude, Michèle de la Clergerie, Thierry Costanza.

Also Fred Conserti, Bernard Cornée, Valérie Coutant, Frédéric Croisier, Nida Darkasanli, Cécile Daycard, Daniel Debaye, Hannah Delamarre, Denis Demangel, Jacques De Place, Jacques Desangle, Sylvain Deschamps, Hubert Tissier De Mallerais, Ivan de Pontcharra, Amaury De Varax, Chickie Dioguardi, Edward O. Douglas, Christian Drouin, Paule Dubuis, Henri Ducret, Richard Duvauchelle, Louise Elliott, Christian Fleith, Jean-Michel Foisnet, Véronique Forgeot, Robert Friaux, Monique Garnier, Jean-Michel Garrigou, Christian Gauthier-La Faye, Yannick Gautier, Daniel Genève, Joseph A. Giacoponello, Pierre Gouirand, Boubakar Guindo, Linda C. Gwinn, Bruce Haxthausen, Odile Hébert, Catherine Henry, Pascale Hervé, Mary Homi.

Also Françoise Jacquet, Marc Julia, Dr. Richard Katz, Virginia Kelly, Jeffrey E. Kriendler, Suzanne Lannes, Marie-Thérèse La Paillerie, Remi Lassaigne, Marie Laure, Danielle Leblais, Robert Lefort, Annie Le Goff, Neeltje Le Grip, Jean-Louis Leimbacher, François Lizeray, Florence Lorentz, Mary Lyons, Maguy Macario, Al Madocs, George Maillet, Jean-Pierre Marcus, Alain Martinez, Richard P. McGinnis, Christiane Menhinick, Josiane Merino, Daniele Micand, Denys Michel, Gérard Minard, Olivier D. Mollin, Mary D. Ockay, Evelyne Orban, Emmanuelle Ott, Claude Paccard, Michel Palmer, Dominique Paravisini, William Peper, Philippe Perichon.

Also Laurence Petit, Guy Planchette, Agnès Porte, Robert Pouchol, Michel Poulain, Pierre Rabany, Wolfgang Rattmann, Fred Reid, Merle W. Richman, Richard Riehm, Robin Rue, Daniel San Giorgio, Marie-Thérèse Sauvayre, Bob Schaeffer, Dagobert M. Scher, Rolande Servoz, Morris Silver, André Soulier, Jean Taittinger, Alain Tapié, Michel Techeney, Brigitte Thorin, Catherine Tierce, Ed Tourtellotte, Catherine Vincent, Christian Voyer, Daniel Zanon, and Marc Zuccolin.

—R.S.K.

Index

A

Abbaye aux Dames, 182
Abbaye aux Hommes, 182
Abbeys. *See* Monasteries
Addresses, 1
Adrien-Dubouchée, Musée, 378
Aiguille du Midi, 203-4
Ainay le Vieil, Château, 177-78
Airlines, 10-11
AIX-EN-PROVENCE:
    entertainment, 10, 112; geography,
    107; history, 106; hotels, 109-10;
    restaurants, 110-12; shopping, 112;
    special attractions, 107-9; travel
    information, 112-13
Aix-les-Bains, 121; hotels, 124;
    restaurants, 127
Albi, 395-96
Albi, Musée d', 395
Alpin, Musée, 203
Alpino, Museo, 203
Alsace. *See* COLMAR;
    STRASBOURG
Alsacien, Musée, 386
Amboise, 247-48
Amboise, Château of, 247-48
American Battle Monuments
    Commission, 184
American Cathedral, 49
American Church of Paris, 49
Amiens, 66
Amphitheaters, in Antibes, 192; in
    Arles, 130; in Nîmes, 318; in
    Orange, 140. *See also* Theaters
Ancien Évêché, l', 114
André-Malraux, Conservatoire, 174
ANGERS, 246; entertainment, 118;
    geography, 113-14; history, 113;
    hotels, 116-17; restaurants, 117-18;
    special attractions, 114-16; travel
    information, 118
Angers, Château d', 114

ANNECY: entertainment, 128;
    geography, 120; history, 119;
    hotels, 122-23; restaurants, 125-26;
    special attractions, 120-22; travel
    information, 128
Annecy, Château d', 120
Annecy, Lac d', 120; hotels, 123;
    restaurants, 126-27
Annonciade, Musée de l', 368-69
Antibes, 190, 191-92; entertainment,
    10; hotels, 196; restaurants,
    199-200
Antibes, Cathedral of, 192
Antique, Théâtre: in Arles, 130, 135;
    in Orange, 140
Antiquités, Musée des, 351, 353
Antiquités Nationales, Musée des, 63
Apollon, Salle, 316
Aquariums: in Paris, 44; in St.-Malo,
    360; in Trouville, 218
Aquitaine, Musée d', 166
Arbaud, Musée, 108
Archéologique, Musée: in Antibes,
    192; in Carcassonne, 396; in Dijon,
    223; in Nantes, 343; in Nice, 305;
    in Nîmes, 319; in St.-Émilion, 168;
    in Strasbourg, 386; in Tours, 247
Arènes, Les: in Arles, 130, 135; in
    Nîmes, 318
Argenterie, Tour de l', 341
Arlaten, Musée, 132
ARLES: entertainment, 135;
    geography, 130; history, 129;
    hotels, 133; restaurants, 134;
    special attractions, 130-32; travel
    information, 135
Armée, Musée de l', 34-35
Art Chrétien, Musée d', 131
Art et d'Histoire de Provence,
    Musée d', 192
Art galleries/Museums. *See*
    Museums

Art Moderne, Musée d': in
Les-Baux-de-Provence, 132; in
Cagnes-sur-Mer, 308; in
Strasbourg, 386
Art Moderne de la Ville de Paris,
Musée d', 50
Art Sacré, Musée d', 224
Arts Africains et Océaniens, Musée
des, 50
Arts Décoratifs, Musée des: in
Bordeaux, 166; in Lyon, 261; in
Paris, 51; in Saumur, 116; in
Strasbourg, 385-86; in Tours, 247
Arts et Traditions Populaires, Musée
des, in Nancy, 299
Arts et Traditions Populaires, Musée
National des, in Paris, 55
Art Moderne, Musée National d', 56
Arts, Théâtre des, in Rouen, 357
Assezat, Hôtel d', 395
Association for the Preservation and
Enhancement of Historical Paris,
39
Assy, 204
Atger, Musée, 291-92
Auberge Vaugrain, 64
Auch, 396
Audierne, 342
Auguste et Livie, Temple Romain d',
262
Augustins, Cloître des, 235-36
Augustins, Musée des, 394
Automobile, Musée National de l',
212
Auxerre, 222, 225-26
Auxey-Duresses, 148
AVIGNON: entertainment, 10, 144;
geography, 137; history, 136-37;
hotels, 140-41; restaurants, 142-44;
shopping, 144; special attractions,
137-40; travel information, 144
Aylcamps, Les, 130
Azay-le-Rideau, Château of, 247,
248

B

Ballet, 10. *See also under* Theaters

Balzac, Musée, 51
Bara-Bahau, 376
Barge, cruising by, 3-4
Baron-Gérard, Musée, 183
Bartholdi, Musée, 210
Basque, Musée, 156
Bastion St.-André, 192
Bayeux, 183-84
Bayeux, Tapisserie de, 183-84
Bayonne, 155-56; hotels, 158;
restaurants, 160-61
Beaubourg, Centre National d'Art et
de Culture Georges-Pompidou,
a.k.a. Le, 50
Beaumont, Parc, 326
BEAUNE, 222; geography, 145-46;
history, 145; hotels, 149-50;
restaurants, 150-53; special
attractions, 146-49; travel
information, 153
Beaune, Côte de, 148-49
Beauregard, Château of, 248
Beaux-Arts, Musée des: in Angers,
115; in Beaune, 147; in Bordeaux,
166; in Caen, 181; in Chambéry,
122; in Dijon, 223-24; in Lyon,
260-61; in Marseille, 273-74; in
Nancy, 298-99; in Nantes, 343; in
Nîmes, 319; in Orléans, 251; in
Pau, 325; in Quimper, 341-42; in
Reims, 62; in Rennes, 340; in La
Rochelle, 334; in Rouen, 353; in
Strasbourg, 385; in Tours, 247
Bénédictine, Musée de la, 354
Bénédiction, Chartreuse du Val de,
139-40
Berenger, Château de, 235
Bergerac, 375-76
Bernadotte, Musée, 325-26
Berry, Musée du, 177
Beynac, Château de, 377
Beynac-et-Cazenac, 377
BIARRITZ: entertainment, 162;
geography, 155; history, 154;
hotels, 157-58; restaurants, 159-60;
shopping, 161; special attractions,
155-57; travel information, 162

Bibliothèque Nationale, 42
Biot, 306-307
Blanc, Mont. *See* CHAMONIX
Blois, Château of, 247, 248
Bonnat, Musée, 156
BORDEAUX: entertainment, 174;
  geography, 164; history, 163-64;
  hotels, 169-71; map, 165;
  restaurants, 171-73; shopping,
  173-74; special attractions, 164,
  166-69; travel information, 174
Boucard, Château, 178
Boulogne, Bois de, 43
Bourbon, Palais, 29, 41
Bourdeilles, Château de, 377
Bourdieu, Château le, 168
BOURGES: geography, 176; history,
  175; hotels, 178; restaurants,
  178-79; special attractions, 176-78;
  travel information, 179
Bourges, Cathedral of, 58, 176
Brantôme, Abbaye de, 377
Breakfast, 1-2
Bretagne, Musée de, 340
Breton, Musée Départemental, 342
Brévent, 204
Brissac, Château de, 116
British Embassy Church, 49
Brittany, climate in, 3
Brochon, 225
Bullfights, in Arles, 130, 135
Buses, 2
Bussy-Rabutin, Château de, 222, 226

C

Cabarets, in Paris, 68
Cabourg, 218
CAEN: entertainment, 188;
  geography, 181; history, 180-181;
  hotels, 185-86; restaurants, 186-88;
  special attractions, 181-85; travel
  information, 188
Cagnes-sur-Mer, 308
Calanques, Les, 274
Calvet, 148
Calvet, Musée, 139
Camarguais, Musée, 132

Camargue, 132
Cancale, 360-61
CANNES: entertainment, 200;
  geography, 190; history, 189-90;
  hotels, 193-96; restaurants,
  197-200; shopping, 200; special
  attractions, 190-93; travel
  information, 201
Cantini, Musée, 273
Capitole, Le, 394
Capitole, Théâtre du, in Toulouse,
  401
Carcassonne, 396
Carnavalet, Hôtel, 39
Carnavalet, Musée, 51-52
Carrée, Maison, 318
Carrousel, Arc du, 36
Casinos, 2; in Aix-les-Bains, 121; in
  Cannes, 200; in Deauville, 217-18;
  in Évian, 122; in Monaco, 281-82;
  in St.-Malo, 366
Cassis, 274
Castles. *See* Chateaux
Castre, Musée de la, 190-91
Castries, Château de, 293
Cathedrals. *See* Churches
Cavaye, 149
Céramiques, Musée de, 353
Cernuschi, Musée, 52
Cézanne, Atelier de, 108
Chablis, 225-26
Chagall, Musée, 306
Chaillot, Théâtre National de, 67
Chaîne, Tour de la, 332
Chambéry, 121-22; entertainment,
  128; hotels, 124; restaurants,
  127-28
Chambolle-Musigny, 225
Chambord, Château de, 247, 249,
  255-56
CHAMONIX: geography, 203;
  history, 202; hotels, 205-206;
  restaurants, 206-207; special
  attractions, 203-204; travel
  information, 207
Champ-de-Mars, 44
Champs-Élysées, Théâtre des, 67

Chancellery, 36
Chantilly, 58
Chapelle l'Anguillon, Château, 178
Charles-Dullin, Théâtre, 128
Chartres, 58-59
Chartres, Musée de, 59
Chasse et de la Nature, Musée de la, 52
Château, Le, 359
Château, Musée du: in
    Cagnes-sur-Mer, 308; in
    Strasbourg, 385-86; in Vitré, 341
Châteaux: in Aix-en-Provence,
    106-107; in Amboise, 247-48; in
    Angers, 114; in Anjou, 116; in
    Annecy, 120; in Azay-le-Rideau,
    248; in Bayonne, 155; in
    Beauregard, 248; in Bergerac,
    375-76; in Beynac-et-Cazenac, 377;
    in Biarritz, 156; in Blois, 248; in
    Bourges, 177-78; in Caen, 183; in
    Chambord, 249; in Chambéry,
    121-22; in Chenonceaux, 249; in
    Cheverny, 250; in Chinon, 247,
    249; in Combourg, 361; in
    Compiègne, 59-60; in Crémieu,
    235; in Dijon, 226; in Grenoble,
    235; in Kaysersberg, 211-12; in
    Langeais, 250; in Malmaison, 62;
    in Montpellier, 292-93; in Nancy,
    298; in Nantes, 343; in Orléans,
    250; in Paris, 38; in Pau, 324-25; in
    Périgueux, 377; in Rambouillet,
    62-63; in Riquewihr, 211; in Sarlat,
    375; in Saumur, 115-16; in
    Vaux-le-Vicomte, 64; in Versailles,
    64-66; in Villandry, 250. *See also*
    Palais
Chemin de Fer, Musée Français du, 212
Chenonceaux, Château of, 247, 249
Cheverny, Château of, 247, 250
Chinon, Château of, 249
Chocolaterie Poulain, 248
Churches: in Aix-en-Provence, 107,
    109; in Albi, 395; in Amiens, 66; in
    Angers, 114-15; in Annecy, 120; in
Antibes, 192; in Arles, 131; in
    Assy, 204; in Auch, 396; in
    Auxerre, 225-26; in Avignon, 138,
    139; in Bayeux, 183; in Bayonne,
    155-56; in Beaune, 147; in Biarritz,
    155, 156-57; in Biot, 307; in
    Bordeaux, 164, 166, 167; in
    Bourges, 176, 177; in Caen, 182; in
    Cancale, 360; in Cannes, 190; in
    Carcassonne, 396; in Chablis, 225;
    in Chambéry, 121-22; in Chantilly,
    58; in Chartres, 58-59; in Colmar,
    209, 210; in Dijon, 223, 224-25; in
    Dol de Bretagne, 361; in Fécamp,
    354; in Fougères, 341; in Grenoble,
    234; in Honfleur, 242; in
    Les-Baux-de-Provence, 132; in
    Limoges, 378; in Lourdes, 326; in
    Lyon, 258, 260, 262; in Monaco,
    283; in Montpellier, 292; in
    Mulhouse, 212; in Nancy, 299; in
    Nantes, 343; in Nice, 303, 305; in
    Nîmes, 320; in Paris, 29, 32, 34-35,
    45-49; in Pau, 326; in Périgueux,
    375; in Pérouges, 263; in Pézenas,
    293; in Poitiers, 331-32; in Reims, 61;
    in Rennes, 339, 340; in Rouen,
    351-52; in St.-Malo, 360; in
    St.-Thibault, 227; in Sarlat, 374; in
    Sauveterre-de-Béarn, 327; in
    Semur-en-Auxois, 227; in
    Strasbourg, 384-85, 386; in
    Toulouse, 393-94; in Vence, 307;
    in Versailles, 65; in Vézelay, 226;
    in Vienne, 262-63; in
    Villeneuve-lès-Avignon, 140; in
    Vitré, 341
Cimiez, Church of, 303
Cité, Île de la, 29, 32
Civilisation Gallo-Romaine, Musée
    de la, 258
Clairefontaine, Hippodrome de, 217
Claude-Debussy, Théâtre, 200
Clemenceau, Musée, 52
Climate, 2-3
Clos de Vougeot, 225

Clos-Luce, 248
Clothes, 3
Cognacq-Jay, Musée, 52-53
Collégiale Church, 168
COLMAR: entertainment, 215;
geography, 209; history, 208-209;
hotels, 212-13; restaurants, 214-15;
special attractions, 209-12; travel
information, 215
Combarelles, Les, 376
Combourg, Château de, 361
Compiègne, 59-60
Concerts, 10. See also under Theaters
Conciergerie, 32, 38-39
Concorde, Place de la, 35-36
Continental Waterways, 4
Cordeliers, Church of the, 299
Cordeliers' Cloister, 169
Cordeliers, Couvent des, 299
Corneille, Musée, 353
Côte d'Azur, 3
Côte des Basques, Plage de la, 155
Country houses. See Châteaux
Crazy Horse, 68
Credit cards, 3
Crémieu, 235-36
Creuilly, Château de, 183
Croisette, Palais, 200
Cruising by barge, 3-4
Culan, Château, 178
Culture, Maison de la, in Grenoble,
239
Currency, 4
Customs, 4-5

D
Dauphinois, Musée, 234
David d'Angers, Musée, 116
DEAUVILLE: entertainment, 221;
geography, 217; history, 216-17;
hotels, 218-19; restaurants, 220-21;
shopping, 221; special attractions,
217-18; travel information, 221
Débarquement, Musée du, 185
Delphinal, Château, 235
Deux Guerres Mondiales, Musée
des, 35

Diane, Temple de, 319
DIJON: entertainment, 10, 231;
geography, 223; history, 222-23;
hotels, 227-28; restaurants, 228-31;
shopping, 231; special attractions,
223-27; travel information, 231
Dinard, 360
Dives-sur-Mer, 218
Docks Romains, Musée des, 272
Dogs, 2
Dol de Bretagne, 361
Dome, Church of the, 35
Dominicans, Church of the, 210
Domme, 377
Driving, 5
Ducs de Bretagne, Château des, 343
Ducs de Savoie, Château des, 121-22

E
École de Nancy, Musée de l', 299
Écologique, Aquarium, 218
Église Grecque, 49
Église Paroissiale: in Avignon, 140;
in St.-Malo, 362
Église Polonaise, 48
Église Reformée, 115
Église Russe, 49
Eiffel Tower, 29, 34, 44
Electric current, 5
Éléphants, Fontaine des, 122
Élysée, Palais de l', 36, 40-41
Entertainment: ballet, 10; casinos, 2;
concerts, 10; festivals, 10; opera,
10; Son et Lumière, 16
Épernay, 62
Esplanade, l', in Montpellier, 296
Esterel, 198
Été, Casino d', 217, 221
Eugène Boudin, Musée Municipal,
241
Europe, Colline d', 140
Europe, Palais de l', 386
Évian-les-Bains, 122; hotels, 124-25;
restaurants, 128
Exotarium, 44
Expiatoire, Chapelle, 45
Éyzies, Les, 376

Èze, 283
Èze-Bord-de-Mer, 283

F

Fabre, Musée, 291
Faure, Musée, 122
Festivals, 10; in Aix-en-Provence,
    112; in Avignon, 144; in Lyon,
    270. *See also under* Amphitheaters;
    Theaters
Fécamp, 354
Fernand Léger, Musée National, 306
Festivals et des Congrès, Palais des,
    190, 200
Flagey-Echézeaux, 225
Flaubert, Musée, 353-54
Flaugergues, Château, 293
Flégère, La, 204
Floral, Jardin, 44
Flotte, La, 333
Folies-Bergère, Les, 68
Font de Gaume, 376
Fontaine, Jardins de la, 319
Fontainebleau, 60
Fontaine-Henry, Château de, 183
Fontenay, 222
Fontenay, Abbey of, 226
Foods: breakfast, 1-2. *See also*
    Restaurants
Fort Antoine, Théâtre du, 288
Fortified Monastery, 191
Fougau, Musée, 292
Fougères, 340-41
Fragonard, Musée, 192
Française, Académie, 42
Française, Comédie, 67
French Revolution, Museum of the,
    235

G

Gardens, in Paris, 43-45. *See also*
    Châteaux
Garnier, Salle, 288
Gassin, 369
Gaveau, Salle, 68
Geography, 6
Gevrey-Chambertin, 225

Giverny, 60-61
Glace, Stade de, 234
Golf: in Chamonix, 204; in Monaco,
    288
Grande Chartreuse, La, 234-35
Grand-Palais, Galeries Nationales
    du, 50
Grand Théâtre: in Bordeaux, 164,
    174; in Nantes, 348
Granet, Musée, 108
Grasse, 190, 192; restaurants, 200
GRENOBLE: entertainment, 239;
    geography, 232-33; history, 232;
    hotels, 236-37; restaurants, 237-38;
    shopping, 239; special attractions,
    233-36; travel information, 239
Grobet-Labadie, Musée, 273
Guénégaud, Hôtel de, 39
Guimet, Musée, 53

H

Haubergier, Maison, 58
Hautefort, Château de, 377
Haut Koenigsbourg, Château, 211-12
Histoire de France, Musée de l', 53
Histoire de la Ville, Musée d', 359
Histoire de Marseille, Musée d', 272
Histoire et d'Art Réligieux, Musée
    d', 283
Histoire Locale, Musée d', 306
Histoire Naturelle, Musée d', 108
Historique, Musée: in
    Dol-de-Bretagne, 361; in Lyon,
    258, 260; in Orléans, 251; in
    Strasbourg, 386
History, 6-7
Hiver, Casino d', 217
Holidays, 7
Homme, Musée de l', 53
HONFLEUR, 183; geography, 241;
    history, 240-41; hotels, 242-43;
    restaurants, 243-44; special
    attractions, 241-42; travel
    information, 244
Hospices Civils, Musée des, 261
Hôtel-Dieu, l', 146-47
Hôtel Lallemant, Musée de l', 177

Hotels, 7-9; in Aix-en-Provence, 109-10; in Aix-les-Bains, 124; in Amboise, 252; in Angers, 116-17; in Annecy, 122-23; in Arles, 133; in Avignon, 140-41; in Azay-le-Rideau, 252; in Bayonne, 158; in Beaune, 149-50; in Biarritz, 157-58; in Blois, 253; in Bordeaux, 169-71; in Bourges, 178; in Caen, 185-86; in Cannes, 193-96; in Cap d'Antibes, 196; in Carcassonne, 398; in Chambéry, 124; in Chamonix, 205-206; in Colmar, 212-13; in Deauville, 218-19; in Dijon, 227-28; in Évian-les-Bains, 124-25; in Grenoble, 236-37; in Honfleur, 242-43; in Juan-les-Pins, 196; in Les Éyzies, 379-80; in Lourdes, 327; in Luynes, 252; in Lyon, 263-65; in Marseille, 274-76; in Monaco, 283-86; in Montpellier, 293-94; in Mont-St.-Michel, 363; in Nancy, 300; in Nantes, 345-46; in Nice, 309-13; in Nîmes, 320-21; in Onzain, 253; in Orléans, 253; in Paris, 69-82; in Pau, 327; in Périgueux, 379; in Poitiers, 334; in Quimper, 344; rates, 11; in Rennes, 343-44; in La Rochelle, 335; in Rouen, 354-55; in St.-Jean-de-Luz, 158-59; in St.-Malo, 362-63; in St.-Paul-de-Vence, 312; in St.-Tropez, 369-70; in Sarlat, 378-80; in Strasbourg, 387-88; in Talloires, 123; in Toulouse, 397-98; in Tours, 251; in Veigné, 252; in Vence, 312
Hugo, Maison de Victor, 57-58

I

Imprimerie et de la Banque, Musée de l', 262
Institut Musulman et Mosquée, 49
Invalides, Les, 34-35
Israélite, Temple, 49

J

Jacobins, Church of the, 394
Jacquemart-André, Musée, 53-54
Jacques-Coeur, Palais, 177
Jardin des Vestiges, Museum of, 272
Jean-Moulin, Centre National, 167
Jeanne d'Arc, Maison de, 251
Jeanne d'Arc, Tour, 351
Joli, Mont, 242
Juan-les-Pins, 190, 191-92; hotels, 196; restaurants, 200
Jules-Chéret, Musée, 306
Jules Verne, Musée, 343
Jussy-Champagne, Château, 178
Justice, Ministry of, 35
Justice, Palais de: in Dijon, 224; in Grenoble, 234; in Paris, 38-39; in Poitiers, 332; in Rennes, 339-40; in La Rochelle, 333; in Rouen, 352

K

Kaysersberg, 211-12

L

Lanessan, Château, 168
Langeais, Château of, 250
Langlois, Le Pont de, 129
Language, 9
Lanterne, Tour de la, 332
Lantheuil, Château de, 183
Lapidaire, Musée: in Aix-les-Bains, 121; in Arles, 131; in Avignon, 139
Lapin Agile, Au, 68
Lascaux II, 376-77
Les-Baux-de-Provence, 132
Lescar, Cathedral of, 326
Légion d'Honneur et des Ordres de Chevalerie, Musée National de la, 54
Léonce Bocquet, 148
Lérins, Abbaye de, 191
Lérins, Îles de, 190, 191
Libraries, in Paris, 42-43
Lido, Le, 68
Limoges, 378
Locronan, 342
Loctudy, 342

Logis Tiphaine, 362
LOIRE VALLEY: entertainment, 255-56; geography, 246-47; history, 245; hotels, 251-53; restaurants, 253-55; special attractions, 116, 247-51; travel information, 256
Long-Cours Cap Hornier, Musée International du, 360
Lorraine, Musée de, 299
Louis XIV, Maison, 156
Lourdes, 326
Louvre, Musée National du, 32-34
Louvre, Palais du, 28
Lumière Grand Auditorium, 200
Luxembourg, Jardin du, 44
Luxembourg, Palais du, 41
LYON, 146; entertainment, 10, 270; geography, 258; history, 257; hotels, 263-65; map, 259; restaurants, 265-69; shopping, 269-70; special attractions, 258, 260-63; travel information, 270
Lyon, Musée Historique de, 258
Lyon, Opéra de, 270

M

Mâcon, 149
Madeleine, Church of La, 28, 47
Magne, Tour, 319
Magnin, Musée, 224
Major, Cathédrales de la, 272
Malmaison, 62
Mammouths, Les Cent, 376
Manufacture Nationale des Gobelins, de Beauvais et de la Savonnerie, Atelier de la, 49
Maurice-Ravel, Auditorium, 270
Marais, Le, 39
Marbella, Plage, 155
Margaux, 168
Marine, Musée de la: in Honfleur, 242; in Marseille, 273; in Paris, 54; in St.-Tropez, 369
Marle, Hôtel de, 39
Marmotton, Musée, 54, 60
Marsannay-La-Côte, 225

MARSEILLE, 222; entertainment, 10, 277; geography, 271-72; history, 271; hotels, 274-76; restaurants, 276-77; shopping, 277; special attractions, 272-74; travel information, 278
Marseille, Opéra de, 277
Massabielle, Grotte de, 326
Masséna, Musée, 305-306
Matisse, Musée, 303, 305
Médoc, 168-69
Meillant, Château de, 177-78
Menetou-Salon, Château, 178
Mer de Glace glacier, 204
Mer, Musée de la, 155
Mémises, Plâteau des, 122
Meursault, 148
Milady, Plage de, 155
Militaire, École, 29, 42, 44
Milleu, Château de, 249
Miramar, Plage, 155
Mogère, Château de la, 292-93
MONACO: entertainment, 288; geography, 281; history, 279-81; hotels, 283-86; restaurants, 286-88; shopping, 288; special attractions, 281-83; travel information, 288-89
Monaco, Cathedral of, 283
Monasteries: in Brantôme, 377; in Caen, 182; in Crémieu, 235-36; in Dijon, 226; in Grenoble, 234-35; in Mont.-St.-Michel, 361-62; in St.-Honorat, 191; in Villeneuve-lès-Avignon, 139-40
Monceau, Parc, 52
Monet, house of, 61
Monolithic Church, 168
Montbazillac, Château de, 375
Mont-Dol, 361
Monte-Carlo, Ballet de, 288
Monte-Carlo, Casino de, 36, 281-82
Monte-Carlo, Orchestre Philharmonique de, 288
Monte-Carlo Sporting Club, 288
Montgeoffrey, Château de, 117
Montignac, 376
Montmartre, 37

MONTPELLIER: entertainment, 10, 296; geography, 290-291; history, 290; hotels, 293-294; restaurants, 294-295; shopping, 295; special attractions, 291-293; travel information, 296
Montreuil-Bellay, Château de, 117
Monuments Français, Musée des, 55
Morey St.-Denis, 225
Moulin Rouge, Le, 68
Mouthe, Caves of La, 376
Mouton-Rothschild, Château, 168-69
Movies, in Paris, 68
Mulhouse, 212, 215
Mure, Chemin de Fer Touristique de La, 236
Musée Municipal: in Bergerac, 375; in Côte de Beaune, 148; in Fécamp, 354; in Limoges, 378; in Orange, 140; in Pérouges, 263; in Semur-en-Auxois, 227; in Vallauris, 192-93
Museums: in Aix-en-Provence, 107, 108-109; in Aix-les-Bains, 121; in Albi, 395-96; in Amiens, 66; in Angers, 115; in Antibes, 193; in Arles, 131-32; in Avignon, 138-39; in Bayeux, 183-84, 185; in Bayonne, 156; in Beaune, 147; in Bergerac, 375; in Biot, 306; in Bordeaux, 166; in Bourges, 177; in Cagnes-sur-Mer, 308; in Cannes, 192-93; in Carcassonne, 396; in Chambéry, 122; in Chamonix, 203; in Chantilly, 58; in Chartres, 59; in Colmar, 210; in Compiègne, 59-60; in Dijon, 223-24; in Fécamp, 354; in Grenoble, 233-34; in Honfleur, 241, 242; hours, 9; in Les-Baux-de-Provence, 133; in Les Éyzies, 376; in Limoges, 378; in Lyon, 258, 260-62; in Marseille, 272-74; in Monaco, 283; in Montpellier, 291-92; in Mulhouse, 212; in Nancy, 298-99; in Nantes, 343; in Nice, 305-306; in Nîmes,

319-20; in Orange, 140; in Paris, 32-34, 34-35, 36, 49-58; in Pau, 325-26; in Périgueux, 375; in Pérouges, 263; in Poitiers, 332; in Quimper, 341-42; in Reims, 61, 62; in Rennes, 340; in La Rochelle, 333-34; in Rouen, 353-54; in St.-Germain-en-Laye, 63; in St.-Malo, 359, 360; in St.-Tropez, 368-69; in Sarlat, 374; in Semur-en-Auxois, 227; in Sèvres, 63; in Strasbourg, 385-386; in Toulouse, 394, 395; in Trouville, 218; in Vallauris, 192-93; in Versailles, 65-66; in Villeneuve-lès-Avignon, 141
Music. See under Theaters

N

NANCY: geography, 298; history, 297-98; hotels, 300; restaurants, 300-301; special attractions, 298-300; travel information, 301
Nancy, Cathedral of, 299
Nantes, 222, 343
Naval et Napoléonien, Musée, 192
NICE, 189; entertainment, 316; geography, 303, 305; history, 302-303; hotels, 308-13; map, 304; restaurants, 313-15; shopping, 315; special attractions, 305-308; travel information, 316
Nice, Opéra de, 316
NÎMES: geography, 318; history, 317-18; hotels, 320-21; restaurants, 321-22; special attractions, 318-20; travel information, 322
Nissim-de-Camondo, Musée, 55-56
Normandie, Musée de, 181
Normandie, Musée Mémorial de la Bataille de, 184
Normandy, climate in, 3. See also ROUEN
Normandy American Cemetery and Memorial, 184
Normandy landing beaches, 184-85
Notre-Dame, Basilique de, in

Beaune, 147
Notre-Dame, Cathedral of: in
  Bayeux, 183; in Chartres, 58-59; in
  Grasse, 192; in Grenoble, 234; in
  Paris, 29, 32, 68; in Rouen, 351-52;
  in Senlis, 58; in Strasbourg, 384-85
Notre-Dame, Church of: in
  Bordeaux, 167; in Dijon, 224; in
  Dives-sur-Mer, 218; in
  Semur-en-Auxois, 227; in
  St.-Thibault, 227; in Vitré, 341
Notre-Dame, Crypte Archéologique
  de, 32
Notre-Dame-de-Bon-Secours,
  Church of, 300
Notre-Dame-de-Grace, Chapel, 242
Notre-Dame-de-l'Espérance, Church
  of, 191
Notre-Dame-de-Locmaria, Church
  of, 342
Notre-Dame-de-Paris, Musée de, 32
Notre-Dame-des-Doms, Cathedral
  of, 139
Notre-Dame-des-Tables, Crypte, 292
Notre-Dame de Toute Grace,
  Church of, 204
Notre-Dame-la-Grande, Church of,
  331
Nouveau Monde, Musée du, 333
Nuits St.-Georges, 225

O
Obernai, 211
Odéon, Théâtre National de l', 67
Oeuvre Notre-Dame, Musée de l',
  385
Oies, Marché aux, 374-75
Olympia, 68
Open hours, 9-10
Opera, 10. See also under Theaters
Opéra, Place de l', 28
Opéra, Théâtre de l', 36
Orange, 140; entertainment, 10
Orangerie des Tuileries, Musée de l',
  56
Orangerie, Musée de l', 61
Oratoire, Chapelle de l', 145-46

Oratoire, Temple Protestant de l', 49
Oratoire, Tour de l', 341
Orbigny-Bernon, Musée d', 334
Orchestre National de France, 68
Ordre National de la Libération,
  Musée de l', 35
Orléans, 246
Orléans, Château of, 250-51
Orsay, Musée d', 56, 57

P
Palais: in Avignon, 138-39; in
  Bourges, 177; in Dijon, 224; in
  Fontainebleau, 60-61; in Monaco,
  282-83; in Paris, 40, 41-42; in
  Poitiers, 332. See also Châteaux
Palais de Tokyo, Musée du, 50, 56
Palais Ducal, 298
Palais Lascaria, Musée du, 305
Palais-Royal, 40
Palais-Royal, Théâtre du, 67
Palavas-les-Flots, 293
Pan American World Airways, 10-11
Panthéon, 40
Papes, Palais des, 137, 138-39, 144
PARIS: climate in, 3; entertainment,
  10, 66-68; geography, 23, 28-29;
  history, 23-28; hotels, 69-82; map,
  30-31; restaurants, 82-96;
  shopping, 96-102; special
  attractions, 32-66; travel
  information, 103-105
Paris, Opéra de, 66-67
Paris, Orchestre de, 68
Paris, Théâtre Musical de, 67
Paroissiale, Église, 141
Passports, 11
Patriarche Père et Fils, 148
PAU: geography, 324; history,
  323-324; hotels, 327; restaurants,
  327-28; shopping, 328; special
  attractions, 324-26; travel
  information, 329
Pau, Château de, 324-25
Pauillac, 169
Paul-Mistral, Parc, 234
Pavié, Château, 167-68

Peinture et de Sculpture, Musée de, 233-34
Pénitents-Blancs, Chapelle des: in Les-Baux-de-Provence, 132; in Vence, 307
Pénitents-Blancs, Musée de la Chapelle des, 374
Pénitents-Noirs, Chapelle des, 139
Pépinière, Parc de La, 300
Père Lachaise, Cimetière du, 49
Perigord. See SARLAT
Périgord, Musée du, 375
Périgueux, 375; entertainment, 10
Pérouges, 263
Petit-Palais, Musée du: in Avignon, 139-40; in Paris, 57
Pézenas, 293
Picardie, Musée de, 66
Picasso, Musée: in Antibes, 192; in Paris, 57; in Vallauris, 192
Pie X, Basilique, 326
Pigalle, Place, 37
Pincé, Hôtel, 115
Plantes, Jardin des, 44
Plessis-Bourré, Château du, 116
Pleyel, Salle, 68
Pointe du Raz, 342
POITIERS: entertainment, 10; geography, 331; history, 330-31; hotels, 334; restaurants, 335-36; special attractions, 331-32; travel information, 337. See also ROCHELLE, LA
Pommard, 149
Pont du Gard, 320
Pont l'Abbé, 342
Port Grimaud, 368
Postal, Musée, 211
Préhistoire, Musée National de, 376
Prieuré-Lichine, Château, 169
Princes, Maison des, 263
Princier, Palais, 282-83
Psalette Cloister, 247
Puligny-Montrachet, 149
Puymartin, Château de, 375
Pyramide, La, 263
Pyrénées, Parc National des, 326

Q

Quai-d'Orsay, Palais du, 42
Quic-en-Groigne, Galerie, 359
Quimper, 341-42
Quimper, Faïenceries de, 342

R

Railroads, 15-16
Rainier III, Auditorium, 288
Ramatuelle, 369
Rambouillet, 62-63
Réattu, Musée, 132-33
Reims, 61-62
Remparts, Les, 359
RENNES: entertainment, 348; geography, 339; history, 338-39; hotels, 343-46; restaurants, 346-48; special attractions, 339-41; travel information, 348-49
Renoir, Maison de, 308
Résistance, Musée de la: in Lyon, 261; in Grenoble, 234
Restaurants, 12-14: in Aix-en-Provence, 110-12; in Aix-les-Bains, 127; in Amboise, 254; in Angers, 117-18; in Annecy, 125-26; in Antibes, 199; in Arles, 134; in Avignon, 142-44; in Azay-le-Rideau, 254; in Bayeux, 187-88; in Bayonne, 160-61; in Beaune, 150-53; in Biarritz, 159-60; in Biot, 314; in Blois, 255; in Bordeaux, 171-73; in Bourges, 178-79; breakfast, 1-2; in Caen, 186-88; in Cannes, 197-200; in Chambéry, 127; in Chambord, 255; in Chamonix, 206-207; in Colmar, 214-15; in Deauville, 220-21; in Dijon, 228-31; in Évian-les-Bains, 128; in Grasse, 200; in Grenoble, 237-38; in Honfleur, 243-44; in Juan-les-Pins, 200; in Limoges, 382; in Lyon, 265-69; in Marseille, 276-77; in Monaco, 286-88; in Montpellier, 294-95; in Nancy, 300-301; in Nantes, 348; in Nice, 313-15; in

Nîmes, 321-22; in Orange, 144; in Orléans, 255; in Paris, 82-96; in Pau, 327-28; in Périgueux, 381; in Poitiers, 335-36; in Quimper, 347-48; in Rennes, 346-47; in La Rochelle, 336-37; in Rouen, 355-57; in St.-Jean-de Luz, 161; in St.-Malo, 363-65; in St.-Paul-de-Vence, 315; in St.-Tropez, 371-72; in Sarlat, 380-82; in Strasbourg, 388-90; in Talloires, 126-27; in Toulouse, 398-401; in Tours, 253-54; in Vence, 315; in Villeneuve-lès-Avignon, 143-44

Revard, Mont, 122

Riquewihr, 211

Riviera. See Cannes; Monaco; Nice; St.-Tropez

ROCHELLE, LA: geography, 332-33; history, 330-31; hotels, 335; restaurants, 336-37; special attractions, 333-34; travel information, 337. See also POITIERS

Rochepot, La, 149

Rochers-Sévigné, Château des, 341

Rodin, Musée, 51

Rohan, Museums in the Château des, 385-86

Romain, Théâtre: in Lyon, 270; in Vienne, 263

Rosaire, Chapelle du, 307

ROUEN: entertainment, 357; geography, 351; history, 350-51; hotels, 354-55; restaurants, 355-57; shopping, 357; special attractions, 351-54; travel information, 357

S

Sabatier-d'Éspeyran, Musée, 292

Sacré-Coeur, Church of, 37, 48

St.-Agricole, Church of, 139

St.-André, Cathedral of, 164, 166

St.-André, Church of, 234

St.-André, Fort, 139

St.-André-le-Bas, Church of, 262-63

St.-Antoine, Chapelle de, 236

St.-Augustin, Church of, 45

St.-Bénigne, Cathedral of, 223

St.-Bonaventure, Church of, 262

St.-Castor, Cathedral of, 320

Ste.-Catherine, Church of, 242

Ste.-Catherine, Clocher de, 242

Ste.-Cécile, Cathedral of, 395

Ste.-Chapelle, Church of, 29, 32, 45, 58, 122

St.-Corentin, Cathedral of, 341

Ste.-Croix, Cathedral of, 250-51

Ste.-Croix, Chapelle de, 283

Ste.-Croix, Church of, 167

Ste.-Croix, Musée, 332

St.-Denis, Church of, 45

St.-Didier, Church of, 139

St.-Émilion, 167-68

St.-Émilion, Maison du Vin de, 168

St.-Estèphe, 168

St.-Étienne, Cathedral of: in Auxerre, 225-26; in Bourges, 176; in Limoges, 378

St.-Étienne, Temple, 212

St.-Étienne-de-la-Cité, Church of, 375

St.-Étienne-du-Mont, Church of, 46

St.-Eustache, Church of, 46

St.-François-de-Sales, Cathedral of, 121

St.-Front, Cathedral of, 375

St.-Gatien, Cathedral of, 247

St.-Georges-de-Commiers, 236

St.-Georges, Chapel of, 181

St.-Germain, Church of, 225

St.-Germain-des-Prés Church: in Paris, 29, 46, 68

St.-Germain-en-Laye, 63

St.-Germain-l'Auxerrois, Church of, 46

St.-Gervais–St.-Protais, Church of, 39, 46

St.-Hilaire, Church of, 332

St.-Honorat, 191

St.-Honoré, Church of, 130

St.-Jean, Baptistry of, 331

St.-Jean, Cathedral of, 258, 260

St.-Jean, Chapelle de, 138
St.-Jean, Church of, 181, 293
St.-Jean, Fort, 272
St.-Jean, Hôpital, 115
St.-Jean-Baptiste, Church of, 156-57
St.-Jean-Cap-Ferrat, 308
St.-Jean-de-Luz, 156-57; hotels,
  158-59; restaurants, 161
St.-Jean-de-Malte, Church of, 109
Ste.-Jeanne-d'Arc, Church of, 352
St.-Julien, 168
St.-Julien-le-Pauvre, Church of, 46
St.-Laurent, Tour, 341
St.-Léonard, Church of, 242
St.-Louis, Cathedral of: in Blois, 248;
  in La Rochelle, 332-34
St.-Louis, Île, 29, 32
St.-Louis-des-Invalides, Church of,
  35
St.-Louis-en-l'Île, Church of, 47
St.-Maclou, Church of, 352
Ste.-Madeleine, Basilica of, 226
Ste.-Madeleine, Church of, 307
ST.-MALO: entertainment, 366;
  geography, 359; history, 358-59;
  hotels, 362-63; restaurants, 363-65;
  shopping, 365-66; special
  attractions, 359-62; travel
  information, 366
Ste.-Marguerite, 191
Ste.-Marie, Cathedral of: in Auch,
  396; in Bayonne, 155
Ste.-Marie, Temple Protestant de, 49
Ste.-Marie-Madeleine, Church of,
  263
Stes.-Maries-de-la-Mer, 132
St.-Martial, Chapelle, 138
St.-Martin, Church of: in Biarritz,
  155; in Chablis, 225; in Colmar,
  209
St.-Martin, Collégiale of, 210
St.-Mathieu, Temple, 209
St.-Maurice, Cathedral of: in Angers,
  114; in Vienne, 262
St.-Maxime, 368
St.-Méen, Church of, 360
St.-Merri, Church of, 47, 50

St.-Michel, Basilica of, 167
St.-Michel, Church of, 225
St.-Michel, Mont, 361-62
St.-Nazaire, Basilica of, 396
St.-Nicholas, Fort, 272
St. Nicolas, Tour, 332
St.-Nicolas-des-Champs, Church of,
  47
St.-Nicolas-de-Chardonnet, 47
St.-Ouen, Church of, 352, 357
St.-Paul, Church of, 260
St.-Paul-de-Vence, 307-308
St.-Paul–St.-Louis, 39
St.-Philippe-de-Roule, Church of, 47
St.-Pierre, Cathedral of: in Annecy,
  120; in Montpellier, 292; in
  Poitiers, 331-32; in Rennes, 340
St.-Pierre, Church of: in Avignon,
  139; in Caen, 182; in Chartres, 59;
  in Vienne, 262
St.-Pierre-de-Montmartre, Church
  of, 37, 47
Sts.-Pierre-et-Paul, Cathedral of, 343
St.-Pierre-le-Guillard, Church of,
  177
St.-Pierre-le-Vieux, Church of, 386
St.-Raymond, Musée, 395
St.-Rémi, Basilique de, 61
Ste.-Réparate, Cathedral of, 305
St.-Roch, Church of, 48
St.-Romain-en-Gal, 263
St.-Sacrédos, Cathedral of, 374
St. Samson, Cathédral, 361
Saint-Sauveur, Cathedral of, 107
St.-Serge, Church of, 115
St.-Sernin, Basilica de, 393
St.-Séverin Church, 46, 48
St.-Sulpice, Church of: in Fougères,
  341; in Paris, 48, 68
St.-Thibault, 222, 227
ST.-TROPEZ: geography, 368;
  history, 367-68; hotels, 369-70;
  restaurants, 371-72; shopping, 372;
  special attractions, 368-69; travel
  information, 372
St.-Trophime, Church and Cloister
  of, 130, 131

St.-Ursule, Church of, 293
St.-Victor, Basilica of, 272
St.-Vincent, Cathedral of, 360
St.-Vincent, Church of, 132
Sales taxes, 14
Santenay, 148
SARLAT: geography, 373-74;
    history, 373; hotels, 378-79;
    restaurants, 380-81; special
    attractions, 374-75; travel
    information, 382
Sassenage, 235
Saumur, 115-16
Sauveterre-de-Béarn, 327
Savoie, Palais de, 121
Savoisien, Musée, 122
Schools, in Paris, 29, 42-43
Second Empire, Musée du, 59-60
Secq des Tournelles, Musée, 353
Semur-en-Auxois, 222, 227
Sèvres, 63
Sèvres, Musée de, 63
Shaking hands, 14-15
Shopping, 5; hours, 9-10
Ski Français, École de, 207
Société Nationale de Chemins de
    Fer Français, 15-16
Son et Lumière, 16, 255-56
Sorbonne, Church of La, 48
Sorbonne, La, 43
Sorcier, Du, Caves of, 376
Soubise, Hôtel de, 39
Soutard, Château, 167-68
Souvenir Napoléonien, Musée du,
    283
Sports, Palais des, 68, 234
Stanislas, Place, 298
Steamship service, 16
Stendhal, Musée, 234
STRASBOURG, 208, 224;
    entertainment, 10, 391; geography,
    384; history, 383-84; hotels,
    387-88; restaurants, 388-90;
    shopping, 390-91; special
    attractions, 384-86; travel
    information, 391
Suquet, Le, 190-91

Sylvia Montfort, Théâtre, 39

T
Talloires, 120-21; hotels, 123;
    restaurants, 126-27
Tapisseries, Musée des, 107
Tau, Palais de, 61
Taxes, sales, 14
Telephones, 16
Tennis, in Monaco, 289
Terreaux, Promenade des, 263
Theaters: in Aix-en-Provence, 112;
    in Angers, 118; in Arles, 130, 135;
    in Avignon, 144; in Bayonne, 162;
    in Bordeaux, 164, 174; in Caen,
    188; in Cannes, 200; in Chambéry,
    128; in Deauville, 221; in Dijon,
    231; in Grenoble, 239; in Lyon,
    270; in Marseille, 277; in Monaco,
    288; in Montpellier, 296; in
    Mulhouse, 215; in Nantes, 348; in
    Nice, 316; in Paris, 36, 39, 67; in
    Rouen, 357; in Strasbourg, 391; in
    Toulouse, 401; in Trouville, 221.
    See also Amphitheaters
Théâtre National Populaire, 67
Thermal spas: in Aix-les-Bains, 121;
    in Évian, 122
Thermes et de l'Hôtel de Cluny,
    Musée National des, 36
Thermes Nationaux, 121
Thollon, 122
Thomas Dobrée, Musée, 343
Tipping, 16-17
Tissus, Musée Historique des, 261
TOULOUSE: entertainment, 401;
    geography, 393; history, 392-93;
    hotels, 397-98; restaurants,
    398-401; shopping, 401; special
    attractions, 393-95; travel
    information, 401
Touques, Hippodrome de la, 217
Tour guides, 3
Tours, 246-47; entertainment, 10
Tours/Tour operators, 17
Touvet, Château de, 235
Toy Soldiers, Museum of, 60

Travel agents, 17
Trémolat, 378
Trinité, Eglise Abbatiale de la, 354
Triomphe, Arc de, 34, 36
Trouville, Casino Municipal de, 217-18, 221
Trouville, Musée de, 218
Tuileries, Jardin des, 28, 44-45

U

UNESCO, Maison de l', 42
Universities. *See* Schools
Unterlinden, Musée d', 209-10

V

Val-de-Grace, Church of, 49
Vallauris, 190, 192-93
Vaux-le-Vicomte, 64
Vence, 307
Vendôme, Pavillon, 107
Vendôme, Place, 29, 35
Vernon, 61
Verrerie, Château de la, 178
Versailles, 64-66
Veyrier, Mont, 120
Vézelay, 222, 226
Vieil-Aix, Musée du, 108
Vienne, 262-63; entertainment, 10
Vierge, Rocher de la, 155
Vieux, Château, 155
Vieux-Grenoble, 234
Vieux-Honfleur, Musée du, 242
Vieux-Lyon, 258, 260
Vieux-Marseille, Musée du, 272-73
Vieux-Montpellier, Musée du, 292
Vieux-Nice, 305

Vieux-Nîmes, Musée du, 319-20
Vieux-Toulouse, Musée du, 395
Vignerons des Côtes Mâconnaises et Beaujolaises, Les, 149
Villandry, Château of, 250
Ville, Hôtel de: in Compiègne, 60; in Lyon, 262; in Paris, 40; in La Rochelle, 333
Villeneuve-lès-Avignon, 139-40
Vin, Maison du, 167
Vin, Musée du, 147
Vin, Route du, 210-11
Vincennes, Bois de, 44
Vincennes, Château de, 38
Vins, Marché aux, 147-48
Vitré, 340-41
Vitré, Château de, 341
Vivenel, Musée, 60
Vizille, Château de, 235
Vosges, Place des, 36-37
Vosne Romanée, 225
Vulliod St.-Germain, Musée du, 293

W

Wineries: in Auxey-Duresses, 148; in Beaune, 147-48; in Bordeaux, 167; in Cavaye, 149; in Colmar, 210-11; in Dijon, 225; in Médoc, 168-69; in Meursault, 148; in Pommard, 148; in La Rochepot, 148; in Santenay, 148; in St.-Émilion, 167-68
Wines, 17-22

Z

Zoos, in Paris, 44

ABOUT THE AUTHOR

Robert S. Kane's initial writing stint was as editor of the [Boy Scout] *Troop Two Bugle* in his native Albany, New York. After graduation from Syracuse University's noted journalism school, he did graduate work at England's Southampton University, first making notes as he explored, in the course of class field trips through the Hampshire countryside. Back in the United States, he worked, successively, for the *Great Bend* (Kansas) *Daily Tribune, Staten Island Advance, New York Herald Tribune,* and *New York World-Telegram & Sun* before becoming travel editor first, of *Playbill,* later of *Cue* and *50 Plus* magazines; he writes regularly for *Travel & Leisure* and leading American and Canadian newspapers, and frequently discusses travel on TV and radio talk shows. *Africa A to Z* was the progenitor of his acclaimed 14-volume A to Z series, which in turn led to creation of the current World at Its Best Travel Guides. A past president of both the Society of American Travel Writers and the New York Travel Writers' Association, Kane makes his home on the Upper East Side of Manhattan.